Commanders & Command

in the Roman Republic and Early Empire

STUDIES IN THE HISTORY OF GREECE AND ROME

Robin Osborne, James Rives, and Richard J. A. Talbert, editors

Books in this series examine the history and society of Greece and Rome from approximately 1000 BC to AD 600. The series includes interdisciplinary studies, works that introduce new areas for investigation, and original syntheses and reinterpretations.

Commanders & Command

in the Roman Republic and Early Empire

FRED K. DROGULA

The University of North Carolina Press   Chapel Hill

Complete cataloging information can be obtained online at the
Library of Congress catalog website.
ISBN 978-1-4696-2126-5 (cloth: alk. paper)
ISBN 978-1-4696-2127-2 (ebook)

For my mother and father

Contents

Acknowledgments

Many years ago I determined to undertake a major project on Roman governors, but at the time I had little idea how difficult this subject would be, or how many different threads of research would be needed to understand it fully. Much has been written on individual aspects of Roman governors, and many scholarly debates about Roman government involve questions about its governors, but I wondered if a single comprehensive study of the provincial governor would reveal new information about ancient Rome. I decided to attempt this task, which turned out to be a rabbit hole that grew only more complex and daunting the further I proceeded. As a result, this work has been many years in the making, as I struggled to determine the best questions to ask and the right way to build my arguments and structure the book. Entire chapters were taken out or reconceived, and the whole work has been repeatedly restructured and rewritten as I discovered new and important lines of inquiry. Through every step of this process, I have been fortunate to have the friendship and counsel of Elizabeth A. Meyer, whose knack for asking the right question — which all-too-often forces you to rethink your entire position — is unparalleled. I am deeply grateful for her guidance, her suggestions, her criticisms, and her comments on several drafts of this book. I also owe a great debt to J. E. Lendon, Richard Talbert, and A. J. Woodman, who have generously assisted me over the years by reading drafts of my work, by pointing me in the direction of valuable evidence, by identifying weaknesses in my arguments, and by suggesting improvements. While these scholars and friends have made important contributions to my thinking and have been invaluable to me in my work, all errors of fact or interpretation in this book remain exclusively my own. I am also grateful to the anonymous readers at the UNC Press, who offered many suggestions and constructive criticisms of my work, and to Charles Grench, the editor at UNC Press who accepted my book for publication in this prestigious series and who provided the needed support to get this book to press. I would also like to thank my employer Providence College for its financial assistance in producing this work and for providing an exceptional Interlibrary Loan staff, whose tireless efforts have facilitated my research. Finally, I owe an eternal debt to my parents Betty Ann and Fred Drogula, who have always supported me and encouraged me to follow my heart (even when it led to the study of ancient history), and most especially to my beloved wife Anne, who not only offered translation suggestions but whose patience and support have made this work — not to mention my happiness — possible.

INTRODUCTION

The history of the Roman Republic is, to a large extent, the history of its military commanders and the campaigns they led. This is partially the result of poor records, since the first ancient historians to write about Rome's early history had little more than lists of consuls, campaigns, and triumphs at their disposal, which they fleshed out with folklore and family traditions that celebrated the military glory won by their ancestors. At the same time, the Romans were a famously militaristic people who cherished and publicly displayed their military decorations, and whose very calendar was organized around military festivals and the cycle of war. While the Greeks tore down sections of their walls for Olympic athletes, the greatest celebrations in Rome were the military triumphs, when victorious generals marched their armies through the streets of the city, hauling their plunder and captives with them. To become a noble in early Rome, a man first had to serve in the army for ten years, and if he acquired a reputation for bravery, he might win election to the praetorship and be given a small military command. Only if he distinguished himself in that campaign might he win election to the consulship and a large command, which would be considered the pinnacle of his career, especially if he won the hoped-for honor of a triumph. Nobility, status, honor, and public office all depended upon one's performance as a soldier and commander. The most important men in the Roman senate had commanded Rome's legions in battle, so commanders and ex-commanders formed the leadership of the state. To the Romans, therefore, their history was indeed the long story of bloody conquests, at first near the city, then throughout Italy, and finally across the seas in every land around the Mediterranean. The story of provincial command *was* the story of Rome.

This book seeks to contribute to modern discussions on the Roman Republic and early empire by studying the nature and development of provincial command. This topic is difficult because its origins lay in the republic's legendary beginnings, for which we have little reliable evidence. In the earliest days of Rome, provincial command was simply military command. It was one of

1

the oldest and most fundamental concepts in Roman civilization and predated accurate records by many centuries. When the Romans of the later republic set about reconstructing and writing down their history — using records of questionable reliability, as well as manifestly false information — they understandably used contemporary values and practices to describe events in their past, creating anachronisms that imposed a false image of continuity and consistency upon the military practices of early Rome. Lacking techniques of critical historical analysis and the basic assumption that their past had been different from their present, the Romans created for themselves origins and an early history that looked remarkably similar to their present. In their traditional accounts, the republic's first military commanders — the consuls — appear no different from the consuls who held office in the late republic, and the military campaigns of the fifth century BC appear little different from those conducted hundreds of years later. This static representation gives the impression that Rome's concepts and practices of military command barely changed during the republic, which can dissuade one from looking for development and innovation. The early republic, therefore, was written to look much like the late republic, making it difficult to study and appreciate the evolution of provincial command.

The best-educated Romans of the late republic knew there were problems with their early history, but these problems never shook their fundamental belief that their practice of provincial command had been basically unchanged since the founding of the republic. Thus they knew that the earliest consuls were actually called praetors, but they were not concerned that this fact contradicted their traditional belief that the praetorship was not created until the Sextian-Licinian Rogations of 367 BC, nearly 150 years *after* the supposed creation of the consulship. They even struggled to understand the exact relationship between these officials: though defined as colleagues under augural law, in the late republic consuls and praetors performed such different functions that they were seen as entirely separate magistracies. The literary record further complicated the issue, because ancient writers — making the incorrect assumption that the differences between the two magistracies in the late republic must have been original to the early republic — presented entirely different origins for the two offices and ascribed different purposes and functions to each. Although Roman religious history stressed the connections between the praetorship and consulship, their literary history emphasized the differences, which has proved to be a difficult knot for modern historians to unravel.

Adding a further layer of complication, Augustus brought about fundamental and far-reaching changes to Rome's concept of provincial command during his rise to power, changes that would strongly influence the manner in which his contemporaries and their descendants would understand the past. Because of these extensive reforms, writers in the early empire conceived of military command in different terms from their colleagues in the republic, and they innocently, but uncritically, inserted contemporary concepts into their accounts of earlier periods. Naturally, most of these ancient historians were intelligent thinkers who had an honest curiosity about Rome's past, and working amid these conflicting ideas and traditions they did their best to put together a narrative of their early history. This tradition — with all its benefits and flaws — is still the foundation of most modern discussions about provincial command. While modern scholars have made great strides to analyze and interpret this tradition, the subject of provincial command as a whole has not yet been given enough attention to pull it free from traditions and folklore that alter its appearance.

Another problem that has hindered the study of provincial command is the failure of many authors — ancient and modern — to appreciate that early Rome did not use the same legalistic mentality and jurisprudence that flourished in the late republic and in the imperial era, and that still influences modern thought today. This mistake has induced scholars of early Rome to look for rigid legal structures and to expect clear legal explanations for military practices rather than conventional but flexible methods of operation. Although it is well known that ancient Rome did not have a constitution in the modern sense of the word, most historians from Livy to the current day have been tempted to use constitutionalist thinking when studying early Rome, assuming that the authorities and responsibilities of early commanders were stable and fixed according to clear and logical principles of law. The rise of jurisprudence in the late republic gradually transformed the exercise of authority from something malleable (although guided by traditional practice) into something fixed by statute or legal precedent, and Western scholars have tended to think in similar legal/constitutional terms ever since.[1] As a result, there has been (and still is) a strong tendency to look for constitutional explanations for the operation of provincial commanders in the early and middle republic, a tendency that can lead one to see legal principle where only convention existed. This is obviously problematic, because legal principles do not change or evolve as readily as conventions, and presupposing that some aspect of Roman government was based on legal principle imposes on it a fixedness that blinds us to the possibility of change or development. When ancient authors presented

1. See the recent work by Schiavone (2012).

the consulship as being created all at once in 509 BC with its familiar authority and prerogatives, they endowed the office with an original and unchanging constitutional quality that blinded them to its actual development and transformation. As many scholars are coming to realize, however, this is far too simplistic a view of the republican consulship, which seems to have evolved and changed significantly over time.

Furthermore, misconceptions about the nature of early Roman military thinking tend to exert an inappropriate influence on the study of provincial command. In the modern world, the military is usually the most orderly and structured part of any society, where soldiers and officers exist in a rigid hierarchy of ranks that are clearly indicated on their uniforms and that instantly define the relationship between any two individuals. For the past century, it has been normal for men in the Western world to have firsthand experience serving in their country's military (many nations have even employed compulsory military service), and this experience can predispose scholars to expect or assume that modern military structures — which seem so logical and traditional — must have existed in ancient armies. Such expectation can be dangerous, because it induces historians to look for modern concepts and structures in ancient armies and can even lead to the anachronistic imposition of modern ideas on Roman culture. The clear logic and universal use of rank in the modern military, for example, can obscure the possibility that Rome, rather than employing certain paradigmatic structures like constitutionalism and military hierarchy, may have used other systems or mechanisms to differentiate its commanders.

In an effort to break new ground, this book focuses on the fundamental concepts that defined a provincial commander in the republic, prioritizing an analysis of the underlying ideas that shaped provincial command. Rather than producing a narrative of Roman warfare and territorial conquest, this inquiry looks through ancient sources searching for the underlying concepts and vocabulary the Romans used to describe their understanding of commanders and their commands. In other words, this inquiry is less concerned with exploring the Romans' own explanations and rationalizations of their early practices and more focused on the way they spoke about provincial command and the ideas and concepts they used to express its development. This entails reading the sources in a different way and looking for clues in the subtext of an author's discussion. Whereas the primary details of a story (such as who, what, where, and when) are readily open to influence, error, or deliberate manipulation, the cultural values and concepts that underlie the story and make it recognizable and comprehensible to its intended audience are less malleable and provide better information regarding the broad ideas — if not necessarily the bare facts — of early provincial command. Rather than study individual provincial commanders, this book approaches them by examining the concepts that defined them, including different types of authority and fields of responsibility given to commanders. Because these basic ideas are common to all ancient writers, they provide a specialized vocabulary and approach for studying provincial command.

The position of the provincial commander, one of the most important officials in the republic, had tremendous scope and was defined and influenced by different legal, social, political, and religious ideas. In short, the study of the provincial commander encompasses a great deal of ground, and this book would have been impossible without the extensive research that has been conducted by other scholars in a number of different areas. Over the years, scholars have explored the individual aspects that contribute to the definition of a commander or a command, but no effort has yet been made to step back and examine the subject as a whole.[2] The consulship and praetorship have individually received significant attention in recent years: Pina Polo's *The Consul at Rome* and the collection of essays edited by Beck, Duplá, Jehne, and Pina Polo have both provided important insights on the consulship, and Brennan produced his essential two-volume study of the praetorship over a decade ago.[3] These books are invaluable sources of research for scholars working on either magistracy, but their focus on a single magistracy makes it difficult for them to treat the concept of provincial command as its own particular field of study (which is admittedly not their primary interest). Similarly, Richardson and Kallet-Marx have studied the development of Spain and Macedonia respectively as Roman provinces, and Richardson, Rüpke, and Wesch-Klein have each produced important book-length discussions of fundamental concepts like *imperium*, *provincia*, and the distinction between *domi* and *militiae*.[4] So many historians have studied these and other aspects of provincial command in their books and articles that a list of even essential works would be too long to produce here (see bibliography). Because of the broad and far-reaching nature of the subject, modern scholars have generally focused on discrete slices of provincial command, examining a single magistracy, an individual province, a par-

2. Vervaet's forthcoming work *The High Command in the Roman Republic* (Stuttgart 2014) was not yet available when this manuscript went to press.

3. Pina Polo (2011), Beck, Duplá, Jehne, and Pina Polo (2011), Brennan (2000).

4. Richardson (1986), (1996a), and (2008), Kallet-Marx (1995), Rüpke (1990), and Wesch-Klein (2008).

ticular war, or a distinct concept. Standing on the shoulders of these scholars who have worked out individual problems and questions about ancient Rome, I have attempted to pull together various topics into a single study.

By approaching provincial command as its own subject, this book argues that it is more than the sum of its parts. Combining the study of several individual topics, this book explores how different aspects of provincial command interacted with one another, making provincial command a more fluid and flexible idea than has hitherto been appreciated. The first three chapters explore the early origins of military leadership in the republic and identify the fundamental concepts that defined provincial command in Roman thought, including magisterial authority (*potestas*), military authority (*imperium*), religious authority (*auspicium*), the commander's field of responsibility (*provincia*), and the separation of military and civilian spheres (*domi militiaeque*). Because these concepts are highly significant to many aspects of Roman society, government, and religion, the new definitions proposed in these chapters have far-reaching consequences for fields beyond provincial command, but examination of these consequences must be left for future investigation. Although most of the texts used in this investigation come from later periods in Roman history, it is contended that cautious and judicious examination of these sources can reveal fundamental cultural concepts that are much older than the texts in which they appear. Such analysis of these concepts, their use in primary texts, and their interconnections with one another enables us to draw reasonable conclusions about the early development of Roman military command and commanders. The last four chapters of this book use the fundamental definitions established in earlier chapters to explore how the various underlying concepts that defined provincial command changed and developed over time. The result is not a narrative of Rome's military conquests but a thematic study using the vocabulary established in the first three chapters to examine how the Romans deliberately (and sometimes accidentally) manipulated individual aspects of provincial command. While these changes or developments were usually made for short-term advantage, they often had a long-term effect on the nature of provincial command as a whole.

Looking at important developments in Rome's system of provincial command — and in particular by offering new explanations for those developments — this study demonstrates that military command was not a single, monolithic idea in the Roman mind but was defined by different and malleable attributes, and that a change in one of those attributes had the ability to change the entire concept of the commander. Some of these changes were formalized by law or by religious practice, but others were merely the product of traditional practice and not codified or legally defined. As the Roman Empire grew and conventional practices and routines became enshrined in tradition, Rome's system of military command became increasingly regular as if based on some kind of constitution, but nevertheless the office of the provincial commander remained a sum of its parts—any one of which could be altered. Because some aspects of military command were defined by habitual practice or routine (rather than by law), they could be changed without recourse to law. Indeed, the structure and administration of Rome's empire grew as a result of changes in the Roman concept of military responsibility. Although many of these changes were unintentional or unplanned, in the late republic powerful men deliberately used their resources to manipulate ideas of provincial command for their personal advantage, such that several confusing phenomena of the period can be explained by understanding how such manipulation occurred. Finally, it is argued that Augustus was able to create an entirely new position for himself by reinterpreting basic concepts like *imperium* and *provincia*. Instead of introducing an alien idea, such as making himself an Eastern monarch, he rearranged the traditional component parts of military command to achieve his ends through reorganization rather than innovation. In this way, Augustus's actions were merely a late stage in a long evolution of the basic ideas of provincial command, and it was the inherent flexibility of the traditional ideas that enabled him to maintain his successful domination of the empire.

1

CONCEPTS AND TRADITIONS OF
MILITARY LEADERSHIP IN EARLY ROME
(TO 367 BC)

The early Roman Republic is a notoriously difficult period to study: accurate historical data are exceedingly rare, and later Greek and Roman historians freely combined legend and folklore with whatever archival sources were available to them. Modern scholars have worked to reconstruct good narratives of the major events in Rome's early history, but despite excellent historical research, controversy on basic questions continues.[1] On the most fundamental level, scholars disagree sharply over the value and reliability of the traditional account of early Rome, which was assembled by annalistic historians in the third and second centuries BC from questionable sources and was subsequently reworked by a series of later historians. This disagreement is tremendously important, because these stories and related documents like the *fasti* (the historicity of which is also questioned) provide most of our information for this early period. Although the traditional account of early Rome was long accepted as fact, it has come under attack by scholars who argue that much of it was a literary creation of the late republic and that archaeological data and an anthropological approach (which give a substantially different interpretation of early Rome) should be preferred. Alföldi is a leading voice in this movement, arguing that the literary tradition is unreliable and contradicted by new archaeological data:

---

1. A select list includes Beloch (1926), von Fritz (1950), Gjerstad (1953–73), de Sanctis (1956–67), de Martino (1958), Alföldi (1965), Werner (1963), Palmer (1970 [2009]), Heurgon (1973), Drummond (1974), Ferenczy (1976), Ogilvie (1976), Giovannini (1983), Hölkeskamp (1987) and (2004), Campanile (1988), Cristofani (1990), Eder (1990), Mitchell (1990), Ungern-Sternberg (1990) and (2005), Pallottino (1991), Holloway (1994), Forsythe (1994), (1999), and (2005), Cornell (1995) and (2005), Kunkel and Wittmann (1995), Wiseman (1995), Smith (1996), Grandazzi (1991 [1997]), Stewart (1998), Brennan (2000), Sandberg (2001), and Beck, Duplá, Jehne, and Pina Polo (2011).

The faithful believers in the narrations of Livy's predecessors were able to repeat over and over again the proud yet imaginary story of Roman chroniclers. It is only quite recently that modern archaeology revealed the superior strength of the conquering Etruscans, the power of Praeneste, Lavinium's priority over Rome as centre of Latium, and the true date of the rise of Rome as leading power, which came only after other Latin centres had held this place.[2]

Alföldi is certainly not alone in this position: Ungern-Sternberg more recently went so far as to state "almost none of Livy's and Dionysius's stories can confidently be claimed as 'historical tradition,'" and that "the first books of Livy and the parallel account of Dionysius cannot retain much value for our attempts at reconstructing early Roman history."[3] In this view, those stories were largely the product of later annalists, who created Rome's early history from unreliable evidence and under the influence of other historical and literary narratives, especially Greek stories that were absorbed and transformed into Roman stories by early writers. Miles has even argued that Livy never intended his work to be an accurate historical account of early Rome but was exploring Roman identity and character.[4] Flower sums the problem up well:

> Few can now doubt that earlier times tended, both consciously and unconsciously, to be re-created by a succession of Roman writers in light of conditions in the third and second centuries. This was true even before the crisis of 133 gave rise to a new political climate in which historians had more urgent motives to project the political concerns and conflicts of their own times onto earlier Roman history.[5]

Although this argument continues to gain traction, the traditional account is still widely accepted by modern historians, who—while acknowledging the problems—believe the annalists had access to more and better sources than are available today and that the general narrative should be accepted as having solid historical value. Cornell has argued that the original sources used by an-

2. Alföldi (1972) 788, written in a review of Palmer (1970), in which Alföldi gives a good assessment—up to the date of the review—of this debate over the interpretation of the literary tradition.

3. Ungern-Sternberg (2005) 75 and 82.

4. Miles (1995) 74, and 220–25.

5. Flower (2010) 38. See also Rich (1997) 12, who points out that annalists were responsible for a good deal of distortion and invention in their works.

cient historians (but now lost) were generally reliable, although they may have been misinterpreted by the annalists:

> The problem is that the Romans themselves did not necessarily comprehend the difficulties of interpretation that faced them, and were not always able to account adequately for the data at their disposal. This happened not so much because they were not trained in the techniques of historical criticism as because they were not in fact engaged in the process of historical research at all. The Romans' approach to their own early history was uncritical because it was not founded on the basic principle of historical criticism, which is that the past is different from the present.[6]

While Cornell points out that "there can be no doubt that the surviving accounts present a highly contrived and unrealistic picture of the early age of Rome," he nevertheless maintains that the basic structure of Roman history given by these accounts is fundamentally sound, and that "the balance of the argument, however, seems to favour the view . . . that the traditional picture of Rome's development is at least as credible as any of the modern hypotheses that have been designed to replace it, and that radical theories such as Alföldi's create more problems than they solve."[7] While Cornell is certainly correct that the early annalistic historians had access to records that are now lost, this may not improve their historical reliability. Bruun has pointed out that nearly all of the annalists we know by name were senators and that their ancestors figure prominently in the republican *fasti*, which may indicate that the traditional account of early Rome was intended more to glorify certain families than to preserve an accurate account of Rome's past.[8] Because we do not know the names of all the annalists who contributed material to the early history of Rome, we must be cautious in accepting details that may be fictional or anachronistic interpolations intended to celebrate (accurately or not) the ancestors of some unknown annalist. On the other hand, we should not discount entirely the cultural memories that early writers were able to access or the early monuments in Rome that preserved the memory of certain deeds.[9]

---

6. Cornell (2005) 59.

7. Cornell (1989) 249.

8. Bruun (2000) 60–61. He cautions that the members of famous *Furii* clan were also "objects of 'the expansion of the past' and the writing of fictive history." See also Vansina (1985), Ungern-Sternberg (1988) and (2006).

9. See Flower (1996) and (2004), and Hölkeskamp (2001).

Recognizing the problems with the annalistic accounts, Cornell suggests identifying the structural facts that are present in these stories and that have real historical value and separating them from the narrative superstructure, which is unreliable and probably fictional material woven into the tradition.[10] Some scholars, however, have argued that even this approach is insufficiently critical of the ancient sources, so the debate on the reliability and utility of the traditional stories remains active and unresolved.[11]

As a general principle, this chapter takes the position that the annalistic tradition for the earliest republic is often unreliable, in particular its presentation of the origins of provincial command. Yet unreliable does not mean useless, since the traditional account possesses a wealth of information about Roman values and ideas. In fact, with the use of careful scrutiny, much can be said about Roman belief in these early traditions and practices. Although Rome's system of provincial command evolved and changed throughout the republic, this scrutiny of the sources reveals important trends in Roman command. This chapter, not seeking to write a new history of early Rome, will engage in the debate over the accuracy of the annalistic tradition only tangentially. Its goal is to explore a narrower topic: the concepts and traditions held by later Romans about the exercise of military command in the early republic. These pages are not trying to determine the accuracy of events described in the traditional accounts but to extrapolate from the language and details used by later authors the ideas they held about early Roman military traditions. In usefully describing this methodology, Grandazzi notes that it is necessary

> to abandon the notion of reading the tradition literally, but without challenging it as a whole. This means not hesitating perpetually between condemnation and acquittal, but rather taking into account the tradition as an element that is historically significant by its very existence, and seeking to explain it in terms of its progressive formation and elaboration.[12]

As a result, this chapter seeks to examine how later Romans remembered and wrote about the military leadership in early periods of their history, and how subtle changes in their accounts reveal changes in provincial command. Rather than attempting to demonstrate that any particular event in the early republic was factually true, such as determining the details of what an early commander

---

10. Cornell (1982) 206 and (2005) 47–74.
11. Wiseman (1983), Ungern-Sternberg (1988) 242, Forsythe (2005), Raaflaub (2005a) 1–46.
12. Grandazzi (1991 [1997]) 130–31.

did, these chapters will use broader strokes to look at major developments in provincial command that appear in tradition.[13]

If one may paraphrase Cornell's system of looking for structural facts, this chapter is looking for structural themes: traditions or concepts about military leadership that survived in tradition from early periods in Rome's history. As Millar points out, "The traces of the archaic Roman community, even that of a still earlier stage, are quite clear enough in the record of its institutions in the historical period."[14] Thus, while one might mistrust a statement that cattle-rustling led a particular consul to lead the Roman army against a particular neighbor in a particular year, the fact that Dionysius and Livy both portray reciprocal raiding as a recurring practice in early Rome should lead us to believe that such raids were common enough in general and that they constituted a good portion of Rome's early military activity. Although any single fact that appears in a story of early Rome might be suspect, some unusual themes do continue to reappear throughout the sources. Thus, it would be naïve to accept that 306 members of the Fabian clan really died while fighting against overwhelming enemy force in a famous last-stand against Veii in 477 BC, since the number and timing of this event seems strangely reminiscent of the 300 Spartans who died at Thermopylae only three years earlier.[15] On the other hand, the odd fact that the Fabii were fighting as a single clan against hostile neighbors fits within a recurring theme of private battles fought between clan-based war bands in early Rome, which contradicts the traditional picture that Roman military command was a highly organized and regulated state endeavor from the foundation of the republic. By reading between the lines of the fundamental sources, one can identify themes and concepts that likely remained relatively stable in the transmission of stories, because a major change without explanation would be contrary to logical expectation. Raaflaub recently articulated this process of careful analysis needed to study the early republic:

> We should not despair of forming concrete and somewhat reliable views about Rome's development in the previous period [i.e., before the second half of the fourth century BC]. But we need to proceed cautiously, to apply a broad range of critical interpretive methods, and to scale our expectations down. Most of all we need to understand the methods the Roman histori-

13. In this respect, these chapters are adopting the method established by Flower (2010), who acknowledged the problems with the sources and suggested studying early Rome as a series of republics rather than as a single republic.

14. Millar (1989b) 139.

15. See Forsythe (2005) 195–200.

ans used to fill the thin framework of memories and accepted "facts" available to them with dramatic content and to shape a continuous, interesting and instructive story.[16]

Using this approach, we can recover important details about the early republic that help us understand the origins of military leadership and command. In particular, this chapter attempts to establish that military authority was originally a vague concept that only gradually came to be monopolized by the state; as such, military authority was defined less by law than by tradition. Since the sole focus of this chapter is the study of the practice and tradition of military leadership in the early republic, it does not engage with debates about the development of Rome's urban, civilian government and society except where these topics touch on generals and command. Although some of the points made in this chapter have relevance to the study of domestic government and society, such applications are left for future consideration elsewhere.

Private and Public Military Leadership in the Early Republic

According to Roman tradition, because the exercise of military authority had been invested in the highest state officials from the foundation of the city, military and civilian authority were thought to have been linked from the very beginning. The Romans attributed the foundation of their state to the legendary Romulus, who established himself as king over the new city and exercised supreme authority over all aspects of civic life. A succession of kings was believed to have ruled over Rome for more than two centuries, when a revolution brought about the end of the monarchy and the establishment of a unique system of government known as the republic (*res publica*). Although the term *res publica* (public possession) suggests a substantial shift away from monarchical government, Roman tradition emphasizes the similarities between Rome's new, elected chief magistrates (two officials called consuls) and its exiled kings. Later ancient writers were explicit that the consuls wielded the authority of the ancient kings, which included the possession of royal symbols (twelve *fasces*, the ivory curule chair, and the purple bordered toga), the right to consult the gods on behalf of the state (*auspicium*), and the authority to give commands to free citizens (*imperium*).[17] Although some of the exiled kings' au-

---

16. Raaflaub (2010) 128.

17. Cic. *Leg.* 3.3.8, *Rep.* 2.56, Livy 2.1.7–8. On the royal Etruscan origin of Roman consular regalia, see Bonfante-Warren (1970a) 57–60 and Barker and Rasmussen (2000) 89.

thority was shared among a senate, citizen assemblies, and certain priesthoods, the two consuls wielded the highest authority in both civilian governance and military command.[18] First and foremost, therefore, the Romans believed that their earliest republican generals were annually elected magistrates, and their two different sets of responsibilities — those of the military general (*imperator*) and of the civilian magistrate (*magistratus*) — were combined in a single office, as they no doubt had been under the monarchy. Naturally, the Romans were not unique in their practice of combining military and civilian responsibilities in a single office: most Etruscan states seem to have had monarchical governments in which the king held supreme authority over the state in a way similar to Rome's kings, and many Latin states were originally governed by two annually elected officials similar in competence to Rome's consuls.[19]

The combination of general and magistrate is an important starting point, because it was a defining aspect of the concept of military command held in the late republic. Roman tradition emphasizes the tremendous power and authority of its early leaders, which in large part derived from their combination of civilian and military prerogatives. The fact that the word magistrate (*magistratus*) is derived from the word master (*magister*) demonstrates the highly unequal relationship between magistrates and citizens; the same root was used originally to describe the dictator (*magister populi*) and master of horse (*magister equitum*), illustrating a close linguistic association between civilian and military offices. Similarly, the title tribune (*tribunus*) described both a military officer (*tribunus militum*) and a civilian magistracy (*tribunus plebis*), and even — for a period in Rome's early history — the highest elected official in the state (*tribunus militum consulari potestate*). Polybius mentions the tremendous authority exercised by Rome's two consuls in both military and civilian functions, and he compared their office to the Spartan dual monarchy.[20] Since the Romans believed that military and civilian authority had always been intrinsically linked in their senior magistrates, the unity of these two types of authority is an important first step in the investigation of the Roman commander.

<hr>

18. The structure and development of the Roman government is beyond the scope of this work. On this topic, see Millar (1984a), (1986), (1989b), and (1995), Finer (1997) 385–441, Lintott (1999a), Brennan (2000) 31–65, Hölkeskamp (2010), Pina Polo (2011).

19. Alföldi (1965) 179, Salmon (1967) 85–87 and (1982) 5 and 27, Campanile and Letta (1979) 34–35, Pallottino (1991) 85–92, Cornell (1995) 230–32, Dillon and Garland (2005) 180, Holloway (2008) 117–18.

20. Polyb. 6.10.1–4 and 11.11–12.10. See Hahm (2009) 178–98.

This traditional account of early Rome provides a clear and neat explanation of the origins of Roman military command. Ancient Greek and Roman historians accepted this foundation story without much difficulty, in part because it was recognizable (it reflected well their knowledge of the consulship in the late republic, with which they were familiar), and because it provided an orderly and straightforward narrative linking the later republic to its early history. Unfortunately, it is highly unlikely that this traditional account is accurate. To begin with, the Romans themselves knew that their early magistrates were called not consuls but praetors: Livy tells his audience that in the fifth century BC "it was not yet the custom for a consul to be called a 'judge,' but rather a 'praetor,'" and elsewhere he records an ancient inscription in which Rome's chief magistrate was called the *praetor maximus*; Cicero notes the confusion of terms when he states that the two highest magistrates in Rome hold the three titles "praetors, judges, and consuls"; Festus also refers to "the praetors, who are now consuls"; and references to the Twelve Tables made by Gellius and Pliny the Elder record praetors but no consuls.[21] Furthermore, since other early Latin states had chief magistrates called praetors, the Romans likely used this designation as well for their original leaders.[22]

The anachronistic identification of the republic's earliest magistrates as consuls is more than a mere problem in terminology. Roman tradition was adamant that the praetorship was not created until 367 BC and then as a singular office and one of secondary importance to the original dual consulship. This creates a fundamental contradiction, since it establishes two entirely different dates for the introduction of the praetorship: at the foundation of the republic (traditionally dated to 509 BC), or 142 years later in 367 BC. If the former is accepted, then we must explain how and why the dual praetorship that existed from 509 to 367 BC was reduced to a single officeholder and supplanted as Rome's chief magistracy by the consulship in 367 BC. If the traditional date of 367 BC is accepted for the creation of the praetorship, then we must explain how it could be that the consuls were called praetors 142 years before the creation of the praetorship.

21. Livy 3.55.11–12: *iis temporibus nondum consulem iudicem sed praetorem appellari mos fuerit*; Livy 7.3.5: *lex vetusta est, priscis litteris verbisque scripta, ut qui praetor maximus sit idibus Septembribus clavum pangat*; Cic. *Leg.* 3.8: *regio imperio duo sunto, iique praeeundo, iudicando, consulendo praetores, iudices, consules appellamino*; Fest. 249L: *initio praetores erant, qui nunc consules, et hi bella administrabant*; for the Twelve Tables, see Gellius (11.18.8, 20.1.47) and Pliny (*NH* 18.12).

22. Including Praeneste (*CIL* 14.2890, 2902, 2906, 2960, 2994, 2999, 3008), Lavinium (*CIL* 10.797, *CIL* 14.171–72), Cora (*CIL* 10.6527), and perhaps Velitrae (*CIL* 10.6554).

Another conundrum is the reliability of the *fasti*—the ancient lists that record Rome's senior magistrates from the foundation of the republic to the rise of the Augustan principate. The *fasti* provide much of our knowledge for the early republic, and rejecting their accuracy means losing much of our literary information for that period. As we have them, the *fasti* are fairly late: although earlier versions may have existed (Livy and Dionysius of Halicarnassus seem to have consulted versions with slight variations), the *Fasti Capitolini*—which includes the list of senior magistrates (*Fasti Consulares*) and a list of triumphators (*Fasti Triumphales*)—were composed under Augustus, and their content may well have been influenced and even adapted to fit his policy priorities. Equally problematic is the source(s) from which the names and dates in the *fasti* were assembled, the most important of which was the *Annales Maximi*, the official records supposedly kept by Rome's priests and stored in the state archives. Defenders of the *Annales Maximi* and the *fasti*, including Beloch and Drummond, suggest that the records were kept in good order from the sack of Rome in 390 BC and that records of previous years that were destroyed in the sack of the city could have been reassembled to some degree, enabling the annalists in the third and second centuries BC to use these records to write their histories, which in turn became the primary source material for later authors such as Cicero, Livy, and Dionysius.[23] Yet even the ancient authors recognized that there were problems in the traditional lists of Roman magistrates and that Rome's history had been distorted by the insertion of fictitious or exaggerated details by later families interested in creating or augmenting the glory of their ancestry. Dionysius refers to variations and inconsistencies among different annalistic accounts, and Livy complains in three different places about the challenges of finding good information on Rome's past:

> [Book Two] One is involved in so many uncertainties regarding dates by the varying order of the magistrates in different lists that it is impossible to make out which consuls followed which, or what was done in each particular year, when not only events but even authorities are so shrouded in antiquity.

> [Book Six] The history of the Romans from the founding of the city of Rome to the capture of the same . . . I have set forth in five books, dealing with matters which are obscure not only by reason of their great an-

---

23. Beloch (1926) 1–61 and 86–95, and Drummond (1978b) 80–108 and (1980) 57–72. On the publication of the *Fasti Capitolini*, see Nedergaard (2001) 120.

tiquity—like far-off objects which can hardly be descried—but also because in those days there was but slight and scanty use of writing, the sole trustworthy guardian of the memory of past events, and because even such records as existed in the commentaries of the pontiffs and in other public and private documents, nearly all perished in the conflagration of the city.

[Book Eight] It is not easy to choose between the accounts or the authorities. The records have been vitiated, I think, by funeral eulogies and by lying inscriptions under portraits, every family endeavouring mendaciously to appropriate victories and magistracies to itself—a practice which has certainly wrought confusion in the achievements of individuals and in the public memorials of events. Nor is there extant any writer contemporary with that period, on whose authority we may safely take our stand.[24]

Cicero encountered the same problem in published copies of funeral orations for famous men, which exaggerated the achievements of long-dead ancestors in order enhance the status and claims of their living descendants: "Yet by these laudatory speeches our history has become quite distorted; for much is set down in them which never occurred, false triumphs, too large a number of consulships . . ."[25] Paulus Clodius was more critical, saying that "those [records] which are now put on display were put together fraudulently by men gratifying certain people who were trying to force their way into the leading families and the most distinguished houses, though their ancestors had no connection with them."[26] Cicero also complains that nothing is as dry as the *Annales Maximi* (*nihil potest esse ieiunius*), and that nothing is more unsubstantial or thin (*exilis*) than Rome's early annalists, including Fabius, Cato, Piso, Fannius, and Vennonius.[27]

Scholars are continually reevaluating the accuracy of the earliest periods of the *fasti*, questioning the nature and reliability of records kept in that early period, and whether those records could have survived the Gallic sack of the city in 390 BC and later fires that destroyed public buildings in which records were probably stored.[28] Many have recognized that family records and

---

24. Dion. Hal. *AR* 11.62.3, Livy 2.21.4, 6.1.1-2, and 8.40.3-5 (Foster, trans.). For commentary on Livy, see Oakley (1997-2004) 1.30-33, who concludes (33) that, "although there is good evidence for the unreliability of family records, there is no reason to believe that this undermines utterly the credibility of L.'s record for the years 389-293."

25. Cic. *Brut.* 62 (Hendrickson and Hubbell, trans.).

26. Clodius fr. 1C = 1P (Cornell, trans.).

27. Cic. *Leg.* 1.6.

28. See in particular Ungern-Sternberg (2000) 207-22.

folklore—which were intended to glorify families rather than preserve accurately the progress of Rome's history—are thoroughly interwoven into the versions of the *fasti*. Frier has even argued that surviving citations of the *Annales Maximi* actually derive from Augustan editions of those records, which may have no resemblance to the original republican records.[29] This debate remains an active one: although there is a strong tendency to accept that the *fasti* for early Rome were based on generally reliable sources, a growing number of historians have argued that the *fasti* are an unreliable product of the late republic whose accuracy regarding the early republic is minimal.[30] While the *fasti* remain an invaluable resource, questioning the reliability of the earliest periods covered by those lists is no longer imprudent.[31] On the other hand, discarding the *fasti* as altogether false would be foolish, since we have no way to prove *or disprove* most of the information contained therein, but understanding the problems with the data provided by the *fasti* enables us to reconsider how we interpret and evaluate that information. Knowing the *fasti* are in error regarding the title of Rome's earliest chief magistrate-commander, one may fairly question other details about the original nature of that office, such as whether it was truly a dual office (held by two men at a time), whether early military commanders were also civilian magistrates, and whether the authority of commanders was all-encompassing or more narrowly focused.

If republican military tradition was not based on a smooth transition from monarchy to the dual consulship, what are the origins of Roman generalship? Although ancient Romans imagined their republican constitution spontaneously appearing full-formed at the expulsion of the monarchy, such a belief is too organized, legalistic, and deterministic to be believed. As Flower argues:

> The concept of one long republic is especially unhelpful as a tool for understanding the complex debates and political experiments that characterized

---

29. Frier (1999) esp. 179–200, and see Bispham (2010) 29–50.

30. A full discussion of this debate would take up too much room and is beyond the scope of the current work, but see Alföldi (1965) 80, Heurgon (1973) 244–50, Pinsent (1975) esp. 33 and 42–60, Ogilvie (1976) 17–19, 79–86, Ridley (1983), Ungern-Sternberg (1988) 237–65 and (2005) 75–97, Bucher (1987), Drews (1988), Billows (1989) esp. 125–33, Culham (1989) 100–115, Poma (1990) 139–57, Rüpke (1993), (1995a), and (1995b), Oakley (1997–2004) 1.24–28 and 30–41, Mora (1999), Forsythe (2000) 6–11, Richard (2001) 19–25, Cornell (2005) 47–74, Itgenhorst (2005) 9–12, 219–23, Forsythe (2005) esp. 155–56, Feeney (2007), Holloway (2008) esp. 108 and (2009) esp. 75 n. 23, Östenberg (2009) 54, Bispham (2010) 30–35, Flower (2010) 37–38, Raaflaub (2010) 127–35, and Smith (2011) 19–40.

31. Oakley (1997–2004) 1.39–40 is surely correct that the list of consuls is more reliable starting in 366 BC.

the first two centuries after the end of the monarchy. During these centuries there was no single political system at Rome, nor did politics operate in the same way as it would later in the third and second centuries.[32]

Surely some period of experimentation and instability must have followed the collapse of the monarchy, and powerful clans probably struggled to acquire as much power and authority as possible. Archaeological evidence demonstrates that considerable wealth and resources had been consolidated in the hands of a few families during the regal period, and these clans no doubt sought to take advantage of the temporary power vacuum caused by the expulsion of the monarchy by asserting their own authority as leaders of the state, particularly in the all-important sphere of military command.[33] This finds support in Polybius, who pointed out that corrupt monarchies are usually overthrown and replaced by aristocracies.[34] Moreover, there is every indication that the government of the early republic was not as organized and structured as ancient authors would have us believe, and so one should expect that military command took different forms in those early days. We can probably accept that Rome's earliest commanders were commonly called praetors, but these archaic praetors were different from the officials who would later be called praetors after the passage of the Sextian-Licinian Rogations in 367 BC.[35] Indeed, it would be a grave mistake to equate the two simply because both positions shared the same name, as is demonstrated by the different types of tribunes that existed in the republic. While the praetorship may have been a recognizable and legally defined public office in the early republic, Holloway has pointed out that the term praetor in this context may not have meant anything more than leader

32. Flower (2010) 56. Likewise, Alföldi (1965) 145–46 argues that ancient historians imposed too much legalistic structure and organization in their descriptions of early Rome, and Magdelain (1968) points out that early magistrates in Rome did not have clearly and legally defined powers and responsibilities and that such legalistic definition emerged only later in Rome's history.

33. On the archaeological evidence for wealthy Roman clans, see Gjerstad (1953–73), Richard (1978) ch. 4 and (1986 [2005]) 107–27, Torelli (1974–75) 3–78, Ménager (1980) 147–235, Richard (2003) 110–13, Cornell (2005) 54–58. On the probability that clans took over military authority following the expulsion of the monarchy, and that there was a period of uncertainty in the governance of Rome following the expulsion, see Last (1945) 30–48, Momigliano (1963) 117, Heurgon (1973) 161–65, Richard (1978), Ogilvie (1976) 59, Mitchell (1990) 132–34, Flower (2010) 47, and Schiavone (2012) 80.

34. Polyb. 6.7.9–8.4.

35. See Oakley (1997–2004) 2.77–80, who supplies considerable evidence for accepting that Rome's chief magistrate was originally called a praetor rather than a consul. See also Urso (2011) 41–60, and Smith (2011) 33.

in the most basic sense.[36] It may have been a term simply given to (or claimed by) those who exercised military command but did not necessarily imply possession of a public office or even authority over the state as a whole.[37] The term most likely derives from *praeire* (to precede) or perhaps from *praeesse* (to be preeminent), and its primary association with military command is apparent in other Roman military vocabulary: a general's tent (even a consul's) was referred to as the *praetorium* (as were meetings of a general's council), his bodyguard and flagship were called praetorian, and the main gate of a military camp — through which the army marched out to war — was called the *praetoria porta*.[38] Saying that Rome's earliest commanders were praetors, therefore, does not obligate us to envisage any kind of official, legally defined, or even elected magistracy. A gradual and less-deterministic evolution is more likely, in which an oligarchy seized control of Rome following the exile of its last monarch, and members of that oligarchy took on the task of military leadership under the generic title of praetor. The archaic term praetor could denote an aristocrat leading his own men in a private military foray of some sort, but it could also refer to a man leading a large army that incorporated the military resources of several — or even all — of the aristocracy. It is worth taking time to see how this may have worked, and whether there is evidence for it in Roman tradition.

THE ROMANS OF THE early republic lived in constant expectation of enemy attack, and they had to be ready to defend themselves and their property by any means possible. Whereas the city and its immediate environs were fairly secure in the late republic, protected by an organized government and several large field armies that fought enemies in distant lands, Romans in the early republic lived within a day's march of enemies — some lived within sight of them — and the farms of most Romans probably lay within easy striking range of enemy raiding parties. In such a situation, self-help was the best means of defense, and many wealthy elites must have taken personal responsibility for the defense of their property (and the ransacking of others' property), using their own mili-

36. Holloway (2009) 71–72 demonstrates that the word praetor could be used independently of Rome's normal magistracies simply to signify the idea of leader. See also Badian (1964) 74.

37. Mitchell (1990) 135–36 and 150 has even suggested that consuls were not originally civilian magistrates but only military commanders (he argues that their civilian authority developed later), a position that Forsythe (2005) 176 also holds.

38. Tent (Cic. *Verr.* 2.4.65, *Div.* 1.72, Caes. *BC* 1.76, Sall. *Jug.* 8.2, Livy 21.43.15, 54.2, 26.15.6, Fest. 249L), bodyguard (Cic. *QFr* 1.1.12, *Verr.* 2.1.36, *Fam.* 15.4.7), flagship (Livy 21.50.8), camp gate (Fest. 249L).

tary resources made up of their family and retainers or dependents. The traditional account reflects this; although Livy and Dionysius tend to present most early campaigns as state-run operations complete with legionary armies that seem to reflect the second century better than the fifth, their accounts nevertheless emphasize the constant reciprocal raids that took place between Rome and its neighbors.[39] The close proximity of enemies made small-scale raids a constant part of life, and the Romans no doubt responded to (and initiated) such attacks in various ways. While large armies might be put together for campaigns of conquest or major punitive actions, it was probably more usual for clans (*gentes*) to defend their own territory and possessions with private war bands. Dionysius even records that Roman territory was dotted with defensive fortresses, each of which had its own commander.[40] Rather than true wars organized and led by the state, much of Rome's earliest military activity may have involved small-scale raids in which individual Roman clans or war bands engaged in what amounted to private wars.[41] Livy writes that by 479 BC Rome and its neighbor Veii were locked in a perpetual state of small-scale raids against one another, in which private bands from each city would launch raids on one another's territory. Since these incursions were private forays to loot and ransack, not official wars, Livy describes the two cities being neither at war nor at peace but existing in a state of freebooting or brigandage.[42] According to Roman legend, this situation led the Fabian clan to conduct a prolonged private war against Veii, and although Livy presents this as an outstanding act of civic virtue and loyalty to the state, the reality was probably different: Fabian lands bordered the territory of Veii, suggesting that the Fabii were actually fighting to defend their own property in a private, self-interested feud with their non-Roman neighbors.[43] This suggests a state in which the leaders of

39. For example: Livy 2.50.1, 3.1.8, 3.2.13, 3.26.2, 3.38.3, 5.45.4, 6.5.4, 6.31.8, 7.15.11, 7.42.8, Dion. Hal. *AR* 3.37.2, 3.39.2–3, 5.42.1, 5.44.5, 5.45.1, 5.50.3, 7.19.1. The annalist Q. Fabius Pictor records Romulus and Remus as young men leading bands of supporters on raids to fight Rome's neighbors over cattle and contested fields (Pictor fr. 4C = 5P). Alföldi (1965) 403 points out that Rome was surrounded by hostile and angry neighbors in its early history.

40. Dion. Hal. *AR* 4.15.2, 5.44.1–2, 5.45.3.

41. See Cornell (1988) 89–100, Rawlings (1999), Rich (2007) 15–16, MacKay (2004) 44, Forsythe (2005) 190 and 198, Serrati (2011) 13–16.

42. Livy 2.48.5–6: *ex eo tempore neque pax neque bellum cum Veientibus fuit, res proxime formam latrocinii venerat.*

43. Diod. 11.53.6, Livy 2.48.8, 2.49.5, Dion. Hal. *AR* 7.19, 9.15.2–3, Fest. 451L. See Alföldi (1965) 314–15, Heurgon (1973) 181, Ogilvie (1965) 359–62 and (1976) 81, 115, Richard (1990) 174–99, MacKay (2004) 44.

powerful clans could lead military forces privately and free from state control. The story of the Fabii is not unique: the famous story of the battle of champions between the three Roman Horatii brothers and the three Alban Curatii brothers—who lived close enough to be intermarried—may also have its origins in clan warfare.[44] Livy's account of 397 BC is also illustrative: when enemies launched raids into Roman territory, two of Rome's consular tribunes, "without holding a regular levy—for this the plebeian tribunes hindered—but with a company consisting almost solely of volunteers whom they had induced to join by exhortations, marched out by cross-country ways."[45] Irregular forces led by powerful men seem to have been normal in early Rome.

Accounts of private war bands are common in this period: Roman tradition held that one of their kings (Tarquinius Priscus, originally called Lucumo) had migrated to Rome with a large band of followers; another future king, Servius Tullius, came to Rome as part of a war band in the company of the Vibenna brothers; the founder of the ancient Claudian clan was a Sabine leader named Attus (or Attius) Clausus, who immigrated to Rome with a huge force of 5,000 families (which is, curiously, the approximate number of men in a later Roman legion); Cn. Marcius Coriolanus left Rome in anger to join the Volscii, taking with him a large private army of clients; and in 460 BC the Sabine Ap. Herdonius was said to have led a war band consisting of either 2,500 (Livy) or 4,000 (Dionysius) men in an effort to seize the Capitol and make himself master of Rome.[46] In later periods, Roman patricians are described as forming private war bands made up of their families and clients to undertake various types of military action, and there is widespread agreement among scholars that early Italy was full of such small, private companies that probably undertook much of the fighting in the early republic.[47] Perhaps the most interesting example of this type of war band is found in the *lapis Satricanus*, which seems to be a dedication from the end of the sixth century BC to the god Mars by a

---

44. Livy 1.24.1–25.14, 5.16.5–6 and Dion. Hal. *AR* 3.13.4–22.10. Alföldi (1965) 312 suggests that the Horatii and Curiatii may have lived close to each other.

45. Livy 5.16.5 (Foster, trans.).

46. Tarquinius: Dion. Hal. *AR* 3.47.2 (cf. Livy 1.34.1–12). Servius Tullius: *ILS* 212, see Gjerstad (1967) 270–75, Ogilvie (1976) 88, Cornell (1995) 133–38, and Raaflaub (2010) 131. Attus Clausus: *ILS* 212, Livy 2.16.4–5, Gell. 13.23.8, Dion. Hal. *AR* 5.40.3, Tac. *Ann.* 11.24, App. *Kings* 12, Plut. *Popl.* 21.2–3, and see Alföldi (1965) 160 and Ogilvie (1976) 90. Cn. Marcius Coriolanus: Livy 2.35.6. Appius Herdonius: Livy 3.15.5, Dion. Hal. *AR* 10.14.1–17.7, and see Cornell (1995) 145.

47. Dion. Hal. *AR* 6.47.1, 7.19.2–3, 10.43.2. See Momigliano (1963) 103–7, Gjerstad (1967) 270–74, Cornell (1995) 143–50 and (2003) 86–88, Rawlings (1999) 104–6, Oakley (2004) 20, Serrati (2011) 12–13.

war band (a group of *sodales*) led by a Publius Valerius, who may be the famous Roman hero and four-time consul nicknamed Publicola.[48]

Garlan has discussed how the initiation rites by which a boy became a man in ancient societies encouraged displays of bravery and bloodletting through raids and battle: "'Private' wars were . . . characteristic of an archaic world in which 'politics' were not yet the effective reality and often withdrew before natural principles of organization."[49] Furthermore, since victims of an attack were almost certain to seek revenge for the damage and insult they suffered (what Garlan called the right of reprisal), one attack would probably stimulate similar retaliation and so on. Because private raids and wars of varying scale were endemic in the early republic, a great number of men probably operated as military commanders (albeit in a private capacity) in any given year, all of whom may have used the title praetor to describe their leadership role. Holloway has pointed out that, "if we could consult the family records which formed the basis of early Roman history, we would surely find many individuals who had commanded in war but had never occupied a magistracy."[50] This is an important clue to understanding the origin of Roman military command — early Rome seems to have made extensive use of small war bands, the leaders of which did not necessarily hold any official magistracy in civilian life. Military authority was not necessarily connected to civic life in the city, and most praetors may have simply been private citizens leading private armies.

While war bands probably worked well for local defense and private raids against enemies, the early Romans must have also worked together to put large armies into the field — probably Greek-style phalanxes at first and eventually legions. Although one cannot place too much faith in the accounts of Rome's early wars, certain recurring themes are helpful for understanding the origins of Roman military thinking. Roman citizens were organized into tribes (among other units), and this social structure may have evolved out of their early military organization. Such was the case in Athens, where the citizens began electing ten annual generals (στρατηγοί) — one from each of their citizen tribes — in 501 BC to supplement their original archaic war leader (πολέμαρχος). By 487/6 BC, the πολέμαρχος seems to have lost most of his military functions,

48. Stibbe, Colonna, de Simone, and Versnel (1980) 19 fig. 1: *ieisteterai Popliosio Valesiosio suodales Mamartei* ("the companions of Publius Valerius erected to Mars"). See Versnel (1980) 97–150, Bremmer (1982), Holloway (1994) 149–55 and (2008) 122 n. 5, Cornell (1995) 144, Forsythe (2005) 198–200.

49. Garlan (1972 [1975]) 26–40 (31 cited).

50. Holloway (2008) 122.

after which the tribal στρατηγοί were the primary Athenian military leaders; each tribe elected a στρατηγός, but the στρατηγοί cooperated in leading the combined forces of Athens.[51] The early Romans may have used their tribes similarly for military organization before adopting the later centuriate structure. Although the later tribal assembly (*comitia tributa*) was primarily concerned with the governance of domestic affairs, the tribes were self-contained administrative units that — among other things — organized their own recruitment of soldiers, and because they were organized geographically, it should be assumed that tribes frequently organized their own military actions, including coordinating with other tribes to fight full-scale wars.[52] Military tribunes were important officers in the later Roman army, and their title is certainly derived from the word tribe (*tribus* → *tribunus*), which may suggest that military tribunes originally commanded tribal units in Rome's army. The title tribune was common in the republic and referred to civilian and military officials, and Forsythe has pointed out that "since the consular tribunes were initially three in number, the title 'tribune' is likely to have derived from the three archaic tribes of the Titienses, Ramnenses, and Luceres, which could still have been used in some form as the basis of military recruitment."[53] If he is correct, then perhaps individual tribes originally picked their own war leaders (tribunes or praetors) and organized their own military campaigns, and they combined when faced with particularly strong enemies.

The distinctiveness and independence of the early tribes may have been the result of archaic Rome's tendency to create new and separate tribes to accommodate immigrants: it was said that, when Attus (or Attius) Clausus (the future Appius Claudius) brought his five thousand retainers to Rome in 504 BC, a new tribe — the Claudia — was created for them within the Roman state.[54] In this tradition, Attus Clausus was obviously the leader of the

51. See Hamel (1998) 79–83.

52. Polyb. 6.20.1–4, Livy 4.46.1, Val. Max. 6.3.4, and Taylor (1960) 8–9. Alföldi (1965) 314–15, argues that in the fifth century BC, "before the geographical areas became the organizatory basis of recruitment, tax-paying, and casting of votes, the *tribus* were the organization of clans for the purpose of war and collective hunting and for the distribution of the pastureland."

53. Forsythe (2005) 236. See also Mitchell (1990) 140. Dionysius of Halicarnassus (*AR* 4.14.1–2) indicates that, when Servius increased the number of tribes from three to four, he appointed commanders (ἡγεμόνας) for each tribe. Smith (2011) 24 argues that each of these three original tribes may have been commanded by a praetor.

54. Livy 2.16.4–5, Dion. Hal. *AR* 5.40.3–5. The Romans believed that twenty-one of their tribes existed by 495 BC, and this number increased by four in 387 BC, and by two in 358, 332, 318, 299, and 241 BC, reaching its final total of thirty-five in that last year (Taylor [1960] 3–7). Early Rome was traditionally portrayed as a loose amalgamation of different peoples: when the Sabines merged their

Claudia tribe, and he would have led the members of his tribe (i.e., his retainers) in military campaigns either individually or on behalf of the entire Roman people. Cornell also supports the view that early tribunes may have originally been tribal leaders, and points out that most of the early tribes were named after clans or *gentes*, suggesting that many tribes were dominated by aristocratic leaders.[55] Because these tribes must have differed in their manpower and resources, commanders may not have had the same degree of force available to them, so their relative influence and clout must have been unequal. Tribal leaders, whether they were tribunes, praetors, dictators, or some other title, could have used their personal resources and those of their clan and tribe to influence the decisions and actions of other clan leaders.[56] Although war was common enough in early Rome, the waging of war was not yet a standardized and uniform operation; military activities varied in scale from small raids to the sacking of cities, and the relative weakness of Rome's early government made it easy for clan- and tribe-based armies to exist simultaneously with the larger, state-controlled field armies.[57] While this cannot be confirmed or refuted, it seems to be further evidence that Rome originally used a fairly diffused system of military command.

Rome's odd experimentation with military tribunes with consular power (*tribuni militum consulare potestate*) may also have bearing in this inquiry. According to their tradition, the Romans chose to elect military tribunes with consular power in place of consuls as their chief magistrates in fifty-one of their seventy-three elections between 444 and 367 BC (70 percent of the time), and between 408 and 367 BC these consular tribunes were preferred in thirty-nine of the forty-one years (95 percent of the time).[58] According to the annalists, therefore, after sixty-four years of using consuls, the Romans abruptly began a period of seventy-seven years in which they used both consuls and consular tribunes (although favoring the tribunes heavily). This flip-flopping of state leadership seems strange, and Livy tried to make sense of this stark departure from the supposedly normal use of two annual consuls by offering two possible explanations: it was a reaction to increasing demands for military

people with the Romans, they are said to have settled on a different hill — the Quirinal — and some scholars have even argued that early Rome was a double state (Livy 1.13.4–5, 17.1–11).

55. Cornell (1995) 174–82.

56. Urso (2011) 41–60, has argued that Rome's early praetors did not — in fact — possess equal powers and authority.

57. Rawlings (1999) 97–111 discusses the scale of wars and the coexistence of aristocratic and state armies.

58. See *MRR* vol. 1 for references. No curule elections were recorded between 375 and 371 BC.

leadership, and it was a domestic political tactic by patricians to prevent men of plebeian family from holding the consulship by substituting a less prestigious office.[59] Neither explanation is particularly satisfying, so modern scholars have suggested that this so-called consular tribunate was a literary fabrication by later annalists, who found far too many men identified as generals in the years between 444 and 367 BC and explained this problem in their evidence by suggesting that a new magisterial college with a variable number of annual commanders temporarily and erratically replaced the consulship.[60] Rather than discard their assumption that the consulship was original to the republic, the annalists created consular tribunes to make their data fit their preconception of Rome's early history.[61] Livy preserves an example of this rationalization of unexpected anomalies in his evidence when he suggests that the Romans elected six consular tribunes in 397 BC because they were simultaneously at war with six different states.[62] It stretches credulity too far to imagine that Rome elected six chief magistrates and gave each a field army at this early date. More likely, several of these six consular tribunes were simply powerful aristocrats leading private war bands in small-scale raids for personal advantage, but Livy's annalist sources assumed they must have been elected officials and so called them consular tribunes to explain the perceived deviation from the wrongly assumed republican government of two consuls. If one considers that military leadership was not merely a state activity in early Rome but could be undertaken by any aristocrat with a sufficient number of family and retainers, then the tradition of the consular tribunes makes much more sense: military command was a private as well as public undertaking in early Rome, so any number of powerful men might have led forces of varying sizes in a given year.

If early Rome did have a varying number of public and private commanders rather than two annual chief magistrate-commanders, other anomalies found in later histories may have been caused by annalists massaging their evidence to make it fit their preconceptions about the structure of Rome's early gov-

59. Livy 4.6.1–12.

60. Pinsent (1975) 29–61 presents this argument well. For discussion of consular tribunes, see also Beloch (1926) 247–64, von Fritz (1950) 3–44, Staveley (1953), Adcock (1959), Boddington (1959), Sealey (1959), Ogilvie (1965) 539–50, Ridley (1986), Richard (1990), Cornell (1995) 334–39, Oakley (1997–2004) 1.367–76, Stewart (1998) 54–95, Forsythe (2005) 234–39, and Holloway (2008) 107–25.

61. Mitchell (1990) 137: "The appearance of different titles in different documents created confusion in our sources over who was in charge and what his actual position was."

62. Livy 5.16.2–3 (cf. Diod. 14.85.1). On the use of increasing numbers of consular tribunes to meet Rome's military needs, see von Fritz (1950) 37–44 and Forsythe (2005) 236–39.

ernment. Livy found three men recorded as military commanders in 464 BC (before the supposed introduction of military tribunes in 444 BC), and to resolve this inconsistency in the data and to preserve the dual consulship as Rome's original government, he made sense of the extra commander by calling him a proconsul in spite of the fact that he later stated clearly that the Romans did not use promagistrates until 327 BC.[63] Dionysius of Halicarnassus does the same thing, identifying extra Roman commanders as proconsuls long before the introduction of prorogation.[64] Such anachronisms suggest that Livy and Dionysius (or their annalistic sources) were perplexed when they found more Roman commanders identified in a given year than they believed possible under their working assumptions about Rome's early government. They sought to explain this anomaly by calling one of the commanders a proconsul (literally *pro consule*, someone acting as a consul), a distortion caused by a compelling need to make the evidence fit their preconceived notions that the dual consulship was original to the republic.

ALTHOUGH MUCH OF THE fighting in early Rome may have been conducted by clans and their leaders, wars certainly arose of sufficient magnitude to require the Romans to band together in a large state army, which may have been called a *classis*. Such an army, made up of men able to provide hoplite armor for themselves, certainly existed under the monarchy and was generally led by the king, but who was given command of it in the early republic? Perhaps the appointment of a supreme commander was originally sidestepped by sending several generals (perhaps clan leaders like tribunes) who shared or rotated supreme command of their combined forces; this was the command structure adopted by the Athenians in 501 BC (they used ten tribal leaders called στρατηγοί to lead their armed forces each year), and the Romans continued to assign similar joint commands well into the second century BC. On the other hand, we know of two archaic titles that may have denoted an individual selected to exercise supreme military authority over the Roman state: *praetor maximus* (highest leader) and *magister populi* (master of the people — an older, alternative title for the dictator).[65] These may have been two different

---

63. Livy 3.4.10, 8.23.10–12.

64. Dion. Hal. *AR* 9.16.3–4, 9.17.5, 9.63.2. Similarly, he also (11.62.1) refers to military tribunes with consular power as having "proconsular power" (ἀνθύπατον ἀρχὴν).

65. *Praetor Maximus*: Livy 7.3.5 and Fest. 152L. Livy (26.6.13) also mentions a *medix tuticus* as a similar office to a *praetor maximus*. See Oakley (1995–2005) 2.77–80 and discussion in chapter 3. *Magister populi*: Cic. *Rep.* 1.63, *Leg.* 3.9, *De Fin.* 3.75, Varro *LL* 5.82.

types of office, or they may have been two different names for the same office because there is nothing inconsistent in referring to a master of the people as the highest leader at a particular time.[66] If any aristocrat with a strong body of retainers could call himself a praetor in early Rome, the title *praetor maximus* or *magister populi* may have been used for the man chosen to exercise authority over Rome's full levy, much as leaders of early Germanic clans would band together under a war chief in times of military necessity.[67] Some scholars have argued that, at the expulsion of their kings, the Romans appointed two praetors to govern their city, but these praetors had unequal authority: the senior was called a dictator (*magister populi*) and his assistant a master of horse (*magister equitum*).[68] This suggestion is attractive and may be correct (especially since other Latin towns are known to have used chief magistrates called dictators),[69] but it still imposes a greater degree of formal structure and organization than early Rome may have possessed, and it creates a system in which supreme authority was always invested in one man, which seems contrary to the fundamental Roman value of sharing powers within magisterial colleges. If such a system was used, it probably appeared later when the Romans were centralizing their control over military leadership.

Rome's authority over the so-called Latin League may have forced the Romans to appoint some kind of supreme commander on occasion. The league was a federation of states in Latium that shared linguistic, cultural, and religious ties with one another and that occasionally cooperated in military campaigns.[70] Although initially opposed to Roman expansion, it was thought to

---

66. Cornell (1995) 228: "It is largely a matter of taste whether one wants to regard *praetor maximus* as an alternative title for the dictator."

67. Heurgon (1973) 161 suggested something similar. Taking praetor as a generic term for magistrate, he suggested that "the departure of the Tarquins left in charge of affairs several of these assistants or ministers to whom the kings had delegated some part of their duties; they made up a rather ill-organized body of *praetores*, analogous to those that we find functioning in the Etruscan republics. There the government was carried on by collegia of *zilah* (in Latin *praetores*), presided over by a *zilath purthne*, the president or *prytanis*. The title corresponds exactly to *praetor maximus*."

68. Beloch (1926) 225–36, de Martino (1972b) 235–49 and (1988) 356–57, Alföldi (1965) 81, Guarino (1969) 199–201, Ogilvie (1976) 47. *Contra*: Heurgon (1973) 162–63. For a recent summary of the discussion with extensive references, see Holloway (2009) 71–73, where he suggests (74) that a single consul, rather than a dictator, governed Rome after the monarchs.

69. Aricia: *CIL* 14.2169, 2213, 4195; Lanuvium: *CIL* 10, 3913, 12.1428, 2121, 14.2097, 2110, 2112, 2121, Cic. *Mil.* 27 and 45; Nomentum: *CIL* 14.3941, 3955; Tusculum: *CIL* 14.212, Livy 1.23.4, 3.18.2, 6.26.4, Dion. Hal. *AR* 5.74.4; Sutrium: *CIL* 10.3257; Fabrateria Vetus: *CIL* 10.5655. See also the Etruscan colony of Caere: *CIL* 11.3593, 3614/5.

70. On the Latin League, see Alföldi (1965) esp. 1–46 and Liou-Gille (1997) 729–64 for discus-

have been brought under Roman control by Tarquinius Superbus; after a brief revolt, it was again subdued and bound to Rome by the Cassian Treaty in 493 B C.[71] Rome was not a formal member of the league,[72] but the Latins were required to serve in Rome's wars under a Roman commander, which means the Romans either had supreme commanders on hand or had a system for appointing a special supreme commander when needed. That the latter was the case is suggested by a passage of L. Cincius (pr. 209 BC) that is preserved by Festus and gives some idea of how the Romans selected a general to assume command over the Latins:

> *Praetor ad portam nunc salutatur is qui in provinciam pro praetore aut [pro]-*
> *consule exit: cuius rei morem ait fuisse Cincius in libro de consulum potestate*
> *talem: "Albanos rerum potitos usque ad Tullum regem: Alba deinde diruta*
> *usque ad P. Decium Murem consulem populos Latinos ad caput Ferentinae,*
> *quod est sub monte Albano, consulere solitos, et imperium communi consilio*
> *administrare: itaque quo anno Romanos imperatorem[73] ad exercitum mittere*
> *oporteret iussu nominis Latini, conplures nostros in Capitolio a sole oriente*
> *auspicis operam dare solitos. Ubi aves addixissent, militem illum, qui a com-*
> *muni Latio missus esset, illum quem aves addixerant,[74] praetorem salutare*
> *solitum, qui eam provinciam optineret praetoris nomine."[75]*

He is now saluted praetor at the gate who leaves the city for a *provincia* acting as a praetor or [acting] as a consul. In his book on consular *potestas*, Cincius said such was the custom of this office: "The Albans held authority up to the time of King Tullus, but then when Alba had been destroyed, up to the consulship of P. Decius Mus the Latin people were accustomed to

---

sion and bibliography. The title Latin League is a modern term for this league; Livy generally referred to this coalition as "the Latin name" (*nomen Latinum*), whereas Dionysius of Halicarnassus used the vague Greek word κοινόν.

71. Dion. Hal. *AR* 3.34.1–5, 4.45.3–46.4, Livy 1.50.1–52.6. See Cornell (2000) 219–20. On the Cassian Treaty: Cic. *Balb.* 53, Livy 2.33.4 and 9, Dion. Hal. *AR* 6.95.1–2.

72. Cornell (1995) 297 makes this point most clearly: "The consistent and unequivocal view of our sources [is] that Rome was never a member of a general Latin alliance. In fact, the traditional account maintains that the League was a political coalition of Latin states formed in opposition to Rome. Its meetings took place outside Roman territory at the grove of Ferentina near Aricia, and its purpose was to organize resistance to the growth of Roman power."

73. The manuscript reads *imperatores*, but Coli (1951) 163 has rightly amended this to *imperatorem*.

74. The repetition of the phrase *aves addixerant* is probably an interpolation from the line above.

75. Cincius Alimentus in Fest. 276L (trans. Drogula). For commentary, see Ogilvie (1976) 103–4, Cornell (1995) 299–301, and Oakley (1997–2004) 1.340.

take counsel at the headwaters of the Ferentina, which is under the Alban Mount, and to administer *imperium* by common council. Yet in a year when it was appropriate for the Romans to send a general to the army by order of the Latin name, many of our men were accustomed to consult the *auspices* on the Capitol from the rising sun. When the birds were favorable, that army, which had been sent by the Latin community, was accustomed to salute as "praetor" that one whom the birds had approved, who would undertake that *provincia* with the title "praetor."

As this passage indicates, when Rome sent out a major expedition and summoned its Latin allies to serve in its army, the soldiers required by treaty assembled at Rome, where a commander was chosen to lead them. Although one does not want to make too much out of a single passage, the need to select a commander after the Latin allies had already arrived suggests that Rome did not have supreme magistrate-commanders on hand at this time. If each year began with the inauguration of two consuls (as the traditional accounts state), there would be no need to select a general as described here, since the two consuls would have been already inaugurated and available to take command. Cincius cannot be referring to consular elections (because only one praetor was chosen) or to the allotment of the command to one of the two consuls (since he states that there were many candidates for the command). De Sanctis offered a different interpretation of this passage, suggesting that this ceremony was used to select a supreme religious general, who was different from Rome's normal magistrates in that he was created to perform important religious actions, much like the Latin dictator found in several ancient sources.[76] While his suggestion emphasizes that dictators may have been somewhat different from praetors because of their greater religious significance, it does not seem to apply particularly well to Cincius's statement, which — although religion is involved — seems to address the selection of a regular praetor to exercise active command. Furthermore, there is no indication in later times that a special religious leader was needed to command the Latin League. Ziolkowski has argued that this auspication ceremony as described by Festus is entirely unique in our knowledge of Roman auspication practice and that the *complures nos-*

---

76. De Sanctis (1967) 94 and n. 29. On the Latin dictator, see Cato (fr. 36C = 58P): *lucum Dianium in nemore Aricino Egerius Baebius Tusculanus dedicavit dictator Latinus. Hi populi communiter: Tusculanus, Aricinus, Lanuvinus, Laurens, Coranus, Tiburtis, Pometinus, Ardeatis Rutulus.* Other references to Latin dictators: *CIL* 10.5655, Livy 1.23.4, 3.18.2, 6.26.4, Dion. Hal. *AR* 5.74.4. See also Alföldi (1965) 42–56, Ridley (1979) 303–9, Cornell (1995) 227–30 and 297–98, and Green (2007) 94–95.

tros cannot refer to magistrates or augurs.[77] If correct, this demonstrates that military commanders were not necessarily regular annual magistrates in early Rome but were specially chosen when and as needed to exercise military command only. This passage seems to record an archaic practice dating to before the establishment of the consulship, whereby men wishing to exercise command over Rome's entire army and its allies would attend a religious ceremony in which one of them would be selected through auspication.[78] It hints at a period in the early republic before military command over all Roman citizens was centralized in the hands of the chief elected magistrates.

The pattern that emerges from the early republic is an oligarchic state in which individual aristocrats could and did use their own military resources, either alone or in combination with those of other aristocrats, to conduct military campaigns independent of any kind of state control. These campaigns existed along a scale of magnitude from private raids led by a single aristocrat or clan to either major campaigns when the full levy of the city was called out or full-scale wars when Rome summoned soldiers from its Latin allies. Although the evidence allows few solid conclusions, it seems most likely that praetor became the default title for all types of military commander, although this term did not necessarily signify someone who held a magistracy. In fact, many (or even most) commanders were probably acting in a private capacity and leading personal military resources in small-scale raids for personal profit or advantage. Furthermore, all of this took place in the countryside, where wealthy aristocrats ruled and their activities could not be regulated by the nascent state as effectively as the conduct of public affairs inside the city, where mobs of citizens could limit the ability of aristocrats to use coercion.

All of this seems to challenge the traditional assumption that the republic's first military commanders were also civilian officials. Instead, some modern scholars see a sharp division between military command and civilian governance in early Rome: Mitchell has suggested that consuls did not exercise regular civilian authority in Rome until the later republic, while Sandberg and Forsythe separately have argued that tribunes of the plebs may have supervised

77. Ziolkowski (2011) 465–71. He rejects the possibility that they were magistrates (469) because no obvious rules exist for determining the results of this type of auspication contest, and he rejects the possibility that they are augurs because that priesthood was not used for political matters, and because multiple augurs are not known to have taken the auspices at a single time.

78. Ziolkowski (2011) 469 acknowledges this possibility: "Yet even if anything like this would be practicable in real life, this would not be an *auspicium* before the departure to a province, but the gods' deciding the assignment of the said province, i.e., something entirely different, which in truly historical times was managed through *sortitio*."

civilian affairs in the city, while the consulship was narrowly focused on military affairs outside the city.[79] Although he notes the limitations of the evidence, Sandberg has made the case that "the prevailing notion that consuls and other curule magistrates were important law-makers in the Middle Republic has ... no foundation in the sources for the period."[80] These arguments are strong, and despite the Roman insistence that their republican government emerged from the monarchy and remained largely unchanged for centuries, the mounting evidence suggests that a significant period of transition existed between the expulsion of the monarchy and the emergence of the classical republic.

Several points support the arguments of Mitchell, Sandberg, and Forsythe that Rome's early military commanders were not also chief civilian magistrates. In the first place, the ancient sources record early military commanders who held no civilian office, such as Caeso Fabius, who led his clan in a private war against the city of Veii after the end of his consulship in 479 BC.[81] Second, the fact that tribunes of the plebs and consuls originally entered office on significantly different dates suggests that military and civilian officials were seen as fundamentally different in nature: tribunes entered office on December 10, but consuls (at least from the late third century until 153 BC) entered office on the Ides of March, when the military campaigning season began.[82] Quaestors, who were primarily civilian officials, also entered office in December like the tribunes.[83] Third, the nature of a military commander's authority (*imperium*) was different from that of a civilian magistrate (*potestas*), indicating a sharp distinction between the two. In the city, where population density diluted the aristocratic monopoly of authority and created rivalry among aris-

79. Mitchell (1990) 135–36 and 150, Sandberg (2000) 121–40 and (2001) 97–113, and Forsythe (2005) 176.

80. Sandberg (2000) 140.

81. Livy 2.48.8–51.3, Dion. Hal. *AR* 9.14.1–15.7 and 18.1–22.6. Caeso Fabius called proconsul: Dion. Hal. *AR* 9.16.3, ἐξουσίᾳ κοσμηθεὶς ἀνθυπάτῳ. Livy (8.23.11–12) describes Q. Publilius Philo (cos. 327 BC) as Rome's first proconsul.

82. When consuls entered office in early Rome is highly problematic—no doubt because consuls did not exist in early Rome, and later annalists were confronted with significant variation in their sources recording consuls entering office in six different months in the fifth and fourth centuries BC. The first reliable information we have indicates that by 217 BC consuls were entering office on the Ides of March, which was the start of the Roman year (Livy 22.1.4–5, 23.30.17, 26.1.1 and 26.5, 44.19.1). This was normal practice until 153 BC, when the Romans moved the start of their calendar year to January 1 and consuls began entering office on that day (Livy *Per.* 47).

83. Botsford (1909) 195. Quaestors normally entered office on December 5, and although a quaestor might be assigned to assist a consul on military campaign as a financial officer, they were primarily civilian officials.

tocrats, a formal system of religious and civilian officials probably developed more quickly, but the countryside — at least for a time — probably existed in a quasi-feudal state, granting powerful aristocratic landholders free rein to use military force when and as they wished, in accordance with their resources, needs, and abilities.

Institutionalization of Military Command

As the political structures of the republican government grew following the expulsion of its monarchy, the Roman citizenry as a whole (or the Roman state) was eventually able to acquire a monopoly on the appointment of military commanders. When this happened cannot be known, but as Rome solidified its control over its neighbors in and around Latium, the opportunities for individual aristocrats to lead retainers in private raids would have decreased sharply. As all neighbors within an easy march from Rome became friends and allies, and as Rome began to contend with larger and more dangerous enemies beyond Latium, private small-scale skirmishing probably became less common. At first, the aristocracy that formed Rome's senate would select — from among their own number — several men each year to exercise official military authority, and the armies they led would be made up of levies from all Roman tribes, but eventually the Roman citizens in their assemblies acquired the prerogative to select their magistrate-commanders.

To bring the waging of war firmly under official control, the increasingly centralized state exerted greater efforts to subdue private wars. The use of *recuperatores* to mediate disputes and of fetial priests to control the declaration of war was probably a part of this, making it more difficult for individual Romans to declare war against Rome's neighbors.[84] Similarly, the establishment of the magisterial oath of office should be seen as part of the assertion of public authority over magistrates: it became compulsory for magistrates to take an oath within five days of entering office that they would obey the laws, and failure to take this oath within the allotted period resulted in an automatic forfeiture of office.[85] Similarly, the concept of *imperium* (legal military

---

84. Garlan (1972 [1975]) 39–40, 48–55, Ridley (1986) 460, Watson (1993) 1–10, and Rawlings (1999) 113. Rich (2011) 187–242 argues that later authors overemphasized the role the fetials played in ensuring the just conduct of war.

85. Livy 31.50.6–8. The oath is attested in 200 BC, but was clearly a well-established requirement by that time. Millar (1989b) 145 sees this oath as an assertion of authority by the Roman people over the magistrates they elected.

authority) was probably introduced or expanded during this period. Romans in later periods believed that *imperium* had been the all-encompassing authority of the kings that had been transferred to the two consuls at the birth of the republic, and henceforth it became the defining civilian and military authority of Rome's chief magistrates. Modern scholars accepted this time-honored principle uncritically until Heuss delivered a powerful blow against it, arguing that *imperium* was introduced at some point in the republic to describe the military authority—and only the military authority—wielded by Rome's chief magistrates.[86] Although Heuss's argument has been challenged or neglected by many scholars, it remains a persuasive explanation for the development of Rome's system of military command. Perhaps as the de facto power of the patrician clans began to give way to the centralized power of the growing republican state, sources of legitimate authority like *imperium* became increasingly important to explain and justify patrician exercise of authority.[87] The origins and nature of *imperium* will be considered at length here, but it stands to reason that not every man who led military forces and called himself praetor in the earliest republic was invested with *imperium* as the term would be defined in the later republic. In the early republic, men often exercised military authority simply because they could command the allegiance of a group of warriors, and it was only later in Rome's history that the concept of *imperium* became the absolute and defining quality of military commanders.

How the state acquired the sole prerogative to authorize military command is unknown, but two important events stand out in Roman tradition as moments of tremendous change for the republican government. The first involves the so-called *decemviri consulari imperio legibus scribundis*, who (according to tradition) were removed from office in 449 BC. In the ancient sources this episode is portrayed as a simple interlude within the consular lists: the use of consuls as chief magistrates was suspended in 451 BC so that a board of ten men might be appointed with full powers to revise the constitution, and when in 450 BC they arrogantly sought to retain power indefinitely, they were forced out of office, and the government reverted to consular elections in 449 BC.[88] Only five years after this restoration of the consulship as Rome's chief magistracy, however, the Romans are said to have changed their government again,

86. Heuss (1944) 57–133. *Contra*: de Francisci (1948) 1.29–40 and (1953) 1.399–432, who argued that *imperium* was too deeply ingrained in the Roman psyche to have been a creation of the republic.

87. See Richard (2005) 117 and Schiavone (2012) 82–102.

88. Cic. *Rep.* 2.61–63, Livy 3.33.1–37.8, 43.1–54.15 and 58.1–11, Diod. 12.23.1–25.2, Dion. Hal. *AR* 10.56.1–2 and 59.1–60.6, 11.45.1.

introducing the military tribunate with consular powers discussed previously, and for a period of seventy-seven years (444 to 367 BC) they decided annually whether to elect consuls or consular tribunes as the chief magistrates of the state. Despite the smooth narration of these events by ancient authors, it is actually a garbled account of erratic shifting between different types of chief magistrates. Roman authors knew there were problems, and Zonaras (following Cassius Dio) tried to reduce the confusion by arguing that praetors were *first* referred to as consuls in 449 BC.[89] While Zonaras portrays this simply as a change of title, some modern scholars have argued that the changes of 449 BC were much more substantial. Ungern-Sternberg has argued that later Romans saw the expulsion of the decemvirate as the true birth of the classical republican government, and Urso (accepting Zonaras) maintains that Rome was originally governed by a college of unequal praetors, but in 449 BC a new college of two equal consuls was established to operate as Rome's chief magistrates.[90] These arguments are persuasive and rightly draw attention to the critical importance of these reforms to the structure of Rome's government, but some historical problems continue to linger. For one, they do not explain why the Romans created the new consulship in 449 BC, only to put it aside five years later and embark on a seventy-seven-year period in which consular tribunes were generally preferred to consuls. This near abandonment of the consulship so quickly after its establishment is so strange that one is inclined to doubt whether the consulship existed at all during this period. Another lingering problem is why the Romans would have dropped the military title praetor in 449 BC (using instead the new title consul) only to reintroduce it in 367 BC as the title for a magistracy that Livy says was primarily judicial in nature. If, however, we remove the consulship altogether from the events of this period, the story becomes much clearer: if there was no fixed number of annual magistrate-commanders before 367 BC, we can dismiss the erratic juggling of different types of chief magistrate as a literary product of later annalists who adjusted their evidence to fit their preconceived notions.

Still, it seems clear that some major reform occurred between 451 and 449 BC: the Romans (probably the plebeians in particular) felt the need for reform strongly enough that they appointed a panel of lawgivers, and when that group devolved into an aristocratic coup and was squashed, they began

89. Zon. 7.19.1 (cf. Livy 3.55.11–12).

90. Ungern-Sternberg (1990) 92–102, Urso (2011) 41–60. See also Heurgon (1973) 164 and Oakley (1997–2004) 2.78–79. Some scholars have even dated the expulsion of the monarchy to 449 BC, but this seems improbable (see Oakley [1997–2004] 2.79).

appointing between two and six military commanders each year, who may or may not have exercised some degree of civilian authority within the city as well. It is perhaps relevant that the Romans believed a *lex Valeria de provocatione* had been passed in 449 BC, which reinstated the citizens' right of appeal from magistrates (which is said to have been suspended under the decemvirate).[91] Although the historicity of this *lex* is widely rejected, the connection between a *lex* regulating *imperium* and a reorganization of Rome's chief magistrate-commanders is tantalizing. The tribunes of the plebs were said to have been active in trying to impose greater limits on the senatorial elite in the decade leading up to the decemvirate: in 462 BC they began demanding that a special commission be created to draw up laws regarding the use of *imperium*; in 457 BC they succeeded in increasing their college from five to ten; in 456 BC they passed the *lex Icilia de Aventino publicano*, which gave the Aventine Hill over to plebeian occupation and made it a center for plebeian political organization; and in 454 BC they coerced the senate into sending an embassy to Greece to study Greek laws in preparation for the rewriting of Rome's laws by the decemvirate.[92] Although all of this must be embraced only with caution, Roman tradition connects the original mission of the decemvirate to the tribunician efforts to curb patrician authority, in particular the use of *imperium* by high officials. The decemvirate may have been appointed (among other things) to reform Rome's military structure, and in particular to curb the ability of the patrician aristocracy to use violence and military force independent of state control. In other words, one result of the decemvirate may have been to establish fixed guidelines defining—perhaps for the first time—a military commander as a praetor elected and invested with *imperium* by the state, thereby prohibiting the use of military force by private individuals.[93] If so, the reforms of 449 BC may have required for the first time that all military commanders be confirmed by a popular assembly that represented the Roman people. To see these reforms as requiring the conferral of *imperium* by the *comitia curiata* for a man to be recognized as a legitimate military commander is not a great step.[94]

91. Cic. *Rep.* 2.54, Livy 3.55.4–6; cf. 3.55.14. Only the *lex Valeria* of 300 BC is accepted generally.

92. 462 BC: Livy 3.9.1–13, Dion. Hal. *AR* 10.1.1–2; 457 BC: Livy 3.30.5–7, Dion. Hal. *AR* 10.26.4–30.6; 456 BC: Livy 3.31.1 and 32.7, Dion. Hal. *AR* 10.31.1–32.5; 454 BC: Livy 3.31.7–8.

93. See Heuss (1944) 57–133. Humm (2012) 83 has also argued that the curiate law was created after the monarchy had been expelled from Rome.

94. Although the *comitia curiata* was largely superseded by the *comitia centuriata* and the *concilium plebis* in early Rome, the *comitia curiata* continued to hold many important responsibilities, and the people continued to meet in *curiae* as late as 209 BC (Livy 27.8.3). See chapter 2 for a full discussion of the role played by the *comitia curiata* in authorizing military command.

Thus, the authority of the state became a *sine qua non* in defining a man as a commander. This may have involved the creation or establishment of *imperium* as an essential legitimizing source of military authority, or perhaps it was merely a moment when the Roman people asserted their right to give and withhold the military authority of *imperium*. The sudden rise in the number of annual commanders after 444 BC may have been caused by increased competition among Rome's aristocracy for generalships: sanctioned by the state, they were now harder to achieve and thus more desirable and important. Furthermore, a new requirement that commanders be authorized by the state would have increased the chances of their names being recorded and remembered, further explaining the sudden increase in the number of military commanders found in the *fasti* after 444 BC. Long ago, Meyer rejected Livy's assertion that the consular tribunate was a product of the Conflict of the Orders and instead suggested that increasing competition among patrician families drove up the annual number of commanders, an argument that was revisited by Kirby and Ridley.[95] This suggestion is supported by the preceding arguments, because new regulations on the exercise of military command may have made it more important to aristocrats that they be officially recognized as a legitimate commander. This event may represent an important stage in the development of state control over the exercise of military authority, but it does not seem to have been the origin of the consulship or the classical republican constitution in which two annual consuls governed the state.

The decisive date for that classical government must be 367 BC, when Roman tradition said the Sextian-Licinian Rogations[96] opened the consulship to men of plebeian families and created two new curule offices: the praetorship, which would provide a judicial official for the city, and two curule aedileships, which would oversee certain festivals and help manage the infrastructure of the city.[97] Livy and other ancient historians describe these rogations as a part of the so-called Conflict of the Orders, a century-long struggle in which ple-

95. Meyer (1924) 303, Kirby (1976) 24–29, and Ridley (1986) 460–61.

96. So-called because the Plebeian Assembly did not yet possess the legal capacity to pass a *lex*, nor would it have this capacity until the *lex Hortensia* of 287 BC. Livy generally refers to this bill put forward by the plebeian tribunes L. Sextius and C. Licinius as a *rogatio* (e.g., 6.35.6–8, 38.10–12), although he does occasionally refer to it as a *lex* (e.g., 6.35.4, 37.7, and 38.1).See von Fritz (1950) 18–28.

97. Livy 6.42.9–11, Diod. 12.25.2, Plut. *Cam.* 42.1–5, Gell. 17.21.27. A full discussion of these rogations — particularly the aspects pertaining to civilian governance — is beyond the scope of the current work. Recent discussions, with full bibliographies to earlier analyses, may be found in von Fritz (1950) 3–44 (who provides a discussion of earlier views), Hölkeskamp (1987) 62–109, Cornell (1995) 334–37, Brennan (2000) 59–69, Forsythe (2005) 262–67, Bergk (2011) 61–74.

beians sought to gain access to magistracies and priesthoods that had always been monopolized by the patrician families. As a result, these rogations were long interpreted within the context of social reform (allowing men of plebeian families access to the consulship), but von Fritz demolished this interpretation of the rogations and demonstrated that they were not motivated by the Conflict of the Orders.[98] He argued instead that they were primarily intended to provide a greater number of annual magistrates to satisfy Rome's increasing demand for government. While this is undoubtedly correct, von Fritz did not explore the important role these rogations played in changing Rome's military structure. The Sextian-Licinian Rogations dramatically *reduced* the number of official military commanders the state recognized each year, bringing an end to the flexible system of appointing as many as six (or more) consular tribunes annually and instead establishing a fixed system in which three — and only three — military commanders were selected each year. This was a remarkable cutback: in the preceding forty years (407 to 367 BC), the Romans had elected six-or-more consular tribunes 75 percent of the time, which means the reforms of 367 BC actually cut in half the average number of annual military commanders they appointed. What should we make of this dramatic change? Since it seems unlikely that the consulship existed before 367 BC (eliminating the explanation that the Romans were reestablishing their ancestral government), two possibilities seem to remain: this was either a strategic decision (reflecting a reduction in Rome's military needs) or a regulatory decision (indicating a desire to limit — perhaps for the first time — the number of annual commanders). Since no other reduction or elimination of annual magistrates is known during the republic (expansion was the norm), the latter explanation seems far more likely, indicating that a main goal of the Sextian-Licinian Rogations was to establish (and therefore limit) the number of men who could hold military commands in any given year. If a reform in 449 BC had required that commanders receive official recognition from the state through a vote of the *comitia curiata* conferring *imperium*, the rogations of 367 BC seem to have placed a hard limit on the number of men who could receive such recognition each year. This new limitation on the annual number of commanders would have increased the exclusivity (and importance) of military commanders and command in the Roman state, which may explain why Oakley identified 366 BC as the date when surviving consular lists become significantly more reliable.[99]

98. Von Fritz (1950) 3–44.
99. Oakley (1997–2004) 1.39: "Whereas the [consuls'] names relating to the late sixth and early

Since soldiers in ancient armies often had some say over the selection of their commander, the *comitia centuriata* may have acquired the sole prerogative of selection or election of commanders at this time.[100] Although the *comitia centuriata* had certainly played an important role in selecting military commanders from the founding of the republic (or earlier), these rogations probably enhanced the power of the *comitia* by making it the *only* way a man could become a commander.

Although they wrote much later, Livy and Dionysius understood from their sources that the Roman people had acquired much more power over elections after the Sextian-Licinian Rogations. As the excerpt of L. Cincius (quoted in full earlier) indicates, patricians had long claimed that plebeians had no right to consult the auspices, and therefore they could not select military commanders but only approve (through acclamation) the commanders chosen by the patricians.[101] If true, this would mean that originally the *comitia centuriata* merely approved the choice of the patricians, although it might get to make a choice if the patricians supplied more candidates than needed. Dionysius makes it clear that patricians had many opportunities for controlling the results before and after the actual vote was taken: "In order that the voting [by the people] in the curiate assembly might be valid it was necessary that the senate should pass a preliminary decree and that the plebeians should vote on it by *curiae*, and that after both these votes the heavenly signs and omens should offer no opposition."[102] Furthermore, Livy indicates that — until 339 BC — the results of a consular election had to be ratified by the senate in order to be valid.[103] The requirement of a preliminary decree (προβούλευμα or *senatus consultum* or *patrum auctoritas*) enabled the senate to control consular elections in early Rome by making the pool of approved candidates as narrow

fifth centuries have long been one of the *causes célèbres* of classical scholarship, little controversy attaches to their counterparts in the fourth and third."

100. For example, the Macedonian army traditionally had the right to approve a new king by acclamation. See Potter (1996a) 133–34, esp. n. 13.

101. Livy 4.6.1–3, 6.41.4–12. Botsford (1909) 100–103, Linderski (1990b) 34–48, and Beard, North, and Price (1998) 1.64. On the patrician use of religious authority to dominate political affairs in early Rome, see Palmer (1970 [2009]) 191–280, Raaflaub (2005b) 198, Schiavone (2012) 66–79. Magdelain (1968) 30–35, emphasized the power of the aristocrats in the *comitia curiata* to choose commanders and invest them with *imperium*.

102. Dion. Hal. *AR* 9.41.3 (Cary, trans.) (cf. 9.42.3 and 9.49.4–5).

103. Livy 8.12.15. Although such ratification had always been necessary (see 6.42.10), a *lex Publilia* of 339 BC required the senate to ratify all measures proposed at the *comitia centuriata* in advance of the meeting in which the vote would be taken.

as it liked, even leaving the people with no choice at all.[104] Livy and Dionysius both record early elections in which only two candidates were put forward by the senate as candidates for the consulship, leaving the plebeians no choice but to approve those men the senators had chosen or to leave the assembly without casting any vote.[105] Even if the plebeians wished to vote for some other candidate, the centuriate assembly was designed to favor the votes of the wealthy, which was usually sufficient to guarantee that elections in the early republic followed the expectations of the rich patrician elites.

The Sextian-Licinian Rogations seem to have changed this. Although the aristocratic elite would continue to influence — and even dominate — elections in the middle republic, limitation of annual commanders to three praetors made selection by the *comitia centuriata* far more important, desirable, and competitive. As Stewart has suggested, "The Licinio-Sextian reforms redefined capacity for leadership as a political abstraction, a property of the citizen defined by comitial decision, and not a sacrally defined aura of the patriciate."[106] The Sextian-Licinian Rogations were said to have enabled plebeians to hold the consulship, but the patricians were wealthy and influential enough to retain a virtual monopoly over the three annual praetorships for many years, until the plebeians forced through the *lex Genucia* of 342 BC, which seems to have required that one of the annual praetors be reserved for a man of plebeian family.[107] This increasing strength wielded by the plebeians may have derived from the increased importance of the *comitia centuriata* in choosing (and not

104. Nicolet (1980) 237 points out the inability of the people in early Rome to elect anyone other than the candidates presented to them by the presiding magistrate: "It is probable that for a long time the people assembled by the magistrate in office had no right other than that of accepting or rejecting his proposed successor or successors"; and 239–40: "Originally the power of the presiding magistrate to designate his own successor was practically absolute: his task, according to the formula, was to 'ask (*rogare*) the people' to appoint the next holder of the office, by presenting them with one or several names to accept or choose from." See also Oakley (1997–2004) 2.525: "*Patrum auctoritas* must originally have been connected with patrician control of the auspices and denoted the opinion of the patricians that a legislative or electoral act of the *comitia curiata* or *centuriata* was auspicious."

105. Livy 1.43.10–12, and Dion. Hal. *AR* 4.21.1–3, 7.59.3–10, 8.82.6, 10.17.3, 11.10.4 give clear description of how the wealthy controlled elections in the centuriate assembly.

106. Stewart (1998) 136.

107. Livy 7.42.2. According to tradition, the Sextian-Licinian Rogations of 367 BC required that one of the consuls elected each year must be a plebeian, and *lex Genucia* of 342 BC enabled plebeians to hold both consulships (367 BC: Livy 6.35.5 and 40.18, Val. Max. 8.6.3, Plut. *Cam.* 39.1, Auct. *Vir. Ill.* 20; 342 BC: Livy 7.42.1–2, Zon. 7.25.9). As Billows (1989) 112–33 argues, however, the patterns in office holding do not support these statements but suggest that the Sextian-Licinian Rogations permitted plebeians to hold the consulship, while the *lex Genucia* required that one of the annual consulships be held by a plebeian.

just approving) military commanders. Thus, the rogations of 367 BC gave the people considerably more power in selecting their annual commanders.

The full significance of the Sextian-Licinian Rogations was obfuscated by later Greek and Roman writers, whose mistaken assumption that the consulship was original to the republic led them to describe the rogations as merely restoring the traditional consulship (albeit with the addition of two new magistracies) rather than establishing something new. Several scholars have recognized that the traditional description of the reforms brought about by these rogations is inaccurate, and two alternate interpretations of what happened have been suggested: at first, de Martino argued that the consulship was actually created (rather than restored) in 367 BC,[108] but now scholars increasingly view the Sextian-Licinian Rogations as establishing a college of three (and only three) praetors, two of whom eventually developed into the historical consuls.[109] Unfortunately, epigraphical evidence provides little illumination on the titles of Roman commanders in the fourth century BC. The earliest known appearance of the title consul is the tombstone of Scipio Barbatus, who held the consulship in 298 BC — nearly seventy years after de Martino believes the consulship to have been created.[110] More problematic: scholars believe this inscription was actually carved in the second half of the third century BC, meaning Barbatus may actually have been called praetor in 298 BC, but his descendants substituted the newer title consul to make clear to their contemporaries that he had held the highest office in Rome. So whether Barbatus was called praetor or consul when he was in office is unknown. The only other epigraphical evidence is equally vague: an inscription first published by Cristofani records a *C. Cenucio Clousino prai(tor)*, which probably refers to C. Genucius Clepsina, who was consul in 276 and 270 BC.[111] Since honorary inscriptions normally list a man's highest office first, and since Genucius is known to have

108. De Martino (1972a) 1.406–15 argued that the republic was originally governed by an annual dictator, which gave way to the decemvirate, which in turn gave way to a government by two unequal praetors or by three to six military tribunes with consular power, which (in 367 BC) finally gave way to the dual consulship.

109. For example: Heuss (1944) 69, de Sanctis (1960) 391–93, Stewart (1998) 95–126, Bunse (2001) 145–62, (2002a) 416–32, and (2002b) 29–43, Beck (2005) 63–70.

110. *CIL* 1^2 7 = *ILS* 1, in which Barbatus's career is listed as *consol censor aidilis*. See Coarelli (1972) 36–106, Wachter (1987) 301–42, Van Sickle (1987) 42–43 and n. 9, Flower (1996) 171–75. Oakley (1997–2004) 2.78 n. 2 points out that — according to Livy (4.20.5–7) — Augustus claimed that Cornelius Cossus had been a consul when he dedicated the *spolia opima* in ca. 437 BC. Augustus based this claim on his assertion that the title consul was evident on the dedication itself, which he had seen in the Temple of Jupiter Feretrius. Oakley is surely correct to imagine that Augustus was lying.

111. Cristofani (1986) 24–26.

held the consulship, this inscription may indicate that the title consul was not yet in use as late as 276 or 270 BC if—and only if—the *prai* in the inscription stands for *praitor* as Cristofani believes (Torelli has suggested the restoration *praifectos*).[112] Sometime after his consulship in 264 BC, however, M. Fulvius Flaccus set up two statues in the Forum Boarium, the bases of which were inscribed "M. Fulvius, the son of Quintus, as consul dedicated this with Volsinii captured" (*M. Folvio Q. f. cosol d. Volsinio capto*).[113] Without better evidence, we can only say that the title consul was being used in or shortly after 264 BC; it is not indisputably attested earlier.

Taken together, the events of 449 and 367 BC probably represent stages by which the Roman people imposed greater controls on the exercise of military command by their aristocracy. If this reconstruction is correct, these events represent a process in which the Roman people in their assemblies gradually claimed authority over the selection of military commanders and the authorization of their *imperium* and *auspicium*; thus, their concept of a commander moved closer to—and eventually merged with—the concept of magistrate. By establishing that only three praetors would be elected each year, the Sextian-Licinian Rogations inherently established (if such had not been the case previously) that those praetors served a full year in office. Before these rogations, Roman commanders probably exercised military command only for the duration of their campaign, which might last no more than a few days or weeks in the early republic. This is probably reflected in the strange fact that dictators were not permitted to hold office for more than six months, which must represent the maximum usual duration of a military command—namely, the summer campaigning season—in the early republic.[114] Rome's early generals may have originally held command only for as long as necessary, which is manifestly different from the year-round work performed by civilian magistrates. The determination in 367 BC that annual elections would choose praetors, and that men would be praetors for an entire year and not only when on active campaign, probably started the Romans thinking about what tasks other than military command a praetor might undertake for the state. As discussed previously, several scholars believe that Rome's military commanders were not originally involved in civilian governance, but this probably began to change in 367 BC as elected praetors began exploring ways to involve themselves in domestic affairs, and as the Roman people began looking to praetors as magistrates who

112. Cristofani (1987) 167 and Torelli (2000) 141–76.
113. Torelli (1968) 71–76.
114. Palmer (1970 [2009]) 216.

might supply desired government services. Although they were military commanders, the regular availability of the praetors (when not on campaign) — and the fact that selection by election conferred clear legitimacy — made them obvious choices to exercise certain administrative tasks in and around Rome, including jurisdiction and the leadership of the senate and certain citizen assemblies.

While the Sextian-Licinian Rogations guaranteed praetors a full year in office, it also limited them to that single year. In the early republic, aristocrats leading military campaigns (especially private war bands of retainers) probably acknowledged no temporal limit on their exercise of command, since their authority over their soldiers was more social and economic than legal. Some of these aristocrats probably led their war bands of retainers in private conflicts whenever necessary for as long as necessary, and their recurrence in Rome's records was interpreted by later annalists as an iteration of office. After 367 BC, however, aristocrats were faced with a stronger legal argument that their position as commander automatically expired at the end of their year, when the citizens elected new praetors to lead them in war. At first, the reckoning of a praetor's term may not have been precise, but as time went on and praetors acquired a regular role in domestic governance, the time limits on their authority became rigidly enforced; praetors (later, consuls) immediately lost their office at the end of the year even if no successors had been elected, in which case the senate had to appoint a special, short-term magistrate — the interrex — to hold the elections.[115] The new importance of elections also meant that commanders in the field could be replaced by successors, which placed new pressure on them to complete their assigned campaign within their allotted term; if they did not, they were compelled either to return to Rome with their task unachieved or to hand their army over to a successor.[116]

In the fourth century BC, the proximity of Rome's enemies normally gave commanders time to fight a major battle, and they could even conduct two entirely separate campaigns in one season.[117] Still, the competition for military

---

115. Cic. *Rep.* 2.23, Livy 1.17.5–11, 1.22.1, 4.43.7, Dion. Hal. *AR* 2.57.1, 8.90.4.

116. For example, in 340 BC the senate instructed the sitting consuls to resign early so their successors could take office immediately and have a full year to deal with a major Samnite uprising (Livy 8.3.4).

117. For example, in 341 BC the consul C. Plautius was assigned as his *provincia* two proximate but different enemies to subdue — the Privernates and Volscian Antiates — whom he defeated in separate battles (Livy 8.1.3). Likewise, in 335 the consul M. Valerius Corvus defeated the Ausonians in Cales, returned to Rome to celebrate a triumph for this victory, and then was given a second campaign against the Sidicini (Livy 8.16.4–11).

command after 367 BC, and the threat that one's command might run out before goals were achieved, probably added a level of urgency to the task. Since a military command was the best opportunity most aristocrats had for enhancing their family's social and political status among the glory-loving Romans, praetors were highly motivated to engage with the enemy, and the failure to achieve something noteworthy — whether from bad luck or poor strategy, or because of the strength of their enemy — was considered a major loss for the commander and his family.[118] Furthermore, the increasing domestic responsibilities of praetors (and, later, consuls) might have interfered with their opportunity to command: in 167 BC, the demand for civil governance was so high that the senate not only instructed a consul to delay leaving for his *provincia* until he had attended to certain affairs of state but it also commanded a praetor to remain in Rome to preside over the courts.[119] Any significant delay — even for good, strategic reasons — could result in the expiration of a man's military command before he had obtained his full measure of glory, and aristocrats who failed to cover themselves with glory in their first command rarely got a second chance.[120] This meant that Rome's aristocracy probably viewed military command in two different but complementary ways: the annual turnover of commands must have instilled a powerful sense of cohesion among the aristocracy, since they shared direct control of Rome's armies in turns, but the strict time limits on an individual's possession of a command must have driven generals to be extremely aggressive with their armies and jealous of their own opportunities for glory and honor.

Conclusion

The nature of our evidence on military commanders in the early republic is insufficient to make many definitive statements, but underlying themes in later sources suggest that the origins of Roman military command do not lie in the traditional account of a joint consulship that was established at the founda-

118. Livy (38.42.1, 40.53.4) sums up such inglorious campaigns with the simple statement that the commander achieved "nothing worthy of memory" (*nihil memoria dignum*).

119. Livy 45.16.4 and 17.6–7.

120. The Roman people had little respect for a commander who delayed engaging with his assigned enemy, even if such delay was beneficial for the state. The most famous example of this was the popular rejection of the delaying tactics that Q. Fabius Maximus "The Delayer" employed against Hannibal in the Second Punic War. Despite the success and wisdom of his tactics, the Romans were eager to replace Fabius with more aggressive commanders (Polyb. 3.103.1–4 and 106.1, Livy 22.8.6–7 and 22.34.1–35.7).

tion of the republic. Rather, two underlying trends are visible: military command was originally a separate sphere from civilian governance, and so the commander was originally understood to be different from the magistrate; and the early Romans understood military command to be a decentralized activity that could be undertaken simultaneously by several independent praetors or other commanders. The first is important because it suggests that military authority was originally different from civilian authority and that these sources of authority developed separately and independently of one another in the republic. Most studies of early Rome have begun with the understanding that military and civilian authority were fundamentally linked in the highest magistrates, a belief that has shaped discussions about the source, nature, and use of those authorities. By separating these two ideas, a different image of Rome appears, one in which military and civilian authorities are separate and unique. The conceptual distinction between commander and magistrate that prevailed in the early republic is critical for understanding the sometimes-conflicting nature of the consulship and praetorship in later periods, a topic that is considered in later chapters.

The diffuse nature of military command in the early republic is a revision to the traditional (and still widespread) view that two consuls were always Rome's generals. Much of our understanding of early Roman military command is based on the assumption that it had always been a centralized concept that originated with the kings and passed directly to two chief magistrate-commanders at the foundation of the republic. This assumption has prevented us from seeing clearly how Rome's ideas of military authority and command expanded and developed over time. Understanding that the republic started with a far less centralized and regularized system of command enables us to view later political and military phenomena in a better light and to make sense of long-standing problems. Because military command was not a single, unitary idea in the early republic but took several forms and was brought under state control only gradually, we need to view Roman provincial command as a developing concept that evolved easily. Whereas the traditional accounts portray a concept of military command that remained basically unchanged from the foundation of the republic, the arguments in this chapter show a far more dynamic set of concepts that could change and develop. The foundation of Roman military thinking was based not on a constitutional government that took shape immediately after the last king was exiled but on the flexibility and independence of the republic's early patrician elite.

2

FUNDAMENTAL CONCEPTS
OF AUTHORITY IN EARLY ROME
(TO 367 BC)

The study of early Rome is challenging not only because of the poverty of the primary source material but also because it requires chasing a moving target. Roman social, political, and military practices were not static monuments but dynamic concepts that evolved over time, making it difficult to know where to place the snippets of information we have. As the previous chapter demonstrated, the military commander was a changing and developing idea in the early republic, and although the Romans would eventually develop what we know as their classical republican government, their military commanders would continue to be influenced by earlier traditions, and the nature of military command would continue to evolve as Rome's empire grew. Although historians writing in the late republic had access to older sources and information, they often did not understand the proper context for that material and had no reason to believe that Roman culture and practices had changed over the centuries, with the result that their misinterpretations have been passed on to modern scholars to sort out. As Cornell points out,

> The preservation and transmission of traditional stories of the city's past should in no sense be seen as an attempt to understand the archaic period as it really was. Rather, the Romans of the late Republic saw the remote past as an idealized and exemplary model of their own society. They seem to have been almost totally unaware of the gulf that separated them from the archaic world of the fifth century BC.[1]

This shortcoming of the ancient writers, combined with the limited material that survives, makes it difficult to discuss what happened in the early republic.

1. Cornell (2005) 59.

Indeed, scholars are increasingly realizing how much of our information on early Rome comes from folklore, which, although not necessarily false, was subject to alteration and adjustment over time.[2] This does not render the early republic unrecoverable, but it requires that the sources be evaluated carefully and judiciously to see what clues they can give for reconstructing the concept and practice of military command in that early period. This chapter examines the most basic and fundamental concepts of authority that defined the early military commander in Roman tradition, and it attempts to create a foundation from which to chart the evolution of military command in later periods. First, the traditional separation of Roman space into the spheres *domi* and *militiae* is examined, since these definitions of space greatly influenced Roman thinking on authority and its application, use, and limits. Then, the chapter looks at the three most fundamental types of authority exercised by military commanders: the *potestas* they (eventually) held as civil magistrates, the *auspicium* they possessed as intermediaries between the state and its gods, and the *imperium* they wielded as military commanders. As absolutely fundamental components of authority in Roman thinking, these three types served to define Roman magistrates and military commanders throughout the republic. The intent of this chapter is not to write a history of the early republic but to examine how later Romans remembered and wrote about these core principles of military command and to argue that these accounts reveal trends and concepts that illustrate the development of the Roman commander. This chapter limits itself to looking at the application of these core principles for understanding military commanders; although they also have relevance for understanding the civilian role played by Rome's chief magistrates, this aspect of *potestas*, *auspicium*, and *imperium* is examined only tangentially and in reference to Rome's generals. By studying the core components that defined a man as a military commander, this chapter both defines a commander in Roman thought and establishes a starting point from which to study the evolution of the commander and ideas of provincial command.

Domi Militiaeque

The Romans had several ways of conceiving of space, but one of the most basic divisions was to distinguish between the civilian and military spheres, which they denoted by the locatives at home and at war: *domi* and *militiae* (although

2. Ungern-Sternberg (1988), Wiseman (1989) 129–37, (1994), and (1998), Flower (1996), Hölkeskamp (1996), Blösel (2003).

for the latter concept *belli* is sometimes used).[3] Although this division had several applications in Roman society, one of the most important was the role it played in defining the authority and competences of magistrates and military commanders. Within the sphere *domi*, civil law prevailed, which meant that the rights and privileges of citizens (*cives*) were normally protected and given precedence over the broad authority and prerogatives of the magistrates. In the sphere *domi*, the citizen body in its assemblies was considered the highest authority and had the right to prohibit its elected magistrates from taking a particular course of action, and all elected magistrates had to swear to obey the laws of the Roman people.[4] Even the highest regular magistrates (consuls or military tribunes) were not permitted to order summary scourging or execution of citizens *domi* without due process of law, and citizens had the right to seek protection against the judgments of the magistrates by making an appeal to the People or to the tribunes of the plebs, whose sacrosanctity was backed and guaranteed by the citizen body as a whole, which enabled them to hinder magisterial action through intercession and formal veto. *Domi* thus referred to the sphere in which the authority of the citizen body was paramount and elected magistrates were expected to respect the rights and privileges of each individual citizen, the sphere that in earliest Rome would have comprised only the city proper and the immediate countryside.

The sphere *militiae*, on the other hand, signified the military sphere where Rome's armies fought bloody wars of conquest and Rome's generals possessed the unlimited and unrestrained authority to punish citizens (brutally and mercilessly if necessary) who were guilty of military negligence or cowardice. In the zone *militiae*, Rome's commanders were permitted to exercise what we might think of as martial law, which meant that they could suspend or ignore the civil rights of Roman soldiers if necessary to guarantee the effectiveness of Rome's armies. As Brand describes it:

> By reason of the requirements of command the organization of an army, as a community, is vastly and fundamentally different from the organization of a civil community. The civil community is ordinarily conceived of as existing for the benefit of the individuals that compose it, and its organization and standards of conduct prescribed by its laws and customs are de-

3. Mommsen (1887–88) 1.61–75, Rüpke (1990) 29–41, Woolf (1993) 173, Taylor (2000) 24–25, Sandberg (2001) 119–23.

4. Oath: Livy 31.50.6–10. That the citizen body held the exclusive prerogative to elect magistrates, to pass laws, and to judge capital law cases (Polyb. 6.14.1–12) is also an indication of their supremacy in the civil sphere. See also Botsford (1909), Staveley (1955), Millar (1998) 204, Hölkeskamp (2010) 60.

signed primarily to promote the happiness and well-being of its individual members. In an army, on the other hand, individuals exist for the benefit of, and as a part of, the organized fighting group.[5]

In the sphere *militiae*, Roman citizens were treated differently by their leaders, and soldiers enjoyed few to none of their normal civil protections. Indeed, a Roman general could order the summary execution of up to 10 percent of his army, with the result that hundreds of Roman citizens could be immediately killed without recourse to appeal.[6] Although some checks seem to have been placed on the general's authority to punish his soldiers in later periods (such as the *lex Porcia*, which was supposed to protect soldiers from the harshest penalties), the vital importance of maintaining military discipline in war meant that generals were free to subordinate civic rights to martial law when needed.[7] Since the term *militiae* designated a military sphere in which Roman commanders conducted warfare, the physical location of the spheres *militiae* changed constantly as Rome contended with different enemies (see the discussion of *provincia* in the next section). The Romans, therefore, had two very different ideas about magisterial authority: the power of magistrates was to be subordinate to the citizens in the civilian sphere, but in the military sphere the rights of citizens were subordinated to the authority of the commander.

The conceptual distinction between *domi* (the sphere of civil law) and *militiae* (the sphere of martial law) is fairly clear. But how did Romans distinguish between the two spheres in practice? One aspect is easy to determine: the city of Rome was always considered *domi*. This identification is obvious and may go back to the regal period, because Livy states that the original census established by Servius included only the four urban tribes, indicating that the city and its immediate environs may have been the entirety of the state.[8] The city

5. Brand (1968) x–xii.

6. Polyb. 6.37.1–38.1, Livy 2.59.10–11, Dion. Hal. *AR* 9.50.6–7, Plut. *Crass.* 10.2–3. See Lintott (1999b) 41–43.

7. Lintott (1972) 251: "At best a *lex Porcia* mitigated the severity of a military flogging"; and Hölkeskamp (2011) 174: "And even when in the wake of the *leges Porciae*, Roman citizens formally came to enjoy the right to *provocatio* outside Rome herself, the privilege could easily turn out to be rather precarious when a power-conscious and arrogant magistrate and an ordinary citizen met anywhere else, especially in the provinces." On the *lex Porcia* and the limited use of *provocatio* in the provinces, see also Heuss (1944) 121–24, McDonald (1944) 18–20, Bleicken (1959), Martin (1970) 87–91, Rüpke (1990) 41–43, Jehne (2002), Brennan (2004) 46–47.

8. Livy 1.43.13. See Nicholls (1956) 225–54, Taylor (1960) 5, and Ogilvie (1965) 175. In early Rome, most of the urban population could likely fit within the city boundary (the *pomerium*) and the walls, so these barriers probably marked the limits of the territorial sphere *domi* (the Campus

was where Roman citizens were best able to enforce their civil rights, since the tribunes of the plebs were available to intercede against magisterial abuse, and mobs of citizens were at hand to whom one could likewise appeal for help. For this reason, a citizen's civilian rights were best protected in Rome because the city was full of civilians willing to defend those rights.[9] Furthermore, military persons and powers were forbidden inside Rome's ancient boundary, the *pomerium*. Although the original purpose of the *pomerium* is not clear, there is no doubt that it was a sacred boundary and that it served to mark the city — which originally fit entirely within its circle — as a civilian sphere into which military authority (martial law) could not reach.[10] The ancient sources are clear that military authority and all things military could not cross the *pomerium* and enter the city: generals could not use their military authority in the city or bring soldiers in the city without special authorization; a departing general could not put on his military uniform until he had exited the city; and the centuriate assembly had to meet outside the *pomerium* because it was organized in military units (centuries).[11] Even after the city of Rome expanded over and beyond the circle of the *pomerium*, that boundary continued to represent an absolute line across which martial law and all things military simply could not cross without the specific permission of the state.

Because of the absoluteness of this regulation, modern historians reasonably posit that the *pomerium* marked the border between the spheres *domi* and *militiae*, but this is probably a mistake. Giovannini is surely correct that the sphere *domi* extended beyond the *pomerium* and that — with the exception of the city of Rome — the terms *domi* and *militiae* were not simply geographic dis-

---

Martius, which was adjacent to the city and where the army and the militarily structured *comitia centuriata* met, was *militiae*). By the late republic, however, the city had expanded beyond its walls and *pomerium*, so the physical space of the city that was considered *domi* was expanded to include all territory within one mile from the *pomerium* (*RS* 24 l.20, Livy 3.20.7, Dio 51.19.6, Gaius *Inst.* 4.104).

9. A full discussion of early *provocatio* within the *pomerium* is beyond the scope of the current work, but see Bleicken (1955) and (1959) 324–77, Staveley (1955) 413, Martin (1970) 87–91, Bauman (1973), Ogilvie (1976) 127, Develin (1978a) 45–60, Nicolet (1980) 317–24, Hölkeskamp (1987) 143–45 and 199–200, Mitchell (1990) 169–74 and 199, Rüpke (1990) 41–43, Cornell (1995) 276–78, Sandberg (2001) 119, 103, and 127, Jehne (2002).

10. On the sacred nature of the *pomerium*, see Livy 1.44.3–4, Plut. *Rom.* 11.4 and *QR* 27, Gell. 10.15.4, 13.14.1–15.4, Varro *LL* 5.143. See also Mommsen (1887–88) 1.63–70, Richardson (1975) 58–60, Magdelain (1976) 155–91, (1977b) 71–109 and (1990) 209–11, 224, 228, Nippel (1984) 20, Linderski (1986) 2156–57, Rüpke (1990) 29–41, Liou-Gille (1993) 94–95, Cornell (1995) 202–4, Beard, North, and Price (1998) 1.177–81, Sandberg (2001) 119–23, Fraschetti (2005) 36–38.

11. Gell. 15.27.5: *centuriata autem comitia intra pomerium fieri nefas esse, quia exercitum extra urbem imperari oporteat, intra urbem imperari ius non sit.*

tinctions but expressions of magisterial operation: *domi* signified the sphere of civilian life and governance, whereas *militiae* indicated the sphere of war and military activity.[12] While the pollution connected with war was forbidden inside the *pomerium* (making the city inside that barrier definitively *domi*), both spheres (*domi* and *militiae*) existed outside of the *pomerium*, and they distinguished and separated the two fundamental notions of authority that defined the relationship between magistrates and citizens. In peaceful, civilian affairs (*domi*), it was understood that the citizens collectively exercised the highest authority and possessed certain fundamental rights; but in military endeavors (*militiae*), the citizens suspended these rights and yielded supreme authority to their highest magistrates to ensure an effective army and the survival of the state. For this reason, Roman soldiers when enlisting in the army swore sacred oaths of obedience that suspended all of the protections they regularly enjoyed as citizens.[13] Cicero explained this distinction well:

> But just as the sailor, when the sea suddenly grows rough, and the invalid when his illness becomes severe, both implore the assistance of one man, so our people, that in times of peace and while engaged at home wield authority, threaten even their magistrates, refuse to obey them, and appeal from one to the other or to the people, yet in time of war yield obedience to their rulers as to a king, for safety prevails over caprice.[14]

Domi thus represented the sphere of civilian law, whereas *militiae* was the sphere of military or martial law.

For the Romans, the default status was *domi*, which meant that citizens normally expected to possess certain privileges and protections against the magistrate's authority and powers of coercion. In other words, anywhere in the world that a Roman magistrate might go, he was expected to allow any private Roman citizens he encountered the full protections and rights they enjoyed under civil law.[15] Thus citizenship itself gave a man certain protec-

---

12. Giovannini (1983) 1–26, esp. 13: "Si l'on acceptait la définition que Mommsen a donnée de l'opposition entre *domi* et *militiae*, il faudrait admettre que les habitants de la ville de Rome se trouvaient *domi* de leur vivant, mais *militiae* après leur mort, que pour aller vénérer leurs ancêtres, ils devaient passer du domaine *domi* au domaine *militiae*, que leur habitation se trouvait *domi*, mais que leur terre se trouvait *militiae*."

13. Polyb. 6.21.1–3, Livy 3.20.3, 22.11.8, 22.38.1–5, 28.27.4 and 12, Dion. Hal. *AR* 10.18.1, 11.43.2.

14. Cic. *Rep.* 1.63 (Keyes, trans.).

15. When Cicero prosecuted C. Verres on behalf of the Sicilians in 70 BC, one of this most serious allegations was that Verres as governor of Sicily had illegally beaten and executed Roman citizens (Cic. *Verr.* 2.5.72 and 161–63). Although Verres was a provincial commander invested with *imperium*,

tions against magisterial abuse of authority, even if he happened to be outside of Rome. This protection was useful because a magistrate's civilian authority (*potestas*) — that is, his ability to exercise his official prerogatives within the restraints of civil law — was in no way diminished or changed when he left the city of Rome. Senior magistrates could summon the senate and conduct state business outside of the *pomerium* as well as within, and strictly civilian officers like quaestors (who were not invested with military authority) regularly exercised their authority away from the city.[16] Crossing the *pomerium* by either entering or exiting the city had no notable effect on the civilian authority of the magistrate since the sphere *domi* existed inside and outside the *pomerium*. Thus a private citizen on his farm could expect to enjoy the protections of his civil rights, although his distance from Rome (and from the tribunes and mobs of his fellow citizens) reduced his ability to obtain help against a magistrate's authority if he felt himself unjustly treated. *Domi* not only was the sphere of civil law but could also be taken as shorthand for the status of a private citizen, who was entitled to the traditional protections (particularly the right of appeal) when confronted by the authority of a magistrate. For this reason, a commander was not permitted to use the absolute power of his military authority (*imperium*) within the sphere *domi* unless specifically instructed to do so by the state (as discussed below). In practical terms, most citizens away from Rome might have great difficulty asserting their rights in the face of a Roman commander who was determined to violate those rights, but this does not diminish the fundamental distinction of the spheres *domi* and *militiae*. The *pomerium*, therefore, marked the city as *domi*, thereby excluding *imperium* from the city but not precluding other areas outside the city from being *domi* as well.

In addition, the *pomerium* was also a religious boundary that was intended to protect the state against enemies, and the Romans were meticulous in maintaining the *pomerium* as a secure religious barrier around the city.[17] Evidence

---

the civilian citizens he killed on Sicily were understood to possess the same protections against beating and execution that citizens enjoyed in Rome.

16. Consuls returning from military command could summon the senate to meet outside of the *pomerium* (Livy 28.9.5, 31.47.7, 33.22.1, 36.39.5); quaestors served as financial officers in consular armies every year (Polyb. 6.31.2, 39.15, 10.19.1, Cic. *Verr.* 2.1.40, 2.3.177, *Fam.* 2.15.4, *Mur.* 18, *Vat.* 11–12, Sall. *Jug.* 29.5–6, Livy 22.49.16) and as supervisors of the granaries of Ostia (Cic. *Mur.* 18 and *Sest.* 39) and elsewhere in Italy (Cic. *Vat.* 12, *Sest.* 39, *Har. Resp.* 43, *Mur.* 18, *Att.* 2.9.1). Although tribunes and aediles were normally expected to remain in Rome — tribunes in particular were not supposed to go beyond the first milestone from the city — they are nevertheless recorded being sent on missions away from Rome (Livy 29.20.4–5 and 22.1).

17. Cicero (*ND* 3.94) refers to Rome being encircled by religious protections even more than by

for this is found in Gellius, who cites a second-century AD work by Laelius Felix that preserved a passage by M. Antistius Labeo:

> A *comitia calata* is an assembly that is held before the college of pontiffs, for the sake of inaugurating either the king or the flamens. Moreover, some of these assemblies are "curiate" and others "centuriate"; the "curiate" are convoked by a curiate lictor — for *"calari"* here means "convoke" — and the "centuriate" by a trumpeter.[18]

Why should some flamens be inaugurated by the *comitia calata curiata* and others by the *comitia calata centuriata*? Botsford pointed out that the *flamen Martialis* was inaugurated outside the *pomerium*, because all shrines to the war god Mars were located outside the *pomerium*, and the most important shrine was in the Campus Martius.[19] Cicero made it plain that crossing the *pomerium* while performing the auspices violated augural law and automatically caused the invalidation of those auspices, demonstrating that the *pomerium* was an absolute barrier in Roman religious thought and practice.[20] The *pomerium* thus divided two fundamentally different religious spheres: *auspicia urbana* and *auspicia militiae*.[21] *Auspicium* was the practice of consulting the gods on important matters, and the *pomerium* marked the city as a unique augural zone that was specifically created to enable magistrates and certain priests to consult

---

walls (*vos pontifices ... diligentiusque urbem religione quam ipsis moenibus cingitis*). Beard, North, and Price (1998) 1.177–81, esp. 178: "Rome could never allow another Remus to cross the *pomerium*; at times of threat the boundary had to be purified and strengthened."

18. Antistius Labeo in Gellius 15.27.1-2: *"calata" comitia esse quae pro conlegio pontificum habentur, aut regis aut flaminum inaugurandorum causa. Eorum autem alia esse "curiata," alia "centuriata"; "curiata" per lictorem curiatum "calari," id est "convocari," "centuriata" per cornicinem.* In this context, *regis* should be taken to signify the *rex sacrorum*. The *pontifices* also summoned and presided over the *comitia curiata* for the process of adoption known as *adrogatio* (Gell. 5.19.6).

19. Botsford (1909) 153–56.

20. Cic. *Div.* 1.33 and 2.75, *ND* 2.10–12. Cicero explains that the auspical ceremony conducted by Tiberius Gracchus during the consular elections for 162 BC had been invalid because Tiberius had crossed the *pomerium* before completing the auspices.

21. Varro *LL* 5.143: ([discussing the *pomerium*] *post ea qui fiebat orbis, urbis principium; qui quod erat post murum, postmoerium dictum, eo usque auspicia urbana finiuntur*); Cic. *Div.* 1.95 (*omitto nostros, qui nihil in bello sine extis agunt, nihil sine auspiciis domi externa videamus*); and 2.77: (*ubi ergo avium divinatio? quae, quoniam ab eis, qui auspicia nulla habent, bella administrantur, ad urbanas res retenta videtur, a bellicis esse sublata*). See also Cic. *ND* 2.10–12, Gell. 13.14.1 and 13.15.4, Varro *LL* 6.53. See Mommsen (1887–88) 1.64 n. 6, Develin (1977) 57–59, Magdelain (1977a) 13, Giovannini (1983) 55–56, Stewart (1998) 124, Sandberg (2001) 121–22 and n. 14. Brennan (2000) 253 n. 89 argued that the distinction between *auspicia urbana* and *auspicia bellica* is not attested, but points to Cic. *Div.* 2.77 (*auspicium militare*).

the gods on the public affairs of the Roman people. Whereas a Roman magistrate might use his civilian authority (*potestas*) anywhere he went, the exercise of *auspicium* was fundamentally and necessarily dependent on the definition of religious space. As Beard, North, and Price clearly defined it,

> Augural expertise, therefore, concerned not just the interpretation of signs but the demarcation of religious space and its boundaries. . . . One of the most important lines of division was the *pomerium*, the sacred and augural boundary of the city; it was only within this boundary that the "urban auspices" (*auspicia urbana*) were valid; and magistrates had to be careful to take the auspices again if they crossed the *pomerium* in order to re-establish correct relations with the gods.[22]

The *pomerium* was first and foremost a religious boundary that distinguished spheres of religious activity. It did not limit or have an effect on the civilian authority (*potestas*) of magistrates, and although *imperium* was normally forbidden inside the sphere marked by the *pomerium*, exceptions to this prohibition could be made by the people, indicating that this was a legal or social prohibition that was created and managed by the citizens. Thus, the religious nature of the *pomerium* did not block *imperium* from entering the city; rather, the *pomerium* was a marker that defined a sphere in which *imperium* (and therefore the sphere *militiae*) was normally forbidden by law or customary practice. In this way, the *pomerium* itself did not create a distinction between the spheres *domi* and *militiae*, because the former existed both inside and outside the *pomerium*, and the latter could exist inside the city when the people wished.

While the sphere *domi* extended anywhere a Roman magistrate might go, the sphere *militiae* was much more specific. The sphere *militiae* indicated the legal relationship that existed between a commander and his soldiers: martial law made the commander the supreme legal authority in his sphere of operation, enabling him to override the normal protections of civil law, including the all-important right of appeal. Such monarchical authority is necessary in the conduct of war, where it is usually considered acceptable to devalue democratic process and civil law to ensure an effective military and the survival of the state.[23] Such overriding authority applies only to those specifically under

---

22. Beard, North, Price (1998) 1.23.

23. Cicero (*Man.* 60) indicates this Roman willingness to make concessions when faced with the necessity in war: "I forbear to mention here that our forefathers always bowed to precedent in peace but to expediency in war" (*non dicam hoc loco maiores nostros semper in pace consuetudini, in bello utilitati paruisse*) (Grose Hodge, trans.).

the authority of the commander—not to any other citizens the commander happened to encounter. When enlisting in the state's legions, Roman soldiers took an oath and implicitly placed themselves under the absolute authority of their commander and understood that martial law superseded their peacetime rights. Private citizens, on the other hand, retained the protections of civil law even if they were outside of the city, and Roman commanders were expected to show restraint and not impose the full weight of martial law on such private citizens. Thus the sphere *militiae* indicated the legal relationship between a commander and his soldiers during the conduct of a military campaign, and not a specific geographic region. If the sphere *domi* signified the normal civilian relationship between Roman citizens and their magistrates, the sphere *militiae* represented an exception to the general rule—a particular and defined activity or endeavor in which citizens yielded their civic rights by becoming soldiers. Rome's citizen assemblies demonstrate this distinction well: the *comitia centuriata* met in military units (centuries) outside the city under the leadership of a magistrate with *imperium*, and in these meetings the authority of the presiding commander was absolute.[24] Matters of civilian governance, on the other hand, were normally handled by the *comitia tributa* or the *concilium plebis*, both of which met inside the city where *imperium* was normally forbidden and where tribunes could use their veto to block the actions of senior magistrates. This indicates that the division between *domi* and *militiae* penetrated to the core of Roman government, so that decisions in each sphere were handled by different assemblies of citizens.

The sharp distinction between *domi* and *militiae* suggests that in early Rome the authority and activity of the military commander were understood to be fundamentally different things from the authority and activity of civilian magistrates. This is corroborated by the *pomerium*, a religious boundary that— among other things—placed constraints on military authority without having a noticeable effect on civilian authority. Taken together, this suggests that military commanders were originally different from civilian officials and were excluded from the civilian sphere. As commanders began performing more tasks of civilian administration in the fourth and third centuries BC, the distinc-

---

24. In the consular elections of 215 BC, the consul Q. Fabius Maximus threatened to use physical violence and perhaps execution to silence opposition to his management of the elections (Livy 24.9.1–3). Only magistrates with the military authority of *imperium* (consuls, praetors, and dictators) were supposed to convene the centuriate assembly, while tribunes of the plebs and even aediles (as well as consuls, dictators, and praetors) could convene the tribal assembly (Gell. 13.15.4, Botsford [1909] 465).

tion between commander and magistrate became blurred and even conflated, although the prohibition on *imperium* in the city remained clear. Although these archaic praetors (and, later, consuls) became increasingly important as civilian magistrates within the city, they remained hybrids of two distinctly different traditions (military and civilian), a mixed nature that would characterize them throughout the republic.

The Influence of Magisterial Office on Military Command

Although the association of military leadership and magisterial office may not have been original to the republic, it was certainly the case that by 367 BC (if not earlier) the Roman people had determined that legitimate military authority would only be invested in magistrates selected by the state. While this practice did not erase the older traditions of military leadership, it did impose greater limitation and definition on the concept of the military commander. Rome was certainly not unique in deciding to unite military command and civilian magistracy, but there were other possibilities: its enemy Carthage separated civilian and military authority, enabling its generals to wield a different type of authority and to operate in a separate administrative structure from the civilian leaders of state.[25] While a detailed study of Rome's civilian magistracies is beyond the scope of the current work, it is necessary to consider briefly how the definitions of magisterial office shaped the position and activity of the military commander. In particular, this section intends to show that the civilian authority wielded by consuls and praetors in the late Republic was fundamentally different from their military authority.

There has long been a tendency in modern scholarship to see consular authority over civilian and military affairs as deriving from a single source of authority— *imperium*. This belief stems from the ancient tradition that the consulship was created in 509 BC to act as Rome's supreme magistrate-commanders, inheriting the all-encompassing regal authority of the exiled king. As discussed in chapter 1, however, this portrayal is almost certainly incorrect. Lacking accurate information and the inclination to imagine their past as having been substantially different from their present, the annalists inaccurately presented the early consulship as virtually identical to the consulship of the late republic, which did indeed exercise both military and civilian authority. Acceptance of the traditional account has led many scholars to be-

25. Lazenby (1998) 7, Hoyos (2003) 30.

lieve that the consulship was created to exercise universal authority in both of these areas. This established a common misunderstanding that military and civilian authorities were somehow related and intertwined into a singular consular authority, causing some misinterpretation of each. Commanders and magistrates, however, were originally different and distinct figures in the early republic, and each possessed a unique type of authority. Only in the fourth century BC did the roles of the commander and magistrate merge in a single official, but even then these two functions (and the authorities that enabled them) remained fundamentally separate. By demonstrating that civilian and military authorities were separate and distinct, we can understand the nature of the provincial commander more clearly.

Potestas was the most fundamental and basic authority invested in all Roman magistrates. It permitted them to perform various duties of government under the aegis of civil law, which limited the amount of force magistrates could use in domestic governance, thereby providing protection to citizens against excessive mistreatment.[26] As I have argued elsewhere, *potestas* was the only legal authority any magistrate needed to fulfill his civilian responsibilities in the city.[27] Since all Roman citizens in the republic theoretically enjoyed freedom (*libertas*) from despotic rule, only a magistrate invested with *potestas* had the right (in varying degrees) to give orders and otherwise impose his will on free citizens. Because of the considerable prerogatives and legal capacities of Roman magistrates, the Roman people normally controlled the bestowal of *potestas* through their assemblies, as only elected officials normally held magisterial *potestas*. Thus official *potestas* (i.e., *potestas* conferred by the state) was the most fundamental trait that defined a man as a civilian magistrate, but this was not necessarily the case for military commanders, who in the early republic

26. Mommsen (1887–88) 1.22–24, 116–18, Staedler (1942b) 116, Hellegouarc'h (1972) 240, 309–10, Kunkel (1973) 15–17, Lowenstein (1973) 48, Schiller (1978) 174, Stephenson (1992) 142, Kunkel and Wittmann (1995) 21–28, Lintott (1999a) 95–96, Buonauro (2002), and Brennan (2004) 38. *Contra*: Bleicken (1981) 266, who calls *potestas* "ein abstrakter Begriff zur Bezeichnung und Verdeutlichung eines Bezugssystems." On the other hand, he does recognize the importance of this idea for the functioning of a magistrate (278–87). Bleicken is correct that *potestas* is an abstract idea in itself, but when it is used in reference to a specific magistracy, such as the phrase tribunician *potestas*, it then conveys a specific set of concrete powers and attributes. See also Giovannini (1983) 34, who believes that *potestas* was less important than *auspicium* for defining a magistrate. For the limitations on magisterial use of force, see Staveley (1955), Bleicken (1959), Brunt (1961), Martin (1970), Lintott (1972) and (1974), Bauman (1973), Develin (1979), Jehne (2002).

27. Drogula (2007) 419–52, where I demonstrate that *potestas* provided sufficient authority to enable all magistrates to perform their civilian duties, and where I refute the widely held belief that the highest magistrates also used *imperium* to perform civilian responsibilities inside the *pomerium*.

were often clan leaders and aristocratic strongmen leading private war bands. Such commanders had authority over their private military resources outside the city, but they held no official status or authority over civilians inside the *pomerium*. Even those men chosen to lead Rome's combined forces did not necessarily have *potestas* within the city during the early republic; they were chosen to perform a military task only. As the Romans increasingly subordinated military commanders to state control, however, there can be no doubt that those commanders gained the status of magistrates and thus began possessing and using *potestas* for administrative activities within the city.

Because *potestas* was the legal authority that enabled a man to act as a civil magistrate, it also empowered him to impose and enforce the law through the exercise of jurisdiction over those aspects of law entrusted to the care of his office. According to the accounts of the early republic, all of the normal magistrates—consuls, praetors, quaestors, tribunes of the plebs, and the aediles—exercised some degree of judicial authority. Although consuls were certainly thought to be the highest magistrates, and praetors frequently ran the lawcourts, tribunes of the plebs carried out most of the important prosecutions in the republic, while quaestors, aediles, and *tresviri capitales* dealt with smaller offenses.[28] Because the word quaestor probably comes from the Latin *quaerere* (to seek), this office may have even been created specifically to inquire into legal disputes.[29] Consuls, on the other hand, were the only magistrates who did *not* exercise judicial authority on a regular basis: de Martino even argued that consuls never possessed jurisdiction in Rome, a position that is difficult to prove or refute because of the absence of any ancient evidence to the contrary.[30] The exercise of jurisdiction is one of the most common attributes of all major magistrates and was not unique to those entitled to take up *imperium*.

Modern historians overwhelmingly believe that the *iurisdictio* of consuls

28. *The Twelve Tables* 9.4, Cic. *Verr.* 2.1.12–14, 5.173, *Sest.* 95, Livy 2.41.11, 3.24.3 and 7, Dion. Hal. *AR* 6.90.2–3, 8.77.1–2, 10.1.3, Fest. 247L, Gell. 4.2.1–12, 14.2, 10.6.3–4. The quaestors seem to have lost many of their judicial responsibilities in the second century BC as standing courts (with praetors as judges) were established. On *tresviri capitales*, see *RS* 45 = Gell. 468L. See Mommsen (1887–88) 2.543–44, Botsford (1909) 245, Lintott (1999b) 102–6.

29. Varro *LL* 5.81: *quaestores a quaerendo, qui conquirerent publicas pecunias et maleficia.* See also Cic. *Rep.* 2.60, Livy 2.41.11 and 3.24.3–7.

30. De Martino (1972a) 1.420–22. While scholars generally agree that there is no evidence for consuls exercising jurisdiction over civilian affairs in Rome (although extraordinary criminal *quaestiones* are recorded), they believe possession of *imperium* automatically conferred jurisdiction on consuls, whether or not they used it. See Leifer (1914) 206–24, Brennan (2000) 63, and Pina Polo (2011) 122.

and praetors derived from their *imperium domi*,[31] but this view generally derives from two mistaken assumptions. First, Byzantine law, and in particular Justinian's *Digesta*, makes a clear connection between *imperium* and *iurisdictio*, and the clarity and precision of these documents have persuaded many scholars to assume this connection derived from early republican practice, but this fails to take into account the considerable development of Rome's legal system, including the rise of legal thinking and jurisprudence, that took place between the early and middle republic and the high empire. In particular, the establishment of the imperial monarchy brought about tremendous changes in Roman thinking about the nature of *imperium*, which took on nuances that were unheard of in the republic.[32] Schiavone, a legal historian, has articulated the substantial revisions, modifications, and changes the compilers of the *Digesta* made in its composition:

> Since the *Digesta* were to appear for so many years as a code, and not as an anthology, over the centuries the constituent texts would not only be viewed (almost always) outside of any historical perspective, but also in a light that compromised the perception of their very quality. They would be seen not for what they truly were — fragments of literary works that needed to be reintegrated into their original context, as historians do with every other aspect of ancient cultures when faced with incomplete and gap-riddled transmissions — but rather as well-framed and carefully sorted articles of a unitary legislative apparatus.[33]

Richardson also articulates this problem clearly in his important study on *imperium* and the *provincia*:

> The citations in the *Digest* are short and thus sometimes lack content. Perhaps more important, however, is the uncertainty as to the content of the citations, since the collection was edited and interpolated by the com-

31. For example: Mommsen (1887–88) 1.22, Lauria (1930) 479–538, esp. 486–93, Jolowicz and Nicholas (1972) 45, 49, 226, Hoffman (1976) 358, Schiller (1978) 179, Rüpke (1990) 41, Robinson (1997) 4, Lintott (1999a) 96–97, Brennan (2000) 63, Mousourakis (2007) 12, Pina Polo (2011) 122.

32. For example, Justinian's *Digest* (2.1.3.pr [Ulpian]) recognized three different types of *imperium*: pure (*merum*), mixed (*mixtum*), and greater (*maius*), all of which would have been completely alien to a Roman of the middle republic. Mousourakis (2007) ix notes that "during its long history Roman law went through a remarkable process of evolution. It passed through different stages of development and underwent important transformations, both in substance and in scope, keeping up with changes in society, especially with those changes brought about by Rome's expansion in the ancient world."

33. Schiavone (2012) 5–41 (33 quoted).

pilers on the instructions of the emperor, in order to make the sense clear and bring the material up to date. The extent of these interpolations has been a matter of dispute among scholars for over a century, but there is no doubt that there has been some considerable editorial work. The uncertainty that this creates adds to the problems always present in determining exactly what an ancient author wrote and requires extra care when tracing the usage of particular words.[34]

Despite the apparent clarity of later legal thinking, imperial conceptions of *imperium* are shaky evidence at best for its original definition and usage, and a reliance on the *Digesta* and similar legal texts can mislead as well as inform.

Second, Livy states that the praetorship was created in 367 BC to administer justice in the city (*qui ius in urbe diceret*),[35] and historians have assumed that it was the praetor's *imperium* that conferred his *iurisdictio*. Yet nothing in Livy's statement requires us to make this connection between *imperium* and the exercise of *iurisdictio*, especially since Livy is almost certainly wrong that the praetorship was created in 367 BC (see chapters 1 and 4). Bergk has even pointed out that praetors did not receive jurisdiction between citizens in Rome until the passage of the *lex Plaetoria*, which may have dated to the First Punic War, more than a century *after* Livy believed the office was created to administer justice.[36] As should be obvious, Livy made a serious-but-understandable mistake: because praetors held the most important jurisdictions in the late republic, he reasonably assumed they had been created for this purpose. It compounds Livy's error, however, to make the false assumption that praetors exercised jurisdiction *because* they possessed *imperium*; Livy's testimony does not support this false analogy, nor does it indicate that *imperium* enabled jurisdiction over citizens.[37] If *imperium* was all that was needed to exercise jurisdiction, the Romans could have resolved their occasional backlogs of judicial business simply by appointing dictators to hear cases, but instead they would rearrange important provincial assignments to keep praetors in the city to

34. Richardson (2008) 206–7.
35. Livy 6.42.11.
36. Bergk (2011) 73–74.
37. A similar false analogy is often made with regard to summoning the senate: because this was normally done by dictators, consuls, and praetors, it is tempting to imagine that—because all three magistracies possessed *imperium*—that *imperium* was the authority that enabled this action. Yet nothing could be further from the truth, since Cicero, Dionysius of Halicarnassus, and Gellius are explicit that tribunes of the plebs (who never possessed *imperium*) had the authority to convene the senate (Cic. *Leg.* 3.10, Dion. Hal. *AR* 10.31.1–2, and Gell.14.7.4).

exercise jurisdiction.[38] The *potestas* of the praetor, rather than the *imperium* of the dictator, was needed in these cases.

Several scholars have pointed out that the origins of *iurisdictio* are obscure at best and have emphasized the problems in imagining it a derivative of *imperium* during the republic. Jolowicz and Nicholas tried to sidestep the issue by concluding that "it is probably best to regard *iurisdictio* as a part of *imperium* which can nevertheless be attributed independently," while Stewart simply said that "no literary source explicitly connects *imperium* and praetorian jurisdiction."[39] Several other scholars have likewise emphasized that *imperium* and *iurisdictio* were originally different and unrelated types of authority, although the two ideas gradually became conflated at some later point in Rome's history.[40] Furthermore, Valgaeren has recently argued not only that *iurisdictio* was originally a priestly prerogative in early Rome but also that the priests retained this legal prerogative into the second century BC.[41] Bleicken pointed out that the growth of Rome's government — including the development of legal and judicial structures — was slow and that concepts of civilian authority probably evolved independently from those of military authority (*imperium*), so that it was only in the late republic that *imperium* came to comprise civilian (as well as military) authority.[42]

It is tempting to interpret the exercise of jurisdiction by promagistrates (who no longer held office) in the provinces as evidence that jurisdiction flowed from *imperium*, but this comparison is faulty. While the unrestrained authority of *imperium* enabled a military commander to enforce his will however he wished in the zone *militiae*, the exercise of jurisdiction within the civilian sphere (*domi*) was different. A commander on campaign exercised martial law and could pronounce summary judgments without appeal or reference to a citizen jury, but the civilian authority of a magistrate *domi* was far more circumscribed. Even in the modern world, military and civilian courts usually operate under different legal principles, so it is presumptuous to assume that

38. For example, after the peregrine praetor in 167 BC had left to take up a command in Illyria, the senators realized that a huge backlog of cases remained unheard before his court, and therefore they forced another praetor to forgo his command in Sardinia and instead take up the peregrine praetor's jurisdiction in Rome (Livy 45.12.13).

39. Jolowicz and Nicholas (1972) 47 n. 9, Stewart (1998) 203 (cf. 113).

40. Lauria (1930) 2.479–538, de Martino (1972a) 1.420–25 (420 n. 45 gives further references), Kaser and Hackl (1996) 43 and 186, Forsythe (2005) 211.

41. Valgaeren (2012) 107–18. See also Wieacker (1988) 310–40, Forsythe (2005) 211–13, Tellegen-Couperus (2006) 31–44.

42. Bleicken (1967), (1975) 115–15, and (1981).

jurisdiction by military commanders with *imperium* in the provinces was the same thing as jurisdiction by magistrates (many of whom never possessed *imperium*) in Rome. As Rome's empire grew overseas and its commanders began to exercise jurisdiction in the provinces regularly, they would adopt similar legal forms as were used in Rome (such as the edict), but their legal authority did not derive from civilian authority. The difference between jurisdiction enforced by *imperium* in the sphere *militiae* and jurisdiction enforced by *potestas* in the sphere *domi* created real problems for provincial commanders in the second and first centuries BC, and the Romans gradually had to produce a new body of legislation to control commanders' use of their authority (see chapter 5). Jurisdiction in Rome and in the provinces would eventually come to look alike, but as part of a long process of development and legislation.

This process is well illustrated by the *lex de provinciis praetoriis* (ca. 100 BC), which stipulated that, should a provincial governor of Asia or Macedonia abdicate his magistracy, he should continue to exercise jurisdiction "just as it existed in his magistracy" until his return to Rome.[43] The whole point of this requirement in the *lex* is to establish something that had not clearly been the case before: commanders returning from their provinces should continue to exercise jurisdiction, which should follow the forms of the exercise of jurisdiction in Rome. If this had always been the case, and jurisdiction exercised by commanders in the field had always been the same as jurisdiction exercised by magistrates in Rome, there would have been no purpose for this section of the *lex*. Another piece of evidence is this: if possession of *imperium* alone conferred jurisdiction, why did no promagistrate lingering outside the *pomerium* in hopes of celebrating a triumph ever convene lawcourts to hear cases by citizens? In the late republic, some commanders retained their *imperium* and lived just outside the city for years as they waited for a triumph—why did no one of them ever try to exercise jurisdiction if they could gain the advantages of doing so? The tremendous authority of *imperium* certainly enabled commanders to enforce their will in their provinces, but this is a far stretch from saying that their exercise of jurisdiction was the same as that of civilian magistrates in Rome, or that military commanders and civilian magistrates used the

---

43. *RS* 12, Cnidos Copy col. IV ll. 31–39 (Crawford, trans.): "If the praetor or proconsul to whom the province of Asia or Macedonia shall have fallen abdicate from his magistracy, as described in his *mandata*, he is to have power in all matters according to his jurisdiction just as it existed in his magistracy, to punish, to coerce, to administer justice, to judge, to appoint *iudices* and *recuperatores*, <registrations> of guarantors and securities, emancipations, and he is to be <immune from prosecution> until he return to the city of Rome."

same type of authority when supervising lawcourts in different spheres (*domi* and *militiae*).

Imperium was not required for normal civic judicial proceedings in the republic, since tribunes, aediles, quaestors *parricidi, decemviri stlitibus iudicandis, tresviri capitales*, and (probably) *quinqueviri cis Tiberim* all exercised legal authority without *imperium*, and aediles even possessed the power to pronounce a legal edict.[44] Lintott points out that private citizens in the republic could inflict the punishment for some crimes — even capital offenses — with merely the assent of a magistrate.[45] Cicero states in his *De Legibus* that all magistrates should possess judicial power, and when he speaks of praetors as judicial magistrates, he specifically refers to them as holding *potestas*.[46] Cicero likewise draws a distinction between an urban magistrate with *potestas* who exercised judicial powers (*iudicassit inrogassitve*) and a military commander who exercised military authority (*imperabit*).[47] Indeed, Sandberg has argued persuasively that tribunes of the plebs took charge of legal affairs in early Rome, while consuls generally limited themselves to military command.[48] Whether or not this was the case, praetors certainly were expected to exercise jurisdiction in the late republic, but often their role in a lawsuit was limited to approving the merits of a prosecution and appointing a judge (*iudex*) who would oversee the trial and pronounce the actual sentence.[49] These *iudices* exercised jurisdiction on behalf of the praetor. It seems highly improbable that the praetor transferred or otherwise delegated his *imperium* to every *iudex* he assigned to

44. The judicial functions of tribunes, aediles, and quaestors *parricidi* are well known. References to minor judicial officials include: Cic. *Caec.* 97, *Clu.* 38, *Dom.* 78, *Phil.* 9.7, *Leg.* 3.6, Livy 3.55.7, *Per.* 11, 39.14.10, Varro *LL* 5.81, Gell. 4.2.1, Fest. 468L, *Dig.* 1.2.2.31 (Pomp.), 21.1.1 (Ulpian) and 21.1.44.1. See Heuss (1944) 100–104, Kunkel (1962) 71–79, Jolowicz and Nicholas (1972) 50, Nippel (1995) 22–26, Kaser and Hackl (1996) 243, Cascione (1999), Lintott (1999a) 137–44, Mousourakis (2003) 185 and (2007) 52, Forsythe (2005) 361, Gaughan (2010) 90–98, and Schiavone (2012) 137.

45. Lintott (1999b) 25–26.

46. Cic. *Leg.* 3.10: *Omnes magistratus auspicium iudiciumque habento*; and *Leg.* 3.8: *Iuris disceptator, qui privata iudicet iudicarive iubeat, praetor esto; is iuris civilis custos esto; huic potestate pari, quotcumque senatus creverit populusve iusserit, tot sunto*. While the *De Legibus* is a literary work, its obvious correspondence to Roman law gives it considerable weight, especially since Cicero openly rated the Twelve Tables as the finest of all law codes (*De Or.* 1.44).

47. Cic. *Leg.* 3.6: *magistratus nec oboedientem et noxium civem multa vinculis verberibusve coherceto, ni par maiorve potestas populusve prohibessit, ad quos provocatio esto. quom magistratus iudicassit inrogassitve, per populum multae poenae certatio esto. militiae ab eo, qui imperabit, provocatio nec esto, quodque is, qui bellum geret, imperassit, ius ratumque esto*.

48. Sandberg (2001) 97–131.

49. Mousourakis (2007) 37.

hear a case, nor am I convinced that his *imperium* was needed simply to grant the legal action—the key importance of legal authority lies in the resolution of a legal dispute and the authority behind the decision, not simply in approval of the complaint. There is no good evidence that magistrates needed *imperium* or anything other than *potestas* to exercise jurisdiction, and even scholars who maintain the opposite are forced by the dearth of evidence to conclude that *imperium* was rarely employed for coercive force in Rome by magistrates.[50] Although consuls might make use of their *imperium* in Rome during extraordinary circumstances, such occasions were inherently unusual and cannot be taken as evidence for normal judicial practice.[51] *Potestas* provided all of the authority that magistrates needed to exercise jurisdiction.

The fundamental distinction between civilian and military authority demonstrates that civilian governance was originally seen as being separate and different from military command. *Imperium* was originally a complete and absolute idea that admitted no fragmentation or differentiation (see chapter 4). *Potestas*, on the other hand, existed in a variety of types and degrees. Every magistracy had the *potestas* to perform the specific responsibilities expected of it: the phrase tribunician *potestas* conveys a particular list of prerogatives (e.g., the all-encompassing veto, *intercessio*, summoning the *concilium plebis* and proposing legislation, arresting and fining citizens), and a different list could be produced for each Roman magistracy. If one college of magistrates refused to perform the responsibilities of its office, no other magistracy might have the *potestas* to perform those duties.[52] *Potestas* also existed in a range of strengths or degrees. The fundamental policy of collegiality within a magisterial college rested on the fact that all members of a magisterial college had the same, or equal (*par*), *potestas*, but different colleges had different levels of *potestas*, so that the praetorship had greater *potestas* (*potestas maior*) than a quaestor, but lesser *potestas* (*potestas minor*) than a consul.[53] Many ancient authors speak of

50. For example, see Brennan (2004) 42: "When push came to shove, in the city at least, members of the same college almost never used *imperium* to check *imperium*"; Lintott (1999a) 99: "It was not an everyday weapon"; and Frier (1985) 246: "The urban praetor's *imperium* was regarded mainly as a device of last resort."

51. See subsequent discussion for extraordinary uses of *imperium* within the *pomerium*.

52. For example, the census could only be performed by censors (Plut. *Crass.* 13.1–2 and Dio 37.9.3). Likewise, in 320 BC the consuls were reportedly so angry with the senate that they refused to act *pro magistratu*, which caused public business to come to a virtual halt (Livy 9.7.12).

53. Collegiality: Cic. *Leg.* 3.6, 3.8, 3.10, 3.11; Livy 2.18.8, 3.51.9–10, 10.26.2–4. See Bleicken (1981) 279: "Die *par potestas* ist identisch mit der römischen Kollegialität," and Abbott (1901) 154–56 for discussion on the application of *par potestas*. More than a century ago Abbott (153–56) identified the

the *potestas maior* of the dictator, of the consul, and of the praetor.[54] Cicero—who rarely passed up an opportunity to invoke *imperium*—states that magistrates are ranked by different levels of *potestas* (*vis in populo abesto, par maiorve potestas plus valeto*), and both Cicero and Aulus Gellius state that the action of a magistrate can only be hindered by the intercession of a magistrate of equal or greater *potestas*.[55] Suetonius and Valerius Maximus both record that an office with higher *potestas* could take precedence over one with lower *potestas*, which Valerius specifically refers to as *potestas maior* taking precedence over *potestas minor*.[56]

This hierarchy of offices by *potestas* is also found in inscriptional evidence: in the *lex repetundarum* (most likely by Gaius Gracchus), the ranking of magistrates is listed in descending order as dictator, consul, praetor, master of horse, censor, aedile, tribune of the plebs, quaestor, *triumvir* for capital crimes, *triumvir* for assigning land, and military tribune of one of the first four legions.[57] The *lex Latina Tabulae Bantinae*—although published as much as two decades later—provides the exact same hierarchical order, as does Crawford's "Rome Fragment A," which dates to the middle of the first century BC.[58] In all of these inscriptions, the basis for the order must be *potestas*; it cannot be *imperium* because most of the magistracies listed never possessed *imperium*, and it cannot be *auspicium* because Gellius (citing Messala) specifically states that differences in *auspicium* separated (rather than subordinated) one magistracy from another—censors could not vitiate or hinder the *auspicium* of the praetors and consuls, and consuls and praetors could not vitiate or hinder the *aus*-

hierarchy of *potestas* as dictator, consul, praetor, aedile, and quaestor and noted that no magistrate exercised *maior potestas* over the censor. He did not, however, argue that *potestas* was the primary determinant of magisterial rank. Giovannini (1990) 431 also takes note of the existence of the *maior potestas* of certain magistrates but argues that their rank derived instead from their *auspicia*. See also Mommsen (1887–88) 1.25, Bleicken (1981) 266, 278, and 293, Kloft (1977) 72, Kunkel and Wittmann (1995) 41–43, 201–2, 212 n. 391, 221–24, Brennan (2004) 38.

54. Dictator: Livy 2.18.8, 4.17.11, 6.11.9–10, cf. Vell. 2.28.2, Suet. *Iul.* 76.2; consul: Livy 2.1.7–8, 2.30.6, 27.5.17, Val. Max. 2.8.2; praetor: Livy 8.32.3, 36.11.8, Suet. *Iul.* 17.2.

55. Cic. *Leg.* 3.6, 3.10, 3.11; Gell. 14.7.6.

56. Val. Max. 2.8.2 (descriptions of offices as having higher or lower *potestas*) and Suet. *Iul.* 17.2 (Caesar, as praetor, sends a *iudex* to jail for offending his *maior potestas*).

57. *RS* 1, ll. 2, 8.

58. *Tabulae Bantinae*: *RS* 7, ll. 14–15. The only discrepancy is the omission of the office of military tribune and the inclusion, at the end of the list, of the *iudex*: Dictator, consul, praetor, magister equitum, censor, aidilis, tribunus plebis, quaestor, IIIvir capitalis, IIIvir agreis dandeis adsignandeis, ioudex. This *lex* probably dates to the very end of the second century BC (see *RS* 195–97). "Rome Fragment A": *RS* 341–42. The fragment twice supplies the order: *dictator, consul, praetor, magister equitum*.

picium of the censors.[59] Thus both *potestas* and *auspicium* differentiated magistracies from one another, but *auspicium* did not place magistrates into a clear hierarchy beyond the simple distinction between offices holding *maxima* and *minora auspicia. Potestas* was the only common feature of magistrates that had sufficient variation in scope and degree to generate distinctions and a hierarchy among magistrates.

While *potestas* determined the hierarchy or relative importance of each magistracy, it did not in general make lower magistrates the subordinates of higher magistrates. In this respect, Roman magistrates did not exist in a chain of command, in which a higher magistrate had authority over (and responsibility for) lower magistrates, or in which a lower magistrate might automatically assume the duties of an absent superior. The closest we see to such a ranking (*ordo*) is an early ranking of priests (*ordo sacerdotum*) given by Festus:

> the first is the *rex sacrorum*, then the *flamen Dialis*, after this the *flamen Martialis*, then in fourth place the *flamen Quirinalis*, and in fifth place the *pontifex maximus.* Therefore on the benches the *rex* is permitted to sit above all the others, the *Dialis* above the *Martialis* and the *Quirinalis*, the *Martialis* above the next, and all above the *pontifex.* The *rex*, because he is the most powerful, the *Dialis* because he is the priest of the whole world, who is called "*Dium*," the *Martialis* because Mars is the father of the city founder, the *Quirinalis* because Quirinus was approved by the Cures as an ally of the Roman Empire, and the *pontifex maximus* because he is held to be the judge and arbiter of all divine and human things.[60]

As is immediately obvious, this *ordo* or ranking is in no way a chain of command in the modern sense but a system of precedence based on prestige; it is a hierarchy of honor but not of authority. Nothing in this passage leads one to believe that the *flamen Martialis* answered to the *flamen Quirinalis*, or that either of these was under the authority of the *flamen Dialis.* Each priest had his own sphere of authority, although it was recognized that each enjoyed a different level of respect or *honos* relative to one another. Similarly, a consul had

59. Gell. 13.15.4.

60. Fest. 198–200L (Drogula, trans.), *maximus videtur Rex, dein Dialis, post hunc Martialis, quarto loco Quirinalis, quinto pontifex maximus. Itaque in soliis Rex supra omnis accumbat licet; Dialis supra Martialem, et Quirinalem; Martialis supra proximum; omnes item supra pontificem. Rex, quia potentissimus: Dialis, quia universi mundi sacerdos, qui appellatur Dium; Martialis, quod Mars conditoris urbis parens; Quirinalis, socio imperii Romani Curibus ascito Quirino; pontifex maximus, quod iudex atque arbiter habetur rerum divinarum humanarumque.* See Cornell (1995) 232–36 for discussion on the *ordo* of priests, which he thinks may predate the foundation of the republic.

no authority over other magistrates in the modern sense and did not supervise their activities or have the ultimate responsibility of ensuring that they performed their responsibilities; and lower magistrates did not derive their authority from the consul or function as his subordinates. To be sure, a consul had the highest *potestas* in the state and could (in certain contexts) give commands to lower magistrates, but such an occurrence was so rare that it highlights how Rome's magisterial colleges normally operated independently of one another.[61] This is demonstrated by the fact that, most often, the orders given to a lower magistrate consisted of a prohibition rather than an authorization; consuls could prohibit or veto the action of their colleague or of a lower magistrate, but they normally did not order a lower magistrate to perform civil duties, nor did lower magistrates answer to the higher magistrates. It would be a mistake to think the consuls exercised positive control over Rome's other magistracies. The quaestorship illustrates this well: most quaestors were responsible to the senate for their actions, and only those quaestors assigned to operate as financial officers in a commander's army might be considered subordinates of the higher magistrate while on campaign.[62]

Because different magistracies normally had different governmental responsibilities, the relative *potestas* between two offices was not relevant to the normal day-to-day administration of the state, but in case of a serious conflict the *potestas* of a higher or more senior magistrate enabled him to intercede in the actions of a lower or more junior magistrate. Still, the greater *potestas* of senior magistrates did not constitute a chain of command in the modern sense: the plebeian tribunate, which was considered a lower office than the praetorship and consulship, was able to veto the actions of any praetor or consul, demonstrating that some lower magistrates (tribunes) could even constrain or hinder the actions of higher magistrates.[63] When the praetor P. Decius refused to rise at the approach of the consul M. Aemilius Scaurus in 115 BC, Scaurus angrily tore the praetor's clothes, smashed his curule chair, and ordered that no one was to bring legal cases before him, but the consul did not order Decius himself to do anything or otherwise illustrate any control over the lower mag-

61. Livy 27.5.17 (a consul orders a praetor to disregard instructions given by the senate) and 43.15.4–5 (a consul refuses to be subject to the judgment of two praetors, as the senate instructed).

62. Mousourakis (2003) 95. Naturally, the relationship was different for those quaestors assigned to serve as a financial officer in a consul's army, the military nature of which (and the consul's possession of *imperium*) usually made the quaestor the second-in-command of the consul's army (see Cic. *Att.* 6.3.1 and 6.4.1, and Lintott [1999a] 114–15, 136 n. 65).

63. Censors also seem to have existed outside the normal hierarchy in that one could be vetoed only by his colleague and not by any other official (Gell. *NA* 13.15.4).

istrate.[64] The disrespect Decius showed to Scaurus indicates that the praetor believed himself to be sufficiently independent of the consul that he did not need to rise from his chair in the latter's presence, probably because he did not recognize Scaurus as his superior. Each college of magistrates possessed its own sphere of responsibilities, and it was highly unusual for a higher magistrate to interfere in the official activities of any other magistrate. The result was a certain vagueness regarding the precise hierarchical relationship of one college to another in the early and middle republic; even the superiority or seniority of the consulship to the praetorship was not firmly established until the *lex Villia Annalis* of 180 BC.

The difference between the civilian authority of *potestas* and the military authority of *imperium* indicates a sharp separation and distinction between civilian magistrates and military commanders in the early republic. In fact, *potestas* may have been the older of the two concepts, since the Romans probably began organizing the civilian governance of their city before they were able to subordinate aristocratic war bands to state control. As the exercise of military authority became institutionalized and commanders became annually elected magistrates, the two different types of authority came to be invested in the most senior magistrates, although they did not merge into a single type of authority. Instead, both consuls and praetors performed two different types of activities, using different types of authority: *potestas* to fulfill their civilian responsibilities, and *imperium* to lead Rome's armies in war.

The Religious Authority of the Provincial Commander: *Auspicium*

Auspicium was the capacity or right to take the auspices (*auspicia*): to request from the gods some portent indicating their support or disapproval of an intended action, to observe and interpret any divine signs, and to perform the intended action if the results of the divination were positive.[65] While everyone

---

64. Auct. *Vir. Ill.* 72, *Publium Decium praetorem transeunte ipso sedentem iussit assurgere eique vestem scidit, sellam concidit; ne quis ad eum in ius iret, edixit.* Another praetor, almost certainly C. Servilius Glaucia in 100 BC, even had his curule chair smashed by a tribune of the plebs (Auct. *Vir. Ill.* 73), but since the tribune was probably his political ally L. Apuleius Saturninus, the significance of this act is unclear and may even be imaginary or a confusion with the earlier altercation between Decius and Scaurus.

65. The focus of this section is the role of *auspicium* in defining a commander, but for more on *auspicium*, see Botsford (1909) 100–118, Magdelain (1964b), (1968), and (1977a), Dumézil (1966 [1996]) 618–19, Versnel (1970) 350, Liebeschuetz (1979) 10–16, Giovannini (1983), Linderski (1986)

had the right to consult the gods on their own private affairs (*auspicia privata*), only magistrates and certain priests had the authority to consult the gods on public matters of state (*auspicia publica*).[66] In this latter case, *auspicium* gave magistrates the authority to act as intermediaries between the *res publica* and the gods, which included making vows to the gods that were binding on the entire state.[67] *Auspicium* was absolutely essential to military commanders, who needed to consult the will of the gods before committing their armies to war or other dangerous undertakings that would have a critical effect on the well-being of the state. Even the election and inauguration of a military commander needed to be performed with the consent of the gods, so *auspicium* both created a commander and — once he was in office — was used by the commander.

In an oft-quoted passage, Gellius — citing Messala — says that the auspices were divided into two powers or strengths (*in duas potestates*): consuls, praetors, and censors had *maxima auspicia* (greatest *auspicia*), while the other magistrates had *minora auspicia* (lesser *auspicia*).[68] Bleicken and Giovannini took this to mean that *auspicium* was the underlying authority that determined the rank of different magistracies, but they may be only partially correct: possession of *auspicia maxima* did distinguish the consulship, praetorship, and censorship from all other offices, but the hierarchical utility of *auspicia* probably ends there.[69] Furthermore, the difference between *maxima* and *minora auspicia* had little practical function in the late republic, so there is no reason to suppose that Gellius had a clear idea of what Messala's passage meant.[70] Gellius indicates not that *auspicia* created an absolute hierarchy or ranking between magisterial colleges but simply that the auspices of those invested with *maiora auspicia* are regarded more highly than the auspices of others: *maiora autem dicuntur auspicia habere, quia eorum auspicia magis rata sunt quam aliorum.*[71]

(who includes an excellent bibliography on *auspicium*) and (1990b) 36–47, Mitchell (1990) 21–22, Rüpke (1990) 41–51, Beard, North, and Price (1998) 1.21–22, Lintott (1999a) 103–4, Brennan (2000) 12–18, Baumgarten (2002) 95, Scheid and Lloyd (2003) 112–23, Rasmussen (2003) 149–68, Konrad (2004) 195, Develin (2005) 299–300, Palmer (1970 [2009]) 197–200, and Guichard (2011) 29–52.

66. Cic. *Div.* 1.28; Livy 4.6.2–3 and 10.8.9. Cicero complains (*Div.* 2.76) that Romans of his day no longer consulted the auspices except by votes of the citizen assemblies.

67. Cicero (*Leg.* 3.10–11) states that all magistrates had *auspicium*. See also Mitchell (1990) 21 and Humm (2012) 71–72.

68. Gell. *NA* 13.15.4.

69. Bleicken (1967), (1975) 115–21, and (1981) 257–300, Giovannini (1983) and (1990). Their argument was challenged by Badian (1990) 458–75.

70. Stewart (1998) 101.

71. Gell. 13.15.7.

As Rüpke has rightly pointed out, Roman religion was a "range of cultural practices,"[72] not a monolithic entity or idea, so one should not imagine that Roman religion was so all-encompassing and ordered as to be able to establish a fixed hierarchy for all of Rome's different magistracies. Gellius makes this clear when he notes that "in the edict of the consuls by which they appoint the day for the centuriate assembly it is written in accordance with an old established form, 'Let no minor magistrate presume to watch the skies.'"[73] The obvious purpose of this decree is to prevent another magistrate from announcing signs that might hinder the comitial meeting, but the fact that such an edict was necessary indicates that a minor magistrate *could indeed* use his *auspicium* to disrupt a meeting under the auspices of a consul unless forbidden to do so in advance. Since consular *auspicium* was insufficient to overwhelm the *auspicium* of a minor magistrate, consuls used their superior *potestas* to prohibit other magistrates from taking the auspices in the first place. Thus, *auspicia maxima* did not make a consul the superior officer of a quaestor.

The taking of *auspicia* was an absolutely essential responsibility of a Roman magistrate, so much so that any flaw in the auspices taken during a magistrate's inauguration was sufficient to invalidate his entire magistracy and to necessitate his immediate resignation from office.[74] The fundamental importance of *auspicia* lay in the deep religiosity of the Romans, who were famously scrupulous when it came to the observance of their gods and who normally consulted the will of their gods before any major action was taken. Since magistrates were leaders of state activity, their *auspicium* was necessary to authorize them to speak to the gods on behalf of the entire state. For this reason, the major decision-making bodies of the state—the senate and the citizen assemblies—could not meet unless the presiding magistrate first used his powers of *auspicium* to ensure that the omens were favorable for that meeting.[75] Magisterial *auspicium* and the reading of omens were understood to ensure divine favor and support (or at least neutrality) for all of Rome's public undertakings, so any magistrate whose relationship with the gods was suspect might be compelled to resign office: in 387 BC the Romans were said to have lost faith in the *auspicia* of their consuls, who were forced to abdicate, and an interrex was

---

72. Rüpke (2004) 179.

73. Gell. 13.15.1: *in edicto consulum, quo edicunt quis dies comitiis centuriatis futurus sit, scribitur ex vetere forma perpetua: "Ne quis magistratus minor de caelo servasse velit"* (Rolfe, trans.).

74. Livy 4.7.3, 6.38.8–9, 8.15.6 and 23.14, 23.31.13, 21.63.5.

75. Livy 5.52.15 and 41.16.5, Varro *LL* 6.91, Gell. 13.15.1.

appointed whose new and untainted *auspicium* would ensure that divine favor shone on the next consular elections.[76]

There is a debate among scholars over how a magistrate received his *auspicium*, which is important because it helps define the relationship—or lack thereof—between the military commander and the civilian magistrate. Some scholars have argued that *auspicium* was conferred by a *lex* passed in the *comitia curiata* (a *lex curiata*) after a man took office, whereas others have maintained that it was conferred earlier by the process of election in the *comitia centuriata* or the *comitia tributa*.[77] Support for this first position is found in a statement by Cicero in his speech *de lege agraria*, where he states:

> Your ancestors wished you to cast your votes twice for each single magistrate . . . so that the capacity for withdrawing the votes would exist if the people regretted the benefit [it had bestowed]. Now, Quirites, you hold those *comitia* as the chief—namely the *centuriata* and *tributa*—while the *curiata* remains only for the sake of the auspices.[78]

The interpretation of this passage requires caution, since it appears in his *de lege agraria*, a speech Cicero gave specifically to defeat a proposed bill that (among other things) would enable an extraordinary commander with *auspicium* and *imperium* to be created without a *lex curiata*. Because his primary goal was to prevent the sidestepping of the *comitia curiata*, Cicero certainly would have stressed—and even exaggerated—the importance of the *lex curiata* in the creation of a magistrate. In fact, there is no evidence that a vote of the *comitia curiata* was ever used as Cicero says to cancel a vote by the *comitia centuriata* or *tributa*,[79] so he is probably inventing this use of the *lex curiata* to suit his purposes. He emphasizes here that "each single magistrate" (*de singulis magistratibus*) was required to receive a *lex curiata*, but this should not be taken to mean *every* Roman magistrate, although Cicero may have hoped that

76. Livy 6.5.6.

77. *Auspicia* through a *lex curiata*: Staveley (1956) 89, Magdelain (1964a), (1964b), and (1968), Develin (1977) 49–65, Giovannini (1983) 53, Palmer (1970 [2009]) 212, and Humm (2012) 65–68. *Auspicia* through election in the *comitia centuriata* or the *comitia tributa*: Nicholls (1967) 257–78, Lintott (1999a) 103, Versnel (1970) 328–29 and 384.

78. Cic. *Leg. Agr.* 2.26–27: *maiores de singulis magistratibus bis vos sententiam ferre voluerunt . . . ut esset reprehendendi potesta, si populum beneficii sui paeniteret. Nunc, Quirites, prima illa comitia tenetis, centuriata et tributa, curiata tantum auspiciorum causa remanserunt.* He makes a similar comment later (2.31): *illis [comitiis] . . . per XXX lictores auspiciorum causa adumbrates constituti.*

79. See Humm (2012) 61.

his listeners would understand it this way. Indeed, we know for certain that censors did not receive a *lex curiata*, and yet they had *auspicium maximum*, demonstrating that investiture with *auspicium* (at least for some magistrates) was available from some source other than the *comitia curiata*.[80] Furthermore, Botsford pointed out that Cicero was describing his understanding of the rule as it was currently practiced in his day (or how Cicero wanted his audience to think the rule *should* be practiced in his day), so there is little reason to suppose he was preserving archaic practices from early Rome.[81] At most, this phrase can only mean that individual magistrates — but not *every* magistrate — required a *lex curiata* for the sake of the auspices. This is supported by Versnel, who argued that censors and all lower magistrates did not receive a *lex curiata*, a position that is likely correct given the absence of any clear evidence to the contrary.[82] Ancient authors frequently mention the absolute requirement that consuls and praetors receive a *lex curiata*, which makes it hard to understand why such an essential *lex* should never be mentioned for any other magistrate. Develin tried to respond to this by suggesting that consuls arranged for a *lex curiata* to be passed on behalf of all magistrates in Rome, but this seems impossible because the various magistracies took office at different times of year.[83]

Other evidence suggesting all magistrates required a *lex curiata* simply does not hold up to scrutiny. First, Dionysius of Halicarnassus writes that Romulus established the custom that no king or magistrate of Rome should accept office without favorable auspices, but this passage has too many problems to be useful:

> He was chosen king by them and established it as a custom, to be observed by all his successors, that none of them should accept the office of king or any other magistracy until Heaven, too, had given its sanction. And this custom relating to the auspices long continued to be observed by the Romans, not only while the city was ruled by kings, but also, after the over-

80. Instead of a *lex curiata*, censors seem to have received a *lex centuriata* (Cic. *Leg. Agr.* 2.11.26 and Gell. 13.15.4). See Magdelain (1968) 13–14.

81. Botsford (1909) 185: "The orator, it is urged, could not himself know the original intention of the usage; and his interpretation is contradicted by the fact that the person who proposed the *lex curiata* was already a magistrate, the voting on this *lex* being subsequent to the election and forming no part of it." See Dionysius of Halicarnassus (*AR* 2.6.1–2), who remarks that the practice of taking the auspices in the late republic was no longer conducted as it had been in earlier periods.

82. Versnel (1970) 329 and n. 2 has decisively argued that minor magistracies did not receive a *lex curiata*, and he provides a bibliography on the debate. *Contra* Brennan (2000) 20 and Humm (2012) 66, who accept Messala's statement (in Gellius) to mean that all magistrates required a *lex curiata*.

83. Develin (1977) 60. See also Oakley (1997–2004) 3.492 n. 1.

throw of the monarchy, in the elections of their consuls, praetors and other legal magistrates; but it has fallen into disuse in our days except as a certain semblance of it remains merely for form's sake. For those who are about to assume the magistracies pass the night out of doors, and rising at break of day, offer certain prayers under the open sky; whereupon some of the augurs present, who are paid by the State, declare that a flash of lightning coming from the left has given them a sign, although there really has not been any.[84]

As was the case with Cicero, Dionysius is here recollecting how he believed the auspices were conducted in an idealized past, so taking such moralization factually is dangerous. Even if his account were accurate, however, he does not mention the *comitia curiata*, and clearly his comments are not about the *lex curiata* but about the auspices that individuals took on their own — separate from any *comitia* — before assuming office. In Dionysius's account, Romulus takes the auspices privately himself and reports the results to the people, and magistrates-elect in the republic likewise take the auspices themselves, albeit in the presence of augurs. Thus Dionysius is not describing the *lex curiata* but simply the auspices a magistrate-elect took when entering office (οἱ τὰς ἀρχὰς μέλλοντες λαμβάνειν).[85] Indeed, since this passage goes on to discuss how neglect of these auspices has caused numerous military disasters for the Romans, Dionysius may be referring only to Rome's highest magistrates (those with *imperium*) in this passage.[86] Whether or not this was the case, this passage by Dionysius seems to say nothing about the *lex curiata*.

84. Dion. Hal. *AR* 2.6.1–2 (Cary, trans.): καὶ τὰ μαντεῖα δηλώσας βασιλεὺς ἀποδείκνυται πρὸς αὐτῶν καὶ κατεστήσατο ἐν ἔθει τοῖς μετ' αὐτὸν ἅπασι μήτε βασιλείας μήτε ἀρχας λαμβάνειν, ἐὰν μὴ καὶ τὸ δαιμόνιον αὐτοῖς ἐπιθεσπίσῃ, διέμεινέ τε μέχρι πολλοῦ φυλαττόμενον ὑπὸ Ῥωμαίων τὸ περὶ τοὺς οἰωνισμοὺς νόμιμον, οὐ μόνον βασιλευομένης τῆς πόλεως, ἀλλὰ καὶ μετὰ κατάλυσιν τῶν μονάρχων ἐν ὑπάτων καὶ στρατηγῶν καὶ τῶν ἄλλων τῶν κατὰ νόμους ἀρχόντων αἱρέσει. πέπαυται δ' ἐν τοῖς καθ' ἡμᾶς χρόνοις, πλὴν οἷον εἰκών τις αὐτοῦ λείπεται τῆς ὁσίας αὐτῆς ἕνεκα γινομένη ἐπαυλίζονται μὲν γὰρ οἱ τὰς ἀρχὰς μέλλοντες λαμβάνειν καὶ περὶ τὸν ὄρθρον ἀνιστάμενοι ποιοῦνταί τινας εὐχὰς ὑπαίθριοι, τῶν δὲ παρόντων τινὲς ὀρνιθοσκόπων μισθὸν ἐκ τοῦ δημοσίου φερόμενοι ἀστραπὴν αὐτοῖς σημαίνειν ἐκ τῶν ἀριστερῶν φασιν τὴν οὐ γενομένην.

85. See Linderski (1986) 2169–70, who also interprets this passage as referring to the auspices a magistrate took when entering office.

86. Dionyius (*AR* 2.6.2) says Romulus's custom was long retained by "consuls, praetors, and all ἄρχοντες chosen in accordance with the law." Although ἄρχοντες can refer to the abstract notion of magistrate, it more usually signifies a chief magistrate, and in this case may refer to dictators, masters of horse, *decemviri*, military tribunes with consular power, *privati cum imperio*, and *triumviri rei publicae constituendae* legally appointed to exercise military command in the republic. This reading is supported by Dionysius's focus in this passage on neglect of the auspices by military commanders, especially by M. Licinius Crassus's neglect of the omens before his ill-fated Parthian campaign.

Similarly, a passage in Dio describing Clodius's aedileship in 56 BC seems to suggest that all magistrates needed a *lex curiata*, but this too falls apart on close inspection. Dio records that "Clodius, in order to embarrass [Pompey] the more, would not allow the *lex curiata* to be introduced; and until that was enacted no other serious business could be transacted in the state or any suit instituted."[87] While some might point to this as an example of the absolute necessity for all magistrates to receive a *lex curiata*,[88] that simply cannot be the case. In the first place, this passage states that only serious business (ἄλλο τι τῶν σπουδαίων) was prevented, which one could easily interpret as indicating only the highest affairs of state, which were supervised by consuls and praetors. Second, Brennan argues that Dio's statement is simply a temporal (not causal) clause, and signifies no loss of magisterial capacity.[89] Brennan must be correct, because we know of at least one consul who successfully completed his administrative duties in Rome without the benefit of a *lex curiata*. In 54 BC, the consul Appius Claudius Pulcher spent the entire year performing his duties in Rome without ever receiving a *lex curiata*, and no one — not even the great lawyer Cicero — doubted the legitimacy of his consulship and his actions as consul.[90] Although Appius's capacity to exercise military command would come into question, his civilian authority as consul does not seem to have derived from a *lex curiata*. It would appear, therefore, that not even a consul needed a *lex curiata* in order for his magistracy to be legitimate in Rome.

In this light, the *comitia curiata* may have conferred *auspicium* on some magistrates and not others, although even this may not be the case. Versnel argued strenuously that Cicero's assertion that the *comitia curiata* remained important "only for the sake of the auspices" (*tantum auspiciorum causa*) means not that the *lex curiata* bestowed *auspicium* on individuals but that this as-

87. Dio 39.19.3 (Cary, trans.).

88. So Develin (1977) 60: "When Clodius obstructed the passage of the *lex curiata*, no major business was possible; no-one had *potestas*."

89. Brennan (2000) 18: "What we have here is only a temporal sequence, not implying causality: for that matter, a consul could not set out for the field before he held the Latin Festival, but no one would hold that this ceremony actually entitled him to start his campaign."

90. Cic. *Att.* 4.17.2–3, *Fam.* 1.9.25, *QFr* 3.2.3. Staveley (1956) 84–88 argues that C. Pomptinus (pr. 63 BC) had also failed to obtain a *lex curiata*, based on a passage of Cicero (*Att.* 4.18.4): "Pomptinus wants to celebrate his triumph on 2 November. Praetors Cato and Servilius are stopping him at the city gate with Tribune Q. Mucius. They say that no enabling law has been brought in (*negant enim latum de imperio*), and it's true that the manner of its bringing in was less than tactful" (Shackleton-Bailey, trans.). Cicero's own words, however, indicate that Pomptinus did indeed receive a *lex curiata*, albeit in a "less than tactful" manner that gave others grounds to challenge the validity of Pomptinus's triumph.

sembly took the auspices officially and validated the magistrate's election.[91] This may be supported by Cincius's story that praetors sent to lead the Latin League in the early republic were selected by a taking of the auspices on the Capitoline Hill, a story that may preserve the early working of the *comitia curiata*.[92] Further evidence that may support Versnel's position is a passage by the augur M. Valerius Messala (cos. 53 BC) preserved in Gellius: "When the lesser magistrates are elected, they are made magistrates by the assembly of the tribes, but due measure (*iustus*) is given by a *lex curiata*; the higher magistrates are made magistrates by the assembly of the centuries."[93] The meaning of this passage is vague and highly debated, such that von Lübtow and Bleicken have both suggested that this passage needs emendation.[94] Particularly problematic is the intended meaning of *iustus*; it could be a synonym for *auspicium*, indicating that the *lex curiata* gave *auspicium* to lower magistrates, or it could simply indicate some kind of ratification or sanctioning of the electoral results.[95] Some scholars have argued *iustus* cannot be a synonym for *auspicium* because consuls are believed to have presided over the meetings of the *comitia curiata* in which they received their own *leges curiatae* and so must have possessed *auspicium* before convening the *comitia curiata* (which required the taking of the auspices).[96] If this is correct, Messala's use of the term *iustus* must refer to some kind of sanction—albeit not a grant of *auspicium*. On the other hand, in the late republic (if not earlier) the *pontifex maximus* was also able to convene the *comitia curiata*, but he is known to have done so only for matters like inaugurating priests and executing certain types of adoptions and wills, in which case the *comitia curiata* was often referred to as the *comitia calata*, which may not have been responsible for the *lex curiata de imperio*.[97] Although he is not at-

---

91. Versnel (1970) 328–29: "The explanation *auspiciorum causa* as 'for the sake of granting the *auspicia* to the new magistrate' can be read in this text only by the person who sets out to do so, and who, in addition, is prepared to twist the meaning accordingly."

92. Cincius Alimentus in Fest. 276–77L, quoted in full in chapter 1 at note 75.

93. Gell. 13.15.4 *minoribus creatis magistratibus, tributis comitiis magistratus, sed iustus curiata datur lege; maiores centuriatis comitiis fiunt* (Drogula, trans.).

94. Von Lübtow (1952) 154–71 and Bleicken (1981) 15–21.

95. Humm (2012) 66 has suggested that *iustus* should be taken as "legal" and that a magistracy became legal with the passage of the *lex curiata*, but this does not seem quite right since it was possible for a consul to perform his magisterial duties in Rome without having the sanction of a *lex curiata* (see my subsequent discussion of Ap. Claudius [cos. 54 BC]).

96. Staveley (1956) 88–90, Badian (1990) 467, Brennan (2000) 19.

97. Gell. 5.19.6. See Botsford (1909) 153–55, Taylor (1966) 4–5, and Oakley (1997–2004) 3.492. Humm (2012) 63–64, points out that the term *lex curiata de imperio* is a made-up term and does not appear in ancient sources, but the following pages will accept it as a convenient shorthand expres-

tested doing so, the *pontifex maximus* could have presided over the meeting of the *comitia curiata* that passed a *lex curiata* granting *auspicium* to consuls, but the fact that the dictator seems to have presided over the meeting of the *comitia curiata* that passed his own *lex curiata de imperio* probably indicates that consuls acted similarly.[98] Magdelain suggested that a consul's *lex curiata* was passed by the *comitia curiata* under the presidency of his predecessor, but this seems unlikely since many consuls entered office and even set out on military commands before their predecessors returned to Rome.[99] The only way to salvage Messala's comment about a *lex curiata* making lesser magistrates *iustus* is to accept that this does not refer to the conveyance of *auspicium* or any other type of authority on civilian magistrates; rather, it was some kind of *pro forma* vote that lower magistrates were expected to obtain from the *comitia curiata*, but the neglect of which did not prevent a magistrate from legitimately performing the responsibilities of his office.

Thus we know that the *lex curiata* had something to do with the auspices, it was desirable (but not required) for magistrates to perform their civilian duties, but it was absolutely mandatory for those wishing to exercise military authority. These factors support those scholars who have separated *auspicium* into two types — *domi* and *militiae* — and suggested that a magistrate received only his *auspicium domi* through his election to office in the *comitia centuriata* or *comitia tributa*, but that military commanders (consuls and praetors) received their *auspicium militiae* by a subsequent *lex* passed by the *comitia curiata*.[100] This is suggested by Livy's statement that the *comitia curiata* dealt with military matters (*comitia curiata, quae rem militarem continent*), and especially by his report that in 390 BC Camillus was not able to take the military auspices until he had received a *lex curiata* (*nec nisi dictator dictus auspicia in exercitu habere — lex curiata lata est dictatorque absens dictus*).[101] The religious authority of *auspicium* was flexible: it could be private or public, greater or lesser, magisterial or priestly, and it had a strong spatial context. The early history of military leadership also helps to make sense of this. As noted above there was originally a distinction between generals and magistrates, a distinc-

---

sion for the vote of the *comitia curiata* that authorized a commander to take up *imperium* outside of the *pomerium*.

98. Livy 8.23.13–15 and 9.38.15–39.1.

99. Magdelain (1968) 26–28.

100. Mommsen (1887–88) 1.116, Badian (1990) 467, Brennan (2000) 18–20 and 57 and (2004) 41, Smith (2006) 221–22.

101. Livy 5.46.11 and 52.16.

tion that continued to exist in the case of lower magistrates. Since generals received a special type of military authority (*imperium*) that non-commanders never received, they would likewise receive a special type of religious authority (*auspicium militiae*) that civilian magistrates lacked. Furthermore, since the *pomerium* was a religious boundary that (at one level) separated the military and civilian spheres, there is every reason to believe that the *auspicium* held by those civilian magistrates inside the *pomerium* were different from the *auspicium* held by generals outside.[102]

One final point seems critical: if we give any credence to Roman tradition, the *comitia curiata* was Rome's original assembly for selecting magistrates and endowing them with the legal capacity to perform the responsibilities for which they were chosen. A story in Livy has it that, at the birth of the republic, the selection of the first consuls was made by the army voting in units called centuries, so the *comitia centuriata* constituted Rome's second citizen assembly after the *comitia curiata*.[103] The *comitia centuriata* retained its responsibility for electing Rome's military commanders (consuls and praetors), but those elected also required a second positive vote in the ancient *comitia curiata*, which was expressed by the promulgation and passage of a *lex curiata*. This double vote is certainly strange, and Cicero's explanation that it gave the Romans a chance to rescind a man's election seems neither logical nor practical. The Romans believed that, in the regal period, the *comitia curiata* had been used to select kings, so Roman conservatism may have preserved a role— even if only *pro forma*—for the *comitia curiata* in the investiture of consuls.[104] It must surely be significant that this second round of approval by the *comitia curiata* was truly relevant only to those magistracies that exercised military

102. This was clearly demonstrated in the consular elections in 163 BC. When a disturbing omen occurred during the election, the presiding consul (Tiberius Gracchus) suspended the election to cross the *pomerium* and reenter the city in order to consult with the senate, and in doing so he forfeited the *auspicia militiae* he had possessed to hold the elections. When he exited the city to resume the elections in the Campus Martius, he neglected to renew his *auspicia militiae*, and therefore the elections he supervised were later found to be invalid (Cic. *Nat. D.* 10–11, *Div.* 1.33, *QF* 2.2.1, Val. Max. 1.1.3).

103. Livy (1.60.4) records this election of consuls as the first constitutional act of the *comitia centuriata* in the republic. See Ogilvie (1965) 733–34, who suggests that the *comitia curiata* assumed authority for investing and delegating power to magistrates after the expulsion of the kings, although the growing democracy in Rome eventually caused the selection of men who would be invested with magisterial power to be made by the *comitia centuriata*.

104. Cic. *Rep.* 2.25, 31, 33, 35. Of course, many kings were selected without a vote of the *comitia curiata*. See Botsford (1909) 182–84.

command. Cicero emphasizes the military nature of this recognition by the *comitia curiata*, stating that a man elected to the consulship in the *comitia centuriata* was forbidden to exercise military authority unless he also obtained the approval of the *comitia curiata*.[105]

The contrast with purely civilian magistrates is illustrative. When the tribunate of the plebs was created (traditionally in 494 BC), men were originally chosen for this office in the *comitia curiata*, but when the plebeians grew frustrated with patrician domination of that body, they are said to have arranged the establishment of the *comitia tributa* for (among other things) the selection of plebeian magistrates.[106] This distinction between military and civilian offices is significant: the election of plebeian tribunes and aediles was said to have been transferred to the *comitia tributa* from the *comitia curiata* and *comitia centuriata* respectively in the year 471 BC, and the quaestors—although perhaps originally appointed by consuls—began to be elected in the *comitia tributa* in 446 BC.[107] In other words, the election of civilian magistracies was deliberately given to the *comitia tributa*, while military magistracies—the consuls and praetors—remained with the *comitia centuriata* and required the additional sanction of a *lex curiata*. The one exception to this division was the election of censors, which took place in the *comitia centuriata* but did not require the additional *lex curiata*, no doubt because their office was purely civilian in nature. Thus magisterial elections were divided into two basic groups: military offices in the *comitia centuriata* that required an additional *lex curiata*, and civilian offices in the *comitia tributa* that did not require an additional *lex curiata*. This demonstrates that election in one of the *comitia* was sufficient to make a man a magistrate and invest him with the civilian authority requisite for his office (his *potestas* and *auspicium domi*), but to exercise military authority he required the addition of a *lex curiata*, which conferred *imperium* and *auspicia militiae*. This makes sense in light of both the republic's separation of civilian and military spheres and its ancient distinction between generals and magistrates. Thus the evolution of comitial elections supports the thesis that the *comitia centuriata* and the *comitia tributa* had the ability to create magistrates, but the additional sanction of the *comitia curiata* remained necessary to confer military authority.

105. Cic. *Leg. Agr.* 2.30: *consuli, si legem curiatam non habet, attingere rem militarem non licet.*

106. Original election in the *comitia curiata*: Ascon. 76.13–20C, Livy 2.56.1–5, Dion. Hal. *AR* 6.89.1–2, 9.41.3. Establishment of the *comitia tributa* in 471 BC: Livy 2.56.2–3, 2.57.4–58.2, Dion. Hal. *AR* 9.41.4–5, 9.49.3–5.

107. Dion. Hal. *AR* 9.41.2–43.4 and 46.4; Tac. *Ann.* 11.22.4–5.

The duration of a commander's *auspicium* is subject to some debate. Cicero stated that promagistrates did not have *auspicium*, which seems to mean that *auspicium* was specifically linked to the tenure of magisterial office, and that both expired together at the end of a man's official term.[108] Since early Roman commanders completed their military commands within their terms of office (prorogation — extending a general's time in command — was not an option until 327 BC), Cicero's statement seems logical, but there are reasons to doubt him on this point. For one, most military campaigning in Cicero's day was conducted by promagistrates who (according to Cicero) did not possess *auspicium*, but this seems patently impossible, because possession of *auspicium* was an absolute requirement for a man to exercise legitimate military command. The simple fact that most triumphs in the late republic were celebrated for victories generals won as promagistrates would seem to overturn Cicero's comment, since it was an ironclad rule that generals could only triumph for victories won under their own *auspicium*.[109] On the other hand, the question may never have been absolutely decided in law or religion. The introduction of prorogation was originally conceived as an exceptional and makeshift solution to a particular problem (see chapter 4), so the fine details of prorogation, such as whether a magistrate's *auspicium* was extended along with his command, may never have been worked out in absolute legal or religious terms.

An example from 195 BC illustrates this problem. In that year, M. Helvius (pr. 197 BC) had turned his *provincia* of Farther Spain over to his successor and was departing from the region when he fought and defeated a group of Celtiberians in a substantial battle. When he requested a triumph for this victory back at Rome, he was refused on the grounds that, because he had already handed the *provincia* over to his successor at the time the battle was fought, he had fought "under another's auspices and in another's *provincia*" (*quod alieno auspicio et in aliena provincia pugnasset*).[110] He was, however, given the lesser form of the triumph known as an ovation. While this demonstrates that a commander's *auspicia* were conceptually linked to the *provincia* he held, the passage cannot mean that Helvius's *auspicium* automatically expired when he handed over his *provincia*, because he did in fact celebrate an *ovatio* and did receive recognition for his victory. Since the ovation was simply the lesser form of a triumph (they differed in scale and prestige, but not in basic require-

108. Cic. *Div.* 2.76. See Lintott (1999a) 103.

109. *Auspicia* essential to triumph (Livy 8.12.6; 27.44.4; 28.9.9–10, 12.12, 16.14; 40.52.5–6; 41.17.3 and 28.8). See Versnel (1970) 319–39.

110. Livy 34.10.5. See Sumner (1970) and (1977), Develin (1980), and Stewart (1998) 90–93.

ments), it is not at all clear why Helvius qualified for an ovation when he had been refused a triumph. Perhaps he received the ovation for a different victory that he had won sometime before handing over his province (he fought a major revolt in 197 BC before falling ill for much of 196 BC), although Brennan has also suggested the intriguing possibility that he may have won the concession of an ovation by threatening to celebrate a triumph outside of Rome on the Alban Mount.[111] Whichever the case, the award of an ovation demonstrates that he possessed *auspicium* as a promagistrate. The charge that he had fought *in alieno auspicio* is strange, because it is just another way of saying he had fought *in aliena provincia*. Because this repetitious statement seems otherwise unnecessary, perhaps the emphasis should be taken to mean that Helvius fought the Celtiberians not in Farther Spain (which he had held as his *provincia*) but while passing through Nearer Spain as he returned to Rome.[112] Since the consul M. Porcius Cato (cos. 195 BC) was holding Nearer Spain at the time, the emphasis that Helvius had trespassed into the consul's *provincia* would make more sense.

The authority to take the auspices on behalf of the state was an absolute necessity for Roman commanders, since the high stakes of the military commands made it essential that they consult the will of the gods before committing Roman citizens to battle. Long before the republican state was able to assert its monopoly on military authority, early commanders — many of whom were private citizens leading war bands of personal retainers in campaigns of self-interest — had probably consulted the auspices privately, as every citizen was permitted to do. As a part of Rome's institutionalization of military command, however, the state probably established its right to control who was authorized to consult the gods on behalf of the Roman people as a whole, which enabled the senate and people to determine whose campaigns were *iustus* and whose were not. Since *auspicium* was fundamentally connected to the execution of particular tasks, commanders were given *auspicium militiae* over their campaigns, whereas civilian magistrates had *auspicium domi* over their assigned domestic tasks. Commanders not only took the auspices before leaving Rome on campaign but were expected to watch for signs during their march, to make sacrifices to acquire and retain divine favor, to consult the will of the gods before key actions (like battle), and even to make vows that obligated the

111. Livy 33.21.7–8, App. *Ib.* 39. Brennan (2004) 44. See my subsequent comments for the prerogative of Roman commanders to celebrate unauthorized triumphs on the Alban Mount.

112. Develin (1980) 367 and Richardson (1986) 181–83 suggested this possibility, although Brennan (2000) 167 maintains that Helvius probably fought the battle in Farther Spain.

Romans to perform some future action if divine favors were needed to secure a victory.[113] Roman military disasters were often attributed to the failure of the commanders to interpret divine signs properly, including the famous Roman defeats at Drepana (when the Roman commander drowned the sacred chickens for giving unfavorable omens before battle) and Lake Trasimene (when the commander's horse stumbled, the standard-bearer could not lift the legionary standard, and there were even earthquakes throughout Italy).[114] Possession of *auspicium* was also a fundamental requirement in any application for a triumph, and in literary usage it became virtually synonymous with a general's authority. In fact, there was a deep connection in the Roman mind between *auspicium* and *imperium* (military authority), and the two terms are frequently combined to represent the power of the military commander, a rapport that illustrates the fundamental importance of both types of authority.[115] The Romans were a highly religious and ritualistic people, so *auspicium*'s status as a fundamental aspect of military command is not at all surprising.

The Military Authority of the Provincial Commander: *Imperium*

Richardson has recently undertaken a valuable study of the use of the word *imperium* by ancient authors, and he concludes that it mainly signified "magisterial power" down to the time of Sulla, although in Cicero's writings it begins to take on a broader meaning of "state."[116] While he is undoubtedly correct, this section argues that magisterial power had different aspects or types and that *imperium* was only one type of official authority that could be invested in Roman magistrates. While *potestas* conferred the authority necessary for a magistrate to perform the functions of his office related to civil governance, *imperium* was the military authority a general needed to exercise martial law over the citizens in his army. *Potestas* and *imperium* were fundamentally different types of authority, which is emphasized by the tendency of inscriptions to include both terms rather than allow one to stand for (or imply) the other.[117]

---

113. Taking auspices before leaving Rome (Cic. *Verr.* 2.5.34, Livy 21.63.9); taking auspices before battle (Cic. *Div.* 2.76, Val. Max. 2.7.4); taking auspices to divide forces (Livy 41.18.8). Rüpke (1990) 44–47 and Magdelain (1977a) 17.

114. On Publius Claudius Pulcher at Drepana: Cic. *ND* 2.7–8, Val. Max. 1.4.2–3. On Flaminius at Lake Trasimene: Cic. *Div.* 1.77, *ND* 2.8, Livy 22.3.4–13, Plut. *Fab. Max.* 2.4–5.

115. For example: Plaut. *Amphit.* 192, 196; Livy 10.8.9–10, 22.30.4, 27.44.4–5, 28.27.4, 29.27.2, 41.28.8; Val. Max. 2.8.2.

116. Richardson (2008) 61, 77–79.

117. *Lex agraria* (*RS* 2, clause 87): *magistratus prove magistratu queive pro eo imperio iudicio potes-*

Unlike *potestas*, which operated under the fundamental principle that magisterial authority was subordinate to the will of the citizens, *imperium* was the absolute authority to command (*impero*) that recognized no higher authority than the general himself. That *imperium* was originally the authority of a commander to lead an army is suggested by its possible derivation from the verb *parare* (to prepare or make arrangements).[118] Cicero emphasized its military nature in repeated statements emphasizing that *imperium* was absolutely necessary for legitimate command of a Roman army, and he asked Brutus the rhetorical question, "What is an army without *imperium*?"[119] Furthermore, the fact that after 215 BC one could create a legal military commander simply by investing a private citizen with *imperium* is sufficient to demonstrate that *imperium* was military authority.[120] Even the title *imperator*, which was given to a victorious general by acclamation of his soldiers, was exclusively a military honor.

The difference between *potestas* and *imperium* was well demonstrated during the consular elections in 215 BC. The presiding consul Q. Fabius Maximus had returned to Rome to hold the elections, but he avoided entering the city itself, and instead he camped outside the *pomerium* on the Campus Martius until the elections, no doubt wishing to retain his *imperium*.[121] When the first century voted for T. Otacilius, Fabius stopped the voting and spoke against his candidacy, telling the Romans to elect a more experienced commander (they ultimately reelected Fabius himself). When Otacilius loudly protested this interference in the election, Fabius sent his lictors to surround the candidate, and he ominously warned Otacilius that those lictors still had axes in their *fasces*, indicating that Fabius was still in possession of *imperium* and had the power to inflict summary punishment without appeal.[122] Livy's emphasis on

---

tateve erit . . . ; Falerio fragment II (*RS* 18): *imperio potestateve*; *lex coloniae Genetivae* (*RS* 25, l. 94): *neve quis pro quo imperio potestateve facito*; *lex Gallia Cisalpina* (*RS* 28, col. 1, l. 51): *neive quis, pro quo imperio potestateue erit*. Cf. *lex Rubria* (*CIL* 1.200 = 11.1146). *Contra* Mommsen (1887–88) 1.90, who saw *imperium* and *potestas* as concepts that largely overlapped.

118. Bleicken (1981) 37 and n. 38, Brennan (2004) 37.

119. Cic. *Phil.* 5.45: *imperium . . . sine quo res militaris administrari, teneri exercitus, bellum geri non potest, Agr.* 2.30 . . . *consuli, si legem curiatam non habet, attingere rem militarem non licet*; and *ad Brut.* 1.15.7: *quid enim est sine imperio exercitus?* Since Pompey did not have *imperium* when — as a private citizen — he formed an army of clients to fight for Sulla, Cicero refers to his authority simply as *praeesse in exercitu* (*Leg. Man.* 61).

120. Livy 23.30.19 (Marcellus given *imperium* in 215 BC because his military skills and leadership are needed against Hannibal).

121. Livy 24.7.10–9.4.

122. The citizen's right of appeal (*provocatio*) extended to the first milestone from the city and

Fabius's retention of *imperium* for the election demonstrates that this was un-usual and noteworthy, no doubt because consuls normally conducted elections solely by virtue of their *potestas*. Consuls *could* take up their *imperium* when exiting the city to hold elections, but this was not necessary and — to judge from Livy's story — it would have been unusual. In less tumultuous times, a consul might have been prosecuted (once out of office) for using his *imperium* in this high-handed way, but at the end of 215 BC the Romans were still reel-ing from losses to Hannibal, and Fabius was their hero of the hour. Thus Livy's story emphasizes that *imperium* normally was not used for civilian responsi-bilities like elections, even those held in the *comitia centuriata*, which voted in military units.

While *potestas* represented the civil law of domestic governance, *imperium* was the absolute and untrammeled authority of martial law. In the early re-public, a general invested with *imperium* and commanding an army in the sphere *militiae* could freely ignore the civil rights of his soldiers — even their fundamental right of appeal — as required by military necessity.[123] The best ex-ample of this unqualified authority was decimation (also called the *fustua-rium*), a form of punishment in which a Roman general could order the sum-mary execution of up to 10 percent of a legion by having those condemned beaten to death by their fellow soldiers at the general's order. Roman legend was filled with such brutal uses of unrestrained power: Appius Claudius (cos. 471 BC) scourged and executed all of his soldiers who had lost their weapons in a rout and decimated the remainder of his soldiers; Manlius Torquatus exe-cuted his own son without trial for disobeying military orders; Cornelius Sci-pio scourged and executed mutinous soldiers; M. Licinius Crassus decimated his army that retreated from battle against Spartacus; Julius Caesar executed the ringleaders of a munity in his army; and Mark Antony executed even more than 10 percent of his army for cowardice.[124] Polybius describes well the un-checked authority of a commander in the field:

therefore encompassed the Campus Martius (Livy 3.20.7, Dio 51.19.6), but as this event demon-strates, *provocatio* was effective only against *potestas* and *coercitio*, not against *imperium*.

123. Polyb. 1.7.11–12, 6.37.7–38.4, 11.29, 9.16.17–19; Livy 2.49, 9.16; Dion. Hal. *AR* 9.50.6–7, 11.43.2–3; Front. *Strat.* 4.1; App. *BC* 1.13.109; Zon. 7.17. Cicero (*Leg.* 3.6) and Livy (3.20.7, 3.55.4) make clear that soldiers had no possibility of appeal from a commander on campaign. Eckstein (1995) 173 notes that Roman commanders had considerably more authority to punish soldiers than Greek generals possessed. See Magdelain (1968) 45 n. 4 and Richard (2005) 119–20. Eventually, a *lex Porcia* would place some limits on a commander's use of *imperium* in the field.

124. Appius: Livy 2.59.11; Torquatus: Livy 8.7.13–22, Dion. Hal. *AR* 2.26.6, Sall. *Cat.* 52.30, Val. Max. 2.7.6, Gell. 9.13.20; Scipio: Polyb. 11.30.2, Livy 28.32.11–12, App. *Ib.* 35–36; Crassus: Plut. *Cras.*

As for the preparation for war and the general conduct of operations in the field, here their power is almost uncontrolled (αὐτοκράτορα τὴν ἐξουσίαν ἔχουσι); for they are empowered to make what demands they choose on the allies, to appoint military tribunes, to levy soldiers and select those who are fittest for service. They also have the right of inflicting, when on active service, punishment on anyone under their command; and they are authorized to spend any sum they decide upon from the public funds.[125]

Ancient sources are clear that, in the field, a Roman commander had the authority to impose summary execution on his soldiers without regard for their rights as citizens. Although generals on military campaign were expected to respect the civil rights of any private Roman citizens they encountered (whose private status meant that they were — technically — in the civilian sphere *domi*), the unchecked authority of *imperium* was the closest a Roman came to exercising the autocratic power of a king.

There is little doubt among scholars that *imperium* was the fundamental and defining authority of the provincial commander, but most would reject that *imperium* was *only* a source of military authority. There is a broad consensus among researchers that *imperium* comprised civilian as well as military authority and that high magistrates used *imperium* to perform their governmental responsibilities in Rome. This amalgamation of the military and civilian authority of consuls and other magistrates *cum imperio* is a mistake caused by ancient writers, who failed to recognize that Roman concepts of *imperium* and provincial command had changed over time, and by modern historians, who have occasionally misconstrued ancient authors' use of the word *imperium* and based some of their arguments on faulty assumptions about the nature of *imperium* and its relationship with civilian authority. As a result, there has been a tendency to confuse the two types of authority wielded by consuls (military *imperium* and civilian *potestas*) and blend them into a single idea, which makes it difficult fully to understand either. Just as earlier in this chapter an effort was made to distinguish *potestas* as the main source of civilian authority, so this section examines *imperium* strictly as the authority of the military commander. By situating *imperium* in its proper context, many problems that have bedeviled scholars of the republic can be resolved.

10.2, App. *BC* 1.118; Caesar: Suet. *Iul.* 69.1, App. *BC* 2.47, Dio 41.35.5; Antony: Cic. *Phil.* 3.14, App. *BC* 3.43, 3.53 and 56, Plut. *Ant.* 39.7, Dio 49.27.1. See Phang (2008) 123–27.

125. Polyb. 6.12.5–8 (Paton, trans.).

In his magisterial *Staatsrecht*, Mommsen pronounced that *imperium* had been the total and all-encompassing power of the exiled kings and that it was transferred intact to the consuls at the founding of the republic, although the collegiality and term limits of the consulship imposed certain checks on magisterial use of *imperium*.[126] This idea followed traditional Roman belief regarding the origin of consular power, but it suffered from an inherent contradiction, because consular authority, although absolute and unchallenged in war, was obviously restricted with regard to civilian governance. How could regal authority—which by nature was complete and unlimited—be circumscribed in one sphere but not another? To solve this, Mommsen further posited that regal *imperium* was divided into two different and separable component parts: the limited and restrained authority exercised over citizens in the domestic sphere (*imperium domi*) and the absolute and unrestrained military authority exercised over soldiers in war (*imperium militiae*).[127] In the republic, consuls (and later, praetors) used only their *imperium domi* inside the *pomerium*, whereas on campaign outside the *pomerium* they used their full *imperium militiae*. This reconstruction was logical and reasonable, and it made sense of several known facts, including:

1. Magisterial use of authority within the *pomerium* is known to have been restrained and limited by certain factors, including the citizen's right of appeal and the tribunician veto.

2. A military commander's use of authority outside the *pomerium* is known to have been absolute and unrestrained in the early republic.

3. Ancient authors use phrases like *consulare imperium* in reference to magistrates both inside and outside the *pomerium*.

4. The word *imperium* is found (albeit rarely) modified by the words *domi* and *militiae* in the surviving literature, and the phrase *imperium domi militiaeque* is attested.

5. Many ancient authors refer to the *imperium* of Rome's ancient kings.

126. Mommsen (1887–8) 1.1–24, 116–36.

127. Mommsen (1887–8) 1.61–75. Mommsen *also* believed that a consul could override *provocatio* if he wished (see 1.140–42, and 150–51). On these restraints on *imperium domi*, see Bleicken (1959), Brand (1968) 66, Martin (1970), Jolowicz and Nicholas (1972) 12–13, 305–17, Lintott (1972) and (1999a) 32–34, Kunkel (1973) 15–16, Magdelain (1990) 210–11, Jehne (2002), Beck (2011) 77–96. Giovannini (1983) 19–26 argues that the right of *provocatio* even extended outside the *pomerium* and beyond the first milestone from Rome.

Mommsen's reconstruction of known facts has been tremendously influential and has dominated scholarly discussion of Roman law and government for more than a century, and modern historians have generally (but not universally) accepted that consuls and praetors derived their civilian authority from their *imperium domi* and their military authority from their *imperium militiae*. Because no detailed description of the working of *imperium* survives from the ancient world, however, the nature of *imperium* in the republic continues to be a matter of debate among scholars.

While Mommsen's reconstruction of the working of *imperium* is clear and legally sensible, modern scholars often encounter difficulty when trying to apply it to particular situations in Roman history. Despite the neatness of the distinction between *imperium domi* and *imperium militiae*, it often creates difficult puzzles for historians, such as:

1. How can consular *imperium* be absolute but also weakened by the right of appeal?

2. Why did a sitting consul awaiting a triumph have to remain outside the city if he possessed *imperium* inside it?

3. If consuls already possessed the complete and unlimited *imperium* of the exiled kings, how could it be that the *imperium* of the dictator was somehow greater (*maius*) than the supposedly complete and unlimited *imperium* of the consul—that is, how could a dictator's *imperium* be more complete or more unlimited?

4. If *fasces* were the symbols of consular *imperium*, why did only one consul possess them at a time when in Rome, since the sources are explicit that the consuls were equal colleagues?

Questions like these bedevil historians, who often have trouble explaining how Mommsen's definition *actually worked*, and they often must ascribe to *imperium* some kind of magical or quasi-magical power.[128] Since the neatness of Mommsen's theory often breaks down when applied to specific aspects of Roman history, some scholars soon began doubting its accuracy. Heuss made the most important challenge and argued that *imperium* was not original to the monarchy or to the foundation of the republic, but was introduced later as a means of describing the military authority—and only the military authority—of Rome's senior magistrates, and gradually it came to signify civilian authority

---

128. See Versnel (1970) 356–57, Lowenstein (1973) 44–48, Richardson (1986) 9 and (1991) 1–2, Badian (1990) 469. Brennan (2004) 36–42 even refers to the "theology" of *imperium*.

as well.[129] Although this argument contradicts Roman tradition sharply, it has been adopted by several prominent scholars, including Bleicken, Versnel, and Kunkel.[130] Daube and Mitchell have also argued that *imperium* originally conferred military authority only and was used primarily outside the *pomerium*.[131] No one (to my thinking) has successfully refuted the position maintained by these scholars regarding the purely military nature and use of *imperium*, but inexplicably their arguments have been unable to crack the authoritative aura cast by Mommsen, although no less a scholar than Lintott has pointed out the highly theoretical nature of the *Staatsrecht*.[132] Most recently, Pina Polo has noted that "Mommsen casts a long shadow, and it is difficult to uproot opinions which have been repeated for decades."[133] The following pages make another assault on one of the most widely held but poorly documented ideas in the study of Roman government: that Mommsen's *imperium domi* existed and was used in civilian governance.

ONE OF THE REASONS why scholars have encountered so much difficulty in the study of *imperium* lies in the broad usage of the word in surviving sources. In addition to the specific military authority vested in Rome's highest magistrates (which is the primary concern of this chapter), the word *imperium* was also commonly used to denote the Roman Empire (*imperium Romanum*), the simple word order or command (*imperiis consulis*), and the vague and abstract notion of power.[134] This last usage is the most troublesome. Sometimes the abstract use of *imperium* is obvious, such as when Plautus mentions the *imperium* of a slave, Cicero refers to the *imperium* of the mind and to the *imperium* of a Spartan king, Caesar talks about the *imperium* of Gallic chieftains, Livy mentions the *imperium* of the Syrian king Antiochus, Varro describes the

129. Heuss (1944) 57–133.

130. Bleicken (1967), (1975) 80–83, and (1981) esp. 21–24 and 41–43, Versnel (1970) 352–55, and Kunkel (1973) 15.

131. Daube (1969) 3–4. Mitchell (2005) 157 n. 14: "As to *imperium*, I believe it was always confined to command and was applicable only in the military, not the urban, sphere"; and (1990) 135–36: "In reality, magistrates with *imperium* held military commands; their authority was confined to areas outside the city."

132. Lintott (1999a) 8: "It is significant that the best known and fundamental modern attempt to give an account of the [Roman] constitution, Theodor Mommsen's *Römisches Staatsrecht*, is highly theoretical, in spite of the assembly of source-material in the footnotes."

133. Pina Polo (2011) 228.

134. On the wide and varied use of the word *imperium*, see Richardson (1991) 2 and (2008), Baronowski (1991) 174, Yavetz (1991) 5–6, Giovannini (1990) 432–33, Awerbuch (1981) 162–76, Béranger (1977), Versnel (1970) 313–19, and Nicolls (1967) 257–58.

imperium of bees, Velleius Paterculus and Livy both speak of the *imperium* of the tribunes, Cicero speaks of the *imperium* of the whole world, and the Urso Charter refers to the *imperium* of the municipal *duoviri* and aediles.[135] Lintott illustrated the problem precisely when he said of this last usage (in the *Tabulae Herculanenses*) that "this should not be taken too strictly to refer to the full *imperium* of a consul or praetor, but to the more limited *coercitio* and *iudicatio* which the aediles enjoyed in specific fields."[136] While *imperium* is obviously meant to be taken as the abstract notion of power in these examples, how is one to determine whether the phrase *imperium consulis* means the official military authority of a consul, or the order of a consul, or even the (abstract) power of a consul? The intended meaning of an author is often difficult to ascertain: when Livy writes that the Roman cavalry obeyed its decurion "like the *imperium* of a consul" (*omnium turmarum equitibus velut ad consulis imperium motis*), or that an officer "ignored the *imperium* of a consul" (*ab eo quoque spretum consulis imperium est*), should we translate *imperium* in each case as power, order, or military authority?[137] Often, there is not enough context in a passage to make a definitive determination, especially given the tendency of ancient authors to identify post and power: Livy uses *imperium* almost as a synonym for the consulship.[138] The wide range of meanings conveyed by *imperium* is also evident in Greek texts, where the word ἀρχή can refer to the military authority (*imperium*) of a commander, the physical empire of the Romans, the office of the consulship, a Roman prefecture, and the territory of a specific Roman province, while the word ἐξουσία can refer to the military authority (*imperium*) of a commander but also to the general concept of power (*potestas*) including legal right (*ius*).[139] Because it is easy to misconstrue the intended meaning of an ancient writer when translating, the range of meanings conveyed by *imperium* necessitates caution and attention.

Furthermore, the challenge in translating *imperium* is made even more difficult when it is paired with suggestive adjectives like *summum*, *maximum*, and *totum*. Are these efforts at legal precision or merely sonorous rhetorical flour-

---

135. Plaut. *Cist.* 235, Cic. *Rep.* 1.60 and 2.50, Caes. *BG* 7.4 and 33, Livy 36.2.2 (Antiochus), Varro *Rust.* 3.16.6, Vell. 2.2.3 (cf. Livy 2.54.5), Cic. *Mur.* 74, and *lex Coloniae Genetivae* (*RS* 25) 94.30, 125.14, 128.12–13.

136. Lintott (1999b) 99–100.

137. Livy 4.38.3, 41.10.9.

138. Livy frequently uses *consulare imperium* as a shorthand term for the general idea of consular power, and often describes the Conflict of the Orders as a clash between consular *imperium* and tribunician *potestas*: 2.27.11, 2.55.2, 3.6.9, 3.9.2, 3.9.8, 3.9.10, 3.17.7, 3.30.4.

139. See Mason (1974) 26 and 44 for examples and citations.

ishes that are devoid of legal significance? Cicero frequently refers to the *summum imperium* of consuls, which certainly sounds like a clear-cut statement that consuls possessed a higher degree of *imperium* than other magistrates, but this idea collapses instantly when one notes that he *also* refers to the *imperium* of the propraetor Verres as *summum*.[140] A praetor was the lowest-ranking magistrate invested with *imperium*, so describing the *imperium* of a propraetor like Verres as *summum* must be either an enormous and obvious error or an indication that *summum imperium* was merely a decorative phrase devoid of any legal or technical significance. Cicero's use of hyperbole is obvious: he describes the *imperium* of the *decemviri* of 451 BC as *summum* (and their *potestas* as both *summa* and *maxima*), but since the consuls and tribunes had resigned their offices before the appointment of the *decemviri*, it seems strange that the *decemviri* should have had or needed *summum imperium* when they were the only *imperium*-bearing magistrates in the state.[141] Why was *summum imperium* needed when there was no other type of *imperium* in use at the time? In a similar manner, Livy describes the *imperium* of dictators as *summum*, which might be taken as an unambiguous statement of the dictator's superiority if Livy did not also describe consular *imperium* as *summum*.[142] Even more confusing: in some places Livy refers to dictatorial authority as being merely *imperium* (i.e., not *summum*), which seems to imply a lower level of authority than the consular *summum imperium* mentioned elsewhere.[143] Given this prolific and indiscriminate use of the phrase *summum imperium*, we must accept either that all *imperium* was *summum* (and therefore *summum imperium* was just *imperium*) or that the use of the modifier *summum* was simply a rhetorical flourish. Indeed, Livy often uses such modifiers for rhetorical effect when describing *imperium*, even in later periods when different types of magistrates possessed *imperium*.[144] *Imperium* is a tricky word to translate, and any discussion of this concept must focus not only on vocabulary but also on how the Romans described military authority working in their society.

140. Consular *summum* imperium: Cic. *Rab. Perd.* 3, *ND* 2.11, *QFr.* 1.1.37, *Mur.* 74, *Phil.* 3.10 (*totum imperium*), and *Phil.* 5.44 (*maximum imperium*). Verres: Cic. *Verr.* 2.3.45 and 2.5.134.

141. Cic. *Rep.* 2.61.

142. Dictators: Livy 6.38.3, 8.32.3; Consuls: 4.1.3, 4.5.1.

143. Livy 4.4.3.

144. For example, Livy (4.26.10) records that in 431 BC the consuls angrily stated that "the authority (*ius*) of the *summum imperium* had been betrayed by the senators and the consulship placed under the yoke of tribunician *potestas*," but because the consulship was the only regular magistracy *cum imperio* at the time, the use of the modifier *summum* can be only a rhetorical flourish, and not a technical term.

A short example illustrates the challenge posed by the word *imperium*. In 211 BC when Hannibal was advancing on the walls of Rome, Livy reports that the senate in a panic declared that all former dictators, consuls, and censors should have *imperium* in the city (*omnes qui dictatores, consules censoresve fuissent cum imperio esse, donec recessisset a muris hostis*).[145] Taken uncritically, this statement suggests that a dozen or more men — in addition to the two consuls and a proconsul en route to Rome — were invested with *imperium* to face Hannibal. This seems highly improbable. Most Roman armies operated perfectly well with only one *imperium*-bearing commander, and having so many men in one place invested with *imperium* would have been a confusing liability because it created too many possibilities for conflict and disagreement. In all likelihood, Livy is actually describing a *tumultus*, which was an emergency situation in which consuls were given freer rein to protect the state but one that stopped short of imposing martial law by allowing the use of *imperium* in the city.[146] In this light, Livy must surely have meant that men with experience in the highest offices were given special commissions for the defense of the city, but *imperium* was hardly necessary for them to set watches and organize defenses. Because only the two consuls and the proconsul led Rome's soldiers against Hannibal on this occasion, we should not imagine that the ex-magistrates were actually given *imperium*.

Another piece of evidence that crumbles quickly is the phrase *imperium domi militiaeque*. To begin, the words *domi* and *militiae* are locative forms, and their use with *imperium* does not express a change in the nature of *imperium* (i.e., domestic *imperium* vs. military *imperium*) but indicates different locations in which the singular *imperium* existed (i.e., *imperium* used at home and at war).[147] Unlike the phrase *auspicia urbana*, which seems to clearly identify a particular type of *auspicia* different from other types of *auspicia*, *imperium domi* simply indicates a place where *imperium* might be used in particular circumstances. *Imperium domi militiaeque*, therefore, should demonstrate not the existence of two different types of *imperium* but simply the use of *imperium* in two different places. Furthermore, the phrase *imperium domi militiaeque* appears only three times in Latin sources, and these actually refute — rather than support — the idea that a weakened form of *imperium* was a normal type of civilian authority in the city. The first of these refer-

145. Livy 26.10.9.
146. On the *tumultus*, see Oakley (1997–2004) 2.126–28, Lintott (1999b) 91–92, and Golden (2013) 42–86.
147. See Sandberg (2001) 119–20.

ences is quickly dispensed with because close inspection makes clear that the author intended the word *imperium* to refer to the Roman state rather than magisterial authority, and furthermore it refers to the regal period, which predates the supposed creation of *imperium domi* in the republic.[148] Second, in his account of 300 BC Livy composed a speech to illustrate plebeian discontent with the patrician monopoly of the consulship and priesthoods, and he makes one plebeian say: "These same things are always heard: *auspicia* reside in you alone, and you alone have a heritage, and you alone have *iustum imperium* and *auspicium* in the city and in war (*iustum imperium et auspicium domi militiaeque*)."[149] The structure of this sentence may suggest a *chiasmus*, in which the phrase *domi militiaeque* modifies only *auspicium*, while *iustum* modifies *imperium*, but even if Livy intended for *domi militiaeque* to modify *imperium* (and for *iustum* to modify *auspicium*), the context of these words is not a clear legal description of the working of *imperium* but an accusation put into the mouth of an angry protester against patrician privilege in a piece of heated dialogue. In point of fact, the speaker here is clearly wrong, since plebeians had held the consulship (with *imperium* and *auspicium*) by that time, so his statement is meant to be provocative rather than factually accurate.

Similar problems arise in the third and most famous reference to *imperium domi militiaeque*, which appears in Sallust's description of the *senatus consultum ultimum* (SCU) passed in 63 BC:

> *Itaque, quod plerumque in atroci negotio solet, senatus decrevit darent operam consules ne quid res publica detrimenti caperet. Ea potestas per senatum more Romano magistratui maxuma permittitur, exercitum parare, bellum gerere, coercere omnibus modis socios atque civis, domi militiaeque imperium atque iudicium summum habere; aliter sine populi iussu nullius earum rerum consuli ius est.*

Therefore, as is often done in an emergency situation, the senate decreed that the consuls should see to it that the republic suffer no harm. That power that—by Roman custom—is entrusted to a magistrate by the senate is the greatest: to prepare an army, to wage war, to coerce by all means allies and citizens, and to hold the command and highest jurisdiction both

---

148. Livy 1.pr.9: *ad illa mihi pro se quisque acriter intendat animum, quae vita, qui mores fuerint, per quos viros quibusque artibus domi militiaeque et partum et auctum imperium sit.*

149. Livy 10.8.9, *semper ista audita sunt eadem, penes vos auspicia esse, vos solos gentem habere, vos solos iustum imperium et auspicium domi militiaeque* (Drogula, trans.). See Oakley (1997–2004) 4.112–16 on the *gentes*.

at home and in military affairs. In other situations, a consul has authority in none of these areas without the command of the people.[150]

As a careful reading should make clear, Sallust is not talking about two distinct types of *imperium* — one type used in the sphere *domi* and another (different) type used in the sphere *militiae*. Rather, he is saying that the SCU authorized a magistrate to use his *imperium* both in the sphere *domi* and in the sphere *militiae*; the same *imperium* was used in two different spheres. There were no *imperium militiae* and *imperium domi*, but simply the single and indivisible *imperium*, which was the total and autocratic authority of martial law. Second, Sallust is also explicit that the SCU authorized consuls to perform those actions that involved the exercise of highest power (*potestas maxuma*), actions they were normally forbidden to undertake without a special vote of the people: preparing an army, waging war, coercing citizens and allies *by all means*, and holding *imperium* and *iudicum* both inside and outside Rome. Although many of these actions were common, all required a specific vote of the people, and none could be undertaken simply because a man was inaugurated as consul.[151] More specifically, a commander could not hold and use *imperium* in the city (*domi*) or in the field (*militiae*) without a vote of the people. It was normal for the Roman people to authorize their commanders to use *imperium* in the sphere *militiae* by assigning them a particular military campaign as a *provincia* (see chapter 3), but authorization to use *imperium* in the city was extraordinarily rare. Thus, Sallust's passage demonstrates clearly that consuls did not use *imperium* within the city except in dire national emergencies, and even then only when they were specifically ordered to do so by the state. There is no good literary evidence to support the contention that a weakened form of

---

150. Sall. *Cat.* 29.2–3 (Drogula, trans.). See McGushin (1977) 175–78 and 305–8.

151. McGushin (1977) 177 restated Sallust's point as: "Except in the case of the Senate using its prerogative to issue the ultimate decree, the consul has no *ius* to do any of these things except by order of the people." McGushin is surely correct: Roman commanders could recruit an army and wage a war only if instructed to do so by the state, and they could only use the soldiers assigned to them and fight the enemies declared as their *provincia*. Similarly, the ability to take up *imperium* and (with it) coerce citizens and allies *by all means* required a vote by the *comitia curiata*, and permission of the state was needed for a commander to use his *imperium* in the sphere *domi* (e.g., to hold a triumph). Finally, the highest degree of jurisdiction (*iudicium summum*) almost certainly refers to the fact that a commander *cum imperio* acted under the aegis of martial law and therefore could ignore the citizens' right of appeal and impose any judicial sentence he wished, including summary execution. Since commanders normally could not use their *imperium* in the city, consuls could exercise *iudicium summum* in Rome only if they received special authority (from the people or through a *senatus consultum ultimum*) to use their *imperium* inside the *pomerium*.

imperium was the basis of the consuls' civilian authority. If anything, Sallust's use of the phrase *imperium domi militiaeque* actually refutes this idea and indicates that there was only a singular and complete *imperium*.

In lieu of any actual statement that *imperium* was normally used in the city, supporters of Mommsen's theory point to the *fasces* as evidence that consuls held *imperium* within the *pomerium*. The *fasces* were bundles of rods that symbolized the office of high magistrates and accompanied them during their term in office, carried by special attendants called lictors. During the republic, magistrates who had the right to possess *imperium* outside the city could insert axes (*secures*) into their *fasces* once they had crossed the *pomerium* and exited the city, but the axes were normally forbidden in the city.[152] According to Mommsen's theory, the *fasces* with axes originally represented the absolute authority (*imperium*) of Rome's early kings, and when the monarchy was exiled, the *fasces* were transferred (along with the king's *imperium*) to the new consulship. He reasoned that the *fasces* with the axes removed represented *imperium domi*, whereas the inclusion of the axes in the *fasces*, which could happen only outside the *pomerium*, symbolized the unrestricted power of *imperium militiae*. This is an attractive argument that seems to work neatly, but the fundamental assumption on which it is based — that the *fasces* represent or symbolize *imperium* — is flawed.

The underlying cause of this assumption is the fact that ancient authors referred to the *fasces* as *insignia imperii*. Staveley produced one of the strongest arguments for this association, citing eleven references to the *fasces* as *insignia imperii*,[153] but under scrutiny his examples fail to prove his point and instead suggest that *imperium* was strictly an extra-urban authority and that *imperium domi* did not exist. In the first place, nearly half of his evidence (five references) comes from literary descriptions of the regal period or the first part of 509 BC, before the supposed creation of *prorogatio* and before any distinction between *imperium domi* and *militiae* could have been made.[154] These five references

---

152. Livy (3.36.4–5) says *decemviri* had axes in their *fasces* because the citizens' right of appeal had been suspended. See also Cic. *Rep.* 2.31–32 and 2.55; Dion. Hal. *AR* 5.19.3, 5.75.2, 10.59.4–5; Livy 2.1.8; Val. Max. 4.1.1; Plut. *Publ.* 10.5–6.

153. Staveley (1963) 459, cites Cic. *Rep.* 2.55, *Leg. Man.* 32, *Lig.* 22, *Verr.* 2.5.39, 5.97, 5.167; Sall. *Cat.* 36.1; Livy 1.8.2, 1.17.6, 2.7.7; Dion. Hal. *AR* 3.61.1–2. See Mommsen (1887-8) 1.373–75, Marshall (1984) 130–38, Schäfer (1989), and Hölkeskamp (2011) 169–71.

154. Dion. Hal. *AR* 3.61.1–2, Cic. *Rep.* 2.55, Livy 1.8.2, 1.17.6, 2.7.7. All of these predate Mommsen's hypothetical division of regal *imperium* into republican *imperium domi* and *imperium militiae*. Furthermore, the reference from Dionysius of Halicarnassus includes all curule trappings — including a royal crown — as *insignia imperii*.

merely indicate that writers of the late republic believed that the early kings and first consuls had possessed the *fasces*, which could have been accurately called *insignia imperii* until the introduction of *provocatio* that forced the removal of the axes from the *fasces* in the city. Of Staveley's remaining six references to *insignia imperii*, three refer to the *fasces* as they appear outside the city (i.e., with axes included), two do not actually mention the *fasces* or *imperium*, and one refers to the *imperium* of the Roman people (and not the authority of the consuls).[155] One of these references (from Sallust) even specifies that Catiline had several types of *insignia imperii* outside of Rome other than his *fasces*.[156] None of Staveley's evidence demonstrates that the *fasces* represented *imperium* in the city, although three of his references do show that the *fasces* could be called *insignia imperii* outside of Rome, once axes had been added to the rods. This reading is supported by another reference to *insignia imperii* that Staveley curiously does not cite, namely Livy 28.24.14, which again refers to the *fasces* fully equipped with axes (*fasces securesque*) as *insignia imperii* outside of Rome.[157] All of this suggests that the *fasces* represented or symbolized *imperium* only when they were completed by the addition of axes inserted into them, which could happen only outside the *pomerium* when a consul was acting in the sphere *militiae*, where no one has ever doubted that *imperium* existed and was complete. Dionysius of Halicarnassus gives further support to this. In his description of the foundation of the republic, he specifically connects the axes (πελέκεις) to the royal power of the exiled kings that was transferred to the first two consuls in 509 BC:

> After the consuls had settled these matters, fearing, as I suspect, that the masses might gain a false impression of their new form of government and

---

155. Cic. *Verr.* 2.5.39 and *Lig.* 22, and Sall. *Cat.* 36.1 all refer to the appearance of *fasces* outside the *pomerium*, which was different from the their appearance inside the city, since axes were added to the *fasces* when the magistrate left the city. At best, these passages indicate that the *fasces* represented *imperium* when they included the axes, which they only did in the provinces. Cic. *Leg. Man.* 32 does not actually mention lictors and *fasces* as *insignia imperii*, and *Verr.* 2.5.167 does not mention *imperium*. Cic. *Verr.* 2.5.97 has an imprecise meaning in its reference to *imperii populi Romani nomen ac fasces*, but it seems to refer to Rome's empire.

156. Sall. *Cat.* 36.1 [*Catilina*]: *cum fasces atque aliis imperi insignibus in castra ad Manlium contendit* ("With the *fasces* and the other insignia of *imperium*, Catiline rushed into the camp to Manlius") (Drogula, trans.).

157. Staveley also does not mention the use of the phrase *insignia imperii* in Cic. *Har. Resp.* 3, probably because the intended meaning and use of the phrase is vague. Even in the Campus Martius—which lay outside Rome's *pomerium*—a consul or praetor was entitled to insert axes into his *fasces* (Livy 24.9.2).

imagine that two kings had become masters of the state instead of one, since each of the consuls had the twelve axes, like the kings, they resolved to quiet the fears of the citizens and to lessen the hatred of their power by ordering that one of the consuls should be preceded by the twelve axes and the other by twelve lictors with rods only, or, as some relate, with clubs also, and that they should receive the axes in rotation.[158]

Later that year, the consuls would remove the axes from their *fasces* altogether when in Rome, but until that time Dionysius is clear that absolute royal power was represented by the axes. Thus, for symbols of *imperium*, we should probably look to the axes consuls held outside the city rather than to the bundle of rods carried by consuls in the city. While the *fasces* (devoid of axes) that accompanied consuls in the city were certainly symbols of consular power in the abstract sense, the literary evidence provides no support for the assumption that they represented the consuls' specific legal authority of command until the axes were inserted into the *fasces*, which only happened outside the city.

Other evidence undermines the notion that the *fasces* without axes represented *imperium*. In the *de lege agraria*, Cicero associates the *fasces* not with *imperium* but with *iudicium* and *potestas*, and in the *pro Cluentio* he refers to *fasces* as only one of many symbols of magisterial honor.[159] Cicero also wrote to his brother that the *fasces* were insignia of *potestas* and *dignitas*, a definition that he and Valerius Maximus repeat elsewhere.[160] Furthermore, lictors (per-

158. Dion. Hal. *AR* 5.2.1 (Cary, trans.): ὡς δὲ κατεστήσαντο ταῦτα, δείσαντες, ὡς ἐμοὶ δοκεῖ, μὴ δόξα τοῖς πολλοῖς ἐγγένηται περὶ τῆς καινῆς πολιτείας οὐκ ἀληθής, ὅτι δύο βασιλεῖς κύριοι γεγόνασι τῆς πόλεως ἀνθ᾽ ἑνὸς ἑκατέρου τῶν ὑπάτων τοὺς δώδεκα πελέκεις ἔχοντος, ὥσπερ εἶχον οἱ βασιλεῖς, ἔκριναν τό τε δέος ἀφελέσθαι τῶν πολιτῶν καὶ τῆς ἐξουσίας μειῶσαι τὸν φθόνον, τοῦ μὲν ἑτέρου τῶν ὑπάτων τοὺς δώδεκα κατατάξαντες προηγεῖσθαι πελέκεις, τοῦ δ᾽ ἑτέρου δώδεκα ὑπηρέτας ῥάβδους ἔχοντας μόνον, ὡς δέ τινες ἱστοροῦσι, καὶ κορύνας, γίνεσθαι δὲ τῶν πελέκεων τὴν παράληψιν ἐκ περιτροπῆς ἕνα μῆνα κατέχοντος αὐτοὺς ἑκατέρου παραλλάξ.

159. Cic. *Agr.* 1.9 (speaking of a proposal to create ten grain commissioners with extensive powers): *quorum cum adventus graves, cum fasces formidolosi, tum vero iudicium ac potestas erit non ferenda; licebit enim, quod videbitur, publicum iudicare, quod iudicarint, vendere.* Cic. *Cluent.* 154: *quodque permulta essent ornamenta, quibus eam mitigare molestiam posset, locus, auctoritas, domi splendor, apud exteras nationes nomen et gratia, toga praetexta, sella curulis, insignia, fasces, exercitus, imperia, provinciae.*

160. Cic. *QFr* 1.1.13: *maioraque praeferant fasces illi ac secures dignitatis insignia quam potestatis.* See also 1.1.35, where Cicero urges his brother: *ut remoto imperio ac vi potestatis et fascium publicanos cum Graecis gratia atque auctoritate coniungas.* Although the phrase *insignia potestatis* does not appear as frequently as *insignia imperii*, the two terms are used in the exact same manner. For example, Cicero (*Agr.* 2.32) says that the *decemviri* proposed by the *lex Agraria* of 63 BC were to have the *insignia potestatis* in Rome, which he identifies as consisting of scribes, lictors, criers, and chicken keepers. Valerius

haps bearing *fasces*) were given to other persons who did not possess *imperium*, such as magistrates, senators, priests, and ambassadors, which is hard to reconcile with the claim that lictors and *fasces* necessarily represented *imperium*.[161] Indeed, even the *duumviri* of Capua are recorded as possessing lictors bearing *fasces*, which Cicero remarks as being highly unusual for a colony and a sign of great presumption and haughtiness, although he does not indicate that it was improper for *duumviri* who lacked *imperium* to have *fasces*.[162] Even dead aristocrats were accompanied by *fasces* during their funeral processions.[163] Finally, when Caesar's lieutenant Curio visited Cicero in April of 49 BC, Cicero asked why Curio was in possession of six laureled *fasces*.[164] Curio responded that he only had six because he had not wanted the full consular twelve, although he added that he could have had the full number had he wished. This seems ample evidence that the number of a commander's *fasces* had nothing to do with his authority and prerogatives but merely with prestige and honor. Otherwise, it is hard to believe that Curio would have passed up holding still greater authority and power had it really been freely available for him to claim.

Finally, the fact that the two consuls traditionally alternated possession of the *fasces* when in Rome illustrates that the *fasces* cannot represent possession of *imperium*: if they did, then the alternation of the *fasces* in Rome would require us to accept that only one consul held *imperium* at a time, which would undermine the fundamental principle that the two consuls were colleagues with equal authority.[165] Some scholars have tried to escape this obvious di-

---

Maximus (6.5.2) describes the ornaments of a consul's office as *insignia potestatis*. Cicero (*Pis.* 23) also refers to lictors (but not *fasces*) as the ornaments of the consulship.

161. Mommsen (1887–88) 1.384 notes that the former aedile acting as *iudex quaestionis inter sicarios* was assigned two lictors and points out (389–92) that several Roman priests were also attended by lictors. Festus (82L) even specifies that the *flamen Dialis* was accompanied by a lictor. Cicero also refers to legates and quaestors possessing lictors when abroad in the provinces (Cic. *Verr.* 2.1.67, 2.11, *Planc.* 98), while Livy (1.20.2) and Plutarch (*Quaest. Rom.* 113) both point out that some priests possessed the same *sella curulis* used by consuls and praetors. Staveley himself (1963) 470 acknowledges that lictors with *fasces* were given to ambassadors and senators visiting the provinces in the first century BC and can offer no better explanation than that, in those cases, the *fasces* were merely tokens of prestige and not *imperium*, a statement that seems to undermine much of his argument.

162. Cic. *Agr.* 2.93: *deinde anteibant lictores non cum bacillis, sed, ut hic praetoribus urbanis anteeunt, cum fascibus bini.*

163. Polyb. 6.53.8.

164. Cic. *Att.* 10.4.9–10. If Curio claimed he had been given the *fasces* by the state, they should not have been laureled (because he had not yet won any victory of his own). If he claimed he had them as Caesar's *legatus pro praetore*, he probably should have had twelve *fasces*, since he was merely partaking of Caesar's own *imperium*.

165. By tradition, consuls rotated possession of the *fasces* in alternate months (Cic. *Rep.* 2.55, Livy

lemma by maintaining that one consul's *imperium* and *auspicium* were somehow dormant except for the purpose of obstructing his colleague, but this seems overly contrived: if consuls did indeed use their *imperium* for civilian governance within the *pomerium*, this suggestion would reduce the dormant consul to a mere sinecure, since he could do little without the fundamental authority of his office. Furthermore, this idea of dormancy contradicts Livy's clear statement that only the symbols of authority (but not the authority itself) alternated monthly; he emphasized that both consuls possessed the full authority of their office, although only one of them was permitted to hold the *fasces* at any given time in Rome: *omnia iura, omnia insignia primi consules tenuere; id modo cautum est ne, si ambo fasces haberent, duplicatus terror videretur.*[166] Lictors bearing *fasces* were certainly important and awe-inspiring symbols of power, but like *imperium* they were merely aspects or traits of certain magistracies or officials, which explains why Cicero frequently refers to *imperium* and *fasces* as separate things, and Gellius indicates that the ability to take up and possess the *fasces* was something that lay within the *potestas* of the consulship.[167] Taken altogether, the idea that *fasces* can be used as evidence for the use of *imperium* as a civilian authority inside the *pomerium* seems extremely unlikely.

LIKE THE *FASCES*, other historical phenomena have been suggested as implying the existence of *imperium domi*, but all tend to collapse quickly upon inspection. Foremost among these is the belief that republican consuls and (especially) praetors needed *imperium domi* to exercise jurisdiction in the city, but as has already been argued, this assumption is based on errors in Livy's text and the assumption that definitions of jurisdiction devised and used in the high empire (or even in the Byzantine era) were equally valid many centuries earlier in the middle republic. It is a shaky argument to insist that praetors in the third century BC needed *imperium domi* to exercise jurisdiction

---

2.1.8, 8.12.13, 9.8.2, Dion. Hal. *AR* 5.2.1; see Lintott [1999a] 100). This practice may have been discontinued for a period in the middle republic (Staveley [1963] 461–62), but in the late republic is was certainly in force and obeyed even by Caesar (Suet. *Iul.* 20.1).

166. Livy 2.1.8. Furthermore, although it is rare to find consuls obstructing one another, it was certainly possible: in 95 BC the consul Q. Mucius Scaevola vetoed his colleague's request for a triumph (Cic. *Pis.* 62, Ascon. 15 C). On the dormancy of one consul's *imperium* and *auspicia*, see Linderski (1986) 2179 n. 115.

167. Cic. *Rep.* 2.31, *Cluent.* 154, *Agr.* 2.45, *Lig.* 22, *Phil.* 11.20.17, *QFr* 1.1.35 (cf. Livy 9.34.2, Mart. 8.66). See also Gellius (*NA* 2.15.4): *legis Iuliae priori ex consulibus fasces sumendi potestas fit, non qui pluris annos natus est, sed qui pluris liberos quam collega aut in sua potestate habet aut bello amisit.*

just because praetors four hundred or five hundred years later were described as using *imperium* in their administration of justice. For example, the *Institutes* of Gaius (second century AD) refer to certain judicial actions as *iudicia imperio continentia*, which certainly seems to demonstrate that *imperium* was used for jurisdiction in Gaius's time, but how useful is this passage for understanding jurisdiction in the mid-republic? Because *imperium* had undergone considerable change by the time Gaius and other jurists were writing in the imperial era, their works were intended to present current practice and legal thought rather than an accurate description of Roman law as it had been practiced centuries earlier. Close examination reveals problems: Gaius points out that the *iudicia imperio continentia* were used for cases involving foreigners or for cases *held outside of Rome*, and he differentiates these cases from those legal actions (*iudicia legitima*) held between Roman citizens inside the city of Rome or within one mile of it.[168] Buckland has emphasized that *imperium* "played no part" in the *iudicia legitima*, which means that *imperium* was not used for the exercise of jurisdiction between citizens in Rome.[169] What then to make of the *iudicia imperio continentia*? Unlike his definition of the *iudicia legitima*, Gaius does not actually describe *iudicia imperio continentia* as actions that took place in Rome; he defines them only as legal actions taking place outside the city or involving a foreigner as a judge or litigator. Roman commanders were obviously free to use their *imperium* in their exercise of jurisdiction outside of Rome. Did Gaius mean that *iudicia imperio continentia* included cases involving a foreigner *in Rome*, such as those before the peregrine

---

168. Gaius 4.104–5 (Drogula, trans.), *legitima sunt iudicia quae in urbe Roma vel intra primum urbis Romae miliarium inter omnes cives Romanos sub uno iudice accipiuntur; eaque <e> lege Iulia iudiciaria, nisi in anno et sex mensibus iudicata fuerint, expirant. Et hoc est quod vulgo dicitur e lege Iulia litem anno et sex mensibus mori. Imperio vero continentur recuperatoria et quae sub uno iudice accipiuntur interveniente peregrini persona iudicis aut litigatoris. In eadem causa sunt, quaecumque extra primum urbis Romae miliarium tam inter cives Romanos quam inter peregrinos accipiuntur. Ideo autem imperio contineri iudicia dicuntur, quia tamdiu valent, quamdiu is qui ea praecepit imperium habebit.* "*Legitima iudicia* are those actions which are taken up in the city of Rome or within the first milestone of the city of Rome among all Roman citizens, under one *iudex*; and under the *lex Julia iudiciaria* these expire unless they are adjudicated within one year and six months. This is the reason why it is said by the commons that under the *lex Julia* a lawsuit dies in one year and six months. Legal actions authorized by *imperium* are those taken up under *recuperatores*, or under a single *iudex* if a participating party — either the judge or a litigator — is a foreigner. In the same classification are those taken up outside the first milestone of the city of Rome whether the case is between Roman citizens or between foreigners. Moreover these actions are said to be authorized by *imperium* because they are valid only so long as he who initially received the action had *imperium*."

169. Buckland (1963) 687.

praetor? This question is—at best—unclear, but the fact that Gaius describes *iudicia imperio continentia* as including cases in which *a judge* might be a foreigner suggests that he is referring to court cases held not Rome but in provincial cities. It makes no legal sense that judges in Rome required *imperium* to exercise jurisdiction over foreigners in *iudicia imperio continentia* but not over Roman citizens in *iudicia legitima*. Why did jurisdiction over foreigners require greater authority and force than jurisdiction over citizens? Roman law underwent substantial change between the middle republic and the high empire, and by the time Gaius was writing in the second century AD *imperium* probably was used to conduct *iudicia imperio continentia* in or near Rome, but there is no compelling reason to believe this was a republican practice rather than a subsequent development.

Some might think that praetors needed *imperium* in order to possess enough authority to impose the most serious penalties on condemned citizens, but this was not the case. All magistrates possessed *coercitio*, which invested them with the authority to coerce or otherwise compel citizens to obey their instructions and decisions.[170] *Coercitio*, as a source of civilian authority, was subject to certain limitations, which made it different from the terrible and unrestrained power conferred by *imperium*. Nippel provides a detailed discussion of the coercive authority of civilian magistrates, and describes *coercitio* as

> the general term for a number of measures a magistrate could use to enforce obedience without instituting legal proceedings. It covers scourging and execution (by decapitation with an axe), arresting and carrying a disobedient person to prison, imposing a fine up to a *multa maxima* limit or seizing a pledge (*pignoris capio*). The gravest form of *coercitio*—scourging and execution—was banned by the *provocatio* laws.[171]

Nippel's analysis demonstrates the extensive coercive powers available to Rome's civilian magistrates, since tribunes of the plebs, aediles, quaestors, and *tresviri capitales* all needed to be able to enforce their authority and judgments, but none of these magistrates possessed *imperium* at any time. Although Nippel refers to scourging and execution as forms of *coercitio*, he also describes them as punishments "exclusively associated with the *imperium* of the chief

---

170. Cic. *Leg.* 3.6, Frontin. *Aq.* 129, Livy 4.53.7, 26.36.12, Suet. *Claud.* 38.2. Nippel (1995) 5–12 gives a detailed discussion of *coercitio*, although he believes that the highest forms of punishment (flogging and execution) could only be performed by magistrates with *imperium*. See Jolowicz and Nicholas (1972) 305–20.

171. Nippel (1984) 22–27 (22 quoted) and (1995) 5–12.

magistrates," and since scourging and execution were banned by *provocatio*, it seems likely that *imperium* was likewise banned within Rome.[172] Because all magistrates had some level of coercive force, it seems convoluted and unnecessary to imagine their *coercitio* came from any source other than *potestas*. Indeed, there is no reason to imagine that magistrates needed *imperium* to enforce their authority in Rome, since *coercitio* authorized considerable use of force, although it was subject to the restraints of civil law. While *coercitio* precluded the use of martial law and military forces against citizens, it did enable an official to set watches, form a *praesidium* of armed guards, or even mobilize an armed mob of friends and retainers.[173] Livy, Velleius Paterculus, Suetonius, and Gellius all refer to the effectiveness of magisterial use of *coercitio* in Rome, and Tacitus mentions *coercitio* as enabling aediles to perform their police functions in Rome.[174]

Naturally, higher magistrates possessed higher levels of *coercitio*, so that it was apparent who had the greater authority of compulsion in case of a conflict between magistrates.[175] Caesar as praetor used his *potestas* and *coercitio* to imprison an official inquisitor into the Catilinarian Conspiracy who had falsely charged him (a superior magistrate) with complicity in the conspiracy.[176] In fact, *coercitio* seems to have provided more force than most magistrates needed, and there is little evidence of magistrates resorting to compulsion in the performance of normal civilian governance.[177] The fact that magistrates resorted to force so rarely in their civilian duties brings into question why civilian magistrates would need *imperium* to govern in the city. This is well

172. Nippel (1995) 5.

173. See also Lintott (1999b) 74 n. 5 and (1999a) 99.

174. Livy 4.53.7–8, Vell. 2.47.3, Tac. *Ann.* 3.52.2–3, Suet. *Aug.* 45.3, Gell. 13.12.9. Tacitus was so accustomed to the idea of *coercitio* being used to enforce domestic order that he described priests as having the *ius coercendi* during assemblies among the German tribes (*Ger.* 11.4).

175. Cic. *Leg.* 3.6: *magistratus nec oboedientem et noxium civem multa vinculis verberibusve coherceto, ni par maiorve potestas populusve prohibessit*, Mil. 89 *an consules in praetore coercendo fortes fuissent?* Livy (3.55.9) records that an aedile could be arrested by a higher magistrate, but this de facto use of force was not appropriate or legal (*non iure fiat*) because magistrates were not supposed to be harmed while in office.

176. Suet. *Iul.* 17.2: *[Caesar] coniecit in carcerem; eodem Novium quaestorem, quod compellari apud se maiorem potestatem passus esset.*

177. Nippel (1984) 22, notes that most reported cases of *coercitio* being used in the middle and late republic were cases of a conflict between two magistrates or between a magistrate and a senator. It is likely that commoners, who individually had no hope of resisting magisterial *coercitio* (unless a tribune intervened), readily obeyed magisterial orders. Lintott (1999a) 97 also notes magistrates in Rome did not use their coercive authority on fellow magistrates.

demonstrated by C. Pomptinus (pr. 63 BC): although there was some doubt as to whether he had properly received a *lex curiata* (and therefore may not have been authorized to possess *imperium*), he was able to arrest and hold Catiline's co-conspirators in Rome by virtue of the *coercitio* invested in his office.[178] Even though Brennan accepts the existence of *imperium domi*, he admits that it generally was not used for coercive force against fellow magistrates: "When push came to shove, in the city at least, members of the same college almost never used *imperium* to check *imperium*"; and "it is significant that for the later Republic we do not have a single secure instance of a praetor in the city using his *imperium* to veto a current colleague's actions, even in the realm of civil law."[179] In the normal performance of civilian governance in the sphere *domi*, the *coercitio* included within a magistrate's *potestas* gave him all the authority he needed to enforce his will.

The notion that magistrates needed *imperium* to perform these civil tasks probably derives from a passage of Varro preserved by Gellius indicating that consuls and "others possessing *imperium*" have the power of summons (*vocatio*):

> In a magistracy . . . some have the power of summons, others of arrest, others neither; summoning, for example, belongs to the consuls and others possessing the *imperium*; arrest, to the tribunes of the commons and the rest who are attended by a messenger; neither summoning nor arrest to the quaestors and others who have neither a lictor nor a messenger.[180]

Obviously, nothing in this passage indicates that *vocatio* derived from *imperium*, nor should such a notion be inserted into Varro's words. All that can safely be said is that the phrase "others possessing *imperium*" is a logical shorthand abbreviation for Rome's senior magistrates, a literary device that Varro

---

178. Cic. *Cat.* 3.5 and 14, *Flacc.* 102, *Prov. Cons.* 32, Sall. *Cat.* 45.1–4.

179. Brennan (2000) 42–43 (cf. 447). He is able to find only one incident in Roman history, when the consul Q. Mucius Scaevola vetoed the *senatus consultum* that his colleague, L. Licinius Crassus, should celebrate a triumph (Cic. *Pis.* 62). Nothing in the sources indicates that Scaevola used his *imperium* to exercise his veto; all magistrates — including those without *imperium* — were able to veto the actions of their colleagues, so the prerogative of veto did not depend on *imperium* (tribunes, who possessed the most potent veto of all, did not possess *imperium* but could block the actions of consuls and praetors).

180. Varro in Gell. *NA* 13.12.6: *in magistratu . . . habent alii vocationem, alii prensionem, alii neutrum; vocationem, ut consules et ceteri qui habent imperium; prensionem, ut tribuni plebis et alii qui habent viatorem; neque vocationem neque prensionem, ut quaestores et ceteri qui neque lictorem habent neque viatorem* (Rolfe, trans.).

uses again in the same sentence to attribute the power of arrest to those magistrates who "have a messenger." If one is unwilling to accept that messengers conferred the power of arrest on magistrates, he should hesitate before accepting that *imperium* conferred the power of summons. Badian demonstrated that Varro's statement cannot logically be reversed to equate the *ius vocationis* with *imperium*, so this passage provides no evidence for magistrates using *imperium* in the city.[181]

Another argument against the existence of *imperium domi* is the surprising weakness of sitting consuls (and, later, praetors) to enforce their will and defend themselves against attacks by others. Tribunes of the plebs—despite being considered lower magistrates and having no part of *imperium*—were able to prosecute sitting consuls: in 172 BC the tribunes forced both consuls to leave the city and set out for their provinces, threatening the consuls with prosecution and punishment if they remained any longer within Rome.[182] In fact, tribunes could and did arrest consuls and throw them into prison, which seems beyond belief if the consuls really did possess *imperium* within the *pomerium*.[183] Likewise, tribunes could summon consuls to appear before them, consuls could not raise soldiers and take command of military units unless authorized by the senate, and the senate could order the consuls to name a dictator and even abdicate their office before the expiry of their term.[184] Praetors fared no better: in 168/7 BC a tribune dragged one praetor off the rostra, and another was compelled by senatorial vote to remain in Rome and preside over the lawcourts rather than set out for the military command that had been assigned to him previously.[185] A praetor in 159 BC was even fined while in office for illegally opposing the pontifex maximus in some matter, and Gaius Marius as tribune in 119 BC forced the senate to rescind an edict by threatening to imprison both consuls.[186] In accounts of early Rome, the plebs are fre-

181. Badian (1990) 468–69.
182. Livy 42.21.4–5 and 8.
183. Ancient sources record that tribunes imprisoned both consuls in 151 BC (Livy *Per.* 48) and in 138 BC (Cic. *Leg.* 3.20, Livy *Per.* 55). In 431 BC the tribunes threatened to imprison both consuls if they refused to obey a senatorial order to name a dictator (the consuls obeyed) (Livy 4.26.9–11), and in 60 BC the tribune L. Flavius imprisoned the consul Q. Caecilius Metellus Celer for his opposition to legislation favorable to Pompey (Cic. *Att.* 2.1.8, Dio 37.50.1). Cicero (*Agr.* 2.101) also remarks that consuls could be arrested by tribunes.
184. Livy 3.64.6, 5.31.8, 8.12.13, 8.15.5, 10.39.4, 27.38.9, 28.45.1–11, 42.10.11–14. On the inability of the consuls to compel the senate, see also Livy 32.28.8, 40.26.6, and 42.9.6.
185. Polyb. 30.4.6, Livy 45.16.4.
186. Livy *Per.* 47 and Plut. *Mar.* 4.2–4.

quently said to have stymied consuls utterly by refusing to enlist in the army, and plebeians might even attack a consul physically if they were sufficiently aroused: in 456 BC, a consul did not have sufficient authority to save his own lictor from being hurled off the Tarpeian Rock by a tribune (the lictor was spared by the tribune at the last minute, but the consul had been powerless to intervene).[187] Even more remarkable was Caesar's need — despite being the urban praetor — to satisfy his creditors before he could leave for his praetorian province in Spain in 62 BC.[188] If *imperium domi* existed, it must have been so weak and degraded that a sitting consul or praetor was not able to protect himself from prosecution and imprisonment by tribunes and moneylenders. Possession of *imperium* outside of Rome was known to be ironclad protection against all forms of prosecution and interference, so the legal liabilities of consuls in Rome make it seem impossible that they possessed even the slightest shred of *imperium* that Cicero said so terrified citizens outside of the city (*est in imperio terror*).[189]

Two exceptions to the normal ban on *imperium* within the city help demonstrate the rule. First, Roman tradition held that a panel of ten extraordinary magistrates ruled Rome from 451 to 449 BC, and it seems likely that these *decemviri* used *imperium* within the city. The *fasti* refer to these men as *decemviri consulari imperio legibus scribundis*, which seems to equate their use of *imperium* to that of the consuls, but other sources are less clear: Dionysius refers to them simply as lawgivers (νομογράφοι or νομοθέτας), whereas Cicero and Livy indicate they had *imperium* and that there was no appeal from their orders.[190] This last point is the most important, because it clearly illustrates a critical difference between the *decemviri* and the consuls: whereas consular authority inside Rome was subject to appeal, the authority of the *decemviri* was absolute and not subject to appeal. This must surely mean that — while the consuls were limited to their civilian authority (*potestas*) within the city — the *decemviri* were especially authorized to possess and use *imperium* within the city. The salient point that Dionysius, Cicero, and Livy all empha-

187. Refuse enlistment: Livy 2.24.1–8 and 27.10, 6.27.10, 31.5, and 32.2, Dion. Hal. *AR* 6.23.2, 25.1, 27.2–3, 8.81.3; consuls attacked by mobs: Dion. Hal. *AR* 6.26.2–3, 9.39.1–3; lictor nearly executed: Dion. Hal. *AR* 10.31.4–6.

188. Suet. *Iul.* 18.1.

189. Immunity to prosecution: *RS* 12 Cnidos Copy Col. 4, ll.31–39 and Delphi Copy Block C, ll.4–8, *RS* 1, ll.8–9. Caesar attempted to retain his *imperium* after his Gallic command to avoid prosecution (see Suet. *Iul.* 30.3–5). See Weinrib (1968) 32–56. Cic. *Leg. Agr.* 45–46.

190. *Fasti Capitolini* for 451 and 450 BC, Dion. Hal. *AR* 10.56.2 and 57.1, Cic. *Rep.* 2.61, and Livy 3.32.5–33.1.

sized was that the *decemviri* were extraordinary magistrates with highly exceptional authority and responsibilities, which means they cannot be taken as
being representative of the normal operation of consular *imperium*. Indeed, it
may have been their exceptional (and objectionable) use of *imperium* within
the city that drove the people to rise up against the *decemviri*. Thus the phenomenon of the *decemviri* says nothing about the normal exercise of consular
authority in Rome, although it does suggest that the possession of *imperium*
inside the city was extraordinary.

Second, it is tempting to take the unauthorized triumph of the consul Ap.
Claudius Pulcher in 143 BC as a sign that consuls held *imperium* in the city,
but the incident actually demonstrates the opposite. After being denied permission to celebrate a triumph for his mediocre victory over the Salassi, Appius
dared the unthinkable and — using his daughter (a vestal virgin) as religious
protection against protest or tribunician veto — he marched his army in triumph through the streets of Rome.[191] While this was a clear display of military
authority and activity within the *pomerium*, the entire point to the story is that
his triumph was *illegal* because he had not received the necessary public authorization to use his *imperium* inside the *pomerium*. Without that authorization,
his possession of *imperium* automatically terminated when he crossed the *pomerium* and entered the city. According to Valerius Maximus, when Appius
mounted his triumphal chariot and tried to cross the *pomerium* and enter the
city, he was instantly attacked by the people of Rome and dragged physically
from his chariot in spite of being a sitting consul. It was publicly understood
that Appius did not have *imperium* in the city, and so he was nearly killed by
the citizens for acting as if he did. It was only then that his daughter Claudia
interceded and placed herself between her father and his attackers, and because vestal virgins were inviolable, Appius's enemies could not continue their
assault against the consul without committing tremendous impiety, nor could
the tribunes interpose their veto. Thus Appius was indeed able to triumph in
Rome, but his triumph was patently illegal and only made possible because
his daughter physically protected him from assault by a mob incensed at his
action. Had Claudia not been a vestal virgin, the Roman people would have
prevented Appius from celebrating his triumph, demonstrating that even sitting consuls normally did not possess *imperium* within the city.

All these factors urge us to accept that *imperium* was the authority of military command — and *only* of military command — and that it was invested in
Rome's highest magistrates for exclusive use in the sphere *militiae*. Not only

191. Cic. *Cael.* 34, Val. Max. 5.4.6, Suet. *Tib.* 2.4.

was *imperium* completely unnecessary for magistrates to perform their civil responsibilities, but also the presence of any kind of military authority or activity within the *pomerium* was anathema to the early Romans. Successful military commanders had to make their requests for a triumph outside the *pomerium* (usually in the Temple of Apollo or the war god Bellona), and the *comitia centuriata* was forbidden to meet within the *pomerium* because it was organized by military units.[192] A Roman commander setting out on campaign was not permitted to put on his military garments until he had left the city, and if he received the honor of a triumph on his return, he wore not the military uniform of a general (*paludatus*) but the tunic and toga of a Roman citizen.[193] Furthermore, ambassadors from enemy peoples were not permitted inside the *pomerium*, and even the temples to the gods of war and destruction like Mars and Vulcan were forbidden within the *pomerium*.[194] Across the board, the Romans seem to have enforced an absolute ban on hostile authority, forces, persons, and even gods within the *pomerium*, which makes it hard to imagine that any part of *imperium* could have been tolerated within the *pomerium*, especially since it was not necessary for civilian governance.

THE LONG-STANDING DEBATE over the nature and purpose of the *lex curiata* also becomes easier if one understands *imperium* as military authority and nothing more.[195] That the *lex curiata* conferred military authority on Roman commanders is clearly demonstrated by Cicero's statement that "it is not permitted for a consul to engage in military affairs if he does not have a *lex*

192. Temple of Bellona: Livy 26.21.1, 28.9.5 and 38.3, 31.47.7, 33.22.1 and 24.6, 36.39.5–6, 42.21.6–7; Temple of Apollo: Livy 34.43.2, 39.4.2, 41.17.4; centuriate assembly: Gell. 15.27.5 (*centuriata autem comitia intra pomerium fieri nefas esse, quia exercitum extra urbem imperari oporteat, intra urbem imperari ius non sit*). See Taylor (1966) 5–6, Magdelain (1968) 57–67, (1977a), and (1977b), Catalano (1978) 422–25 and 479–91, Rüpke (1990) 29–57, and Sandberg (2001) 123–31.

193. Cic. *Pis.* 55, Caes. *BC* 1.6, Livy 41.10.5, 42.49.1–2, 45.39.11, Varro *LL* 7.37, Dio 53.13.3–4. See Versnel (1970) 183 and Humm (2012) 74.

194. Ambassadors: Livy 30.21.11–12 and 30.40.1, Brennan (2000) 135. Temples: Scheid and Lloyd (2003) 62. Only in 2 BC were temples to these gods permitted inside the *pomerium* (Sandberg [2001] 122). Also related may be the ban on cremating and burying dead bodies within the *pomerium* (Cic. *Leg.* 2.58; see Patterson [2000] 265).

195. Almost every modern historian who studies Roman government gives consideration to the connection between *lex curiata* and *imperium*, so a complete bibliography would be too massive to include here. Leading opinions and representative discussions may be found in: Greenridge (1901) 48 and 251–53, Botsford (1909) 190–99, Staveley (1956) 84–90, Catalano (1960) 461–87, Magdelain (1964b) and (1968), Nicholls (1967), Ogilvie (1969), Versnel (1970) 319, Bleicken (1975) 72–73, Develin (1977), Hermon (1982), Rüpke (1990) 41–51, Richardson (1991), Cornell (1995) 196, Brennan (2000) 13–20 and (2004) 35–42, Sandberg (2001) 135, Smith (2006) 217–23, Pina Polo (2011) 17–18.

curiata."[196] Many scholars agree that the *lex curiata* conferred *auspicia militiae*, but what about *imperium*? Because most historians have accepted Mommsen's distinction between *imperium domi* and *imperium militiae*, it has been widely assumed that election in the *comitia centuriata* conferred *imperium domi* on magistrates, who subsequently received their *imperium militiae* through a *lex curiata*. Yet this explanation should seem quite odd, since it creates an overly contrived process through which two different citizen assemblies are independently responsible for conferring two halves of what was supposed to be a single type of authority (*imperium*). Believing in the existence of *imperium domi* is a primary mistake that tends to create secondary errors, because introducing *imperium domi* into one's interpretation of Roman government requires one to find a source for this authority where none is attested, an exercise that has occupied the talents of many historians.[197] If, however, *imperium* is understood as strictly a military authority that normally did not exist within the *pomerium* (i.e., if the whole idea of *imperium domi* is rejected), then these problems seem to resolve themselves: magistrates received their *potestas* through election in the *comitia centuriata* or *comitia tributa* to a particular office (which defined their *potestas*), but senior magistrates had to receive a further *lex curiata* if they were to receive *imperium* outside Rome and to exercise military command over Roman citizens. Even Cicero's description of Rome's kings seems to reflect this: he says Numa had already been appointed king by the people in the *comitia curiata*, when he took the subsequent and separate step of carrying another *lex curiata* conferring his *imperium*.[198] It seems clear that the *lex curiata* was the essential action that enabled a commander to take up and use *imperium* once he had performed the necessary rituals and exited the *pomerium*.

Two famous cases demonstrate that *imperium* was conferred in this way.

196. Cic. *Leg. Agr.* 2.30: *consuli, si legem curiatam non habet, attingere rem militarem non licet.* See also Livy 5.52.16: *comitia curiata, quae rem militarem continent.*

197. Staveley (1956) 84–90, for example, argued that—if *imperium* was the essential source of civilian authority used by consuls and praetors—it needed to be conferred by some entity before men assumed these offices. Magdelain (1964) and (1968) argued that the *lex curiata* somehow defined the magistracy, Nicholls (1967) thought that the *lex curiata* was just a ratification of authority previously conferred through election, Versnel (1970) 340–49 suggested that the *lex curiata* was properly an acclamation of a magistrate as *imperator* and that (355) it was a rite performed immediately before the army marched out to war, and Develin (1977) 51–63 suggested *imperium* came only from election in the *comitia curiata* and that censors, who possessed the *auspicia maxima* like consuls, also possessed some kind of *imperium*.

198. Cic. *Rep.* 2.25: *qui ut huc venit, quamquam populus curiatis eum comitiis regem esse iusserat, tamen ipse de suo imperio curiatam legem tulit* (cf. 2.31, 2.33, 2.35).

The first involved the C. Pomptinus (pr. 63 BC) mentioned earlier, who may have neglected to secure a *lex curiata* during his praetorship, although he had been able to take up his *provincia* in Transalpine Gaul and hold it for three years. When he returned to Rome in 60 or 59 BC and demanded a triumph for his victories, he was refused, and Pomptinus waited outside the *pomerium* for more than five years in hopes of having his petition approved. In a letter to Atticus in 54 BC, Cicero explained that two praetors and a tribune claimed that Pomptinus was ineligible to triumph because no law had been carried about his *imperium* (*negant enim latum de imperio*), although Cicero himself enigmatically says that Pomptinus's method of acquiring a *lex curiata* had been inelegant (*est latum hercule insulse*).[199] Pomptinus clearly had not followed the traditional manner of receiving a *lex curiata*, but whatever steps he took met the minimum legal requirement in Cicero's eyes, although several prominent magistrates believed that the irregularity disqualified Pomptinus from celebrating a triumph. In the end, it took the intervention of powerful friends to obtain that triumph for Pomptinus: the praetor Ser. Sulpicius Galba rigged the vote by approving the triumph in a secret, predawn vote when all the opponents to the bill were absent, and the consul Claudius Pulcher used his *auctoritas*, *potestas*, and perhaps *coercitio* to quash opposition to the triumph.[200] Still, those claiming the illegitimacy of the triumph were determined, and their efforts to block Pomptinus led to bloodshed. Cicero emphasizes that Pomptinus's *imperium* was the point of contention in this event, and the belief by some that he lacked *imperium* because of the irregularity of his *lex curiata*.

The role of Appius Claudius in this affair further illuminates the importance of the *lex curiata*. The praetor Galba aided Pomptinus out of friendship, but why did the consul Appius Claudius support a triumph that seems to have been patently improper and against traditional practice? In fact, he was in a similar situation as Pomptinus: Appius Claudius had also failed to obtain a *lex curiata de imperio* from the curiate assembly at the start of his consulship in 54 BC, and was concerned about his own legitimacy as a military commander. How a sitting consul could commit such an oversight is not known, although Appius certainly made enemies who may have somehow blocked his *lex curiata*, perhaps because of a tribunician veto, bribery by political opponents, or mob violence initiated by Clodius and Milo.[201] Like Pomptinus, Appius

199. Cic. *Att.* 4.18.4 (cf. *Prov. Cons.* 32 and Livy *Per.* 103).

200. Cic. *Att.* 4.18.4, *QFr* 3.4.6, Dio 39.65.1–2.

201. Claudius had been present at the meeting of the so-called first triumvirate at Luca in 55 BC and perhaps was politically aligned with the triumvirs (Cic. *QFr* 2.5.4, 2.14.3). During his consulship,

had been able to fulfill all the civilian responsibilities of his consulship despite lacking a *lex curiata* (and therefore *imperium*). Toward the end of 54 BC, however, he became concerned that his failure to obtain a *lex curiata de imperio* would invalidate his ability to take up a military command, since—without the *lex*—he did not possess the *imperium* and *auspicia militiae* that were absolutely necessary to exercise military command. The sight of Pomptinus waiting outside the *pomerium* year after year in hopes of a triumph may have frightened him more. To avoid losing his opportunity to command, Appius bribed some augurs to swear falsely that he had indeed acquired the necessary *lex*, but this forgery was revealed.[202] His efforts to secure this forgery demonstrate that *imperium* had not been necessary to exercise civilian authority in Rome, but it would be needed if he wanted to exercise military authority in a *provincia*. After his attempt at forging a *lex curiata* failed, Appius argued that he did not need the *lex* to acquire *imperium* because the senate had already assigned to him the *provincia* of Syria, and a *lex Cornelia* of 81 BC allowed him to hold *imperium* until he returned to Rome from his *provincia*.[203] In other words, Appius argued that the *lex Cornelia* automatically invested him with *imperium* (even without a *lex curiata*) because he had a *provincia*. This was a highly imaginative interpretation of the *lex Cornelia*, and the lawyer Cicero expressed doubts about the legitimacy of this legal claim, but nevertheless Appius would take up his command in Cilicia.[204] Two months before his departure, however, the case of Pomptinus became a major topic of concern. Pomptinus's hopes of a triumph had been quashed for years because he lacked a *lex curiata*, and Appius could see his own future in Pomptinus's frustration. To

---

however, Claudius was pulled away from the triumvirs, reconciled with Cicero and his circle, and began actively attacking Gabinius (Cic. *Fam.* 1.9.4 and 19, *QFr* 2.11.2–3, 3.7.3, *Scaur.* 31–37), indicating that Claudius had perhaps switched sides and was an active player in the biggest political question of the day. Cicero (*leg. agr.* 2.30) also mentions tribunes interfering with the *lex curiata*.

202. Cic. *Att.* 4.17.2: (*tres augures . . . dicerent cum lex curiata ferretur quae lata non esset*); and 4.18.4: (*negant enim latum de imperio*); *Fam.* 1.9.25: ([Appius] *dixit . . . sese, si licitum esset legem curiatam ferrem sortiturum esse cum collega provincias; si curiata lex non essent, se paraturum cum collega tibique successurum; legem curiatam consuli ferri opus esse, necesse non esse . . .*); *QFr* 3.2.3: (*Appius sine lege curiata confirmat se Lentulo nostro successurum*).

203. Cic. *Q.fr.* 3.2.3, *Att.* 4.18.4, and *Fam.* 1.9.25. The content of Sulla's *lex Cornelia* is unknown. Sumner (1982) 136 points out that Appius's colleague L. Domitius Ahenobarbus also lacked *imperium* but was unwilling to push the issue as far as was Appius, and he believes that Ahenobarbus would not have proceeded to a province without a *lex curiata*. If correct, this suggests that Appius's intentions were—at best—reprehensible.

204. Several of Cicero's letters are addressed to Appius during the latter's provincial command (*Fam.* 3.6–3.13).

establish precedent for his anticipated demand to triumph without a *lex curiata*, Appius decided to support Pomptinus's claims, using his consular *potestas* and *auctoritas* to subdue Pomptinus's enemies. The cases of Appius and Pomptinus both demonstrate that *imperium* was not needed to perform the civilian duties of the praetorship and consulship, but was absolutely required to take up a *provincia*.

Once an elected magistrate had assumed office and received a *lex curiata de imperio*, he could take up *imperium* at any time he wanted by performing requisite ceremonies, crossing the *pomerium*, and exiting the city. The importance of these actions demonstrates that *imperium* was normally kept outside the city. First, the magistrate had to make certain vows and take the auspices in the sanctuary on the Capitoline Hill to ensure that he possessed the favor of the gods, and when this was complete, the magistrate could exit the city by crossing the *pomerium*, where he could change into the military clothing of a Roman general.[205] Once he was properly arrayed in his military uniform (*paludatus*), he was understood to be invested with *imperium* and to possess full military authority.[206] Naturally, a high magistrate did not have to perform these ceremonies every time he exited the city, but if he did not, it was understood that he did not possess *imperium*.[207] When the consul C. Claudius (cos. 177 BC) neglected these requisite ceremonies in his haste to reach his military command in Gaul, the proconsuls he had been sent to replace and the soldiers he had been ordered to command all refused to acknowledge his authority over them.[208] Such refusal to obey a sitting consul is extraordinary and can be

205. Cic. *Att.* 4.13.2, *Pis.* 55, Caes. *BC* 1.6; Livy 21.63.5–13, 36.3.14, 37.4.2, 41.10.5, 41.17.6, 42.49.1–2, 45.39.11; Varro *LL* 7.37; Dio 53.13.4. This may also have involved a ceremony with the spears and shields of Mars, housed in the Regia (Serv. *Ad Aen.* 8.3, 7.603).See Versnel (1970) 181–85, Magdelain (1977b) 76, Giovannini (1983) 16–19, Marshall (1984) 121–22, Rüpke (1990) 125–43, Stewart (1998) 124–26, Sumi (2005) 35–41, Mousourakis (2007) 7, and Hurlet (2010) 45–72.

206. Because only one who was *paludatus* could properly exercise military command, Cicero virtually equated the two ideas, such as his statement that two consuls feared to be sent *paludati* (i.e., in command) against the Parthians (*Fam.* 8.10.2).

207. It is unlikely that consuls performed the necessary ceremonies to take up *imperium* every time they exited the city to officiate a meeting of the centuriate assembly, which met in the Campus Martius outside of the city. This is suggested by the previously mentioned meeting of that assembly in 215 BC when the presiding consul — Q. Fabius Maximus — took the unusual step of using his *imperium* to threaten a candidate (Livy 24.7.11–12 and 9.1–2). Livy's attention to Fabius's retention and use of *imperium* here suggests that it was unusal and that consuls normally did not possess *imperium* when officiating in the centuriate assembly.

208. Livy 41.10.5–13: *non votis nuncupatis, non paludatis lictoribus . . . nocte profectus.* The proconsuls replied that they would only obey his orders once he had returned to Rome and performed

explained only by the fact that Claudius, having neglected the necessary rituals, did not have *imperium*. Stymied, Claudius had no choice but to return to the city, perform the appropriate rituals, and return to Gaul, now properly invested with *imperium* and able to command the soldiers (who now recognized his authority as legitimate). Similarly, at the end of 218 BC the consul-elect C. Flaminius suspected that his political enemies would hinder his departure for his command against Hannibal, so he secretly left the city early and officially entered office in Gaul, a move that not only outraged the senate but also drew charges that he was not exercising legitimate military command because he had failed to receive the auspices, to make sacred vows on the Capitol, and then to put on the commander's uniform and set out from Rome *paludatus* and accompanied by lictors.[209] The senate demanded that he return to Rome and perform the rituals necessary to exercise legitimate command, but he engaged Hannibal and was killed at the Battle of Lake Trasimene. Finally, Caesar ridiculed some of his foes for making a big display of taking up *imperium* at the *pomerium* when (he asserted) they had never received the right to take up *imperium* in the first place. This joke was intended to show that his foes were all show and no substance, but nevertheless it emphasizes that *imperium* was taken up only when crossing the *pomerium* and exiting the city.[210]

Whereas the assumption of *imperium* by commanders was carefully regulated both by rituals and in space (i.e., only outside the *pomerium*), the removal or cancellation of a commander's *imperium* was an automatic process that required no willful action on his part beyond stepping across the *pomerium*. Because *imperium* was normally forbidden inside the *pomerium*, the simple act of a commander crossing the *pomerium* and entering the city triggered the automatic and unavoidable termination of his *imperium*.[211] Naturally, a sitting consul or praetor who thus laid down his *imperium* could take it up again as many times as he wished during his term in office, although each time he had to repeat the necessary rituals.[212] Cicero argued that C. Verres's entire

---

the necessary rituals: *tum consulis imperio dicto audientes futuros esse dicerent, cum is more maiorum, secundum vota in Capitolio nuncupata, lictoribus paludatis profectus ab urbe esset.*

209. Livy 21.63.8–10.

210. Caes. *BC* 1.6: *Neque exspectant, quod superioribus annis acciderat, ut de eorum imperio ad populum feratur, paludatique votis nuncupatis exeunt.* Caesar's comment was intended to invalidate the legitimacy of his enemies' commands by pointing out their failure to receive a *lex curiata*.

211. Cicero as proconsul in 50 BC indicated (*Att.* 7.7.4) the ease of this automatic process by saying that—if his retention of *imperium* became a nuisance to him—he would "use the first gate I see" (*utar ea porta quam primam videro*) to get rid of it.

212. In 333 BC, for example, a consul attacked and defeated one enemy and then returned to Rome

governorship over Sicily had been invalid because—after exiting the city and taking up his *imperium*—Verres had snuck back into the city at night to meet with his mistress, thereby forfeiting his *imperium* and with it his authority to command.[213] Military authority simply could not exist within the city under normal conditions, so *imperium* automatically expired if its holder crossed the *pomerium* and entered the city.

IF ONE ACCEPTS THAT *imperium* was not possessed or used inside the city under normal circumstances, several hitherto-unsolvable problems disappear. Foremost among these is the question of why a Roman general could not cross the *pomerium* and enter the city without forfeiting his right to claim and celebrate a triumph. The triumph was the greatest honor that most commanders could hope for in Roman culture,[214] but it was highly unusual among military awards because it violated the normal prohibition of *imperium* within the *pomerium*. Everything about the triumph was military in nature: the celebrant entered the city in his role as *imperator* rather than as *magistratus*; he wore the royal all-purple toga referred to as *picta* or *triumphalis*; he painted his face to resemble the statue of Jupiter; and he led his soldiers on a military parade through the heart of the city, using his military authority (*imperium*) to exercise command over them during the march. The whole spectacle was very regal, and modern scholars have emphasized that this triumphal military march into the city was descended from the royal practice of Rome's early kings, whose possession of absolute *imperium* both inside and outside the *pomerium* represented their complete authority over citizens.[215] Consuls and praetors in the republic were forbidden to exercise military authority in Rome under normal circumstances, so the triumph was a remarkable evocation of Rome's earliest days as a monarchy.

Because the triumph entailed such a tremendous violation of the traditional

---

and celebrated a triumph (at the end of which his *imperium* would have expired), and at a subsequent meeting of the senate in that same year he was given a second military campaign, which meant he would have taken up his *imperium* at least twice during his year in office (Livy 8.16.11).

213. Cic. *Verr.* 2.5.32–34. See Rüpke (1990) 32 n. 31.

214. The dedication of the *spolia opima* was Rome's highest military honor (see chapter 7), but it was so rare that the triumph was the highest military award that most men could hope to achieve. Much has been written about the triumph: Mommsen (1887–88) 1.126–34, Deubner (1934) 316–23, Durante (1951) 138–44, Payne (1962), Versnel (1970), Bonfante-Warren (1970a) and (1970b), Gagé (1970) and (1973), Richardson (1975), Develin (1978b), Künzl (1988), Rüpke (1990) 223–34, Itgenhorst (2005), Beard (2007).

215. Bonfante-Warren (1970a) 49–66, Versnel (1970) 201–303, 352–55 and (2006) 291–92.

prohibition of *imperium* within the city, all triumphs had to be approved in advance by the state. When a victorious military commander returned to Rome, he took great care not to cross the *pomerium* and enter the city, but instead summoned the senate to a meeting outside the *pomerium* where he presented his claim for a triumph (strictly speaking, the approval of the people was necessary to hold a triumph, but the senate gradually assumed regular exercise of this prerogative).[216] If the senate approved his request (or granted the lesser form of a triumph known as an ovation), it originally requested that the tribunes of the plebs bring a bill (*rogatio*) before the people that authorized the prospective triumphator to possess *imperium* in the city on the day of his triumph.[217] Livy gives examples of what this process might have looked like in his accounts of 211 and 167 BC:

> On the authority of the senate, the tribunes of the plebs brought a bill before the people that there should be *imperium* to M. Marcellus on that day in which he should enter the city celebrating an ovation.

> A triumph was decreed to all three commanders by the senate, and to the praetor Q. Cassius the task was assigned that he work with the tribunes of the plebs so that — on the authority of the senate — they would bring to the people a bill that *imperium* should be to those commanders on that day when they should enter the city celebrating their triumph.[218]

If the senate rejected his request, the general could take his case directly to the people, who alone could authorize the temporary grant of *imperium* necessary to lead the victorious army through the streets of Rome.[219] If the consul was denied by the people as well, his only alternative was to celebrate an unofficial

216. Cic. *Att.* 4.18.4, 7.1.5, *QFr.* 3.2.2; Livy 26.21.1–5, 28.9.5–7, 31.47.7, 33.22.1, 38.44.9–11, 39.4.2, 39.29.4, 42.21.6–7, 45.35.4; Vell. 1.10.4; Plut. *Caes.* 13.1 and *Cat. Min.* 31.2–3. This meeting was usually held in the Temple of Apollo or the Temple of Bellona. See Cotton and Yakobson (2002) 199 and Beard (2007) 201.

217. Richardson (1975) 59–60. Although the senate seems to have appropriated the prerogative to grant or refuse triumphs by the late republic, the originally public (as opposed to senatorial) control over the authorization of a triumph suggests that the prohibition on possessing *imperium* within the *pomerium* was primarily a matter of law rather than of religion. On the approval process of the triumph, see Beard (2007) 187–218.

218. Livy 26.21.5 (Drogula, trans.): *tribuni plebis ex auctoritate senatus ad populum tulerunt ut M. Marcello quo die urbem ovans iniret imperium esset*; and 45.35.4: *tribus iis omnibus decretus est ab senatu triumphus mandatumque Q. Cassio praetori, cum tribunis plebis ageret, ex auctoritate patrum rogationem ad plebem ferrent, ut iis, quo die urbem triumphantes inveherentur, imperium esset.*

219. Livy 3.63.7–11 and Dion. Hal. *AR* 11.50.1 (449 BC), Livy 7.17.9 (356 BC), 10.37.6–12 (294 BC).

triumph outside the city (the Alban Mount, a short distance north of Rome, was the usual choice).[220] If a commander's request for a triumph was approved, he had to remain outside the city until the actual celebration of the triumph; if he reentered Rome at any time before his triumph, his *imperium* and the auspices connected to it automatically lapsed and he irreversibly forfeited his right to triumph.[221] At the end of the triumphal celebration, the triumphator laid aside his status as *imperator* and (if he was a sitting magistrate) returned to his civil status as *magistratus*, which meant he could continue to perform his assigned duties and he could even take up *imperium* again — under new and different auspices — by performing the necessary ceremonies.[222] If the triumphator was a promagistrate (see chapter 4), all of his official authority expired at the end of his triumph, and he became once again a private citizen (*privatus*). The careful regulation of the triumph demonstrates that it was a special and unusual exception to the normal rule that *imperium* was forbidden inside the *pomerium*.

While these basic facts about the triumph are clear, those who accept the existence of *imperium domi* are confronted with the difficulty of explaining why a sitting consul or praetor who had won a great military victory could not enter Rome without forfeiting his claim to a triumph. If he possessed *imperium* inside the city as well as outside, why did his right to triumph dissolve automatically if he crossed the *pomerium* and entered the city before the celebration of the triumph? So awkward is this problem that Develin suggested that sitting magistrates actually did not have to remain outside the *pomerium* while awaiting a triumph, but could enter the city if they wished, and could even use their *imperium* to hold a triumph in Rome on their own authority without obtaining any kind of permission from the state.[223] This suggestion was a considerable departure from the evidence (Liou-Gille called such a notion "un sacrilège abominable"),[224] but it indicates the challenge this problem poses to the (unattested) concept of *imperium domi*. Other scholars suggested that sitting magistrates needed a special extension of their *imperium*

---

220. *Act. Trium.* for 231, 197, 172, and 44 BC. Livy 26.21.6, 33.23.3, 42.21.7, 45.38.4.

221. Plut. *Caes.* 13.1: ἐπεὶ δὲ τοὺς μὲν μνωμένους θρίαμβον ἔξω διατρίβειν ἔδει (cf. *Cat. Min.* 31.2–3).

222. The triumph itself ended (and with it the authorization to hold *imperium* in the city) after the conclusion of the parade and sacrifices, although the feasts and other celebrations surrounding the triumph might continue much longer: *RS* 1.12, Cnidos 4, ll.38–39 and Delphi C, l.3, Polyb. 16.23.7. See Beard (2007) 257–63.

223. Develin (1978b) 437. See the earlier discussion of the illegal triumph held by Ap. Claudius Pulcher in 143 BC.

224. Liou-Gille (1993) 102.

militiae into the sphere *domi* in order to triumph,[225] but this does not resolve the problem. Richardson sums up the quandary:

> Certain magistrates returning to demand a triumph, namely a dictator, consul or praetor in their years of office, can scarcely have needed an extension of *imperium*, for they already held *imperium domi* in virtue of their magistracy; and yet in these cases too the senate met outside the city, nor did the general cross the *pomerium* before the day of his triumph. Attempts to conjecture an additional grant of *imperium militiae* to the returning magistrate ... cannot explain those examples already noticed.[226]

In other words, there seems to be no legal reason why a sitting magistrate awaiting a triumph could not enter the city without forfeiting his right to a triumph, and yet this was clearly the case. In the absence of a legal explanation, Richardson suggested ceremonial or religious reasons:

> It is better to explain the undoubted desire of a potential *triumphator* to avoid crossing the *pomerium* by some other ceremonial inhibition than the need for an extended *imperium*. Perhaps the most satisfactory is the idea that the triumph was in part an "entry" ritual, and that once he had crossed the *pomerium*, it was no longer possible for the general to make the formal entry *triumphans* or even *ovans*.[227]

While this suggestion is possible, it does not explain how commanders could be forcibly delayed from celebrating a triumph. In 60 BC Julius Caesar was confronted with a serious dilemma, because he was granted a triumph to be celebrated after the date by which candidates for the consulship needed to declare their candidacy inside the *pomerium*. By assigning this date for his triumph, the senate knowingly prevented Caesar from crossing the *pomerium* and entering Rome to announce his candidacy if he wished to keep his triumph (he famously forfeited his triumph in order to stand for election). If Caesar had been free to perform the proper entry ritual and celebrate his triumph when he wished, then he certainly would have done so rather than forfeit the triumph altogether. Bonfante-Warren pointed out that the original Etruscan triumph was largely a purification ceremony for the army, although she noted that this meaning was lost early in Rome's history (she also believed that a triumphator needed a special grant of *imperium* in the *pomerium* in

---

225. Last (1947) 160, Versnel (1970) 191–92.
226. Richardson (1975) 59–60.
227. Richardson (1975) 60.

order to triumph).[228] While this might have been the purpose of the triumph in its earliest form, it does not explain why later generals forfeited their right to a triumph if they crossed the *pomerium* early, since most Roman commanders and armies returning from war just walked into the city without a purifying triumph, and they experienced no hindrance or delay despite being polluted with the carnage of war.[229] In short, scholars have been unable to reconcile the belief that magistrates possessed *imperium* inside the city with the fact that consuls and praetors were unable to enter the city without forfeiting their claims on a triumph — claims based primarily on their possession of *imperium*.

If one rejects the theory of *imperium domi*, this conundrum is quickly and logically resolved: a consul or praetor lost his *imperium* completely when he entered the city, and with it any claim to a triumph he had achieved with that *imperium*. Although a sitting consul or praetor could lay down and take up his *imperium* any number of times, the fact that each taking-up of *imperium* required a consultation of the auspices meant that each possession of *imperium* was uniquely auspicated in the eyes of Rome's gods. Every time a consul or praetor wanted to take up his *imperium*, he used his *auspicium* to consult the gods regarding his proposed undertaking, and those auspices sanctioned and marked that particular tenure of *imperium*. When a commander laid his *imperium* down, the divine favor attached to that tenure of *imperium* also came to an end; so if that commander took up *imperium* once again, it was under different auspices. Because the triumph was a religious ceremony to honor the gods for a particular victory that a commander won under the unique divine sanction they had granted him, it was essential that a man triumph under the same auspices with which he had won his victory. For this reason, commanders celebrating a triumph were not granted *imperium* anew on the day of their triumph — previous possession of *imperium* was a fundamental requisite even to request a triumph. Rather, the *rogatio* that authorized the triumph granted the general a temporary exemption from the normal ban on *imperium* within the *pomerium*, and probably specified the date on which this exemption would be in effect.[230] Since the commander had to possess the same *imperium* that

228. Bonfante-Warren (1970a) 49–66, esp. 56 n. 49. See also Magdelain (1977b) 76, Develin (1977) 58, Marshall (1984) 121–22, Rüpke (1990) 125–43, 215–34, Beard, North, and Price (1998) 1.177–81, Stewart (1998) 124–26.

229. In the republic, the Romans used different types of purification ceremonies for their army, like the Quinquatria, the Armilustrium, and the Tubilustrium. See Phang (2008) 89–90.

230. This is emphasized by the passages (Livy 26.21.5 and 45.35.4) given in note 218 above, which do not mention a conferral of *imperium* on triumphators, but simply state that triumphators would have *imperium* in the city on the date of their triumphs.

had been auspicated when he set out for his campaign and under which he had achieved his victory, it makes no sense that the *rogatio* would have given him a new grant of *imperium*, which would have required a new set of auspices. This case demonstrates how belief in *imperium domi* has created serious problems and misconceptions for modern historians, but by rejecting the idea, these problems are easily and logically resolved.

There is, therefore, no good reason for believing that *imperium domi* existed as something different from *imperium militiae*, or that *imperium* was normally used in Rome for civilian governance. *Imperium* operated differently from the civilian authority of *potestas* that magistrates employed in Rome: while *potestas* was unalterably intertwined with the idea of the magistrate, *imperium* was an independent idea separate from (but related to) the fundamental concept of the magistrate. A magistrate could have *imperium* in some places and not in others, and some magistrates (but not others) could have *imperium*. Whereas different magistracies possessed different types and degrees of *potestas*, *imperium* was originally a single, fixed, and unchanging idea; it was not adjusted to confer some prerogatives but not others but was a blanket authority that empowered a commander to do whatever had to be done in time of war. Messala (quoted by Gellius) illustrated this distinction between *imperium* and *potestas* when he identified the major magistracies with *auspicia maxima* as the consulship, praetorship, and censorship, but added the qualifier that consuls and praetors are colleagues, but the censors are not colleagues with them.[231] Why is *imperium* not even named in this explanation of magisterial authority, especially if (as many have suggested) *imperium* was the fundamental authority of consuls and praetors? Why does Messala go into minute detail to explain how the *auspicia* of consuls and praetors differed from that of censors, and how this tiny difference explains why censors are not colleagues with consuls and praetors, when he could have made this point much more clearly by pointing out that consuls and praetors had *imperium* but censors did not? Clearly, Messala is discussing the civilian qualities of magistrates here — hence his inclusion of the censorship and minor magistracies — and *imperium* had no place in a discussion about civilian governance.

Although scholars have struggled to make Mommsen's neat theory work, there is insufficient evidence to accept that any idea of *imperium domi* actually existed in the Roman Republic, and the preponderance of the evidence actually argues against this possibility. The ancient sources seem to confirm

---

231. Gell. 13.15.4. Develin's efforts ([1977] 63–65 and [2005] 309 n. 21) to show that censors possessed some kind of *imperium* are unconvincing.

that *imperium* was not permitted within the *pomerium* during normal circumstances, and attempts to impose the idea of *imperium domi* into reconstructions of Roman government cause more confusion and contradictions than they solve. Furthermore, the idea that *imperium* should somehow be a source of civilian authority within the city is an outdated concept that derives from a time when modern historians were inclined to accept the traditional foundation myth of the republic, which held that the dual consulship was created on the first day of the republic and was the direct inheritor of the regal authority (*imperium*) of the exiled monarch. More and more, historians are realizing that this classical republican government did not spring fully formed from the collapse of the monarchy, as Livy and Dionysius of Halicarnassus depict it, but was the result of a gradual evolution and considerable experimentation. If one releases the preconceptions about *imperium* that are imposed by the inaccurate myths about the republic's foundation, it becomes clear that *imperium* was not the primary and all-encompassing authority of the magistrate but simply a source of military authority that was strictly prohibited inside the *pomerium* under normal conditions. Although this would change in the early imperial era, there is no evidence or reason to believe that *imperium* was anything but military authority in the Republic.

NATIONAL CRISIS: *IMPERIUM* WITHIN THE WALLS OF ROME

Other than during the celebration of a triumph, there was one exception to the normal prohibition on possessing and using *imperium* in the city. On rare occasion, a national crisis that threatened to destabilize or destroy the state erupted within the walls of Rome, and the elected magistrates were unable to suppress the trouble with the civil powers available to them.[232] As we have seen, the magistrates were limited to their *potestas* and *coercitio* in the civilian sphere, and although these gave potent authority and the capacity to use force, they were strictly limited by certain fundamental protections afforded to citizens in the sphere *domi*, namely the freedom from summary beating and execution. When the authority invested in magistrates under civil law was insufficient to resolve widespread armed violence by citizens in the city, however,

---

232. Consuls and praetors had considerable powers of coercion even without *imperium*, and this civilian authority could be augmented in emergencies by the declaration of a *tumultus*, which involved a suspension of the courts (*iustitium*), the authorization of leaders to wear military dress, a suspension of military exemptions, and a levy of soldiers (Cic. *Phil.* 5.31, 5.53, 6.2, 6.9, 8.2–4, 13.23; Livy 8.20.2, 34.56.3–13; Fest. 486L; Dio 41.3.3, 46.29.5, 46.44.4). Despite the authorization of military dress, however, it is unlikely that consuls were permitted to use their *imperium* within the city during a *tumultus*; such use of martial law within the *pomerium* required special authorization.

the Roman state (usually represented by the senate) took the highly unusual step of authorizing the emergency use of *imperium* within the city. This step was conceptually related to the state's authorization of a triumph, by which the senate or the assembly granted the successful commander a temporary exemption from the ban on the possession and use of *imperium* within the *pomerium*, enabling the triumphator to operate as a military commander within the civilian sphere. National emergencies were addressed in the same manner when the state granted a particular commander a similar short-term exemption that enabled him — but not other commanders — to use his *imperium* in Rome. By allowing the use of military authority in the civilian sphere, these emergency decrees were effectively — if not legally — a declaration of martial law within the sphere *domi*. Depending on the desires and priorities of the senate, this could take two forms: the appointing of a dictator and the pronouncement of the *senatus consultum ultimum* (*scu*).

According to Roman tradition, the dictatorship was first created in 501 BC because civil violence and widespread domestic upheavals within the city, and a military crisis without, were threatening to topple the young republic.[233] Although the consuls were present and had attempted to quell the unrest, their civilian authority (*potestas* and *coercitio*) was insufficient to compel obedience from the rioters, and they were forbidden to employ martial law (*imperium*) within the city. Although the senate might have authorized the consuls to use their *imperium* within the city, both magistrates were known to be supporters of the exiled king Tarquin and therefore were not to be trusted with absolute power within the city. To restore the peace, the Romans created a new, emergency magistrate, a dictator who was invested with extraordinary authority for a period of not more than six months.[234] Livy — no doubt using his imagination to recapture the Roman response to the unprecedented sight — writes that the rioters were so intimidated by the appearance of this new dictator, and so frightened by his obvious power and authority, that they immediately stopped their improper behavior.[235] The sources are unanimous

233. The origin of the Roman dictatorship is a debated question that does not have immediate bearing on the present discussion, but a solid foundation may be found in Ogilvie (1965) 281–82, Kaplan (1977), Ridley (1979) 303–9, and Golden (2013) 11–41.

234. Like the consuls, the dictator received his *imperium* from a *lex curiata* (Livy 5.46.11 and 9.38.15).

235. Livy (2.18.1–11) records that the first dictator was created in 501 BC specifically to quell domestic strife within Rome and that the appearance of his *fasces* with axes *inside* the city struck terror into troublemakers (cf. Dion. Hal. *AR* 5.75.2, 6.39.2, 8.81.3–4). *Contra*: Ridley (1979) 303, who sug-

that the dictator's power in Rome was unique because his orders were not subject to appeal (*provocatio*) and he had no colleague who could interpose a veto.[236] The appointment of a dictator did not dissolve *provocatio*, since it was still invoked occasionally against dictators;[237] rather, the dictator could simply refuse to allow any appeal from his decisions, something consuls did only at their peril. A military commander in the sphere *militiae* could similarly ignore any appeal made by his soldiers while they were on campaign, but the dictator could also ignore the appeal of a civilian in Rome, and he could even disregard the veto of a tribune.[238] Such behavior was possible because—unlike regular magistrates—the dictator could possess and use *imperium* within the *pomerium*. This was visibly displayed by the dictator's unique ability to place axes in his *fasces* while he was still in the city, an event that Dionysius describes as filling the Roman citizens with terror:

> Desiring to show how great was the extent of his power (τῆς ἐξουσίας τὸ κράτος), he ordered the lictors, more to inspire terror than for any actual use, to carry the axes with the bundles of rods through the city, thereby reviving once more a custom that had been observed by the kings but abandoned by the consuls after Valerius Publicola in his first consulship had lessened the hatred felt for that magistracy. Having by this and the other symbols of royal power terrified the turbulent and the seditious . . .[239]

Because the dictator was acting under military rather than civilian law, he was under no requirement to allow any appeal from his decisions, which made him particularly effective at suppressing civil unrest. For this reason, the senate

---

gests that the internal strife was only significant because it threatened Rome's ability to respond to a threat posed by a Latin uprising.

236. Livy 2.18.8, 3.20.8; Dion. Hal. *AR* 5.70.2–3, 6.58.2; Plut. *Fab.* 9.1.

237. Cic. *Off.* 3.112; Livy 2.30.5, 7.3.9, 8.32.1–33.8, 9.26.7–16.

238. Livy 2.18.8: *Neque enim, ut in consulibus qui pari potestate essent, alterius auxilium, neque provocatio erat neque ullum usquam nisi in cura parendi auxilium*; 3.20.8: *dictatore opus esse rei publicae, ut qui se moverit ad sollicitandum statum civitatis sentiat sine provocatione dictaturam esse* (see also 2.29.11, 3.41.7, 8.35.5; Dion. Hal. *AR* 6.58.2; Plut. *Fab.* 9.1). See Lintott (1972) 236–37 and 251, (1999a) 111–12.

239. Dion. Hal. *AR* 5.75.2–3 (Cary, trans.). While the majority of ancient authors agrees that the dictator was entitled to twenty-four lictors (Polyb. 3.87.7, Dion. Hal. *AR* 10.24.2, Plut. *Fab.* 4.2, App. *BC* 1.100, and see also Mommsen [1887–88] 1.383 n. 3), John Lydus states that they were to use only twelve (*de Mag.* 1.37) and Livy's epitomator says that Sulla was the first to use twenty-four (*Per.* 89). Since the dictatorship had been in abeyance for 120 years before Sulla revived it in 82 BC, it is possible that he made some innovations to the office, which might have included a greater number of lictors. Still, it was not the number of a dictator's *fasces* that was so terrifying but the inclusion of axes in the *fasces* within the city. See Staveley (1963), Magdelain (1990) 579–82, and Brennan (2000) 41–43.

later even appointed dictators to overwhelm political opposition by plebeian tribunes.[240] Dionysius actually praised a dictator for resolving a domestic crisis without resorting to executions and banishments, which were entirely within his prerogative. While Livy speaks of consuls as being weak and powerless before the urban mob, he invariably describes the plebs as being submissive and obedient to the unrestrained might of the dictator.[241] Possession of *imperium* within the *pomerium* subordinated all citizens and magistrates in that sphere to the dictator's authority, which probably led Polybius to make the incorrect statement that all regular magistrates ceased to hold office once a dictator was appointed.[242] The dictator was liable to prosecution for his actions once he left office, but this seems to have been rare.[243] Eventually, the Romans started appointing dictators to perform nonemergency tasks (see chapter 3), but the origin of the office seems to have derived from the need to quell domestic emergencies through the exceptional use of *imperium* inside the city.

Two further examples illustrate that dictators were uniquely able to use their *imperium* in the city. First, when Sp. Maelius formed a plot against the state in 439 BC, the consuls claimed they were unable to suppress the domestic crisis because their *imperium* had been dissolved or annulled (*dissolvendum imperium*) by the laws of appeal. They called for the appointment of a dictator, who, unlike the consuls, would be free from all laws and be able to inflict summary execution.[244] Once appointed, the dictator immediately brought military units into the city to terrify the citizens into obedience, and he praised his master of horse for killing Maelius in the streets of Rome without trial or appeal. Second, in 325 BC the dictator L. Papirius Cursor ordered the summary execution of his popular but disobedient master of horse, Q. Fabius Maximus Rullianus. Rullianus not only was inside the civilian sphere of the city but also

240. Dionysius of Halicarnassus (*AR* 5.70.1–5, 75.2, and 77.2) wrote that only a dictator could stop civil unrest and portrays the senate's creation of dictators specifically to suppress political opposition by plebeian tribunes. See Mommsen (1887–88) 1.165–66 and 2.141–72.

241. Livy 2.55.9, 6.16.3, 6.28.4.

242. Polyb. 3.87.6–9 (cf. App. *Hann.* 12). In all known cases, magistrates continue to hold office under a dictator.

243. The *lex repetundarum* (*RS* 1.8–9) specifically states that dictators are liable to prosecution once out of office, but only one such prosecution is recorded (Livy 9.26.17–22).

244. Livy 4.13.11–14.7, Dion. Hal. *AR* 12.2.1–4.6. Lintott (1970) 13–18 has argued that the dictator in this story may have been a later addition (perhaps post-Gracchan). Whether or not this is correct, I believe we may still accept that Livy's account describes the notions Romans held about the power of the traditional (pre-Sullan) dictatorship. See Ogilvie (1965) 550–51 for more on the historicity of the event.

invoked his right of *provocatio* and appealed to the tribunes and urban mob for help. They were helpless to resist the authority of the dictator, however, and were reduced to begging for mercy on the young man's behalf. Only when Cursor's anger was assuaged by the sustained pleas of the tribunes, senators, and citizens alike did he agree to withdraw the death sentence.[245] In normal situations, tribunes could prosecute and even arrest sitting consuls, but before the dictator they were dumbfounded and powerless to do anything but beg for the life of Rullianus.[246] These two cases illustrate clearly that dictators were able to use their *imperium* within the *pomerium*, but the exceptional nature of their office and their ability to impose martial law within the civilian sphere proves the general rule that *imperium* was forbidden in Rome under normal circumstances.

The second way the senate could resolve a crisis in the city was to pass the *senatus consultum ultimum*, which gave the consuls the blanket authority to do whatever was necessary to ensure "that the state suffer no harm" (*ne quid res publica detrimenti caperet*, or some variation thereof).[247] As discussed earlier, Sallust gives the best description of the *scu*, in which he specifically states that it authorized the magistrates "to have the *imperium* and the highest *iudicium* both *domi* and *militiae*" (*domi militiaeque imperium atque iudicium summum*

---

245. Livy 8.33.3–35.9. Chaplin (2000) 114 argues this episode is an annalistic rehearsal for the more famous conflict between the dictator Q. Fabius Maximus and his master of horse M. Minucius Rufus, but even so the details of the story reflect Livy's understanding of a dictator's authority. Lintott (1999a) 111 believes that this incident suggests that *provocatio* was effective against a dictator because the disobedient master of horse, Q. Fabius Maximus Rullianus, had appealed to the people for protection (Staveley [1955] 427–28 also believed the tribunician veto was valid against the dictator's *imperium*). As Livy makes clear, however, Papirius Cursor was not forced to relent, nor was Rullianus in any way saved from execution. Rullianus's fate remained continually in the hands of the dictator, who—perhaps to avoid prosecution after resigning his office—chose to forgo the execution. Brennan (2000) 47 holds the same opinion: "It was only special pleading by the Senate, army, and People which saved him from execution by his dictator L. Papirius Cursor, whose orders he had disobeyed."

246. Livy 8.35.1–2: *stupentes tribunos et suam iam vicem magis anxios quam eius cui auxilium ab se petebatur . . . tribuni quoque inclinatam rem in preces subsecuti orare dictatorem insistent ut veniam errori humano, veniam adulescentiae Q. Fabi daret; satis eum poenarum dedisse.*

247. For example: Cic. *Rab. Perd.* 20, *Fam.* 16.11.2, *Cat.* 1.4, *Mil.* 70; Caes. *BC* 1.5, 1.7; Sall. *Hist. Frag. Phil.* 22; Livy 3.4.9 and 6.19.3–4. The current discussion is interested only in demonstrating how the *senatus consultum ultimum* was an exceptional use of *imperium* within the city. See Rödl (1968), Ungern-Sternberg (1970) 79–80, Mitchell (1971), Raaflaub (1974) 79–97, Kaplan (1977) 10–17, Duplá (1990) 113–14, Drummond (1995) 79–113, Kunkel and Wittmann (1995) 230–38, Nippel (1995) 57–69, Lintott (1999a) 90–92 and (1999b) 156, Gaughan (2010) 109–25, and Golden (2013) 104–49.

habere).[248] Sallust emphasizes that this was a highly unusual and extraordinary conferral of authority on the consuls (*sine populi iussu nullius earum rerum consuli ius est*), in particular because it instructed consuls to use their *imperium* in the sphere *domi*. Ancient authors state clearly that the SCU authorized the exercise of military authority (*imperium*) in the city: Cicero emphasizes the military actions enabled by the SCU, including the arming of citizens within the city and the execution of citizens without trial; Caesar claimed that his enemies declared a state of emergency to empower Pompey and the consuls to use military force against him and his supporters in Rome; and Dio wrote that Clodius believed the entire senate was equally guilty of the death of Catiline's co-conspirator Lentulus because his execution without trial had been authorized by a SCU.[249] The passage of the SCU unleashed the full and unrestrained force of *imperium* into the city, which otherwise was normally forbidden.

Because any *senatus consultum* was merely an opinion of the senate and not a law, the SCU was not a legal authorization for the consul to hold *imperium* in the city (as was the triumph, which received or presumed ratification by the people). Rather, it was the suggestion by the senate that the consuls should take up their *imperium* in the city despite the illegality of such action, and it probably contained the senate's implicit promise to use its full *dignitas* and *auctoritas* to support the consuls should they be prosecuted for this action.[250] Similar to the appointment of a dictator, the passage of the SCU was in effect a declaration of martial law, instructing the consuls to ignore the constraints of civil law that they were normally required to observe, and to use the full military might of their *imperium* within the city. Indeed, Plutarch describes L. Opimius (cos. 121 BC) — who was directed by an SCU to suppress the actions of Gaius Gracchus — as the first consul to exercise the power of a dictator.[251] Livy shows this similarity between the dictator and the SCU in his account of 384 BC: when M. Manlius Capitolinus appeared to be planning a coup to take over the city, the senate recognized it needed a leader "who would not provoke a public enemy by ordering him thrown in chains, but who would end an in-

248. Sall. *Cat.* 29.2–3, the passage is quoted in greater length earlier in this chapter at note 150.

249. Arming citizens: *Rab. Perd.* 20; summary execution of citizens: *Cat.* 1.3–4, *Mil.* 70; Caesar's statement: *BC* 1.5; Dio's report on Clodius: 38.14.4.

250. Cicero states clearly that the *senatus consultum ultimum* used to authorize the murder of Gaius Gracchus was contrary to the law (Cic. *De Or.* 2.132–35, 165, 169; cf. Livy *Per.* 61). As it happened, when Opimius was tried for the murder of C. Gracchus in 120 BC, the sitting consuls undertook his defense and secured his acquittal (*MRR* 1.523). See Gaughan (2010) 117–21.

251. Plut. *C. Gracc.* 18.1.

ternal war by laying low a single citizen."[252] The emphasis here is on summary execution made possible by ignoring *provocatio*. Because the *scu* was not actually legal, however, the consuls could be punished after the fact if the Roman people were not satisfied with the results of their illegal use of martial law in the city: when the consul L. Opimius (cos. 121 BC) used the passage of an *scu* to execute Gaius Gracchus and his supporters in Rome without trial, he was prosecuted as soon as he was out of office for violating the citizens' right of appeal. Opimius was acquitted of this charge, but the fact that he was prosecuted in the first place indicates that Gracchus's right of *provocatio* had been in force when he and his supporters were executed and that Opimius had felt emboldened to ignore their right of appeal. Because the *scu* was not a *lex* and conveyed no new legal prerogatives to the consuls, it was probably a vaguely understood concept in the mind of most Romans, and its validity rested solely on the *auctoritas* of the senate.[253] Like the dictatorship, the *scu* is an important exception that proves the general rule that *imperium* was forbidden in the civilian sphere of the city under normal circumstances.

When considering the role of *imperium* in the republic, one should keep in mind that the dictatorship and the *scu* were highly exceptional phenomena that do not reflect the normal operation of civilian governance in Rome. The purpose of both was to enable a magistrate to ignore the usual prohibition on *imperium* within the *pomerium* in order to resolve some domestic crisis — their *raison d'être* confirms that *imperium* was the authority of military command outside the city. In fact, the dictatorship and *scu* seem to be two different solutions, established at different times, to the same political problem of how to authorize the use of martial law in the civilian sphere. The dictatorship was the original mechanism that enabled *imperium* to be brought into the city to subdue violent uprisings, but something happened around 300 BC that made the dictatorship dramatically less common: forty-seven dictators are recorded in the fourth century BC, but only twenty-five are known in the third century.[254] The resolution of the so-called Conflict of the Orders in the late fourth and early third centuries may have greatly reduced the frequency of domestic strife in Rome, but a *lex Valeria de provocatione* passed in or around 300 BC may have also greatly reduced the powers of the dictatorship in the city. Although we do

252. Livy 6.19.2: *qui non in vincla duci iubendo inritet publicum hostem sed unius iactura civis finiat intestinum bellum* (Drogula, trans.).

253. Drummond (1995) 79–95.

254. Kaplan (1977) 103 and 169–73.

not know the content of the *lex*, several scholars have argued that it asserted or affirmed the validity and force of *provocatio* in the sphere *domi*, even against the *imperium* of a dictator.[255] The dictator was still able to use his *imperium* within the *pomerium*, but he had to allow citizens their right of appeal against his decisions.[256] This new regulation would also have greatly reduced the effectiveness of the dictatorship in suppressing major civilian upheavals, which may explain why the use of dictators dropped by nearly 50 percent in the third century BC, and stopped altogether after 202 BC.[257]

With the dictatorship thus defanged and in abeyance, the senate had no way to authorize the use of *imperium* to crush the popularist uprising of the tribune Tiberius Gracchus in 133 BC. Although the senate had used dictators in the past to get around tribunician vetoes, and it might have revived the dictatorship at this time to quell the insurrection, it instead chose a different means for achieving this same end, and it passed the SCU encouraging the consuls to use any means to resolve the current crisis, including bringing their *imperium* inside the city.[258] Perhaps the *lex Valeria* did not restrain consular use of *imperium* in the city as clearly as it did dictatorial use of *imperium* (because consuls were normally forbidden to use *imperium* in the city at all, such oversight would have been understandable), or perhaps the senate simply ignored the *lex Valeria* and trusted in its ability to protect its consuls from punishment for their actions. Whichever was the case, the SCU became the senate's preferred method for enabling magistrates to use *imperium* in the city to crush large-scale uprisings,[259] although two senators — Sulla and Caesar — would revive the dictatorship as a means of using *imperium* in the city for their personal ends. Thus the dictatorship and the SCU were two different senatorial methods

255. Bauman (1973), Kaplan (1977) 103, Develin (1978a) 47, Hartfield (1982) 249, Lintott (1999a) 111–12, Oakley (1997–2004) 4.520–21.

256. Sulla obviously violated this requirement when he became dictator in 82 BC, which explains why his dictatorship was seen as more brutal than his predecessors in that office, and why the dictatorship became a particularly hated office after Sulla's abuse of authority.

257. Kaplan (1977) 103 and 169–73 identifies forty-seven dictators appointed in the fourth century BC, but only twenty-five in the following century after the passage of the *lex Valeria* in 300 BC.

258. It is also possible that Tiberius Gracchus's obstruction of public business — either through a *iustitium* or with his tribunician veto — deprived the senate of other traditional methods of responding to his legislation (Plut. *Tib. Gracc.* 10.5–6; see Lintott [1999a] 125 and Golden [2013] 88–89). Livy (3.4.9 and 6.19.3) records the *senatus consultum ultimum* being used in 464 and 384 BC, but the early dates and the convoluted nature of the stories (neither is recorded as accomplishing anything in Rome) suggest that both are fiction.

259. Kaplan (1977) 174–75, identifies nine different occasions between 133 and 49 BC when a *senatus consultum ultimum* was passed.

for enabling magistrates to bring *imperium* inside the city, and this underlying purpose demonstrates that—in normal circumstances—*imperium* was absolutely forbidden inside the *pomerium*.

LIMITS ON COMMANDERS' USE OF *IMPERIUM*

There were four different checks on a commander's use of *imperium* in the early republic. First, as has already been discussed, he was absolutely forbidden to possess *imperium* inside the *pomerium*, unless given a special exemption to this restriction by the state. Second, his *imperium* could be abrogated (removed) by a vote of a citizen assembly. This was rare, but if it was done, the commander's military authority was nullified, thereby releasing his army from his control.[260] Third, he could use the full force of his *imperium* only in his assigned sphere *militiae*, which the state could restrictively define, change, and revoke as it wished (see chapter 3). Fourth, he could be prosecuted for any mistakes or abuses he committed once he had reentered the city and laid down his *imperium*. While this liability could not hinder a commander from using his *imperium* to carry out illegal actions (such as executing private citizens or violating treaties with Roman allies), the possibility of prosecution, even after the fact, probably imposed a powerful curb on bad behavior, especially since his soldiers—who were eyewitnesses to any abuses he committed—could be among his jurors back in Rome.[261]

In this way, commanders could be punished for a range of misdeeds or abuses of *imperium*: the consuls of 455 BC were prosecuted and condemned to a fine for failing to share the spoils of war fairly with their soldiers (a consul of 219 BC was convicted on the same charge); in 212 BC a praetor was fined because his poor leadership led to his defeat by Hannibal; in 170 BC C. Lucretius Gallus (pr. 171 BC) was successfully prosecuted for his mistreatment of allies while on command; in 136 BC a consul of the previous year was successfully prosecuted for his poor leadership against Numantia; in 104 BC M. Junius Silanus (cos. 109 BC) was prosecuted for illegally starting a war with the Cimbri; and in 103 BC Cn. Mallius Maximus (cos. 105 BC) and Q. Servilius Caepio (cos. 106 BC) were both prosecuted and condemned for their disastrous

---

260. Efforts were made (successful or not) to abrogate the *imperium* of Fabius Maximus in 217 BC (Livy 22.25.10); M. Claudius Marcellus in 209 BC (Livy 27.21.4); P. Cornelius Scipio (Africanus) in 204 BC (Livy 29.19.6); A. Manlius Vulso in 177 BC (Livy 41.6.1–3 and 7.4–10); Q. Servilius Caepio in 105 BC (Livy *Per.* 67; Ascon. 78C). Vishnia (1996) 82–85 and 139 discusses several examples.

261. Rosenstein (1990) 12 n. 14 and 179–204, identifies twelve to fourteen commanders prosecuted for military defeats between 390 and 49 BC.

leadership at the Battle of Arausio in 105 BC.[262] Even if an abusive general escaped judicial punishment, he still risked the social and political backlash from his fellow citizens, since unpopular commanders could be denied triumphs and additional offices, and such public rebukes could damage a man's standing in Roman society. Such was the lot of M. Aemilius Lepidus, who won "universal disapproval" (*adversa omnium fama*) for leaving his praetorian *provincia* early, and as a result he was passed over in the consular elections for 189 BC.[263] These restraints demonstrate that Roman commanders enjoyed absolute authority in the field, and within their assigned spheres (*provinciae*) they were allowed broad discretion in their use of that authority, but commanders were expected to show restraint and self-control in their exercise of *imperium*; the state gave each commander tremendous freedom of action, but it was ready to strip him of his *imperium* and punish him judicially and socially if he failed to show the self-discipline expected of him.

Imperium was fundamentally different from civilian authority in that it did not automatically expire once granted.[264] Whereas a magistrate's *potestas* was directly linked to his tenure of office and therefore expired automatically after an established term (normally one year), the *imperium* of a commander in the field was not subject to any temporal limitation. Unless a commander deliberately relinquished his *imperium* by performing a special ceremony or by crossing the *pomerium* and entering Rome, or unless the people voted to cancel (abrogate) his *imperium*, he was able to retain it indefinitely. Even after a man's military command (*provincia*) had been completed or transferred to another general, he was able to retain his *imperium* as long as he wished by remaining outside the city. In early Rome there was little reason for a man to retain his *imperium* for long after the completion of his military command, since the proximity of Rome's enemies enabled its commanders to fight, return, and potentially triumph all within a short period. Furthermore, remaining outside Rome would have been unattractive for most senatorial elites, since it rendered the man a virtual exile and prevented him from participating fully in civilian life or in the political business of the senate. Although a commander with *imperium* was entitled to retain his impressive curule symbols (lictors, *fasces*, and

262. 455 BC: Livy 3.31.4–6, Dion. Hal. *AR* 10.48.3–4; 219 BC: Front. *Strat.* 4.1.45 (*de vir. ill.* 50 indicated he may have been condemned for peculation); 212 BC: Livy 26.2.7–12; 170 BC: Livy 43.8.2–10; 136 BC: App. *Ib.* 80; 104 BC: Cic. *Corn.* 2, fr. 7, *Verr.* 2.2.118, Ascon. 80–81C; 103 BC: Auct. *Ad Herenn.* 1.24, Cic. *De Or.* 124–25, 197–203, *Balb.* 28, Val. Max. 4.7.3, 6.9.13.

263. Livy 37.47.6.

264. Lacey (1996) 17–18, 21–23, 35–37 has provided one of the strongest arguments for this. See Linderski (1986) 2204, Beck (2005) 349 and (2011) 93.

curule chair) so long as he remained outside Rome, he was not entitled to exercise his military authority without a command (*provincia*).[265]

Because of these disadvantages, there was not much point to retaining *imperium* after returning to Rome, unless one hoped to receive a triumph. In the late republic, however, political infighting among senators occasionally led to a commander's request for a triumph being blocked (at least temporarily), but if he was optimistic that his allies in the senate could force his request through, he would remain outside the *pomerium* and retain his *imperium* and *auspicium militiae* in order to maintain his claims on a triumph. Two famous examples of this are Q. Caecilius Metellus Creticus and Q. Marcius Rex, both of whom lingered outside the *pomerium* for more than three years, all the time retaining their *imperium* in hopes of eventually acquiring permission to triumph.[266] That their *imperium* never expired during this time is demonstrated by the fact that Creticus was eventually able to triumph, and also because the senate was able to reactivate and use both men as fully competent military commanders simply by giving them new *provinciae* against Catiline's forces in Italy—no new grant of *imperium* was needed. Cicero likewise avoided laying down his *imperium* in hopes of receiving a triumph for his victories in Cilicia, but he eventually regretted this decision and complained that his retention of *imperium* made him an unwilling player in the political struggles between Caesar and Pompey.[267]

The fact that *imperium* did not automatically expire was in large part responsible for Pompey's early career: although he was too young to hold the praetorship (which was the most junior office to which *imperium* was normally added), in 77 BC he convinced the people to give him an extraordinary grant of *imperium* to help suppress Lepidus and Brutus.[268] Swiftly accomplishing this goal, he refused to lay his *imperium* down as was expected of him and instead kept his army encamped right outside of Rome to pressure the senate into giving him another *provincia* to undertake with the *imperium* he was

265. Jones (1951) 115 states this well: "*Imperium* without any *provincia* in which to exercise it was a tenuous conception—it was in fact merely the capacity to assume a *provincia* when assigned without waiting for a law conferring *imperium*. It could only be actualized by the grant of a *provincia*."

266. Both Metellus Creticus and Marcius Rex had just claims for a triumph, but their petitions were obstructed by supporters of Pompey, who wished to steal the credit for their victories. Metellus Creticus waited at least three years (65–62 BC) before being permitted to triumph, but Marcius Rex died without ever receiving permission, having waited at least three years (66–63/2 BC) (Cic. *Att.* 1.16.10, Sall. *Cat.* 30.3–4, App. *Sic.* 6).

267. Cic. *Att.* 7.3.3, 7.7.4–7, 8.1.3.

268. Plut. *Pomp.* 17.3–4.

retaining.[269] He received a *provincia* in Spain from the senate, and because his *imperium* was not subject to time limits, he was able to operate as a military commander for the next seven years, the whole time possessing only the extraordinary grant of *imperium* he had received from the state in 77 BC. The military authority conveyed by *imperium* was not conferred for a fixed period of time, nor was it subject to involuntary expiration except by abrogation or crossing the *pomerium* and entering the city. Once taken up, a commander could retain his *imperium* indefinitely, demonstrating that the Romans conceived military authority very differently from civilian authority.

One final attribute of *imperium* was the immunity to prosecution it conferred on its holder. While sitting magistrates might be arrested in office, possession of *imperium* was an ironclad defense against any kind of prosecution, so a retiring commander who anticipated legal troubles back in Rome could remain outside the city and retain his *imperium* in the hope that his political enemies would abandon their efforts to prosecute him. In 187 BC Cn. Manlius Vulso (cos. 189) returned from a command in the East, but managed to delay the celebration of his triumph until the very end of the year, because he feared prosecution by one of the sitting praetors and wished to keep his *imperium* until there was too little time left in the praetor's term for him to preside over any prosecution.[270] C. Cassius Longinus (cos. 171 BC) likewise sought to avoid prosecution by retaining his *imperium* long after he had laid down his campaign, but instead of lingering outside the *pomerium*, he accepted a place as a tribune of soldiers in the army of A. Hostilius Mancinus, which allowed Longinus to say he was away from Rome "on state business" (*absens rei publicae causa*) rather than simply evading prosecution.[271] Of course, not every commander who retained his *imperium* after laying down his command did so for nefarious reasons: when Ti. Sempronius Longus laid down his *provincia* in 194 BC, he did not return to Rome and lay down his *imperium*, but instead remained in the *provincia* and helped his successor by acting as his legate and providing his knowledge and experience of the region.[272] The immunity to prosecution provided by *imperium* was obviously intended to protect commanders while on campaign and prevent legal preoccupations from reducing their military effectiveness, but the fact that *imperium* did not automatically

269. Plut. *Pomp.* 17.1–4.
270. Livy 39.6.3–6.
271. Livy 43.1.4–12 and 5.1–2.
272. Livy 34.42.3, 35.5.1 and 8.6.

expire enabled ex-commanders to retain their immunity beyond the completion of their campaigns.

Imperium, therefore, represents a different concept of authority from *potestas*. Not only do the two ideas represent different types of authority (military vs. civilian), but also they pose different notions of how authority worked: *imperium* was absolute authority within a specific sphere and — once given — did not automatically expire, whereas *potestas* endowed each magistracy only with those prerogatives appropriate to its civilian responsibilities, but this authority could be used more broadly than *imperium* (inside and outside of Rome), although *potestas* automatically expired at the end of a set period. These differences are so fundamental that they support the argument that *imperium* evolved as an entirely separate concept from the practice of civilian governance. Indeed, they support the contention that military commanders and civilian magistrates were originally entirely different and separate concepts in early Rome. Although *imperium* and *potestas* eventually combined in certain magistracies, the fundamental nature of each type of authority remained unique and separate.

Conclusion

Given *imperium*'s overwhelming importance in Roman thinking, the lack of a description surviving from the republican period is perhaps surprising. In all likelihood, the idea was so pervasive and obvious in Roman society that authors never even thought to define it. Without such a definition, modern historians must build a composite picture made up of many small pieces of evidence. Mommsen began with the assumptions that *imperium* was a static concept during the millennium from the foundation of Rome to the law codes of the late empire, and that *imperium* must have been used for civilian governance as well as military command in the early republic. Working from these assumptions, he built a logical argument to explain how *imperium* was weakened and limited in the sphere *domi* but absolute and unchecked in the sphere *militiae*. This complicated reconstruction is logical and systematic, but the underlying assumptions on which it is built fall apart too easily when applied to real incidents in Roman history. As this chapter has argued, there is no good evidence that *imperium* was a normal source of civilian authority in the republic, and there is much evidence suggesting the opposite. This is not a new revelation — many historians have recognized problems with Mommsen's ideas over the years, but his scholarly *auctoritas* and the reasonableness and clarity of his theories have proved resilient to challenge. The definition presented in this chapter of *imperium* as the singular and indivisible authority of military command that was forbidden within the civilian sphere of Rome except in dire emergencies fits the evidence better. Although there is insufficient evidence to say conclusively that this definition must be true, it corresponds with the known facts, does not depend on underlying assumptions, and is not contradicted by what evidence we have as readily as is Mommsen's theory. In example after example, the evidence shows that there was no need for *imperium* to be a source of civilian authority, that there were strong taboos against the holding of *imperium* in the city, and that there is no good evidence that a weakened *imperium domi* ever existed. Furthermore, accepting that *imperium* was strictly the extra-urban authority of military command enables us to unlock several confusing questions from Roman history, including the nature of the dictator's authority and his relationship to the consuls, and the nature of the relationship between the consuls and praetors.

3

THE CONCEPT OF
PROVINCIA IN EARLY ROME
(TO 367 BC)

The previous chapter argued that *imperium* conferred the absolute (but vaguely defined) authority to give orders and to enforce one's will but that its use was normally confined to a specific sphere *militiae*. That sphere was referred to as the commander's *provincia*, which defined the purpose for which the commander's *imperium* was to be used, but it did not define or limit how the commander was to use his *imperium* within the pursuit of that purpose. Unlike *potestas* and *auspicium*, the conferral of *imperium* on a magistrate was thus qualified by the stipulation that its full force was to be used only in the sphere or *provincia* designated by the state.[1] As such, the *provincia* focused a commander's use of his *imperium* because it was a restricting assignment that defined his official military responsibilities, thereby establishing how his *imperium* was to be used: to impose martial law and to enforce one's orders by any means necessary in the specific responsibility or sphere that defined (and therefore limited) the purpose(s) for which the commander's otherwise-absolute *imperium* could be used. The two concepts were inextricably linked, so a man with *imperium* but no *provincia* could not act as a commander.

The *provincia* was originally a specific task given to a Roman commander, a point on which most scholars agree, although the meaning of *provincia* slowly evolved to signify a specific territory as well as a task.[2] These tasks were usually

1. Certain aspects of a commander's *imperium* — such as his immunity to prosecution — were active outside of his *provincia* as well as inside, but the full force of his authority to give orders and compel obedience (and punish non-obedience with the severest penalties) could only be used in pursuit of the *provincia* assigned him.

2. Richardson (2008) has recently published a thorough analysis demonstrating this evolution in the way the term *provincia* was used by surviving authors. See also Badian (1965) 110–21, Jolowicz and Nicholas (1972) 66–71, Bertrand (1982), Richardson (1986) 6–10 and (1996) 2–6, Bertrand (1989),

military campaigns against specific enemies, and ancient authors make it clear that a man needed both *imperium* and a *provincia* in order to exercise legitimate command.[3] Because of this symbiotic relationship between the two concepts, a commander's *provincia* defined and limited the sphere within which he could use the full force his *imperium*.[4] While *imperium* authorized an early consul to impose summary execution on disobedient or cowardly soldiers while he was on campaign fulfilling his military *provincia*, he certainly would have been prosecuted and condemned if he had executed a citizen (or even a soldier) while marching with *imperium* in a triumph through the streets of Rome. Possession of *imperium* was to be used only in the fulfillment of a commander's assigned *provincia*, and there could be consequences if it was used arbitrarily. For example, the consul L. Postumius in 291 BC was prosecuted and condemned to pay a heavy fine for using his *imperium* to coerce his soldiers into working as laborers on his farm while on military campaign.[5] His authority (*imperium*) was legitimate and in force, but he was condemned for using that authority in a pursuit other than the responsibility (*provincia*) given him by the state. A consul could possess his *imperium* anywhere outside the domestic area encircled by the *pomerium*, but that authority was supposed to be used only within the sphere of his assigned responsibility. Cicero accurately called it "stupid" (ἀβδηριτικόν) that Pompey had asked him to take command of Sicily in 50 BC, since he (Cicero) had no authorization from the senate or people to exercise the *imperium* that he had received for his Cilician *provincia* in Sicily. In other words, he did not have that *provincia*:

> I hear from many places that it has been decided by Pompey and his council that I be sent to Sicily because I have *imperium*. This is stupid, for neither had the senate instructed me to hold *imperium* in Sicily, nor has the people ordered it.[6]

Ando (1999) 16, Lintott (1999a) 101–2, Ferrary (2008) 8, Wesch-Klein (2008), Beck (2011) 92. For a discussion of terms used by Greek authors, see Freyburger-Galland (1996).

3. Military command was described as holding a *provincia* with *imperium*: Cic. *Verr.* 2.4.8, 2.5.46, *Flacc.* 85, *Sest.* 128, *Fam.* 3.2.1, 8.8.8; Caes. *BC* 1.31; Livy 28.28.14, 29.13.3; Suet. *Aug.* 29.2; Gell. 5.14.17, 12.7.1. The absence of a commander from his command was referred to as a *provincia* without *imperium*: Cic. *Att.* 7.7.5, Caes. *BC* 1.31, Livy 39.21.4. See also Jones (1951) 115, Lowenstein (1973) 46, Lintott (1981a) 54 and (1993) 22, Giovannini (1983) 51 and (1999) 97–98, Hurlet (1994) 257, and Richardson (2008) 8.

4. On the way in which a *provincia* defined the *imperium* of a commander, see Giovannini (1983) 27 and Jones (1951) 114–15.

5. Livy *Per.* 11 and Dion. Hal. *AR* 17–18.4.3–4.

6. Cic. *Att.* 7.7.4: *a multis audio constitutum esse Pompeio et eius consilio in Siciliam me mittere*

Cicero had returned from his *provincia* in Cilicia and understood that he had no right to exercise his *imperium* elsewhere than where he had been authorized to do so by the state. The necessity of legal possession of a *provincia* was made painfully clear to L. Licinius Lucullus in 67 BC: when the *lex Manilia* stripped him of his *provincia* fighting Mithridates, his disgruntled soldiers immediately became insubordinate, claiming he no longer had any right to command them — without a *provincia*, his *imperium* seems to have meant little to his soldiers.[7] Naturally, a military commander had considerable liberty to determine what actions did and did not fall within his military *provincia*, a potential that would be exploited by greedy or ambitious commanders. Nevertheless, the *provincia* was an important qualifier that gave shape and definition to the otherwise vaguely defined concept of *imperium*; a commander's *provincia* defined the specific sphere in which (and *only* in which) he was free to use the full force of his *imperium*.

Because the *provincia* played an essential role in defining how commanders would use their *imperium*, one of the first orders of business that the senate undertook at the start of each year was to determine what *provinciae* the new consuls (and, later, the new praetors) would undertake. Livy's descriptions of these senate meetings are regular and rarely display variation, illustrating a long-standing customary practice. The following from 203 BC is typical:

> When the consuls Cn. Servilius and C. Servilius — whose year was the sixteenth of the Punic War — had related to the senate the situation regarding the republic and the war and the *provinciae*, the Fathers decided that the consuls should either arrange amongst themselves or determine by a drawing of lots which of them would have the *provincia* of the Bruttii against Hannibal, and which should have the *provincia* of Etruria and the Ligurians, and that the consul who received the Brutii should command of the army of P. Sempronius.[8]

Although the consuls were the highest regular magistrates and acted as the presidents of the senate, it was not within their authority to determine where or for what purpose they would use their *imperium*, although they could cer-

---

quod imperium habeam. id est Ἀβδηριτικόν; nec enim senatus decrevit nec populus iussit me imperium in Sicilia habere (Drogula, trans.).

7. Plut. *Luc.* 35.2–4, App. *Mith.* 90, Dio 36.14.4–15.1.

8. Livy 30.1.1–3 (Drogula, trans.): *Cn. Servilius et C. Servilius consules — sextus decimus is annus belli Punici erat — cum de re publica belloque et provinciis ad senatum rettulissent, censuerunt patres ut consules inter se compararent sortirentve uter Bruttios adversus Hannibalem, uter Etruriam ac Ligures provinciam haberet; cui Bruttii evenissent exercitum a P. Sempronio acciperet.*

tainly try to influence the decision.[9] It is likely that provincial assignment and the requirement that commanders use the full force of their *imperium* only in their assigned *provincia* developed as part of the process by which the early Roman state asserted its authority over its aristocratic warlords and eventually acquired its monopoly on the conferral of military authority. It was the prerogative of the Roman citizens voting in their assemblies to determine which *provinciae* were given to which commanders, probably because the citizens composed Rome's army and had demanded some say in how they were used.[10] In normal practice, however, the people were content to allow the senate to determine the best allocation of Rome's military forces each year, although particularly contentious decisions might be referred to the people for their approval.[11] Still, it was ultimately the prerogative of the Roman citizens to determine what tasks its commanders would perform with the authority invested in them, as Julius Caesar demonstrated in 59 BC when he arranged to have the *comitia tributa* annul the *provincia* given him by the senate (the highways of Italy) and instead give him the *provincia* of Cisalpine Gaul and Illyricum.[12] Provincial assignment was of fundamental importance for two reasons: it determined what opportunities a commander would have to win glory and profit, and it simultaneously determined the limits of the sphere within which

9. In 205 BC, for example, the consul P. Cornelius Scipio (later Africanus) was determined to have Africa and the war against Carthage as his *provincia*, a command that would immeasurably increase his own reputation, but turned out to be in Rome's best interests as well (Livy 28.45.1–2). Likewise, in 74 BC the consul L. Licinius Lucullus had received the *provincia* of Cisalpine Gaul but worked behind the scenes to have this changed to the *provincia* of the Mithridatic War (Plut. *Luc.* 5.1–2 says he was given Cilicia and the Mithridatic war, but Vell. 2.33.1 says he was given Asia plus the war).

10. See Livy 38.45.4–11, where he emphasizes the authority of the senate and people of Rome to declare wars and assign *provinciae*.

11. In 202 BC, for example, the incoming consuls very much wanted the *provincia* of Africa so they could replace Scipio (Africanus) and claim credit for ending the war. The senate could not (or would not) come to a decision itself, so it referred the question to the tribunes and the tribal assembly, which voted that the *provincia* should stay with Scipio (Livy 30.27.1–4).

12. Cic. *Vat.* 36, *Prov. Cons.* 36–37; Vell. 2.44.5; Suet. *Iul.* 22.1; Plut. *Caes.* 14.9–10, *Pomp.* 48.3, *Crass.* 14.3, *Cat. Min.* 33.3; App. *BC* 2.13; Dio 38.8.5. Other cases of the Roman citizens asserting their supreme control over provincial assignment: in 205 BC P. Scipio (Africanus) threatened to have recourse to the people if the senate did not give him Africa as his *provincia* (Livy 28.45.1–11); the people insisted that Scipio Aemilianus receive Africa in 147 BC (Livy *Per.* 51, Val. Max. 8.15.4, App. *Pun.* 112); Gaius Marius uses the popular assemblies to receive the command in Africa against Jugurtha in 107 BC (Cic. *Prov. Cons.* 19, Sall. *Jug.* 73.7); Clodius as tribune arranged provinces for Piso and Gabinius in 58 BC (Cic. *Sest.* 24–25 and 53; *Dom.* 23–24, 55, and 70; *Prov. Cons.* 3–9; *Pis.* 28 and 49); in 55 BC the tribune Trebonius arranged for Pompey and Crassus to receive provinces from the people (Livy *Per.* 105, Vell. 2.46.2, Plut. *Pomp.* 52.3–4, *Crass.* 15.1–2, *Cat. Min.* 43, Dio 39.33.2).

he was able to use the full force of his *imperium*. The *provincia* was an important tool of state control over the exercise of military command.

When the senate met to determine *provinciae* for its military commanders, it prioritized Rome's offensive and defensive goals and balanced these with any other pressing needs.[13] Although the *provinciae* were almost always military in nature, other types of tasks could be assigned: in 207 BC a consul was sent (without an army) to investigate suspicious activities among the Etruscans or Umbrians, and in 173 BC a praetor-elect was sent to combat a locust plague in Apulia.[14] Once the senate had determined one or more *provinciae* it wished (or needed) undertaken, the consuls would normally draw lots to determine which of them would take command of which *provinciae*, although the senate could assign the *provinciae* to the consuls by decree, or it could allow the consuls to divide the *provinciae* among themselves.[15] The process also allowed for adjustments: in 210 BC the consuls drew lots for their *provinciae*, but on reflection the senate decided that an exchange would be desirable, and it asked the consuls to switch *provinciae* (which they did).[16] Such a switch could also be required by law: in 192 BC both the senate and the *concilium plebis* voted that the *provinciae* assigned to two praetors by lot should be changed.[17] A political arrangement was also possible: Cicero had been assigned the *provincia* of Macedonia during his consulship in 63 BC, but he offered to trade commands with his colleague C. Antonius Hibrida in exchange for the latter's political support against Catiline.[18] On occasion—particularly in the early years of the republic—a single military command could be given to both consuls, which would require the two men to share authority for that responsibility. In addition to deciding the *provinciae* commanders would receive, the senate also determined

13. On the senate's decision-making process, see Rich (1993) 55–64 and Vervaet (2006a) 625–32.

14. Livy 28.10.4–5, 42.10.6–8.

15. *Sorte provincia evenit* or *sortiri* (Livy 4.37.6, 4.43.1, 7.6.8, 7.38.8, 10.11.1, 21.17.1, 28.45.9, 30.1.2, 30.40.12, 32.8.1, 37.1.7, 38.35.9, 42.31.1 43.12.2, 45.17.5). Dion. Hal. *AR* (9.36.1) uses the term ἐκληρώσαντο. In a passage of Cincius preserved by Festus (276L—cited in full earlier), the Romans in the early republic also used augury to determine which praetor would receive a particular command. *Provincia extra sortem decreta est* or *provincia sine sorte data est* (Livy 3.2.2, 6.30.3, 8.16.5, 10.24.3, 10.24.18, 28.10.9, 28.38.12). *Consules partiti provincias* (Livy 3.10.10, 3.22.3, 3.57.9, 8.20.3, 9.12.9, 9.31.1, 9.41.2, 10.12.3). See Rosenstein (1995) 43–75, Stewart (1998) 12–94, and Vervaet (2006a) 625–32.

16. Marcellus had received the *provincia* of Sicily by lot, but when the Sicilians complained about the poor treatment they received during his previous command on that island, enough senators were swayed by their fear of reprisals that agreed to ask the consuls to trade commands (Livy 26.29.1–10, Plut. *Marc.* 23.1–5).

17. Livy 35.20.11–13.

18. Cic. *Pis.* 5, *Fam.* 5.2.3, Sall. *Cat.* 26.4, Plut. *Cic.* 12.4, Dio 37.33.4.

what military forces and funding each commander would have for his *provincia*, and commanders could recruit soldiers only if authorized to do so by the senate. Thus in 205 BC the consul Scipio (Africanus) had to recruit an army of volunteers, because the senate had refused to allocate soldiers and resources to his Sicilian *provincia*.[19] Once the assignments had been made and all essential civil and religious responsibilities were carried out, the consuls were at liberty to take up *imperium* on exiting the city and to assume command of their designated *provinciae*, although the senate or assembly could order them to accelerate or delay their departure.[20]

Even after a commander exited the city and took up his *imperium* and *provincia*, the senate and people of Rome retained the ability to adjust, change, and dissolve his *provincia*, which meant they were able to redefine the sphere in which a commander could use his *imperium*. In the earliest period of the republic, military campaigns were probably too short to need much adjustment, but in later years it was common for the senate to change, add to, or remove a commander's *provincia* as it deemed appropriate. In 218 BC, for example, the senate recalled the consul Ti. Sempronius Longus (who was en route to his *provincia* of Sicily and Africa) and directed him instead to march against Hannibal in northern Italy.[21] The senate could also make adjustments to a commander's *provincia*, as occurred in 174 BC when the senate added Corsica to the *provincia* of the praetor dispatched to Sardinia.[22] The senate could even dictate what routes a commander was to take to reach his *provincia*.[23] While

---

19. Zon. 9.11, Livy 28.45.14. On the role of the senate to finance military *provinciae*, see Polyb. 6.13.1 and 15.4–8, and Pina Polo (2011) 240.

20. Consuls had to perform certain religious duties (Livy 27.23.1); a consul who was also the *flamen Martialis* was forbidden to take up his *provincia* by the *pontifex maximus* in 242 BC because he was needed in Rome to tend to his religious duties (Livy *Per.* 19, Val. Max. 1.1.2; cf. Livy 37.51.1–7). In 167 BC a praetor was ordered forgo his *provincia* and remain in Rome and tend to legal jurisdiction (Livy 45.16.4), and in that same year a consul was ordered to complete certain matters of domestic governance before leaving for his *provincia* (Livy 45.17.6–7). On the other hand, when C. Popillius Laenas, a consul of 172 BC, refused to leave for his *provincia* because he wished to remain in Rome to protect his brother from prosecution, two tribunes forced him with threats of prosecution to depart for his *provincia* (Livy 42.21.4–5 and 8).

21. Polyb. 3.61.9, Livy 21.48.7. Similarly, when M. Valerius Laevinus, a praetor holding the *provincia* of Lucania and Apulia in 215 BC, intercepted messengers traveling from King Philip of Macedon to Hannibal in Italy, the senate directed Laevinus to hand his army over to a legate and to take command of a fleet based at Tarentum (Polyb. 8.1.6, Livy 23.38.10–12). And when one consul suffered a serious loss fighting the Histrians in 178 BC, the senate instructed his colleague to leave his own *provincia* and instead hasten to his defeated colleague's *provincia* in Gaul (Livy 41.5.5).

22. Livy 41.21.1–2.

23. See Brennan (2004) 45 and Pina Polo (2011) 240.

it was generally understood that commanders could retain their *provinciae* for up to a year, the senate could cancel or transfer a provincial assignment at any time and recall a commander to Rome.[24] The senate could also make adjustments to the military forces under their commanders while they were in the field.[25] If proximity allowed, the senate could even micromanage some aspects of a commander's *provincia*, such as when it instructed the consuls laying siege to Capua in 212 BC to allow Campanians to leave the city unharmed and with their possessions if they wished.[26] If necessary, the senate could have its decisions (*senatus consulta*) backed by the legal weight of a vote by the people, but in general Livy portrays the senate as qualifying its instructions to commanders with the phrase "if it seems good to you" (*si ei videretur*) — a polite request, but one that was difficult to ignore.[27] Taken altogether, the senate (and people) had the ability to define and redefine the *provincia* that a commander held, meaning that the vast power of his *imperium* was to a large extent confined within the limits implicit in the provincial command he received.

While the senate and people of Rome retained full control over a commander's *provincia*, it was notoriously difficult to control a commander with *imperium* in a *provincia* who did not want to acknowledge the senate's authority. Since a commander with *imperium* enjoyed absolute authority over the *provincia* given him by the state, he was not required to obey the senate or any other authority so long as he retained his *imperium* and *provincia*, although he might pay a heavy price later for refusing to heed the instructions of the state. Still, if ignoring the senate's instructions for a brief period might bring lasting glory and sociopolitical advancement for a commander and his family by enabling him to complete the subjugation of the enemy or to engage in an imminent battle, the potential repercussions might be acceptable. In 223 BC the consuls C. Flaminius and P. Furius Philus were on the verge of

24. Examples include: recalling for elections (Livy 35.24.2, 44.17.3); recalling to name a dictator (Livy 7.19.9); transferring command to successors (Livy 8.3.4); dissolving a *provincia* altogether (Livy 38.42.8–13).

25. In 172 BC the senate instructed one of the consuls to send a large portion of his army — including one of his legions — to another commander (Livy 42.27.5–6). Other examples of such adjustments of a commander's *provincia*: Livy 27.38.9 and 40.14.

26. Livy 25.22.11. Similarly, commanders near Rome might seek the input of the senate regarding the conduct of their campaign (Polyb. 3.107.6–8).

27. Livy 22.33.9, 25.41.9, 26.16.4. Henderson (1957) 85 pointed out that the senate normally did not use the imperative mood when communicating with its magistrates and interprets it as a stylistic tradition in which social equals did not use the imperative when addressing one another. On the other hand, Daube (1956) 37–41 demonstrates that *senatus consulta* could use imperative forms if they were conveying a *lex* of the people.

fighting a great battle, and so refused to obey a letter from the senate instructing them to return to Rome and abdicate their office because of bad omens
and auspices.[28] Fortunately for the consuls, they won a great victory over the
Gauls, but the indignant senate refused them a triumph (although the people
overrode this decision). Six years later in 217 BC, Flaminius was again recalled
from a second consulship on account of bad omens and neglected auspices,
and a senatorial commission was sent to bring him back to Rome, but he defied this recall and died in the Battle of Lake Trasimene.[29] In 173 BC the consul M. Popillius Laenas disobeyed senatorial instructions to free Roman allies
he had illegally enslaved, and he refused to return to Rome until forced to do
so by the tribunes.[30] In 78 BC the consul M. Aemilius Lepidus refused to heed
the senate's instructions that he should return to Rome from his *provincia* in
Transalpine Gaul in order to hold elections. Aemilius wanted more time to
win glory and plunder to enhance his status back in Rome, but he was finally
declared an enemy of the state as a result of his refusal to obey the senate.[31]
It even happened that consuls in Rome would take up their *imperium* and
provincia and leave the city in order to avoid obeying instructions of the senate,
as happened in 210 BC when the consul M. Valerius Laevinus refused to name
a dictator as the senate requested and left Rome secretly at night in order to
put himself beyond the ability of the senate, tribunes, and assembly to coerce
him into obedience.[32] Eckstein has demonstrated that commanders in the field
had tremendous independence and freedom from senatorial control, such that
their decisions in the field often dictated Roman foreign policy.[33] It was always
open for the senate and people either to revoke a commander's *provincia* or
to abrogate his *imperium*, but short of this there was no way to coerce a commander in the field beyond the threats of prosecution once he returned to
Rome.

Once the senate had defined a commander's *provincia*, it fully expected that

28. Plut. *Marc.* 4.2–3.

29. Livy 21.63.1–11, Val. Max. 1.6.6, Plut. *Fab.* 2.3–3.1. See Broughton (1951) 1.242 and Beck
(2005) 245.

30. Popillius sold the allied tribe of the Statelliates into slavery (Livy 42.7.3–9.6), and the tribunes
carried a bill in the assembly forcing him to return to Rome to face prosecution for his misconduct
(Livy 42.22.2–8). Fortunately for Popillius, the *praetor urbanus* was a friend and postponed the trial
long enough for Popillius to escape punishment (Livy 42.22.7–8).

31. App. *BC* 1.107.

32. Livy 27.5.14–19.

33. Eckstein (1987).

he would remain within that assigned sphere. Since early *provinciae* were normally tasks rather than specific places, commanders were expected to limit their use of military authority to the pursuit of the task to which they had been assigned. Commanders were free to move around as necessary to subdue the enemies assigned to them, but they were not permitted to use their *imperium* for purposes other than those defined by the state. Those commanders who exceeded the bounds of their assigned *provinciae* received sharp rebukes from the senate: in 294 BC the senate refused to grant a triumph to the consul L. Postumius Megellus because he had left his *provincia* against the Samnites to fight needlessly in Etruria; in 188 BC much of the senate attempted to block Cn. Manlius Vulso's request for a triumph over Galatia on the grounds that the Galatians had lain outside his assigned *provincia* in Asia; in 178 BC the senate sharply rebuked the consul A. Manlius Vulso for leaving his *provincia* in Gaul to launch an unauthorized attack on Histria; in 171 BC the senate sent three envoys to prevent the consul C. Cassius Longinus from interfering in his colleague's *provincia*, and these envoys delivered such a stern message that Cassius took a position as a military tribune in his successor's army to avoid returning to Rome until the senate's anger had cooled; in 80 BC the senate was angered when Cn. Cornelius Dolabella left his *provincia* in Cilicia in order to assist the illicit dealings of his legate C. Verres in Asia; and in 55 BC Cicero sharply rebuked A. Gabinius for leaving his assigned *provincia* of Syria in order to restore the Egyptian king Ptolemy to his throne.[34]

Of course, the restriction against leaving one's *provincia* might be set aside if the result of the transgression were sufficiently glorious or strategically necessary to Rome's interests: in 218 BC no one doubted that the consul P. Cornelius Scipio had done the right thing when he broke off from his march to his assigned *provincia* in Spain in order to intercept Hannibal's march to Italy.[35] Although he had been assigned the *provincia* of fighting the Carthaginians in Spain, he may have reasoned that his *provincia* authorized him to pursue Carthaginian forces from Spain into Italy, or he may have felt that military necessity justified his exercise of military command outside his assigned *provincia*. Likewise, in 207 BC the consul C. Claudius Nero won a triumph for leaving

---

34. Livy 10.37.1–12 (Megellus: the popular assembly gave him a triumph in spite of the senate's objection), 38.45.1–50.3 (Cn. Vulso: he ultimately received a triumph through his powerful connections), 41.7.4–10 (A. Vulso), Livy 43.1.4–12 and 5.1–9 (Longinus), Cic. *Verr.* 2.1.73 (Dolabella), *Pis.* 50 (Gabinius).

35. Polyb. 3.49.1–4, Livy 21.32.1–5 and 39.3, App. *Hann.* 5.

his own *provincia* in southern Italy in order to help his colleague destroy Hasdrubal's army, which had arrived in northern Italy.[36] Livy portrays Claudius as understanding that his action was a violation of established practice, but he (Claudius) justified the action by saying that "the situation of the state was not such that they should carry on the war by routine methods, each consul within the bounds of his own *provincia*, operating with his own armies against an enemy prescribed by the senate."[37] In such cases, the interpretation of what was and was not in the best interests of the state could vary according to one's perspective: at the end of 44 BC Cicero castigated Dolabella for attempting to assume command of a *provincia* not assigned to him (Syria), but he praised Brutus and Cassius for doing the same thing in order to deny Dolabella and other Caesarians access to important resources.[38]

The expectation that commanders were to remain in their assigned *provinciae* was so strong that some men might pass up military opportunities: in 191 BC the consul P. Cornelius Scipio Nasica was criticized because, having subdued the Boii within his own *provincia*, he returned to Rome to request a triumph rather than using his army to aid the proconsul Q. Minucius Thermus in Liguria. In Livy's description, Scipio, after responding properly that Liguria had not been his *provincia*, was permitted to triumph over the Boii.[39] Livy and his audience clearly understood that each Roman commander was expected to remain in his own *provincia*. This expectation explains the unusual provincial assignment given to P. Cornelius Scipio (Africanus) in 205 BC: Sicily, but *with permission* to cross over into Africa in order to attack the Carthaginians directly (*permissumque ut in Africam, si id e re publica esse censeret, traiceret*).[40] This demonstrates that a commander assigned to Sicily was normally expected to remain on the island (or at least in the immediate vicinity of it, if he held a naval command), but Scipio had received special permission to leave his assigned *provincia* (the conquest and defense of Sicily) in order to engage a different enemy (Carthage itself in Africa) in a different place. Thus the *provincia* not only identified what a commander was expected to achieve with his *imperium* but also limited his use of military authority to a specific pursuit or purpose.

36. Livy 27.43.8–51.13; Val. Max. 3.7.4, 7.4.4; Frontin. *Str.* 1.1.9, 1.2.9, 2.3.8, 2.9.2 (cf. Polyb. 11.1–3 and App. *Hann.* 52–54).

37. Livy 27.43.6: *non id tempus esse rei publicae ratus quo consiliis ordinariis provinciae suae quique finibus per exercitus suos cum hoste destinato ab senatu bellum gereret* (Moore, trans.).

38. Cic. *Phil.* 11.26–28.

39. Livy 36.39.3–40.9.

40. Livy 28.45.8–9 (cf. Plut. *Fab.* 25.1–26.2, App. *Hann.* 55, *Pun.* 7).

Most of early Rome's *provinciae* were campaigns against enemies who lay within a few days' march of the city, so there must have been an expectation that a commander could defeat his assigned enemy, and thereby complete his *provincia* (task), within a single campaigning season. Most of these *provinciae* involved one or more pitched battles rather than a prolonged multiyear siege, so the *provincia* was normally a short-term assignment. When a commander holding a specific *provincia* left office, his *provincia* ceased to exist or have relevance, although the senate might assign that same task to one of the incoming commanders for the following year, in which case the task was the same, although it was a new assignment to a new commander. In general, commanders were expected to complete the *provincia* assigned to them within the present campaigning season. If a commander did this (normally by conquering his assigned foe), he would immediately bring his army back to Rome and hope for permission to triumph — the two consuls of 266 BC returned to Rome so swiftly after completing their shared *provincia* that they were able to triumph and receive a second shared *provincia*, which they completed quickly enough to celebrate a second triumph each within a single year.[41] Once a commander completed his *provincia*, the *provincia* itself automatically ceased to exist; the task of defeating a particular enemy was no longer pertinent or meaningful once that enemy had been defeated. Commanders were expected to remain in the field until they completed their *provincia* or until the campaigning season ended, and returning to Rome early without accomplishing their assigned tasks probably brought shame on them as quitters or failures. In 205 BC the army of P. Licinius Crassus Dives was disabled by a plague and could not continue its campaign. Fearing the stigma of being a quitter, Crassus did not return to Rome until he had first written the senate, explained the situation, and asked its permission to return to Rome with his *provincia* unaccomplished.[42] If a commander remained in the field until the end of the campaigning season but was unable to complete his *provincia* by defeating his assigned foe, he could return to Rome (without shame, but also without much glory), or the senate could send a successor to keep Rome's army in the field if necessary. In this way the Romans supposedly maintained their legendary siege of Veii for ten years (405 to 396 BC), which required the introduction of pay for soldiers and a succession of military commanders.[43] Thus the *provincia* was originally

41. *Act Tr.* for 266 BC.

42. Livy 29.10.1–3. See also 28.9.1–3, where a consul of 207 BC communicated with the senate before leaving his *provincia*.

43. The siege begun in 405 BC (Livy 4.61.2) and was completed in 396 BC by the famous dic-

a temporary assignment that lasted only until the commander to whom it had been assigned completed it or until he left office.

The *provincia* was thus an essential qualifier that identified the specific purpose or responsibility a commander was expected to undertake with his *imperium*. The relationship between a commander's *imperium* and *provincia* was symbiotic; he could not exercise the full force of his *imperium* outside the sphere defined by his *provincia*, so a man with *imperium* but lacking a *provincia* could not exercise the military authority necessary to be fully defined as a commander. Because it delimited the use of *imperium* and restricted it to a specific purpose or responsibility, the *provincia* and the practice of provincial assignment probably arose in the early republic as one method by which the developing state achieved a monopoly of control over the exercise of military authority by its aristocracy. Rather than weaken the effectiveness of their generals by reducing the authority conferred on commanders by *imperium*, the Romans instead chose to define and limit the use of that absolute authority to tasks identified by the state. The *provincia* was a concept of fundamental importance in the definition of a military commander, but it was inherently different and separate from other defining concepts like *imperium* and *auspicia*. The ideas were interconnected with one another in that they defined both commander and command, but because they were separate ideas they could also change or develop independently of one another.

Military Hierarchy Determined by Provincial Assignment

It seems an obvious notion that early Roman commanders must have existed within some kind of hierarchical structure, because a vertical system of ranks and a clear chain of command are among the most basic and defining aspects of armies. This is obvious within a Roman army: the commander with *imperium* was the supreme commander, supported by senior officers (military tribunes) and junior officers (centurions) who lacked *imperium* but nonetheless were recognized authorities within the army. Within his army, the commander with *imperium* was the uncontested supreme authority. But how did the Romans determine superiority of authority between two or more commanders, each of whom possessed *imperium* and his own command? Because every Roman commander possessed the exact same *imperium*, there was no legal distinction or hierarchy of military authority among commanders; each

---

tator M. Furius Camillus (Livy 5.19.1–23.12; Diod. 14.93.2–3; Dion. Hal. *AR* 12.14.1, 13.3.1–2; Val. Max. 4.1.2; Plut. *Cam.* 5.2–6.1). Pay for soldiers: Livy 4.59.11, Diod. 14.16.5, Flor. 1.6.8, Zon. 7.20.

commander had absolute authority in his command, so no commander out-ranked another in the modern sense. Since Rome had two or more command-ers in chief in the field each year, there was a serious danger that disagreements or disputes between them could hinder effective action or even endanger the armies.[44] In the civilian sphere, such an impasse between or among magisterial colleagues (such as a consul exercising his *potestas* to veto his colleague) could bring the civilian legal system to a standstill, which was certainly an annoyance, but generally not a fatal one for the state.[45] In military affairs, however, such a stalemate between the *imperium* of commanders could be lethal for the army as well as for the state if it prevented necessary military action, so a system was needed to prevent paralyzing conflict by establishing which colleague's authority took precedence in any given endeavor.

In modern armies, two basic mechanisms are used to determine hierarchy of authority: authority and responsibility.[46] Authority refers to the specific au-thority of military command, which is invested in a commander by the state and is different from other types of authority the state might invest in its offi-cials.[47] This modern command authority exists in different ranks or levels, and military personnel are placed into a fixed number of ranks that exist in verti-cal hierarchy; each of these ranks possesses a different level of command au-thority in such a way as to form a chain of command in which each rank can give orders to lower ranks and must obey orders from higher ranks. For ex-ample, generals have authority over captains, but two colonels are equal and (absent other factors) possess no authority over one another.[48] Such a hierar-

44. Consuls commanding in the same sphere did frequently disagree on tactics: Livy 10.19.1–9, 21.52.1–2, 22.42.8, 22.44.5–45.9.

45. Cicero remarks (*Leg.* 3.42) that Rome's legal system was more concerned to prevent bad ideas than enable good ideas: *parere iubet intercessori, quo nihil praestantius; inpediri enim bonam rem me-lius quam concedi malae.*

46. For example, the U.S. Army's Command and Rank source document (AR 600-20, Army Command Policy), paragraph 1-5b states: "*Elements of command.* The key elements of command are authority and responsibility."

47. AR 600-20, Army Command Policy, paragraph 1-5a: "A civilian, other than the President as Commander-in-Chief (or National Command Authority), may not exercise command."

48. In the modern U.S. army, precedence between two officers of equal rank is determined by the length of time they have spent in that rank (AR 600-20, Army Command Policy, paragraph 1-6). In the early Roman Republic, however, regular commanders entered office at the same time and held military authority for no more than a year, preventing any hierarchy by length of time in command (although men who had held previous consulships generally had greater prestige). Indeed, proconsuls (who held extended terms in command) actually had less prestige and status than the new sitting consuls.

chical system of authority is so basic to the modern mind that we automatically expect it in other societies, but the early Roman Republic does not seem to have employed this type of thinking. The early Romans are recorded as using only one type of regular commander at a time, such as archaic praetors (called consuls in the texts) or consular tribunes; dictators were used irregularly. Because the early Romans normally used only a single type or rank of commander at a time, to assume that they conceived of military command authority (*imperium*) existing in different levels or degrees is illogical; because all of their normal commanders possessed the same rank, they would have possessed the exact same level of *imperium*. To imagine that one (archaic) praetor with *imperium* could give orders to another praetor with *imperium* on the basis of military authority alone is likewise illogical. This is supported by the preceding argument that military authority in early Rome was not divisible into different levels or degrees — *imperium* was originally an absolute idea that did not admit gradations of authority and could not have provided the basis for determining the respective level of command authority held by two men. The *imperium* held by all commanders in early Rome was equally absolute and provided no method of differentiation between commanders. The idea of military rank is so basic and prevalent in the modern world that historians must be careful not to assume the necessity of its existence in ancient times.

The Romans did, however, employ the second modern method (responsibility) for establishing a hierarchy of military authority, and this idea of responsibility was their primary safeguard against a deadlock of *imperium* between military commanders. In modern usage, responsibility refers to a military task or responsibility that is placed under the authority of a specific individual, who exercises primary authority over that task or responsibility.[49] Thus a particular brigade could be placed under the authority of a particular colonel as his command, and that colonel would exercise greater authority over that brigade than any other colonel. Naturally, a higher authority could direct the colonel in how he was to use his brigade, but so long as it was his command, the colonel exercised primary and direct authority over that brigade. The ancient Roman equivalent of the English term "command" was the *provincia*, which was the task or responsibility in which a Roman commander was to use his *imperium*. When the state assigned a *provincia* to a particular commander, that assign-

49. AR 600-20, Army Command Policy, paragraph 1-5a: "A commander is, therefore, a commissioned or WO who, by virtue of grade and assignment, exercises primary command authority over a military organization or prescribed territorial area that under pertinent official directives is recognized as a 'command.'"

ment not only determined how the commander would use his *imperium* but also established that his *imperium* was to take priority in that sphere. This was demonstrated in the previous chapter by the senate's refusal in 195 BC to give M. Helvius a triumph for the victory he had won over the Celtiberians in Farther Spain: because he had already turned the *provincia* over to his successor at the time of his victory, the senate rejected his request for a triumph on the grounds that the victory had been won in another man's *provincia* (*quod alieno auspicio et in aliena provincia pugnasset*).[50] The senate did not weigh or even consider the level of Helvius's authority but simply asked whether Helvius had been in command (i.e., whether he had held the *provincia*) of Farther Spain at the time of the victory.

Because the authority conferred by *imperium* was absolute and complete and did not establish different levels of authority between commanders or subordinate one commander to another, the early Romans were dependent on the idea of commands or *provinciae* to determine which commander exercised primary authority in what theater of war. Ancient authors occasionally use the phrase *provinciae praeesse* ("to be in charge in a *provincia*") to describe the command of a *provincia*, an expression that clearly defines a particular commander as being preeminent in a particular *provincia* without any reference to higher or lower levels of *imperium*; supreme command of a *provincia* was easily defined and expressed without reference to *imperium*.[51] As Badian pointed out, "*Imperium* itself, of course, could not be conditional. . . . But the *provincia* to which its exercise was limited could be and was conditional."[52] In this way, provincial assignment determined not only which commander would undertake which action but also which commander's *imperium* took priority in which *provincia*.

Cicero demonstrated this function of provincial assignment in his prosecution of Verres. In one of his speeches, Cicero makes the point that Sicilian farmers had been on the point of giving up planting their fields, since they expected to make no profit under Verres's corrupt practices. Back in Rome, the praetor L. Caecilius Metellus had been appointed to succeed Verres as commander of Sicily, and when he learned of the dire situation of the island's economy, he took the extraordinary step of writing the communities of Sicily to promise them that his administration would be superior to that of Verres.

50. Livy 34.10.1–6. Briscoe (1981) 71 states that Helvius was refused a triumph because "he was not fighting in the province where he could legitimately operate [his *auspicia*]."

51. See Cic. *Att.* 6.5.3, *Fam.* 3.5.5; Sall. *Cat.* 42.3; Livy 27.7.10, 28.46.14, 31.10.5, and 39.54.10.

52. Badian (1965) 112.

Cicero emphasizes that Metellus did something entirely unprecedented (*quod nemo umquam post hominum memoriam fecit*) by sending official letters in advance into another man's *provincia* (*in alienam provinciam mittat litteras ante tempus*).[53] Although Metellus was a sitting praetor, and he had already been assigned the *provincia* of Sicily, actual possession of the *provincia* gave the propraetor Verres precedence of authority in that sphere. Metellus would assume command upon his arrival in Sicily, but until that time Verres's legal possession of the *provincia* made him the supreme commander over it.

Provincial assignment was the usual method by which the state prevented conflicts between commanders, since it not only placed a particular task under the primary authority of a specific commander but also removed that task from the authority of all other Roman commanders. According to Lintott, "the Roman concept which lay at the root of the separation of magistrates in space was *provincia*."[54] By thus separating and isolating commanders from one another, the Romans had no need to think about questions of rank or hierarchy, because if one commander happened to enter the *provincia* of his colleague, it was clearly understood that the *imperium* of the commander who held the *provincia* should take precedence.[55] When the consul L. Postumius Megellus (cos. 291 BC) trespassed into the *provincia* of a proconsul and refused to acknowledge the proconsul's precedence in that sphere, Megellus was prosecuted and condemned to pay a large fine for interfering with another man's command.[56] The Battle of Metaurus in 207 BC also demonstrates well how provincial assignment established priority of command. Days before this battle, the consul C. Claudius Nero learned that Hasdrubal Barca was arriving in Italy with an army to reinforce Hannibal. Without orders and entirely on his own initiative, Nero left his own *provincia* in southern Italy and raced to reinforce his colleague M. Livius Salinator in the north where Hasdrubal was to arrive.[57] With their combined forces, the two consuls crushed Hasdrubal's army in Salinator's *provincia*. Although both consuls were awarded a triumph for the victory, Nero — who had devised the winning strategy — refused to accept equal credit; he declined to triumph on his own, and instead took the secondary honor of riding on horseback in his colleague's triumph while

53. Cic. *Verr.* 2.3.44.

54. Lintott (1999a) 101.

55. Stewart (1998) 196–219 has put forward a similar point, arguing that the assignment of specific civilian duties (*provinciae*) to magistrates in Rome obviated the need for hierarchy, although she maintains (208, 210) that consuls and praetors held different degrees of *imperium*.

56. Dion. Hal. *AR* 17–18.4.4–5.4.

57. Livy 27.43.1–12, Val. Max. 4.1.9.

Salinator drove the triumphal chariot. As Livy and Valerius Maximus both emphasize, Salinator had been the holder of the *provincia* in which the victory had been won, so Nero was only following proper procedure when he allowed his colleague to receive primary credit for their joint victory.[58] While both men were consular colleagues and had the exact same *imperium*, Salinator had been the unquestioned commander in chief at the Battle of Metaurus because he was operating in his own *provincia*; possession of the *provincia* was the sole attribute that determined which consul was actually in command.

This method for establishing precedence was particularly relevant on occasions when one commander summoned the aid of a colleague. In the early republic, when Rome was occupied with conquering Italy and both consular armies were operating within a short distance from one another, it was not uncommon for one consul to summon the aid of his colleague when faced with a stronger-than-expected enemy.[59] Ideally, the two commanders would cooperate in a collegial manner, as occurred in 214 BC when the consul M. Claudius Marcellus came to the aid of his colleague Q. Fabius Maximus Verrucosus, and together the two commanders crushed Casilinum and several other Campanian cities.[60] While relations between these two commanders appear to have been friendly, it is likely that only Fabius would have received the official credit for the victories, since they were won in his *provincia* (Marcellus had been assigned to Nola).[61] This was certainly how matters had been arranged ninety years earlier: in 306 BC the consul Q. Marcius Tremulus answered his colleague's call for aid and left his own *provincia* against the Hernici and Anagnini to join P. Cornelius Arvina facing the Samnites.[62] Together, the two consuls crushed the Samnites in battle, but despite his essential contribution to this victory over the Samnites, Tremulus would not receive the credit for the victory he made possible over the Samnites, and would triumph only over the Hernini and Anagnini.

One final case further demonstrates this essential role of the *provincia*: when the consul Ap. Claudius Caecus encountered trouble fighting the Etrus-

58. Livy 28.9.10, Val. Max. 7.2.6a. Livy stresses Nero's generosity in allowing Salinator — an older man — to receive primary credit for the victory, especially since the two men had been bitter enemies before their consulship. It is possible that Livy was trying to honor his patron (Augustus), whose two stepsons belonged to the same branch of the *gens Claudia* as had C. Claudius Nero.

59. For example: Dion. Hal. *AR* 9.14.5, 9.63.1–2, 10.23.4–5.

60. Livy 24.19.1–20.2.

61. Livy does not mention whether either commander received a triumph, and this year is missing from the *Fasti Triumphales*.

62. Livy 9.43.8–24.

cans in 296 BC, he seems to have summoned his colleague's assistance only to spurn that aid when it arrived, accusing his colleague (L. Volumnius Flamma Violens) of improperly interfering in his (Caecus's) *provincia*. As Livy presents the encounter, Caecus denied having requested Volumnius's assistance and rebuked him for having left his own *provincia* to interfere in the *provincia* of a colleague.[63] Livy's description of this encounter portrays Caecus as a liar and poor general, but he makes it clear that Volumnius *would* have been in the wrong if he had he entered Caecus's *provincia* unbidden (Volumnius responds to Caecus's disavowal of the letter by offering to leave the *provincia* immediately). Livy even addresses his audience directly to assure it that three different authorities confirmed Caecus's call for help, thereby freeing Volumnius of the charge of interference in a colleague's *provincia*. Caecus probably would have been wise to accept Volumnius's assistance because (as the holder of the *provincia*) Caecus would have been entitled to claim all of the glory, but Livy presents him as being made to look the fool by comparison to a better commander. Rome's preferred method for avoiding crippling conflicts between commanders, therefore, was based not on rank or levels of authority but on separating them into different *provinciae*.

On occasion, the Romans dispatched two commanders into the same general territory or against the same enemy. This may have been done because that territory or enemy was considered especially dangerous, or because the senate was unable to judge the extent of the threat and so sent two commanders. Although this is usually portrayed as two commanders being assigned to a single *provincia*, it was normal practice for the commanders to assess the situation and to divide their *provincia* in such a way as to enable each commander to conduct an independent campaign; the single *provincia* was thus divided into two separate *provinciae*, giving each commander his own *provincia* in which he could operate with complete autonomy.[64] In such situations, each commander maintained his own camp separate from his colleague, and if joint action was needed against a single foe, each commander might lead his own army (under his own *imperium*) and attack the enemy from a different direction, thereby maintaining a distinction between each commander's sphere of authority.[65] This sharing of a *provincia* was especially common during the Roman conquest

63. Livy 10.18.7–22.

64. Polyb. 1.18.2, 1.40.1, 2.34.5–6; Livy 8.13.5, 9.44.6, 10.14.1–4, 32.29.5–6, 33.36.1–37.1, 35.22.4, 39.2.1–11, 39.32.1–4, 41.18.7; Diod. 20.25.2.

65. Separate camps: Dion. Hal. *AR* 5.39.1 and 41.1; two consuls draw lots to determine which of them would attack an enemy from what direction: Livy 41.18.7–8.

of northern Italy in the early second century BC, when Rome frequently dispatched both consuls to the Po Valley and each would operate against a different enemy. Livy gives several examples of this, but his account of the consular *provinciae* in 197 BC is particularly revealing because it shows his underlying understanding of how provincial assignment worked. Both consuls in that year had been given northern Italy as their *provincia*, which they separated so that one fought the Insubres and Cenomani, while the other fought the Boii and Ligurians. Livy's account of their request for a triumph is worth quoting at length:

> At about the same time the consuls returned to Rome; when they summoned the senate to meet in the temple of Bellona and demanded a triumph for their successes in the war, Gaius Atinius Labeo and Gaius Afranius, tribunes of the people, insisted that the consuls offer separate motions regarding the triumph: they would not allow a common motion to be voted on, lest equal honour be bestowed upon unequal merit. Quintus Minucius replied that the province of Italy had fallen to the lot of both consuls and that he and his colleague had acted in accordance with a common policy and plan of campaign, and Gaius Cornelius added that the Boii, who were crossing the Po against him, to aid the Insubres and Cenomani, had been called away to defend their own homes when his colleague laid waste their towns and farms. To this the tribunes rejoined that they agreed that Gaius Cornelius had accomplished in the war results of such magnitude that there was no more question of his triumph than there could be of paying honour to the immortal gods; yet neither he nor any other citizen was so powerful in influence and resources that, when he had obtained a well-earned triumph, he could bestow the same unmerited honour upon a colleague who had the effrontery to demand it. Quintus Minucius, they continued, had fought some unimportant battles in Liguria, hardly worthy of mention, and in Gaul had lost a great number of his men . . . the surrender of small towns and villages had taken place, but this was fictitious, manufactured for the occasion, and without guarantees. These debates between the consuls and the tribunes continued for two days, but at last, overcome by the stubbornness of the tribunes, the consuls offered separate motions.[66]

66. Livy 33.22.1–10 (Sage, trans.). Likewise, in 193 and 192 BC the consuls of each year separated northern Italy into two different *provinciae* — one against the Boii and the other against the Ligurians (Livy 34.55.6, 35.22.3–4). In 121 BC the consul Q. Fabius Maximus (later Allobrogicus) received a *provincia* in Gaul where the proconsul Cn. Domitius Ahenobarbus was already engaged in fighting Gallic tribes. Fabius did not supersede Domitius or become his superior; rather, the two men divided

Livy's passage clearly indicates that although the two consuls had been given a single *provincia* of Italy, everyone understood that they had operated separately and independently and could not submit a single request for a joint triumph because they had effectively divided their shared *provincia* into two different commands, and each had acted within his own *provincia*. There is no doubt that both commanders had the right to request a triumph—both were acting with their own *imperium*, under their own *auspicium*, and in their own *provincia*—but Minucius was turned down because his accomplishments were found lacking.[67] Minucius had clearly anticipated this and sought to share a triumph with his colleague (a shared triumph was better than none), but the tribunes saw through this ploy.[68]

The preference to divide a shared *provincia* into two separate and independent parts is seen in other types of commands as well. If the provincial assignment contained a naval component, it was normal for one consul to take command of the fleet, and the other of the army, once again voluntarily creating two *provinciae* out of one. This is frequently done in the Roman campaigns on Sicily and in Africa during the first two Punic Wars, and consuls are even found dividing the Roman navy into two distinct fleets so that each could be the exclusive *provincia* of one consul.[69] Even the siege of a single city could be divided into two separate spheres, as happened in the First Punic War when the two consuls established themselves in different camps and attacked the city at different points, thereby allowing each consul to operate independently of his colleague.[70] By dividing a single *provincia* into two distinct *provinciae*, each commander could enjoy absolute authority in different and separate spheres, enabling each to claim personal glory for his own accomplishments, and the possibility of debilitating conflict was removed.

If two commanders were assigned to a single *provincia* that for some reason could not be divided into two separate *provinciae*, it was normal practice for the commanders to alternate supreme command of their shared *provincia*

---

the *provincia* by selecting different enemies—Fabius fought the Allobroges and Domitius the Arverni (Livy *Per.* 61, Vell. 2.10.2).

67. Minucius celebrated a triumph on the Alban Mount (Livy 33.23.1–8).

68. Gaius Marius and Q. Lutatius Catulus celebrated a single triumph for their defeat of the Cimbri in 101 BC, probably because Marius wanted to deny Catulus a triumph of his own (Cic. *Tusc.* 5.56, Livy *Per.* 68, Plut. *Mar.* 27.5–6).

69. Consuls or praetors divide a *provincia* into land and naval commands: Polyb. 2.11.1, 2.11.7–8, 8.1.4, 8.1.6–7, 8.3.1; Livy 23.26.1–2, 24.12.7–8, 30.27.5. Consuls divide the navy into two fleets: Polyb. 1.26.10–16.

70. Polyb. 1.18.2, 1.38.9, 1.42.8, 8.3.1–2; Livy 25.22.8–9.

daily. Instead of dividing the *provincia* spatially, they divided it temporally. This occurred most frequently when Rome needed to send an exceptionally large and powerful army against a single, particularly dangerous foe, so two commanders (usually consuls) cooperated but still avoided the possibility of conflict by alternating supreme command of their joint army daily.[71] This alternation of supreme command was probably a voluntary agreement backed by customary practice; no legal transfer of authority actually took place in the alternation, because no Roman commander could adjust or change the authority conferred by his *imperium*. *Imperium* was absolute and did not increase or decrease—or turn on or off—at a commander's whim. Instead, the commanders alternated priority of command, which enabled one consul to yield to his colleague without creating any imparity between them.

Although this use of priority among equals may seem unusual to the modern audience, it was common in the Roman Republic. The most famous example is the monthly alternation of priority between the two consuls in Rome, which was visually expressed by the alternation of the *fasces*. Each month, the consul holding priority—the *prior* or *maior consul*—was preceded in public by his twelve lictors bearing *fasces*, whereas the consul who was not *prior* was preceded only by a single attendant while his lictors and *fasces* followed behind him.[72] The *prior* or *maior consul* was certainly not the superior of his colleague, since both consuls retained full, simultaneous, and equal authority, and either could veto the actions of his colleague, but the *prior* consul enjoyed sole possession of the *fasces* and priority in executive actions, such as presiding over the senate. Cicero specifies that it was only the insignia of power that exchanges hands,[73] so we should not imagine that a real change in the authority held by the consuls took place. Thus priority was intended to promote efficiency, since

71. Polybius (3.107.14) emphasized that this type of shared command was rare.

72. *Lex de provinciis praetoriis* (*RS* 12 Cnidos III 28); Cic. *Rep.* 2.55; Livy 2.1.8, 8.12.13, 9.8.1–2; Dion. Hal. *AR* 5.2.1, 9.43.4; Fest. 154L; Val. Max. 4.1.1; Dio 53.1.1; Suet. *Iul.* 20.1; Plut. *Popl.* 12.5. On the importance and advantages of the *prior consul*, see Taylor and Broughton (1949) 3–14 and (1968), Linderski (1965) 423 and 433, Drummond (1978b) 81–83, Lintott (1999a) 100. Linderski (1986) 2179 suggests that "only the actual holder of the *fasces* had the right to independent action, whereas the *imperium* and *auspicium* of his colleague were dormant at that time (however, it is important to realize that in any case the *auspicium* was dormant only as far as independent action was concerned, and not obstruction)." This argument seems too convoluted and contrived, and even contradictory in that it suggests *imperium* and *auspicium* could be simultaneously active and dormant. It is far more likely that each month one consul simply adhered to customary practice by allowing his colleague to exercise priority of action.

73. Cic. *Rep.* 2.55.

it enabled one consul to have primary charge of affairs at a time without reducing the status or authority of his colleague.

Priority was used in other aspects of the Roman state: in the army, the senior centurion in each of the legion's three lines (*hastati, principes, triarii*) was referred to as *prior* (*hastatus prior, princeps prior*, and *pilus* [*triarius*] *prior*); in the senate, the *princeps senatus* was given priority of speaking over his colleagues; and in the *comitia centuriata* the *praerogativa* vote (the vote of the century selected to cast its ballot first) was considered more weighty than the subsequent votes.[74] Likewise, the Romans frequently gave precedence to older members of a group — such as a consul allowing his older colleague to speak first on official matters — which was a voluntary prioritization of one colleague over another that did not indicate or imply an imbalance of legal authority between them.[75] The use of priority rather than superiority was a common feature of Roman thinking, and it was attractive to them because it permitted one member of a group of equals to take precedence over his colleagues without subjecting them to the demeaning position of being an inferior or subordinate. Commanders sharing a *provincia* would be expected to use this traditional practice to avoid conflict and to enable each man to enjoy full command on alternate days by establishing whose authority would take priority in a shared *provincia* at any given moment.

Although the accuracy of Livy's account of early Rome is certainly open to debate, he clearly understood the long-standing practice by which priority enabled two commanders to alternate supreme command without actually changing the *imperium* or *auspicium* invested in either man. He believed that the consuls of 446 BC were the first to use this method for alternating command, which he described as follows:

> Although the two consuls were of equal authority in the Roman army, yet they made an arrangement which is extremely advantageous in the administration of important measures, by which Agrippa yielded the supreme command to his colleague. The latter, thus preferred, responded courteously to the ready self-effacement of the other by admitting him to a share in his plans and his achievements, and treating him as an equal, despite

---

74. On the army, see Keppie (1984) 174; on the *princeps senatus*, see Gell. 14.7.9 and Ryan (1998) 293–314; on the *praerogativa centuria*, see Cic. *Planc.* 49, Livy 5.18.1, 9.38.15, 10.22.1, 24.9.3, 26.22.2, 26.22.13, 27.6.3, Botsford (1909) 211–12, 389, 463, Taylor (1949) 56, Brunt (1988) 524 n. 2, and Yakobson (1999) 52.

75. Polyb. 36.6.5.

his inferiority (*imparem*). In the battle-line Quinctius held the right wing, Agrippa the left.[76]

In his passage on 418 BC, Livy emphasizes how this alternation of authority was an important means for enabling two men who hated each other to share a single command:

> The bickerings which had commenced between them in the city grew much hotter in the camp, from the same eagerness to command; they could not agree on anything; each strove for his own opinion; each desired his own plans and his own orders to be the only valid ones; each despised the other and was in turn despised by him, until at last, reproved by their lieutenants, they arranged to exercise the supreme command on alternate days.[77]

When describing this type of alternation of authority in a *provincia*, Livy occasionally uses the phrase *summum imperium* or *dies imperii* to express the thing being exchanged or alternated between the two commanders, but how should this be interpreted?[78] It is tempting to take such passages as legal terminology expressing some kind of change in the relative *imperium* of the two consuls, but this seems unlikely. There is no indication that *imperium* existed in greater or lesser degrees in Rome's early history, and even if it did, the comparative adjective *maius* would have been more appropriate and accurate than the superlative *summum*.[79] But because *imperium* was a singular and absolute concept until the end of the republic, there cannot have been any notion of changing *imperium*; a man either had *imperium* or did not, but *imperium* itself did not change. Furthermore, even if there had been different levels or degrees of *imperium*, it seems impossible that a consul in the field could somehow increase and decrease his *imperium* on his own authority and on his own schedule — how could the simple exchange of *fasces* make one consul's *im-

76. Livy 3.70.1–2: *in exercitu Romano cum duo consules essent potestate pari, quod saluberrimum in administratione magnarum rerum est, summa imperii concedente Agrippa penes collegam erat; et praelatus ille facilitati summittentis se comiter respondebat communicando consilia laudesque et aequando imparem sibi. In acie Quinctius dextrum cornu, Agrippa sinistrum tenuit* (Foster, trans.).

77. Livy 4.46.2–3: *coepta inter eos in urbe certamina cupiditate eadem imperii multo impensius in castris accendi; nihil sentire idem, pro sententia pugnare; sua consilia velle, sua imperia sola rata esse; contemnere in vicem et contemni, donec castigantibus legatis tandem ita comparatum est ut alternis diebus summam imperii haberent* (Foster, trans.).

78. Livy 3.70.1 (*summa imperii concedente*), 4.46.5 (*dies imperii erat*), 22.27.6 (*alterius summum ius imperiumque esse*), 22.27.9 (*dies imperii*), 22.41.3 (*eo die — nam alternis imperitabant — imperium erat*), 22.45.4 (*summa imperii eo die fuerit*).

79. Compare with Cic. *Att.* 4.1.7, *Phil.* 11.30, Tac. *Ann.* 2.43.1.

perium greater and his colleague's *imperium* lesser? *Imperium*, like *auspicium* and possession of a *provincia*, was authority and responsibility conferred on a consul by the Roman people, and the Roman state alone had the prerogative to make changes in the *imperium, auspicium*, and *provincia* they had granted. It defies legal principle that two consuls out on campaign could bring about a real and legal increase or decrease in the *imperium, auspicium*, or *provincia* invested in their office simply by mutual agreement and without some kind of authorization or confirmation of that adjustment by the state, which was the sole source of all authority held by Roman magistrates. It is far more likely that Livy is using the phrase *summum imperium* not to indicate a change in the level or degree of *imperium* held by either consul but simply to signify that one of the two consuls held supreme command at a time.[80] This understanding fits well with Livy's emphasis that this alternation was a *voluntary agreement* made by the consuls, not a legislated action.

Livy demonstrates this further in his description of the famous conflict between Q. Fabius Maximus and M. Minucius Rufus in 217 BC, when the senate ordered the two men to determine how they would share their *provincia* of fighting Hannibal.[81] Livy's portrayal of this discussion—although a creation of his own mind—nevertheless demonstrates the normal Roman understanding about the discretion commanders had to choose the method by which they would cooperate in a *provincia*. It also demonstrates that Livy knew that possession of a *provincia*, and not variations in levels of authority, determined supreme command:

> Therefore, on the day when [Minucius] first met with Q. Fabius, he said that the first thing of all to establish was in what way they would use their shared command: he himself thought it best either to lead on alternate days or, if longer periods were desirable, to hold supreme authority and command for alternating periods of time. . . . This was not at all pleasing to Q. Fabius . . . [who said that] his command had been shared with another,

80. This seems supported by Polybius's description (3.110.3–4) of the alternation of authority used by L. Aemilius Paullus and C. Terentius Varro at Cannae: τῆς δ' ἡγεμονίας τῷ Γαΐῳ καθηκούσης εἰς τὴν ἐπιοῦσαν ἡμέραν διὰ τὸ παρὰ μίαν ἐκ τῶν ἐθισμῶν μεταλαμβάνειν τὴν ἀρχὴν τοὺς ὑπάτους. The use of the word ἡγεμονία suggests that the prior commander of the day held superior leadership but not necessarily authority. The term ἀρχή frequently refers to Latin *imperium* in Greek documents but could also refer to the terms *potestas* and *ius*—see Mason (1974) 44, 133 and Dmitriev (2005) 238.

81. Although ancient sources suggest that the Roman people took the unique step of naming Minucius co-dictator with Fabius (Polyb. 3.103.1–5, Livy 22.25.10–11, Val. Max. 5.2.4), Walbank (1957–79) 1.434 points out that he may have shared authority with Fabius without actually being a co-dictator.

not taken away from him: he would not divide the army with him for time periods or days of command, and by his own counsels he would save what he could, since it was not possible for him to save everyone. In this way he brought it about that the legions were divided between them as was the custom among consuls.[82]

Livy here illustrates the two common methods voluntarily used by Roman commanders to share command: the temporal alternation favored by Minucius, and the division into separate *provinciae* demanded by Fabius. Although one does not want to press the details of Livy's account too far, Fabius got his way probably because the negative vote normally prevailed among magisterial colleagues:[83] since Minucius could not get Fabius to agree to the temporal division, he settled for the division of the *provincia* into two separate Roman operations. The conflict between Fabius and Minucius illustrates that commanders were expected to work out for themselves how they would share authority over a single *provincia*, a voluntary and autonomous action that would seem to preclude the notion that any real change in their authority (*imperium* and *auspicium*) or responsibility (*provincia*) took place.

Although this alternation of priority in a *provincia* was voluntary, it was backed by custom and treated as binding, so men willingly acknowledged the precedence of their *prior* colleagues. The best example of this is the ill-fated campaign of the consuls L. Aemilius Paullus and C. Terentius Varro, who were jointly assigned the *provincia* of fighting Hannibal in 216 BC. From the beginning, the two commanders are portrayed as holding opposite views on the proper strategy for defeating Hannibal: Aemilius favored the Fabian tactics of delay and attrition, whereas Varro would accept nothing less than a single decisive battle. Because such a disagreement could paralyze Rome's army in a dangerous moment, the two commanders followed the practice of alternating priority of command daily. Although each consul loathed the strategy followed by his colleague, neither denied his colleague's right to follow whatever strategy he wished while he held priority. When Aemilius Paullus—fearing

---

82. Livy 22.27.5–10: *Itaque quo die primum congressus est cum Q. Fabio, statuendum omnium primum ait esse quem ad modum imperio aequato utantur: se optimum ducere aut diebus alternis, aut, si maiora intervalla placerent, partitis temporibus alterius summum ius imperiumque esse ... Q. Fabio haudquaquam id placere ... sibi communicatum cum alio, non ademptum imperium esse: nec se tempora aut dies imperii cum eo, exercitum divisurum, suisque consiliis, quoniam omnia non liceret, quae posset servaturum. Ita obtinuit ut legiones, sicut consulibus mos esset, inter se dividerent* (Drogula, trans.). See also Polyb. 3.103.7–8.

83. Cic. *Leg.* 3.42.

one of Hannibal's famous traps — prevented his army from following up a small victory with headlong pursuit, Varro shouted out in angry protest but did not attempt to act contrary to Paullus's instructions.[84] Later, when it was Varro's day to hold priority over the army, he ordered a full attack against Hannibal near the town of Cannae, which would become one of Rome's greatest military disasters. Paullus is portrayed as being vehemently opposed to this action, but he was powerless to prevent it since Varro happened to have priority that day.[85] There is no reason to imagine that Paullus possessed weaker *auspicium* or *imperium* than Varro, or that his claim on the *provincia* was lesser; Varro simply took priority over his colleague in all of these areas on that day.

As the case with Fabius and Minucius demonstrates, the Romans usually left it up to their commanders to determine how they would share a *provincia* when necessary, which required a minimum level of cooperation between commanders. At the very least, the two commanders had to agree on how their *provincia* would be split or shared, because neither one could force his colleague to yield. This was demonstrated in the disastrous Battle of Arausio in 105 BC, when two consular armies were annihilated because their commanders failed to follow traditional methods for sharing a *provincia*. In this year, the threat of imminent Gallic invasion drove the senate to send the consul Cn. Mallius Maximus to Gaul, where he was to operate in conjunction with the proconsul Q. Servilius Caepio (cos. 106 BC), who had been campaigning in that region for many months.[86] Orosius suggests that the Rhone River was the boundary between their respective *provinciae*, but this was probably a makeshift distinction, since there is ample evidence that Cisalpine and Transalpine Gaul were not clearly organized as separate entities until after Sulla.[87] It is not clear whether Mallius and Servilius ever met or came to some agreement about how to share the *provincia*, or whether they simply ignored and avoided each other, each operating in different territories (Caepio in Transalpine Gaul, and Mallius in Cisalpine Gaul). By all accounts, these two men disliked each other greatly, mainly because Servilius (a blueblood from an ancient family) looked down on the new man Mallius. When Mallius intercepted the main force of

---

84. Livy 22.41.3. Livy (22.41.3, 42.8–9, 43.8, 44.5–7) and Polybius (3.110.3–4) portray the two consuls arguing bitterly over questions of strategy and tactics, but there is no indication that either consul considered acting contrary to the wishes of whoever held priority that day.

85. Polyb. 3.110.3–4, Livy 22.45.5–6, Val. Max. 3.4.4, and App. *Hann.* 18.

86. Livy *Per.* 67, Dio 27 fr. 91.1–4; Vell. 2.12.2–5; Plut. *Mar.* 19.2, *Sert.* 3.1–2. The relationships between magistrates and promagistrates is considered in the next chapter.

87. Oros. 5.16.1–4: *provincias sibi Rhodano flumine medio diviserunt.* On the absence of a formal separation of Cisalpine and Transalpine Gaul at this time, see Konrad (2004) 193–94.

Gauls, however, he sent a letter asking that Servilius come to help him defeat the powerful enemy. Dio describes Servilius's arrival and behavior as follows:

> Servilius became the cause of many evils to the army by reason of his jealousy of his colleague; for, though all other things had been entrusted to him equally, his rank was naturally diminished by the fact that the other was consul. After the death of [Mallius's legate] Scaurus, Mallius had sent for Servilius; but the latter replied that each of them ought to guard his own affairs. Then, anticipating that Mallius might gain some success by himself, he grew jealous of him, fearing that he might secure the glory alone, and went to him; yet he neither encamped in the same place nor entered into any common plan, but took up a position between Mallius and the Cimbri, with the evident intention of being the first to join battle and so of winning all the glory of the war. . . . The soldiers forced Servilius to go to Mallius and consult with him about the situation. But far from reaching an accord, they became as a result of the meeting even more hostile than before; for they fell into strife and abuse, and parted in a disgraceful fashion.[88]

Because these two commanders could not agree on a way to determine precedence among themselves, both of their armies were destroyed by the Gauls. This passage illustrates that neither commander had any kind of real authority over the other; in spite of being a sitting consul, Mallius was unable to compel the proconsul Caepio to obey orders, demonstrating that commanders (at least consuls and proconsuls) did not operate within a hierarchy of rank or authority.[89] For this reason, Dio and Orosius made a point of informing their audiences that Caepio had entered into Mallius's *provincia*, a statement intended to establish Mallius's precedence of authority. Since this claim on precedence seemed clear, Livy and Dio placed the blame for the debacle squarely on

---

88. Dio 27.91.1–4 (Cary, trans.): Ὅτι ὁ Σερουίλιος ὑπο τοῦ πρὸς τὸν συνάρχοντα φθόνου (τὰ μὲν γὰρ ἄλλα ἐξ ἴσου οἱ ἐπετέτραπο, τῷ δὲ δὴ ἀξιώματι οἷα ὑπατεύοντος αὐτοῦ ἠλαττοῦτο) πολλῶν καὶ κακῶν αἴτιος τῷ στρατεύματι ἐγένετο. καὶ γὰρ ὁ Μάλλιος μετὰ θάνατον Σκαύρου τὸν Σερουίλιον μετεπέμψατο· ὁ δὲ ἀπεκρίνατο τὴν ἑαυτοῦ ἑκάτερον δεῖν φυλάττειν. εἶτα ἐλπίσας τὸν Μάλλιον καθ᾽ ἑαυτόν τι κατορθώσειν, ἐφθόνησεν αὐτῷ, μὴ μόνος εὐδοκιμήσῃ, καὶ ἦλθε μὲν πρὸς αὐτόν, οὔτε δὲ ἐν τῷ αὐτῷ χωρίῳ ηὐλίσατο οὔτε τι βούλευμα κοινὸν ἐποιήσατο, ἀλλ᾽ ὡς καὶ πρότερος αὐτοῦ τοῖς Κιμβροις συμμίξων, τήν τε δόξαν τοῦ πολέμου πᾶσαν ἀποισόμενος, ἐν μέσῳ ἱδρύθη . . . Ὅτι οἱ στρατιῶται τὸν Σερουίλιον ἠνάγκασαν πρὸς Μάλλιον ἐλθεῖν καὶ μετ᾽ αὐτοῦ βουλεύσασθαι περὶ τῶν παρόντων. τοσούτου δὲ ὁμοφρονῆσαι ἐδέησαν ὥστε καὶ ἐχθίους ἢ πρόσθεν ἦσαν ἐκ τῆς συνουσίας ἐγένοντο· ἔς τε γὰρ φιλονεικίαν καὶ λοιδορίας προαχθέντες αἰσχρῶς διελύθησαν.

89. See chapter 4 for discussion on the status of the promagistrate and its relationship to magistrates.

Caepio's greed and arrogance, which prevented him from yielding to the consul's obvious prior claim on the *provincia*.[90] Was this as clear-cut to the Romans in 105 BC? The vague definition of Gaul as a *provincia* probably gave Caepio some flexibility to claim (at least in his own mind) that he shared the Gallic command with Mallius, giving both men equal right to exercise supreme command. The Roman people may have accepted this argument, since they prosecuted, condemned, and exiled both commanders.[91] The fact that the Romans held both men responsible for the disaster indicates that neither had a legal (or better) claim on the *provincia*; otherwise, only one should have been found guilty of improper action. When two commanders needed to operate in the same *provincia*, the Roman people expected them to find a method of sharing, and their punishment of Mallius and Caepio was a salutary lesson for their successors: when Gaius Marius and Q. Lutatius Catulus shared the same Gallic *provincia* in 102 and 101 BC, they managed to work together effectively despite loathing each other.[92]

In addition to instructing two commanders to share possession of a single *provincia*, the Romans could also assign one commander with *imperium* to operate in another man's *provincia*. In other words, two commanders with *imperium* could be directed to operate in a single *provincia*, but only one of those commanders actually held the *provincia*. In such cases, the man who held the *provincia* was the sole commander in chief of that sphere, and he did not alternate priority of command with the other general(s) who had been assigned to work with him. Although both commanders held the exact same *imperium*, because only one of them had been given the *provincia* by the state, that commander held primary authority over it. The commander who did not hold the *provincia* but operated within it was usually called a "helper" (*adiutor*) to the commander in chief, a title that did not imply inferiority but clearly indicated that the *adiutor* was not in primary command of the *provincia*. Unlike the normal military officers who appeared in a general's army (centurions, tribunes of the soldiers, quaestors, legates), the *adiutor* was not truly a subordinate or inferior to the commander in chief (*imperator*); he was a helper who held equal status and authority to the man he helped, but he did not hold the status of

90. Livy (*Per.* 67) places the blame squarely on Caepio (*Caepionis, cuius temeritate clades accepta erat*), while Dio (note 88) emphasizes that the soldiers urged Caepio to consult with Mallius, indicating that they believed the consul was owed deference, if not obedience.

91. Auct. *Ad Herenn.* 1.24; Cic. *De Orat.* 2.124–25, 197–200, *Brut.* 135, *Balb.* 28; Livy *Per.* 67; Val. Max. 4.7.3.

92. Livy *Per.* 68, Vell. 2.12.4–5, Plut. *Mar.* 15.4–27.6.

commander in chief because he did not have a *provincia* of his own. Thus the *imperator* and the *adiutor* held equal authority, but the *imperator* held primary responsibility (*provincia*), and his decisions always took priority in that sphere.

The idea of an *adiutor imperatoris* may well have its origin in the relationship that existed between a dictator and his master of horse: both held the exact same *imperium*, but the dictator was clearly in charge of whatever task they were given. In Livy's (questionable) account of early Rome, *adiutores* began to be used when Rome had unusually large colleges of commanders. The first such use is in his description of the decemvirate's division of *provinciae* in 449 BC: "[The *decemviri*] assigned Spurius Oppius as an *adiutor* to Appius Claudius in looking after the City with equal *imperium* as all the other *decemviri*."[93] As this passage demonstrates, both men held the same *imperium*, but Appius Claudius had primary responsibility for the assigned *provincia*, while Spurius Oppius was assigned to help his colleague. In the years when Rome was said to be appointing large numbers of military tribunes with consular power, *adiutores* again appear: in 381 BC, L. Furius Medullinus was chosen by lot to act as an *adiutor* to M. Furius Camillus in his campaign against the Volscii, and after the victorious conclusion of that *provincia* Camillus chose Medullinus again to be his *adiutor* in a new campaign against the Tusculans.[94] As Livy portrays these cases, the Romans did not want the two commanders to share command of a *provincia* but preferred that the more senior or experienced man be the commander in chief of the *provincia*, supported by a helper who possessed *imperium*. Since these uses of *adiutores* occurred in years when Rome had a large number of commanders (ten in 449 BC, six in 381 BC), perhaps such doubling-up was necessary to find enough assignments for all commanders. Still, the use of *adiutores* continued long after Rome did away with the so-called military tribunes with consular powers: in 295 BC Q. Fabius Maximus Rullianus was given as his *provincia* a major uprising of Samnites, Gauls, and Etruscans and requested an *adiutor* to help in such an important campaign. Fabius was not asking to split or share this *provincia* with another man, but he wanted a helper who could assist (but not share) in the command of the *provincia*. He asked first for his consular colleague P. Decius Mus, with the caveat that he would next choose a consul from the previous year should Decius refuse.[95] Decius ac-

---

93. Livy 3.41.10: *Sp. Oppium Ap. Claudio adiutorem ad urbem tuendam aequo omnium decemvirorum imperio decernunt.*

94. Livy 6.22.6 and 25.5–6.

95. Livy 10.26.2–3: *ceterum si sibi adiutorem belli sociumque imperii darent, quonam modo se oblivisci P. Deci consulis per tot collegia experti posse? Neminem omnium secum coniungi malle; et copiarum*

cepted the assignment to fight as his colleague's *adiutor*, and famously devoted himself and died in the battle to secure a Roman victory.[96] Since Fabius and Decius were colleagues in the consulship, they held the exact same authorities of *imperium* and *auspicium*, but Fabius alone held the *provincia*. Instead of alternating command, Fabius held supreme authority every day of the campaign, and Decius simply deferred to his colleague's decisions.

The use of *adiutores* probably had two important benefits for the Romans. First, it enabled the state to prevent an alternation of command by appointing only one commander to hold the *provincia*, thereby ensuring that the preferred commander held supreme authority every day of the command. It is likely, however, that this could only be accomplished when there was a significant difference in the social status of the two colleagues that mitigated the insult the *adiutor* might otherwise feel. Second, the use of *adiutores* was a way to send two commanders with *imperium* into a particularly dangerous campaign, which could be an important advantage if (as often happened) one commander was killed in battle. When the consul P. Cornelius Scipio (cos. 218 BC) set out for his *provincia* in Spain at the start of the Second Punic War, he took his brother Gnaeus (cos. 222 BC) with him, but Gnaeus's actual title is unclear. He is usually considered Publius's *legatus*, which would mean he possessed no independent authority (*imperium* or *auspicium*) and held no *provincia* from the state; when he commanded soldiers, he legally did so as his brother's lieutenant and under the aegis of his brother's *imperium*. Although this is consistent with normal Roman practice, Livy adds a complication by describing Gnaeus with the vague term *imperator* and suggests he was prorogued in 212 BC, both of which suggest possession of *imperium*, but Livy also describes Gnaeus as being under his brother's auspices, indicating that Publius was in complete command of the *provincia*.[97] If Gnaeus did receive an independent grant of *imperium* from the state but did not have possession of the *provincia* in which he was operating, then he would have been his brother's *adiutor* and, as such, was entitled to exercise *imperium* in his brother's *provin-*

---

satis sibi cum P. Decio et nunquam nimium hostium fore; sin collega quid aliud mallet, at sibi L. Volumnium darent adiutorem.

96. It is possible that Decius was not an *adiutor* to Fabius but held the *provincia* jointly with him, since Livy (10.26.5–7) is suspicious of some of his sources regarding the provincial assignment in this case. In either case, there is no reason to doubt that Livy's underlying understanding that *adiutores* were used and that his account of Fabius and Decius reflects how one consul could have been assigned to act as an *adiutor* to his colleague.

97. *Imperator* (Livy 25.32.1, 37.9, 26.2.5, 27.4.6), prorogued (Livy 25.3.6), under brother's auspices (Livy 21.40.3).

cia, albeit subject to his brother's *auspicium*, and he was required to yield to his brother's prior authority when so instructed.[98]

The evidence clearly indicates that it was provincial assignment and not any variation in *imperium* or *auspicium* that determined which commander possessed supreme authority in what sphere or campaign. Because all commanders possessed the exact same *imperium* and *auspicium*, these attributes did not provide the variation or differentiation necessary to enable one commander to take priority over another. Since their concept of military authority was absolute and invariable, the Romans avoided the possibility of conflict between commanders by assigning each to a different *provincia*, an assignment that defined the sphere in which each commander held supreme authority. Possession of a *provincia* conferred priority of *imperium* within that sphere to the holder of the sphere, so any other commanders who entered that sphere were expected to defer to the holder of the *provincia*. Appian represents this well in his description of the dispute between Mark Antony and Decimus Brutus over possession of the *provincia* of Gaul in 44 and 43 BC, when he makes Antony say, "The people gave me the Gallic *provincia* by a law, and I will attack Decimus for not obeying the law."[99] In this way the provincial assignment gave priority in a specific sphere to the orders of one commander, without diminishing or changing the *imperium* of any other commanders in that sphere. Unless two commanders were specifically instructed to share a single (and usually indivisible) *provincia*, the process of provincial assignment normally established a single supreme commander for each sphere.

The Extraordinary Provincial Commander: The Dictator

The importance of the *provincia* in establishing priority of *imperium* within particular spheres or activities can also help explain the unusual authority of

98. The same may also have been the case with M. Junius Silanus, who was an *adiutor* to P. Cornelius Scipio (Africanus) (cos. 205 and 194 BC) in Spain. Silanus had been praetor in 212 BC, and for his provincial assignment the senate instructed him to assist Scipio as *propraetor adiutor ad res gerendas* (Livy 26.19.10). Since Silanus had been a praetor the previous year and was given the assignment by the senate, there is no reason to doubt that he possessed *imperium* just like Scipio and all other commanders. This is supported by a speech Livy attributes to Scipio (28.28.14), in which Silanus is said to have assisted Scipio *eodem iure eodem imperio*, and by Polybius's reference (10.6.7) to Silanus as συνάρχων with Scipio. In all likelihood, Silanus had *imperium* just like Scipio, but Scipio was in supreme command because he had sole possession of the *provincia*. See Eckstein (1987) 189–98 and 209–10, Brennan (2000) 157–58, Richardson (1986) 56, and Pittenger (2008) 57.

99. App. *BC* 3.63 (Drogula, trans.).

dictators. Unlike the regular magistrates, who were elected annually in colleges and who held office for an entire year, the dictator was an extraordinary magistrate who was appointed only when needed, who held office for no more than six months, and who had an assistant called a master of horse, but no colleague. According to tradition, the dictator was a powerful magistrate, but there is significant debate surrounding many details of his office, no doubt because it went out of use in 202 BC, and later authors may have had difficulty finding reliable information about the nature of the office.[100] Certain points are widely agreed upon: the dictator held *imperium* like the consuls, but he was able to ignore the citizens' right of appeal (*provocatio*) even within the city. The dictator also seems to have occasionally superseded the consuls: Dionysius refers to dictators taking charge of consuls and even forcing a consul to resign his office.[101] The creation of a dictator was also unusual: when it was decided that a dictator was needed, the senate instructed one or both consuls to appoint as dictator someone who had held the office of consul, and the consul named his choice for the dictatorship in a special nighttime ceremony.[102] A dictator took office as soon as he was informed of his appointment, although he was expected to choose for himself a colleague to be his master of horse, and (like the consuls) he had to secure the passage of a *lex curiata* to confer his *imperium* and *auspicium militiae*.[103] While in office, the dictator was probably entitled to possess twenty-four lictors, which was double the number given to consuls.[104] Dictators could hold office for a maximum of six months, although they frequently resigned their office before the end of their term, after first requiring their master of horse to resign his office. The dictator was usually created to deal with some emergency or other problem facing the state, but he could be given any task to accomplish.

Beyond these simple facts, however, much about the office and authority of

---

100. See Staveley (1956) 101–7, Cohen (1957), Henderson (1957) 82–87, Jehne (1989), Mitchell (1990) 136–39. The dictatorships of Cornelius Sulla and Julius Caesar in the late republic probably did more to mislead ancient writers about the nature of the dictatorship than it did to inform them.

101. Dion. Hal. *AR* 10.24.3–25.2.

102. Livy 4.21.10, 7.19.9, 8.12.2–3, 9.38.13–4, 27.5.14–19; Dion. Hal. *AR* 10.23.5–6. Exceptions were possible: the first dictator may have been elected (Fest. 216L) or at least confirmed (Dion. Hal. *AR* 5.70.4) by the people, and when the consuls were unavailable after the Battle of Lake Trasimene, the Romans seem to have elected Q. Fabius Maximus Verrucosus dictator (Polyb. 3.87.6 and 9, Livy 22.8.5–7, App. *Hann.* 11).

103. Livy 3.26.10 (Cincinnatus hailed dictator on the spot) and 9.38.15–39.1 (dictator must secure a *lex curiata*).

104. Polyb. 3.87.7–8, Dion. Hal. *AR* 10.24.2, Plut. *Fab.* 4.2, App. *BC* 1.100.

the dictator is uncertain, largely because of problems with the sources. Even Polybius, who is normally one of our most reliable sources of information on the republic, gives a description of the dictatorship that is manifestly incorrect, in particular his statement that other magistrates cease to hold office on the appointment of a dictator.[105] The dictatorship had not been in use for thirty-four years by the time Polybius came to Rome in 168 BC, so popular tradition had probably given the obsolete office some traits or characteristics it had not possessed in reality. Furthermore, when L. Cornelius Sulla revived the dictatorship in 82 BC, he claimed for it much broader and absolute authority than had ever been granted to early dictators, and Caesar's dictatorships from 49 to 44 BC substantially followed Sulla's model.[106] Authors of the late republic and early empire were heavily influenced by those exceptionally powerful (and highly unpopular) recastings of the original dictatorship, making it difficult to reconstruct the office as it had been used before 202 BC. Dionysius echoes Polybius's statement that consuls resign their office at the appointment of a dictator, but then he contradicts himself by depicting consuls retaining their commands after a dictator takes office.[107] Even worse, he records that dictators could and did appoint new consuls when resigning their office, a considerable error perhaps influenced by the tremendous prerogatives exercised by Sulla and Caesar as dictators.[108]

There is also an apparent contradiction in the nature and use of the dictatorship. On the one hand, ancient authors are unified in emphasizing the vast power and authority of the dictator: Polybius and Dionysius defined him as an autocrat (αὐτοκράτωρ) who is free from the need to consult with others, Dionysius describes him as a monarch (μόναρχος) and as an elected tyrant (αἱρετὴ τυραννίς), and Livy speaks of the power of the dictator instilling fear in all who saw him and says that the dictator was the judge, jury, and executioner in all matters.[109] In many accounts, the dictator's authority seems all encompassing, as if he was in charge of everyone and everything for the duration of his office. On the other hand, the dictatorship often appears as nothing more than a substitute or proxy for an absent consul, since it often happened that consuls who could not (or would not) leave their campaigns and return

105. Polyb. 3.87.8–9. In his description of ideal laws (which are closely modeled on Rome), Cicero states (*Leg.* 3.3.9) that a dictator should have "the same right" as the two consuls (*idem iuris quod duo consules teneto*), but this is too vague to be helpful.

106. See Jehne (1989).

107. Consuls resign (Dion. Hal. *AR* 5.70.4); consuls do not resign (6.2.2, 6.42.1, 12.2.2).

108. Dion. Hal. *AR* 5.77.1 (cf. 8.90.3–4).

109. Polyb. 3.86.7 and 87.7–8; Livy 2.18.8, 8.32.9–33.23; Dion. Hal. *AR* 5.73.1–3.

to Rome to perform necessary civilian functions would instead appoint a dictator to complete the needed function. Such dictators certainly do not seem intimidating and all-powerful; rather, they are mere understudies, appointed to deal with those duties that the consuls could not be troubled to perform.

Some of these inconsistencies may be the result of mistakes in the sources used by early annalists. Mitchell points out that ancient authors are occasionally confused and contradict one another regarding the offices and titles held by commanders at different periods, making it difficult to tell whether a particular commander was a consul, proconsul, or dictator.[110] This problem is highlighted by the contradictions ancient historians occasionally found in attributions of military victories when dictators were involved. Livy struggles with these problems in his account of 322 BC:

> Some writers hold that this war was waged by the consuls, and that it was they who triumphed over the Samnites; they say that Fabius even advanced into Apulia and thence drove off much booty. But that Aulus Cornelius was dictator in that year is not disputed, and the doubt is only whether he was appointed to administer the war, or in order that there might be somebody to give the signal to the chariots at the Roman Games — since the praetor, Lucius Plautius, happened to be very sick — and whether, having discharged this office, which is, to be sure, no very noteworthy exercise of power, he resigned the dictatorship.[111]

This not only illustrates the difficulty in properly identifying a man's office but also shows how some dictators were appointed to undertake minor tasks. Not much later in his account Livy encounters a similar problem:

> Not very long after this Nola was captured, whether by Poetelius the dictator or the consul Gaius Junius — for the story is told both ways. Those who ascribe the honour of capturing Nola to the consul, add that Atina and Calatia were won by the same man, but that Poetelius was made dictator on the outbreak of a pestilence, that he might drive the nail.[112]

It is possible (and perhaps probable) that later annalistic writers mistakenly identified some early commanders as dictators. Since a variable number of men exercised military command each year in the early republic, later annalists may have tried to make sense of this by calling two of those commanders

---

110. Mitchell (1990) 137.
111. Livy 8.40.1–3 (Foster, trans.). See Oakley (1997–2004) 1.30–38, 41–44, and 2.770–72.
112. Livy 9.28.5–6 (Foster, trans.).

consuls and the others dictators. Such confusion makes it all the more difficult to distinguish between the regular and the extraordinary military commander, making the dictatorship an elusive subject.

What was the nature of a dictator's power and authority? Many ancient authors refer to dictators as having *maius imperium, summum imperium, maximum imperium*, or even *omne imperium*, which has given rise to a general assumption that the dictator held a greater degree or level of *imperium* than the consuls and praetors.[113] This idea is based on the underlying assumption that such phrases are being used in a precise legal manner to express differentiations in the official authority invested in each office, rather than as general expressions of power. Such an assumption cannot stand: the same ancient authors refer to consular *imperium* as *summum*, and Cicero specifies that consuls and dictators held the same *imperium*.[114] Dionysius demonstrates the looseness of such terms as well: in one section of his work he defines dictators as having "superior power than the consuls" (κρείττονα ἐξουσίαν ἔχοντα τῶν ὑπάτων), but later in his work he defined the consuls as governing Rome with "the greatest power" (αὗται δύο ... ἀρχαὶ Ῥωμαίων αἱ τὸ μέγιστον ἔχουσαι κράτος ἐγένοντο).[115] Some scholars have also suggested that the dictator held a higher degree of *auspicium* than the consuls, but this is unlikely since Gellius (citing the augur Messala) specifically states that there are only two types of *auspicium*—the *maxima auspicia* of consuls, praetors, and censors and the *minora auspicia* of the lesser magistrates—and it is hard to imagine that dictators had *auspicium* greater than maximum.[116] Furthermore, the fact that ancient scholars writ-

---

113. Cic. *Rep.* 1.63 (*omne imperium*), Livy 6.38.3 and 8.32.3 (*summum imperium*), Livy 7.3.8 (*maius imperium*), Cic. *Phil.* 5.44 and Livy 6.7.5 (*maximum imperium*).

114. Cic. *Rep.* 2.56: *magnaeque res temporibus illis a fortissimis viris summo imperio praeditis, dictatoribus atque consulibus, belli gerebantur*; and *Leg.* 3.3.9: *si senatus creverit, idem iuris quod duo consules teneto, isque ave sinistra dictus populi magister esto.* See also Cic. *Rab. Perd.* 3, *ND* 2.11, *Verr.* 1.1.37; Livy 4.26.10, 22.53.3–4; Val. Max. 2.2.4.

115. Dion. Hal. *AR* 5.70.4 and 11.62.3.

116. Gell. 13.15.1–7. Linderski (1986) 2181 n. 124 believes that a passage of Livy (4.41.11 [although Linderski cites it as 4.41.3]) proves that dictators had greater *auspicium* than consuls, but this is not so. In the passage, Livy writes that a consul in 431 BC had served under the auspices of a dictator (*T. Quinctium ... quia et in Volscis consul auspicio dictatoris Postumi Tuberti ... res prospere gesserat*), but this does not necessarily mean that the dictator's *auspicium* was greater than the consul's. All that can be securely said about this passage is that the dictator's *auspicium* was preeminent in the command against the Volscii, but this most likely derived from the dictator's possession of the *provincia*. Indeed, if a dictator's *auspicium* was greater than the consuls', one would expect that no consul could receive a triumph while a dictator was in office, since all commanders would have been fighting under the *auspicium* of the dictator, yet this was obviously not the case, since consuls could and did triumph while dictators were in office.

ing in Greek chose the word ὁ ὕπατος—a contraction of the superlative adjective ὑπέρτατος, meaning "highest, uppermost, first"—to render the Latin word consul emphasizes that the consul was Rome's highest or most important magistrate. Dionysius specifically states that Greeks called the Roman consuls ὕπατοι "in accordance with the greatness of their authority, since they command everyone and they hold the highest position."[117] It seems unlikely that a dictator outranked a consul or was a higher magistrate than the highest magistrate.

Two passages in Livy have done a great deal to fuel speculation about the nature of a dictator's *imperium*, although on closer analysis they actually tell us very little. First, Livy pauses his account of 363 BC to inform the reader that an ancient law in archaic lettering had required that the *praetor maximus* should drive a nail into the Temple of Jupiter Optimus Maximus every year on the ides of September and that this duty had been performed by consuls at one time but was eventually transferred to the dictators because they had higher authority (*imperium maius*). This religious observance had fallen into abeyance before 363 BC, when the Romans decided to revive it in an effort to stop a plague that had broken out in the city. A dictator was appointed to perform the ceremony, although Livy does not indicate whether this was done because a dictator was considered the *praetor maximus* or simply because the consuls were unavailable.[118] Although this passage seems to demonstrate the existence of *imperium maius*, it has far too many problems to be accepted. Not only is Livy talking about the distant past (363 BC), but he is referring to a practice that had been defunct for a long time before 363 BC, so he compounds confusion. Oakley remarks about this story that it "is not supported by any other reference to such an appointment," and Brennan even calls it "an annalist's or antiquarian's rationalization."[119] Most modern scholars who have studied this passage have found it confusing and problematic,[120] so it cannot be used with any confidence to demonstrate that dictators possessed *imperium*

117. Dion. Hal. *AR* 4.76.2: ὕπατοι δ' ὑφ' Ἑλλήνων ἀνὰ χρόνον ὠνομάσθησαν ἐπὶ τοῦ μεγέθους τῆς ἐξουσίας, ὅτι πάντων τ' ἄρχουσι καὶ τὴν ἀνωτάτω χώραν ἔχουσι.

118. Livy 7.3.5–8: *lex vetusta est, priscis litteris verbisque scripta, ut qui praetor maximus sit idibus Septembribus clavum pangat . . . M. Horatius consul ea lege templum Iovis optimi maximi dedicavit anno post reges exactos; a consulibus postea ad dictatores, quia maius imperium erat, sollemne clavi figendi translatum est. Intermisso deinde more digna etiam per se via res propter quam dictator crearetur.*

119. Oakley (1997–2004) 2.74 (cf. 4.547) and Brennan (2000) 39.

120. Alföldi (1965) 44 and 78, Pinsent (1975) 24, Hartfield (1982) 155–56, Oakley (1997–2004) 2.73–80, Brennan (2000) 21 and 39, Forsythe (2005) 151, Holloway (2008) 111–13 and (2009) 73–75, Pina Polo (2011) 35–40, Smith (2011) 33–34 and 38–40.

maius. Second, Livy relates that the dictator Q. Fabius Maximus was chosen to vow a temple to Venus Erycina in 217 BC because the Books of Fate (*libri fatales*) indicated that this temple should be vowed by the one who held the greatest authority in the state (*ut is voveret cuius maximum imperium in civitate esset*).[121] While it is tempting to take this as demonstrating an actual difference in the dictator's military authority, doing so is a pure assumption lacking good grounding. The passage does not say that dictators have *maximum* or *maius imperium*, but that whomever happened to have the greatest *imperium* at the time should make the vow. Most obviously, the *libri fatales* were supposedly of Etruscan origin and may well have predated the republic, in which case they cannot have referred to any republican magistracy.[122] Even in the early republic, the Romans normally used only one type of regular military commander at a time (archaic praetor or consular tribune), and gradations of *imperium* would have been senseless in a system in which all commanders held the same title and rank. At best, the *libri fatales* must be referring to the most important praetor and not signifying that dictators possessed *imperium maius.*

Some scholars have argued against the outdated notion that a dictator had *imperium maius* or *auspicia maior*: Brennan delivered a forceful refutation of these ideas, stating that "the dictator's primitive, anomalous status, with precedence over all other magistrates, is never adequately explained to us by our ancient sources," "the Romans of the Classical Republic never accepted the concept of *imperium* which was greater than the regal power [of the consuls]," and "it would be most surprising if the dictator possessed anything qualitatively greater than consular *imperium*. The consul had the *imperium* and *auspicia* of the kings of Rome. Logically, the dictator could have no more."[123] Lintott also noted this problem, pointing out that "how absolute the power of the dictator was, seems to have been an issue which was determined not by statute or by any clear rule, but by casuistry."[124] Gardner concurs: "Despite some traditions to the contrary, these powers [of the dictator] do not seem in practice to have been regarded as absolute, nor as overriding those of other magistrates," and Henderson refers to the entire notion of *imperium maius* as "a hazy idea

121. Livy 22.10.10.

122. Cic. *Div.* 1.100, Livy 5.14.4. Livy mentions the *libri fatales* in his account of 398 BC, which means he believed the books predated the creation of the praetorship as an office separate from the consulship (trad. 367 BC). In other words, Livy himself dates the books to a period when Rome used only one type of military commander at a time, so no difference in *imperium* could have existed. On the antiquity of the *libri fatales*, see Cancik (1983) 549–76, Harris (1991) 154, and Takács (2007) 69.

123. Brennan (2000) 38–43 and 599 (40, 43, and 599 quoted above).

124. Lintott (1999a) 112.

in the minds of annalists."[125] Despite such strong arguments to the contrary, the belief in a dictator's *imperium maius* continues to pervade modern scholarship, no doubt because it is an easy and logical explanation for the obvious precedence of the dictator in the Roman Republic. To imagine that magisterial precedence must be based on relative levels of official authority is a common predilection of the modern mind, but this was not how the early Romans organized their most senior magistrates.

The main difference between the dictator and consul was not in the degree of their *imperium* or *auspicium* but in the fact that the dictator could take up and use his *imperium* inside the *pomerium*, whereas consuls were absolutely forbidden to do that (although exceptions could be made). Whereas consuls were limited to the use of *potestas* and *coercitio* and operated under the restraints of civil law within the city, the dictator's ability to use *imperium* inside the *pomerium* meant he could impose the absolute authority of martial law even within the civilian sphere. This was the exact same *imperium* that consuls and praetors used outside the city, but it enabled the dictator to use military force to suppress major domestic uprisings (see chapter 2). The Greek writers emphasized this when they chose the word αὐτοκράτωρ (or στρατηγός αὐτοκράτωρ) to describe the dictatorship, a term that indicates the *sole use* of power and authority rather than the possession of a special type of authority. Polybius provides a good example, describing the great power of the dictator as deriving from his ability to make and enforce decisions without the need to consult anyone on the legitimacy and appropriateness of his actions:

> A dictator has this difference from the consuls: while there are twelve *fasces* for each of the consuls, for the dictator there are twenty-four, and while the consuls in many areas have need of the senate's cooperation to accomplish matters, the dictator is an autocratic commander.[126]

Free from the need to consult with (or defer to) any person or body, and armed with *imperium* to authorize the scourging and summary execution of citizens, the dictator could easily impose his will on anyone within the city, even consuls. Livy has the consuls of 439 BC specifically state that they could not use harsher measures to suppress Maelius because the citizens' right to appeal had

125. Gardner (2009) 57 and Henderson (1957) 83.
126. Polyb. 3.87.7–8 (Drogula, trans.): ὁ δὲ δικτάτωρ ταύτην ἔχει τὴν διαφορὰν τῶν ὑπάτων· τῶν μὲν γὰρ ὑπάτων ἑκατέρῳ δώδεκα πελέκεις ἀκολουθοῦσι, τούτῳ δ᾽ εἴκοσι καὶ τέτταρες, κἀκεῖνοι μὲν ἐν πολλοῖς προσδέονται τῆς συγκλήτου πρὸς τὸ συντελεῖν τὰς ἐπιβολάς, οὗτος δ᾽ ἔστιν αὐτοκράτωρ στρατηγός.

dissolved their *imperium,* so they called for a dictator who would not be subject to such restrictions.[127] Within the city, therefore, the supremacy of the dictator is easily explained by his unique possession of *imperium;* he did not have greater power than the consuls in the sphere *domi* but had a *different type* of power (*imperium*).

If Roman tradition is accurate, the dictatorship was originally created to suppress dangerous internal strife, and for this purpose it was uniquely authorized to possess and use *imperium* inside the *pomerium.* What we do not know, however, is how much freedom dictators had in their use of *imperium* in Rome: Could they take any action they wished, or was their use of *imperium* limited to the performance of particular tasks, as was the case with consuls and praetors? In other words, did dictators have *provinciae?* Although later writers did not use the word *provincia* to describe the actions undertaken by dictators, they normally identified each dictator as being created for a specific purpose (*causa*). The more common of these purposes were holding elections (*causa comitiorum habendorum*), holding games in the city (*causa faciendorum ludorum*), driving a sacred nail into the Temple of Jupiter Optimus Maximus (*causa clavi fingendi*), establishing a festival (*causa feriarum constituendarum*), holding a *lectio* of the senate (*dictatorem . . . creari placuit qui senatum legeret*), and celebrating the Latin Games (*causa Latinarum feriarum*).[128] Dictators were also commonly created in order to undertake military campaigns, which were usually described by the general phrase of "doing things" (*causa rei gerundae*), although more specific assignments do appear (e.g., *causa belli Gallici*).[129] Some scholars suggest that these different purposes indicate different types of dictators, so the office or authority of a dictator *causa rei gerundae* was somehow different from that of a dictator *causa clavi fingendi,* but this seems im-

127. Livy 4.13.11.

128. *Causa comitiorum habendorum* (Livy 7.24.10–11, 7.26.11–12, 8.16.12, 8.23.13, 9.44.1–2, 22.33.11–12, 25.2.3, 27.5.14, 27.33.6–8, 29.11.9, 30.26.12, 30.39.4–5; *Fast. Cap.* for 348, 280, 246, 231, 224 BC), *causa faciendorum ludorum* (Livy 8.40.2, 9.34.12, 27.33.6), *causa clavi fingendi* (Livy 7.3.4, 9.28.6, 9.34.12; *Fast. Cap.* for 363, 331, 263 BC), *causa feriarum constituendarum* (Livy 7.28.7–8), *lectio* of the senate (Livy 23.22.10), Latin Games (*Fast. Cap.* 257 BC).

129. Livy 7.3.9 (*qua de causa creatus L. Manlius, perinde ac rei gerendae ac non solvendae religionis gratia creatus esset, bellum Hernicum adfectans dilectu acerbo iuventutem agitavit*), 8.29.9 (*iussusque dictatorem dicere rei gerendae causa*), 8.40.2 (*id ambigitur, belline gerendi causa creatus sit*), 22.31.8 (*omnium prope annales Fabium dictatorem adversum Hannibalem rem gessisse tradunt*), and 23.23.2 (*nec dictatori, nisi rei gerendae causa creato, in sex menses datum imperium*). In the *Fasti Capitolini,* most dictators were created *causa rei gerendae,* but see also Livy 7.9.5 (*belli Gallici causa dictatorem creatum*).

probable, since dictators obviously differed in their responsibilities rather than in their authority or office.[130]

There is an obvious parallel between the purpose or *causa* assigned to a dictator and the *provincia* assigned to regular magistrates with *imperium*; in both cases, the Roman state defined the specific actions its *imperium*-bearing magistrates were to undertake with their military authority. Although it may not have been called a *provincia*, the *causa* for a dictator was a specific task or purpose that defined (and limited) his full exercise of *imperium*. The distinction between a dictator's *causa* and other commanders' *provinciae* may lay in the different processes by which dictators and consuls/praetors were assigned their tasks: dictators were specifically created to perform a particular task, whereas (until 123 BC)[131] consuls and praetors were normally elected before the state determined what *provinciae* would be assigned that year. In other words, the *causa* existed before and therefore caused the creation of a dictator, whereas a consul's or praetor's *provincia* was (originally) determined and assigned only after he had already entered office. Still, the effect of both types of assignment was the same: the dictator was not free to do whatever he wanted with his *imperium* like a true autocrat, but—like all those invested with *imperium*—his use of authority was limited to the task or purpose assigned to him by the state.

Despite the emphasis given by ancient writers to the tremendous power of the dictator, there is substantial evidence that dictators were expected to confine their full use of their *imperium* to the *provincia* or *causa* assigned to them by the state, just as consuls and praetors were required to do. Livy certainly seems to have understood this to be the case: in his account of 353 BC, he specifies that the dictator T. Manlius Imperiosus Torquatus undertook the war against the Caerites only when authorized to do so by the senate and people of Rome.[132] Likewise, he portrays Q. Fabius Maximus (dict. 217 BC) as summoning the senate to ask what resources he was to be allowed for his command, and he points out that Fabius opened himself up to censure that year by failing to consult the senate before ransoming Roman captives from Hannibal,

---

130. Cohen (1957) 304, Kaplan (1973-74) (although in [1977] 4 he seems to consider them assignments rather than types of dictators), Drummond (1978a) 570, Hartfield (1982).

131. Legislation by the tribune Gaius Gracchus in 123 BC imposed a requirement that consular *provinciae* be determined before the election of the consuls who would hold those *provinciae* (Cic. *Dom.* 24, *Prov. Cons.* 3, *Balb.* 61, *Fam.* 1.7.10; Sall. *Iug.* 27.3—see chapter 6).

132. Livy 7.19.10: *consulari exercitu contentus ex auctoritate partum ac populi iussu Caeritibus bellum indixit.* Oakley (1997-2004) 2.204 questions whether this dictator existed and notes that his activities are rather curious, but this does not undermine Livy's understanding that dictators received their *provincia* from the state.

as a result of which the senate delayed sending the money he requested.[133] Livy also portrays the dictator M. Junius Pera (dict. 216 BC) being recalled to Rome to update the senate on the progress of the war so that the senate could decide how to adjust provincial assignments if needed.[134] When the dictator M'. Valerius Maximus (dict. 494 BC) tried to carry a bill securing debt relief for the plebs, the patrician senators rebuffed his efforts, and he was forced to resign his office without achieving his goal.[135] Sixty years later, Mam. Aemilius Mamercinus was named dictator to suppress an anticipated Etruscan uprising in 434 BC, but when this upheaval did not happen, Livy wrote that he was powerless to obtain an alternate military command for himself.[136] Despite holding the awesome authority of a dictator and reportedly being desperate to find something great to achieve with his office, Mamercinus was unable to acquire a new military command or to take over for himself the *provincia* of another commander. Unable to achieve anything else with his dictatorial authority, he settled for proposing legislation reducing the censorship's term of office from five years to eighteen months. A similar thing happened to the dictator C. Julius in 352 BC: when the military emergency for which he had been created turned out to be a false report, he was unable to acquire a different command or to achieve anything else with his vast authority except push for the election of patrician candidates to the consulship.[137] The dictatorships of Mamercinus and Julius undermine any idea that dictators held unusually vast or all-encompassing authority; having lost the specific commands for which they had been created, both dictators clearly lacked the authority to recruit an army and attack some other enemy, or even to take over the *provincia* of another commander, which one would expect if dictators really had greater authority than consuls. Although Livy emphasizes the tremendous power dictators wielded in Rome, he presents them as being little different from other commanders outside of Rome, where their full use of authority was confined to their assigned *provincia* or *causa*.

Furthermore, why did none of the dictators created to perform relatively minor civilian tasks in Rome ever try to use their dictatorial authority to obtain a military command? It can safely be taken for granted that most Roman

133. Livy 22.11.1 and 23.5–10.
134. Livy 23.24.1–2.
135. Livy 2.31.8–11, Dion. Hal. *AR* 6.43.1–45.1.
136. Livy 4.23.4–24.9.
137. Livy 7.21.9–22.2. Oakley (1997–2004) 2.213 accepts this dictator as historical, although he notes that some scholars have doubted it.

aristocrats were eager to exercise military command, so why do we not find dictators named for domestic purposes using their authority to demand (or take) military commands? The answer must be that dictators — like regular magistrates — could use the full force of their *imperium* only in the tasks or purposes assigned them by the state. In 363 BC, L. Manlius Imperiosus was appointed dictator simply to perform the ceremony of driving a nail into the Temple of Jupiter Optimus Maximus (*causa clavi figendi*), but when he attempted to take up a military command as well, he was compelled to resign the dictatorship by the tribunes of the plebs because he was trying to use his authority in an activity that had not been assigned to him.[138] Thus the concept of the *provincia* (if not the word itself) applied to dictators, and their full exercise of authority was limited to the *causa* for which they had been created.

Because the dictator's full use of his *imperium* was channeled into (and limited by) his *provincia* or *causa*, it seems likely that provincial assignment determined where and when a dictator's authority took precedence over that of another commander. The dictator always took precedence in Rome, because he was fully invested with *imperium* in the city, whereas consuls and praetors were limited to their *potestas*. Outside of Rome, however, the situation was probably different: since there was no such thing as *imperium maius* until the end of the republic, dictators outside the *pomerium* possessed the exact same *imperium* as did consuls (and later, praetors), so dictators did not possess more military authority than other commanders in the field. Because the dictatorship carried great prestige and normally went to senior senators, other commanders might willingly defer to the greater *auctoritas* of the dictator, but this was a voluntary recognition of social status and not compulsory obedience to superior authority. Like all commanders, a dictator in the field could claim priority of *imperium*, and therefore supreme authority, only in a *provincia* given him by the state.

A dictator had no authority over other commanders unless they fell within his assigned *provincia*, as is indicated by the fact that several consuls celebrated triumphs for victories won while a dictator was in office, which would not have been possible if they had been fighting under the dictator's authority. At least eight such triumphs are known,[139] but most striking is the episode in 360 BC,

138. Livy 7.3.9: *[causa clavi figendi] qua de causa creatus L. Manlius, perinde ac rei gerendae ac non solvendae religionis gratia creatus esset, bellum Hernicum adfectans dilectu acerbo iuventutem agitavit; tantemque omnibus in eum tribunis plebis coortis seu vi seu verecundia victus dictatura abiit.*

139. In the fourth century BC alone, the *Fasti Triumphales* identifies at least eight consuls who triumphed while there was a dictator in office, in 361, 360 (*bis*), 358, 340, 322, 314, and 312 BC. Consuls

when a consul was given a triumph for a victory he won in what should have been a dictator's *provincia*: when returning from a victorious *provincia* against Tibur, the consul encountered and defeated a group of Gauls who were fleeing from the destruction of their army by the dictator, and the consul was permitted to triumph over both Tibur and the Gauls, while the dictator received no triumph at all, although the Gallic army had been his *provincia*.[140] While Livy suggests the dictator allowed the consul this privilege, this explanation is not possible since a fundamental requirement for a triumph was that the commander must have fought under his own *imperium* and *auspicium* and in his own *provincia* (which explains why tribunes prevented the consul C. Cornelius Cethegus from sharing a triumph with his less successful colleague Q. Minucius in 197 BC). In the opinion of the Romans at the time, the fleeing Gauls must have entered the consul's *provincia* as they neared Tibur, thereby allowing the consul to receive the official credit for their defeat.

When a dictator was sent to replace a consul in the field, he did not outrank the consul, nor was he a superior officer in the modern sense; rather, he took over possession of the *provincia* as ordered by the state, just as one consul might take over command of a *provincia* from his predecessor. An argument against this is usually found in the famous tale of L. Quinctius Cincinnatus, who was called from his plow in 458 BC and made dictator in order to save the army of the consul L. Minucius Esquilinus Augurinus, which had been trapped by the Aequi at Algidus. After defeating the Aequi and saving the trapped army, Cincinnatus ordered the disgraced consul to act as his *legatus*; Minucius is said to have done this and also to have resigned as consul in a voluntary action.[141] The sources do not identify the legal grounds that enabled Cincinnatus to order Minucius to act as his *legatus*, but two possibilities seem obvious: the dictator possessed greater *imperium* than the consul, or the dictator had been given command of the consul's *provincia* when he had been

---

are frequently found exercising independent command of their *provinciae* while a dictator is in office, as was the case in 494 BC (Livy 2.30.9–31.5 and Dion. Hal. *AR* 6.42.1), in 360 BC (Livy 7.11.2–9), and in 353 BC (Livy 7.19.6–20.9).

140. *Act. Trium.* for 360/59 BC, Livy 7.11.3–9. Brennan (2000) 39–40 discusses this incident to demonstrate that dictators cannot have possessed greater *imperium* and *auspicium* than consuls.

141. Livy 3.26.6–29.6; Dion. Hal. *AR* 10.23.5–25.2, 11.20.1–4; Val. Max. 2.7.7. Livy (3.29.2–3) makes Cincinnatus say: "You, L. Minucius, until you begin to have a consular spirit, you will command these legions as a *legatus*," after which Minucius resigned the consulship but remained with the army as ordered (*iussus*) (cf. Dion. Hal. *AR* 10.25.1–2 and Val. Max. 2.7.7). Ogilvie (1965) 444 pointed out that this event may be a fictional literary duplication of the more famous dispute between the dictator Fabius Maximus and his master of horse Minucius in 217 BC.

created. While there are no good grounds for accepting the existence of *imperium maius* at this time, there is every reason to believe that the appointment of Cincinnatus entailed the transfer of the *provincia* against the Aequi from Minucius to the dictator. As the new holder of the *provincia*, Cincinnatus became the commander in chief of the campaign, so his *imperium* took priority over Minucius's *imperium*.

Another occasion illustrates this well: in 217 BC, both consuls had been given the *provincia* of campaigning against Hannibal, but when one of the consuls was killed along with his army at Lake Trasimene, Q. Fabius Maximus was named dictator and sent to take charge of the campaign against Hannibal.[142] When Fabius took the field, the remaining consul (Cn. Servilius Geminus) appeared before him without lictors, which is the same display that consuls in Rome made when they did not hold priority in the monthly alternation of the *fasces*. There is no reason to assume that Fabius possessed *imperium maius*, since his assignment to take over the command against Hannibal (i.e., Geminus's *provincia*) would have given him supreme authority in that sphere. Because the senate had effectively stripped Geminus of his command against Hannibal, it assigned him a new *provincia* commanding Rome's fleet, which he undertook as a fully independent and self-directing commander; it was his *provincia* alone, and he is not known to have answered to the dictator in any way.[143] If Geminus had remained with Fabius, however, he would have been the dictator's *adiutor*—an *imperium*-bearing commander in another man's *provincia*. When Fabius stepped down at the end of his six-month dictatorship, the *provincia* of fighting Hannibal was transferred back to Geminus, who continued to hold it until the start of the next year (216 BC), when it was transferred to the two incoming consuls. When his successors took command of the *provincia*, Geminus remained with them and acknowledged their priority of *imperium* by following their orders, which included fighting and dying at the Battle of Cannae.[144] These transfers of command emphasize that it was possession of the *provincia*—given at the discretion of the senate—that determined priority of authority between commanders. Like all commanders, dictators in the field enjoyed supreme authority only in the *provincia* assigned to them by the state, so they could not assume command of a *provincia* not given to them. Thus, when a dictator is found assuming the command of a *provincia*

142. Polyb. 3.87.6–88.9, Livy 22.11.2–12.1, Plut. *Fab.* 4.1.
143. Polyb. 3.96.8–14, Livy 22.31.1–7. Livy makes clear that Geminus received his naval *provincia* from the state, and not from the dictator.
144. Polyb. 3.106.1–114.8, Livy 22.32.1.

from a consul, this is explained by the transfer of the *provincia* to the dictator and not by any superiority of his *imperium*.

The fact that dictators held the same *imperium* and *auspicium* as consuls and praetors, and were assigned to a specific *provincia* or *causa* just like any other commander, creates a different picture of the dictatorship from the one normally given in the surviving sources. There can be no doubt that the dictator was uniquely powerful in Rome because of his ability to use *imperium* and impose martial law in the civilian sphere of the city. For this reason, the tradition that the dictatorship was originally created to suppress large-scale domestic uprisings may well be correct. Outside of the city, on the other hand, the dictator enjoyed no more or less military authority than any other commander; he possessed *imperium* that gave him absolute authority within his assigned *provincia* or *causa*, but the same could be said of any consul or praetor in the field. A dictator's use of his *imperium* was also liable to review by the people just like any other commander, and dictators could be (and were) prosecuted for any abuses of authority they committed.[145] Although the extraordinary nature of the dictatorship — and the fact that only experienced ex-consuls were chosen for the office — conferred a degree of seniority and *auctoritas* on its holder, the legal authority of a dictator and his ability to exercise military command seem to have been no different from the authority and ability of a consul.[146] Since dictators were no more or less effective as military commanders in the field than consuls, it stands to reason that dictators were not some kind of super commander, but merely extra commanders. That is, the appointment of a dictator provided Rome with an additional military commander whose authority in the field was every bit the same as the two annual consuls. Until the introduction of prorogation in 327 BC, the Romans had a limited number of annual magistrates who could exercise military command each year, so the dictatorship was probably used simply to increase the number of legal commanders when needed.

145. For example, in 362 BC a tribune of the plebs prosecuted the former dictator L. Manlius Capitolinus Imperiosus (dict. 363 BC) on a number of charges, including (among other things) that he had made excessive use of force in conducting a levy of soldiers. Manlius escaped condemnation only by the intervention of his son (Cic. *Off.* 3.112; Livy 7.4.1–7; Val. Max. 5.4.3, 6.9.1; App. *Samn.* 2). Likewise, Q. Publilius Philo (dict. 339 BC) and C. Maenius (dict. 314 BC) were both prosecuted after they abdicated the dictatorship because their actions had been considered excessive by the Roman nobility (Livy 9.26.20–22).

146. Hartfield (1982) 151–53 argues that the dictator had greater religious significance than a consul, but since they performed the same ceremonies to receive their authority as consuls and praetors, this argument seems uncertain.

A close look at the actual use of dictators in the field demonstrates that they were normally used simply as supplemental commanders. In the first place, dictators were appointed to suppress military threats that became apparent only after the departure of the consuls for their own campaigns. If a new threat appeared and it was undesirable or impossible to recall one or both consuls, an extra commander (the dictator) was created to undertake the new campaign.[147] Second, men were named dictator in order to replace (but not outrank or supersede) a consul who was too sick to continue in active command, so the dictator was a replacement commander, not a superior.[148] Third, a dictator might be appointed to assist a consul (or a consular tribune) against a particularly difficult enemy, but in such cases it often happened that the dictator and the consul would split the *provincia* into two separate and independent commands (just as two consuls might) rather than for the dictator to act like the sole commander of the whole *provincia*.[149] In such cases, the dictator was effective not because he had a higher level of authority, but because the addition of an extra commander and an extra army gave the Romans greater tactical flexibility and effectiveness. Dictators were indeed created on occasion to take over a *provincia* from a sitting consul, but for the most part dictators in military commands acted like the colleagues of the consuls rather than as their superiors. Thus when Q. Fabius Maximus was named dictator in 217 BC following the Roman disaster at Lake Trasimene, he was assigned the *provincia* of fighting Hannibal, which enabled the senate to assign Geminus to a new *provincia* commanding Rome's fleet. The appointment of Fabius to the dictatorship did not change the command structure of Rome's military disposition: Geminus remained an independent commander with his own *imperium*, *auspicium*, and *provincia*, and Fabius replaced the deceased consul in facing Hannibal. Fourth, the six-month maximum tenure of the dictatorship is suspiciously similar to the six-month extension of command originally given to the first promagistrates, a correlation that suggests the dictator and the promagistrate were similar ideas in the Roman mind; they were both short-term solutions to provide an extra commander.[150] The dictator simply filled any gaps in Rome's slate of active commanders.

147. In 333 BC, for example, a dictator was appointed to deal with an unexpected threat while the consuls continued the campaigns they had been assigned at the start of the year (Livy 8.17.2–4).

148. In both 325 and 312 BC, a dictator was appointed to fill the responsibilities of a consul who was seriously ill (Livy 8.29.9, 9.29.3), and in 322 BC a dictator may have been appointed to direct the chariot races at the Roman Games in place of an ill praetor (Livy 8.40.2–3).

149. Livy 4.27.2, 6.2.7–8, 6.6.12–15, 7.11.5–9, 7.15.9.

150. The length of the first prorogation in 327 BC is not given (but was probably meant to last

Because the appointment of a dictator did not necessarily change the disposition of any other Roman commander in the field, the dictatorship enabled the senate to place a particular man in a particular command if and when desired. Whereas consuls were men who had won the most recent election, dictators were men who were specifically chosen to perform a particular task. When the senate instructed the consuls to name a dictator, the nominating consul could select any current or former consul for the office.[151] Although it was his decision, one must assume that the senate could express its preferred candidate for the dictatorship, particularly if the nominating consul was in Rome and subject to the full influence of the senate. It often happened that the senate used the naming of a dictator to arrange for a particularly capable or experienced senator to be given an especially important command: reports of serious military setbacks against the Samnites in 310 BC led the senate to arrange for L. Papirius Cursor—five times a consul and the foremost military man of his day—to be named dictator even though the Roman consul in Samnium was alive and capable of continuing to hold the *provincia*.[152] Since the authority and capacity of the dictator as a military commander were no different from those of a consul, the decision to name Papirius dictator was done to supply the *provincia* not with a higher-ranking commander but with a more talented, experienced, and trustworthy commander. Likewise, when a consul died while on campaign in 299 BC, the senate wanted to have one of its best commanders at that time—the five-time consul M. Valerius Maximus Corvus—appointed dictator but then changed its mind when this same Valerius was elected suffect consul.[153] Clearly, the situation had not called for a dictator per se but for a particular man, and the dictatorship was just a convenient way to place a talented (but private) citizen in command of a *provincia*. This episode demonstrates that a commander's title (consul or dictator) was not particularly important, since Valerius the consul was every bit as capable and powerful as Valerius the dictator. Thus in 337 BC the senate called for the appointment of a dictator merely because it was disgusted with the inefficiency of the sitting consuls.[154] Similarly, in 215 BC the suffect consul Q. Fabius Maximus Verrucosus spoke against the candidacy of T. Otacilius Crassus for election to the consulship

---

only a few days or weeks at the most), although six months was the normal extension given to other early proconsuls (see Brennan [2000] 74–75).

151. Livy 2.18.5–6 (only men of consular rank can be dictators) and 28.10.1–5 (consul names colleague dictator).

152. Livy 9.38.9–14.

153. Livy 10.11.1–6, Val. Max. 8.15.5.

154. Livy 8.15.4–6.

on the grounds that Otacilius was a poor commander. Fabius warned that the senate would have to propose the appointment of a dictator if Otacilius was elected consul, indicating that the senate used dictators not merely in response to emergencies but also in an attempt to prevent crises by using the dictatorship to replace unsure commanders with more capable men.[155] On the other hand, it also happened that the Romans would deliberately avoid appointing a dictator if a particularly capable consul was available to take charge of a disaster. Thus Livy writes that fear of a war with the Etruscans in 386 BC would have led the Romans to make M. Furius Camillus dictator if he had not already been a military tribune with consular power, and later that they did not name a dictator to replace a deceased consul because his colleague was the respected L. Furius Camillus (son of the famous hero).[156] In all of these cases, the senate's decision whether or not to have a dictator appointed depended mainly on the individual abilities and reputations of the men involved.

In addition to being used as extra or supplemental commanders, a dictator was often appointed to fill in for absent consuls by performing their civilian responsibilities. Rather than being awe-inspiring magistrates with unlimited power, these dictators were often assigned to perform the humdrum, unexciting domestic tasks that consuls in the field could not be bothered to return to Rome to perform. The best example of this is curule elections. It frequently happened that consuls were unwilling or unable to leave their military campaigns and return to Rome to hold the annual elections, so they appointed a dictator instead to perform this routine responsibility for them. Nearly 25 percent (20 out of 85) of all recorded dictators between 501 and 202 BC were appointed simply to hold elections, so they were substitutes more than super commanders.[157] Dictators appointed to perform such civilian duties could not take up a military command unless instructed to do so by the state; as stand-ins for the absent consuls, they did not have the authority to encroach on the military commands the consuls were currently undertaking. The above-mentioned case of L. Manlius Imperiosus illustrates well that dictators—when used as consular substitutes—were not particularly powerful or intimidating: having completed the nail-driving ceremony for which he had been named dictator, he was forced to resign his office when he tried to do something more with his *imperium* (and this was in 363 BC, before the *lex Valeria* of 300 BC limited the scope of a dictator's use of *imperium* in Rome). Even within the domestic

155. Livy 24.8.17.
156. Livy 6.6.6, 7.25.10–13.
157. Kaplan (1977) 169–73 gives a list of all recorded dictators.

sphere, the dictatorship was frequently used simply as a supernumerary chief magistrate to perform whatever tasks the consuls were neglecting, so a dictator was not necessarily the frightening and all-powerful autocrat so frequently depicted in surviving sources.

Why did ancient sources (Livy in particular) tend to portray the dictator as being more powerful and intimidating than he really was? Four reasons probably explain this. First, because the dictatorship went out of use in 202 BC, our chief sources on republican history had never witnessed the traditional dictatorship firsthand and were reliant on older sources, folklore, and legend. Second, the fact that the dictatorship had been held by so many of early Rome's greatest and most celebrated heroes, such as Cincinnatus, Fabius Maximus, Furius Camillus, Manlius Torquatus, Valerius Publicola, Papirius Cursor, and Valerius Corvus (among others), probably gave the office a luster and aura of power and authority not based in any legal reality. The power and actions of such heroes are easily exaggerated by folklore and become difficult to separate from historical truth. Third, the fact that the dictator had no colleague must have distinguished his office as even more monarchical than the consulship, as did his possession of *imperium* in the city. In a culture where the most important magistracies were also the most exclusive, the singular position of the dictator must have given that office tremendous prestige. The Greek term for the dictator, στρατηγός αὐτοκράτωρ, catches this unique authority well. Fourth and most important, the dictatorships of Sulla and Caesar in the first century BC forever changed the idea of the dictatorship in the Roman mind. Both men used the office to act tyrannically in Rome and, in doing so, probably exercised far more real power than any of their predecessors in the early republic (see chapter 6). They also had extraordinary *provinciae*: Sulla was *dictator legibus scribendis et rei publicae constituendae*, and Caesar was *dictator perpetuus*. Indeed, Dionysius said that Sulla was the first dictator to abuse his authority, and scholars are agreed that Sulla and Caesar made the dictatorship far more powerful than it had been in earlier centuries.[158] Under these two men, the dictatorship became such an implement of tyranny that it was banned entirely by Mark Antony in an effort to please the people.[159] When writers of the late republic sat down to write histories of earlier periods, their minds were too ready to connect the dictatorship to a frightening level of absolutism that was anachronistic to the early republic.

The dictatorship, therefore, was probably not as powerful or remarkable

---

158. Dion. Hal. *AR* 5.77.4–6. Santangelo (2007) 9, Jehne (2010) 187–211.
159. Cic. *Phil.* 5.10.

an office as tradition depicts. Because it possessed the highly unusual ability to possess and use *imperium* inside the *pomerium*, the dictatorship may well have been created to suppress dangerous rebellion within the city, but this use would have been greatly limited by the *lex Valeria* of 300 B C. Outside the city, dictators possessed the same *imperium* and *auspicium* as the consuls (and, later, the praetors), and their use of authority was defined and limited by the *provincia* or *causa* given them by the state, so the authority and military capacity of the dictator were no different from any other commander. The real importance of the dictatorship seems to have been its ability to provide the Romans with an extra magistrate or military commander quickly. Through a simple nighttime ceremony, a consul could easily appoint his choice of dictator, who could undertake any military or civilian task that the state needed performed. Although Sulla and Caesar would turn the dictatorship into something much more fearsome in the late republic, the classical dictatorship seems mainly to have been used to provide a supplemental commander and magistrate rather than an exceptionally powerful one.

Conclusion

The *provincia* was a term of fundamental importance in the definition and development of military command in the Roman Republic. On the most basic level, the *provincia* defined the task that any military commander was to undertake and gave purpose and definition to his *imperium*. On a deeper level, by defining the area in which a commander's use of his *imperium* was supreme and unrestricted, the *provincia* also limited the sphere in which his *imperium* could be used with full effect. Because the *provincia* imposed a restriction or limitation on the commander's use of his *imperium*, it probably evolved as part of the early republic's efforts to constrain the freebooting tendencies of its warrior aristocracy and to assert the state's absolute control over the authorization and use of military force. As such, the concept of the *provincia* became inextricably linked to the concept of *imperium*, because the *provincia* qualified a commander's *imperium*, and *imperium* could not be used to full force outside of the commander's *provincia* (but passive aspects, like immunity to prosecution, could operate). The state's ability to determine the *provinciae* of its commanders gave it some control over the activity of those commanders, but it did so by circumscribing the use of *imperium* without reducing *imperium* itself: *imperium* continued to confer the full and absolute authority of martial law, but the *provincia* limited the full use of that authority to a specific sphere.

Because the *provincia* and provincial assignment defined the sphere in which each commander's *imperium* was absolute and unchallenged, there was no need to establish different degrees of *imperium* between different commanders; the notion of rank was unnecessary because each command was clearly defined. Instead of placing its commanders into a hierarchy of rank or a chain of command, the Romans gave each commander a different *provincia*, thereby establishing whose *imperium* took priority or precedence in what sphere. Thus there was no idea of *imperium maius* or *minus* in early Rome, because such an idea would have been nonsensical and unnecessary. Since *imperium* was a singular and absolute idea, all Roman commanders—dictators, masters of horse, consuls, and praetors—had the exact same authority and capacity to use military force and martial law within their respective *provinciae*, but each commander enjoyed priority of *imperium* in his own *provincia*. This explains the use of the dictatorship down to 202 BC: although the dictator was unique in his ability to use *imperium* inside the *pomerium*, his *imperium* outside the *pomerium* was no different from that of any other commander, and he could claim precedence or priority of *imperium* only within the *provincia* (*causa*) assigned to him by the state. Since the senate occasionally used the dictatorship to send an experienced man (as dictator) to replace a less capable consul, the dictatorship appears to have possessed greater authority (*imperium*) than the consulship, but this was not the case. The dictator did not have the power to take over a consul's *provincia* on his own authority, but in an emergency the senate often transferred a consul's *provincia* to a dictator (perhaps to put a more experienced commander in a critical military zone), thereby giving priority of authority in that sphere to the dictator. The *provincia* and provincial assignment, not *imperium*, created a distinction between two *imperium*-bearing commanders, a distinction that determined which commander took precedence in what sphere.

4

THE DEVELOPMENT OF
THE CLASSICAL CONSTITUTION
(367 TO 197 BC)

According to Roman tradition, Rome's system of provincial command remained unchanged for nearly 150 years after the founding of the republic, during which time annual consuls (archaic praetors) or consular tribunes, with
the occasional addition of a dictator, were sufficient to fulfill Rome's need
for military commanders. Because the accuracy of this tradition cannot be
tested, Rome's system of military command may have been substantially different from the image of continuity and constitutionalism put together by later
historians. As suggested in chapter 1, the early Romans may have employed
not two different types of senior magistrate — consuls or consular tribunes —
during this period but a varying number of praetors. It is also possible that the
archaic praetorship was not at first an elected magistracy but simply the general
name for any military commander in early Rome from the leader of a raiding
party to someone who united the fighting men of several clans or tribes under
his authority. While the poverty of the evidence prevents any solid conclusions
being drawn, the government of early Rome was a work in progress rather than
a fixed creation of the founders of the republic. In or around 367 BC, however,
a major change in Rome's system of military command seems to have taken
place, which should probably be considered the birth of the classical system of
military command, which included two consuls, a growing number of praetors, and the occasional dictator and master of horse. This chapter explores
the development of this familiar classical system and argues that it took shape
over a long process of experimentation and innovation through which Rome's
structure of military command gradually evolved. The Roman government
and its practice of military command was not a static structure but a changing
and evolving system that underwent considerable development as the Romans
sought solutions to new problems and experimented with new ideas.

Three key developments between 367 and 197 BC played an essential role in the development of Rome's system of provincial command. First, the chapter explores the division of Rome's command structure into senior (consular) and junior (praetorian) commanders, and it argues that consuls and praetors held the same legal authority as military commanders, but the greater prestige of the consulship led to a difference in status that only gradually made the praetorship a less desirable office. Second, the introduction and use of prorogation is studied as a product of experimentations with the idea of *provincia*. The creation of the promagistrate was an important conceptual change for the Romans because it separated the military commander from the civilian magistrate, reversing what had probably been an important consolidation of authority under state control in the early republic. Thus prorogation loosened the controls on aristocratic use of military authority by separating possession of *imperium* from the restraints placed on sitting magistrates. Finally, the stresses of the Second Punic War would lead the Romans to begin investing private citizens (i.e., nonmagistrates) with *imperium*, an action that was expedient in the short run but would establish a precedent for further separating military command from magisterial office. More immediately, the use of *privati cum imperio* would give rise to new thinking about the idea of military rank, as these nonmagistrate commanders began to consider whether they were acting like consuls or praetors. Each of these developments would have a substantial influence on the way Romans conceived of provincial command and would create the system of provincial command that was familiar to writers of the late republic.

The Praetorship

According to Roman tradition, the familiar two-tiered system of provincial commanders, in which two consuls were the senior military commanders and an increasing number of praetors were secondary or junior commanders, was established in 367 BC by the Sextian-Licinian Rogations. In this year (the Romans believed) the office of the praetorship was first created, as a different and separate magistracy from the consulship.[1] Livy describes the creation of the praetorship as a by-product of the so-called Conflict of the Orders: the patrician families that ruled Rome agreed to allow plebeians to hold the consulship if another magistracy (the praetorship) was created that would be

---

1. Livy 6.42.9–14, *Fast. Cap.* For discussion of these reforms, see von Fritz (1950), Billows (1989) esp. 129, Hölkeskamp (1993) 22–23, and Flower (2010) esp. 50.

open only to patricians.[2] The only other motive Livy gives for the creation of the praetorship was the need to relieve the two consuls of their responsibility to administer justice in the city, since the increasing demands placed on Rome's court system called for a full-time judge to exercise jurisdiction.[3] According to Messala (as quoted by Gellius), the praetor was the colleague to the consuls and had all the same capacities and privileges as the consuls, except that a praetor could not preside over consular elections.[4]

Despite the clarity of Livy's statements, however, few modern historians today would accept his account as written.[5] As discussed in chapter 1, ancient writers like Livy and Cicero knew that the consuls were originally called praetors in early Rome, which means that the praetorship cannot have been created in 367 BC. Second, Livy's emphasis that the praetorship was created to be a judicial magistrate is overly simplistic. The new praetorship was almost identical in capacity and prerogatives to the consulship, and it was clearly a military office: it possessed *imperium* and its very name (*praetor*) was a military title. The praetor's power and authority seem inappropriately great and broad in relation to the task he was supposedly created to perform. A comparison is useful: when the censorship was created to provide regular magistrates to take over the consuls' traditional responsibilities of the census, the new office was strictly civilian; it did not possess *imperium*, nor was a censor considered a colleague to the consul, nor did the prerogatives of the censors overlap in any way with the remaining responsibilities of the consuls.[6] Even the name of the office (*censor*) demonstrated the specific purpose for which it was created. The praetorship, on the other hand, was virtually identical in authority and capacity to the consulship, so Livy's description of the creation of the praetorship is unlikely to be accurate. There is no reason to doubt that Rome underwent some kind of important governmental change around that time, but Livy (or his sources) does not seem to have preserved an accurate description of the nature of those changes.

As suggested in chapter 1, the word praetor was probably the normal catch-all title given to a military commander in early Rome, and until 367 BC it was common for a large and variable number of men to exercise military command

2. Livy 6.35.1–42.14 (cf. 7.1.1).
3. Livy 6.42.11.
4. Messala in Gellius 13.15.4, cf. Livy 3.55.11, 7.1.6.
5. Brennan's two-volume work (2000) provides a thorough discussion of the scholarly debates on the origin and development of the praetorship, and Bergk (2011) 61–74, provides further discussion and bibliography since the publication of Brennan's volumes.
6. Livy 4.8.2–7, Zon. 7.19.

in any given year. In the twenty-five years preceding the Sextian-Licinian Rogations in 367 BC, the Romans are never recorded as using fewer than four military commanders in a single year, and six annual commanders are regularly listed toward the end of that period. After 367 BC, however, only three regular commanders were elected annually, which Roman tradition held to be two consuls and a single praetor. This is certainly a mistake. That any office was first created in 367 BC is highly unlikely: the praetorship cannot have been created at that time because the title praetor was older than the title consul and must have existed before 367 BC, and the consulship cannot have been created in 367 BC because it seems impossible that the Romans would have created a new magistracy to supersede their original praetors as Rome's commanders in chief. Furthermore, the creation of the praetorship as a singular office (tradition held that there was only one annual praetor from 366 to ca. 241 BC) would have been a tremendous violation of Roman practice, in which all regular magistracies — and most priesthoods — were created in colleges consisting of at least two colleagues.[7] If a consul died or was otherwise removed from office, a dictator was named or elections were held for a substitute (*suffectus*) as soon as possible, and if a censor died in office, his colleague was compelled to resign rather than continue to hold the office alone.[8] Only the extraordinary dictator lacked a colleague, and his unique freedom from collegial intervention was one of the primary aspects that made his office so frighteningly effective and different from all other Roman magistracies. Romans did not allow regular magistrates to hold office without a colleague, so it makes no sense that the praetorship should have been a singular office for 125 years, especially since the praetor was invested with *imperium* and (according to tradition) had authority over jurisdiction. Thus the traditional version that the praetorship was created in 367 BC to perform jurisdiction in Rome cannot be accepted.

The suggestion of chapter 1 seems far more likely: three praetors were probably established as Rome's chief military commanders in 367 BC, and the consulship gradually evolved out of the praetorship, rather than being a separate constitutional development. In the first place, the consuls and praetors were always understood to be colleagues and created under the same auspices, which signifies that they were originally members of a single magisterial college, although by the late republic they had come to be treated as substantially

7. Caes. *BC* 3.20, *Dig.* 5.1.58. See Mommsen (1887–88) 1.27–61, Lowenstein (1973) 48–51, Bleicken (1975) 315, Schiller (1978) 176–78, Stewart (1998) 52–94, Forsythe (2005) 150–55. Several scholars have argued that the early republic originally employed two unequal commanders.

8. Livy 27.6.18, Plut. *Rom. Q.* 50.

different and separate magistracies.[9] Even in the late republic, the praetor was in every way the colleague (albeit a lesser one) to the consuls. Not only was he elected in the same meeting of the centuriate assembly and therefore under the same auspices as the consuls, but he also performed the same basic duties as the consul: he could preside over the senate and public assemblies and introduce legislation, he acquired *imperium* and *auspicium militiae* through a *lex curiata* just like the consuls, he could raise and command armies, and had the right (if approved) to celebrate a triumph over his enemies.[10] Indeed, praetors had even broader responsibilities in Rome than the consuls, since the praetors also exercised the highest levels of jurisdiction, which the consuls did not.[11] That the Romans did not recognize a substantial difference between the two offices is also indicated by the fact that it was common practice for men to hold the praetorship after a consulship (until the passage of the *lex Villia Annalis* in 180 BC).[12] Thus it was not considered a demotion or a diminution of a senior senator's status and *dignitas* to move from a consulship to a praetor-

9. Cic. *Att.* 9.9.3: *Nos autem in libris habemus non modo consules a praetore sed ne praetores quidem creari ius esse idque factum esse numquam; consules eo non esse ius quod maius imperium a minore rogari non sit ius, praetores autem cum ita rogentur ut collegae consulibus sint, quorum est maius imperium;* Gellius 13.15.4 (referring to Messala): *conlegam esse praetorem consuli docet, quod eodem auspicio creantur;* Livy 3.55.11, *fuere qui interpretarentur eadem hac Horatia lege consulibus quoque et praetoribus, quia eisdem auspiciis quibus consules crearentur, cautum esse;* and 7.1.6: *praetorem quidem etiam iura reddentem et collegam consulibus atque iisdem auspiciis creatum.*

10. With the exception of holding elections for consuls (Gell. 13.15.4) and certain religious responsibilities (such as holding the Latin Games), praetors could perform most any function normally undertaken by consuls, including military command (Polyb. 2.23.5–6, 3.40.14), summoning and presiding over the senate (Cic. *Leg.* 3.10, Livy 8.2.1, Gell. 14.7.4), perform certain religious observances (Livy 22.9.11 and 33.8, 27.33.8), convening and introducing legislation to the public assemblies (Livy 8.17.12), and triumphing (Harris [1979] 262–63).

11. Mommsen (1887–88) 2.233, struggled with the fact that — because of their responsibilities over the highest courts — praetors seem to have exercised even more authority in Rome than the consuls: "Das militärische Imperium mangelt dem Prätor keineswegs wie dem Consul das jurisdictionelle, vielmehr ist sein Imperium zwar schwächer, aber vollständiger als das consularische."

12. P. Valerius Poplicola (cos. 352, pr. 350) (*MRR* 1.128), M. Valerius Corvus (cos. 348, pr. 347, cos. 345, 343, 335, pr. 308, cos. 300, 299) (*MRR* 1.130 and 164), Q. Publilius Philo (cos. 339, pr. 336) (*MRR* 1.139), Ap. Claudius (cos. 307, pr. 297, cos. 296, pr. 295) (*MRR* 1.175), P. Sempronius (cos. 304, pr. 296) (*MRR* 1.176), M. Atilius (cos. 294, pr. 293) (*MRR* 1.180), L. Papirius Cursor (cos. 293, pr. 292, cos. 272) (*MRR* 1.182), L. Caecilius (cos. 284, pr. 283) (*MRR* 1.188), Q. Marcius Philippus (cos. 281, pr. 280) (*MRR* 1.191), A. Atilius Caiatinus (cos. 258, pr. 257, cos. 254) (*MRR* 1.208), L. Postumius Megellus (cos. 262, pr. 253) (*MRR* 1.211), L. Postumius Albinus (cos. 234, pr. 233, cos. 229, pr. 216, cos. 215) (*MRR* 1.225), M. Claudius Marcellus (cos. 222, pr. 216, cos. 215, 214, 210, 208) (*MRR* 1.231), P. Furius Philus (cos. 223, pr. 216) (*MRR* 1.231), Q. Fulvius Flaccus (cos. 237, 224, pr. 214, cos. 212, 209) (*MRR* 1.254). See Bergk (2011) 67.

ship, since holding the praetorship after a consulship was simply a method of holding *imperium* for a second year. The two offices were so similar that the order in which they were held was unimportant, even to the status-conscious Roman aristocracy.

While it is tempting to read Livy's statement that the praetorship was created to take over the exercise of jurisdiction in Rome as an indication that the praetors (post-367 BC) were primarily civilian officials, nothing could be farther from the truth. The first two praetors on whom we have any information are found commanding armies away from the city, and while the praetorship certainly exercised jurisdiction in Rome in later periods, several modern scholars have emphasized that it was primarily a military office from the beginning.[13] If a particular praetor did not exercise military command during his year in office, this was not the result of any deficiency of authority or capacity; rather, the state simply did not choose to give him a *provincia* in that year or preferred to keep him in Rome for the defense of the city. The praetorship originally held the exact same military authority and capacity for command as the consulship.

Thus the Sextian-Licinian Rogations of 367 BC probably established a college of three equal praetors to exercise military command, but these somehow became differentiated into consuls and praetors in the later republic. This change must have been gradual, since there is no indication that the magistracies underwent any such change after 367 BC, but it was certainly complete by 180 BC, when the *lex Villia Annalis* established a younger minimum age for the praetorship than the consulship, thereby emphasizing the seniority of the consulship.[14] As discussed in chapter 1, the title consul is first attested sometime in the third century BC. Furthermore, Beck is certainly correct that the creation of a second praetorship around 241 BC was a landmark moment in

13. Livy 7.23.3–4 (350 BC) and 7.25.12–13 (349 BC). The first of these praetors is identified in 366 BC, but his activities are not recorded (6.42.11). Brennan (2000) 58–73 argues (61) "the early appearances of the praetor in Livy are outside of Rome, in a military capacity . . . when we do see the praetor acting in the city in Livy Books 7–10, he is doing practically everything accorded to him by virtue of his *imperium* except hearing cases at law." Bergk (2011) 67 also points out the high number of military commands given to praetors before the start of the Second Punic War, and Mitchell (1990) 185 has argued that the early praetorship was essentially military in nature.

14. Cic. *Phil.* 5.47, Livy 40.44.1. See Astin (1958), Develin (1979) 81–85, Richard (1982) 31. The one exception is the fact that, by the late republic, praetors possessed only six *fasces*, whereas consuls possessed twelve. I know of no evidence that explains why this was so, although the fact that praetors usually commanded one legion (i.e., one-half of a consular army) is perhaps a tempting clue to explain why praetors were given only one-half of consular *fasces*.

the separation of the consulship from the praetorship, since a new *cursus hono-rum* is distinguishable after 241 BC that seems to separate the praetorship and consulship as different stages in a man's career.[15] The aedileship of the Ogul-nii brothers in 296 BC may also be a clue to the differentiation of the offices. In their aedileship the two brothers set up Rome's first statue of Romulus and Remus suckling a she-wolf.[16] Since Remus was not a part of Rome's earliest foundation narratives, some scholars believe his introduction in the late fourth or early third century represented the union of patricians and plebeians in the joint consulship, which — if true — would also indicate that the two consuls (one patrician, one plebeian) were seen as distinct from the single praetor by the start of the third century BC.[17]

Over a period of roughly 125 years, the college of three annual praetors established as Rome's military commanders in 367 BC became differentiated into two distinct groups, although their fundamental authority and preroga-tives remained the same. As other scholars have suggested, this process of sepa-ration and distinction was certainly the result of the extreme importance of military glory, and the growing role of wealth, in Roman society.[18] Although all three praetors established in 367 BC held equal capacity for military com-mand (i.e., equal *imperium* and *auspicium*), it was in these years normal Roman practice to reserve one commander in or near the city for purposes of defense and (eventually) for civilian administration.[19] Since the praetors who received military campaigns away from the city had by far the best opportunities to win glory, prestige, and wealth, it became more desirable and prestigious to be one of these two praetors rather than the single praetor who normally remained in the city. As a result, the two praetors sent to fight wars probably acquired the nickname consuls because they consulted (*consulere*) with one another about military matters (especially about the raising of armies, which was organized

---

15. Beck (2011) 82–86. He also suggested ([2005] 64) the fact that a plebeian reached the praetor-ship in 336 BC reduced the desirability of that office for patricians, but this has been challenged by Bergk (2011) 63 n. 16.

16. Livy 10.23.11–12. See Wiseman (1995) 72–76.

17. Wiseman (1995) esp. 103–28. This fits well with the first appearance of the title consul on the tomb of Scipio Barbatus, who was consul in 298 BC, although his epitaph may have been inscribed much later.

18. Hölkeskamp (1993) 26–31, Bunse (1998) 189, Stewart (1998), Beck (2005) 63–70 and (2011) 82–91, Bergk (2011) 61–74, Rosenstein (2011).

19. For example: Livy 3.4.10 and 5.3, 4.27.1 and 45.7–8, 9.22.1 and 42.4, Dion. Hal. *AR* 6.2.3, 6.28.3, 6.91.1, 8.64.3.

jointly by the two consuls),[20] whereas the single praetor who remained in the city came to be known as the *praetor urbanus* or "city commander" because he generally remained in or near Rome. This division or transformation emerged from traditional usage rather than legal definition, so the praetorship was not *made* a lesser office by any official change to its legal authority or capacity, but rather its lesser desirability gradually gave it lower status.

Thus the relationship and the relative status of the two offices changed over time; the praetorship was originally equivalent to the consulship, but by the early second century its popularity relative to the consulship had dropped considerably, forcing the Romans to pass the *lex Baebia* and the *lex Villia annalis* to increase the desirability of the praetorship.[21] Because this was a gradual and mainly social change, the praetorship was never actually demoted or reduced in authority relative to the consulship, meaning that the secondary nature of the praetorship was traditional rather than constitutional. While the consulship developed greater status than the praetorship, it did not possess greater legal authority.

While traditional usage seems to have differentiated the consuls from praetors in this manner, there is little reason to assume that this gradual and informal development was accompanied by a real change in the *imperium* each group possessed as military commanders. There can be no doubt that consuls in the late republic enjoyed considerably more *dignitas*, *auctoritas*, and *honos* than praetors — and one should not underestimate the power and importance of these social forces — yet it would be wrong to assume that this imbalance in the prestige of two magistracies was accompanied by a real and legal difference in their *imperium*. There is a near consensus among modern scholars that the difference in status between the consul and the praetor derived from the relative strength or degree of their *imperium*: the *imperium* of the consul was considered greater (*maius*) to that of the praetor, whose *imperium* was considered lesser (*minus*) to that of the consul. This belief is based on the evident dis-

---

20. Varro *LL* 5.80, Polyb. 6.19.5–21.5 and 26.1–5.

21. Livy 40.44.1–3. He mentions the *lex Baebia* (probably promulgated in 180 BC) that stipulated that the Romans would alternate electing four praetors one year and six praetors the next. This was probably done because most Spanish praetors needed at least two years in command (and therefore a Spanish pair of praetors was only needed in alternate years), but by reducing the overall number of praetors, the exclusivity and prestige of the office would have been increased. Likewise, the *lex Villia Annalis* of 180 BC established a younger minimum age for the praetorship than for the consulship, thereby increasing the attractiveness of the praetorship by making it an office men could hold *before* becoming eligible for the consulship.

parity between the offices within Roman government in later periods: since it is widely (but erroneously) believed that consuls and praetors used *imperium domi* in the exercise of their civilian duties in Rome, the seniority of the consul in all aspects of the Roman government and military is assumed to be the product of a real difference between consular and praetorian *imperium*. The strongest evidence for this point of view comes from two passages, one found in Cicero and the other in Aulus Gellius. Complaining to Atticus that Caesar intended to have a praetor supervise consular elections in 49 BC, Cicero wrote:

> But we have it in our books that it is illegal not only for consuls but even praetors to be elected under a praetor, and that such a thing is without precedent — illegal for consuls because it is illegal for a higher authority (*maius imperium*) to be proposed by a lower (*a minore*), and for praetors because they are proposed as colleagues of the consuls, who possess higher authority (*maius imperium*).[22]

Nearly two hundred years later, Aulus Gellius inserted into his *Attic Nights* a passage that he claimed was a quotation from the text *De Auspiciis*, written in the first century BC by the augur M. Valerius Messala, which supports Cicero's original statement:

> As we have learned it from our ancestors or as it has been preserved before these times, and as it appears in the thirteenth book of the *Commentaries* of C. Tuditanus, the praetor, although he is a colleague of the consul, is not able to propose the election of a praetor or consul legally, because the praetor has *imperium minus* and the consul *imperium maius*, and it is not legally possible for the election of *imperium maius* to be promulgated by *imperium minus*, nor for the election of a greater colleague to be promulgated by a lesser colleague.[23]

These statements seem clear, and they have induced modern scholars to accept that the praetors held a different and lesser form of *imperium* than that which had been possessed by Rome's military commanders before 367 BC. Indeed,

22. Cic. *Att.* 9.9.3 (Shackleton Bailey, trans.): *Nos autem in libris habemus non modo consules a praetore sed ne praetores quidem creari ius esse idque factum esse numquam; consules eo non esse ius quod maius imperium a minore rogari non sit ius, praetores autem cum ita rogentur ut collegae consulibus sint, quorum est maius imperium.*

23. C. Sempronius Tuditanus fr. 2C = 8P (Drogula, trans.): *praetor, etsi conlega consulis est, neque praetorem neque consulem iure rogare potest, ut quidem nos a superioribus accepimus aut ante haec tempora servatum est et ut in Commentario tertio decimo C. Tuditani patet, quia imperium minus praetor, maius habet consul, et a minore imperio maius aut maior a minore conlega rogari iure non potest.*

Last — whose article has long been essential reading for any discussion of *imperium maius* — thought these comments by Cicero and Messala were entirely sufficient to demonstrate the distinction between *imperium maius* and *minus*, and he based much of his argument on the basic assumption that Cicero and Messala were historically accurate.[24]

Despite the apparent strength of this evidence, however, there are good grounds to suspect that Cicero and Messala/Tuditanus were not entirely correct. In the first place, a simple and obvious contradiction in their statements seriously undermines their reliability on this question. Both Cicero and Messala/Tuditanus are explicit that a lower magistrate (*imperium minus*) cannot oversee the creation of a greater magistrate (*imperium maius*), but the falseness of this statement is obvious from the fact that consuls normally appointed dictators, which — if one believes in the distinction between *imperium maius* and *minus* — was certainly a case of *imperium maius* (a dictator) being appointed by *imperium minus* (a consul). As further evidence, Bergk has also pointed to the unusual election of a dictator in 217 BC, during which a praetor must have presided over the assembly that elected the dictator.[25] This error by Cicero and Messala/Tuditanus is too substantial to disregard, since it demonstrates that they did not understand the real reason why praetors were not supposed to supervise consular elections in the late republic but were simply making a logical but incorrect guess. Linderski has effectively dismantled the reliability of Cicero and Messala/Tuditanus in this matter, pointing out that their explanations drew more on custom and tradition than on authoritative sources, that there may have been no real legal foundation to their explanation, and that most Romans in the late republic seem to have accepted that even a praetor (the lowest or most junior type of commander) could appoint a dictator.[26]

---

24. Last (1947) 157–58.

25. Bergk (2011) 66 n. 40. Since both consuls were unavailable to name a dictator after the Battle of Lake Trasimene, the senate asked the people to elect a dictator, and only the *praetor urbanus* would have been available to preside over the election.

26. Linderski (1986) 2182: "Cicero intimates that the theory he expounds was enshrined in the ritual books of the augurs. This must be taken *cum grano salis*. Cicero and Messala subscribed to the same doctrine, and yet Messala, who wrote extensively on the subject, was not able to find anything more authoritative as his source than the *commentarii* of C. Sempronius Tuditanus. And it is quite characteristic that both Cicero and Messala stressed the authority of custom and tradition. . . . Also Caesar recognized the strength of the argument, and he chose the legally and augurally least objectionable way, namely to be appointed dictator by a praetor. The procedure was carefully thought out." See also Stewart (1998) 99, who argues that Cicero's understanding of the collegiality of the praetor and consul, which prohibits a praetor from electing another praetor, is "vague and general," and that Cicero was writing about matters of which he had no real understanding.

Furthermore, because Cicero and Messala were both augurs, their main interest in these passages was probably the traditional lore surrounding *auspicium*, and their references to *imperium* may have been intended to signify nothing more than the general and abstract concept of magisterial power.

Two other mistakes demonstrate that Cicero did not truly understand the legal or religious grounds for consular precedence over the praetor: his statement that a consul could go into whatever *provincia* he wished, and his claim that all provinces are under the jurisdiction (*iure*) and command (*imperium*) of the consuls. Both of these statements are obviously incorrect, which seriously erodes confidence in the accuracy of his earlier comments on consular *imperium*.[27] How could these authors have made such a mistake? The nature of their errors suggest that, while all informed Romans understood that the consulship was a greater and more important office than the praetorship, no one knew the legal grounds (if there were any) for this difference, and their efforts to surmise or produce such grounds seem to fail miserably. Cicero and Messala admit that their obscure (and apparently incorrect) claims were rejected by their respective colleagues in the college of augurs, which also seriously undermines the strength of those claims.[28] Since the difference between consuls and praetors had been a gradual social development, there was no constitutional difference between the two, although Cicero and Messala thought there should be one. Although there can be no doubt that the conceptual distinction of *imperium maius* and *minus* existed by the end of the republic (see chapter 6), these passages in Cicero and Gellius/Messala provide no evidence that such a distinction existed earlier in the republic and, in particular, at the creation of the praetorship in the fourth century BC.

---

27. Cic. *Att.* 8.15.3: *ipsi consules, quibus more maiorum concessum est vel omnes adire provincias*; and *Phil.* 4.9: *omnes . . . in consulis iure et imperio debent esse provinciae*. Henderson (1957) 82–83 easily dismantled Cicero's claims, pointing out that the first passage (*Att.* 8.15.3) was a simple statement that consuls, like legates and other commanders *cum imperio*, can leave Italy and travel into the provinces, and the second statement (*Phil.* 4.9) was made out of political necessity in a speech before the senate and cannot be taken as constitutional law. Giovannini (1983) 57–71 tried to sustain the argument that consuls were in supreme command of all *provinciae*, but this has been toppled by Crook (1986) 286–88.

28. Cicero (*Att.* 9.9.3) points out that many augurs (some of them admittedly Caesar's supporters) accepted the legitimacy of Caesar's claims that a praetor could run elections, and Messala (in Gell. 13.15.4) points out that praetors did indeed supervise the election of praetors in his day, which is in direct contradiction to the augural opinion he cites (Messala himself says that he abstains from overseeing the auspices at such elections, but other augurs did not see any problem in participating year after year).

Arguments against the Existence of *Imperium Maius/Minus*

Given the general resistance among modern scholars to the idea that *imperium* was absolute and did not exist in greater or lesser levels or degrees, it is worthwhile to review briefly several passages or phenomena that have been used to demonstrate the existence of *imperium maius* or *minus* to illustrate how rapidly they fall apart on close inspection. Efforts to use these passages or phenomena as evidence of *imperium maius/minus* strain credulity too much, especially since other (better) explanations are usually available.

VIS IMPERII

In his account of 169 BC, Livy makes two praetors say that their office had less authority and force of *imperium* (*vis imperii minor*) than the consulship, which is easy to interpret as a reference to praetorian *imperium minus* if one is predisposed to assume that *imperium* was fragmented into different levels.[29] Such an interpretation is a mistake. Livy's point in this passage is not to explain Roman legal thinking but to provide a moral lesson that unjustifiable arrogance among the aristocracy is self-defeating: after the consuls had been unable to carry out a military levy because their pride and callousness had alienated the citizenry, two praetors offered to complete the recruitment, boasting that they would do better than the consuls despite having *vis imperii minor*.[30] The story is not a statement of the relative authority invested in different magistracies but a moral that moderate and restrained treatment of the plebs is more successful than the arrogant use of force. Livy uses the phrase *vis imperii* in only two other places, once to describe a commander's disciplining his men and another to describe the Roman Empire (*imperium Romanum*).[31] Both of these are nonspecific and offer no suggestion that they are used in a technical sense to measure relative degrees of military authority between commanders.

A passage by Festus should also discourage us from interpreting Livy's words as evidence for *imperium maius* and *minus*: he writes that seniority within the college of praetors was determined by the relative *vis imperii* of

---

29. Livy 43.14.4: *praetores se, quibus vis imperii minor et auctoritas esset*.

30. Livy 43.14.2–5 presents a dramatic scene in which the haughty and arrogant consuls claimed to be unable to complete the levy. Upstaging the consuls, two praetors—who were known for their moderation—assert to the senate that they will succeed where the consuls had failed, even though the praetors held *vis imperii minor et auctoritas*.

31. Livy 9.16.16: *et vis erat in eo viro imperii ingens pariter in socios civesque* (a consul in the field uses his *vis imperii* to discipline troops); and 42.44.4: *quanta esset vis et fortuna imperii Romani* (a reference to the might of the Roman Empire).

each praetor.[32] If one believes the phrase *vis imperii* illustrates differing levels of *imperium*, Festus's use of the phrase must indicate that each praetor held a different level or degree of *imperium* from his colleagues. This is obviously an impossible notion, because it suggests that some praetors held *imperium maius* and others *imperium minus*, and it eradicates the fundamental republican principle of collegiality on which the republican government was based.[33] Indeed, Festus himself admitted that augurs disagreed with his explanation for precedence within the college of praetors, indicating that some augurs believed that precedence was determined by age (the eldest took priority), while others thought that the *praetor urbanus* was always the senior praetor.[34] Pinsent has even suggested that this passage in Festus may be Augustan, because Cicero and Valerius Maximus both believed that seniority among praetors was determined by age.[35] Obviously, none of these writers understood the legal principle for a hierarchy of praetors, probably because there was no legal principle—the hierarchy of praetors (if there even was such a thing) was a conventional practice. It seems best either to accept the phrase *vis imperii* as an abstract term signifying power in the general sense or to dismiss it as an anachronism from the later Augustan era, as Pinsent suggests.

THE INVITATION LIST TO A TRIUMPHATOR'S BANQUET

A passage in Valerius Maximus has also tempted scholars to see it as evidence of *imperium maius/minus*, but careful reading demonstrates that this is not the case. Valerius observes that "it is the custom for the consuls to be invited to dinner by a commander about to celebrate a triumph, and then for them to be asked to refrain from coming lest, on that day on which he triumphs, there might be someone of greater *imperium* at the same dinner party."[36] Staveley questioned the accuracy of this passage,[37] but the practice it describes makes perfect sense in the imperial era. Valerius lived and wrote under Emperor Tibe-

---

32. Fest. 152L: *Maximum praetorem dici putant ali eum, qui maximi imperi sit; ali, qui[a] aetatis maximae. Pro collegio quidem augurum decretum est, quod in Salutis augurio praetores maiores et minores appellantur, non ad aetatem, sed ad vim imperii pertinere.*

33. See Linderski (1986) 2177–80.

34. Fest. 152L (note 32) and 154L (*praetorem autem maiorem, Urbanum: minores ceteros*).

35. Pinsent (1975) 25 n. 28, he cites Cic. *Rep.* 2.55 and Val. Max. 4.1.1 and points out that elsewhere Gellius (2.15.4) suggests that age had been the criterion up to the passage of the *lex Julia*.

36. Val. Max. 2.8.6 (Drogula, trans.): *his illud subnectam: moris est ab imperatore ducturo triumphum consules invitari ad cenam, deinde rogari ut venire supersedeant, ne quis eo die quo ille triumpharit maioris in eodem convivio sit imperii.* See Versnel (1970) 390 and Beard (2007) 262.

37. Staveley (1963) 476–77.

rius, when there can be no doubt that *imperium maius* existed, so the tradition he mentions is probably a product of the imperial age and does not date back to the republic. In Valerius's day, only the emperor or members of his house celebrated triumphs, so this practice of uninviting consuls to the celebratory dinner may have been an effort to avoid embarrassment on all sides. Consuls were supposed to be the leaders of the state and were expected to receive seats of honor at all public events, but a triumphal banquet celebrating the glory of the imperial house would draw attention to the consuls' obvious inferiority to the emperor and his heirs, which would have been awkward for the emperor and humiliating for the consuls.

Everything about this passage from Valerius indicates that it refers to his current day rather than to the republic: it is awkwardly inserted (*his illud subnectam*) without explanation or relevance into descriptions of republican triumphs, and the conspicuous use of the present tense (*moris est*) contrasts with the past tense used in the preceding and following sections. Even if the practice were republican in origin, it was probably intended to protect the honor of the consuls rather than to shield the triumphator from *imperium maius*. This interpretation is clear in a passage from Plutarch, who also reports this particular custom of the Romans. In his account he suggests that the custom existed to protect the superior honor of the consuls from being upstaged by the greater glory of the triumphator; since it was imperative that the triumphator receive the place of honor at the dinner table and a special escort home after the banquet, this special treatment would make the consuls appear less important by contrast.[38] Plutarch further illustrates this aspect of Roman social dynamics when he points out that "Lucullus had been consul before Pompey, and was older than he; but Pompey's two triumphs gave him a greater dignity."[39] This tradition of uninviting consuls to certain public banquets was probably a product of social etiquette intended to protect the *dignitas* of the consuls from the dazzling glory of the triumphator; the practice would have been all the more important in the imperial period under Augustus, who took considerable steps to protect the dignity and prestige of the Roman senate. It could simply be that consuls, by virtue of the seniority of their office, were expected to preside at all public functions, but to protect their *dignitas* from being diminished by com-

38. Plut. *Rom. Q.* 80: "Διὰ τί τοὺς θριαμβεύσαντας ἑστιῶντες ἐν δημοσίῳ παρῃτοῦντο τοὺς ὑπάτος, καὶ πέμποντες παρεκάλουν μὴ ἐλθεῖν ἐπὶ τὸ δεῖπνον;" ἢ καὶ τόπον ἔδει τῷ θριαμβεύσαντι κλισίας τὸν ἐντιμότατον ἀποδίδοσθαι καὶ προπομπὴν μετὰ τὸ δεῖπνον; ταῦτα δ' οὐκ ἔξεστιν ἑτέρῳ γίγνεσθαι τῶν ὑπάτων παρόντων, ἀλλ' ἐκείνοις."

39. Plut. *Pomp.* 31.4.

parison to a triumphator, they were politely asked not to attend the triumphal banquet. In sum, this seems like a social convention rather than a constitutional measure of *imperium*.

LACK OF EVIDENCE FOR *IMPERIUM*
MAIUS BEING USED IN ROME

A considerable problem for those who believe in *imperium domi* and that consuls had greater *imperium* than praetors is the fact that consuls never seem to have used their *imperium maius* to overrule or command praetors in Rome. If *imperium maius* was the essential quality that determined the superiority of the consulship, it is striking that no example exists in the long history of the republic of a consul in Rome ever using his greater *imperium* against a praetor. Last attempted to resolve this obvious problem by arguing that the consuls' *imperium maius* existed only as a preventive step against the potential that a consul and praetor might get into a conflict with one another, so the consul did not exercise direct authority over the praetor, although in the event that they disagreed on some point, the command of the consul was to take precedence.[40] While this certainly sounds reasonable, Last himself admitted that there was virtually no evidence that supported his reconstruction and that it was only a theory that could not be demonstrated. Scholars have been able to find only one occasion on which a consul seems to have overruled a praetor: Valerius Maximus writes that the consul Mam. Aemilius Lepidus Livianus (cos. 77 BC) abrogated a praetor's jurisdiction (*praetoriam iurisdictionem abrogavit*) by reversing the praetor's ruling on an inheritance matter.[41] As is immediately obvious, however, this provides no evidence for consular *imperium maius*: the passage does not even mention *imperium*, and magisterial jurisdiction was a separate and distinct type of authority from *imperium*. Furthermore, Valerius indicates that the praetor's ruling was actually reversed by a *senatus consultum* rather than consular coercion, suggesting that Livianus could not have reversed the praetor's ruling on his own authority.[42] Brennan also points out that the use of the verb *abrogare* was probably rhetorical, since the praetor in question did not lose his *provincia* over the court.[43]

Other evidence for the superiority of consular authority over praetors in

40. Last (1947) 158–59.
41. Val. Max. 7.7.6. The praetor had allowed a eunuch to inherit property, which the consul felt intolerable.
42. See discussion in Ryan (1998) 307–8.
43. Brennan (2000) 445.

Rome is scanty and weak at best: in 115 BC a consul insulted a disrespectful praetor by ripping his toga, smashing his chair, and ordering that no one should bring lawsuits before him, and in 67 BC a consul ordered the chair of a praetor who failed to stand at his approach smashed, but in neither case did the consuls in question need their *imperium* to carry out these deeds, since these were simple insults and not legal actions that pitted one magistrate's *imperium* against another's.[44] In neither case did the consul order the praetor to do anything. This is particularly evident in the altercation in 115 BC: since the consul could not order the praetor to stop exercising jurisdiction, he ordered the people not to appear in the praetor's court. In sum, the whole idea that praetors possessed lesser *imperium* (*imperium minus*) or that consuls had greater *imperium* (*imperium maius*) is groundless and based on assumption rather than demonstrable fact.

CONSULS AND PRAETORS ON MILITARY CAMPAIGN

If consuls and praetors did have different levels of *imperium*, one would expect that this measurable inequality in their military authority would be immediately obvious in the relationship between the two types of commanders in the field. The superiority of senior officers over their juniors is readily apparent in modern armies: junior officers automatically give salutes, deference, and obedience to their seniors in the military hierarchy. Such automatic obedience is certainly evident in Roman armies: legates, quaestors, military tribunes, and centurions recognized their commander (whether consul or praetor) as an absolute superior whose orders were to be followed without question. Yet this type of clear hierarchical relationship does not seem to have existed between the consuls and praetors. To be sure: the consulship was certainly considered a more important and prestigious magistracy, and all Romans automatically paid the consuls the honor and deference owed to their high office, but there is a big difference between polite respect and legally required obedience. It would be a mistake to assume that, just because praetors occasionally deferred to the wishes of the consuls, such deference was really obedience compelled from them by consular *imperium maius*. Even tribunes of the plebs, who were completely immune to all legal forms of compulsion, still showed willing respect and consideration to consuls, so why should one imagine that praetors only showed such deference out of legal necessity?

There were certainly occasions when praetors holding independent *provinciae* consulted with consuls and even appear to have followed their instruc-

44. 115 BC: Auct. *Vir. Ill.* 72; 67 BC: Dio 36.41.2.

tions: in his account of 215 BC, Livy says the propraetor M. Claudius Marcellus and the praetor M. Valerius Laevinus respectively heeded the instructions of the consuls Q. Fabius Maximus and Ti. Sempronius Gracchus.[45] In the following year, the consul M. Claudius Marcellus is said to have called for the help of the propraetor Pomponius with his army, in 212 BC the consul Ap. Claudius Pulcher summoned the praetor C. Claudius Nero to assist in military operations around Capua, and in 207 BC the consul C. Claudius Nero instructed the proconsul Q. Fulvius Flaccus to redirect his military activities.[46] These examples leave no doubt that Rome's commanders could and did coordinate their activities when necessary, but it would be a serious mistake to interpret these events as evidence that consuls exercised legal authority over praetors or promagistrates. As discussed in chapter 3, it was common enough for consular colleagues to assist one another in military operations without one of them being subordinate to the other, so there is no reason to suppose that a praetor who cooperated with a consul had to be the subordinate officer of that consul. The greater *dignitas* and *auctoritas* of the consulship — and the dangers an angry consul could pose to one's future political career — ensured that praetors would willingly follow reasonable instructions from consuls, but this was a voluntary display of deference rather than legally required obedience. If a praetor came to the assistance of a consul and entered the consul's *provincia*, the consul naturally enjoyed precedence and priority of *imperium* within his own *provincia* without needing *imperium maius*.

It also happened that a praetor could be given a *provincia* that supported a consular *provincia*, but this did not make the praetor the subordinate of the consul any more than when two consuls cooperated or coordinated in fighting a single enemy. In the second century BC, several praetors are found commanding fleets in support of consular armies, but the praetors were the absolute commanders of their naval *provinciae*, and if they lent support to a consular army on land, they did so as independent commanders.[47] In 168 and 167 BC, the praetor Cn. Octavius held command of Rome's eastern fleet and frequently cooperated with the consul L. Aemilius Paullus, who was campaigning against Perseus in the Third Macedonian War. Clearly this cooperation did not make Octavius the consul's subordinate, since Octavius was granted a naval triumph in 167 BC, which means that he was the supreme and

---

45. Livy 23.39.7–8 and 23.48.3.

46. Livy 24.17.2, 25.22.7, and 27.42.17.

47. 191 BC: Livy 36.2.6, 36.42.1–45.8; 190 BC: Polyb. 21.10.1–14, Livy 37.2.10, 4.5, 14.1–19.8, and 26.9–27.9; 169 BC: Livy 44.1.3–4, 2.1–3, 7.10, and 10.5–13.11.

independent commander of his *provincia*.[48] Naturally, if a praetorian naval commander left his own *provincia* and entered the sphere of a consul's *provincia*, the consul's *imperium* would take priority in that zone: in 202 BC another praetorian fleet commander named Cn. Octavius, who had held the *provincia* of naval operations around Sardinia for four years, moved his fleet to Africa where he took up service as a legate in Scipio Africanus's army at Zama.[49] Although Octavius retained his independent *imperium* and was even prorogued for 201 BC, by entering Scipio's *provincia* he willingly yielded priority of command. So long as they remained in their own *provinciae*, praetors enjoyed priority of *imperium* and complete independence in that zone.

Because a commander's supreme authority over a *provincia* depended on his official possession of that *provincia*, a praetor could be superseded in his command only if his *provincia* was transferred to a consul or other commander. In such cases, the incoming commander did not take over the *provincia* by virtue of a higher level of *imperium* but because the *provincia* itself had been transferred to him by the senate. Livy illustrates this process in his account of 295 BC, when a massive uprising of Samnites, Gauls, and Etruscans broke out, and the praetor holding the *provincia* of Etruria was said to have realized that his army was hopelessly outnumbered. Sending a dispatch to Rome, the senate and people both decreed that the *provincia* of Etruria should be transferred to the consul Q. Fabius Maximus Rullianus.[50] Similarly, when a praetor of 199 BC lost most of his army in an ill-led campaign against the Gauls, his *provincia* was transferred to a consul, who was sent to restore Roman control over the area.[51] Finally, when the praetor L. Julius was given the *provincia* of Gaul in 183 BC, he was instructed to prevent the Gauls from building a city by all means short of war, since — if war became necessary — the senate intended

48. Cooperation: Livy 44.30.1, 32.5-6, 35.8 and 13, 45.6.11-12, 28.8, 29.3, 33.7; triumph: Livy 35.4-5, 42.2-3, Vell. 1.9.5-6, Plut. *Aem.* 26.1-5, *Act. Tr. Cap.* for 167/6 BC.

49. Livy records the major events of Octavius's multiyear command as follows: in 205 BC, he exercised independent command over the fleet guarding Sardinia (28.46.14); in 204 BC he brought supplies to Scipio in Africa (29.36.1-3); in 203 BC he was again guarding the coasts of Sardinia (30.2.4); in 202 BC he was prorogued and ordered to command naval operations around Sicily (30.27.9), but he joined Scipio in Africa and — after the Battle of Zama — took command of Scipio's army while Scipio himself used Octavius's fleet to approach Carthage (30.36.3-6); at the end of 202 BC Octavius's fleet *provincia* was transferred to Scipio, who was authorized to retain Octavius as a legate with *imperium* (30.41.6-7); in 201 BC he served as Scipio's legate for a period of time before returning to Rome (30.41.6-8, 44.13).

50. Livy 10.24.18. Fabius's colleague would later join him in this *provincia*. Oakley (1997-2004) 4.268-302 gives an extensive discussion of this campaign.

51. Livy 32.7.5-8.

to give the *provincia* against the Gauls to one of the consuls.[52] In all of these cases it was provincial assignment, and not *imperium maius*, that transferred the supreme command of a praetor's *provincia* to a consul. This is emphasized by occasions on which the senate instructed a consul to hand over his army and *provincia* to a praetor: in 216 BC, the senate instructed the consul C. Terentius Varro to turn over the survivors of Cannae to a praetor and to return to Rome in order to consult with the senate, and in 200 BC the senate ordered a consul to hand his newly raised army over to a praetor's command if the consul himself could not be ready to depart on military campaign expeditiously.[53] The praetors in these cases took over command of consular armies because the senate (rather than levels of *imperium*) determined which commanders exercised authority over which groups of Roman soldiers. Thus, in 203 BC the praetor P. Quinctilius Varus took over the *provincia* of Ariminum in Cisalpine Gaul from the proconsul M. Cornelius Cethegus (cos. 204 BC), but Cethegus remained in the *provincia* to help Varus fight Mago, and in the critical battle the proconsul yielded supreme command to the praetor and followed his instructions regarding a critical cavalry charge.[54] That a proconsul would obey the orders of a praetor in this manner seems impossible if authority derived from different levels of *imperium*, but it makes perfect sense if Varus's possession of the *provincia* made him the supreme commander in that sphere.

While provincial assignment was normally sufficient to establish superiority of authority in different spheres, it could happen that an unexpected and major development in a commander's *provincia* changed his claim to that *provincia*. In 218 BC, two praetors were holding commands against the Boii in Cisalpine Gaul when the consul P. Cornelius Scipio—who had been en route to his *provincia* of fighting Hannibal in Spain—appeared with the shocking news that Hannibal was on the march and would soon arrive in northern Italy.[55] The praetors handed command of their legions over to Scipio, who led the (unsuccessful) attack on Hannibal when he finally arrived in Italy. What authorized Scipio to assume command of the praetors' armies? In his account of this event, Appian makes Scipio claim that praetors had no right to com-

52. Livy 39.45.6–7.
53. Livy 22.57.1 and 31.11.1–2.
54. Livy 30.18.5.
55. Polyb. 3.56.6: ποιησάμενος δὲ τὴν πορείαν διὰ Τυρρηνίας, καὶ παραλαβὼν τὰ παρὰ τῶν ἑξαπελέκεων στρατόπεδα τὰ προκαθήμενα καὶ προσπολεμοῦντα τοῖς Βοίοις. The praetor L. Manlius had originally been sent to fight the Boii, but when he suffered setbacks, one of his colleagues, C. Atilius Serranus, was dispatched to assist him (Polyb. 3.40.11–14, Livy 21.39.3).

mand when a consul was present,[56] but this is manifestly inaccurate—one need only consider the praetor Falto, who received a triumph for his role in winning the Battle of the Aegates Islands alongside the consul Catulus (as discussed below). As discussed in chapter 3, a commander could exercise the full force of his *imperium* only in the *provincia* assigned to him by the state, so Scipio could not have claimed authority over praetorian legions stationed in Cisalpine Gaul simply by right of his *imperium*, even if it had been *maius* to that of the praetors. It may be that the praetors voluntarily deferred to Scipio because of the seniority of his office and his greater *dignitas* and *auctoritas*, or Scipio may have asserted (rightly or wrongly) that fighting Hannibal fell within his *provincia*, even if Hannibal left Spain.[57] He and the senate had thought this battle between Hannibal and Scipio would take place in Spain, but Scipio may have asserted that Hannibal's unexpected march changed the location of Scipio's *provincia* but not the *provincia* itself. Furthermore, at least one of the legions serving under the praetors had originally been recruited by Scipio for his *provincia* in Spain but had been transferred to the praetors for their campaigns in northern Italy, so he may have had some legitimate claim to taking back what he considered to be his legions.[58] The praetors could have contested Scipio's claim and refused to hand over their legions, but Scipio was both a more senior magistrate and a more experienced commander, and his family was influential enough to threaten the praetors' prospects of political advancement if they made an enemy of him, so it probably did not occur to them to refuse him, even if it had been legally possible. Of course, it is possible that Roman military practice at the time offered no type of standard operating procedure for this extraordinary and unprecedented situation and that the praetors willingly and without legal compulsion deferred to Scipio's higher office, to his

56. App. *Hann.* 5: καὶ Μάλλιον μὲν καὶ Ἀτίλιον, οἳ τοῖς Βοιοῖς ἐπολέμουν, ἐς Ῥώμην ἔπεμψεν ὡς οὐ δέον αὐτοὺς ἔτι στρατηγεῖ ὑπάτου παρόντος.

57. Livy (21.17.1) records that Scipio was assigned the *provincia* of *Hispania*, while his colleague received *Africa cum Sicilia*. This may well be accurate (in which case Scipio may have stretched the truth if he asserted his right to fight Hannibal in Italy), but—since these two *provinciae* were the centers of Carthaginian power and the anticipated theaters of war with the Carthaginians in 218 BC—the provincial assignments may have indicated that the consuls were to engage Carthaginian forces in these areas, in which case Scipio may have had some right to claim that Hannibal's army remained his *provincia* even if it left Spain.

58. Livy 21.26.1–2. One of the praetors (L. Manlius) had encountered difficulties fighting the Boii, so the second praetor (C. Atilius) was ordered to assume command of one of Scipio's legions and march to Manlius's relief. Stewart (1998) 215 suggests that Scipio had been given the northern *provincia* against Hannibal by the senate, and therefore he was merely assuming command of the forces that had been earmarked for his *provincia*.

greater *dignitas* and *auctoritas*, and to the logic of his plan to attack Hannibal while his army was exhausted from its crossing the Alps. While it is tempting to see this event as an example of *imperium maius* in action, more likely it demonstrates the role of the *provincia* and provincial assignment in determining who could claim authority in what sphere.

That only the possession of a *provincia*—and not *imperium maius/minus*—determined precedence of command between consuls and praetors is demonstrated by the debate surrounding the triumph of the praetor L. Furius Purpurio in 200 BC. Furius had been holding the territory of Gaul as his *provincia* when a major uprising of Gauls broke out, and because he had insufficient forces to deal with the threat, the senate assigned the suppression of the revolt to the consul C. Aurelius Cotta.[59] Aurelius raised a new army and sent it ahead to Ariminum, but when the consul was delayed in Rome, the praetor Furius (on his own authority) took command of the consul's army, defeated the Gauls, and returned to Rome to request a triumph. His request was hotly debated because some senators believed that Furius had fought the battle in the consul's *provincia* and with the consul's army (*alieno exercitu*), whereas others supported Furius because he had held the *provincia* of Gaul and had fought *in magistratu suisque auspiciis*.[60]

The question as Livy presents it is a matter of provincial assignment: in whose *provincia* did the battle take place? If (as many think) rank was established by *imperium*, and if praetors possessed *imperium minus*, then Furius's claim for a triumph could not possibly have been taken seriously, since the consul's higher authority would have been obvious and indisputable even if he was not physically present. As things happened, however, their *imperium* does not appear to have been a consideration. The only question that was seriously considered was which commander held the *provincia* when the battle was fought. In the end, the senate judged that Furius had been in the right, because his possession of the *provincia* of Gaul authorized him to exercise his *imperium* in that sphere independent of any other commander, even of the consul who was *en route*. Naturally, if Aurelius had been present with his army in Gaul at the time of the battle, we may assume that his *imperium* and *auspicium* would have taken priority, since the senate explicitly gave him the *provincia* of fighting the Gauls. As it was, however, Aurelius had not yet assumed command of the *provincia*, and the senate (and Aurelius's soldiers and officers) recognized

---

59. Livy 31.10.1–11.3 and 21.1–18.

60. Livy 31.48.1–49.12. Briscoe (1973) 158 only comments that "the politics of the episode are obscure."

that Furius held full and legitimate command of the *provincia* of Gaul; levels of *imperium* were not a consideration.

To be sure, there were occasions when a praetor was clearly serving as a lieutenant or assistant to a consul, but such cases do not indicate that praetors were normally the subordinates of consuls or even that consuls held *imperium maius* and praetors *imperium minus*. While praetors normally received independent *provinciae* of their own, the senate could instruct a praetor to act as the helper or *adiutor* of a consul. A praetor assigned to be an *adiutor* to a consul continued to hold the full and complete *imperium* that all praetors held, but his ability to use his military authority was greatly limited because he did not possess his own *provincia* in which to exercise his *imperium*. A praetor acting in this way as an *adiutor* was operating in the consul's *provincia*, so the consul's *imperium* always enjoyed priority over that of the *adiutor*. Just as it happened that one consul might serve as an *adiutor* to his colleague without becoming a subordinate or having lesser *imperium*, so it should be no surprise that praetors could operate in the same manner. A praetor acting as an *adiutor* brought the same advantages as a consul in the same role: he provided an extra commander in case the consul was wounded or killed, and he provided the consul with an experienced and especially powerful colleague to help lead major campaigns.

There are several examples of praetors serving as *adiutores* in a consul's *provincia*: in 210 BC the propraetor M. Junius Silanus was recalled from his province in Etruria to be the *adiutor* of P. Cornelius Scipio (Africanus) in his Spanish *provincia* against the Carthaginians; in 195 BC the praetor P. Manlius was assigned as his provincial allotment to be an *adiutor* to the consul M. Porcius Cato in Nearer Spain; and in 177 BC the propraetor on Sardinia, T. Aebutius Parrus, was instructed to remain on the island and function there as the *adiutor* to his successor, the consul Ti. Sempronius Gracchus.[61] In all three cases, the consuls were expected to engage in major military operations, and the addition of a praetorian *adiutor* no doubt seemed wise: the great distance between Spain and Italy would make it difficult to replace Scipio or Cato as commander in chief if either were killed fighting enemy forces, and the fact that Aebutius Parrus had already conducted military operations on Sardinia would have made him an invaluable resource for the incoming consul Gracchus. That the praetors acting as *adiutores* were independent commanders fully invested with *imperium* is evident from the fact that two of the preceding examples (Silanus and Aebutius) had been engaged in commanding their own *provinciae* when they were instructed to assume positions as *adiutores* to in-

61. Livy 26.19.10–11, 33.43.5–6, 41.15.6–7.

coming consuls. There is no reason to imagine that their *imperium* changed in any way by becoming an *adiutor*; the only change was that they lost command of their own *provinciae* and took up responsibilities in another man's *provincia*. This was certainly a sensitive situation, since the senate was asking one fully independent, *imperium*-bearing commander to forgo his own opportunities for exclusive military glory by taking up a position in another man's army. The title *adiutor* was likely chosen because it neatly avoided any indication of rank or authority that might imply that the praetor was somehow the inferior or underling of the consul, just as great Roman senators might refer to their less-important supporters by the status-neutral term *amici* (friends). That *adiutor* implied an equal, collegial relationship is also indicated by the fact that a consul could refer to his consular colleague as an *adiutor*.[62] In all cases, the holder of the *provincia* enjoyed priority of *imperium*, so his *adiutor* was a secondary commander, although the *adiutor*'s independent possession of *imperium* made him a uniquely powerful aide.

CATULUS VS. FALTO

A passage in Valerius Maximus that seems to illustrate consular *imperium maius* over praetors is his story about the disputed triumph of 242 BC, but this is also a false lead. In this event, the consul C. Lutatius Catulus had been granted a triumph for his victory over the Carthaginians in the Battle of the Aegates Islands, but the praetor Q. Valerius Falto—who had been sent along with Catulus in an unspecified capacity—demanded this triumph for himself on the grounds that he had been the actual commander in charge of the Roman fleet during the battle, since the consul had been incapacitated by a previous wound.[63] Valerius reports that Falto's judicial challenge (a *sponsio*) was taken seriously, and a judge was appointed to determine the case.[64] When the judge got Falto to admit that Catulus as consul had been invested with greater (*superior*) *auspicium* and *imperium*, Falto's claim was denied. At first glance, Valerius's account of this case seems to indicate that a consul had *imperium maius* and a praetor *imperium minus*, and that this difference in *imperium* accounted for the judge's decision, but this conclusion cannot be supported. To begin with, in this story Falto's claim on the triumph is apparently

---

62. Livy 10.26.2–4.

63. Val. Max. 2.8.2.

64. Richardson (1975) 51 points out that the *sponsio* was no longer used in this manner when Valerius Maximus was writing in the imperial era, which he interprets as evidence that Valerius was citing a reliable source.

taken seriously by all parties, which indicates that there was no clear-cut reason (like the inferiority of his *imperium*) why his claim should have been disqualified. If everyone knew or believed that consuls had more or greater *imperium* than praetors, then Falto would have been acting in an irrational manner by making a claim so obviously false, and no one should have credited that claim or accepted the possibility that he could have been in the right.[65] Furthermore, Valerius's description of this event is demonstrably wrong, since the *Fasti Triumphales* indicate that Falto *did indeed triumph* two days after Lutatius.[66] While Valerius presents the *sponsio* as a fairly clear-cut matter about *imperium* and *auspicium*, the fact that Falto did indeed triumph undermines this reasoning.

The fact that Falto was given a triumph demonstrates that he had possessed his own *imperium* and *auspicium*, that his authority had been entirely separate and independent from the consul's authority, that Catulus had no means (like *imperium maius*) to subordinate the *imperium* of the praetor, and that Falto must have argued successfully that he was holding his own *provincia* during this campaign — otherwise, he could not have triumphed. The senate did not instruct Catulus and Falto to share a single triumph for the victory but gave each of them a triumph, indicating either that both had possessed an independent *provincia* or that some unusual exception was made to allow each to celebrate separate triumphs for the same victory.[67] Perhaps Falto did indeed present enough evidence to demonstrate his claim on the triumph, but the senate — enjoying its great victory over Carthage and not wishing to insult Catulus by revoking his triumph — made the extraordinary concession of authorizing a second triumph for the same battle. Or perhaps Falto had been in command of a different *provincia* against the Carthaginians on Sicily but took command of Catulus's navy when the consul was disabled (similar to the case of Furius Purpurio above). Whether or not this was the case, the fact that Falto did triumph demonstrates that he was a fully competent military commander

---

65. Bergk (2011) 72 points out about this story, "in my view, this clear and seemingly unambiguous decision is striking. The relationship, or more precisely the hierarchy among the military commanders, simply cannot have been so easily determined, otherwise the very discussion (as well as any arbitration) would not have been necessary."

66. *Act. Trium.* for 241 BC.

67. After the Battle of Metaurus (207 BC), the senate likewise offered a triumph to each of the participating consuls in spite of the fact that one of the consuls had no claim on the *provincia* in which the battle had been won. The scope of the victory drove the senate to honor both consuls, but the consul who did not hold the *provincia* declined his own triumph and instead took a lesser role in his colleague's triumph. Falto was less tactful.

and that the consul Catulus had not possessed *imperium maius* or any other type of superior authority that would have enabled him to subordinate Falto's authority and to suppress his demand for a triumph.

M. PORCIUS CATO AND Q. CAECILIUS
METELLUS PIUS SCIPIO NASICA IN 47 BC

After Caesar defeated Pompey at the Battle of Pharsalus in 48 BC, many of Pompey's supporters retreated to Africa where they intended to regroup. The most senior of these fugitives were M. Porcius Cato (pr. 54) and Q. Caecilius Metellus Pius Scipio Nasica (cos. 52), both of whom had probably received special grants of *imperium* as *privati* at the outset of the civil war in 49 BC.[68] In Pompey's absence, it was natural that one of these two men would assume command of the Pompeian forces in Africa, and the process by which Scipio was chosen to do this seems — at first glance — to support the idea of *imperium maius*. Dio describes this action as follows:

> Scipio and Cato, who surpassed all the others by far — Scipio in reputation (ἀξιώσει) and Cato in sagacity (συνέσει) — came to an agreement, and they gained the support of the others and persuaded them to turn over all affairs to Scipio. Cato could have held command equally with Scipio or solely by himself, but he did not wish to do so because he thought it would be most harmful in the present situation, and because he was lesser than the other in political reputation (ὅτι τῷ πολιτικῷ ἀξιώματι ἠλαττοῦτο αὐτοῦ). For he thought it important in military affairs even more than elsewhere that a commander have priority over others by some law (νόμῳ δή τινι τῶν ἄλλων προκεκρίσθαι), and on account of this he yielded command to Scipio willingly, and beyond this he also gave him the army which he had led.[69]

Plutarch also records the decision-making process by which Scipio became the commander in chief:

> Although everyone thought it right that Cato should command — and Scipio and Varus first among these stepped down and handed the command over to him — he refused to break the laws on account of which they were fighting a law-breaker, and with a proconsul being present he refused to place himself (being a propraetor) in command. For Scipio had been ap-

---

68. By senatorial decree, Scipio had been given the *provincia* of Syria in 49 BC (Caes. *BC* 1.6), and Cato had been sent to hold Sicily (Cic. *Att.* 7.15.2, 10.12.2, 10.16.3; Caes. *BC* 1.30; Plut. *Cat. Min.* 53.1–3).

69. Dio 42.57.2–3 (Drogula, trans.).

pointed a proconsul, and many took courage on account of his name, thinking they would be successful with a Scipio holding command in Africa.[70]

If one is predisposed to believe that *imperium maius* existed in the republic, these passages seem to provide ample evidence to support this view: Cary (Loeb edition) translated Dio's comment that Cato as a propraetor was τῷ πολιτικῷ ἀξιώματι ἠλαττοῦτο αὐτοῦ as "he was inferior to the other in official rank," and Plutarch's statement suggests that it was illegal for a propraetor to exercise command in the presence of a proconsul. In this reading, it is easy to interpret Dio and Plutarch as saying that a consul or proconsul held higher or greater *imperium* than a praetor or propraetor, and that a praetor or propraetor was legally required to yield command of his *provincia* to any consul or proconsul who appeared in that sphere. But this understanding depends on certain faulty assumptions.

While Dio's reference to ὁ πολιτικὸς ἀξίωμα can be taken to signify *imperium*, its more usual meaning is a person's dignity, honor, or reputation, for which reason Mason identifies *dignitas* as the primary Latin translation of ἀξίωμα.[71] Under this more usual reading, Dio is explaining that Scipio as an ex-consul held greater *dignitas* than Cato as an ex-praetor, and therefore Cato is following Roman social norms (rather than legal requirement) by handing supreme command to the more prestigious man. Dio goes out of his way to emphasize that Cato *voluntarily* acknowledged Scipio as the supreme commander and that he did so for military efficiency rather than out of legal necessity. Dio does say that Cato believed commanders should have priority over others "by some law" (ἑώρα δυνάμενον τὸ τὸν ἄρχοντα καὶ νόμῳ δή τινι τῶν ἄλλων προκεκρίσθαι), but this statement strongly suggests that there was no *existing law* that determined whether Cato or Scipio should hold supreme command; priority of command needed to be established in some formal way, but the criteria for this determination were not clear to Cato and Scipio. If the criteria had been levels of *imperium* and if proconsuls had held *imperium maius* than propraetors, then Scipio's precedence should have been obvious to all, and Dio's vague phrase "by some law" should have been out of place. Rather, the reason for the

---

70. Plut. *Cat. Min.* 57.3 (Drogula, trans.): ἀξιούντων δὲ πάντων ἄρχειν αὐτόν, καὶ πρώτων τῶν περὶ Σκηπίωνα καὶ Οὔαρον ἐξισταμένων καὶ παραδιδόντων τὴν ἡγεμονίαν, οὐκ ἔφη καταλύσειν τοὺς νόμους περὶ ὧν τῷ καταλύοντι πολεμοῦσιν, οὐδὲ ἑαυτὸν ἀντιστράτηγον ὄντα παρόντος ἀνθυπάτου προτάξειν. ἀνθύπατος γὰρ ὁ Σκηπίων ἀπεδέδεικτο, καὶ θάρσος εἶχον οἱ πολλοὶ διὰ τοὔνομα, κατορθώσειν ἄρχοντος ἐν Λιβύῃ Σκηπίωνος.

71. Mason (1974) 23, who identifies *imperium* only as a secondary meaning of ἀξίωμα (and see *LSJ*).

uncertainty was that neither Cato nor Scipio had been assigned the *provincia* of Africa by the state, so there was no clear mechanism to determine which of the two *imperium*-bearing commanders should have priority of *imperium* in that sphere. In the absence of provincial assignment, some other way was needed to determine precedence, and Cato and Scipio seem to have agreed that the superior *dignitas* of the ex-consul made Scipio the proper commander in chief, an agreement that created a single clear general. Thus, Dio's passage actually reinforces the argument that the superiority of a consul to a praetor on the battlefield was social rather than legal; provincial assignment gave a praetor or propraetor priority of *imperium* in his assigned *provincia*, but he might *willingly* choose to yield supreme command of his *provincia* to a consul or proconsul, who held greater *dignitas* and position in Roman society, who probably had more military experience and a larger army, and who had the *auctoritas* to help or hinder the praetor's future political aspirations.

Plutarch's version of this story likewise undermines the idea of *imperium maius*. Although the passage seems to say that Roman law required that a proconsul always outranked or superseded a propraetor in a military command, this was not at all the case. In the first place, Plutarch is explicit that everyone — including Scipio and Varus (who had been holding Africa for the Pompeians as a *legatus pro praetore*) — automatically assumed that Cato should have the command. If Roman law stated that Scipio should hold command by virtue of his proconsular status, no one in the army seemed to know or care about it, since they all expected Cato to assume command. Second, if Scipio had possessed *imperium maius*, it seems incomprehensible that anyone could have considered making Cato the supreme commander, since this would have been an egregious violation of law. Third, although Plutarch makes it sound like propraetors were not permitted to hold supreme command over proconsuls, this was not at all the case: as discussed earlier, in 203 BC the proconsul M. Cornelius Cethegus (cos. 204 BC) served in Ariminum under the command of the praetor P. Quinctilius Varus, and it was the praetor who exercised supreme command of the *provincia* and who gave combat orders in the critical battle against Mago. There was no legal reason why Cato could not have assumed supreme command of Africa with Scipio present, but the proconsul's greater *dignitas* and social status made it far more appropriate that the senior man should have the command. As the champion of the *mos maiorum* and tradition, Cato was strongly motivated to show proper deference to a man higher up on the *cursus honorum*, and Plutarch points out that he gave equal considerations to the positive effect Scipio's command would have on the morale of the soldiers, since the Cornelii Scipiones had always been successful in Africa. Finally, Plutarch says that Scipio and Varus initially "stepped down and handed the command" to Cato, which must indicate a debate on possession of the *provincia*, and not on relative levels of *imperium*—Scipio was not relinquishing or adjusting his *imperium* but was offering to give priority of *imperium* in Africa to Cato (Varus, as a *legatus*, probably did not have *imperium*). While it is easy for someone looking for evidence of *imperium maius* to point to this episode and interpret Dio's and Plutarch's words as providing evidence to support their assumptions, such an interpretation is not tenable in light of the passages as a whole, which clearly show that Cato could have exercised supreme command in Africa legitimately, but he voluntarily chose to follow social convention and defer to Scipio, who was his social (but not legal) superior.

In summary, the relationship between the consuls and praetors is perhaps the most confusing in all Roman government, because they gradually evolved from a single office (the archaic praetorship) and the differences between them were customary more than constitutional. In strict legal and religious terms, the consul and praetor were virtually identical: both were elected in the *comitia centuriata* and received a *lex curiata*, both exercised the highest levels of *potestas* and *auspicium* in Rome, and both had the right to take up *imperium* outside the city and command a *provincia* assigned to them by the state. Over time, the college of archaic praetors would separate into two consuls and a praetor, but this distinction was never established in constitutional law, and they were not as different as modern historians generally assume. In Rome, the greater *dignitas* and *auctoritas* of the consulship made it the senior office, and praetors usually received smaller armies and lesser commands, but in the field there was no real difference between the *imperium* of a consul and the *imperium* of a praetor.

Prorogation

According to Roman tradition, one of the most important checks placed on magistrates' use of power was their limitation to a single year in office. This meant that the authority of all Roman magistrates—the *potestas* that enabled them to perform their official duties within Rome and (for some) the ability to take up *imperium* outside of the city—automatically and unavoidably expired at the end of their term, rendering them once again private citizens (*privati*). Likewise, if a consul or praetor were in command of a military *provincia* when his term in office expired, his possession of that *provincia* automatically expired along with his office, although he would retain his *imperium* until he reentered the city (crossing the *pomerium*) or until the Roman state voted to strip him of his authority. While consuls and praetors had a strict limit on how long they could retain their office and military command, their ability to retain *imperium* beyond the expiration of their office enabled them to request and hold triumphs as ex-consuls and ex-praetors (i.e., as *privati*). This time limit would have put pressure on early Roman commanders to complete their assigned *provincia* quickly, although the close proximity of Rome's enemies in the early republic probably made it easy for most commanders to conduct their military campaigns within their yearlong magistracy.[72] If a commander could not complete his assigned *provincia* during his magistracy, the command could be reassigned to a successor.

The single-year terms for magistrates, and the automatic expiration of *potestas* and *provinciae*, had three desirable effects. First, it was a powerful motivation for commanders to be aggressive and achieve glory quickly for themselves, which would (or could) translate into positive gains for the state as well. Second, single-year terms were strong protections against magisterial corruption and oppression in the early republic, since officeholders could not escape being held accountable for their actions once their magistracies expired. Third, the strict time limits ensured that opportunities for command would be shared among the aristocracy, and no single aristocrat could monopolize military command. Such limits were also strong checks on the behavior of commanders on campaign, because the imminent expiration of their *provinciae* would restore their soldiers to civilian status, in which capacity they would be able to sit in judgment on their former commander for any misdeeds or abuses he committed while in command.

This traditional practice is said to have changed in 327 BC when the senate ordered the consul Q. Publilius Philo, whose magistracy was about to expire, to continue to perform his duties as a military commander beyond the expiration of his consulship. Normally, the senate would have dispatched one of the incoming consuls to take over the *provincia*, but Philo was on the verge of capturing Palaeopolis and of completing his *provincia*, so it probably seemed imprudent to send a new consul to take over a command that would be completed within days. We have no idea how the senate described and defined this action at the time, or how Philo understood his extension of command, but Livy describes the decision as follows:

72. Polyb. 1.31.4, 18.39.1–4 and 42.1–5 refers to the pressure on commanders to finish their campaigns in a single year.

Therefore, since the days for elections were pressing, and since it was not for the good of the Republic that Publilius — who was already threatening the walls of the enemy — should be called away from the hope of taking the city within days, legislation was moved through the tribunes, who brought the proposal to the people that, when Q. Publilius should step down from the consulship, he should continue to manage the campaign *pro consule* until he should bring the war with the Greeks to an end.[73]

Livy refers to this extension of command as a prorogation of *imperium*, and he specifies that Philo was the first Roman commander to enjoy such an extension (*prorogatio imperii non ante in ullo facta*).[74] Since Philo was performing the military responsibilities of a consul without actually being a consul any longer, he was said to be acting "in place of a consul" (*pro consule*). In other words, he had the military authority (*imperium* and *auspicium*) and responsibility (*provincia*) of a magistrate without actually being a magistrate.[75] Despite the novelty of his position, the legitimacy of his accomplishments *pro consule*

73. Livy 8.23.11–12: *itaque cum et comitiorum dies instaret et Publilium imminentem hostium muris avocari ab spe capiendae in dies urbis haud e re publica esset, actum cum tribunis est, ad populum ferrent ut, cum Q. Publilius Philo consulatu abisset, pro consule rem gereret quoad debellatum cum Graecis esset* (Drogula, trans.). There was a long delay in electing consuls for 326 BC (fifteen *interreges* were needed — Livy 8.23.17), which may have contributed to the decision to prorogue Philo. See Oakley (1997–2004) 2.658–61 for commentary.

74. Livy 8.26.7. Livy (3.4.9–11) and Dionysius (*AR* 9.63.2) refer to an occasion in 464 BC when the senate instructed an ex-consul, T. Quinctius Capitolinus Barbatus, to deliver a force of allies to the consul Sp. Furius Medullinus Fusus, who had suffered a setback against the Aequi. Livy and Dionysius refer to Barbatus as acting *pro consule*, which contradicts Livy's later statement that Philo was the first man to be prorogued *pro consule*. It is likely that — since Barbatus was commanding allied units and not Roman legions, and since he did not have a *provincia* of his own but was delivering soldiers to a consul in the consul's *provincia* — Barbatus should not be considered a true *pro consule* but something closer to a *legatus* or even a *praefectus*.

75. Livy stated (36.39.10) that a proconsul triumphed *non in magistratu* and repeatedly describes promagistrates as men serving beyond the completion of their magistracies (22.22.1, 26.28.6, 30.2.3, 32.8.3); Cicero said (Cic. *Man.* 62) that both Scipio Africanus and Pompey were each, in their day, sent to Spain *non pro consule sed pro consulibus* (emphasizing that *pro consule* was not the title of an office but a job description); and the *lex Agraria* clearly establishes magistrates and promagistrates as separate but related entities (*Lex Agraria* [*RS* 2 ll. 30, 34–36, 72, 87]: *magistratus prove magistratu queive pro eo inperio iudicio potestateve erit*). There is a debate over whether the promagistrate retained his *auspicium militiae*, or whether it lapsed automatically along with his magistracy. Cicero (*Div.* 2.76–77) states plainly that promagistrates did not have *auspicium*, but if this was so, it is difficult to see how any promagistrate could have triumphed, since the celebration of a triumph required the taking of the auspices, which required *auspicium*. Perhaps Cicero was thinking of *auspicium urbana*, which certainly expired along with one's magistracy.

was not questioned: he was awarded a triumph for his capture of Palaeopolis in spite of the fact that he achieved this capture after the expiration of his consulship, indicating that a military victory won *pro consule* was every bit as valid and glorious as those accomplishments achieved while in office.[76] While Philo is the first promagistrate[77] in Roman tradition, the prorogation of retiring consuls became regular practice within a few decades, and by 241 BC (if not sooner) praetors began to be prorogued *pro praetore*.[78] The development and use of promagistrates signifies two fundamental changes in the nature and conception of provincial commanders. First, prorogation made it possible for individual commanders to hold on to their commands indefinitely, thereby weakening one of the fundamental checks the Romans had over their magistrate-commanders. Second, and more important, prorogation created an official who was purely a military commander, which is to say a military commander with no civilian authority or responsibility in Rome. A proconsul or propraetor had only the authority to conduct war in his assigned *provincia*; he had no other concerns or duties.

From a military perspective, prorogation was a simple idea: a commander was instructed to continue doing what he was already doing, so no new authority was needed except for the authorization to continue conducting the same campaign beyond the date at which the commander's magistracy ended. Indeed, the idea of prorogation seems to have been so obvious to the Romans that there was little discussion among them about the conceptual nature of the promagistrate in comparison to the magistrate. As a result, scholars have had some difficulty understanding the legal definition of the promagistrate, because it was something of a legal anomaly: a private individual (a *privatus*)

76. *Act. Trium.* for 326/5 BC (*primus procos.*), Livy 8.26.7.

77. A brief disclaimer is necessary to qualify the terms used in this and later chapters. Strictly speaking, the words "proconsul," "propraetor," "proquaestor," and "promagistrate" are, as this chapter demonstrates, products of the late republic and early empire. Thus the middle republic did not possess *proconsules*, but men acting *pro consulibus*. Likewise, there was no such thing as a *promagistratus*, but a man functioning *pro magistratu*. It would be stylistically disastrous, however, to avoid using the more familiar and convenient (if technically incorrect) terms of proconsul and promagistrate. The reader is kindly requested to forgive the anachronistic use of terms such as "promagistrate" that have been used for readability.

78. Livy 10.25.11, 10.26.12–15, 10.29.3–4, 10.30.1. Although Rome continued to prorogue consuls following the precedent of Philo, it would be eighty-five years before a prorogation would be used to continue a praetor in a *provincia* (in 241 BC: *MRR* 1.220), which is probably further evidence that the distinction between consul and praetor was not firmly established until the middle of the third century BC. The propraetors created in 295 BC had not been prorogued praetors but private citizens empowered to act *pro praetore* by a consul.

invested with military authority that only senior magistrates were permitted to possess. Several scholars have wrestled with this problem, and they have generally come to the conclusion that prorogation was technically a circumvention of the law. Jashemski and Brennan both referred to the use of proconsuls as a "legal fiction" that enabled the senate to provide itself with extra commanders that could not have existed otherwise under strict adherence to traditional legal practice, and Kloft suggested that the Romans themselves probably did not have a clear understanding of the legal difference between a magistrate and a promagistrate.[79] While all three may well be correct, a better explanation is perhaps possible.

A handful of references in ancient texts enable us to draw some conclusions. To begin with, prorogation was a legal process by which a retiring magistrate was authorized to continue his duties and retain certain prerogatives for a fixed time. The word *prorogatio* itself refers to an official vote by the people, since a *rogatio* was a question that was put before a citizen assembly for formal vote. The extension of a consul or praetor in his command was originally authorized by a vote of the people and carried the weight of law, although it eventually became the senate's prerogative to authorize such extensions through *senatus consulta* (which the people could override with a *lex*).[80] The concrete legal nature of prorogation is evident in the way that early cases of prorogation stipulated precise durations for extensions of time in command: early promagistrates were often limited to an extra six months in command, although longer (and even indefinite) periods could be granted, such as when Scipio Africanus was prorogued *rei gerendae fine*.[81] Prorogation did not create a new commander or a new type of commander, but simply enabled a normal commander (a consul or praetor) to continue to perform his consular or praetorian military responsibilities beyond the expiration of his office. This idea of continuation is seen in the use of original promagisterial titles: a consul invariably

79. Jashemski (1950) 2, Brennan (2000) 73 and (2004) 57, Kloft (1977) 62–76. See also Mommsen (1887–88) 636–45, Giovannini (1983) 37–44, and Develin (1975) 716. Most scholars simply call the promagistrate a person who acts like a magistrate while not being one: Stevenson (1939) 55, Jolowicz and Nicholas (1972) 67, Richardson (1976a) 29, Cornell (1995) 360, Kunkel and Wittmann (1995) 15–16, Lintott (1999a) 113, and Brennan (2000) 73.

80. See Livy 8.23.11–12 (cited above), Mommsen (1887–88) 1.643, Jashemski (1950) 11–14, McDonald (1953) 143–44, Hölkeskamp (1987) 147–50, Brennan (2000) 73–75, 187–90.

81. Six-month prorogation: Livy 10.16.1 (*bis*) (see Brennan [2000] 74 and 81). In 203 BC Scipio Africanus was prorogued *rei gerendae fine* (Livy 30.1.10). Livy even remarks that repeated prorogation of a promagistrate is unnecessary, since a single prorogation can empower a former magistrate to retain his command for years (Livy 33.25.11, 40.39.1, 41.14.11).

became *pro consule* and a praetor became *pro praetore*, although the Romans frequently referred to promagistrates simply as consul and praetor.[82] In trying to work out the Roman legal understanding of the promagistrate, the critical question is, What did prorogation actually do that enabled an outgoing magistrate-commander to retain his military command?

Later authors, and Livy in particular, refer to prorogation as *prorogatio imperii*, which would seem to suggest a vote put to the people regarding the *imperium* of an outgoing magistrate. Given the apparent clarity of this statement, most historians have generally accepted that prorogation extended or renewed a commander's *imperium*, thereby enabling him to continue exercising military authority in his *provincia militiae*.[83] Yet this interpretation is contradicted by the solid evidence (discussed in chapter 2) that tenure of *imperium* was not temporally limited and did not automatically expire at the end of a magistrate's year in office. If a man could retain his *imperium* for years while waiting outside of Rome in hopes of a triumph, a retiring consul on campaign would hardly need an extension or reauthorization of *imperium* in order to continue his campaign *pro consule*. *Imperium* did not automatically expire unless a commander crossed the *pomerium* and entered Rome, so *prorogatio imperii* cannot be taken literally to represent a change, extension, or renewal of a man's *imperium*. An ex-magistrate could likewise retain his *auspicium militiae* indefinitely outside of Rome while awaiting a triumph. Despite its apparent clarity, the phrase *prorogatio imperii* must be taken in a more general sense to mean an extension of command. Because consuls and praetors needed military authority (*imperium* and *auspicium militiae*) and a command or field of responsibility (*provincia*) to function as a military commander, and since the general's authority did not expire, it must have been his possession of a command (*provincia*) that needed extension.[84] *Prorogatio imperii* must have been the authorization for a commander to continue holding his *provincia* beyond the expiration of his magistracy.

One need only consider the case of Metellus Creticus and Marcius Rex mentioned earlier: after laying down their consular *provinciae*, both men lingered for years outside of the *pomerium* as proconsuls without *provinciae*, the

82. For example, see Livy 8.23.11–12, 24.10.4 and 31.8.9.

83. For example, see Jashemski (1950), Lowenstein (1973) 163, Develin (1975) and (1985) 37–38, Kloft (1977), Hölkeskamp (1987), Lintott (1999a) 113, Brennan (2000) 73–74 and (2004) 39, Mousourakis (2003) 81, Southern (2007) 66, Beck, Duplá, Jehne, and Pina Polo (2011) 6, Beck (2011) 88.

84. The *provincia* was the only defining aspect of a commander that automatically expired after a fixed period; *imperium* and *auspicium militiae* could be retained for years.

whole time retaining their *imperium* and *auspicium militiae* in hopes that they might receive permission to triumph. When the Catilinarian conspiracy was revealed in 63 BC, however, it took only a decree of the senate for both men to once again become active military commanders.[85] This reactivation was accomplished not by a *lex curiata* (used in grants of *imperium*) but by a simple decree of the senate that the two men were to receive new *provinciae*: Creticus was given Apulia and the surrounding countryside, and Marcius the city of Faesulae. It had been the lack of a *provincia* — and not *imperium* — that had prevented the men from acting as military commanders while they had lingered outside of Rome hoping for a triumph. Whereas the *comitia curiata* voted on grants of *imperium*, the senate determined what *provincia* a particular commander would hold. It was not within the power of the senate to grant, adjust, alter, extend, or revoke *imperium*, nor did the senate need to extend the *imperium* of men like Metellus Creticus and Marcius Rex, who waited year after year outside the city retaining their *imperium* and *auspicium militiae* in hopes of a triumph. Whereas the senate had no control over a commander's *imperium*, his *provincia* was merely an assignment that was given to him by the state (usually by the senate), and it could be changed, expanded, or removed simply by the will of the senate. In other words, the *provincia* was easily adjustable, whereas *imperium* was not subject to alteration (merely cancellation by a vote of the people). That prorogation signified an extension of a military *provincia* is indicated by many passages in Livy (by far the chief source for the phrase *prorogatio imperii*), in which he emphasizes that commanders were prorogued in a specific *provincia*.[86] *Prorogatio imperii*, therefore, was an extension of a general's possession of a *provincia*.

The fact that a commander's *imperium* did not expire at the end of his magistracy provides an important clue for another debated topic about pro-

---

85. Sall. *Cat.* 30.3: *igitur senati decreto Q. Marcius Rex Faesulas, Q. Metellus Creticus in Apuliam circumque ea loca missi — ei utrique ad urbem imperatores erant, impediti ne triumpharent calumnia paucorum, quibus omnia honesta atque inhonesta vendere mos erat.*

86. For example: *et quibus prorogatum imperium erat easdem quas priori anno regiones obtinuerunt* (24.12.8); *et Q. Fulvio Capua provincia decreta prorogatumque in annum imperium* (26.28.6–7); *et P. Sulpicio ut eadem classe Macedoniam Graeciamque provinciam haberet prorogatum in annum imperium est* (27.22.10); *C. Hostilio Tubulo ut Capuam provinciam haberet prorogatum in annum imperium est* (28.10.15); *in eadem provincia et C. Servilio prorogatum imperium si consulem manere ad urbem senatui placuisset* (30.27.6); *Flaminio Fulvioque in Hispaniis prorogatum imperium* (35.20.11); *prioris anni magistratibus C. Laelio cum suo exercitu prorogatum in annum imperium est, prorogatum et P. Iunio propraetore in Etruria cum eo exercitu, qui in provincia esset, et M. Tuccio propraetori in Bruttiis et Apulia* (37.50.13); *P. Cornelio et M. Baebio prorogatum imperium iussique provincias obtinere donec consules venissent* (40.36.7).

magistrates: their rank or status in comparison to magistrates. As has already been argued, there was only one level or type of *imperium* in early Rome, so all military commanders possessed the exact same type of *imperium*. While the preeminence of the consuls might induce one to believe they had a higher degree of *imperium* than promagistrates, this would be a mistaken assumption. Syme noted that the precedence of a consul over a proconsul was only "vague and traditional," and Girardet has demonstrated that all promagistrates had the same *imperium*, which was identical to the *imperium* held by the consuls.[87] A propraetor had the exact same *imperium* as a consul and could wield supreme authority within his own *provincia*, although he might find it expedient and prudent to show voluntary cooperation to a request made by the consul. It seems impossible that a commander's *imperium* could somehow change level or strength when he became a promagistrate, or that some automatic or passive force without agency could bring about a change to the *imperium* that he had received and auspicated through specific ceremonies in Rome. Furthermore, no change occurred to the number of *fasces* and *secures* a commander possessed when he became a promagistrate: proconsuls retained all twelve of the consul's *fasces*, and propraetors all six of the praetor's.[88] If (as some believe) the number of *fasces* a magistrate had represented the degree of his *imperium*, than one would expect any decrease in *imperium* to be visually represented by a decrease in the number of a promagistrate's *fasces*.

The available evidence indicates that proconsuls were understood to hold the same level of authority as consuls. The most famous case might be the dispute in 105 BC between the consul Cn. Mallius Maximus and the proconsul Q. Servilius Caepio. Both men had been assigned *provinciae* against the Gauls, but the two men were unable to find a way to cooperate with one another, with the result that both of their armies were destroyed by the Cimbri and Teutones.[89] If the consul Mallius had possessed greater authority than the proconsul, then surely Caepio would have received most or all of the blame for the defeat because he had refused to acknowledge the orders of a consul with *imperium maius*. As it happened, the Romans blamed Mallius for the defeat as well as Caepio (both men were condemned and exiled), indicating that neither man was required to obey the instructions of the other.[90] Similarly, in

87. Syme (1939) 330 and Girardet (2000) 176–81. See also Kloft (1977) esp. 72–76 and Beck (2011) 86–88.

88. Staveley (1963) 460.

89. Livy *Per.* 67, Flor. 1.38.4, Gran. Lic. 33.12–13, Dio 27 fr. 91.1–4.

90. Auct. *Ad Herenn.* 1.24; Cic. *De Or.* 2.124–25, *Brut.* 135, *Tusc.* 5.14, *Balb.* 28; Gran. Lic. 33.13.

291 BC the consul L. Postumius Megellus was given as his *provincia* one part of the Samnites to campaign against, while the proconsul Q. Fabius Maximus Gurges (cos. 292) was to retain as his *provincia* another part of the Samnite tribes.[91] Out of arrogance, the consul claimed all of the Samnite tribes as his *provincia* and demanded that the proconsul leave, which he did, yielding (as Dionysius explains) to madness rather than authority. Since the consul had no right to command a proconsul in this manner or to deprive him of his *provincia*, two tribunes of the plebs prosecuted Postumius, and he was condemned to pay a large fine, demonstrating that his claim of authority over the proconsul had been illegal. Promagistrates were in no way inferior or lesser commanders than magistrates, which conforms to Rome's general attitude that provincial commanders should exist within a horizontal command structure rather than in a steep vertical chain of command.

Another practice by which a man could be authorized to act in place of a commander (*pro praetore*) requires brief attention. While most promagistrates were created by prorogation (official extension of one's *provincia* by the state), the hazards and vagaries of war required that a Roman commander could in an emergency appoint one of his officers to assume command of part or all of his army. Most obviously, this delegation of authority was necessary to replace a dying commander, but it might also be used if a commander needed to leave or divide his army. The first example of this in Roman tradition appears in Livy's account of 295 BC, when both consuls needed to hand over their armies to a lieutenant: P. Decius Mus, on the verge of devoting himself to death in battle, handed command of his army to M. Livius Denter, while his colleague Q. Fabius Maximus Rullianus left his legate L. Cornelius Scipio (Barbatus) in command of the army while he (the consul) returned to Rome to hold elections.[92] In both cases, the consuls instructed their chosen lieutenant to act *pro praetore* (in place of a *praetor*), a title that has led scholars to believe that the consuls delegated their *imperium* to the lieutenants, such that the *legati pro praetore* actually possessed *imperium*.[93]

While such delegation is possible, it seems unlikely. Given the tremendous controls the Romans placed on the conferral and use of *imperium* — including election by the centuriate assembly, passage of a *lex curiata*, and requisite reli-

91. Dion. Hal. *AR* 17–18.4.4–5.4.

92. Livy 10.25.11–12 (Scipio), and 10.29.3–4 (Denter).

93. For evidence of this title, see *ILS* 37 and Cic. *Att.* 10.8a.pr. See Mommsen (1887–88) 1.680–86, Jashemski (1950) 24–27, 37–39, Kloft (1977) 98–99, Richardson (1986) 35, Lintott (1999a) 114 (who also allows [without explanation] that the senate itself may have been able to delegate *imperium*).

gious ceremonies and auspication on exiting the city — it seems impossible that the Romans would permit their commanders simply to give *imperium* to their subordinates without some kind of state control. The only possible examples of a commander conferring authority in this way are a consul's nomination of a dictator, and the apparent capacity of a praetor in Rome to appoint a commander *cum imperio* to undertake a small or temporary military task when no regular commander was available.[94] The essential difference is that both of these actions were usually authorized by the senate: the senate normally instructed a consul to perform the requisite ritual to name a dictator (although the senate and people could also appoint one), and it was the senate that instructed a praetor in Rome to appoint a commander to carry out a necessary military task (and presumably certain rituals were followed here too; perhaps even a *lex curiata* was passed). The official authorization in these cases undermines the notion that commanders in the field could simply give *imperium* to a subordinate. Some scholars — who accept that *imperium* existed in different levels — have sought to make sense of this problem by arguing that commanders could only delegate a lower degree of *imperium* than they themselves possessed, but this is contradicted by the arguments put forward in chapter 2, and by the examples above of praetors appointing new commanders.[95]

In all likelihood, a commander's instruction that one of his officers should assume command *pro praetore* was not a legal delegation or conferral of *imperium*; rather, it was a type of battlefield promotion intended to maintain the operational capacity of the army. The junior officer was instructed to act "as a commander" (*pro praetore*), but he did so under the aegis of his commander's *imperium*. Thus the officer *pro praetore* partook of his commander's *imperium* but did not possess *imperium* in his own right, nor did he possess *auspicium* or the *provincia* in which he was operating. He was not a commander in chief (an *imperator*), he could not triumph, and he was not kept in command any longer than necessary. Still, the official bestowal of the status *pro praetore* on an officer by the commander in chief was probably sufficient to endow that officer with the de facto (if not de jure) authority to exercise military command, even in the absence of the commander in chief. Since most Roman armies contained

94. The appointment of dictators has been discussed in chapter 2. Praetors selecting a commander: Livy 23.34.13–15 (215 BC): *decreverunt patres ut Q. Fulvius Flaccus [praetor] . . . mitteret . . . [ad provinciam] cum imperio quem ipsi videretur*; and Livy 28.46.13 (205 BC): *et Cn. Servilio praetori negotium datum ut, si e re publica censeret esse, duas urbanas legione, imperio cui videretur dato, ex urbe duci iuberet*. See Vishnia (1996) 68.

95. Brennan (2000) 36–37, 640–47 and (2004) 49, Richardson (1986) 66.

only one commander with *imperium*, the death or absence of that individual could leave his army without an undisputed leader. Naturally, in the heat of battle a respected officer or soldier could rally his men and exercise social authority in the absence of their commander,[96] but this was an *ad hoc* solution, whereas the appointment of an officer *pro praetore* was a necessary form of battlefield promotion that could maintain the command structure of an army.

On the whole, the introduction of prorogation was one of the most important steps the Romans took to provide enough commanders to satisfy the city's growing military needs, but it also eased some of the controls their state had placed on the exercise of military authority. By 367 BC at the latest, the Romans had determined that three — and only three — regular military commanders would be appointed each year (although the dictatorship made short-term emergency appointments possible), but the introduction of prorogation by the senate forty years later reversed this limitation by enabling the Romans to keep commanders active in the field beyond the expiration of their magistracy. This was possible through a manipulation of the concept of the *provincia*, the area of official responsibility that had hitherto been given only to sitting magistrates. Previously, tenure of a *provincia* had always expired automatically at the end of a man's magistracy, so the introduction of prorogation in 327 BC was actually an exception to this rule, enabling Philo to retain his *provincia* longer than was traditionally allowable. As a consequence of this action, the Romans created a new distinction or separation between the *provincia* and the magistrate, enabling the former to exist without the latter. Although earlier commanders had been able to retain their *imperium* indefinitely beyond the expiration of their magistracy, they had been unable to do much with that military authority once their possession of their *provincia* expired. When the Romans began extending possession of *provinciae*, however, men who were no longer magistrates could exercise the full force of their *imperium* in their *provincia* for as long as the people wished. Perhaps the Romans (at the time) gave little thought to the long-term consequences of introducing prorogation, since it was a pragmatic solution that enabled Philo to complete the imminent capture of Palaeopolis, and few could have guessed that this one-time special exception would eventually become normal, annual practice in Rome's empire. Still, by manipulating the basic concept of the *provincia*, the Romans established a new type of military commander; since the promagistrate held no official status or civilian authority in Rome, he was technically a

96. See, for example, *SIG*³ 700, where a quaestor in Macedonia is honored for leading a Roman army to victory after the praetor in command had been killed in battle.

private citizen invested with the full might of *imperium* and could retain and use that *imperium* to full effect within his *provincia* for as long as the state allowed. In what may have been a return to older and abandoned practice, therefore, prorogation loosened the controls on aristocratic use of military authority by enabling citizens to hold and use *imperium* without the restraints imposed by magisterial office.

Privati cum imperio and Experiments with Rank

One final but important experimentation with Rome's methods of provincial command during this period involved the complete separation of *imperium* from magisterial office. In a handful of instances during the Second Punic War, the Roman state decided to invest one of their private citizens (a *privatus*) with *imperium* and *auspicium militiae* and to assign him a *provincia*, which effectively and legally made that *privatus* a military commander, even if he had not yet held a magistracy entitled to possess *imperium* and *auspicium militiae*. This was similar to the battlefield commission of a lieutenant to act *pro praetore*, but these *privati cum imperio* were complete commanders because they possessed a *provincia* as well as independent *imperium* and *auspicium*.[97] Still, the fact that *privati cum imperio* were not permitted to hold triumphs for their victories indicates that they were not seen as entirely legitimate commanders in the eyes of the Romans, probably because they had not held a magistracy.[98] During the many crises of the Second Punic War, this method of quickly creating an extra military commander was a useful tool that enabled the Roman people to select any man — whether or not he had ever been elected to office — and make him the commander of any *provincia* they wished. The Roman people used the legislative authority of their assemblies to authorize the conferral of *imperium* and a *provincia* on a man of their choice, thereby rendering him a fully legitimate and independent provincial commander. In the early republic, the Romans had normally achieved this purpose by having one of the consuls name a dictator, but because dictators were not permitted to leave Italy, the office became less useful as more and more of Rome's battles were fought

97. All promagistrates were technically *privati cum imperio* because they no longer held a public magistracy in Rome, but for the sake of clarity I use the term *privati cum imperio* to refer only to those men who were private citizens when they received *imperium* and their *provincia* (unlike promagistrates, who received *imperium* and a *provincia* while magistrates).

98. Livy 28.38.4 and 31.20.3, Val. Max. 2.8.5, Plut. *Pomp.* 14.1. Versnel (1970) 186–89 demonstrated that *privati cum imperio* possessed *auspicium* as well as *imperium* and a *provincia*, and argued that their inability to triumph was connected to the fact that they had not held a magistracy.

overseas.[99] Furthermore, the choice of man to become dictator had generally been at the sole discretion of the consul who named him, but *privati cum imperio* were selected by the popular assemblies, which would have been much more attractive to the Roman citizens during dangerous days of the Second Punic War. Like the dictator and the promagistrate, the *privatus cum imperio* was another Roman experiment to produce an extra commander in times of emergency.

The first recorded *privatus cum imperio* was created in 215 BC when the Romans, stunned by their incredible losses at Trebia, Trasimene, and Cannae, wanted a thoroughly capable and experienced man to take command when the consul L. Postumius Albinus was killed in battle. They elected M. Claudius Marcellus (cos. 222 BC) as suffect consul, but he was subsequently forced to step down when the augurs detected flaws in his election.[100] Determined to have their choice of commander, the Roman people ordered that Marcellus was to be invested with *imperium* and *auspicium militiae* despite his abdication from office and was to take command of a consular army against Hannibal.[101] Some modern scholars have questioned the constitutional mechanics of this event: Jashemski wondered whether the special grant occurred at all, while Develin and Stewart suggest that, since Marcellus had been praetor in the previous year, he had actually been prorogued for 215 BC and so was a promagistrate and not a *privatus cum imperio*.[102] Another possibility is that Marcellus had retained his *imperium* and *auspicium* beyond the expiration of his praetorship by remaining outside the city, in which case the senate or people only needed to vote him a *provincia* in order to enable him to exercise full military command. Whatever the process, Marcellus was clearly exercising full military command throughout 215 BC, which means he had been given a new *provincia* to undertake with his *imperium*.

The second *privatus cum imperio* may have been Cn. Cornelius Scipio who was sent to Spain with his brother in 218 BC either as an *adiutor* (with *imperium*) or as a legate (lacking *imperium*). His brother Publius held the *provincia* and the *auspicium*, but Gnaeus took command of the army when Publius returned to Italy to face Hannibal, and Publius may have instructed his

99. Dio 36.34.2. One exception is known: the dictator Atilius Calatinus was especially exempted from this restriction to go to Sicily during the First Punic War (Livy *Per.* 19).

100. Livy 23.31.13–14.

101. Livy 23.30.19 and 48.2, Plut. *Marc.* 12.1–2. See Jashemski (1950) 20.

102. Jashemski (1950) 20, Develin (1980) 357, Stewart (1998) 208. Vishnia (1996) 63–64 discusses the possible methods of this special grant, but notes that the national emergency may have made constitutional procedures irrelevant.

brother Gnaeus to act *pro praetore* in the type of battlefield commission discussed previously. This was all quite unexceptional, but two odd comments by Livy confuse the issue: he says the senate prorogued Gnaeus in 212 BC, and after Gnaeus's death Livy has the senate refer to him as a commander in chief (*imperator*).[103] If these statements are accurate, three answers are possible: Gnaeus had received a special grant of *imperium* and *auspicium* before leaving Rome (and therefore was a *privatus cum imperio* and an *adiutor*); Livy is inaccurately portraying Gnaeus's status out of respect for his family, personal accomplishments, and status as an ex-consul; or the senate or people of Rome made some extraordinary allowance or conferral of authority that is not found in surviving records. Since Marcellus and Cn. Scipio were senior senators and had both held the consulship previously, a special grant of *imperium* and *auspicium militiae* to such experienced commanders may not have seemed particularly innovative at the time, especially to Gnaeus, since the senate may have wanted to provide a second commander *cum imperio* for the army that was being sent far away to Spain.

The third known *privatus cum imperio* was from any standpoint much more unusual. The deaths of Publius and Gnaeus Scipio in Spain in 211 BC created a real crisis, because Rome's position in the Iberian Peninsula was shattered and total Carthaginian victory in that military theater seemed likely. No consul or praetor wanted to take up the Spanish *provincia* in such a dire situation, so the Roman people voted to give it to Publius's son, P. Cornelius Scipio (later Africanus), and to invest him with *imperium* and *auspicium militiae* despite the fact that he had yet to hold any magistracy entitled to possess *imperium*.[104] If anyone at the time thought it inappropriate to divorce *imperium* from magisterial office so completely, the popularity of the Scipio family and the lack of other viable options quieted any objections. Once Scipio had forced the Carthaginians out of Spain and was ready to return to Rome in 206 BC, the senate was unable to produce a successor for him from its pool of available commanders. At a loss, the people selected two private citizens who had previously held the praetorship and authorized them to take up *imperium* and assume command of Spain, performing the duties of a consul (*pro consule*) who could not otherwise be produced.[105] Since the Romans remained unwilling or unable to

103. Livy 25.3.6 and 26.2.5–6 (see Broughton [1951] 1.246 n. 10).

104. Livy 26.18.1–14, Val. Max. 3.7.1a, App. *Ib*. 18, Zon. 9.7. See Richardson (1986) 45–46 for further discussion on the election of Scipio.

105. L. Cornelius Lentulus and L. Manlius Acidinus. Although Livy (28.38.1) recorded that Lentulus and Acidinus were Scipio's lieutenants, Sumner (1970) 89 and Develin (1980) 361 have argued

dispatch magisterial or prorogued commanders to take command of the Spanish *provincia*, Spain remained under the command of *privati cum imperio* until the creation of two new praetors in 197 BC made it possible to send annual magistrates instead.[106]

Despite its short-lived use, the *privati cum imperio* would have two important influences on the development of Roman provincial command. In the first place, their creation established a precedent for completely severing military command (possession of *imperium*, *auspicium militiae*, and a *provincia*) from magisterial office. This bond had been weakened by prorogation, but it was completely shattered by the practice of investing a private citizen with *imperium*, *auspicium militiae*, and a *provincia*. Like prorogation, this was something of a return to Rome's ancient practice, since it enabled an aristocrat to exercise military authority outside Rome without holding any kind of official status in the city.

The second, and more lasting, influence of these *privati cum imperio* was the idea that magisterial precedence could be separated from the magistracy to which it properly belonged, thereby creating for the first time something similar to the idea of military rank. Before the Second Punic War, the concept of rank was not truly applicable among Rome's military commanders. The consuls' status as Rome's senior commanders derived from the greater prestige of their office as Rome's primary military commanders, from the larger armies and more important campaigns they received, from their precedence in supervising certain public functions in Rome, from their greater number of lictors and *fasces*, and (after 241 or 227 BC) from the greater exclusivity of their office as the number of annual praetors was incrementally increased to six (by 197 BC). In this respect, one would not say that a consul outranked a praetor, since a consul could not give orders to a praetor (except in particular military situations), and a praetor was not expected to obey a consul's commands. Likewise, rank did not generally apply among promagistrates, or between magistrates and promagistrates, although sitting magistrates normally enjoyed higher prestige and precedence than prorogued ex-magistrates. If a

---

convincingly that they were not, and that Scipio left part of the Roman army in the hands of his legate Marcius, while the propraetor Silanus, who had come to Spain with Scipio in 210 BC, remained in Spain in command of the other part of the army. Only after Scipio's return to Rome were Lentulus and Acidinus sent to Spain, either as *privati pro consule* (Sumner) or as *privati pro praetore* (Develin). Richardson (1986) 64–65 discusses the various emendations of this passage in Livy's text and concludes that Lentulus and Acidinus were elected *privati pro consule* in Rome in 206 BC.

106. C. Cornelius Cethegus (Livy 30.41.4–5, 31.49.7), C. Cornelius Blasio (Livy 31.50.11), and L. Stertinius (Livy 31.50.11).

praetor or promagistrate were assigned to act as an *adiutor* to a consul in the consul's *provincia*, then the *imperium* of the consul would take precedence over that of his *adiutor*, but this is a specific circumstance and does not reflect the normal relationship between two *imperium*-bearing commanders. Because Roman military commanders normally operated in a horizontal structure (one with multiple independent commanders) the idea of rank originally did not apply: supreme military authority came from possession of *imperium*, *auspicium*, and a *provincia*, not from any concept of rank. Thus, consuls were not the equivalent of generals while praetors were merely colonels—all bearers of *imperium* were generals. In this respect, the titles consul and praetor originally had no real legal significance in terms of exercising military command; they indicated different levels of prestige and status but not different levels military authority or capacity for exercising command.

In the second century BC, however, the Romans began experimenting with the titles given to different promagistrates with the apparent intent of making some commanders appear more important than others. The root of this phenomenon lay in the use of *privati cum imperio* during the Second Punic War. Such *privati* were pure military commanders—invested with *imperium* and *auspicium militiae* and assigned a *provincia*—but they were neither magistrates nor prorogued magistrates. Thus they possessed the authority and command that were common to all military commanders, but they did not possess consular or praetorian office, which conferred different levels of prestige (but not authority) on commanders. *Privati* were promagistrates in that they were acting in place of a magisterial commander (*pro magistratu*), but whereas a prorogued consul or praetor simply became a proconsul or propraetor (respectively), *privati cum imperio* did not have an office when they received their *imperium, auspicium militiae*, and *provincia*, so it was not clear whether they were acting in place of a consul (*pro consule*) or a praetor (*pro praetore*). This made no difference in legal terms, since consuls and praetors were equally capable of commanding armies, but in the highly status-conscious Roman society men naturally wanted the most prestigious title when possible. Before the creation of *privati cum imperio*, prorogation involved no real change of status; a consular magistrate became a consular promagistrate, and it would have made no sense for a praetor to be prorogued *pro consule*, since such a change of title would have been manifestly incorrect. Because the first two men appointed *privati cum imperio* (Marcellus and Cn. Scipio) were celebrated senators and former consuls, the Romans no doubt chose the more prestigious of the two titles (*pro consule*) out of respect for their previous accomplishments and because they had (in fact) been consuls most recently.[107] On the other hand, P. Scipio (Africanus) had not yet held the praetorship or consulship when he was made a *privatus cum imperio* in 210 BC, but the prestige and political muscle of his family, his own outstanding reputation as a soldier, and the fact that he was succeeding his father the proconsul drove the people to give him the more prestigious title of *privatus cum imperio pro consule*.

The situation was perhaps less clear, however, when the decision was made in 206 BC that Scipio should be succeeded in Spain by two more *privati cum imperio*. Although the two men selected for the command had only reached the praetorship, they were both given the title *pro consule*, suggesting that a precedent had been established in the minds of the Romans that the commands in Spain were consular in status, which is to say that they were of primary importance and received larger armies than existing praetorian *provinciae*.[108] That the prestigious title was an enticement is also possible, since the senate had encountered difficulty finding talented commanders willing to take up commands in Spain. Whatever the reason, Rome would continue to rely on *privati cum imperio* to supervise and protect its Spanish possessions until 197 BC, and all of these were given the title *pro consule*.

When two new praetors were created in 197 BC to assume command of the Spanish *provinciae*, they would have been keenly aware that their *provinciae* had held an unusual place in Rome's system of provincial command for eight years and that the *privati* they were replacing had enjoyed the prestigious title of *pro consule* despite never having reached the consulship. Although it was common for a Roman *provincia* to be held by a consul one year and a praetor the next, these two praetors and their supporters in Rome were able to exploit the unusual honor that had been given to the *privati* in Spain, no doubt claiming that the praetors in Nearer and Farther Spain deserved the same prestigious title of *pro consule* as the *privati* who had previously held those *provinciae*. In other words, why should praetors be given the less prestigious title of *pro praetore* when *privati* had received the more desirable title of *pro consule*? The senate apparently agreed, and when it prorogued those two praetors for

107. Develin (1980) 357 suggests that the senate sought proconsular rank for Marcellus because "such a man should be proconsul rather than propraetor."

108. Livy initially (28.38.1) refers to these two *privati* (L. Cornelius Lentulus [cos. 199 BC] and L. Manlius Acidinus [pr. 210 BC]) as *propraetores*, probably because both men were had held the praetorship previously (although neither held office at the time). In his next mention of these two men (29.13.7) he twice refers to them as being *pro consulibus*, and explicitly states that the people ordered them to hold the Spanish *provinciae pro consulibus*.

another year in Spain, it gave them the more prestigious title of *pro consule* instead of the title *pro praetore* that ex-praetors had always received.[109] In this way these two praetors in Spain became the first Roman magistrates to receive a promotion or upgrade of their title upon prorogation, and in 196 BC they were ex-praetors with the title *pro consule*.

Historians who believe in the existence of *imperium maius* and *minus* believe that this change of a praetor's title upon prorogation represents a change in the level of *imperium* he possessed and that praetors in Spain regularly had their normal praetorian *imperium* promoted to consular *imperium* (*imperium maius*). This was done, scholars argue, because the nature and challenges of the Spanish *provinciae* required consular *imperium maius* rather than praetorian *imperium minus*,[110] but this simply does not make sense. First, praetors in Spain were usually not promoted to *pro consule* until *after* their first year in command of their province, and the first pair of praetors in Spain was only prorogued *pro consule* after their successors had already been named and were in transit.[111] If command in Spain required consular *imperium*, one would expect the *comitia curiata* to confer it on praetors *before* they set out for their commands instead of waiting until the praetors' second year in their *provincia*.[112] Clearly, ex-praetors could and did command their *provinciae* successfully with the title *pro praetore*, so why should anyone think a promotion to the title *pro consule* was necessary (rather than merely desirable)? Second, not all praetors in Spain were prorogued *pro consule*, which demonstrates that a commander in Spain did not need the augmented title (or *imperium*) to operate. Third, it is illogical to imagine that any commander would require a higher level of *imperium* to conduct his campaign: *imperium* (even the putative *imperium minus*) gave a praetor the absolute authority of martial law over his soldiers, and to think that he might need still greater authority in Spain is

<hr />

109. Livy 33.25.9, *Act. Trium.* for 195 BC.

110. This is a common belief among scholars. For example: MacDonald (1953) 143–44, Sumner (1970) 90 and 100 n. 76, Develin (1980) 361–62, Richardson (1986) 76 and (1996a) 49, Brennan (1994) 430–31, (2000) 398, and (2004) 49, Vishnia (1996) 67, and Girardet (2000) 179–80.

111. The praetors of 196 BC triumphed *pro consule* in 195 BC (*MRR* 1.341), meaning they had only held proconsular rank in Spain for a few months at most.

112. There is one example of this: Plutarch (*Aem. Paull.* 4.1–2) says that Aemilius Paullus, praetor in 191 BC, departed for Spain accompanied by twelve lictors, which suggests that he had already been prorogued *pro consule*. There is no reason to doubt this statement—the Aemilii Paulli were a powerful and influential patrician clan, and quick prorogation to *pro consule* is to be expected—but this can hardly be taken as evidence of normal procedure for all praetors. Most praetors were already in Spain when they were prorogued *pro consule* and could not have departed Rome with twelve *fasces*.

nonsense. I am aware of no example in which the promotion of a praetor to ex-praetor *pro consule* made him a more capable or authoritative commander. To the contrary, regular praetors are frequently found commanding full consular armies (two or more legions) without any difficulty, and when the consul C. Lutatius Catulus was wounded in 242 BC, the praetor Q. Valerius Falto took over command of the consul's fleet and used it to win the decisive victory of the First Punic War (the Battle of the Aegates Islands).[113] Indeed, following the death of the Scipio brothers in Spain in 211 BC, the senate dispatched a propraetor to assume command of the entire Spanish *provincia* until other arrangements could be made, and he was not considered insufficiently powerful or authoritative to command.[114] Even those modern historians who believe in the existence of *imperium maius* and *minus* agree that the difference was intended to resolve questions of seniority, so why would a commander in a Spanish *provincia*—who was operating hundreds of miles from any other Roman commander—need a higher level of *imperium*? Who would challenge the authority of the sole bearer of *imperium* in a Spanish *provincia*? Perhaps the commander with *imperium* in the neighboring Spanish *provincia*, but since it was normal to promote both Spanish praetors to *pro consule*, the promotion would be meaningless, since the promotion of both praetors effectively nullified the relevance of the promotion (i.e., by promoting both, no real effect would be achieved, and no other commanders were near Spain who might have interfered with either commander). The promotion of a praetor to propraetor *pro consule* was not about authority or capacity, but about the honor and prestige derived from the upgraded or enhanced title.

Yet one should never underestimate the importance of honor and prestige in Roman politics. While the enhanced title of propraetor *pro consule* may have added nothing to a man's ability to command a *provincia* in Spain, it could add considerably to his social status and prestige back in Rome. In the first place, a praetor prorogued *pro consule* was probably permitted to double the number of his lictors and *fasces*, employing the full twelve that traditionally represented consular authority; in 191 BC, the praetor L. Aemilius Paullus was given a *provincia* in Spain, and Plutarch writes that he had twelve lictors when he took up his command, so that he would possess consular dignity (ὥστε τῆς

---

113. Falto's victory in 242 BC: Val. Max. 2.8.2. Praetors or ex-praetors *pro praetore* commanding consular armies: Q. Fabius Maximus in Apulia in 214 BC (Livy 24.11.2, 24.12.6, 24.20.8); Hostilius Tubulus in Etruria in 208 BC (Livy 27.22.5); M. Tuccius in Apulia and Bruttium in 190 BC (Livy 37.2.6).

114. App. *Ib.* 17, Livy 26.17.1–3.

ἀρχῆς ὑπατικὸν γενέσθαι τὸ ἀξίωμα).[115] While such visible symbols of status would certainly impress his soldiers, the ex-praetor *pro consule* no doubt looked forward eagerly to returning to Rome with his enhanced symbols of authority, and one can imagine that even praetors denied a triumph might have dallied outside the *pomerium* for a period of time rejoicing in their own magnificence as they walked around the Campus Martius adorned in consular splendor and enjoying the respect from their peers that those symbols demanded. In the second place, it was common practice for ancient writers to refer to ex-praetors *pro consule* simply as proconsuls, and we may guess that this same practice was used in spoken Latin.[116]

These opportunities for praetors to use the consular title and regalia were valuable and desirable. After 197 BC, there were six praetors but still only two consuls per year, which meant that the title *pro consule* was much more rare, and therefore far more desirable, than the title *pro praetore*, and Brennan points out that the proliferation of propraetors during the Second Punic War had probably made that title seem more common and less prestigious.[117] Prorogation *pro consule* would certainly have given the Spanish praetors an edge over other praetors in both politics and society. Not only was possession of the symbols and title *pro consule* highly satisfying in itself, but the increased distinction and the clear implication that the former praetor had reached a higher level of prestige and had performed a consular command could be of substantial assistance in winning a triumph and subsequent election to the consulship. Between 196 and 174, praetors commanding in Spain won at least six ovations and seven triumphs, while praetors elsewhere won only two naval triumphs.[118] For these reasons, it is not surprising that — once the new practice was established — it became common for ex-praetors in Spain to be prorogued

115. Plut. *Aem. Paull.* 4.1–2. Possession of twelve lictors must indicate that Aemilius was prorogued *pro consule* at the end of his year as praetor.

116. Jashemski (1950) 43, Badian (1964) 74. For example: Livy 35.22.6 (M. Fulvius Nobilior in 192 BC), 37.46.7 (L. Aemilius Paullus in 190 BC), Livy 39.29.4 (L. Manlius Acidinus Fulvianus in 185 BC). In the late republic, many ambitious men were called proconsul before they had actually held the consulship. For example: App. *BC* 1.80 (Q. Caecilius Metellus Pius); *IGRP* 4.196 (C. Claudius Nero); Cic. *Verr.* 2.3.212 (C. Claudius Marcellus); Caes. *BG* 3.20 (L. Manlius); Plin. *NH* 2.100 (M. Junius Silanus); Eutrop. 6.7.2 (M. Licinius Crassus); Cic. *Fam.* 5.1pr (Q. Caecilius Metellus Celer); Cic. *Div.* 1.58 (Q. Tullius Cicero); Ascon. 15C (M. Pupius Piso Frugi Calpurnianus).

117. Brennan (2000) 243.

118. Praetors in Spain winning ovations: *MRR* 1.336, 341, 354, 373, 383, 404. Praetors in Spain winning triumphs: *MRR* 1.341, 362 (perhaps doubtful), 376 *bis*, 389, 395, 396, 402. Praetors elsewhere winning naval triumphs: *MRR* 1.362, 366. See Richardson (1975) 52–57.

pro consule.[119] Between 196 and 174 BC at least nineteen praetors in Spain are known to have been prorogued *pro consule*, while only four praetors in Spain are known to have been prorogued *pro praetore* in this same period.[120] This was remarkable, since it had always been normal practice to prorogue ex-praetors *pro praetore*, and this continued to be the standard practice in provinces other than Spain.[121]

As might be expected in a culture obsessed with honor, the special privilege of prorogation *pro consule* did not long remain the unique possession of the praetors in Spain. After Livy's account breaks off in 167 BC, our knowledge of the titles of various promagistrates is poor for a period of fifty years.[122] When this information becomes available again at the end of the second century BC, however, the practice of proroguing praetors *pro consule* had expanded beyond Spain. From 196 to 167 BC only one praetor outside Spain is known to have been prorogued *pro consule*;[123] by the end of the second century BC it had become a common practice to prorogue some praetors *pro consule* regardless of their assigned provinces.[124] In the period following 167 BC the praetors serving in Spain had lost their monopoly on prorogation to a higher rank,

119. Most were prorogued *pro consule* (*MRR* 1.336–37, 341, 351, 353–54, 357, 362–63, 373, 379, 388–89, 395–96, 401–2, 404). Mommsen (1887–88) 2.649, Kloft (1977) 16, Richardson (1986) 76, Kallet-Marx (1995) 343–45, Brennan (2000) 398.

120. P. Cornelius Scipio Nasica (*MRR* 1.348), P. Junius Brutus (*MRR* 1.366), L. Postumius Albinus (*MRR* 1.392), and Ti. Sempronius Gracchus (*MRR* 1.393).

121. Such as Macedonia (*MRR* 1.353), Sicily (*MRR* 1.354, 367), Sardinia (*MRR* 1.357, 401), Corsica (*MRR* 1.412), Illyria (*MRR* 1.434), and various regions of Italy (*MRR* 1.362–63, 367).

122. Livy's last record of a praetor *pro consule* is in 174 BC (41.28.1). Broughton identifies one praetor *pro praetore* in 123 BC (*MRR* 1.514) but otherwise cannot determine the rank of prorogued praetors between 167 and 108 BC. Beginning in 108 BC the ranks of many prorogued praetors can again be regularly ascertained.

123. In 178 BC the peregrine praetor, Ti. Claudius Nero, was assigned the *provincia* of Pisa with one Roman legion and substantial allied units (Livy 41.5.6). Although there is no record of him accomplishing anything unusual during his praetorship, Livy describes him as a proconsul in the following year (41.12.1). While this may be an error on Livy's part, it would be the first one of its kind, since he regularly described all prorogued praetors (except those in Spain) as propraetors. On the other hand, there is no satisfactory reason why Nero received this unique honor, since he neither received a triumph nor is known to have advanced to higher office (*MRR* 1.394). As a member of the Claudian *gens* he may have had some powerful family support, but in light of his otherwise undistinguished career this is mere speculation.

124. Cic. *Div.* 1.58, *Leg.* 1.53; Livy 41.12.1; Val. Max. 6.9.7; *OGIS* 441, 114; *IG* 5.1.1432; *CIL* 1² 2.815 (see *MRR* 1.553) and 2.2662; *I. Délos* 4.1.1679; *Act. Trium.* for 107 BC. Broughton thinks it likely that C. Marius was functioning *pro consule* in Spain in 114 BC, and that T. Didius was *pro consule* in Macedonia in 100 BC, but their titles are unattested (*MRR* 1.534 and 577).

no doubt because other praetors were jealous of this special privilege and demanded equal access to the honor and dignity that came with the prestigious title *pro consule.*

Conclusion

The Roman practice of provincial command was constantly developing and changing in the period between 367 and 197 BC, so it would be wrong to think of it as a fixed system with established and unvarying regulations. Just as Flower has recently argued that the Roman Republic was actually made up of several distinctly different phases or republics, Rome's practice of provincial command evolved and changed over time. These changes were not carefully planned public policy decisions but experiments with individual aspects of military command that over time took on greater importance than was perhaps originally intended. While we may speak of the classical Roman constitution being established by 367 BC, this date is probably far more significant to modern historians than it was to the ancient Romans. In all likelihood, the Romans determined that they would elect three and only three annual praetors in 367 BC, and it took many decades — probably the better part of a century — before the consulship arose as an office distinct from the praetorship. Since this was a gradual and (in all likelihood) an unintentional development, there is no reason to imagine that the consulship and praetorship were ever redefined as legally different offices, or that their authorities and capacities were any different in law. Naturally, the consulship acquired greater prestige and status, which could be used to political and social effect in the republic, but this does not require us to assume a real difference in law.

Prorogation was a similar phenomenon: it originated as a one-time exception to the time limit on holding a *provincia* in order to solve a particular military problem. In this respect, prorogation was not so much created as it came into being; it was a legal exception to provide a useful solution, but because of its utility the Roman people resorted to it again and again. In time, the exception became tradition, but it was never set down in law and no precise explanation of the legal difference between a magistrate and promagistrate had ever been drafted. Although later Romans understood that there was a difference between a consul and praetor, and between a magistrate and a promagistrate, these differences were nowhere defined and codified because they had never been formally defined in law; they were traditional customs only. The consuls were Rome's senior military commanders because they had come to possess greater prestige and wield broader influence, but they did not possess any greater authority in law than praetors. Likewise, magistrates held greater status and prestige than promagistrates, but within their respective *provinciae* every consul, praetor, proconsul, and propraetor possessed the same *imperium*. For this reason, there was originally no real difference in law between a man acting *pro consule* and another *pro praetore*, because both wielded the absolute authority of *imperium* within their assigned *provinciae*. Only at the start of the second century BC, when the use of *privati cum imperio* had separated the concept of military authority from the trappings of magisterial office, did the Romans begin thinking about the idea of rank and hierarchy among military commanders. The ability of ex-praetors to acquire the trappings of the consulship transformed lictors and *fasces* from symbols of office to symbols *of rank*. As with all other examples, this was an informal practice at first; an ex-praetor prorogued *pro consule* gained no new authority or prerogatives, although he enjoyed greater prestige and status than ex-praetors who were only prorogued *pro praetore*. In time, however, this new thinking about rank would take root and would become conventional practice.

5

FROM COMMAND TO
GOVERNANCE

The preceding chapters have argued that the classical Roman "constitution" probably took shape later and more gradually than is portrayed in the ancient accounts. Rather than appearing fully formed at the expulsion of the monarchy, the consulship probably developed over an extended period of time as the military might of wealthy aristocratic clans was gradually brought under the control of the developing Roman state. The familiar republican government slowly took shape in the fifth and fourth centuries BC and was in place by the early third century BC at the latest: the archaic praetorship had divided into consuls and praetors, who exercised military command outside Rome and certain civilian responsibilities inside the city, and purely civilian magistrates (censors, tribunes, aediles, quaestors, and minor magistracies) had also been established to perform a broad range of governmental functions in Rome. The civilian aspects and responsibilities of Rome's military commanders are beyond the scope of this work, but it is worth noting that the basic government structure that developed early in the Roman Republic seems to have served the needs of Rome's citizens for a long time; the civilian government that took shape when Rome was merely an Italian power continued to suit the Romans after they had become the sole superpower in the Mediterranean world. Their concept and practice of military command, however, underwent considerable change in response to Rome's acquisition of its empire. As the Romans conquered more peoples and acquired many overseas territories, they had to adapt their thinking about commanders and command to suit the changing shape and nature of their empire.

In the early republic, the Roman *provincia* was a short-term military task that normally lasted for a single campaign season. If a commander completed his assigned task, his *provincia* ceased to exist and the next year's commanders were given different *provinciae*. This concept of the *provincia* as a temporary military assignment given to a general would continue to exist in the late republic, but alongside it a second definition would develop: a geographically defined territory under permanent Roman control that was maintained by an unbroken series of Roman governors who regularly exercised civilian jurisdiction as well as military authority over the territory. This chapter focuses on the origins and development these new territorial provinces; it explores how the geographic area of administration (the province) came to be different from the traditional military campaign (the *provincia*) and what the consequences of this differentiation were for the Roman understanding of command. Like so many other aspects of Roman provincial command, the expansion of the term *provincia* to encompass a new and different concept (governed territory) was not a deliberate decision but a gradual development that came about as Roman practices changed to meet new problems or challenges. The Romans never passed a law that defined the war *provincia* and the territory-province as two different things, but a distinction gradually took shape in the mind of the ruling aristocracy as it became accustomed to the different opportunities and activities each type of command offered. Furthermore, as the Romans brought more and more territory under their direct control, much of Rome's empire came to consist of territorial provinces: unconquered enemy territory was declared a Roman military theater (*provincia*) and smashed into submission, and when enemy resistance was utterly destroyed, the military theater was transformed into a zone of garrisoning and control, which gradually evolved into a sphere of administration and governance. This does not mean that Rome set out to impose government in these permanent *provinciae*; the demand for governance most likely originated from below, as locals seeking benefits or simple mediation of disputes increasingly turned to their Roman overlords as obvious sources of authoritative pronouncements. Rome sent military commanders to oversee and protect its permanent *provinciae*, and it was probably the demand for order and justice from below that gradually turned those commanders into governors.

This chapter begins by looking at Rome's first overseas *provinciae*—Sicily, Sardinia, Corsica, and Spain—and explores how the acquisition of these territories gradually caused the Romans to expand their concept of the *provincia*. The unique characteristics of these territories, and the ways the Romans chose to manage them, led to the new concept of the permanent *provincia*: a conquered territory that was permanently assigned as a *provincia* by the senate, meaning it would always be under the authority of a high-ranking commander with *imperium* irrespective of the need (or lack thereof) for military action. The permanent nature of these *provinciae* emphasized their character as territories rather than tasks; whereas the traditional *provincia* had normally been an assignment to attack and destroy a particular enemy, the fact that permanent *provinciae* were often peaceful meant they could be defined only as places (not as enemies or targets). In offensive campaigns, it was easy to identify a particular foe to be defeated (such as the Samnites or the Carthaginians, Perseus or Antiochus), but in defensive military assignments where no obvious enemy was present, commanders were normally dispatched to areas rather than against people. Thus a commander could be sent to attack the Carthaginians or the Syracusans on Sicily, but if everything was peaceful on that island, a commander was just sent to Sicily. Although they were military commands given to a military commander, many permanent *provinciae* offered few or no opportunities for serious campaigning, so they were garrisons rather than wars. Second, this chapter argues that the permanent *provinciae* eventually came to be seen as inferior in the eyes of Rome's aristocracy because they were essentially defensive commands that offered few good opportunities to win status-enhancing glory and honor. As a result, the Romans normally reserved major wars or expansionary campaigning for their senior commanders (consuls), while their junior commanders (praetors) were normally given the less attractive garrison responsibilities in permanent *provinciae*. This practice gradually led to an association between praetors and permanent *provinciae*, so the praetorian *provincia* eventually came to be understood as something different from the consular *provincia*.

Turning to the activities of the Roman commanders themselves, the chapter considers what early praetors were doing in their permanent *provinciae* and how they came to exercise civilian responsibilities, in particular legal jurisdiction. Although the paucity of the evidence makes it difficult to say much conclusively, particular qualities of the permanent *provinciae* appear to have been conducive to the rise of provincial governance. Traditional *provinciae*, on the other hand, remained primarily zones of military conquest. As praetors in particular took on greater responsibilities for civilian governance in their *provinciae*, and as the senatorial elite became accustomed to thinking of permanent *provinciae* as zones of administrative responsibility, the Roman government began to take a more direct interest in the activities of their praetors abroad. At first, the Roman state began establishing policies intended to dissuade their commanders from abusing provincials too excessively. Because the state was hesitant to curtail the authority and prerogatives of its commanders in any way, however, these early policies were essentially reactive in nature; they were intended to enable the punishment of commanders who did not show proper self-restraint, but they did not actively prohibit commanders from committing improper actions in the first place, or reduce the force of *imperium* available to provincial commanders.

In time, however, the mounting pressure to acquire glory and profit from military commands made it increasingly difficult for the senate to rely on commanders' self-restraint in the treatment of peaceful provincials in the permanent *provinciae*. To prevent certain abuses of authority by provincial commanders, the Roman government began taking proactive steps, in particular the *lex Porcia* of 100 BC, which set new types of restraints on commanders' use of their authority in their *provinciae*. The promulgation of this *lex Porcia* suggests a new stage in Roman thinking about its empire, because it established new regulations that constrained the actions of praetorian governors of permanent *provinciae* more effectively than they did consular commanders of traditional *provinciae*. The unequal application of these laws was caused by a development in Roman thinking that had come to recognize two distinctly different types of *provincia*: zones of conquest and zones of governance.

Permanent *Provinciae*

Rome's conquest of central and southern Italy down to 264 BC was a process of digestion as Rome absorbed its defeated enemies and integrated them into its network of allies. Rather than rule its conquered foes with an occupying force, Rome incorporated them by extending to them certain rights of citizenship as well as mutual promises of military support. If there was any doubt about the stability and loyalty of a conquered people, the Romans confiscated some of their land and established a colony of Roman citizens to observe and to project Roman power. As Salmon emphasized in his study on the subject, these colonies were strategic and military in nature: "The chief consideration was the defence of Roman soil and the establishment of future bases for military operations."[1] In essence, these colonies were self-sustaining garrison forces (*praesidia*); they were strong enough to subdue small-scale uprisings, and secure enough to withstand major rebellions until Rome's legions could be summoned to the area along the roads Rome built as military highways through Italy. As a result, the Romans did not have to deplete their military resources by using armies to occupy conquered territory. Only when necessary did Rome maintain defensive garrisons as occupying forces, and even then only for short periods. At the start of the Second Punic War in 218 BC, the Romans knew that their conquests in northern Italy (Cisalpine Gaul) were

---

1. Salmon (1970) 15, 40–66 (15 quoted). See also Rosenstein (2012) 91–93.

unstable and the Gauls there likely to revolt, but with a major war starting they did not want to be forced to maintain a *provincia* in the north. Their solution was to send a junior commander with a small force to act as a garrison (*praesidium in Gallia*) while they hastened the completion of two colonies in the region, Cremona and Placentia.[2] This illustrates two aspects of Roman policy: when an uprising was possible, but not probable or imminent, the Romans might assign a commander to watch over the area, which entailed maintaining a garrison (*praesidium*) but not actually leading a campaign (*bellum*). It also shows that the Romans preferred not to occupy their military commanders with such *provinciae* unless necessary, preferring instead to have such garrison duty performed by colonies.

Rome was unaccustomed to occupying conquered territory with armies. Because its commanders were not used for garrison duty in the early republic, *provinciae* were normally wars or other aggressive campaigns, and not simple defensive positions. Thus early *provinciae* were inherently temporary; once a particular enemy was conquered, the commander and his army returned to Rome, and that particular foe ceased to be a *provincia*. If that conquered enemy remained peaceful, it might never again become a Roman *provincia*, but if it rebelled sometime in the future, Rome might again declare that foe a *provincia* until such time as it was once more pacified. Thus commanders and their *provinciae* originally were tools of conquest and aggressive campaigning, not zones maintained by occupying forces. As a result, the Romans did not have to think much about long-term projects like annexing and governing captured enemy territory, since their Italian territory and allies could be controlled effectively from Rome. Down to 264 BC, Rome was a mainly reactive imperial state: it dispatched its commanders and armies from Rome against whatever enemies threatened or defied the Romans in a given year, and the proximity of those enemies meant that individual campaigns rarely lasted more than a few months (although a succession of annual commanders could be sent against particularly difficult enemies). Rome's ability to control and expand its dominion with seasonal campaigns — as well as the predilection among the Roman aristocracy for fighting battles — rendered long-term annexation of enemy territory unattractive beyond the creation of colonies to act as watch posts. As a result, the *provincia* probably remained an inherently temporary concept — a short-term military responsibility given to a particular commander to hold for a fixed period.

At some point, however, the concept of the *provincia* began expanding to

2. Livy 21.17.7 (cf. Polyb. 3.40.3). See discussion in Eckstein (1987) 24–28.

signify a territorial possession of the Roman people as well as a task or assignment given to a Roman commander. The scarcity of sources from the third and second centuries BC makes it difficult to pinpoint when this development occurred. Bertrand argued that the word *provincia* always carried a geographic meaning, but Richardson has challenged this position.[3] Surveying the surviving sources, Richardson argues that, in the years between the Hannibalic War and the death of Sulla, the term *provincia* was used to signify a task or responsibility and that only in the writings of Cicero do we first see evidence that the term could be used to represent a geographic area under the control of a Roman commander or a territorial possession of the Roman people. Richardson gives an excellent analysis of Cicero's use of the term *provincia*, but because his argument is mainly a linguistic study based on literary texts, it is difficult to determine at what point before Cicero's writings the word *provincia* acquired this new territorial definition. Richardson does note that Plautus twice uses *provincia* to signify an area under a commander,[4] so the expansion of the term *provincia* to encompass a territorial command may have been underway during Plautus's lifetime (ca. 254–184 BC) and was in common usage by Cicero's day. This span of time can be narrowed by Brennan's argument that the territories seized from Carthage in the first two Punic wars normally constituted a class of praetorian *provincia* that he calls "fixed," and that these fixed *provinciae* differed somewhat from the other, "special" *provinciae* that could also be given to praetors.[5] Brennan must surely be correct that Rome's overseas territorial acquisitions represented a different definition of the *provincia* from the wars and campaigns traditionally assigned as *provinciae* to consuls and praetors, but it was beyond the scope of his inquiry to focus closely on the development of the *provincia* itself.[6]

In the literary sources, the earliest challenge to the traditional definition of the *provincia* as a task or responsibility seems to have been Rome's acquisition of Campania in 343 BC, which reportedly happened in an unusual manner.

---

3. Bertrand (1989) 191–215, Richardson (2008) 8, 24, 51, 54–55, 61, 79–86, and 183.

4. Richardson (2008) 51. He cites Plautus's *Captivi* 156 and 158, and points out that the other ten times Plautus uses the word, it is used in a mocking sense, generally signifying the responsibility or task of low-class characters like prostitutes and slaves.

5. Brennan (2000) 144–90. Brennan includes the judicial responsibilities of the urban and peregrine praetors as fixed *provinciae*.

6. Since I am only examining military commands in this work, I use the term "permanent *provincia*" for clarity and to distinguish my arguments from those of Brennan, who uses the term "fixed *provincia*" to describe the judicial responsibilities of the urban and peregrine praetors in Rome as well as praetorian commands like Sicily and Sardinia.

When the Samnites began raiding Campania in 345/4 BC, the Campanians sought assistance from the Romans, who declined to send military aid because they had a treaty with the Samnites. In response, the Campanians surrendered themselves unconditionally to the Romans through the process of *deditio in fidem*, thereby making all of Campania a Roman possession.[7] Although Rome had taken over parcels of land for its colonies in the past, this was the first time it had annexed an entire region and its occupants all at once, and the Romans were immediately faced with the problem of what to do with their new subject territory. The consul M. Valerius Corvus was dispatched with an army to defend Campania against the Samnites, but because these mountain tribes could not easily or quickly be defeated, the Romans were forced to garrison Campania with an army in order to protect the territory year-round from enemy incursions. Such garrison duty was a novelty for a Roman soldiery that was unaccustomed to defending territory passively instead of engaging in active campaigning, and the Roman soldiers soon began a conspiracy to seize Campanian property and territory for themselves, a conspiracy that was only barely suppressed by their commanders.[8] A *provincia* without conquest and plunder, it would seem, was alien to the Romans.

After the Samnites were defeated, the Romans were faced with the next problem of deciding how to exercise administration over Campania, especially since many Roman citizens lived in the region and wanted access to Roman lawcourts (which existed only in Rome).[9] According to Livy, Rome began sending a special prefect (*praefectus*) in 318 BC to administer justice in Capua at the request of its citizens living in Campania.[10] This may be an anachronistic error, since Livy also says that Rome began sending prefects to Capua in 211 BC as punishment for its decision to side with Hannibal during the Second Punic War, and several scholars have suggested that Livy confused Rome's two conquests of Capua and inaccurately recorded the city receiving prefects in 318 BC.[11] Oakley and Fronda, however, have defended Livy's statement that

7. Livy 7.31.3–4. Stone (2013) 28: "The appeal of Capua in 343 launches Roman imperialism." This *deditio* may well be a literary invention anticipating Capua's similar surrender in 211 BC. See Frederiksen and Purcell (1984) 190–98, David (1994 [1996]) 38, Oakley (1997–2004) 2.284–89, Forsythe (2005) 284–87, Eckstein (2009) 141–45, Burton (2011) 122–27.

8. Livy 7.38.4–10, Dion. Hal. *AR* 15.3.4–15.

9. Not only were Roman citizens drawn to Campania for its wealth and opportunities, but Rome also gave Roman citizenship to the occupants of Capua — full citizenship to the nobles, and citizenship *sine suffragio* to the lower classes (Livy 8.11.16, Vell. 1.14.3).

10. Livy 9.20.5, Fest. 262L.

11. Livy 26.16.10 (cf. Cic. *Leg. agr.* 2.84 and 88, Vell. 2.44.4, Fest. 262L). On Livy's possible con-

the Romans began sending *praefecti Capuam Cumas* in 318 BC, although they allow that we do not know the frequency with which they were sent until 211 BC, from which time they were dispatched annually.[12] If the 318 BC date is accurate, it represents the first time the Romans were confronted with the need to exercise active governance over conquered territory, and they responded to this need by dispatching civilian judicial officials rather than a military commander with *imperium*. Even if the Romans did not begin sending prefects to Capua until 211 BC, there is no evidence that the Romans ever considered keeping a military commander permanently stationed in pacified Campania as they would later do with their overseas conquests. This treatment of Capua was repeated a few decades later when Rome took control of the *ager Gallicus* in northern Italy: after taking the territory from the Senones, the Romans did not maintain an occupying army in the region but followed their normal practice of establishing a colony (Sena) and sending armies only as needed to maintain control and suppress threats.[13] The treatment of Campania and the *ager Gallicus* indicates that at that time the Romans did not consider the long-term garrisoning of peaceful territory to be an appropriate *provincia* for a Roman commander.

Rome's victory in the First Punic War (264–241 BC) created far greater challenges to its traditional definition of the *provincia* and its concept of provincial command. As part of the peace treaty imposed upon Carthage at the end of the war, Rome took possession of Sicily in 241 BC and three years later demanded Sardinia and perhaps Corsica as well.[14] This represented not only a vast increase in the territory under Roman authority but also the first Roman possessions overseas. Rome had never been interested in such extensive territorial acquisitions before, but the war with Carthage had demonstrated that these islands posed a threat to Roman Italy if they fell into enemy hands.[15]

---

fusion on the original date of the prefects, see Brunt (1971) 529, Heurgon (1973) 203, Sherwin-White (1973) 43–44, Ungern-Sternberg (1975) 57 n. 107 and 96 n. 59, Linderski (1979) 248 and (1995) 144 n. 5, Knapp (1980) 14–38, Salmon (1982) 165, Frederiksen and Purcell (1984) 229, and Oakley (1997–2004) 2.555–56 and 3.266–67.

12. Oakley (1997–2004) 2.555–57 and Fronda (2010) 114–16.

13. Polyb. 2.19.7–21.9. Over time, the Romans would send more colonists and would establish more colonies (Polyb. 3.40.5 and 8–10, Livy 21.25.2), but the *ager Gallicus* never became a permanent *provincia* like Sicily, Sardinia, Corsica, and Spain.

14. Most of Sicily (all except the kingdom of Syracuse) had been surrendered by Carthage at the end of the war in 241 BC, but Rome later demanded Sardinia as well, which was ceded by Carthage a few years later (Polyb. 1.62.8–63.3, 1.88.8–12, 3.27.1–6, 3.28.1–2; Livy 21.41.14; Zonaras 8.17–18 says in 238 BC, Eutropius 3.2 says in 237 BC).

15. The strategic importance of these three islands is widely accepted, as is the fact that Rome's

Furthermore, Carthage remained a formidable enemy even after it surrendered to Rome in 241 BC; it recovered quickly after the war, was expanding into Spain by 237 BC, and was inciting revolts against Rome on Sardinia and Corsica in 234 BC. It was probably out of perceived necessity, rather than out of a desire for conquest or domination, that Rome took possession of these islands. While the strategic need to keep control of the islands is clear, what plan (if any) Rome had for imposing this control is far less certain.

Conceptually, the acquisition of Sicily (and, to a lesser degree, Sardinia and Corsica) must have posed something of a problem for the Romans—what were they to do with this conquered territory? Sardinia and Corsica were more straightforward: they were full of untamed tribes eager to fight, and their close proximity to northern Italy where Rome was expanding into Liguria meant they would remain normal military *provinciae* for years to come, and consular armies would continue to hammer away at these hostile islanders just as they had fought and conquered their Italian neighbors.[16] Sicily, on the other hand, was subdued and peaceful, and while no consular army is found there until the start of the Second Punic War, Rome was afraid to pull out of the island completely as it normally did when military spheres had been pacified in the past. There was no obvious need to incur the expense of maintaining an army and a commander on Sicily, and Rome even had a strong ally on the island (Hiero of Syracuse) to keep watch over Rome's interests. According to traditional Roman thinking, Sicily should have ceased to be assigned as a *provincia* after 241 BC, and this may indeed have happened for a few years.

During the First Punic War, Sicily (in whole or in part) had been the *provincia* of a succession of consuls and praetors, but when the last Roman commanders left the island after the peace treaty with Carthage had been ratified, the Romans seem to have stopped assigning Sicily as a *provincia* because the quiet and pacified state of the island left nothing for a Roman commander and army to accomplish there. It would have been illogical to the Romans to keep a consul and an army in a sphere with no enemy to fight. To help arrange the peace treaty with Carthage in 241 BC, ten senators had been sent to look over Sicily and to advise Rome's commanders on the spot. Whether these advisers were concerned with the postwar organization of Sicily or merely with the crafting the peace treaty is unknown, but the two Roman commanders

possession of them was essential to defend Italy from possible invasion. See Bouchier (1917) 62–66, Errington (1972) 30–34, Harris (1979) 133, Dyson (1985), Brennan (2000) 136, and Prag (2013) 57–59.

16. On the links between the islands and Liguria, see Vishnia (1996) 16–25.

holding the *provincia* of Sicily in that year made some kind of arrangements on the island: Zonaras says they established order (πάντα τὰ ἐκεῖ κατεστήσατο), stripped the local population of its weapons, and thus "enslaved" the Sicilians.[17] At some point the Romans confiscated some land on Sicily and made it public land (*ager publicus*), but the quantity and location of this land is largely unknown.[18] Still, Sicily was a very large, wealthy, and strategically important island, and the Romans probably felt that some official presence was necessary to ensure Rome's interests there. Rome's traditional methods of controlling conquered territory in Italy, such as establishing colonies and winning over the local inhabitants by offering them varying levels of Roman citizenship, do not seem to have been tried on Sicily; no Roman colonies are known to have been established on Sicily until the Augustan era, although one city (Messana) was made a *civitas foederata* and several others were declared *civitates foedere immunes ac liberae*.[19] Otherwise, no Sicilians are known to have been made *socii*, Rome's official allies who possessed military responsibilities to Rome, some Roman legal rights, and freedom from taxation. In short, the Romans did not utilize either of their traditional methods for securing long-term control of conquered territory on Sicily.

There seems little doubt that Sicily's wealth was an important factor in Rome's thinking about what to do with its new island territory. After the end of the First Punic War, the Romans probably thought Sicily was no longer a *provincia* in the normal sense (an active military command), but their interests and financial concerns on the island needed oversight. For this reason, it seems logical and reasonable that their first solution was to dispatch a quaestor to Sicily, probably stationed in Rome's naval stronghold at Lilybaeum.[20] Although he was not a military commander and did not possess *imperium*, the quaestor was an important Roman official and was entrusted with a wide range of significant duties.[21] The decision to dispatch a quaestor to Sicily suggests several things about Roman thinking. First, since the quaestor was not a military commander, Sicily was no longer considered a *provincia* in the sphere *militiae*; the senate did not anticipate military action on the island, so no military commander was sent. Second, quaestors were high-ranking financial offi-

17. Zon. 8.17. See Hoyos (2003) 19.
18. Finley (1979) 130.
19. Finley (1979) 124, Clemente (1988) 111, Serrati (2000b) 120, Prag (2013) 56, 61–64.
20. Ascon. *Div.* 2, Cic. *Planc.* 65, *Verr.* 2.2.22. See discussion in Mommsen (1887–88) 2.572, Pareti (1953) 185, Thiel (1954) 33 n. 90, Harris (1976) 102, Clemente (1988) 111 Brennan (2000) 87–89, Serrati (2000b) 120–23, Vanderspoel (2010), and Loreto (2011) 200–201.
21. For an overview of the quaestorship, see Lintott (1999a) 133–37.

cers, suggesting that Rome's interest in Sicily at the time was mainly financial, such as disposing of territory acquired by the Romans during the war, and collecting the substantial grain tithes levied on the Sicilians.[22] Third, quaestors were often placed in charge of Rome's main port at Ostia — especially the granaries located there — so the decision to place a quaestor in the great port of Lilybaeum may suggest that the Romans were primarily concerned with the shipping of grain and collecting port taxes, since Sicily sat on important seaborne trading routes.[23] Fourth, quaestors were often found managing Rome's fleets in peacetime.[24] Since Rome generally used allies and not its own citizens as sailors and rowers in their fleet, a quaestor was fully capable of giving orders in the Roman navy and had sufficient authority to maintain and operate a fleet (*imperium* was necessary to compel obedience only from Roman citizens; allies had fewer rights before Roman magistrates). Thus the Romans at first may have intended to maintain a presence only at Lilybaeum, since a quaestor there could collect tithes and duties, maintain the city as a Roman stronghold, and keep Rome's navy there in good shape. So important were these duties that this special quaestor continued to be sent to Lilybaeum even after the Romans began sending a regular praetor (with his own quaestor) to manage Sicily,[25] making it the only Roman *provincia* with two quaestors stationed in it — one with the praetor in Syracuse, and the other in Lilybaeum.

At some point, however, the Romans decided that a single quaestor was insufficient to oversee Roman interests in Sicily, and they began sending regular praetors to the island as well. When this happened, however, is a matter is debate. Appian states that after the conclusion of the First Punic War in 241 BC, the Romans "subjected the Sicilians to tribute, assigned naval responsibilities to their cities, and dispatched an annual praetor to Sicily."[26] Solinus, on the other hand, indicates that Rome did not begin sending regular praetors to Sicily (and Sardinia) until 227 BC, when two further praetors were created to provide regular commanders for those islands.[27] Brennan has argued for

22. Polyb. 6.39.15, 10.19.1; Cic. *Verr.* 2.1.40, 2.3.177, *Fam.* 2.15.4, *Mur.* 18; Livy 35.1.2 and 42.31.8.

23. Quaestors were the supervisors of the granaries at Ostia (Cic. *Mur.* 18, *Sest.* 39) and elsewhere in Italy (Cic. *Vat.* 12, *Sest.* 39, *Har. Resp.* 43, *Mur.* 18, *Att.* 2.9.1).

24. *Quaestores classici*: Lydus 1.27. See Mommsen (1887–88) 2.270–72.

25. Cic. *Div. Caec.* 39, 55–56, *Verr.* 2.2.44, 2.5.114, *Planc.* 65.

26. App. *Sic.* 2.2: φόρους τε αὐτοῖς ἐπέθεσαν, καὶ τέλη τὰ θαλάσσια ταῖς πόλεσι μερισάμενοι στρατηγὸν ἐτήσιον ἔπεμπον ἐς Σικελίαν.

27. Solin. 5.1: *Si respiciamus ad ordinem temporum uel locorum, post Sardiniam res uocant Siculae. Primo quod utraque insula in Romanum arbitratum redacta iisdem temporibus facta prouincia est, cum eodem anno Sardiniam M. Valerius, alteram C. Flaminius praetor sortiti sint. Adde quod freto Siculo*

the earlier date, suggesting that the second (peregrine) praetor was created in 241 BC to provide a regular commander of Sicily.[28] While this is a reasonable argument, there is no evidence for a praetor (or consul) on Sicily anytime between 241 and 227 BC, which seems strange if the island was indeed assigned as a praetorian *provincia* in every one of those fourteen years.[29] Our information on praetorian provincial assignments during that period is exceedingly poor, however, and only three are known: one praetor died fighting on Sardinia in 234 BC, and praetors were sent to Sicily and Sardinia in 227 BC.

Although the lack of evidence makes a firm conclusion impossible, the fact that Sicily received an extra quaestor in Lilybaeum suggests (in my thinking) that there must have been some delay in deciding to send regular praetors to Sicily; why was Sicily the only Roman *provincia* to receive two quaestors—each sent to different parts of the island—unless one of them was a relic of an earlier method of administration? There was probably an initial period when the Romans regularly sent only a quaestor to Sicily, but by 227 BC they had decided to establish Sicily (and Sardinia) as a permanent *provincia*, which was a military command that would receive a praetor every year, whether or not military activity was expected or necessary.[30] Since Sicily was generally peaceful with little need for active campaigning, this *provincia* was normally a defensive assignment; rather than a war of conquest, this *provincia* was the defense and maintenance of a guarded area under direct and perpetual Roman control. While it is common to refer to this as the annexation of Sicily, such a term does not quite express Rome's action. Although the island would henceforth be a Roman possession, it remained a separate and distinct sphere from those territories that had received partial or full Roman citizenship in Italy, as is demonstrated by the absence of colonization and the fact that a military commander was continually stationed over the Sicilians.

No ancient source explains why the Romans decided to permanently garri-

---

excipitur nomen Sardi maris. For the creation of two further praetors in 227 BC, see also Livy *Per.* 19; Lydus 1.38 and 45; *Dig.* 1.2.2.28 [Pomponius]. The date for the creation of these praetors is uncertain, but Brennan (2000) 91–93 persuasively argues for the traditional date of 227 BC.

28. Brennan (2000) 85–89 argues that the peregrine praetor was literally sent *inter peregrinos*.

29. Richardson (1986) 7–8 points out that there is no evidence for a Roman presence on Sicily until 227 BC, a fact that Brennan's *fasti praetorii* does not refute. Eckstein (1987) 136–38 also discusses the meager evidence of Roman activity on Sicily from 241 to 225 BC.

30. Eckstein (1987) 21–50 discusses how certain *provinciae* were used as defensive garrisons, and has suggested (112, 122–24) that 227 BC was the true beginning of the province of Sicily. Ferrary (2010) 35 also discusses the possibility that Sicily officially became a permanent province in 228/7 BC, and considers the comital legislation that may have been involved.

son Sicily and Sardinia with praetors in 227 BC, but it probably had to do with military concerns like the Illyrian War of 229 BC or the revival and expansion of Carthaginian power. While Sicily had been peaceful throughout the 230s BC, Rome had spent the majority of that decade (238 to 231 BC) hammering both Sardinia and Corsica with consular armies, and only at the end of 231 BC did Rome stop assigning those islands as consular *provinciae*. From 230 to 227 BC, all three islands were apparently quiet and needed no military supervision, but nevertheless the Romans increased their praetorian college in 227 BC to provide enough annual commanders to make Sicily and Sardinia permanent *provinciae*. External concerns may have provoked this move, such as (perhaps) a new deployment of Rome's fleet: the Romans had equipped two hundred warships in their campaigns against the Illyrians in 229 BC, and after the successful conclusion of that war they may have decided to place many of those ships under the care of praetors at the strategically critical bases on Sicily and Sardinia.[31] Carthaginian conquests in Spain were also a source of concern for the Romans. Following the death of Hamilcar Barca in 229 BC, his son-in-law Hasdrubal was able to consolidate Carthaginian conquests quickly, and his foundation of New Carthage in 227 BC may have induced the Romans to project their power more forcefully by placing praetors and stronger fleets in Sicily and Sardinia.[32]

Whether or not the Romans had dispatched praetors to these islands previously, they were sufficiently concerned about events in 227 BC to expand their praetorian college further to ensure that military commanders were always available for Sicily and Sardinia. The decision not to garrison or colonize territory in Illyria, which they had conquered in 229 BC, demonstrates that the Romans were primarily concerned with projecting power from the islands, and not simply expanding their empire by increasing their administration on the islands.[33] The commitment to making Sicily and Sardinia permanent *provinciae* was a military decision to create garrisons against external threats, not

31. Polybius (2.11.1) discusses the fleet Rome used in the Illyrian War. Lilybaeum on Sicily was one of Rome's most important naval bases at the time, and Hoyos (2003) 115, 118, and 141 emphasizes the importance of Rome's naval bases on Sardinia during the Second Punic War. Brennan (2000) 91–93 discusses the possibility that the Illyrian War spurred the creation of two more praetors for Sicily and Sardinia.

32. Polybius (2.13.1–7) points out that that Carthaginian foundation of New Carthage in Spain particularly troubled the Romans. On the growth of Carthaginian power in Spain and its effect on Rome, see Hoyos (2003) 55–86.

33. See Badian (1952).

to absorb territory. If Rome had previously been uncertain what to do with its new permanent *provincia* of Sicily, by 227 BC it unequivocally committed itself to maintaining it as a military garrison.[34] Whereas the Romans had been content to send a prefect to Campania in 318 BC, the external threat of war probably led them to send praetors to Sicily and Sardinia.

Although important military commanders, the praetors in Sicily and Sardinia had only modest military forces at their disposal. They certainly commanded small fleets, and they may even have had charge of much of Rome's main battle fleet when those two hundred or more warships were not in use elsewhere. In addition, the praetor in Sicily may have had a Roman legion under his command. In his tally of Rome's available forces in 225 BC, Polybius states that a legion was keeping guard over Sicily, but he gives no indication of whether this legion was stationed on the island for the long term, or whether it had been dispatched for a particular short-term mission.[35] Brennan has argued that Sicily began receiving a legion in this year, and Loreto believes this legion was dispatched to guard against a Carthaginian naval attack while both of Rome's consuls were occupied with conquering northern Italy.[36] Loreto may well be right, or it may be that one of the new praetors created in 227 BC brought the legion with him to Sicily, and that legion was still in place two years later. It is hard to imagine that the Romans would have dispatched a praetor to Sicily in 227 BC without having some sizable military force under his command; otherwise, why bother sending a praetor at all? Although praetors would eventually be used to govern peaceful *provinciae* without an army at their backs, in 227 BC it would have been unusual to dispatch a praetor to a *provincia* without an army. As had been demonstrated from 240 to 227 BC, a quaestor was sufficient to supervise a peaceful Sicily and give orders to obedient provincials, so the dispatch of a praetor *in addition to* the regular quaestor at Lilybaeum suggests a new type of military presence on the island. Perhaps Rome did fear a resurgent Carthage, as Loreto suggests, or perhaps the quaestor on Sicily had found his resources insufficient to suppressing piracy

34. On military defense being Rome's priority on making Sicily a permanent *provincia*, see Ferrary (1990) 219, Serrati (2000b) 115–33, Hoyos (2003) 48 (115–18, 128, and 141 discusses how Carthage tried to use Sardinia as a base in the Second Punic War), Loreto (2011) 197–201, and Prag (2013) 54–65.

35. Polyb. 2.24.13: ἔτι γε μὴν κἂν Σικελίᾳ καὶ Τάραντι στρατόπεδα δύο παρεφήδρευεν, ὧν ἑκάτερον ἦν ἀνὰ τετρακισχιλίους καὶ διακοσίους πεζούς, ἱππεῖς δὲ διακοσίους. Walbank (1957–79) 1.196–202 discusses the idea of Sicily as a defensive guard.

36. Brennan (2000) 93 and Loreto (2011) 197–98.

and brigandage in and around the island.[37] It is possible that the first praetor known to be assigned the permanent *provincia* of Sicily in 227 BC brought the legion with him, further emphasizing the Roman intention to maintain the island as a guarded area.

Whatever Rome had been thinking when it claimed permanent control of Sicily in 241 BC (and of Sardinia in 238 BC), the creation of two additional praetors in 227 BC demonstrates that the Romans came to conceive of those islands as somewhat different *provinciae* from the other commands they traditionally assigned to their consuls and praetors. The provision of extra praetors to enable the sustained annual assignment of the islands as military commands gave the concept of the *provincia* a quality of permanence that it had never had before.[38] *Provinciae* had previously been wars or other military tasks that were specifically assigned as responsibilities *to be completed* by a commander, but now some *provinciae* were assigned with the express understanding that they could never be completed — they would always be handed over to a successor at the end of the incumbent's term. Even Campania had ceased to be a *provincia* once it had been become a Roman possession, and the Romans had been content to dispatch civilian officials to oversee judicial affairs there. Sicily and Sardinia, however, became permanent military zones that would receive military commanders long after they had been conquered, pacified, and incorporated into Rome's empire. Although they may not have fully realized it at the time, the Romans had expanded their basic conception of the *provincia* to create something new: a permanent *provincia*.

The acquisition of Sicily (and then Sardinia and Corsica) triggered an irreversible change in Roman thinking about the *provincia*, which would also have consequences for how they understood the commander. Whereas the *provincia* had almost always been an aggressive war in the past, now some of the *provinciae* assigned each year would reliably be defensive assignments overseeing previously conquered territory. The fact that a permanent *provincia* was usually defined as a place rather than a task (such as a war) would have an important influence on the development of Rome's empire. Because such defensive assignments offered less status-enhancing glory and profit, the permanent *provinciae* would necessarily be less desirable in the eyes of Rome's *imperium-*

37. Praetors were (later) responsible for protecting Sicily's shores from pirates and maintaining sufficient land forces to suppress uprisings, brigandage, and slave revolts (Cic. *Verr.* 2.5.18–34).

38. See Richardson (2011b) 9 and n. 46: "Cicero in several places, when he is at pains to emphasise the history of Roman presence in an area, speaks in terms of the *provincia* passing from one magistrate to another in ways which demonstrate its continuity."

holders. That a praetor was seen as the appropriate commander to send to a permanent *provincia*, and that the praetorian college was increased to provide commanders for them, show that by this time the praetor was certainly seen as a secondary commander, and that the task of maintaining a defensive garrison was more appropriate for the praetor than the consul. As was argued in previous chapters, one of the three annual praetors established in 367 BC usually received inferior opportunities for military command in comparison to his two colleagues, with the result that this particular praetorship (the urban praetor) became less desirable — and therefore less prestigious and important — than his two colleagues (the consuls). This lesser status was confirmed by the expansion of the praetorian college in circa 241 and 227 BC; the larger number of praetors made the office more common and therefore less exclusive and desirable than the consulship, which was never expanded beyond the two colleagues. By 227 BC the praetorship held less prestige and a lower status than the consulship, and it was decidedly a secondary military commander despite having the exact same military authority (*imperium* and *auspicium*). The decision to increase the number of annual praetors and use them to command these less desirable permanent *provinciae* augmented and reinforced the perception of the praetorship as a junior or secondary office to the consulship. In this way, the development of Roman thinking about military commands also influenced how they conceived of the commander.

Although it was a slow and gradual process that would take more than a century, the acquisition of Sicily established the idea that a *provincia* could be a place as well as a war. This process was probably accelerated by the fact that Sicily, Sardinia, and Corsica were all islands and therefore had clearly defined boundaries that marked out the exact extent of the territory that made up the command. Although Rome did not (yet) possess all of Sicily, there were clear boundaries marking the separation between Roman and Syracusan territory.[39] Furthermore, the peaceful nature of Sicily probably meant that praetors were assigned the *territory* of Sicily rather than any particular *enemy or task* located in Sicily: since there was no particular enemy to fight, the praetors were just assigned to the region. Although it may have been only slightly noticed at first, the creation of geographically defined *provinciae* enabled a commander to see quite clearly where his *provincia* — and his authority — ended.[40] Naturally,

39. Livy 24.7.9 and 44.4 refers to marked boundaries that defined the Roman *provincia Sicilia* and distinguished it from the kingdom of Syracuse.

40. See Eck (1995) 18 "Dies wurde am Anfang vor allem dadurch erleichtert, weil Sicilia und Sardinia sowie Corsica als Inseln auch territorial präzis erfaßbar waren . . . Je mehr die Zeit fortschritt,

a praetor was not imprisoned on his island *provincia*—he was fully authorized to fight pirates or other enemies in the waters around Sicily—but he was not expected to attack enemies (or potential enemies) outside the Sicilian sphere. When Rome did need a major fleet to accompany its land armies (such as in the eastern campaigns against Antiochus), the naval *provincia* was normally given to a praetor other than the one who held the *provincia* of Sicily, indicating that Rome wanted that praetor guarding the island, rather than using it as a launching pad for expansionary campaigning elsewhere.[41] The shores of the islands, while not representing impermeable or official boundaries, nevertheless functioned to define the island *provinciae* in a geographic manner that was different from the military campaigns that constituted earlier *provinciae*; as such, they forced the idea of the *provincia* to expand and include territorial space as well as a military campaign.

The adjustments Rome made to control and defend Sicily and Sardinia (and Corsica) were probably experiments; although Rome had adapted its traditional notions of provincial command for these new *provinciae*, it would be wrong to think that the Romans fully understood the significance of these experiments at the time, or that they thought of their traditional and permanent *provinciae* as fundamentally different things. This is illustrated by their acquisition of Spain at the end of the Second Punic War in 202 BC: although Rome demanded that Carthage relinquish its claims to the entire Iberian Peninsula, it is not at all clear that Rome knew what it intended to do with the territory.[42] Throughout most of the sixteen-year war (218–202 BC), Spain had been a critical but secondary theater of warfare, generally left to the command of one family (the Cornelii Scipiones). Like all traditional *provinciae*, the command in Spain had been a war, and the commander's task was to defeat the Carthaginians. Richardson has emphasized that the Scipio brothers were sent to

---

desto stärker setzte sich der Aspekt durch, daß unter *provincia* ein genau definierbares Territorium zu verstehen sei, das einem römischen Amtsträger mit *imperium* unterstand."

41. Although the record of praetorian commands on Sicily and with the fleet post-227 BC is often spotty, Brennan's table of Sicilian and Sardinian commanders 218–201 (Brennan [2000] 681–83) demonstrates that the Roman fleet was usually in the hands of consuls or promagistrates, and not of the praetors of the island *provinciae*. Details about the activities of these island praetors for the next decade (200–190) are extremely poor, but when the senate wished a fleet prepared in 192 BC, they instructed the urban and peregrine praetors, and not the island praetors, to undertake the task (Livy 35.21.1). Likewise, when major naval operations were necessary in the Aegean in the following three years (191 to 189 BC), the senate gave a fleet to a separate praetor and not to the island praetors (Livy 36.3.4–6 and 41–45, 37.2.10, 37.4.5, 37.60.1, App. *Syr.* 20, 22, 26–27).

42. On the Roman hesitation, see Richardson (1986) 62–125 and (2011a) 468–70, and Rosenstein (2012) 198.

Spain in 218 BC to conquer an enemy and that their provincial assignment did not represent a Roman claim on (or annexation of) the Iberian Peninsula.[43] When the youngest of these Scipios (the later Africanus) had accomplished this task and forced the Carthaginians out of Spain in 206 BC, he returned to Rome, no doubt believing his *provincia* to be complete—he did not stay to conquer more territory. Furthermore, the Romans did not see fit to hand the *provincia* of Spain over to another consul or praetor, suggesting that they had not yet decided to lay permanent claim to Spain as they had the islands taken from Carthage thirty-five years earlier; the Sicilian model of territorial possession and control under a regular praetor was not yet applied to Spain. Instead, the command of the entire peninsula was handed over to *privati cum imperio*, and it would remain in the charge of *ad hoc* commanders for the rest of the war. Even when the Romans forced Carthage to abandon Spain after the war, they still did not make any change that indicates what they intended to do with the peninsula. Instead of expanding the praetorian college again (as it had done after the First Punic War), Rome left Spain in the hands of *privati cum imperio* for four more years despite the availability of other commanders, both magistrates and promagistrates. This hesitation indicates uncertainty on Rome's part as to what it would do with Spain, and how (if at all) it would impose control and arrange for the defense of the region.[44] That Rome did not immediately reproduce the arrangements it had made for Sicily and Sardinia by creating new praetors suggests that the idea of the permanent *provincia* was still an experiment or evolving concept.

Only in 198 BC did the Romans finally decide to increase the praetorian college by an additional two praetors, bringing the total number up to six in the following year in order to provide regular commanders for the new permanent *provinciae* of Nearer and Farther Spain.[45] As it had done with the island *provinciae*, Rome committed itself to maintaining perpetual garrisons under military commanders in Spain, thereby establishing the two Spanish commands as permanent *provinciae*.[46] Many motives may have contributed to the Roman decision to stay in Spain, but once the decision was made, the Romans

43. Richardson (2011a) 468: "The senate was not, by naming Spain and Africa as *provinciae* [in 218 BC], making a territorial claim on these areas, much less annexing them to a Roman Empire. It was assigning to the two magistrates tasks that they were to carry out."

44. On the general hesitation of the Romans to create new permanent *provinciae* during this period, see Ferrary (2008) 7–18.

45. Livy 32.27.6–7.

46. Richardson (1986) 95–125 has produced the most detailed discussion of the formation of these two Spanish *provinciae*.

moved ahead fairly quickly. In 206 BC Scipio had founded the colony of Italica for his wounded veterans, but otherwise the Romans would use the permanent presence of a praetor — rather than a series of colonies — to control the conquered territory.[47] Taxation was imposed (although it seems to have been irregular at first), and the praetors set about consolidating and expanding Roman control.[48] Unlike pacified Sicily, however, the new permanent *provinciae* in Spain were active military zones.[49] At the start of the second century BC, the Romans controlled only a limited amount of Spanish territory along the Mediterranean coast, so most of the peninsula was unconquered when the Romans established their permanent *provinciae*, giving the praetors there plenty of opportunities for campaigning against untamed tribes. As a result, the Spanish permanent *provinciae* would resemble traditional *provinciae* for many years as praetors gave their primary attention to their military responsibilities, but in fact the two Spains were more like the permanent *provinciae* of Sicily and Sardinia than has previously been recognized.

Like the island *provinciae*, the two Spanish *provinciae* were fundamentally conceived of as garrisoned territory rather than particular campaigns. Whereas the Cornelii Scipiones had been sent to Spain to fight the Carthaginians, and Africanus had returned to Rome as soon as this war was complete, the praetors after 198 BC were sent to the geographic areas of Nearer and Farther Spain regardless of whether a war or other specific military task needed to be accomplished; and, regardless of their accomplishments, they were to remain in the *provinciae* until relieved by a successor. This shift in the conception of the Spanish *provinciae* is evident in the senate's instructions to the first praetors sent to Spain (in 197 BC): they were directed to establish a geographic border that would separate their two *provinciae*, so Nearer and Farther Spain were to be distinguished and separated from one another as two distinct territories.[50] How quickly or thoroughly this was done is unknown, although Livy indicates that the border was in place by 180 BC.[51] Richardson has established that the boundary started south of New Carthage and ran west toward Castulo on the

47. App. *Hisp.* 38. Richardson (1986) 53 and 61.

48. On taxation, see Richardson (1976b) 139–52, Keay (1990) 128–30, and Castro (2013) 74–76.

49. Richardson (1986) 104–5 and (2011a) 470 points out that, of the one consul and twenty-three praetors sent to Spain between 197 and 179 BC, all but four were primarily engaged in military operations, and half of these commanders received a triumph or ovation on their return.

50. Livy 32.28.11: *terminare iussi qua ulterior citeriorve provincia servaretur.*

51. Livy 40.41.10. Richardson (1986) 77–78 argues that the border may not have been put in place immediately.

north bank of the Baetis (Guadalquivir) River.[52] Nearer Spain was defined as the eastern coast of Spain down to (and including) the territory of New Carthage, whereas Farther Spain was defined as the southern coast of Spain from (but not including) the territory of New Carthage to Italica.[53] Apparently, this border existed only in between Rome's two permanent *provinciae*, so it did not fully encircle either *provincia* or define their outer or external boundaries; the praetors were free to march their armies to the Atlantic if possible. In other words, the purpose of the border was not to limit the territorial scope of the two *provinciae* but to separate the two *provinciae* from one another. In this respect, the border in Spain did permanently what Roman commanders had long been doing on an *ad hoc* basis — dividing a shared *provincia* into two separate and distinct *provinciae*. Just as two Roman commanders assigned to northern Italy might divide their shared *provincia* by dividing it into different parts (each attacking different tribes or regions — see chapter 3), the Romans used the border in Spain to differentiate the peninsula into two separate *provinciae*.

This effort to create an artificial definition of territory had not been necessary when the Romans had made Sicily and Sardinia (and Corsica) into permanent *provinciae*, since their insular nature, and the fact that only one commander was normally placed on each island at a time (the Second Punic War was an exception) automatically created a clear boundary that defined the territory over which the commander enjoyed supreme authority.[54] Spain, however, presented a new problem, because the two praetors sent there in 197 BC were given one big region in which to campaign jointly without a clear way to divide it. If the Spanish *provinciae* had been short-term campaigns (like traditional military *provinciae*), the two praetors might have selected different enemies to fight, thereby separating their *provinciae*. Because the Spanish *provinciae* were to be permanent Roman *provinciae*, however, the senate probably did

52. Richardson (1986) 77–78. Livy (40.41.10) mentions the beginning of the border south of New Carthage, and Caesar (*BC* 1.38) describes it running toward Castulo. Also see Dyson (1985) 187, Talbert (1985) 144, Lintott (1993) 23, Brennan (2000) 164–66, and Rosenstein (2012) 199.

53. See Richardson (1986) 42–49, who suggests (49) that Scipio Africanus, while holding the *provincia* of Spain, may have divided his forces to operate against the Carthaginians with two separate armies. If he is correct, then the senate's decision to divide Spain into two separate *provinciae* in 197 BC may originate from the assessment of previous commanders that the nature of the geography required two separate commands. See also Richardson (1996a) 50–51.

54. The Roman *provincia* in Sicily was originally distinguished geographically from the kingdom of Syracuse, which remained an independent ally until it too was incorporated into the Roman *provincia* in 211 BC.

not want to rely on ad hoc methods or enable successive praetors to redefine the *provinciae* each year. The senate wanted a permanent method to distinguish clearly the nearer and farther *provinciae* in Spain from one another, and a fixed border was certainly the most simple and efficient means for achieving this. Since Rome could not divide the Spanish commands by tasks, campaigns, or enemies, it divided them by geography, which was an unusual but effective means for establishing and distinguishing the two spheres of authority. Although the Romans probably did not intend it, their decision to establish two permanent *provinciae* in Spain established the important precedent, following on the example of the islands, that permanent *provinciae* were territories that had to be geographically defined from one another.

This use of an artificial boundary to separate *provinciae* does not, however, mean that the Romans automatically conceived of permanent *provinciae* as entirely defined areas, or that a commander's authority was limited or confined by that boundary. In spite of the existence of a border separating the two Spanish *provinciae*, there is no indication that the praetors in Spain were constrained by it. On several occasions, one praetor is known to have crossed the border and entered his colleague's *provincia* in pursuit of some enemy or to have cooperated with his colleague in a joint attack on a powerful Spanish tribe.[55] Richardson considered it remarkable that two independent commanders—each of whom had his own *provincia* in Spain—should have joined forces in this way,[56] but such cooperation between *imperium*-bearing commanders had not been uncommon during the Second Punic War. Indeed, it was the clear territorial distinction between the *provinciae* of Nearer and Farther Spain that enabled the two praetors to work together, since the separation of their respective spheres of authority made it clear which of them took precedence in which sphere, making conflict between them unlikely (and probably illegal). A praetor in Spain who left his own *provincia* and crossed the border into his colleague's *provincia* did not suffer any diminution of *imperium*, but he was required to yield precedence of authority to his colleague if and when necessary.

55. Livy 39.30.1, 40.39.3–5, 40.47.1, App. *Hisp.* 59–61. See Sumner (1970) 92–98, Richardson (1986) 77–79, 97–104, Lintott (1993) 23, Richardson (1996a) 54–55, 66. Sumner (1970) attempts to disprove Livy's statement that Spain was divided into two areas known as Citerior and Ulterior in or shortly after 197 BC, arguing instead for two unbounded *provinciae*. His main evidence—that the praetors in Spain are occasionally found operating within their colleague's *provincia*—does not, however, disprove the existence of two separate provinces, but only that the border was occasionally transgressed in the pursuit of a highly mobile, tribal enemy. Briscoe (1973) 345 and Develin (1980) 364–67 disagree with Sumner's argument.

56. Richardson (1986) 99–100.

Presumably, if one praetor pursued an enemy into his colleague's *provincia*, the pursuer was fully capable of engaging the enemy without legal impediment, and he experienced no change in authority unless he encountered his colleague who held the *provincia*.

This arrangement is evident in the actions of the two praetors sent to Spain in 186 BC, C. Calpurnius Piso (Farther Spain) and L. Quinctius Crispinus (Nearer Spain), who decided from the outset to combine their forces and work together on their campaigns.[57] They first fought the Lusitanians in the Baetis Valley in Farther Spain, and then they moved north into Nearer Spain, where they defeated the Celtiberians. Livy says that each man received a triumph in 184 BC over the Lusitanians and Celtiberians, but — in strict legal terms — we may suppose that Calpurnius received the primary credit for defeating the Lusitanians, and Quinctius the primary credit for the Celtiberians. Just eleven years earlier in 195 BC, M. Helvius had been denied a triumph for a victory he won *in aliena provincia*, so it is unlikely that a praetor in one Spanish *provincia* could have claimed a triumph for a victory he helped achieve in the other Spanish *provincia*. Thus Livy's description of their triumphs may be erroneous (both victories were wrongly attributed to both commanders), or the two praetors may have willingly shared the credit for both victories, although each would have had to justify his own claim before the senate.[58]

When the Romans decided to establish two permanent *provinciae* in Spain, therefore, they conceived of these commands as being fundamentally geographic in nature, as they had been in the islands. Thus, from their origins the permanent *provinciae* were different from traditional *provinciae*, although the Romans at the time may not have recognized this difference or thought it particularly important or unusual.[59] Nevertheless, the Spanish *provinciae* would serve as a model for future permanent *provinciae*, which would all be defined partly or completely by geographic boundaries. When Rome absorbed developed states like Macedonia, Carthage, or Pergamum, the preexisting borders of those states were adopted (sometimes with adjustments) to define the new Roman *provincia*, and natural boundaries were often used to define conquered territories where no developed state with its own territorial borders had pre-

57. Livy 39.30.1–31.18, 39.42.2–4. Richardson (1986) 98–99 and (1996a) 55 discusses their campaigns.

58. Such had been the case in 197 BC, when the consuls C. Cornelius Cethegus and Q. Minucius Rufus requested a joint triumph over the tribes they had defeated in northern Italy.

59. For a full discussion of the influence the Spanish *provinciae* played in the development of the Roman Empire, see Richardson (1986) and (1996). See also Ferrary's discussion ([2010] 34–38) of the legislation behind the creation of new permanent *provinciae*.

viously existed.[60] As Rome continued its conquest and annexation of the East, the boundaries that had distinguished its *provincia* of Asia from foreign kingdoms came to separate Asia from the new permanent *provinciae* of Bithynia, Cilicia, and Pontus.[61] Cilicia is an excellent example of this process, because it seems to have been enlarged and reduced in size several times during the late republic, but each time by the addition or subtraction of specific and defined territorial regions.[62] Whereas once Rome's *provinciae* had been almost exclusively wars in which a particular enemy was to be beaten regardless of location, the decision to begin acquiring permanent *provinciae* meant that a growing number of Rome's *provinciae* would henceforth be defensive assignments, the supervision of which required a clear understanding of the geographic extent of the territory included in the commander's responsibility.

In summary, it cannot be doubted that Rome's permanent *provinciae* reflect a different purpose or new strategic thinking among the Romans. It was surely no coincidence that all of Rome's permanent *provinciae* as of 197 BC consisted of territory taken from Carthage, suggesting that they were conceived of as being (at least in part) garrisons or watch posts from which Rome could keep an eye on its twice defeated foe from a position of strength.[63] As with its colonies in Italy, these standing *provinciae* were on strategic military routes that controlled access to Rome itself, and Rome may have wanted these permanent *provinciae* to be formidable watch posts acting as its eyes and ears across the sea.[64] Instead of colonies, however, Rome placed high-ranking military

60. Macedonia (*CIL* 1² 2.626, *ILS* 20, Strabo 8.6.23, Val. Max. 7.5.4; the free and allied states of Greece defined the southern border); Carthage/Africa (*ILS* 67, Livy 34.62.8–11, Vell. 2.38.2, App. *Pun.* 135, Plin. *NH* 5.25; its border with Numidia had to be kept clearly defined); Pergamum/Asia (*CIL* 1² 2.646–51, Vell. 2.38.5, Strabo 13.4.2, 14.1.38; its borders with allied eastern kingdoms had to be maintained). Use of natural geographic boundaries: Cisalpine Gaul stretched from the Rubicon to the Alps, whereas Transalpine Gaul consisted of southern France from the Alps to the Pyrenees.

61. Cic. *Prov. Cons.* 31: *ut Asia, quae imperium antea nostrum terminabat, nunc tribus novis provinciis ipsa cingatur.*

62. See Magie (1950) 284–85, 376, 1162–66, and 1245.

63. Rome was a nervous neighbor who liked to keep a close watch for potential trouble. Gruen (1975) gives an excellent account of how Rome paid strict attention to affairs in the East in the second century BC. Even under Augustus provinces would function as watch posts, as Syme wrote of the province of Moesia at that time: "The garrison of Moesia, reduced to two legions, is anxiously intent (and with reason) on the task of keeping watch over Thrace" (Syme [1934] 133).

64. Errington (1972) 236–41, 266–68 has pointed out that Rome's establishment of a permanent *provincia* often followed the loss of an important Roman ally in that region: Spain was annexed after the loss of Saguntum, Africa was made a permanent *provincia* in 146 BC following the death of Massinissa, Macedonia was made a permanent *provincia* following the rebellion of the Achaean League in Greece in 146 BC (although Kallet-Marx [1995] sees a slower process of provincialization). Errington

commanders and formidable armies in its permanent *provinciae* to watch and intimidate Rome's Mediterranean neighbors. Standing *provinciae* served as forward bases, projecting Roman power as much as defending it, and over a century later Cicero would still refer to Rome's *provinciae* as outposts (*pro-pugnaculis*) that protected its allies as well as Rome itself.[65] In the early second century BC Rome's concept of provincial command recognized in practice (if not in formal policy) two different types of *provincia*: the traditional *provincia* that normally constituted a military campaign against a particular enemy; and the new, permanent *provincia* that was characterized by the supervision of a specific (but perhaps only vaguely defined) territory. The recognition of this development probably explains why, sometime in the 190s BC (or shortly thereafter), the senate stopped submitting its decisions on prorogations of permanent *provinciae* to the people for confirmation.[66] Because the permanent *provinciae* needed to receive commanders every year, the senate no longer debated *whether* to send commanders to them, but simply *who* would receive command of each. Since this was basically a staffing issue, rather than a question of war and peace, the people probably cared little that they were no longer consulted in such prorogations. The establishment of permanent *provinciae* created (in practice) two different types of military command.

Patterns in Provincial Assignment

Although permanent *provinciae* were essential to Roman interests, such territorial, garrison-like commands were less attractive to the Roman aristocracy than traditional military campaigns. The division of the archaic praetorship into consuls and (classical) praetors was probably caused by differences in their respective military assignments: the two archaic praetors who generally received the most important military commands each year became known as consuls, while the third archaic praetor — who was generally assigned the protection and supervision of Rome as his *provincia* (although he might also receive a military command of secondary importance) — became known as the urban praetor. This distinction was confirmed and compounded by Rome's

---

also argues (esp. 119–21) that Roman overseas expansion in the second century BC was largely driven by the need to protect good friends and punish bad ones.

65. Cic. *Leg. Man.* 32. Dyson (1985) 250 described the function of Corsica and Sardinia as watch posts over the western Mediterranean.

66. Ridley (1981) 289, Brennan (2000) 187–90 and (2004) 45. This may perhaps be the reason why Ovid (*Fast.* 1.589) claimed that all *provinciae* return to the senate.

acquisition of permanent *provinciae*, which usually went to praetors because they offered no campaigning or less desirable campaigning. Because the desirability of a *provincia* rested heavily on the opportunities it offered commanders for winning glory and reputation, it should not be surprising that the more senior consuls received the best or first choice *provinciae* each year, while praetors received whatever commands were left, which mostly consisted of permanent *provinciae*.[67] Thus the prestige of a military command was directly related to the prestige of the commander who held it; consuls were Rome's senior military commanders because they received the most prestigious commands, and praetors were junior commanders because they received secondary commands.[68]

While permanent *provinciae*—particularly Spain—frequently offered opportunities to conduct military campaigns, such operations tended to be smaller-scale battles against mountain tribes of limited importance. Rich has argued that aggressive warfare was not the primary activity of the commanders in Spain and that few expansionary expeditions were launched outside of Roman territory there in the second century BC.[69] Livy even refers to large parts of Rome's Spanish *provinciae* as pacified land (*agrum pacatum*).[70] While such campaigns were certainly desirable and enhanced the reputation of the successful commander, they could not compare to the glory and prestige to be won by driving the hated Gauls out of Italy, or by conquering the heirs of Alexander the Great in Macedon and Asia.[71] This distinction helps to explain why

67. Edwell (2013) 47–48 argues that Roman ideas of *gloria*, honor, and *virtus* made Roman imperialism more offensive than defensive in nature. If correct, this would suggest that the Romans were psychologically predisposed to prefer offensive *provinciae* over defensive garrison assignments.

68. Rich (1993) 52: "So in most years the best opportunities for winning glory went to consuls, and it was only exceptionally fortunate praetors who had the chance of a triumph." Richardson (1986) 128–32 and (1996a) 62 has argued that the Romans actually changed the calendar for provincial assignments in order to give consuls enough time to reach the best and most important commands, which were increasingly overseas.

69. Rich (1988) 214 points out that "very few of Rome's second-century wars in Spain can be classed as aggressive. Most were fought in areas already under Roman sway, either subduing revolts or repelling invaders. Of the numerous wars fought early in the century all took place in the regions acquired during the Second Punic War, except for the campaigns in the *meseta* in 193–92 and 185 and the conquest of Celtiberia in 182–178. . . . If the commanders' job was to fight wars, how was it that they neglected their duty, with the Senate's acquiescence, for over twenty years?"

70. Livy 37.46.8.

71. On occasion, strategic necessity might require that the consuls be given commands in Italy when more prestigious *provinciae* were available elsewhere: in 196 BC both consuls wanted Macedonia but received Italy (Livy 33.25.4–11) and in 187 BC the consuls, on receiving the Ligurians as their *provincia*, bitterly complained that the proconsular commands of Macedonia and Asia were far

praetors had greater difficulty winning triumphs in the second century BC: the introduction of the permanent *provincia* increasingly forced praetors to hold partially or fully pacified *provinciae*.[72] Furthermore, since permanent *provinciae* were territories, in any given year it could happen that a commander encountered no significant enemy during his tenure, leaving him with no glory and no hope of a triumph. Chance — rather than strategic planning by the senate — usually determined whether a permanent *provincia* offered good opportunities for military campaigning in any given year. For these reasons, the permanent *provinciae* were generally less desirable and prestigious than the major offensive military campaigns the senate usually decreed each year, and it should be expected that second-choice commands were generally assigned to those commanders deemed — by common practice if not by law — to be junior to the consuls. Over time, this difference in consular and praetorian provincial assignments became standard procedure, giving rise to the notion that consular *provinciae* were better than praetorian *provinciae*, even though the same geographic area might be a consular *provincia* one year and a praetorian one the next.[73] While this distinction between the consular/campaign *provincia* and the praetorian/permanent *provincia* was not absolute, the distinction would eventually become very important and would provide the building blocks of Rome's empire in the imperial era.

This subtle distinction becomes obvious when major military threats broke out in a permanent *provinciae*. Since the attractiveness of a particular *provincia* derived mainly from the opportunities for military campaigning it offered, a permanent *provincia* — although normally a second choice for consuls — could become substantially more attractive if it became the theater of a particularly large uprising or other major military threat. If this happened and the military opportunity in a permanent *provincia* was considered to be one of the two most important commands of the year, a consul would normally receive the permanent *provincia* instead of a praetor. In other words, a permanent *provincia* would normally be assigned to a praetor whether or not significant fighting was expected, but if a major war broke out in that region, or if the fighting in that region was better and more important than any other military threats that

more prestigious and demanded to be named as successors to these more desirable provinces (Livy 38.42.8–13).

72. Richardson (1975) 58–63 discusses the lower number of praetorian triumphs and argued that the senate established new regulations making it harder for praetors to qualify for a triumph. While he is certainly correct, the changing nature of the praetorian *provincia* is also an important explanation.

73. Brunt (1971) 567–69, Eckstein (1987) 55. See also Jehne (2011) 211–31, who discusses the rise of the consular as a specific type of senator in Rome.

year, a consul would usually be given the *provincia* instead. Thus, a permanent *provincia* would be given to a consul only if a major uprising or other war made it an offensive assignment with aggressive campaigning rather than a defensive assignment. When Rome decided to take permanent possession of Sardinia, it was assigned to a consul (from 238 to 235 BC) who was given the task of pacifying the island.[74] When this task was complete and war on the island ended in 234 BC, the *provincia* of Sardinia was handed over to a praetor to hold, but when a major revolt broke out later that year and the *provincia* once again had a clear war to win, it was immediately assigned to a consul.[75] Once the island was pacified a second time in 231 BC, control of the island was then returned to praetors, but further revolts in 225 BC would cause the *provincia* to again be given to consuls.[76] In his account of the provincial assignments in 178 BC, Livy wrote that Sardinia had been assigned to a praetor, but because a war of great magnitude broke out on the island, the *provincia* was instead given to a consul.[77]

Clearly, the Romans believed that permanent *provinciae* should be assigned to consuls only when they were the theaters of major wars or uprisings; otherwise they were assigned to praetors who would garrison the region whether or not campaigning was needed. This was certainly the case with the *provincia* of Sicily: it was normally entrusted to praetors, but whenever a major slave revolt broke out on the island, the task of subduing the revolt was given to consuls.[78] The Spanish *provinciae* display the same pattern: in 197 BC the senate established the *provinciae* of Nearer and Farther Spain as distinct geographic territories and created two new praetors to hold them, but when major warfare broke out with indigenous tribes in 196 BC the senate sent the consul M. Porcius Cato with the task of conducting the war.[79] As Livy explained it, the sen-

74. Ti. Sempronius Gracchus occupied the island in 238 BC (Polyb. 1.88.8–12, Livy *Per.* 20, Zon. 8.18), and T. Manlius Torquatus further pacified it in 235 BC (Livy 23.34.15, *Per.* 20, Vell. 2.38.2, Eutrop. 3.3).

75. The praetor P. Cornelius died of illness on the island (Zon. 8.18), and the consul Sp. Carvilius was sent to quell the ensuing revolt in the same year (*Inscr. Ital.* 13.1.76, 549, Zon. 8.18). In 233 BC the consul M'. Pomponius Matho was sent to continue this campaign (*Inscr. Ital.* 13.1.78, 549, Zon. 8.18), and both consuls were sent in 232 BC (Zon. 8.18).

76. Pacified by the consul M. Pomponius Matho in 231 BC (Zon. 8.18). Major revolts in 126 and 115 BC would also be assigned to consuls (*MRR* 1.508 and 531).

77. Livy 41.8.2: *[Sardinia] propter belli magnitudinem provincia consularis facta.*

78. Sicily during the slave revolts between 215 and 11 BC (*MRR* 1.259), 135 and 32 BC (*MRR* 1.490), and 104 and 100 BC (*MRR* 1.571).

79. In 195 BC M. Porcius Cato campaigned as consul in both Spanish provinces (Livy 33.43.5, App. *Hisp.* 39–41, Plut. *Cat. Mai.* 10.1). See Richardson (1986) 80–94.

ate decided to assign Spain to a consul rather than a praetor in 195 BC because "so great a war was raging in Spain that it was now a task for a consular commander and a consular army."[80] When this campaign was complete and the rebellion was extinguished, the Spanish territories were returned to the supervision of praetors, but consuls would again be dispatched whenever substantial campaigns were expected.[81] Later in the second century BC, the same pattern is evident in the *provincia* of Asia: this normally peaceful *provincia* was given to consuls only when major wars were fought there against Aristonicus and Mithridates; otherwise, it was assigned to praetors who faced lesser threats or no threats at all.[82]

That consular and praetorian *provinciae* could be differentiated by the quality or quantity of military campaigning each contained is evident in Livy's descriptions of annual provincial allotments. His account of 184 BC is typical:

> At Rome, in the beginning of this year, when the question of the provinces for the consuls and praetors came up, the Ligurians were decreed to the consuls, *since there was war nowhere else*. Of the praetors, Gaius Decimius Flavus received the civil jurisdiction, Publius Cornelius Cethegus that between citizens and aliens, Gaius Sempronius Blaesus Sicily, Quintus Naevius Matho Sardinia and the additional task of investigating cases of poisoning, Aulus Terentius Varro Nearer Spain, Publius Sempronius Longus Farther Spain.[83]

80. Livy 33.43.1–2: *quoniam in Hispania tantum glisceret bellum ut iam consulari et duce et exercitu opus esset.*

81. Between 153 and 151 BC consuls were sent against a major Celtiberian uprising (App. *Hisp.* 45–55, Polyb. 35.1.1–4.14), and the revolt of Viriathus and the Numantines would draw consuls, not praetors, from 145 to 134 BC (Cic. *De Or.* 1.181; Livy *Per.* 52–57; Diod. 33.1.4, 33.21; Vell. 2.1.3–5; App. *Hisp.* 65, 70–71, 76–80, 83–89; Val. Max. 1.6.7, 2.7.1, 6.4.2b, 9.3.7). See Richardson (1986) 126–32.

82. After the war against Aristonicus was brought to an end in 129 BC, no consul is known to have been assigned to the province of Asia until the war against Mithridates, when Asia was assigned to the consul Sulla in 88 BC (*MRR* 2.40). After Sulla's return to Rome in 84/3 BC, Asia was returned to the supervision of praetors until a new war against Mithridates in 74 BC resulted in Asia being assigned to the consul Lucullus (for references, see *MRR* vol. 2). Furthermore, when the province of Asia was removed from Lucullus's large consular *provincia* of fighting Mithridates in the East (i.e., when Asia was no longer the theater of major warfare), Dio writes that the Romans "restored the province of Asia to the praetors" (Dio 36.2.2: καὶ διὰ τοῦτο τότε τε ἐς τοὺς στρατηγοὺς τὴν ἀρχὴν τῆς Ἀσίας ἐπανήγαγον).

83. Livy 39.38.1–3 (E. T. Sage, trans.; emphasis added): *Romae principio eius anni, cum de provinciis consulum et praetorum actum est, consulibus Ligures, quia bellum nusquam alibi erat, decreti. Praetores C. Decimius Flavus urbanam, P. Cornelius Cethegus inter cives et peregrinos sortiti sunt, C. Sempronius Blaesus Siciliam, Q. Naevius Matho Sardiniam et ut idem quaereret de veneficiis, A. Terentius Varro Hispaniam citeriorem, P. Sempronius Longus Hispaniam ulteriorem.*

As Livy represents the process, the assignment of consular *provinciae* was a military decision determined by Rome's need to conquer its enemies: the consuls were assigned to the only major war that was active at the time (fighting the Ligurians). Praetorian provincial assignment, on the other hand, was largely a staffing issue in which praetors were assigned to fill a list of preexisting permanent *provinciae* or to nonmilitary tasks.[84] Although this difference was nowhere codified in law, the conceptual difference between a consular and praetorian *provincia* was certainly taking shape.

The idea that consular and praetorian *provinciae* could be fundamentally different in nature and quality is also clear in the way Romans spoke and thought about the two types of commands. This is particularly clear in the *lex Sempronia de provinciis consularibus* promulgated by the tribune Gaius Gracchus in 123 or 122 BC, which required that consular (but not praetorian) *provinciae* be announced each year before the elections for the men who would actually hold those commands.[85] Gracchus's purpose was to prevent sitting consuls from using their position to influence provincial assignments improperly (and perhaps to Rome's detriment), but the very fact that he thought to include only consular *provinciae* in his *lex* indicates that he saw an important difference between the two. Gracchus did not feel the need to regulate the assignment of praetorian *provinciae* because praetorian *provinciae* were usually assigned by a drawing of lots from among a fixed and unchanging list of permanent *provinciae*, whereas consular *provinciae* could (in theory) be any military command anywhere in the known world. In other words, by 123 BC the assignment of praetorian *provinciae* had already become a substantially different and better-regulated process than the assignment of consular *provinciae*, so Gracchus included only the latter in his *lex*.

This distinction between consular and praetorian *provinciae* was given greater legal definition in a *lex Julia* passed by Julius Caesar, which established that consular *provinciae* could be held for a maximum of two years, while praetorian *provinciae* could only be held for a single year.[86] Caesar describes the dis-

---

84. Livy frequently describes consular and praetorian provinces in this way; see 39.45.1–7 (183 BC), 40.1.1–5 (182 BC), 40.18.3–7 (181 BC), 40.35.1–4 (180 BC), 40.44.3–7 (179 BC), 41.8.1–3 (177 BC), 41.14.4–9 and 15.5–8 (176 BC). In Livy's day, almost all provincial commands assigned to proconsuls and propraetors were permanent *provinciae*, so his practice of describing consular *provinciae* differently from praetorian *provinciae* may reflect information found in his sources, or may be a deliberate effort on his part to reflect his understanding of earlier practices.

85. Cic. *Dom.* 24, *Prov. Cons.* 3, *Balb.* 61, *Fam.* 1.7.10; Sall. *Jug.* 27.3.

86. Cic. *Phil.* 1.19: *quae lex melior, utilior, optima etiam re publica saepius flagitata, quam ne praetoriae provinciae plus quam annum neve plus quam biennium consulares optinerentur?*

tinction between the two types of *provinciae* when he writes that, at the open-
ing of 49 BC, his enemies in Rome assigned "two consular *provinciae* and the
remaining praetorian *provinciae* to private citizens. Syria goes to Scipio, Gaul
to L. Domitius . . . praetors are sent to the remaining [*reliquas*] *provinciae*."[87]
The fact that Caesar identifies two *provinciae* as consular before identifying
what territories they comprised and to whom they were assigned demonstrates
clearly that the term "consular *provincia*" conveyed a specific meaning to his
audience. On the other hand, Caesar practically dismisses the praetorian provincial assignments as "the remaining *provinciae*" and does not even bother to
name them, no doubt because his readers already knew the fixed and unvarying
list of permanent *provinciae*.

Cicero also described praetorian *provinciae* in this dismissive manner, referring to them simply as the "eight remaining *provinciae*" (*octo reliquas
provincias*).[88] Cicero emphasizes the difference between a praetorian and consular *provincia* in his speech *De Provinciis Consularibus* (56 BC) when he com-
pares "a campaign waged in Sardinia with wretched bandits clad in sheepskins
by a propraetor with a single auxiliary cohort, and a war with the most powerful peoples and rulers in Syria carried through by a consular army and a consular commander."[89] In that same speech, Cicero records a senatorial debate
over which *provinciae* should be consular and which praetorian, and his language makes it clear that they were understood to be significantly different
things.[90]

The emergence of this difference was gradual and perhaps not noticed by
many Romans at first. A conflict in 180 BC between a praetor in Nearer Spain
and his successor provides a rare snapshot of how long it took many Romans
to recognize the distinction between the two types of *provinciae* that would
be obvious by the time of Gaius Gracchus's legislation in 123 BC. In 180 BC

---

87. Caes. *BC* 1.6: *provinciae privatis decernuntur duae consulares, reliquae praetoriae. Scipioni ob-
venit Syria, L. Domitio Gallia . . . in reliquas provincias praetores mittuntur.*

88. Cic. *Fam.* 8.8.8.

89. Cic. *Prov. Cons.* 15 (Gardner, trans.).

90. Cic. *Prov. Cons.* 17. Some senators wanted to supplant Caesar in the two Gallic *provinciae*,
and others (including Cicero) wanted to replace the proconsuls Gabinius and Piso in Macedonia and
Syria. The key issue was that changes to praetorian provincial assignments could be made immediately (but were subject to tribunician veto) whereas consular provincial assignments had to be made
in advance of the consular elections (under the *lex Sempronia*) but could not be vetoed. So assigning
the Gallic *provinciae* to sitting praetors would take effect immediately (but might be vetoed), whereas
assigning them to the next year's consuls could not be vetoed (but would leave Caesar in Gaul for
months).

the praetor in Nearer Spain, Q. Fulvius Flaccus, claimed that he had "completed" his assigned *provincia* (*confecta provincia*) and asked for permission to bring his army with him back to Rome (no doubt to participate in the triumph he intended to seek).[91] This was a substantial request, since the complete subjugation of a *provincia* and the removal of Roman military forces from the area were considered stunning accomplishments that brought tremendous glory and honor upon a commander, and they were traditional expectations for winning a triumph.[92] Flaccus's request indicates that he viewed his *provincia* in Nearer Spain as a war of conquest: he had been given a task to complete, and—having completed it—the *provincia* was finished and the army could return to Rome. One of the loudest voices opposing Flaccus's request in the senate was Ti. Sempronius Gracchus, the praetor of 180 BC who had been appointed to succeed Flaccus in Nearer Spain. Although he was certainly acting out of personal interest (he wanted a veteran army under his own command), Tiberius argued that military forces were still needed in Spain in case the recently pacified Celtiberians once again rose up against Rome. Gracchus argued that the *provincia* of Nearer Spain was a garrison or defensive assignment and needed an army to guarantee the security of Rome's overseas possession. The senate agreed that Nearer Spain was a permanent *provincia*, could not be completed in the foreseeable future, and would continue to be garrisoned and protected no matter how great a victory had been achieved there. Flaccus was given a triumph and was permitted to bring back those of his soldiers who had been serving in Spain for six or more years as well as those who had shown conspicuous bravery under his personal command, but all his other soldiers would remain in Spain for Gracchus, who would receive in addition a new, overstrength legion of fresh recruits as well as seven thousand Italian allies. Thus, while Flaccus wanted to think of Nearer Spain as a traditional *provincia* that could be completed by a major military victory destroying (for a time) his assigned enemy, Gracchus and the senate insisted that Nearer Spain was something different—a perpetual garrison in conquered territory that could never be completed.

Just as the Roman decision to maintain direct control over territories cap-

91. Livy 40.35.10–36.12.

92. In the early and middle republic bringing one's army back to Rome safely was one of the prerequisites for a triumph (until overseas campaigns and the garrisoning of provinces made this impracticable). Thus, in 187 BC the proconsul Cn. Manlius Vulso listed bringing his army back to Rome as one of the reasons why he deserved a triumph (Livy 38.50.3), as did L. Aemilius Paullus in 167 BC (Livy 45.38.14).

tured from Carthage gradually led to the distinction between traditional and permanent *provinciae*, the practice of assigning those permanent *provinciae* to praetors gradually solidified and augmented a divergence in popular thought about what type of command a consul should have and what type of command a praetor should have, accentuating the differences between two magistracies that had once been the same. Without benefit of legal definition or established Roman policy, these distinctions evolved slowly through sustained practice and gradually became the norm: Rome acquired two types of *provincia* instead of one (the task to complete and the territory to defend), and it became expected that consuls would normally receive wars while praetors would normally receive garrison duties. Because of this, consuls and praetors might act somewhat differently in the same permanent *provincia*: a praetor might see his task as the control and protection of a particular territory, whereas a consul might see his task as the destruction of an enemy who might or might not be in the territory to which he was assigned as his *provincia*. Richardson points out that when the consul Cato the Elder was assigned to Nearer Spain in 195 BC to suppress a major uprising, he freely ignored the border with Farther Spain and operated in both permanent *provinciae* without distinction; Cato did a good job of destroying the enemy, but did so by ignoring boundaries and alliances with local tribes that — in the long run — probably destabilized the Spanish *provinciae* as long-term garrisons and zones of control.[93] Eckstein identifies other Roman consuls who similarly ignored geographic boundaries "to *post factum* senatorial approval."[94] In common practice, therefore, consuls continued to understand their *provinciae* to be a particular enemy to destroy (regardless of territorial boundaries), whereas praetors increasingly found their *provinciae* described as specific territories to guard and control.

The Demand for Administration and the Origin of Governance

The praetors sent to hold the permanent *provinciae* were military commanders first and foremost, but the permanent *provinciae* they increasingly received were more than simple military assignments. In addition to protecting their assigned territory and (if applicable) leading raids against hostile neighbors, the praetors exercised authority over a large civilian population that was generally pacified and in need of governance. That the Romans had intended for

93. Richardson (1986) 88.

94. Eckstein (1986) 46–47. He specifically mentions C. Claudius Nero (Livy 27.43.6–7), L. Aemilius Papus (Polyb. 2.31.3–4), and Cn. Servilius Geminus (Livy 22.9.6, Zon. 8.25).

their praetors to become governors of conquered peoples is highly unlikely; the praetors were dispatched as military commanders to protect Rome's interests in hard-won territories, and those military commanders only gradually (and probably unintentionally) evolved into governors. At first, the praetors were probably concerned with responsibilities that served Rome's interests, such as maintaining the peace and the collection of taxes and tithes, but in time the power and authority of the Roman praetor made him the obvious source for governmental services the local provincials wanted, in particular the exercise of jurisdiction.

Rome began to collect tithes and taxes from its territory in Sicily shortly after the end of the First Punic War, and Sardinia and Spain would eventually become important sources of state income as well. Originally, the collection of these funds on Sicily must have been supervised by the quaestor annually dispatched to Lilybaeum, but when the Romans began the regular assignment of praetors to Sicily, these financial responsibilities would have fallen under their authority just like everything else on the island. Although this financial supervision must have been important to Rome, it would be surprising if the praetors gave much of their time to it, since such pecuniary business could be left to the quaestors, who probably adopted whatever preexisting system of tax collection already existed on the island. So long as the proper amount was delivered, the praetors probably had little desire to change the methods of collection.[95] Sicily's other financial obligations to Rome would also have fallen under the (probably uninterested) authority of the praetor, including the collection and purchase of extra grain for Rome as needed, the supervision of Sicily's grain trade, and the collection of a 5 percent duty on all goods passing through Sicilian harbors.[96] How much of this each praetor took upon himself, and how much was left for the quaestors under his command, is unknown, but as the chief authority on the island the praetors were expected to make sure Rome received its due.

It is unlikely that the early praetors on Sicily (or Sardinia) had much interest in exercising civilian duties, such as providing jurisdiction for local provincials. Diodorus (a Sicilian) made a point of emphasizing that the Romans did not interfere with private law: Sicilians continued to use the laws of Diocles that had been established in the fifth century BC and did not adopt Roman

95. Finley (1979) 125: "Lacking any previous experience with provincial rule, Rome simply took over an existing procedure." See Prag (2013) 59–62.
96. Finley (1979) 123.

private law until all the Sicilian Greeks were given Roman citizenship.[97] Although praetors in Rome exercised judicial authority, there is no reason to imagine they would have thought it their responsibility to impose Roman laws on peoples in Sicily or in any other *provincia*, since their assigned task was foreign and military (*militiae*), not civilian and domestic (*domi*). And because one had to be a Roman citizen to enjoy the benefits of Roman law, there was probably little need for Roman law in recently conquered territories that (at least initially) contained only a handful of Roman citizens. Finley described the Roman disposition toward Sicily in these early years well:

> Rome had neither the manpower nor the desire nor any good reason to take on that burden [local administration and local taxation], in Sicily or elsewhere in the empire. What little information we have suggests a great diversity in the details, the end-product in each community of centuries of more or less autonomous development.[98]

Serrati agrees that the Romans made little effort to change anything about the administrative structures of Sicily when they took it over from Carthage — they just replaced the previous rulers at the top of the island's hierarchy.[99] At best, the Romans acted to restore the rich and profitable economy of Sicily, which had been badly damaged by the long First Punic War, in order to maximize their own profits from taxes and tithes. To achieve this, the Romans restored land and possessions to the Sicilians and encouraged them to rebuild their own economy, but we cannot tell from the surviving sources whether this was a major endeavor undertaken by a series of praetors on Sicily or simply a few decrees sent by the senate to the various cities throughout the island.[100] Otherwise, we have no evidence to indicate what the Romans were doing on Sicily between the first two Punic Wars. This silence is particularly frustrating, because it blinds us to Rome's first two decades as an overseas power; but Cicero would later write that possession of Sicily first taught the Romans how good it was to rule over other nations.[101]

---

97. Diod. 13.35.3. When the Sicilian Greeks received Roman citizenship is uncertain. Cicero (*Att.* 14.12) suggests that Mark Antony may have given them the citizenship in 43 BC, but, if so, they seem to have lost it by Augustus's accession.

98. Finley (1979) 126.

99. Serrati (2000a) 112.

100. Pritchard (1971) 227, Verbrugghe (1972) 537–56, and Serrati (2000a) 112–14 and (2000b) 124–25.

101. Cic. *Verr.* 2.2.2.

The Second Punic War interrupted the development of the permanent *provincia*, and Sicily and Sardinia became active war zones that were assigned to consuls or praetors as the necessities of war demanded. When Rome emerged victorious from the war, it acquired two new permanent *provinciae*, demonstrating its determination to continue controlling overseas territories. The praetors sent to these *provinciae* were military commanders first and foremost, so they usually prioritized their military responsibilities (or opportunities) above all else. This was especially true of the two Spanish *provinciae*, where praetors were able to spend a great deal of their time in military campaigning if they wished, and the praetors in Sardinia are found suppressing local uprisings or campaigning on the even more savage Corsica.[102] Sicily was generally peaceful, but even so its strategic location and importance as one of Rome's great naval bases meant it was a critical zone of defense and might also play a role supporting wars in other *provinciae*. Livy indicates that there was still a Roman army on Sicily in 191 BC, when the praetor there was given special instructions to guard the island's shores carefully against the navy of Antiochus, and in 172 BC the praetor of Sicily was ordered to refit the ships under his command and dispatch them to Brundisium.[103] In all permanent *provinciae*, the military identity of the *provincia* continued to be prominent, showing that the differences between the permanent *provincia* and the traditional *provincia* were not pronounced initially.

While Roman generals may not have sought to become governors, their absolute power made them an obvious source for authoritative judgments, so provincials probably began seeking rulings, mediation, and justice from them. This aspect of provincial governance (which was to become central) seems to have developed as a response to demands from below rather than as an imperial imposition from Rome. To some extent, this could have been anticipated by Rome's succession as the supreme power in a region; by displacing the Carthaginians as overlords of Sicily, Sardinia, and (to a lesser extent) Spain, it was only natural that those who had once looked to Carthage for defini-

---

102. Richardson (1986) 104–25 has argued that Roman commanders in Spain were predominantly occupied with military responsibilities between 193 and 155 BC. In the islands, in 181 BC the praetor M. Pinarius Rusca not only fought campaigns with the Ilienses on Sardinia but also crossed over to campaign on Corsica (Livy 40.19.6–8 and 34.12–13); in 178 BC an uprising on Sardinia was great enough that the praetor's forces were inadequate to suppress it (Livy 41.6.5–7); and in 173 BC the Sardinian praetor won a tremendous war on Corsica and imposed tribute on the defeated enemy (Livy 42.1.3 and 7.1–2).

103. Livy 36.2.6–13 and 42.27.2.

tive judgments would now look to Rome's representatives. This bottom-up demand for jurisdiction began long before territories were thoroughly pacified: Scipio Africanus took time out from his conquest of Spain to hear petitions from locals seeking arbitration in disputes; in 191 BC the praetor of Farther Spain, L. Aemilius Paullus (cos. 182, 168), ruled that the slaves who belonged to the Hastenses of Turris Lascutana should be free; M'. Acilius Glabrio, as proconsul with the *provincia* of fighting Antiochus in Greece, responded to reports of corruption at Delphi by establishing regulations and privileges for the sanctuary; sometime after 146 BC the Dionysiac artists secured special privileges from a Roman commander in Greece or Macedonia; in the late second century BC the city of Dyme in Greece called upon the Roman commander in Macedonia to put down internal strife in their city; rival Greek guilds of Dionysiac artists repeatedly sought Roman intervention to resolve their disputes; and a Roman commander in Spain appointed judges and set out the formula for the arbitration of a water dispute between two Spanish communities in 87 BC.[104]

The main appeal of Rome's commanders was certainly their power, since their military authority, their command of soldiers, and their role as Rome's representatives enabled them to wield more authority than any other person in the *provincia*. For this reason, Roman commanders had the ability to back their decisions with force and could rule on critical matters, including the restitution of goods seized in war, the recognition of sanctuaries and the sanctity of entire cities (including tax-exempt status), and the general reorganization of cities disrupted by warfare or party strife.[105] Boundary disputes, which could bring entire cities into conflict with one another, were also likely to be brought to Roman commanders, and Kallet-Marx has argued that Macedonians actively sought Roman involvement and even intervention into their domestic affairs and their disputes with other Greek states.[106] Furthermore, it seems to have been common that the Romans made certain arrangements

104. Scipio: Polyb. 11.33.8, Livy 28.16.10; Paullus: *ILLRP* 514; Glabrio: *RDGE* 37; Dionysiac artists: *RDGE* 44 = *IG* 7.2413; Dyme: *RDGE* 43 = *Syll.*[3] 684; rival guilds of Dionysiac artists: *RDGE* 15; Spain: Richardson (1983) and Birks, Rodger, and Richardson (1984). For discussion of commanders making other such arrangements, see Badian (1964) 72, Richardson (1986), and Eckstein (1987), and Kallet-Marx (1995) 47–53.

105. Restitution of goods: *RDGE* 33 = *Syll.*[3] 593; sanctuaries: Rigsby (1988) 153, *RDGE* 34 = *Syll.*[3] 601; party strife: *RDGE* 2 = *Syll.*[3] 646.

106. Boundary disputes: *CIL* 1[2] 2.633 and 634 (141–116 BC, Cisalpine Gaul), 636 = *ILS* 5945 (ca. 135 BC, Cisalpine Gaul), *CIL* 1[2] 2.823 and 824 (second century BC, Lerida), 840 (ca. 164 BC, Spain), cf. *ILS* 5812, 5813. Kallet-Marx (1995). See Eckstein (2012) 181–229.

when establishing a permanent *provincia*,[107] and Rome's commander on the spot would have been the proper authority to approach about these imperial arrangements. Finally, Roman citizens living or traveling in Rome's permanent *provinciae* certainly took their legal matters to the Roman provincial commander whenever possible, since they hoped to acquire some benefit from their fellow citizens' exercise of *imperium*.[108]

The authority of a commander to resolve disputes in a permanent *provincia* was especially valuable because of the implicit guarantee that his decision would be lasting on account of Rome's permanent possession of the territory; the presence of a Roman praetor could be counted on year-after-year, increasing the likelihood that one praetor's judgment would be upheld by his successors, creating lasting decisions. Furthermore, the fact that the praetor in charge of a *provincia* changed every year or two may have been attractive to locals, since it meant individual Roman praetors were less likely to be biased by long-term local ties. Also, if an applicant failed to achieve his request from one praetor, he could always try again a year or two later with that praetor's successor. Marshall has illustrated this point, arguing that the high frequency of judicial corruption in the Greek world encouraged the Greeks to look to Rome and Roman commanders as a source of fair and impartial judgment.[109] As a result, provincials involved in disputes began looking to Roman generals as powerful (but, it was to be hoped, neutral) third parties whose judgments carried great weight. Lintott notes this probable origin of provincial government as follows: "Thus the early stages of development [of jurisdiction] are a matter of conjecture, but it seems probable that this was a process of casuistry, where there were few, if any, ground rules existing at the beginning, and the growth of jurisdiction was, at least initially, a response to demand."[110]

---

107. Such boards of ten legates were to assist the Roman magistrate in settling territory coming under direct Roman control, including Greece and Macedonia (Cic. *Att.* 13.4.1, 6.4, 30.2, and 32.3; Paus. 7.16.6; Polyb. 39.4.1–5.1), Africa (App. *Pun.* 135), Spain after the fall of Numantia in 133 BC (App. *Ib.* 99.428), Asia (in 129 BC: Strab. 14.1.38; in 67 BC: Cic. *Att.* 13.6.4, Plut. *Luc.* 35.5, 36.1), and perhaps Crete (Livy *Per.* 100). Such procedures were also used to make peace treaties at the ends of the First and Second Punic War (Polyb. 1.63.1–2 and Livy 30.43.4), the Second Macedonian War (Livy 30.44.13), the Third Macedonian War (Livy 45.17.1). For other examples of the uses of boards of ten legates for making treaties, see Hoyos (1973) 47–48.

108. See Wilson (1966) 19–27, Hoffman (1976) 366–74, Richardson (1996a) 43, 77–82, Ferrary (2002) esp. 134–36, and Beltrán Lloris (2011) 131–44.

109. Marshall (1967) 412.

110. Lintott (1993) 55. See also Richardson (1996a) 43: "Taxation and tribute, relations with local communities and the placing of new settlements were all part of the activity of a Roman commander in Spain in the second century BC, and these, along with the legal decisions which accompanied

Most likely, praetors found themselves being approached regularly by provincials with questions about legal disputes. Since praetors were first and foremost military commanders, they made decisions by right of their *imperium* and acted from the perspective of a military commander. Richardson has demonstrated this point, arguing that the early administration of the Spanish *provinciae* grew out of the experience of warfare and included command, administrative arrangements, and relations with indigenous peoples.[111] Kallet-Marx has likewise emphasized that there was a slow and gradual timetable by which *provinciae* developed from conquered peoples to spheres of governance and control.[112] How quickly commanders became accustomed to exercising jurisdiction over local civilians is uncertain, but it would have occurred faster among the praetorian commanders of permanent *provinciae*, who spent more time among peaceful provincials, than did their consular counterparts, who were occupied with wars of conquest.

One may well ask, however, why a powerful Roman military commander would agree to act as a judge or arbiter in local cases when he could be doing other things with his short tenure in a *provincia*. From the praetor's perspective, he was a military commander fully invested with *imperium* in the sphere *militiae*, so why would he spend time on civilian matters as if he was in the sphere *domi*? On a pragmatic level, Prag has pointed out that praetors needed to offer some rewards to provincials in order to acquire local levies for military operations, so the exercise of jurisdiction may have been an effort to win local support.[113] There are also cultural reasons why praetors would have been inclined toward adding regular jurisdiction to their role as provincial commander. First, Rome's aristocracy had a long tradition of voluntarily assisting poorer citizens in legal affairs, since such assistance both established a patron-client relationship between the two and was an expected part of an existing relationship. Exercising jurisdiction helped to create and reinforce an aristocrat's place in Rome's social hierarchy. To any Roman aristocrat, it would have been natural to receive requests for legal assistance from those beneath him, and he would have perceived his acquiescence to such requests as increasing his own status. Praetors most likely did not seek to spend their time exercising jurisdiction, and minor cases involving unimportant people were surely left to local officials, but

---

them, came to make up a large part of what it was to be a governor in a province of the empire, in Spain as elsewhere in the Mediterranean world."

111. Richardson (1986) 55, 123–25 and (2011a) 475.

112. Kallet-Marx (1995) 12–20 and 30.

113. Prag (2011) 15–28.

high-profile cases involving important persons or cities may have been worth their time to hear, since such exercise of authority reinforced the praetors' own prestige and status.[114] Second, this natural inclination of Rome's aristocracy to render judgment on others would have been multiplied by holding the office of praetor, which normally exercised the highest level of jurisdiction in Rome. Although early praetors would have understood themselves to be generals in the sphere *militiae*, it was a natural and expected part of their office to exercise jurisdiction. From the praetor's viewpoint, the exercise of jurisdiction reflected the civilian part of his office, and the prestige inherent in sitting in judgment over others made provincial requests for judicial supervision attractive.[115] Indeed, praetors seem to have simply applied standard Roman legal thinking and terminology to their exercise of jurisdiction of provincials, suggesting an improvised process in which commanders used familiar concepts to satisfy local demands for justice.[116] The prestige a praetor acquired by exercising jurisdiction was far less desirable than the glory he might win commanding Rome's legions in war, but it was still significant and would have been attractive if and when no better way to enhance one's reputation was available.

As the demand for justice increased, praetors seem to have had recourse to issuing edicts, which was a common method judges used in Rome to announce publicly what kind of lawsuits they were willing to hear.[117] Some commanders seem to have put great thought into their edicts, whereas others — who were probably less interested in the law or in exercising jurisdiction for provincials — often adopted the edict of their predecessor or of some other commander. The best example of this is probably Q. Mucius Scaevola, the propraetor of Asia in 97 BC whose edict became famous for its excellence and was adopted by later commanders in other provinces.[118] In this way, the development of pro-

114. Cicero (*Att.* 6.1.15) mentions that Q. Mucius Scaevola, the famous jurist who was propraetor in Asia in 97 BC, normally allowed the provincials to function under their own laws unless his authority was sought to solve a difficult case. See Hoffman (1976) 369–74 and Mellano (1977).

115. On the prestige governors derived from exercising jurisdiction, see Meyer (2006) 167–80.

116. Richardson (2011a) 475 has pointed out that the edict of L. Aemilius Paullus (*ILLRP* 514) freeing slaves in Farther Spain in 191 BC "uses Roman legal terms in non-Roman context."

117. Cic. *Verr.* 2.1.119 (Verres issues edicts of his own devising in Rome) and 3.36–37 (some of the shady edicts of Verres in Sicily). See Buckland (1934), Martini (1969), Jolowicz and Nicholas (1972) 70, and Hoffman (1976) 360–64.

118. When crafting his provincial edict for Cilicia, Cicero based it on the edict of his predecessor in the *provincia*, Appius Claudius Pulcher (Cic. *Fam.* 3.8.4), and of Q. Mucius Scaevola (Cic. *Att.* 6.1.15, Val. Max. 8.15.6). See Buckland (1934) 81–96, Jolowicz and Nicholas (1972) 69–71, 356–59, Hoyos (1973) 48–50, Galsterer (1986) 15–19, Lintott (1993) 28–32, Schulz (1997) 93–98, Ferriès and Delrieux (2011) 207–30.

vincial governance was probably an informal and unplanned process through which praetors reacted to requests for justice from below but rarely tried to impose any organized system of administration from above. One drawback to this developing system of governance was the temporary nature of the provincial commander's authority. A praetor with *imperium* in his *provincia* enjoyed virtually unlimited power, and he could make whatever pronouncements he wanted and impose his will with an iron fist if he so wished. Once he returned to Rome and laid down his *imperium*, however, the authority that had backed all of his decisions in his *provincia* expired. In later periods, locals would hasten to greet every incoming governor and seek confirmation of their predecessors' rulings, thereby renewing the validity of those decisions whose underlying authority (the *imperium* of a previous commander) had expired.[119]

On the other hand, some provincial commanders seem to have laid down lasting regulations called *leges provinciarum*. Because Roman commanders did not have legislative authority (unless their decree was confirmed in Rome and became a formal *lex*), these *leges provinciarum* must have been strictly local arrangements that had force in only a particular *provincia*, but they do seem to have been effective tools of long-term governance. The most famous of these was the *lex Hieronica*, which the Romans adopted from King Hiero of Syracuse when they took over his kingdom, and which was eventually replaced in 132 BC by the *lex Rupilia*.[120] Although we know little about the nature and content of these *leges*, some clues are available: in their settlement of Greece, Pausanius says that the Romans imposed aristocratic governments, established taxes to Rome, forbade Greeks to own property abroad, banned federated leagues, and placed a Roman governor over the *provincia*.[121] More generally, they could include clauses concerning the destruction of enemy towns and the rewarding of friendly ones, the imposition of tribute on land and persons, the status of towns and land, the supervision of local and international relations, regulations about local government, and the extent of the province and its borders.[122] Of course, such *leges provinciae* were not intended to be the final word on the subject, as Hoyos points out:

119. For example, *IGRR* 4.943 records the statement of a provincial governor that it was his general policy to uphold the decisions of his predecessor.

120. Cic. 2.2.32–44. Lintott (1993) 57, Kallet-Marx (1995) 12–18, 30, and 127, Richardson (1996) 70, and Eckstein (2010) 248.

121. Paus. 7.16.6–7. See Gruen (1984) and Baronowski (1988).

122. See Hoyos (1973) 49. A good example is the *lex provinciae* of Asia, which was set down in 129 BC and was still in use (albeit probably in modified form) in the second century AD. When Hadrian wished to reward Aphrodisias in AD 119 by making it free from imperial taxation, he simply

The *lex provinciae* was not an ordinance of a special cast, distinct from and superior to the governors' edicts that followed. It did not always occur at the outset of provincialization, and for a later governor to ignore or to violate it was not illegal. It was the product of administrative convenience; it could be emended if a governor saw fit, and, when circumstances required, it could be scrapped and a new dispensation set up in its place.[123]

This emphasizes that the early governance of a permanent *provincia* was an informal affair; conventions were established and provincials began to expect certain services from the military commander of the *provincia*, but much of provincial governance remained ad hoc in the third and early second centuries BC. Rather than set up new structures or methods to govern provincials, the Roman commanders continued to use the military force of *imperium* to govern, so provincial government was inherently based on the exercise of martial law, under which commanders had to recognize few legal limits or restraints to their authority.

Although the permanent *provinciae* differed from the traditional *provinciae* in many ways, these differences were probably not immediately felt by the praetors assigned to them. Even after the Romans created more praetors to enable the continual assignment of Sicily, Sardinia (often with Corsica), and Nearer and Farther Spain as permanent *provinciae*, the men who received these *provinciae* understood themselves to be military commanders in the sphere *militiae*, and this perspective shaped the rise of provincial governance. Although commanders had always had the prerogative to make arrangements with allies and conquered enemies, the nature of the permanent *provinciae* made it more likely that Rome's commanders there would be drawn into the exercise of jurisdiction over civilians. Because permanent *provinciae* tended to be the supervision and defense of previously conquered territory rather than active wars of conquest, praetors probably had more time and opportunity to engage in governance in permanent *provinciae* than consuls; praetors had more time because they were expected to remain in the permanent *provincia* whether or not campaigning was necessary (they could not leave when they judged their *provincia* complete), and they had more opportunity because the peaceful inhabitants of permanent *provinciae* were more likely to seek the intervention of their regular praetorian commanders. The more praetors provided administration and jus-

---

removed the city from the *formula provinciae*, thus rendering it free from imperial taxation (Reynolds [1982], doc. 15, ll. 8–17).

123. Hoyos (1973) 53. He points out (50) that Verres felt free to ignore the *lex Rupilia*'s rules for selecting witnesses while propraetor in Sicily (Cic. *Verr.* 2.2.40).

tice for provincials, the more provincials were likely to seek these services of government from the annual praetors. Early provincial governance, therefore, was discretionary and reactive, and there were few limits on the commander's use of *imperium* and martial law.

Early Roman Regulation of Commanders and Provincial Government

Originally, Rome had little desire or interest in controlling the activities of its commanders in their *provinciae*. So long as a commander did no harm to Roman interests, he was free to exercise his authority as he thought fit. When a consul or praetor was punished for some misdeed in his *provincia*, the crime was normally incompetence in command or misuse of Roman soldiers for personal profit. Since early *provinciae* were normally military campaigns against Rome's enemies, it was fully expected that a provincial commander would kill and plunder those non-Romans within his sphere of authority. Indeed, consuls and praetors were actively encouraged to devastate their *provinciae*, since the republic's highest military honor (the triumph) was a public display of enemies killed, cities sacked, and plunder taken from the defeated. Thus, commanders were expected to ennoble and enrich themselves through the successful conduct of war in their *provincia*. Rome's aristocratic elites were steeped in this tradition, and they derived much of their identity and social status from their role as military leaders.

That aristocratic commanders were slow to change their conceptions of provincial command as Rome began acquiring permanent *provinciae* is perhaps understandable. The early praetors in peaceful *provinciae* like Sicily probably took up their commands with the same cultural expectations as commanders in traditional *provinciae*: to acquire glory—or at least profit—from their commands. The expansion of the praetorian college to six members in 197 BC would have given praetors even more incentive to derive personal benefit from their *provinciae*, since only two of those six (33 percent) could reasonably hope to win political advancement to the consulship. All praetors would have been eager to profit from their commands, either to enhance their standing in the consular elections or, if they had little hope of winning, to enrich themselves from what would probably be their last chance to make a considerable contribution to their family's wealth. While some praetorian *provinciae* enabled praetors to seek fame and plunder through military campaigning, all permanent *provinciae* had substantial civilian populations under the praetor's jurisdiction that could be squeezed for money.

An underlying problem in the permanent *provinciae* was the blurring of the line between the spheres *militiae* and *domi*. As discussed in chapter 2, the division of the Roman citizen's world into *domi* and *militiae* seems to have been an ancient and fundamental principle that separated the spheres of what would now be called civil and martial law; a Roman citizen had certain rights, privileges, and legal protections when *domi* that he temporarily waived when he took the military oath (*militiae*).[124] Thus the terms *domi* and *militiae* defined the degree of authority a Roman magistrate could exercise over a Roman citizen: *domi* the magistrate had limited authority and could not impose the most severe forms of summary punishment (flogging and execution of citizens), but *militiae* there was originally no limit on the authority of a magistrate with *imperium*. The statuses held by citizens *domi* and *militiae* defined their rights; a soldier in an army was *militiae* and so had little protection from his commander's authority; but once he was discharged, he was *domi* and enjoyed the full protection of Roman citizenship, even in the presence of a Roman commander *cum imperio*. It was probably easy for commanders to distinguish between *domi* and *militiae* in early Rome: since *provinciae* were normally wars against enemies, everyone directly involved in the war was *militiae*, including Roman soldiers and allies as well as enemy combatants and noncombatants. A general might encounter a few private citizens as he marched out to war and returned home again, and those citizens could have been *domi*, but otherwise almost everyone a commander encountered outside of Rome fell under the martial law of his *imperium*.

As Rome began annexing overseas territories, however, the distinction between *domi* and *militiae* became more complex and difficult. A praetor sent to a permanent *provincia* like Nearer Spain was a military commander with *imperium* leading an army of citizen-soldiers and allies who were all in the sphere *militiae*, but there was also a growing number of private Roman citizens living in or traveling to Nearer Spain, all of whom were in the sphere *domi*. When those private citizens approached the praetor for any reason, they had the right to be treated as if in the sphere *domi*, even if the praetor may have thought of himself mainly as a commander in the sphere *militiae*. Unlike consuls in traditional *provinciae*, who rarely encountered Romans *domi* in their wars of conquest in enemy territory, praetors were expected to be alert to the status *domi* of a growing number of Roman citizens living in or visiting their *provinciae*.[125]

124. Livy 2.32.1–2 and 3.20.1–5 makes clear how soldiers bound by the military oath had little protection from their commanders.

125. Cicero (*Verr.* 2.5.144, 170) makes it perfectly clear to the jury that Roman citizens have the equal protections against magisterial violence in the provinces as they do in Rome, and that it is illegal

Thus the praetor of a permanent *provincia* frequently needed to adjust his thinking about his use of *imperium*. The situation was made even more complex because of the large numbers of peaceful, non-Roman provincials who generally had no standing in Roman law (although some might be Roman allies). Only Roman citizens could claim the protections provided by the status *domi*, which left non-Roman provincials in the status *militiae*, meaning they had no rights or protections from a Roman commander's use of *imperium*. This probably created something of a conceptual problem, since it must have seemed unnecessarily harsh to supervise peaceful civilian provincials with the force of martial law. The unrestrained power of a commander in the sphere *militiae* was a military necessity to maintain absolute discipline, but how was it to be applied to peaceful non-Roman civilians? The original Roman division of the world into *domi* and *militiae* had not taken account of noncitizens who were peaceful, obedient Roman subjects. In its conquest and absorption of Italy, the Romans had often granted limited rights to their Italian allies, such as the *ius commercii* that provided the allies some legal protections in making contracts with Roman citizens, but few provincials in the permanent *provinciae* had such clear rights. Without established guidelines, provincial commanders were expected to use their judgment and show restraint in their treatment of provincials, but given the power of *imperium* and the weak protections of provincials, many commanders seem to have had trouble restraining their greed.

Although consuls and praetors had always been entitled to profit from their military commands in the past, the Romans gradually began punishing those who took excessive steps, especially in permanent *provinciae* where restraint was most particularly needed. Roman commanders had always been answerable for their use of authority in their *provinciae*, but this effort to set limits on profiteering was new. There are certainly good reasons why an imperial power would want to limit the abuse of its subjects: angry provincials might be moved to revolt or resist tithe payments, and annoyed subjects or allies could be dangerous in wartime. Rome's main concern, however, may well have been its expectation that commanders show proper self-control in the use of their authority. Roman society was comfortable giving its social and political leaders tremendous power, but it expected these men to show self-restraint in their use of that power. Thus the head of a family (the *paterfamilias*) could kill

---

for a governor to bind, beat, or kill a Roman citizen in the provinces. Of course, exceptions did occur: Cicero states unequivocally (*Verr.* 2.1.7 and 14, 4.24, 5.113–70) that Verres imprisoned, flogged, and executed several Roman citizens during his tenure as governor of Sicily. Brunt (1971) 204–33 discusses the presence of Roman citizens and Italian allies in the provinces during the republic.

any dependent relation who disgraced his family, and a Roman commander could order the summary execution of cowardly soldiers, but in both cases self-control was expected—the *paterfamilias* was expected to consult with other members of the family before killing a relation, and commanders could be prosecuted for unjust executions. Self-control and moderation were expected of those given *imperium*, and the Romans were increasingly willing to punish those who lacked sufficient restraint while invested with *imperium*.

A classic example of this is the complaint by the Sicilians (the Syracusans in particular) in 210 BC that the Roman consul Marcellus had been too harsh when he captured Syracuse the previous year and had plundered Sicilian cities too cruelly. Eckstein provides an excellent analysis of the debate in the senate between Marcellus and the Sicilian envoys, and he points out that Livy composes it as a classic debate over the freedom of the Roman commander in the field.[126] In the end, the senate sided with Marcellus, although Livy (writing two centuries later) gives strong reasons why it is not in the Romans' interest to treat provincials poorly.[127] Marcellus was a consular commander fighting an active war against declared enemies, a situation in which claims on justice and fairness usually fell on deaf ears. In this case, however, Marcellus was operating in Rome's permanent *provincia* of Sicily, which had become a war zone but was still full of cities allied to Rome. This complicated matters for Marcellus (not to mention for the peaceful provincials), since he had to be more cautious in his use of *imperium*. Traditionally, Roman commanders with *imperium* and a *provincia* in the sphere *militiae* had little need to show much restraint, because the main goal of their *provincia* was the destruction of their appointed enemy, preferably in enemy territory, which itself became fair game for plundering. Thus Livy presents C. Flaminius (cos. 187 BC) as saying before the senate that defeated enemies had no right to complain of mistreatment and that the despoiling of enemies brings honor to the conqueror.[128] In short, commanders had traditionally been unleashed against Rome's foes, so restraint was not called for or expected. In Sicily during the Second Punic War, however, the Romans were fighting in their own territorial possessions and plundering their own allies, so the concept of Sicily as a military sphere was somewhat blurred. Although it was assigned to a commander with *imperium* and was considered *militiae*, the fact that the territory was a Roman possession and held many peaceful, obedient provincials meant that commanders

126. Livy 26.29.1–30.10. Eckstein (1987) 169–77.
127. Livy 26.32.1–6.
128. Livy 38.43.7–13.

occasionally needed to act as if they were in the sphere *domi*. This was not a legal requirement (unless Roman citizens were involved as civilians) but rather a phenomenon of the permanent *provincia* that obfuscated the line between military and civilian spheres.

Because of this phenomenon, accusations against Roman commanders were more likely to come from the permanent *provinciae*, so praetors probably felt the burden of restraint and regulation far more than their consular colleagues. Naturally, many praetors (especially those in Spain) were able to win legitimate and praiseworthy plunder by fighting untamed tribes in or near their *provinciae*, but much greater self-control was expected when dealing with the peaceful inhabitants. Since restraint and moderation were normal expectations of all Roman generals, at first no positive laws were established to limit abuses, and there was no fixed procedure for the prosecution of accused senators. In the preceding examples, aggrieved communities brought their complaints against Roman commanders to the senate, which was a cumbersome, difficult, and time-consuming method of seeking justice. When several ex-praetors were accused all at once by a number of Spanish communities in 171 BC, however, the senate took a different approach. Perhaps because of the number of accusations, the senate instructed a praetor to appoint a judicial panel of five judges (*recuperatores*) to hear and judge each case, and the judges permitted the Spanish ambassadors to select whichever Romans they wished to act as prosecutors.[129] This was not a new policy created to improve provincial governance, but simply an adaptation of the old practice of using panels of *recuperatores* to judge disputes between Romans and foreigners (*peregrini*).[130] Since the *recuperatores* in this case were to be drawn from the senatorial order, the ex-praetors would be judged by their peers who were hardly neutral or disinterested, suggesting that the senate was more concerned with evaluating the behavior of its own members than with seeking fair recompense for the provincials (one defendant was acquitted, and the other two went into voluntary exile—presumably without repaying the Spanish communities). Although they were concerned about the behavior of their commanders and expected self-control, the Romans were slow to establish regulations that would prevent those commanders from abusing their authority and instead preferred to rely on peer pressure and social expectations.

A case from 170 BC demonstrates this well. In that year, the Romans were

129. Livy 43.2.1–12. See Richardson (1986) 114–15, Vishnia (1996) 135–36, and Brennan (2000) 172–73.
130. Fest. 342L.

disgusted with the cruelty and greed (*crudelius avariusque*) of their command-ers fighting Perseus in Greece; tribunes railed against the consul and praetor who had held the command the previous year (in 171 BC), and the current praetor who was holding the fleet as his *provincia* appeared to be equally cor-rupt.[131] Ambassadors from the free and allied city of Abdera on Crete ap-peared before the senate to denounce the past actions of C. Lucretius Gallus (pr. 171 BC), who was back in Rome, and the current behavior of L. Hortensius (pr. 170 BC), who was still in his *provincia*. Focusing their complaints primarily against Hortensius, they described his program of extortion, as well as the en-slavement (for profit) and execution of free and allied provincials. Since Hor-tensius was still in his *provincia* and invested with *imperium*, he was immune from prosecution, but the senate instructed two of its members to deliver to him a *senatus consultum* condemning his activities and ordering him to restore to freedom all those whom he had improperly enslaved. Second, ambassadors from Chalcis likewise complained about both Lucretius and Hortensius but turned the full force of their complaint against Lucretius, whom they accused of the same crimes Hortensius was said to be committing against the Abder-ans.[132] After this accusation before the senate, the tribunes hauled Lucretius before the *comitia tributa*, prosecuted him for his deeds, secured his convic-tion by all thirty-five tribes, and imposed a fine of one million *asses* upon him. These cases demonstrate that the Romans expected their commanders to show moderation in their use of their *imperium* and that they were willing to pun-ish those who departed too far from the cultural expectations. Although they had broken no written law, the cruelty and greed of Hortensius and Lucretius were viewed with disgust as a violation of social norms by their fellow citizens and senators. Whether the Romans were truly concerned about the suffering of the provincials is unclear, since the restitution does not quite seem to equal the crime. While Lucretius was subjected to public disgrace, however, Horten-sius was protected at least temporarily by his *imperium*. The senate did send clear instructions that he was to make restitution, but their *senatus consultum* had no legal weight. Although he would have likely paid a high price had he ignored the will of the senate (especially as a praetor with future political am-bitions), no check or limit was imposed on his use of *imperium*.

In time, however, the Roman senate began establishing regulations that di-rectly impinged on and limited commanders' use of *imperium*, albeit in spe-cific ways. One such regulation was a *senatus consultum* of 169 BC that strictly

131. Livy 43.4.5–6 and 8–13.
132. Livy 43.7.5–8.10. See Vishnia (1996) 137–39.

limited the ability of commanders to requisition materials (both men and sup-plies) from provincial cities.[133] This regulation was probably established in re-sponse to an accusation made by the Athenians in the previous year about excessive requisitions of men and grain made by the Roman commanders of 171 BC, who (among other things) abused their authority to requisition sup-plies in order to make personal profit.[134] The senate instructed the cities not to provide any war material to Roman commanders unless the senate had autho-rized the requisition — limiting for the first time what commanders could do with their *imperium*. Whereas the authority of military commanders used to be absolute, it was now qualified by the stipulation that they could not requi-sition men and material for war without the senate's approval. Granted, there was no way for the senate in Rome to enforce its request, and Polybius even records that it was almost immediately ignored by a commander in Greece, but the Greeks themselves were able to use the senate's decree to withhold the requisitioned men and materials.[135]

Other similar restrictions on the use of *imperium* were gradually intro-duced, such as those found in two inscriptions from Colophon suggesting that provincial governors were specifically instructed to respect the autonomy of free states, although the precise dates of these decrees are uncertain; also im-posed was a limit on the number of slaves a provincial commander was per-mitted to take with him to his *provincia* in the second century BC.[136] Although these regulations applied to all Roman commanders, they would have fallen far more heavily on the praetorian commanders of permanent *provinciae*, since they spent much more time interacting with peaceful and allied cities than the consuls. Although these were individual and specific restrictions on the use of *imperium*, they were nevertheless important changes from the traditional practice of allowing commanders absolute authority in their *provincia*.

The *lex Calpurnia de repetundis* of 149 BC was an even greater develop-

---

133. Polyb. 28.13.10–13 and 16.1–2, Livy 43.17.2–4: *ne quis ullam rem in bellum magistratibus Romanis conferret praeterquam quod senatus censuisset.*

134. Livy 43.6.1–3. The consul P. Licinius Crassus and the praetor C. Lucretius Gallus had requi-sitioned the full army and navy of Athens and had demanded sufficient grain (100,000 measures) to feed those men. The Athenians claimed that Crassus and Lucretius had not used the men in the war, so presumably they had pocketed the grain to sell for personal profit.

135. Polyb. 28.13.6–14.

136. On the Colophon decree: Robert and Robert (1989) 13 (Polemaios decree, col. 2, 51–61) and 64 (Menippos decree, col. 2, 1–18), Ferrary (1991) 557–77, Lintott (1992) 12–14 and (1993) 62–63, Ager (1996) 459–61, Eilers (2002) 132–37, Rowe (2002) 127–30. On the limit of slaves: Lintott (1981b) 176.

ment in Rome's attitude toward the occupants of its *provinciae* and toward the Roman commanders who held those *provinciae*. As has been well discussed by many modern historians, the *lex Calpurnia de repetundis* facilitated the recovery of provincial property extorted by Roman commanders by establishing a permanent court (a *quaestio perpetua*) with fixed procedures that made it quicker and easier for wronged provincials to bring prosecutions.[137] Rather than the ad hoc arrangements that had been used previously to hear complaints against former commanders, the establishment of a permanent court was a strong statement that the Romans expected their commanders to show restraint in their supervision of provincials. Its benefit for provincials, however, was probably limited by several factors: litigants had to travel to Rome to present their case, the ex-commanders were tried by Roman juries that were likely to be biased, provincials could achieve no more than the recovery their property (if it was still available), and the ex-commander was not clearly responsible for the misdeeds of his subordinates or of other individuals (such as freedmen, lieutenants, and *publicani*). Since commanders could act illicitly through the agency of such subordinates, proving the culpability of the commander himself could be difficult. The main problem was that, while the *lex Calpurnia* facilitated the prosecution of provincial commanders after the fact, it did little to prevent extortion in advance. Rather than placing proactive restrictions or limitations on commanders' use of *imperium* over peaceful provincials, the *lex Calpurnia* merely offered reactive punishment. The *quaestio perpetua* was a deterrent on bad behavior but did not seek to prevent abuse from occurring in the first place by imposing limits on commanders' use of *imperium*. For this reason, extortion would continue to be a problem in the *provinciae*, and even subsequent efforts to strengthen the *lex Calpurnia*—such as the *lex Junia* (between 149 and 122 BC) and the *lex repetundarum* (122 BC)— were unable to control the problem.

Although the *lex Calpurnia* facilitated the prosecution of any provincial commander, in practice it too fell disproportionately on praetorian commanders of permanent *provinciae*, who usually had more day-to-day contact with peaceful provincials than consuls and therefore greater opportunity to abuse

137. *CIL* 1² 2.583 ll. 74 and 81 (=*RS* 1–2, ll. 74 and 81); Cic. *Brut.* 106, *Verr.* 2.2.15, 3.195, 4.56, *Off.* 2.75; Tac. *Ann.* 15.20.3. This inquiry focuses on the influence the *lex Calpurnia* had on the development of provincial command, but for bibliography on the *lex Calpurnia* itself, see *RS* 39–40. On the development of the standing courts (*quaestiones*), see Gruen (1968), Eder (1969) 58–119, Sherwin-White (1972) 83–99 and (1982) 18–31, Stockton (1979) 230–35, Lintott (1981b) 177–85, and (1999a) 157–62, Williamson (2005) 301–6.

their authority. Furthermore, because the relative peace in the permanent *provinciae* offered fewer opportunities for legitimate plunder, praetors may have been more likely to engage in the illegitimate extortion of provincials in order to obtain the profits they expected from holding a *provincia*. There were many prosperous cities and individuals in Rome's permanent provinces, and their wealth was a powerful temptation to praetors who had few other methods of enriching themselves. For these reasons, praetors were more likely to be charged under the *lex Calpurnia*. At least eight praetors are known to have been prosecuted for extortion between 149 and 100 BC, which is a high number considering that in that period the activities of praetors in their provinces are rarely mentioned in surviving sources.[138] Brennan has argued that the great wealth of Asia and Sicily was a powerful temptation for Roman commanders and that the senate was careful not to let any Roman commander remain too long in those provinces.[139] The fact that the *lex Calpurnia* fell more heavily on praetors than consuls underscores the fact that permanent *provinciae* were evolving into spheres of governance and administration, while the traditional *provinciae* given to consuls generally remained wars of conquest.

Whereas the *lex Calpurnia* attempted to reduce improper peculation by facilitating the prosecution of former governors after the fact, the *lex Porcia* of 100 BC was the first substantial effort known to impose tangible and proactive restrictions on the actions of provincial commanders in their *provinciae*, a critical new development that probably accentuated the distinctions between consular generals and praetorian governors. The *lex Porcia* established fixed regulations that prohibited certain actions in advance, instead of depending on the voluntary self-restraint of commanders and punishing them if they crossed the undefined boundaries of acceptable behavior. While similar to the *senatus consultum* of 169 BC banning the unauthorized requisition of goods from provincials, these restrictions placed on commanders were much more significant and far-reaching. The *lex Porcia* was probably promulgated in 100 BC by an otherwise unknown Roman praetor named M. Porcius Cato. Although no original copy of this *lex* survives and the year in which this Cato held the praetorship is not otherwise attested, the reference to the *lex Porcia* in the *lex de provinciis praetoriis* (which is securely dated to 100 BC) indicates that

138. See Gruen (1968) 304–10.

139. Brennan (2000) 233. He argues that Sicily was usually reassigned annually in the second century BC and that Asia was probably reassigned every two years from its acquisition into the first century BC.

both *leges* were almost certainly passed in the same year.[140] Although no actual text of the *lex* has thus far been discovered, a portion of it has been preserved in the *lex de provinciis praetoriis*:

μήτε τις τούτοις τοῖς πράγμασιν ὑπεναντίως τοῖς ἐν τῶι νόμωι ὃν Μάαρκος Πόρκιος Κάτων στρατηγὸς ἐκύρωσε πρὸ ἡμέρων γ' τῶν Φηραλίων ἐκτὸς τῆς ἐπαρχείας ἐκτασσέτω μήτε ἀγέτω τις ᵛᵛ μήτε πορευέσθω τις δι' ἃ ἑκάσ[τοτε] ἐπάξει εἰδὼς δόλωι πονηρῶι μήτε τις ἄρχων μήτ' ἀντάρχων ἐκτὸς τῆς ἐπαρχείας, <ἐφ'> ἧς αὐτὸν ἐπαρχείας κατὰ τοῦτον τὸν νόμον εἶναι δεῖ ἢ δεήσει, εἰ μὴ ἀπὸ συγκλήτου γνώμης, πορευέσθ<ω> μήτε προαγέτω, εἰ μὴ διαπορείας ἕνεκεν ἢ δημοσίων χάριν πραγμάτων, τούς τε ἑαυτοῦ κωλυέτω {εἰδὼς} ἄνευ δόλου πονηροῦ.

No-one, in contravention of those measures which are in the statute which M. Porcius Cato as praetor passed three days before the Feralia, is knowingly with wrongful deceit to draw up (an army) or march or travel outside his province, for whatever reason or whenever he shall arrive, nor is any magistrate or promagistrate to travel or proceed outside the province in command of which province it is or shall be appropriate for him to be according to this statute, except according to a decree of the senate, except for purposes of transit or for reasons of state, and he is without wrongful deceit to restrain his staff.[141]

In addition, the *lex Antonia de Termessibus* (c. 68 BC) indicates that the *lex Porcia* established limits on the types and amounts of goods that Roman commanders could requisition from Rome's allies:

neu quis magistratus proue magistratu legatus neu quis alius facito neiue inperato, quo quid magis iei dent praebeant ab ieisue auferatur, nisei quod e<o>s ex lege Porcia dare praebere oportet oportebit.

nor is any magistrate or promagistrate or legate or anyone else to see, or order, that [the citizens of Termessus Maior] in fact give or provide any-

---

140. Lintott (1976) 81, (1981b) 192, and (1999a) 212, Ferrary (1977) 645–54, Pohl (1993) 216–24, Crawford (1996) 236 and 260, de Souza (1999) 108 and 114, Brennan (2000) 471 and 525, Gordon and Reynolds (2003) 224–25. *Contra*: Giovannini (2008) 93–100 argues for a date of 99 BC for this *lex*, Ferrary (1998) 151–67 thinks that the *lex Porcia* must date to either 118 BC or circa 121 BC. Daubner (2007) 9–20 concurs with the earlier date (c. 121 BC). For my full argument in dating the *lex Porcia* to 100 BC, see Drogula (2011a) 91–92. For bibliography on the *lex Porcia* and the *lex de provinciis praetoriis*, see Crawford (1996) 231–33.

141. *RS* 12, Cnidos Copy, col. III, ll. 3–15 (Crawford, trans.).

thing or that in fact anything be taken from them, except what it is or shall be appropriate for them to give or provide according to the Lex Porcia.[142]

The content of the *lex Porcia* that we can recover in these fragments places two new and different types of restrictions on provincial commanders.

First, it strengthens significantly the antiextortion regulations of the *lex Calpurnia* by making governors responsible for the actions (in particular, the crimes) of their subordinates and by establishing clear limits on quantities of goods and services governors could requisition from provincials. This closed loopholes in the *lex Calpurnia* that could be (and probably were) used by commanders to avoid prosecution for extortion by demanding money from provincials through intermediaries or in the guise of official requisitions. The fragments indicate that the *lex Porcia* established what was appropriate for magistrates to collect from provincials, thereby indicating that anything beyond that was considered inappropriate and liable to prosecution. The definition itself would ease prosecution. In the past, wronged provincials had to prove *both* that a commander's peculation was criminal *and* that he had actually committed the crime. The first part of this requirement was probably the most difficult, since the line between gifts and extortion was undefined, making it extremely difficult to distinguish between necessary requisitions and theft, and between justifiable plunder and unacceptable extortion. Since the *lex Porcia* identified and defined certain activities as crimes in statute, the prosecution needed to demonstrate only that the crime had been committed and no longer had to prove that the action itself was criminal. Since it was probably much easier to demonstrate that a commander had taken something from provincials than it was to prove that his taking of it was a crime, the *lex Porcia* facilitated the prosecution of ex-commanders. Thus the imposition of limits in statute placed substantial limits — in advance — on the freedom of provincial commanders to requisition goods and services.

Second, the regulations prohibiting a commander from leading his army outside his *provincia*, or even from traveling outside his *provincia* (excepting transit to and from Rome), confined commanders' movements and actions in a completely new and unprecedented manner. In the past, commanders of all *provinciae* had been able to move about as they pleased. Although they were expected to limit their activities to their own *provinciae*, a great deal of latitude and freedom had been given to their physical movements. Even the borders of the permanent *provinciae* had been porous and easily crossed by

142. *RS* 19, col. II, 13–17 (Crawford, trans.). This text is discussed at greater length in chapter 6.

praetorian commanders, but the *lex Porcia* hardened those borders by compelling commanders more forcefully to remain inside their *provinciae*. This would have increased considerably the identification of permanent *provinciae* as fixed territories, such that in 43 BC the praetorian commander C. Asinius Pollio could assure Cicero that he had remained strictly within the boundaries of his *provincia* in Farther Spain (*finibus meae provinciae nusquam excessi*).[143] This new constraint was fairly rigid: although the *lex* allowed commanders to undertake emergency actions "for reasons of state" (δημοσίων χάριν πραγμάτων), this did not necessarily give unscrupulous commanders an easy loophole to exploit. The legal requirement that a commander was to remain in his *provincia* may have shifted the burden of proof against him if he was later prosecuted, so that he had to prove that his departure from his *provincia* was justified, whereas the prosecution merely had to demonstrate the simple fact that the departure had taken place. The *lex Porcia* was a drastic departure from the established tradition of allowing commanders a free hand in their *provinciae*, and it put praetors in particular on notice that if they exited their *provinciae* for any reason, their motives and actions would be subject to review by the state, and improper actions would be punished. As Lintott describes it, "The *lex Porcia*, by laying down rules for the conduct of officials, created a new range of offences."[144] For the first time, provincial commanders had a list of things they could not do in their *provinciae*, which restrained their exercise of authority far more than any previous law.

As occurred with earlier Roman efforts to deter extortion and excessive profiteering in the *provinciae*, the weight of the *lex Porcia* likely fell much more heavily on praetorian commanders of permanent *provinciae* than on their consular colleagues in traditional, campaign-based *provinciae*, and may have been intended to do so. For example, the requirement that a commander had to remain inside the boundaries of his own *provincia* was relevant only if the commander's *provincia* was (in fact) geographically defined. The permanent *provinciae* assigned to praetors could all be roughly defined by geography, whereas the wars and campaigns given to consuls (even if launched from a permanent *provincia*) were rarely defined by geography. In fact, the newest permanent *provinciae*, including Macedonia (between 148 and 146 BC), Africa (146 BC), and Asia (129 BC), had strengthened the identity of permanent *provinciae* as geographically defined areas, because all three had been fully developed kingdoms

143. Cic. *Fam.* 10.32.5.
144. Lintott (1981b) 196.

with well-established borders when they were absorbed by Rome.[145] These borders separated the new permanent *provinciae* from neighboring kingdoms and polities, many of which were allies of Rome and therefore had the right to expect Rome's provincial commanders to keep to their side of those borders. Whereas the praetorian commanders in Spain had only to worry about stepping on each other's toes (they recognized the freedom of no other state in the peninsula), the praetors in Macedonia, Africa, and Asia could provoke serious complaints and international trouble if they marched their armies out of their *provinciae* and into a free state or kingdom whose independence had been guaranteed by Rome. It was important that praetors remain within the spheres assigned to them.

The rules were different for consuls, who normally held wars without established geographic borders as their *provinciae*. In the second century BC, consuls were rarely assigned to a permanent *provincia* unless it contained a major uprising or revolt, or unless it was being used as a base from which to attack and destroy a particular enemy outside of the permanent *provincia*. In both cases, consuls were being sent to destroy an enemy, and often that enemy was to be found outside the permanent *provinciae* to which they had been assigned. In 205 BC the consul Scipio (later Africanus) had been given the *provincia* of Sicily with permission to invade Africa (*permissumque ut in Africam, si id e re publica esse censeret, traiceret*); in 190 BC the consul L. Cornelius Scipio (later Asiaticus) was given as his *provincia* the war against Antiochus in Greece (a Roman protectorate), although he was given permission to pursue Antiochus into Asia (*et adiectum ut, cum in provinciam venisset, si e re publica videretur esse, exercitum in Asiam traiceret*); and the permanent *provincia* of Africa had been used as a launching platform for invasions of Numidia by Q. Caecilius Metellus (later Numidicus) from 109 to 107 BC (*cum exercitum in Africa Iugurthino bello . . . consul accepisset*), a command that C. Marius took over in 107 BC.[146] This expectation that a consular commander could use a permanent

145. The kingdom of Macedonia was traditionally organized into a *provincia* in 146 BC by L. Mummius (*CIL* 1² 2.626, *ILS* 20; Cic. *Att.* 13.4.1, 6.4, 30.2, and 33.3; Strabo 8.6.23; Val. Max. 7.5.4), and its borders with neighboring states must have been established, although the northernmost border — which looked out on unconquered territory — was probably left undefined. The kingdom of Carthage was annexed by Scipio Aemilianus in 146 BC (*ILS* 67, Vell. 2.38.2, App. *Pun.* 135) and bordered the allied kingdom of Numidia. The kingdom of Pergamon was organized into a *provincia* in 129 BC by M'. Aquillius (*CIL* 1² 2.646–51, Strabo 13.4.2, 14.1.38; Velleius [2.38.5] says it was M. Perperna) and bordered several allied kingdoms, including Bithynia and Cappadocia.

146. Scipio Africanus: Livy 28.45.8 (cf. App. *Hann.* 55, *Pun.* 7); Scipio Asiaticus: Livy 37.2.3 (cf.

provincia to attack an enemy outside that *provincia* continued in the first century BC: Roman commanders assigned to conduct wars against Mithridates held a variety of different territories, but their campaigns ranged all over the East, paying no attention to geography or territorial boundaries.[147] Because of this difference in the nature of consular and praetorian provincial assignment, the most important Roman senators — who had held a consular command or hoped to do so in the future — may have felt that the *lex Porcia*'s prohibition on leaving one's *provincia* simply did not apply to consular commanders, since consular *provinciae* were traditionally tasks that were not subject to clear geographic boundaries. Even when a consular command included a permanent *provincia* with clear boundaries, the commander needed and expected the freedom to pursue and attack his assigned enemies across those borders if necessary.[148] In practice, therefore, this new restraint must have been felt most strongly by praetorian commanders, because conventional thinking did not define their *provinciae* as a major campaign but as a geographically defined area with clear (or somewhat clear) boundaries. Naturally, consular commanders were not legally exempt from the *lex Porcia*, but the traditional practice of identifying consular *provinciae* as tasks made it easier for them to claim that their *provincia* extended beyond the borders of the permanent province that they held as part (and only part) of their command.

By requiring commanders (most especially praetorian commanders) to remain inside their *provinciae*, the *lex Porcia* was probably trying to limit the amount of discretionary campaigning undertaken by Rome's commanders. Since consuls were normally instructed to fight wars as their *provinciae*, the senate would have been primarily concerned with discretionary campaigning

---

37.1.7–10); Metellus Numidicus: Val. Max. 2.7.2 (cf. Sall. *Iug.* 43.1–44.1); Marius: Sall. *Iug.* 73.7, 82.2, 86.4.

147. In 88 BC L. Cornelius Sulla received the province of Asia to fight Mithridates, but his campaign was conducted mainly in Greece, and he only crossed into Asia later (for references, see *MRR* 2.40, 48, 55, 58, and 61). In 74 BC, L. Licinius Lucullus received the provinces of Cilicia and (probably) Asia to use as a base to conduct military operations against Mithridates, although his campaigns ranged through Bithynia, Pontus, and Armenia as well, and he even planned an invasion of Parthia (*MRR* 2.101, 111, 118, 123, 129, 133, 139). Finally, in 66 BC Cn. Pompeius Magnus replaced Lucullus, receiving the standing provinces of Cilicia, Bithynia, and Pontus in order to conduct war against Mithridates, although he also led campaigns in Armenia, Syria, Commagene, and Judaea (*MRR* 2.155, 159, 163–64, 169–70).

148. Giovannini and Grzybek (1978) 44–47 believed that the *lex Porcia* was intended to restrain commanders, particularly in the East, but their argument can only be applied to praetorian commanders, since consular commanders like Sulla, Lucullus, and Pompey freely ignored geographic boundaries during their eastern commands without penalty.

or "triumph hunting" by praetors in permanent *provinciae*. As I have argued elsewhere, the military exploits of two praetors between 102 and 100 BC may have provided immediate stimuli for the *lex Porcia*.[149] In these years the praetor M. Antonius (pr. 102) greatly exceeded the boundaries of his *provincia* in Asia by taking over the rich and strategically important region of Lycaonia and (perhaps) Cilicia, and the praetor T. Didius (pr. 101) likewise left his *provincia* of Macedonia to conquer the Caenice and the Chersonese. In all likelihood, both of these campaigns were unauthorized by the state and probably caused tremendous consternation among the senators, since both had entailed great risk at a time of national crisis (the imminent threat of invasion into Italy by the Cimbri). Not only did these unauthorized campaigns by the praetors risk Rome's armies and the security of its territorial possessions, but also Antonius's aggressive use of his Asian command threatened to destabilize Rome's relations with eastern kingdoms. Although both campaigns were successful, the senate had to react quickly and reassure its eastern friends and allies that Antonius's unexpected campaign was not a threat to them. In strict legal terms, neither praetor had done anything wrong by attacking neighboring territory, but their ambition and desire to gain glory and an edge in their upcoming bids for the consulship had driven them to launch unwise campaigns. While the senate and people could be happy with their successes (both men quickly reached the consulship), the senate certainly did not want other praetors following their example and launching risky and potentially disruptive campaigns from every permanent *provincia*. Not surprisingly, the senate immediately responded to Antonius's and Didius's actions by promulgating the *lex Porcia*, which stipulated that commanders were henceforth to remain in their assigned *provinciae* except for particular exceptions. This did not diminish the military capacity of praetorian commanders in any way (it did not lessen their *imperium*), but it did place a strong restraint to hinder praetors from engaging in unauthorized and unnecessary triumph hunting or warfare that did not directly serve Rome's strategic interests.

Another stipulation of the *lex Porcia* that must have weighed more heavily on praetors than consuls was the requirement that commanders were not to leave their *provinciae* before the end of their terms. Since consular *provinciae* were generally understood to be military tasks, consular commanders traditionally had been free to return to Rome as soon as their task was completed (*provincia confecta*).[150] When Q. Caecilius Metellus (Baliaricus) decisively de-

149. Drogula (2011a) 91–124, where full references are given.
150. Livy, for example, frequently refers to province as being completed (*provincia confecta*) when

stroyed the pirates of the Balearic Islands in 123 BC, or when Marius and Catulus ended the threat of Germanic invasion by destroying the Cimbri at Vercellae in 101 BC, these commanders felt free to return to Rome immediately, and they did not have to wait for a successor. The most famous example of a consul completing and leaving his assigned *provincia* was Pompey the Great, who managed to complete his three-year *provincia* against Mediterranean pirates in only a few months, enabling him to receive a different *provincia* fighting Mithridates in the East. The fact that consular *provinciae* could be completed at any time was even used as a political weapon in 51 BC: in his efforts to strip Julius Caesar of his *provincia*, the consul M. Claudius Marcellus claimed that Caesar's tremendous victory at Alesia had completed the Gallic War and thus brought Caesar's *provincia* to an end, so there were no further grounds for keeping Caesar and his army in Gaul.[151] Naturally, if a consular commander was unable to complete his *provincia* by defeating his assigned foe decisively, he would remain in the command as long as possible, until the expiration of his tenure of the *provincia* or the arrival of a successor compelled him to leave, but there is no indication that he was required to stay in the *provincia* regardless of his military successes or failures.

Praetorian commanders, on the other hand, rarely left their *provinciae* before the expiration of their tenure because—unlike consular *provinciae*—praetorian *provinciae* were permanently maintained and therefore could never be completed.[152] This indicates that praetorian commanders were expected to remain in their permanent *provinciae* until relieved, unless they had specific instructions from the senate to do otherwise. Almost all praetors received the protection and supervision of territory as their *provincia*, and such a task was ongoing and did not end. Indeed, because the presence of the praetor was increasingly necessary for the judicial administration of the permanent *provinciae*, the early departure of a praetor would leave one of Rome's possessions without a high-ranking official, which was increasingly problematic as provincials came to rely on the commander for governance. The stipulation in the *lex Porcia* that commanders were not to leave their *provinciae* except for specified

---

the consular commander had vanquished his enemy, thereby accomplishing the goal for which he (and his army) was sent: 26.21.2, 28.24.7, 28.28.7, 37.2.5, 38.50.3, 40.28.8, 40.35.4, 40.35.10, 41.12.3, 45.38.14. There is no evidence that this phrase was a technical term used in the republic, but it correctly expresses the understanding that some *provinciae* could be completed, whereas others were merely handed over to successors.

151. Suet. *Iul.* 28.2.

152. Naturally, the situation would be different if a praetor received a task-based *provincia*, such as the command of a fleet, but such assignments were rare in the final century of the republic.

reasons, therefore, must have been aimed at praetorian commanders far more than their consular colleagues.

Third, the stronger regulations against improper profiteering were also more likely to ensnare praetors than consuls (although consuls were certainly liable to the laws against extortion). Most praetors had significantly fewer opportunities to win legitimate plunder, and their temptation to abuse their authority to seek profit from the peaceful inhabitants of their permanent *provinciae* must have been great.[153] Praetors were under a great deal of pressure, because the competition for advancement to the consulship was fierce; only one-third of praetors was likely to advance, so every man who held a praetorian command had to gain as much advantage as possible for the upcoming elections, while simultaneously preparing for the possibility that he would not advance beyond his current post by accumulating as much wealth as possible to enrich himself and his family. In the five years immediately preceding the promulgation of the *lex Porcia*, four praetors were accused of extortion (two were convicted), whereas only a single consul was charged with the same crime, but acquitted.[154] This number of extortion trials—combined with the unauthorized military activity of the praetors Antonius and Didius—may have created the impression that praetorian commanders needed to be reined in, an impression that produced the *lex Porcia*. Naturally, the extortion law applied to consuls as well as praetors, but the greater ability of consular commanders to seek legitimate plunder through conquest gave them more legal options for self-enrichment; praetors had fewer such options and would have felt the regulations of the *lex Porcia* more acutely. Of course, when it became increasingly common for the senate to assign consular commanders to permanent *provinciae* (see chapter 6), the consuls were every bit as liable to the extortion laws as their praetorian colleagues. In 100 BC, however, the senate seems to have been more particularly interested in changing or limiting the behavior of praetorian commanders.

The *lex de provinciis praetoriis* sheds more light on the evolving conception of the praetorian commander, and it suggests that the senate wanted the praetor to operate more as a governor than as a military commander. Although

153. Harris (1979) 77: "The opportunities for self-enrichment open to provincial governors and their immediate subordinates were very extensive even in peaceful conditions."

154. See Gruen (1968) 306–7, who identifies the following: of praetors, T. Albucius (pr. 105) was condemned in 104 BC, C. Memmius (pr. 104?) was acquitted in 103 BC, L. Valerius Flaccus (pr. 103) was acquitted in 103 BC, and C. Servilius (pr. 102) was condemned in 101 BC; of consuls, C. Flavius Fimbria (cos. 104) was acquitted in 103 BC.

this *lex* is fragmented and even its title is not preserved, it records the senate's assignment of praetorian *provinciae* for 100 BC, including particular instructions that the senate gave to those praetors.[155] Within the context of these instructions, the praetors are especially reminded to obey the terms of the *lex Porcia*, which had just been passed. To supplement the new regulations established by the *lex Porcia*, the *lex de provinciis praetoriis* set down still more instructions to guide and limit the behavior of the praetorian commanders in their *provinciae*. In particular, it specifically instructs the incoming governor of Macedonia to make arrangements concerning tax collection and alliance making, to spend a minimum of sixty days of his term in a particular region of his *provincia* to guarantee that Rome's friends in that area receive no harm, and to establish boundaries for the *vectigal* of the Chersonese.[156] The *lex* also stipulates that, should a praetorian commander of Asia or Macedonia abdicate his office, he is to retain the authority to perform his civilian responsibilities of jurisdiction until he should return to Rome.[157] This statement suggests two things: that it had not previously been allowable or normal for military commanders who had laid down their *provincia* (in the sphere *militiae*) to continue to exercise jurisdiction (presumably in the sphere *domi*), and that the senate increasingly looked at praetors of permanent *provinciae*—at least in Asia and Macedonia—as civilian governors rather than military commanders.

By 100 BC Roman commanders were commonly promagistrates, men whose civilian magistracies had expired, but who were continuing to exercise the military aspects of their office through prorogation. When these promagistrates resigned their *provinciae* and therefore could no longer operate as a commander, their capacity to exercise jurisdiction may have lapsed or at least may have become unclear, since the men were neither magistrates nor (active) commanders. Thus the *lex de provinciis praetoriis* established that they could continue to exercise jurisdiction *domi* even though they no longer held a magistracy or a command *militiae*. Furthermore, the *lex de provinciis praetoriis* took the unusual step of compelling governors to swear an oath to uphold these regulations.[158] This requirement was not really necessary, since *leges* were equally

155. Most scholars believe the *lex de provinciis praetoriis*—which mentions only the *provinciae* of Asia, Cilicia, and Macedonia—is part of a larger document that would have discussed all praetorian *provinciae* for the year. *Contra*: Dmitriev (2005) 85, who defines it more narrowly as a *lex de Cilicia Macedoniaque provinciis*.

156. *RS* 12: Cnidos Copy, col. IV, ll. 5–30.

157. *RS* 12: Cnidos Copy, col. IV, ll. 31–42.

158. *RS* 12: Delphi Copy, block C, ll. 8–19. See Giovannini and Grzybek (1978) 41–42 and Crawford (1996) 267–68.

valid whether or not men swore to obey them and should therefore be taken to indicate the seriousness of the senate's purpose. To emphasize this, the *lex de provinciis praetoriis* (and perhaps the *lex Porcia* as well) laid down new, specific, and serious penalties, including a new fine of 200,000 sestertii, which could be imposed on those who violated the *lex*.[159] Naturally, the fragmented nature of the *lex* means we probably have only a portion of the regulations imposed on incoming praetors, but even the surviving instructions make it clear that praetorian commanders of permanent *provinciae* were expected to provide a great deal of governance and administration in their *provincia*. Developments like this led Giovannini to conclude that the senate distinguished praetorian and consular *provinciae* respectively as zones of jurisdiction and warfare,[160] but this is a slight oversimplification, since praetors engaged in military activity when possible, and consuls could engage in jurisdiction if necessary.

Perhaps the most striking aspect of the *lex Porcia* is that it imposed new regulations on provincial commanders by changing the definition of their *provincia*, rather than of their *imperium*. Unlike the modern world, in which a military commander's authority can be expanded and restricted without confusion or complication, the Romans still did not have any real notion that *imperium* could be limited or restricted in any way. The *lex Porcia* demonstrates this: whereas a modern law might remove a particular action (such as initiating war) from the authority of a military commander, the *lex Porcia* preferred to leave the scope of the commander's *imperium* untouched, although it confined the use of that *imperium* to a particular geographic sphere. Instead of reducing the authority of particular military commanders, the Roman state chose to confine (more or less) that authority within the borders of a particular geographic region. This was no doubt connected to the increasing culture of jurisprudence that pervaded Roman law in the late republic, and in particular the development by which the writings and opinions of jurists created a stronger concept of legal precedence that reduced the freedom of magistrates (especially praetors) to use their authority as they wished.[161] As a result, the authority of a praetor's *iurisdictio* was not reduced, but the growing body of precedent and tradition restrained his ability to deviate or innovate in his exercise of authority.

In a similar fashion, the Romans chose to impose restrictions not on the authority (*imperium*) of their commanders but on the field of responsibility

159. *RS* 12: Delphi Copy, block C, ll. 19–30.
160. Giovannini (1983) 65–72.
161. See Frier (1983) 221–41.

(*provincia*) in which commanders exercised that authority, thereby limiting the field in which his authority was used rather than reducing the authority itself. This process of restriction would continue in the late republic with other laws, most notably the *lex Cornelia de repetundis*, the *lex Julia de pecuniis repetundis*, and the *lex Julia de provinciis*. These laws built upon the *lex Calpurnia* and the *lex Porcia* by establishing more rules and restrictions to confine the provincial commander's use of his authority, but like the *lex Porcia* they did not fundamentally change the nature of *imperium* or the *provincia*. Thus these laws did not reduce the authority a commander possessed, but they sought to restrain his use of that authority by (among other things) establishing limits on how many days a commander could remain in his *provincia* after the arrival of his successor, on how many goods and services he could demand from provincials for the maintenance of his *legati*, and on how many years a consul or praetor could retain his *provincia*.[162] In this manner, positive law was increasingly used to establish limits on a commander's use of his authority, a development that helped transform the commander of a permanent *provincia* from a general into a governor.

Conclusion

The decision to take possession of territory seized from Carthage in the first two Punic Wars would have tremendous consequences not only for the size of Rome's empire but for the way the Romans would think about the concept of the *provincia*. The *provincia* originally had been a short-term task or commission to be completed by a commander and perhaps never assigned again, but the acquisition of overseas territories gradually caused the concept of the *provincia* to expand and to signify a territorial possession as well, which was generally pacified (at least internally) and was perpetually assigned as a *provincia* to a Roman commander. This was surely a gradual process: the territories were simply *provinciae* (tasks) at first, but the continual assignment of those territories year after year made them permanent *provinciae* (the defense of con-

---

162. Cic. *Fam.* 3.6.3 and 6, 3.10.6, *Pis.* 50, *Phil.* 1.19; Dio 43.25.3. The poverty of the evidence on these *leges* makes them difficult to study, but the scraps of surviving information indicate that they followed the general pattern of the *lex Porcia* and *lex de provinciis praetoriis* of imposing regulations on commanders' use of *imperium*. Crawford (1996) 769–70 points out that Caesar, and probably Sulla, incorporated older laws into their own *leges*, so these *leges Cornelia* and the *lex Julia* probably reiterated and updated previous legislation to fit the changing behavior of governors.

quered territory) and finally just provinces (territories). Because these permanent *provinciae* usually offered only limited opportunities for winning glory and profit through military campaigning, they were seen as less desirable assignments and therefore left for praetors, who had already come to be seen as Rome's junior commanders and as an office of lower status than the consulship. The decision that praetors were the appropriate commanders for permanent *provinciae*, and the decision to increase the number of praetors to provide commanders for the increasing number of permanent *provinciae*, further solidified the belief that the praetorship was a junior office to the consulship. Although the process was almost certainly unintentional, the Romans in practice (but not in law) came to have two types of *provinciae* and two levels of commanders.

This distinction of two types of *provincia* was particularly evident in the prosecution of former commanders and the establishment of regulations to limit their bad behavior. While the Romans expected all commanders to show proper moderation while exercising military authority, the different natures of their two types of *provinciae* made it harder for praetors to show such self-control. Consuls in traditional *provinciae* were fighting wars, where the plundering of one's enemies was entirely acceptable and praiseworthy. Praetors, on the other hand, spent much of their time — perhaps all of it — in peaceful territory already subject to Rome, and although some praetors had opportunities to enrich themselves in limited campaigns, it was probably difficult to keep one's hands off the wealth of the cities that were prospering under Roman rule. Even if a praetor had good intentions, there were any number of individuals in his province eager to enrich themselves by aiding (and even encouraging) his abuse of magisterial authority. Furthermore, many praetors had no other way to profit from their permanent *provinciae* except through improper means, and as competition for the consulship increased throughout the second century BC, praetors would have felt tremendous pressure to acquire some advantage from their peaceful provincials, even if it meant resorting to extortion. Furthermore, Rome's allies in permanent *provinciae* were also more likely to complain of bad treatment to the senate, since they — unlike Rome's enemies that were despoiled by consuls — had some right to expect decent treatment from Roman commanders. Even more important: Roman citizens living, working, or visiting Rome's conquered territories would have been able to report the misbehavior of provincial governors to Rome and to pursue their prosecution. As the number of Roman citizens in the provinces rose, governors had to be increasingly careful of how they used their *imperium*;

the most damning charge Cicero would level against Verres was the latter's execution of Roman citizens without trial in Sicily.[163] While consular commanders naturally dealt with peaceful provincials as well, they generally did so on a smaller and shorter scale,[164] since their main preoccupation was the conquest of a particular enemy, after which they returned to Rome.

As it became evident that many commanders (often praetors) were not showing the level of self-control expected of them, the Romans began establishing official policies to improve commanders' behavior and to provide some degree of relief to provincials. At first these policies were reactive, such as helping provincials sue ex-commanders for the recovery of goods illegally seized, but in time the Romans began imposing proactive regulations that forbade certain actions outright by defining them as crimes. Since these restrictions were primarily aimed at forcing commanders to show restraint in their treatment of peaceful friends and allies of Rome, they fell far more heavily on the praetorian commanders of peaceful permanent *provinciae* than on the consular commanders leading campaigns against Rome's enemies, which were usually outside of Roman-held territory in the second century BC. The regulations naturally applied to all commanders, but their nature and purpose had much greater applicability in the permanent *provinciae* than in the traditional *provinciae*. As a result of this process, the permanent *provinciae* increasingly became zones of governance and administration in the second century BC, and the *lex Porcia* and *lex de provinciis praetoriis* of 100 BC formalized this difference by establishing new regulations for (mainly praetorian) commanders that further reduced their role as generals and increased their role as governors. This was not achieved by reducing the authority of praetorian governors, who still possessed full *imperium* and capacity for military command, but rather by defining certain actions as crimes (facilitating prosecution if those actions were committed) and by adjusting the concept of the permanent *provincia* to contain and confine better the praetor's use of his *imperium*. Thus, subtle changes in the concept of the *provincia* transformed the structure of the Roman Empire from 241 to 100 BC.

163. Cic. *Verr.* 2.1.7 and 14, 4.24, 5.113–70.

164. During his Gallic campaigns, Caesar normally tended to the judicial needs of the provincials under his authority only in the winter months (Caes. *BG* 1.54, 5.1, 6.44 and 7.1), but even then he would drop this civilian business if winter campaigning were needed (2.2, 3.7, 4.5–6, 5.1, 6.1, 7.1).

6

THE LATE REPUBLIC

(100 TO 49 BC)

The previous chapters have studied the evolution of certain fundamental Roman concepts of command from the republic's earliest days to the end of the second century BC and have suggested alternative understandings of how these concepts shaped and defined Roman thinking about the military commander and the provincial command. In particular, the importance of the *provincia* has been emphasized as a driving force behind the evolution of Roman military command, which is a departure from previous arguments that focused on *auspicium* and *imperium*. As has been argued, the concepts of *auspicium* and *imperium* were so basic and fundamental in Roman thinking that they admitted no real change; all commanders possessed the exact same *auspicium* and *imperium*. The idea of the *provincia*, on the other hand, was dynamic and easily adjusted. Not only did provincial assignment determine which commanders took precedence in which spheres, but the extension of this assignment (prorogation) extended a man's term in command, which is to say his exercise of *auspicium* and *imperium* within a designated sphere. Most important, the flexibility of the *provincia* in the Roman mind enabled it to be repeatedly reimagined and reconceived in response to the changing needs of Rome's growing empire. As the empire grew, the concept of the *provincia* was adapted to enable Rome to control its conquered territories.

In the late republic, the concept of the *provincia* would continue to evolve and change, driven largely by *popularis* legislative activity. Whereas permanent *provinciae* had normally been less desirable and left for praetors in the late third and second centuries BC, changes in the nature of provincial assignment brought about by Gracchan legislation and the rapid growth of Rome's empire induced consuls to begin seeking out new ways to use permanent *provinciae* as launching pads for military glory. As it became harder for most consuls to acquire campaigns of conquest as their *provinciae*, they instead began seeking out permanent *provinciae* that offered the greatest opportunities for discretionary fighting, such as using a consular army to launch an attack against hostile neighbors. By the mid-first century BC, consuls were regularly receiving permanent *provinciae* as their commands rather than the expansionary warfare in enemy territory that had generally been expected as a consular *provincia* in earlier centuries. This change made it easier for ambitious men to manipulate the process of provincial assignment, using the popular assemblies to receive choice *provinciae* and even to combine multiple permanent *provinciae* into a single command. This manipulation decreased the role that provincial assignment had traditionally played in separating commanders into different spheres of activity, forcing the Romans to begin thinking of alternate ways to establish precedence of command independent of the definition of a man's *provincia*. This thinking would ultimately lead the Romans to begin imagining that military authority (*imperium*) could be defined in greater and lesser terms, providing a new means for establishing precedence of command. This period of rapid development and manipulation of traditional ideas would ultimately produce Augustus and his principate.

Despite the evolution in Roman thinking about *imperium* and the *provincia* that is the focus of this chapter, the fundamental structure of Roman provincial command remained remarkably constant throughout the late republic. While powerful men sought ways to gain personal advantage by experimenting with different forms or interpretations of the *provincia* (and, eventually, with *imperium*), there were strong underlying continuities in the way provincial command worked. Until the final years of the republic, the senate continued to assign *provinciae* on the basis of Rome's military and administrative priorities, continued to give the best or most important commands to consuls and the secondary commands to praetors, generally decided what military resources commanders received and how those resources were to be used, usually decided which commanders to prorogue and which to replace, and judged whether victorious commanders were to be honored with a triumph or not. Consular and praetorian commanders continued to receive the same *imperium* and *auspicium*; the prestige of the consulship (and not its authority or capacity for command) continued to distinguish it from the praetorship; and provincial assignment continued — in most cases — to determine which commander held precedence in what sphere.

These continuities with the earlier republic were so strong that the average Roman probably did not perceive the subtle innovations that were being introduced by powerful and influential men; while the changing patterns in provincial command seem considerable in hindsight, to the contemporary Roman they were probably sporadic and occasional, if they were even detectable. Indeed, change was so gradual that the Romans can be excused for believing that the consulship and Rome's way of making war had been basically unchanged since the establishment of the republic. As this chapter explores the various changes to—and experiments with—*imperium* and the *provincia* that took place during the late republic, it is important to keep in mind that these happened within a system of provincial command that appeared consistent with traditional practice. The late republic is a well-documented period, and this evidence demonstrates that provincial command on the whole continued to operate within the basic parameters established in earlier chapters, but because much of provincial command was based on customary practice rather than on clear legal principle (much less on a constitution), exceptions or innovations remained possible. These exceptions to traditional practice—and not the traditional practice itself—are the subject of this chapter. Although these innovations may have appeared as little more than anomalies at the time, collectively they served to change the very nature of provincial command.

The *Provincia* in the Late Republic

At a first glance, the basic concept of the *provincia* does not seem to have changed much in the late republic: while the Romans continued to create more permanent provinces by converting conquered territory into geographic zones that they kept under the continual authority and supervision of a Roman commander, some *provinciae* also continued to be wars of conquest in enemy territory. At the same time as the senate decreed the routine rotation of commanders for the permanent provinces of Sicily or Asia, it might also declare as a *provincia* a war against Mediterranean pirates or Spartacus's slave uprising or Mithridates of Pontus. Thus the *provincia* could be a task or a territory. In this respect, the experiments with the *provincia* that took place in the third and second centuries BC had become enshrined in traditional practice, so provincial assignment in the late republic was—on the whole—consistent with earlier practices. Yet these underlying continuities cannot entirely mask the experimentation that continued to take place with the concept of the *provincia*, which had always been flexible and dynamic. The following discussion examines several important developments in the *provincia* and provincial assignment that took place in this period, demonstrating that the Roman concepts of the commander and command continued to evolve.

In either 123 or 122 BC, the tribune of the plebs C. Sempronius Gracchus pro-mulgated a law that changed the nature of provincial assignments for consuls. Modern scholars generally accept that this *lex* required the senate to announce consular *provinciae* before the election of the consuls who would hold those *provinciae* and that this *senatus consultum de provinciis consularibus* would not be subject to tribunician veto.[1] When the consuls entered office, they would cast lots for the two previously declared *provinciae*. Certain exceptions to this requirement might be made in the face of national emergency (*rei publicae causa*), but these exceptions did not overturn the general rule.[2] Vervaet has challenged this position, arguing that these exceptions prove the senate was not required to determine consular *provinciae* in advance, and that the *lex Sempronia* simply prohibited tribunician veto of the *senatus consultum de provinciis consularibus* if the senate voluntarily chose to announce it before the elections.[3] Whichever was the case, it became normal practice for the senate to announce consular *provinciae* before consular elections, which had long-term consequences for Rome's system of provincial assignment and command, and indeed for the very concept of the *provincia*. Previous to 123 BC, con-sular *provinciae* had been the greatest variable in the annual assignment of Rome's military forces; each year, the senate prioritized the various military threats facing the state and assigned the two most important commands to the consuls. Consular *provinciae*, therefore, had always been determined ac-cording Rome's military priorities during the consuls' year in office. Naturally, this practice lent itself to corruption, since ambitious sitting consuls could use their considerable *auctoritas* to influence the selection of what *provinciae* they were to undertake, which might or might not have been in the best interests of the republic.[4] The *lex Sempronia* was promulgated to prevent such abuse of

---

1. Cic. *Dom.* 24, *Balb.* 61, *Prov. Cons.* 3, *Fam.* 1.7.10, Sall. *Jug.* 27.3.

2. Marius was given the *provincia* in Gaul after his election *in absentia* in 105 BC (Sall. *Iug.* 114.1–4), and in 60 BC both sitting consuls were assigned to Gallic *provinciae* to face an emergency (Cic. *Att* 1.19.2). Manipulation might be possible after the elections: Lucullus was said to have con-spired to get his provincial assignment changed in 74 BC (Plut. *Luc.* 5.1–3), and Cicero made a deal with his consular colleague C. Antonius, so that Antonius received the *provincia* that had been as-signed to Cicero (Cic. *Pis.* 5, *Fam.* 5.2.3).

3. Vervaet (2006a) 625–54. See comments by Ferrary (2010) 40.

4. Probably the most famous example of this was in 205 BC, when the consul P. Cornelius Sci-pio (Africanus) demanded that the senate assign him the *provincia* of Africa and threatened to use the powers of his office to take the question to the popular assembly if the senate did not give him

consular influence, but this presented an obvious problem: How were *provinciae* to be determined so far in advance, before the senate could have a clear understanding of what Rome's priorities would be when the consuls actually took office some months later?

In the late republic, elections for consuls were normally held in October, which meant consular *provinciae* had to be announced several months before the consuls themselves would be ready to take the field the following spring.[5] Perhaps unrealistically, this required the senate to anticipate in autumn what *provinciae* would be the most strategically critical in the following spring. In other words, by forcing the senate to make consular assignments months in advance, the *lex Sempronia* decreased the ability of the senate to make strategic decisions in a timely manner. Whereas Rome had normally reacted to military needs as they arose in the past, the senate was now required to make provincial assignments before the needs of the campaigning season were entirely clear. Naturally, protracted wars that extended over many years, like those against Mithridates in the East, could be identified as good consular commands in advance, but in most cases the senate probably had to assign consular *provinciae* without knowing clearly what military necessities would be paramount in the coming months. For this reason, it became strategically more prudent to assign consuls to permanent *provinciae* that were near to likely military priorities, like Spain, Gaul, Macedonia, and (eventually) Syria. Instead of guessing what enemies would pose the greatest threat in the next year, the senate placed consular armies in areas where major fighting was likely, but not certain.

After 123 BC, therefore, the tendency to assign consuls to permanent *provinciae* increased dramatically. In the 77 years before the *lex Sempronia* (200 to 124 BC), only 22 percent (24 out of 111) of all consular *provinciae* identified or surmised by Broughton involved a permanent *provincia*, and in most of those cases the permanent *provincia* was assigned to a consul because a major war or uprising in that territory made it a particularly important command, such as the Celtiberians in Spain, slave revolts in Sicily, and the war with Aristonicus

---

what he wanted (Livy 28.40.1–2, Plut. *Fab.* 25.2). Despite fierce opposition from (among others) the *princeps senatus* Q. Fabius Maximus, Scipio received his desired *provincia*, which turned out well for Rome. Four years later in 201 BC, however, the consul Cn. Cornelius Lentulus was eager to steal the credit for ending the Second Punic War from Scipio and demanded that the senate give him Scipio's almost-complete *provincia* in Africa, threatening to block all other business until he received the command (Livy 30.40.7–16). Recourse to the tribunes was needed to prevent Lentulus from carrying out his threat.

5. Balsdon (1939) 58 suggested that consular *provinciae* had to be announced at least six months in advance.

in Asia. On the other hand, in the 69 years following the *lex Sempronia* (122 to 53 BC), 51 percent of all known consular *provinciae* (36 of 70) involved a permanent *provincia*, or 60 percent (42 of 70) if Cisalpine Gaul is accepted as being a permanent *provincia* from 89 to 53 BC.[6] Whereas only one-fifth of consuls had been sent to permanent *provinciae* before 123 BC, after this year three-fifths of all known consular *provinciae* involved holding a permanent *provincia*. Thus permanent *provinciae* became dramatically more attractive to consuls in the decades after the *lex Sempronia*, almost certainly because the necessity of making consular assignments early forced the senate to hedge its bets by assigning consuls to permanent *provinciae* that were *likely* to be active military theaters in the coming year. Instead of sending consuls against the best *enemies*, the senate now began identifying the best military *zones* or *territories* where good fighting was likely or possible. Naturally, the senate could not guarantee that a consul sent to Macedonia or Farther Spain would find a major war to fight, but the proximity of those provinces to untamed tribes ensured that an aggressive consular commander could find or create a good campaign for his army.

This new trend in the nature of provincial assignments was an unintended consequence of the *lex Sempronia de provinciis consularibus*, and it would have a profound effect on the way Romans conceived of provincial command. As discussed in the previous chapter, the different natures of Rome's two types of *provincia*—military conquest and military governorship—eventually became associated with the two different military offices: consuls received military campaigns as their *provinciae*, whereas praetors generally received military governorships. Naturally, some consuls spent time exercising governance, and some praetors spent time leading military campaigns, but nevertheless most consular *provinciae* had been conceived as offensive campaigns whereas praetorian provinces were generally conceived as garrisons or even defensive assignments. In other words, the status of the commander became increasingly

---

6. See *MRR* vols. 1 and 2 for references. A *lex Pompeia* of 89 BC gave Roman citizenship to the inhabitants of Cispadane Gaul and Latin rights to the inhabitants of Transpadane Gaul (*CIL* 1² 709, Ascon. 3C, Plin. *NH* 3.138, Dio 37.9.3). This is often taken to mark the establishment of Cisalpine Gaul as a permanent *provincia*, although this may have happened even earlier (Badian [1966] 906–8). Of the thirty-four consular *provinciae* between 122 and 53 BC that did not include a permanent *provincia*, twenty-five were in Cisalpine and/or Transalpine Gaul (six of those in Cisalpine Gaul after 89 BC), five were commands in the Social War, two were commands against Spartacus, and two were traditional *provinciae* elsewhere (Illyricum and pirates in Crete). Military commands during the civil war of 87 to 82 BC are not counted.

important to defining the nature of the *provincia*. The *lex Sempronia* solidified this trend. By causing the senate to begin assigning consuls to permanent *provinciae* on a regular basis, the *lex Sempronia* had the unintended consequence that the definition and use of a permanent *provincia* was largely determined by the status of the commander who held it. In the hands of a praetor—who tended to be subject to greater restrictions as discussed in the previous chapter—a permanent province was a garrison in which military activity was normally limited to skirmishing and raids rather than the initiation of a full-scale war. In particular, the expectation that praetors would remain inside their *provinciae* limited what they might do with their commands, as did the fact that they were usually given smaller armies and fewer resources. In the hands of a consul, however, the permanent province normally was the theater of major war or a platform from which to launch a major war. Because consuls enjoyed greater latitude and freedom of action in their *provinciae* than praetors and were not subject to the same restrictions that limited the activities of praetors, a consul could easily treat a permanent *provincia* as a platform from which to launch a major offensive campaign into unconquered territory. Whereas permanent *provinciae* in the third and second centuries BC had normally been (at best) secondary military theaters, and therefore had generally been left to praetors, in the first century BC permanent *provinciae* became the forward bases for almost every major consular campaign in major wars. Thus the *lex Sempronia* made the permanent *provincia* a much more flexible concept.

The members of the so-called First Triumvirate are perhaps the best examples of this development. Using their combined influence, Caesar, Pompey, and Crassus could have acquired any *provinciae* they wanted for themselves, but instead of choosing specific wars or other campaigns of conquest, Caesar chose Illyricum and Gaul, Pompey chose Spain, and Crassus chose Syria, all of which were permanent *provinciae* that were (for the most part) internally pacified and peaceful at the time. This would have seemed strange in the third or even second century BC, but it made sense in the first century BC, by which time the *lex Sempronia* had made it common practice for ambitious commanders to seek not just wars but promising military zones that could be reached from permanent provinces. Thus Caesar at first choose the permanent *provinciae* of Cisalpine Gaul and Illyricum as his command because he judged the wild tribes in the Balkans, or perhaps the kingdom of Dacia, to be the best opportunity for aggressive campaigning, but when Transalpine Gaul became available on the unexpected death of its commander, he switched his attention to this permanent *provincia* because—in his estimation—it offered a better theater of war.[7] When Pompey and Crassus decided that they too wanted new military commands, Crassus chose the permanent *provincia* of Syria and used it to launch an invasion of the Parthian Empire, while Pompey chose the two permanent *provinciae* in Spain as good sources of military glory that he could control from Rome through legates.[8] That these men at the height of their power chose permanent *provinciae* for their consular commands demonstrates the change in the conception and use of the permanent *provincia* that had taken place since the passage of the *lex Sempronia*.

Because consuls were increasingly sent to permanent *provinciae* in the late republic, certain problems arose that illustrate the different ways the Romans could conceive of the *provincia*. Although consular *provinciae* had traditionally been tasks to complete or enemies to destroy, a consequence of the *lex Sempronia* was that these military generals were increasingly placed in command of pacified, civilian territory (permanent *provinciae*) that usually expected some degree of administrative supervision from their Romans overlords. Permanent *provinciae* were filled with allies and obedient subjects who had a just claim on Roman *fides*, which was different from the traditional consular *provincia* that had generally consisted of a war in enemy territory. This meant that consular commanders had to adapt their expectations to accommodate the changing realities of provincial assignment. The *lex Antonia de Termessibus* is a good example of this. Passed in or around 68 BC while Lucullus and (perhaps) Marcius Rex were fighting Mithridates in the East, the *lex* declared the citizens of Termessus Maior in Pisidia to be friends and allies of the Roman people.[9] A portion of this *lex* sets out certain privileges Termessus was to enjoy with its new status:

> *nei quis magistratus proue magistratu legatus ne[u] quis alius meilites in oppidum Thermesum Maiorum Pisidarum agrumue Thermensium Maiorum Pisidarum hiemandi caussa introducito, neiue facito, quo quis eo meilites introducat quoue ibei meilites hiement, nisei senatus nominatim, utei Thermesum Maiorum Pisidarum in hibernacula meilites deducantur, decreuerit; neu quia magistratus proue magistratu legatus neu quis alius facito neiue inperato, quo quid magis iei dent praebeant ab ieisue auferatur, nisei quod e<o>s ex lege Porcia dare praebere oportet oportebit.*

7. Caesar had initially begun concentrating his legions in Aquileia with the intention of using Illyricum as his base of operations, but he redeployed those forces when Transalpine Gaul was added to his command (*BG* 1.10.3). See Seager (2002) 89 and Rosenstein (2009) 88.

8. Livy *Per.* 105, Vell. 2.46.2, Plut. *Pomp.* 52.3–4 and *Crass.* 15.5, and Dio 39.33.2–3.

9. *RS* 19. See Sherwin-White (1976) 11–14, Ferrary (1985) 419–57, Griffin (1973) 210–11, and Crawford (1996) 331–32.

No magistrate or promagistrate or legate or anyone else is to introduce soldiers into the town of Termessus Maior in Pisidia or into the territory of Termessus Maior in Pisidia for the purpose of wintering nor see that anyone introduce soldiers thither or that soldiers winter there, unless the senate shall have decreed with mention of the town's name that soldiers be brought into winter quarters in Termessus Maior in Pisidia; nor is any magistrate or promagistrate or legate or anyone else to see, or order, that they in fact give or provide anything or that in fact anything be taken from them, except what it is or shall be appropriate for them to give or provide according to the Lex Porcia.[10]

It is not surprising that this *lex* takes the time to explicitly state the limits on military quartering and requisitioning; the Romans had been waging war against Mithridates in the East for several years, and these military operations were certainly taking a toll on the local inhabitants, including Rome's subjects in its permanent *provinciae* who were supporting Rome's armies. Roman commanders had always been expected to respect the rights and privileges of any Roman allies in their sphere of operations, but in previous centuries consular commanders had been operating mainly in enemy territory and had less need to worry about their treatment of locals in their military sphere. After the *lex Sempronia*, however, most consuls were receiving permanent *provinciae* as a base of operations for their armies and had to take much greater care how they quartered their soldiers and requisitioned supplies. Roman commanders probably expected to be subject to these kinds of restraints during their praetorian commands, but the prominent mention of the *lex Porcia* in this *lex Antonia* suggests that consular commanders were increasingly being subjected to restraints on their exercise of *imperium* within their *provincia*. Indeed, the *lex Antonia* was promulgated and passed when consuls were in command of the East, a potent statement of limitations on consular commands.

Similarly, consular commanders eager to conquer untamed peoples adjacent to their *provinciae* might be annoyed to learn that the inhabitants of their permanent *provincia* expected certain governmental services from them, in particular the exercise of jurisdiction. Even Julius Caesar — who was determined to use his command in Gaul to win as much military glory as possible and often used his winters preparing for the next year's campaigns — frequently took the time to travel through provincial towns administering justice.[11] Whereas con-

10. *RS* 19, col. II, 6–17 (Crawford, trans.).
11. Caes. *BG* 1.54, 5.1–2, 6.44, 7.1.

sular commanders in earlier centuries had been unleashed on enemy territory to destroy and pillage, in the late republic they frequently found themselves based in allied territory and needed to make an effort to respect the rights of their allies and perform expected administrative responsibilities. Thus the changing pattern of provincial assignment caused the role and expectations of the consular commander to change, even if only a little.

C. MARIUS AND THE EFFECT OF POPULAR
LEGISLATION ON PROVINCIAL ASSIGNMENT

Gaius Marius's rise to power introduced a new element in the process of provincial assignment: the use of tribunician legislation in assigning *provinciae* to *popularis* commanders. In theory, the Roman assemblies had always possessed the legislative authority to declare war, but in practice they normally deferred such decisions to the senate, so it is rare to find the assemblies doing anything but approving senatorial decisions about war.[12] Even more unusual was for the popular assemblies to contradict the senate in the process of provincial assignment.[13] The senate was normally able to follow its own procedures for selecting and assigning consular and praetorian *provinciae* and in making decisions about prorogation. In 107 BC, however, the tribune T. Manlius Mancinus used the popular assembly to change the senate's planned provincial assignments. The senate had already decided to prorogue the proconsul Q. Caecilius Metellus (Numidicus) in the *provincia* of Africa with the war against Jugurtha, but the new consul C. Marius arranged for Mancinus (his political ally) to bring the question of this provincial assignment before the people, who overwhelmingly decided they wanted the *popularis* Marius to be given the command.[14] This action was without precedent,[15] but the authority of the people could not be denied, so Marius received the *provincia*.

12. For example: in 264 BC the people are recorded pushing the senate to war against Carthage (Polyb. 1.10.3–11.3); in 200 BC the people resisted the senate's plan to declare war on Philip (Livy 31.6.4–6); and in 167 BC two tribunes vetoed the senate's proposed war against Rhodes (Polyb. 30.4.4–6, Livy 45.21.1–8, Diod. 31.5.3).

13. The most obvious example was the popular decision in 210 BC to give P. Cornelius Scipio (Africanus) the *provincia* in Spain despite objections from the senate that he had never held an office with *imperium* (Livy 26.18.1–11, Val. Max. 3.7.1a, App. *Pun.* 18–19, Zon. 9.7). Of course, the people only nominated Scipio because no other Roman commander wanted the *provincia* in Spain, so they did not actually supersede the senate's provincial assignment.

14. Sall. *Iug.* 73.7.

15. Marius may have been inspired by the consular election in 148 BC, in which the centuriate assembly demanded the right to elect P. Cornelius Scipio Aemilianus to the consulship of 147 BC in spite of the fact that Scipio was too young, had not held the praetorship as a requisite precursor to

Several reasons explain why Marius used this tactic to assume command of Metellus's *provincia*: the rise of *popularis* politics, the importance of the war against Jugurtha, the personal enmity reported between Marius and Metellus, Marius's status as a *novus homo*, the fact that Jugurtha was already nearly beaten, and Marius's own desire for status and reputation. The unintended consequence of his action, however, was subtly to change the process of provincial assignment and the basic conception of what a *provincia* could be. The change in process is obvious. Previously, provincial assignment had been a holistic and empirewide practice — the senate had taken all of Rome's military needs and commitments into a single consideration, and with a unified overview and strategic purpose it had named new *provinciae*, had allocated permanent *provinciae* to new commanders, and had prorogued commanders in the field. Even when unexpected military threats appeared, the senate had the experience, knowledge, and strategic vision to react accordingly, making adjustments to the annual provincial assignment as needed. The ability of tribunes to interfere in this process destabilized the senate's ability to plan. Under the *lex Sempronia*, two *provinciae* had already been set aside for Marius and his colleague, so Mancinus's legislation giving Marius the war with Jugurtha meant one of the two consular *provinciae* for that year was left vacant, which may have been a serious problem since consuls were normally given the most important commands. The senate may have given Marius's original *provincia* to a praetor or prorogued a commander already in the field, but even this would have been a significant disruption to the senate's planning. Although we do not know where the senate had intended to send Marius, perhaps he was supposed to join his colleague in the *provincia* of Gaul, where hostile tribes had recently defeated two consular armies and were quickly becoming Rome's highest military priority.[16] Marius's colleague was killed fighting the Tigurini,[17] and one can only speculate whether the senate had intended Marius to support his colleague with a second consular army. Even if Marius had been intended for another *provincia* altogether, the aggressive use of the popular assemblies in

the consulship, and was only standing for election to the aedileship at the time (see *MRR* 1.462 for references). Astin (1967) 61–69 believes Scipio may have encouraged the Roman electorate to vote for him in violation of law and tradition, but Develin ([1978c] 484–88) sees no reason to reject ancient sources saying Scipio's election was spontaneous. Whether or not Scipio devised his exceptional election, it may have given Marius ideas about how the assemblies could be used to challenge the senate's control of provincial commands.

16. Cn. Papirius Carbo in 113 BC (Livy *Per.* 63, Vell. 2.12.2, Strabo 5.1.8, Plut. *Mar.* 16.5, App. *Celt.* 13) and M. Junius Silanus in 109 BC (Ascon. 68 and 80C, Livy *Per.* 65, Vell. 2.12.2, Flor. 1.38.4).

17. Caes. *BG* 1.7, 12, 13, and 14; Livy *Per.* 65; Tac. *Germ.* 37.5; App. *Celt.* 1.3.

provincial assignment by *popularis* politicians introduced a new and destabilizing element to Rome's system of provincial command.

Marius used the popular assembly to acquire for himself a *provincia* that the senate had already allocated to another commander; the senate had determined that Africa and the war with Jugurtha would continue to be a *provincia* in 107 BC, but the popular assembly overrode the senate's decision about who should hold that command. Later aristocrats would be more innovative with Marius's *popularis* methods and would use the popular assemblies to acquire commands of tremendous size and scope — commands that were custom-tailored to serve the needs of ambitious individuals. In the past, the senate had made some effort to keep consular *provinciae* within the same general parameters, to prevent any one of its members from acquiring so much glory and prestige that he eclipsed the group. Although some wars were naturally greater and more desirable than others, the senators tried to share opportunities for command equitably among themselves, such that consuls rarely received more than two legions and a single permanent *provincia* to use as a base of operations, and it was extremely rare for the senate to prorogue a commander for more than twelve months at a time (decisions were normally made on an annual basis). If a particular enemy required a larger Roman force, multiple commanders were usually sent, or land and naval forces might be assigned to different commanders (see chapter 4). After Marius, however, some commanders would use the popular assemblies not only to obtain particular commands for themselves but to create *provinciae* of unprecedented size and scope: Pompey received his vast piracy command from the *lex Gabinia* in 67 BC and his eastern command against Mithridates from the *lex Manilia* the next year, Caesar received his Gallic command through the *lex Vatinia* in 59 BC, Pompey's Spanish command and Crassus's Syrian command were produced by the *lex Trebonia* in 55 BC, and the commands held by the members of the Second Triumvirate, which together comprised the entire Roman Empire, were conferred by the *lex Titia* in 43 BC.[18] Harnessing the legislative power of the popular assemblies, these men were able exploit the difference between permanent *provinciae* (territories) and traditional *provinciae* (military tasks) to construct massive commands in which multiple permanent provinces were incorporated into a single consular provincial assignment, and they received proportionately larger military and financial resources to command these tremendously large commands. Popular legislation thus created a whole class of

18. For references, see *MRR* 2.144, 153, 190, 217, and 340.

super commands designed to satisfy the goals of one man rather than suit the strategic priorities of the Roman senate.

Pompey's piracy command was the first of these super *provinciae*. After his consulship in 70 BC, Pompey had declined to take a *provincia*, no doubt because none of the available options were sufficiently glorious for his oversized ambition. Three years later, his friendly tribune Gabinius proposed a special naval *provincia* that would be one of the largest commands ever given to a single Roman commander. On the surface, this naval command seemed consistent with recent efforts to suppress piracy in the Mediterranean: in 74 BC the praetor M. Antonius had been given a fleet to suppress piracy, and after his death in Crete in 71 BC the consul Q. Caecilius Metellus (Creticus) was sent to finish off the Cretan pirates in 69 BC.[19] Neither command was unprecedented or truly exceptional for the time. Antonius's command was unusually far-reaching (he was active in the western and eastern Mediterranean), but naval commands had frequently been praetorian assignments in the past, and the two consuls in 74 BC had both been sent to the far more important and prestigious *provincia* of fighting Mithridates in the East, so Antonius's *provincia* was certainly a second choice assignment at the time. Metellus's *provincia* on Crete was also entirely conventional and even rather modest compared to other contemporary consular commands, such as the Mithridatic wars in the East. Pompey's command, however, was far grander than these previous naval commands: in addition to having the suppression of piracy throughout the entire Mediterranean as his *provincia*, he was given authority up to fifty miles inland from the coast to pursue pirates on land, received twenty-four legates with *imperium* to assist him, received a massive fleet of five hundred ships and authorization to raise more from the allies as needed, was granted the authority to recruit sailors from the allies as needed, received seemingly unlimited financial resources, and was to hold this unprecedented *provincia* for three years without need of prorogation.[20] The size and scope of this *provincia*, and the resources dedicated to it, were unprecedented in Roman military history. It was still a traditional *provincia* in that it was a military task to defeat

19. Antonius was active in the western Mediterranean his first year, then spent the next three years around Sicily and Crete (where is died): Cic. *Verr.* 2.2.8 and 3.213–16, Livy *Per.* 97, Vell. 2.31.3–4, App. *Sic.* 6.1, *SIG*³ 748. Metellus's command: Cic. *Flacc.* 30 and 63, *Ad Brut.* 1.8, Livy *Per.* 98, Vell. 2.34.1, Val. Max. 7.6.ex.1, Flor. 1.42.4, App. *Sic.* 6.2, Plut. *Pomp.* 29.1.

20. Cic. *Leg. Man.* 44 and 52–58, *Leg. Agr.* 2.46, Livy *Per.* 99, Vell. 2.31.2–32.6, Tac. *Ann.* 15.25.3–4, App. *Mith.* 94, Plut. *Pomp.* 25.2–3, Dio 36.23.4–5. Gabinius initially proposed a bill with slightly lower resources, but the bill that finally passed had the resources listed here.

a particular enemy, but the massive scale of the campaign — and the resources placed under a single commander — were unprecedented.

Other than the scale of the *provincia*, two other factors made Pompey's piracy command unusual. The first was the way his *provincia* overlapped with the *provinciae* of other commanders: the piracy *provincia* was defined as extending fifty miles inland from the coast, but this fifty-mile coastal strip also fell within many of Rome's permanent *provinciae*. This aspect of Pompey's piracy command was highly unusual and a departure from traditional practice, and its consequences on Rome's conception of provincial command will be examined below. The second unusual aspect of Pompey's command was the fact that he was given his *provincia* for three years, which meant he did not need the senate's authorization (through prorogation) to retain his *provincia* for this period. This was not without precedent: Livy claimed that Scipio Africanus had been prorogued *rei gerendae fine* in 203 BC and that a single prorogation could keep a commander in his *provincia* for more than a single year.[21] There may also have been more recent precedents: M. Antonius Creticus may have received a three-year command against pirates in 74 BC, and Vervaet has argued that the senate gave three-year commands to Pompey in 77 BC and to M'. Acilius Glabrio in 67 BC.[22] Regardless of these precedents, such multiyear commands were virtually unheard of earlier in the republic, no doubt because they detracted from the senate's ability to control provincial assignments. The senate held de facto (but not de iure) control over annual provincial assignments and prorogation, and its traditional prerogative to review each commander's performance, and either extend his command or recall him to Rome (replacing him with another commander if necessary), enabled it to regulate the ambitions of its members. Undermining this senatorial prerogative and thus evading senatorial control became an important tactic of *popularis* politicians: Julius Caesar followed Pompey's example and used the popular assembly to secure for himself a five-year command over the two Gauls and Illyricum in 59 BC (he had this command renewed for another five years in 54 BC), Pompey and Crassus received five-year commands over Spain and Syria respectively from the assembly in 55 BC, and the tribunician *lex Titia* gave the

21. Livy 30.1.10 (Scipio), 33.25.11, 40.39.1, 41.14.11.

22. In describing the details of Pompey's piracy command, Velleius Paterculus (2.31.3) says that M. Antonius Creticus had received "the same" (*idem*) seven years earlier in 74 BC. Without more detail, it is impossible to know whether Velleius meant that the terms of the two piracy commands were identical or merely similar. Vervaet (2009) 419–22 and (2011) 265–90, esp. 279, argued that Pompey received a three-year command against Sertorius and that Glabrio received a three-year command of Bithynia and the war against Mithridates.

members of the Second Triumvirate five-year commands in 43 BC.[23] While the senate seems to have given extended commands to a small number of men in the past, Pompey's use of the popular assembly to give himself a three-year piracy command illustrates how *populares* were finding ways to loosen the senate's authority over provincial assignment.

The senate had done its best to prevent the passage of the *lex Gabinia*, and the *princeps senatus* Q. Catulus argued passionately that the command was too great for one man to control and such a concentration of power was dangerous. Dio makes Catulus observe that Marius and Sulla had both acquired tyrannical power through their long-term possession of many legions and great *provinciae*—a claim that was not exactly accurate but emphasized his concern about Pompey's command.[24] One of Catulus's particular concerns was that such a vast *provincia* was being given to one man instead of being divided up among a number of independent commanders, which would not only safeguard continuity of command should Pompey be killed but also provide more Roman commanders with much-needed military experience. In the past, the Roman senate had carefully controlled the ambitions of its members by sharing military responsibilities among multiple commanders and dividing major wars into several different *provinciae*, each under an independent commander, as it had done in the first two Punic Wars and in the many years when both consuls had been dispatched to Cisalpine Gaul.[25] It was also important to divide those commands that were likely to be highly profitable, since too much plunder could also make an individual commander excessively powerful when he returned to Rome.[26] Catulus realized that Pompey's command—although technically a single *provincia*—was actually an amassing of what would have been several *provinciae* earlier in the republic; by placing one man in overall control of a massive war that comprised several separate and independent armies and fleets, the *lex Gabinia* was breaking with this traditional practice.

23. See *MRR* 2.190, 215–17, and 337 for references.

24. Dio 36.31.1–36.4, esp. 36.31.3–4. Sulla had barely taken up command of his army—and had not even departed for his *provincia* in the East—when he marched on Rome in defiance of the senate and executed political enemies in 88 BC, and Marius had neither legions nor possession of a *provincia* when he started a civil war against Sulla and his supporters in that same year.

25. Rosenstein (2011) 241–53 discusses the control of aristocratic competition.

26. While Sulla had been given the First Mithridatic War to himself, in 74 BC both consuls were assigned the *provincia* of fighting Mithridates, no doubt because the campaign would be as profitable as it was important. One of the consuls, L. Licinius Lucullus, was far more successful than his colleague and became fantastically wealthy, but the senate was certainly not pleased when the *lex Manilia* gave the massive eastern campaign to Pompey alone.

Instead of dividing the pirates into several *provinciae*, each under an independent commander, Pompey was taking all pirates as his *provincia* and controlling sections of it through legates. The senate would never have considered giving such a massive *provincia* with so many resources to a single commander for three years, but Marius's innovation of using the popular assemblies to override senatorial decisions about provincial commands enabled Pompey to construct a command of unprecedented size and scope, which made him far more important and powerful than any previous (or current) commander.

A look at the Mithridatic wars illustrates further this change in the *provincia* and provincial assignment. In 88 BC the senate determined that war with Mithridates was necessary, so it declared that one consul (Sulla) would have the permanent *provincia* of Asia and the war with Mithridates as his *provincia*—command of the war was linked to a permanent *provincia*.[27] When another war with Mithridates seemed imminent in 74 BC, the consul L. Licinius Lucullus—who had already been assigned the *provincia* of Cisalpine Gaul—used his considerable influence to receive instead the *provincia* of Cilicia, whose commander had just died unexpectedly. Lucullus certainly knew that command in the war against Mithridates would be connected to the assignment of a permanent *provincia*, and Cilicia was a logical choice for a base of operations for this war. Lucullus may have also received the *provincia* of Asia, and his successful campaigns brought even more territory under his control, but his command was not fundamentally different from Sulla's command: his foreign war was linked to possession of a permanent *provincia*.[28] Furthermore, the senate did not give Lucullus the entire war as his *provincia*: his consular colleague M. Aurelius Cotta was assigned to the war as well, holding the permanent *provincia* of Bithynia as a base of operations and having command of a fleet with which to fight Mithridates on the sea (although he was soon defeated and Lucullus had to come to his rescue).[29] This sharing of a large command was normal practice to divide responsibility and to prevent any single

27. App. *BC* 1.55 (Σύλλας μὲν ὑπατεύων ἔλαχε στρατηγεῖν τῆς Ἀσίας καὶ τοῦδε τοῦ Μιθριδατείου πολέμου), *Mith.* 22 (ἔλαχε μὲν Κορνήλιος Σύλλας ἄρχειν τῆς Ἀσίας καὶ πολεμεῖν τῷ Μιθριδάτῃ).

28. Vell. 2.33.1 (*L. Lucullus . . . ex consulatu sortitus Asiam Mithridati oppositus erat*), Plut. *Luc.* 6.1–7.1 (ὁ Λούκουλλος Κιλικίας οὐ πολὺν εἶχε λόγον, οἰόμενος δ᾽, εἰ λάβοι ταύτην, ἐγγὺς οὔσης Καππαδοκίας, ἄλλον οὐδένα πεμφθήσεσθαι πολεμήσοντα Μιθριδάτῃ), App. *Mith.* 72 (Λεύκιος δὲ Λεύκολλος ὑπατεύειν καὶ στρατηγεῖν αἱρεθεὶς τοῦδε τοῦ πολέμου).

29. Cic. *Mur.* 33; Livy *Per.* 93; Plut. *Luc.* 6.5, 8.1–3; App. *Mith.* 71. The kingdom of Bithynia had been bequeathed to Rome and organized as a permanent *provincia* in the previous year (75 BC): Cic. *De Leg. Agr.* 2.40; Livy *Per.* 93; Vell. 2.4.1, 39.2; App. *BC* 1.111, *Mith.* 7, 71 (see Magie [1950] 250 and 320).

commander from having excessive power, so each commander was given a permanent *provincia* from which to strike at Mithridates (although Cotta's failure would lead Lucullus to assume command of the entire war). When Lucullus's political enemies started moving against him, their tactic was to remove permanent *provinciae* from his command: Asia was reassigned to a praetor in 69 BC, and Cilicia was transferred to a different commander in the following year.[30] This left Lucullus with the province of Bithynia and the war with Mithridates in Pontus—the permanent *provincia* serving as a base of operations for his campaigns—until these too were reassigned by the *lex Manilia* in 67 BC.[31]

While Lucullus's success and his conquest of territory were exceptional, his *provincia* demonstrates the new pattern that arose as a consequence of the *lex Sempronia*: he had received one (or perhaps two) permanent provinces as a base of operations to conduct a foreign war against a defined enemy. When Pompey conspired to take over the Mithridatic command, however, he worked through the tribune C. Manilius to craft a *provincia* consisting of several different territories that effectively gave Pompey authority over the entire East.[32] Having as his base of operations Bithynia, Cilicia, and Pontus (which together embraced most of Asia Minor), Pompey was able to attack a large number of neighboring peoples, including some that had little to do with his war against Mithridates: in 66 BC he defeated Mithridates as well as Tigranes of Armenia; in 65 BC he subdued the Albanian, Colchian, and Caucasian tribes and negotiated treaties with Armenia and Parthia; in 64 BC he subdued many territories, including Commagene, and marched into Syria, sending envoys to negotiate with Judaea; and in 63 BC he campaigned in Syria and captured Judaea.[33] While Pompey did complete his primary task (the defeat of Mithridates), his possession of multiple permanent *provinciae* and extensive resources enabled him to undertake far greater discretionary campaigns than would have been possible from a single permanent *provincia*: holding Pontus gave him access to northeastern neighbors like Armenia and the Caucasus region, and holding Cilicia gave him access to southern neighbors like Parthia, Syria, and Judea.

The use of popular legislation to manipulate *provinciae* and provincial assignment would also create the armies that brought down the republic. Although the senate had normally assigned Cisalpine Gaul and Transalpine Gaul

30. Dio 36.2.1–2 and 15.1.
31. Cic. *Leg. Man.* 26, Sall. *Hist.* 5.13 M, Plut. *Luc.* 33.5.
32. Vell. 2.33.1–2, Plut. *Pomp.* 30.1–3, App. *Mith.* 97, Dio 36.42.4–44.2.
33. For references, see *MRR* 2.155, 159, 163–64, and 169.

as separate consular *provinciae* previously, Caesar managed to get both of these permanent *provinciae* as well as Illyricum assigned to him for a period of five years with four legions, which was double the size of the normal consular army.[34] Possession of Transalpine Gaul and Illyricum gave Caesar tremendous opportunities for conquest (he would focus on Gaul), and possession of Cisalpine Gaul gave him access to good recruits in the colonies and allied cities of northern Italy, which would enable Caesar to increase his army to ten legions. The size and strength of this army made Caesar far more than a just provincial commander; it made him a tremendous power in Rome despite his absence. For this reason, his enemies fought tenaciously to separate him from his command, while Caesar fought equally tenaciously to keep it as long as possible.

The members of the Second Triumvirate also bundled permanent *provinciae* to take over direct control of the entire Roman Empire: Antony received all of Gaul except Narbonese province; Lepidus held Narbonese Gaul and all of Spain; and Octavian took control of the provinces of Sicily, Sardinia, and Africa.[35] Thus the western empire was divided into three provincial commands, each consisting of a bundle of permanent provinces that would change as the political and military fortunes of each man rose or fell. Thus when Marius used the popular assembly to appropriate the African war against Jugurtha for himself, he undermined the traditional methods of provincial assignment and laid the groundwork for later *popularis* commanders to expand the scope of what a *provincia* might encompass. While Marius had only sought for himself a *provincia* that the senate had already assigned to another commander, Pompey and Caesar would use *popularis* methods to create commands of tremendous scope that the senate would not have assigned to any single commander in the first place. The senate had long served as a check on aristocratic ambition, but Marius's *popularis* tactics enabled future commanders to design and acquire *provinciae* that served their own ambitions rather than the good of the state.

A final aspect of Marius's career requires brief attention: his five consecutive consulships from 104 to 100 BC. This was in violation of a law dated to 342 BC that prohibited anyone from holding the same office twice within a ten-year period, but this law was not always observed, since the popular assembly was able to make exceptions to its own laws.[36] In Marius's case, the people repeatedly elected him consul in these years because they wanted him — and

---

34. Gallic assignments in 60 BC: Cic. *Att.* 1.19.2. Caesar's command in 59 BC: Cic. *Vat.* 36, *Prov. Cons.* 36–37, Vell. 2.44.5, Suet. *Iul.* 22.1, App. *BC* 2.13, Plut. *Caes.* 14.9–11, Dio 38.8.5.

35. App. *BC* 4.2–3, Dio 46.55.4–56.1.

36. Livy 7.42.2 and 10.13.8.

him only—to command Rome's armies against the Gauls.[37] The obvious question is why the Romans felt the need to elect Marius to consecutive consulships in violation of the law, when their purpose could have been achieved simply by voting to prorogue Marius in his command? As we have seen, a proconsul's capacity to command an army and lead a campaign was the exact same as a consul's, so repeated consulships were not necessary to keep Marius in his *provincia*. The people may simply have wanted to honor their chosen hero by giving him the added luster of being a sitting consul, but there was probably something more to it.

Sitting consuls traditionally expected to receive the best or most important wars as their *provinciae*, so Marius and his supporters may have feared that if Marius was merely a proconsul, the new consuls would have a strong case for superseding him in his *provincia*.[38] Marius himself had used his consulship in 107 BC to take the *provincia* of fighting Jugurtha from the proconsul Metellus, and he may have felt that he needed to hold successive consulships to ensure that he kept his command. Indeed, there was certainly pressure from the aristocracy to let other consuls have a share of the *provincia*—in 102 BC the senate succeeded in sending the consul Q. Lutatius Catulus to join Marius in fighting the Germans (they initially divided the *provincia* and fought different tribes). Furthermore, if Marius had been a proconsul in that year, Catulus as a sitting consul might have overshadowed him, since consuls held greater prestige and social status (but not authority) than proconsuls. Consecutive consulships were Marius's method for retaining the *provincia* he very much wanted. His immediate successors did not adopt this technique, in part because Sulla reinforced the law against repeating the same office within a ten-year period,[39] but also because they were more aggressive and innovative in their use of the popular assemblies, which they used to create bigger and grander commands. They also arranged to receive multiyear commands, which enabled them to hold their *provinciae* for three or five years at a time without the need for an-

37. Livy *Per.* 67 (*eique propter metum Cimbrici belli continuatus per complures annos est consulatus*); Plut. *Mar.* 14.6 (ἅμα δὲ καὶ τῶν βαρβάρων ἔτους ὥρᾳ προσδοκίμων ὄντων ἐβούλοντο μετὰ μηδενὸς ἄλλου στρατηγοῦ κινδυνεῦσαι πρὸς αὐτούς).

38. Even the most famous Roman proconsuls had to be on guard against being replaced by their consular successors. A consul of 203 BC very nearly achieved his demand that he be sent to replace the proconsul Scipio (Africanus) in Africa (Livy 30.24.1–4), and the proconsul T. Quinctius Flamininus (cos. 198 BC) took into account the possibility that he could be replaced in his command by the new consuls when he planned his strategy for fighting Philip V of Macedon (Polyb. 18.11.1–12.5, Livy 32.28.4–10, Plut. *Flam.* 7.1–2).

39. App. *BC* 1.100.

nual prorogation (or repeated consulships). Years later, however, the *imperator* Augustus (Octavian at the time) would emulate Marius by holding consecutive consulships from 31 to 23 BC in order to keep control of his provincial command (see chapter 7).

THE SO-CALLED *LEX CORNELIA DE PROVINCIIS ORDINANDIS*

The late republic saw another important change in the nature of Roman provincial command: consuls and praetors started taking up their *provinciae* at the end of their terms in office rather than earlier in their magistracy. In the second century BC and earlier, consuls and praetors normally departed for their *provinciae* as soon as possible after entering office. Their eagerness to exercise military command was so great that compulsion was needed in some cases to keep consuls and praetors in Rome long enough to complete vital civilian duties, and sitting consuls away on campaign frequently needed to be recalled to Rome to conduct elections.[40] In the late republic, however, consuls and praetors often did not leave Rome for their *provinciae* until the end of their terms. While one may attribute this delay among praetors to the dramatic rise in the number of standing courts (supervised by praetors) between 149 and 81 BC,[41] there is no obvious reason why consuls should have delayed their departure, since their workload of civilian duties is not known to have increased significantly. This shift in consular behavior led Mommsen to argue that Sulla had arranged for the passage of a *lex Cornelia de provinciis ordinandis*, which prevented consuls from taking up their *imperium militiae* during their terms in office; they governed the civilian affairs of the state with their *imperium domi* only, and only after the end of their terms could they take up their *imperium militiae* and depart for their *provinciae*.[42]

Although Mommsen supplied no evidence to support this position, his scholarly *auctoritas* was sufficient to sustain his argument in spite of the fact that a series of historians have demonstrated conclusively that this restriction on consuls did not exist and was not included in the *lex Cornelia*.[43] Giovannini

40. Livy 45.16.4 (a praetor being ordered to remain in Rome to exercise jurisdiction), and 45.17.5–6 (a consul is ordered to remain in Rome until he had presided over senatorial meetings).

41. By the end of Sulla's dictatorship in 81 BC, there were seven *quaestiones perpetuae* (for references, see Botsford [1909] 419–20 and *MRR* 2.75).

42. Mommsen (1887–88) 1.57–59, 2.94–95, 214–15, 3.1086–87.

43. See Balsdon (1939) 57–73, Valgiglio (1956) 132–40, Giovannini (1983) 73–101 and (1999) 99, de Martino (1990) 1.415–17, Girardet (1992b) 213, (2000) 176–77, and (2001) 155–61, Bleicken (1995) 177–78, Brennan (2000) 394–96, Ferrary (2001b) 101–54, and Beck (2011) 89. There is no advantage

all but demolished Mommsen's argument by demonstrating that nearly half of all consuls between 80 and 53 BC are known to have departed Rome for their provincial commands during their term in office, and only one consul (Julius Caesar) is known for certain to have delayed setting out for his command until after the end of his magistracy.[44] Pina Polo has (I would hope) brought this debate to a close by providing a better explanation for commanders' delay in setting out for their *provinciae*: the changing nature of politics in the late republic and the changing role of the consulship in the day-to-day governance of Rome drove many consuls — either voluntarily or on the recommendation of the senate — to remain in Rome longer than had their pre-Sullan (or even pre-Gracchan) predecessors.[45] The rise in internal strife and contentious politics made it prudent for consuls to remain in Rome for much or all of their magistracy in order to lend the state (and their own political interests) as much support as possible. This explains the extended presence of the consuls in Rome far better than an undocumented rule of a *lex Cornelia*, and demonstrates that the consuls' actions were voluntary rather than compulsory.

Pina Polo's argument is certainly correct, and the points developed in the preceding chapters lend further support to his position. In particular, the changing nature of the *provincia* and provincial assignment in the late republic further explains why consuls would deprioritize taking up their commands during their year in office, and why many consuls would forgo holding a military command at all.[46] Because the *lex Sempronia* of 123 BC caused a change in the assignment and conception of consular commands, most consular *provinciae* became *opportunities* to win military glory through discretionary campaigning from permanent *provinciae* rather than active wars in enemy territory that required immediate military action. As a result, consuls could afford to delay taking up their commands until the end of their terms in office, since, for most of them, any fighting would be discretionary and could be initiated if and when the commander chose. While an ambitious man like P. Servilius

---

to repeating their arguments here, but for a detailed summary of the discussion (with original contributions), see Pina Polo (2011) 225–48.

44. Giovannini (1983) 83–90. Many other consuls remained in Rome for their entire consulship, but it is unknown whether they took any *provincia* at all after leaving office. See also Ferrary (2001b) 101–54 and Humm (2012) 62 n. 22, who support Giovannini's refutation of Mommsen's position.

45. Pina Polo (2011) 242–48.

46. Consuls known to have refused a *provincia*: Pompey and Crassus in 70 BC (Vell. 2.31.1); Q. Hortensius Hortalus in 69 BC (Dio 36.1a [Xiph.]); M. Tullius Cicero in 63 BC (Cic. *Pis.* 5, *Fam.* 5.2.3).

Vatia Isauricus might wrench a great deal of military glory from the *provincia* of Cilicia, another man — like Cicero — might keep his military activity to a minimum and conduct only those operations necessary for the security of the *provincia*. Furthermore, since permanent *provinciae* were maintained continually under the authority of a commander, a sitting consul rarely needed to rush to his *provincia*, because it was already under the supervision of his predecessor. So sitting consuls after 123 BC often had greater discretion about when they needed to leave Rome and take up their provincial commands than they had had before. Although some consuls would indeed receive a grand war against a powerful foreign attacker like Mithridates, shrewd men knew that such commands were increasingly rare in the late republic, and they were difficult to anticipate under the restrictions of the *lex Sempronia*. Instead, wise consuls sought permanent *provinciae* with the potential for discretionary campaigns; to such ambitious men, the consular *provincia* was the possibility of good campaigning rather than an actual war or campaign. For this reason, most consuls could remain in Rome for their entire term if they wished, enjoying the glory of consular *auctoritas* and *dignitas* and advancing their political interests, and only when they had maximized their opportunities in Rome would they set out for their commands.

Caesar demonstrated the new flexibility of the *provincia* and the potential of discretionary campaigning very well: he initially used the *lex Vatinia* to receive Cisalpine Gaul and Illyricum as his command with a large army of three legions, most likely planning to use Illyricum as a base from which to launch an attack on the kingdom of Dacia, as demonstrated by his concentration of his legions into a single force at Aquileia, which was on the Italian border with Illyricum.[47] When the commander in Transalpine Gaul suddenly died, however, the senate assigned it and an extra legion to Caesar as well, fearing (we are told) that the people would give it to him if the senate did not.[48] With this new acquisition, Caesar shifted his attention and his legions to Transalpine Gaul, planning to launch an invasion of unconquered Gaul from there. Since Transalpine Gaul was quiet at the time, however, there was no rush for Caesar to race to his *provincia*, so he could leave Rome most anytime he wished during his consulship. Thus the flexibility of his command enabled him to spend his consular year in Rome, where he could push through his desired legislation

47. Caes. *BG* 1.10 indicates that Caesar's legions had been concentrated in Aquileia. Seager (2002) 89 and Rosenstein (2009) 88 discuss Caesar's possible plans for Illyricum.
48. Cic. *Att.* 8.3.3, Suet. *Iul.* 22.1.

and keep pressure on his many political enemies. It was not a *lex Cornelia de provinciis ordinandis* that kept Caesar in Rome, but the changing nature of the *provincia* that reduced the need for consuls to take up their commands quickly.

IN THE LATE REPUBLIC, the concept of the *provincia* continued to evolve and change as unusually powerful men manipulated the concept for their own ends. Although Gaius Gracchus had been trying to limit corruption with his *lex Sempronia*, the change in provincial assignment imposed by his *lex* triggered a change in the way aristocrats thought about consular *provinciae*. Because the *lex* made it difficult to ensure that consuls received good wars as their *provinciae*, the senate instead began assigning them permanent *provinciae* that had promising opportunities for discretionary campaigning. While major foreign wars would still be the best and most desirable *provincia*, consuls in permanent *provinciae* like Macedonia, Spain, Gaul, and Cilicia would find that they had ample opportunities to win glory and plunder if they were aggressive enough. As competition between aristocrats continued to rise, men like Marius and Pompey began using tribunes and popular legislation to craft their ideal *provinciae*. Instead of taking whatever the senate had decreed months earlier, these men used their popularity to acquire *provinciae* designed to serve their personal desires and agenda. For centuries, it had been the senate's prerogative to assign *provinciae* to commanders, and in this way it sought to temper the ambitions of the aristocracy by limiting the scope and duration of military command. Exceptionally large commands had traditionally been shared or split between two or more independent commanders, and extensions of command through prorogation had also been regulated by the senators, who were powerfully motivated not to allow one of their members to gain too much personal glory and influence. By using the popular assemblies to acquire special commands, however, Marius and his imitators loosened the reins on this regulation, and crafted commands to glorify and profit themselves first, and serve the state second. Unlike the senatorial aristocracy, the people in the assembly sought to reward their favorite politicians with extraordinary *provinciae*, and were probably not concerned with the possible ramifications of raising their heroes up still higher. For men like Pompey and Caesar, the people ordered commands made up of multiple permanent provinces — any one of which would have been a good consular *provincia* in the eyes of the senate. Beyond just being a military command, the *provincia* could be used as a political tool to gain unprecedented personal power in Rome as well as on campaign.

The Development of *Imperium Maius/Minus*
as a Product of Changes in the *Provincia*

Just like the concept of the *provincia*, the notions and definitions of *imperium* were also manipulated in the late republic to serve the interests of increasingly powerful men. As has been argued in earlier chapters, *imperium* was originally a single and absolute concept and was not differentiated into greater (*maius*) and lesser (*minus*) degrees until late in the republic. Instead of placing its commanders into a hierarchy of rank, the early Romans prevented conflict and deadlock by assigning commanders to different *provinciae*, thereby defining clearly whose *imperium* took priority in what sphere. Greater and lesser degrees of *imperium* were simply unnecessary and would have been confusing and redundant, because Rome's system of provincial command was not a vertical hierarchy of generals and colonels but a patchwork quilt with different spheres of authority. This system of separating commanders into different spheres worked perfectly well, so long as their spheres could be distinguished from one another with some clarity. As the traditional concept of the *provincia* began to expand in the third and second centuries BC, however, the groundwork for future trouble was laid. As Rome's overseas empire grew, it became possible to think of the *provincia* in two different ways: as a task to complete, and as a territory to defend and supervise. This created the possibility that two *provinciae* could overlap in a particular space, so that two commanders could claim precedence of command over the same area on the basis of different qualifications: one because that land itself fell within his territorial *provincia* (e.g., Cisalpine Gaul), and another because the enemy he had been assigned to defeat as his *provincia* (e.g., a war with the Cimbri) had moved into that territory. The possibility that two *provinciae* could overlap in a single space meant that provincial assignment became insufficient to separate commanders into different spheres. As a result, the Romans for the first time needed a new and different method for preventing deadlock and conflict among its commanders: a hierarchy of authority.

The failure of provincial assignment to separate commanders and their spheres of military authority became apparent first in the great pirate commands of the late republic. Before that time, the Romans had encountered little difficulty in keeping naval and land commands separate. Even during the Third Macedonian War, when the consul L. Aemilius Paullus and the praetor Cn. Octavius simultaneously waged war against the Macedonian king and his allies — the consul by land and the praetor by sea — the clear distinction of their *provinciae* enabled them to conduct military operations both jointly and independently without conflict.[49] Both men were fully independent as commanders, and both celebrated triumphs for their victories, but the clear definition of their respective *provinciae* prevented any conflict. Although Octavius must have come on land frequently to attack coastal targets and to rest and resupply his navy, the fact that his *provincia* (naval operations against Perseus) was fundamentally different from Paullus's *provincia* (land campaign against Perseus) meant that the two men's activities rarely overlapped, even when they were cooperating or working within close proximity to one another. The piracy commands assigned to M. Antonius (Creticus) in 74 BC and to Cn. Pompeius in 67 BC, however, created a substantially different situation.

According to Cicero, Antonius's naval command was unusual because it included *imperium infinitum*, a phrase that was long thought to signify a special type of *imperium maius*. Jameson debunked this idea long ago, demonstrating that *imperium infinitum* was a made-up term with no technical, legal, or military significance.[50] While we may certainly believe that Cicero found something about Antonius's command objectionable and untraditional, it cannot be that he had an unusual type of *imperium* legally defined as *imperium infinitum*. Velleius Paterculus was closer to the truth when he wrote that Antonius's naval command granted him *imperium* equal to that of other proconsuls in all other provinces up to fifty miles inland from the sea (*imperium aequum in omnibus provinciis cum proconsulibus usque ad quinquagesimum miliarium a mari*).[51] Like Cicero, Velleius indicates that something about Antonius's military authority was unusual, but it certainly was not his *imperium*, which Velleius specifically describes as being equal to that of all other provincial commanders. Since Velleius lived and wrote under the *imperium maius* of Emperor Tiberius, he was certainly familiar with different levels of *imperium* and was capable of expressing this idea had he wished to do so. In short, Cicero and Velleius recognized that there was something unusual (and perhaps objec-

49. *MRR* 1.427–28, 433–34.

50. Cic. *Verr.* 2.2.8 and 3.213. Jameson (1970) 542. Badian (1980) 105 n. 22 concurred, arguing that the question of Antonius's *imperium* "has been confused by the blunder of taking Cicero's *infinitum imperium* for a technical term and creating a category of *imperium infinitum* for him." See also Béranger (1948) 19–27and Ehrenberg (1953) 117 n. 12. Cicero used the phrase to place Antonius's command in a negative light, as the orator also did (*Dom.* 55) when describing the commands of the pro-Caesar proconsuls L. Calpurnius Piso and A. Gabinius (coss. 58 BC).

51. Vell. 2.31.2–4. This is the description of the *provincia* given to Pompey in 67 BC, which Velleius says was the same as the *provincia* given to Antonius in 74 BC.

tionable) about Antonius's piracy command, but it was not his *imperium*. The oddity must have lain with his *provincia* and the fact that it was specifically defined as overlapping the *provinciae* of other men.

Commanders were supposed to be separated by their provincial assignments, but Antonius's *provincia* was defined as including coastal territory that fell within the *provinciae* of other Roman commanders; Antonius could claim authority along the coastal strip of most permanent provinces, even though those provinces had been assigned to other men. Whereas two commanders had often shared the same *provincia* in the past by alternating supreme command daily, the coastal strip within Antonius's command was different: it was not a shared *provincia* but two separate *provinciae* that partially overlapped in the same space. To the commanders who held the permanent *provinciae* along the Mediterranean coast, Antonius's ability to interfere in their commands and exercise his *imperium* independently within their assigned spheres of responsibility was potentially a great insult. Since two men had legal grounds for claiming sole and unshared precedence within those fifty-mile coastal strips, the traditional methods for sharing a joint *provincia* could not apply, creating the possibility of irresolvable conflict. The shocking thing about Antonius's naval command was not the authority (*imperium*) given to the commander but the unusual sphere of responsibility (*provincia*) that deliberately overlapped with the *provinciae* of other commanders. Although this created the potential for destructive deadlock between two commanders should they fall into conflict within the overlapping area of their *provinciae*, the Romans seem to have chosen their man well—Antonius appears to have acquitted himself well and avoided any conflict with his fellow commanders, and he was likely chosen for this command specifically because he was the sort of man who would respect tradition and the prerogatives of his colleagues and would avoid giving insult to another commander by unnecessarily (or inappropriately) intruding into his *provincia*.[52]

Less prudent and considerate was Pompey, who held the second great piracy command of the late republic. Although Pompey seems to have received far greater resources for his piracy campaign, Velleius emphasizes that he had the same *imperium* and *provincia* that had been given to Antonius seven years earlier: Pompey was to campaign against pirates, and his *imperium* was to be the same (*aequum*) as that of any other commander, within fifty miles inland from the sea. Plutarch and Appian support Velleius in stating that Pompey's

---

52. Velleius (2.31.4) specifically credits Antonius's reasonable personality to explain why he did not abuse his ability to interfere in other men's *provinciae* during his piracy command.

imperium was the same as that of other commanders, although his *provincia* was unusual in that it overlapped with other men's *provinciae*.[53] Only Tacitus suggests that Pompey had an unusual level of authority, but this comment can be safely rejected. In this passage, Tacitus is referring to the special command given to Cn. Domitius Corbulo by Emperor Nero in AD 63:

> The administration of Syria was entrusted to C. Cestius, the military forces to Corbulo; and the Fifteenth Legion, in the process of being led by Marius Celsus from Pannonia, was added. The tetrarchs and kings and prefects and procurators and those praetors who controlled the bordering provinces were written to that they should comply with Corbulo's orders, his power (*potestas*) having been more or less increased to the very considerable limit which the Roman people had given Cn. Pompeius for his conduct of the pirate war.[54]

There is no good reason to take this passage as evidence that Pompey possessed *imperium maius*: Tacitus does not even mention *imperium* in this description, and Pompey is not known to have been given authority over other Roman commanders as was Corbulo (Velleius's testimony even refutes this possibility). If anything, Tacitus was equating the "praetors who controlled the bordering provinces" to the numerous legates Pompey was given in his command — in Corbulo's day, a praetor in a province would have been a *legatus Augusti pro praetore*, an imperial legate who served in the *provincia* and under the auspices of the emperor (governors of public provinces were all called proconsuls — see chapter 7). Such *legati Augusti pro praetore* were lieutenants, and Corbulo's control over so many lieutenants may have reminded Tacitus of the twenty-four lieutenants assigned to Pompey as part of his piracy command. Whether or not this was the case, at best we can only say that Tacitus knew that Pompey had held a large and unusual *provincia*, but nothing in Tacitus's statement requires us to imagine that Pompey had an unusual *imperium*.

This is further supported by Pompey's conflicts in 67 BC with Q. Caecilius Metellus Creticus on Crete and with C. Calpurnius Piso in Gaul, in which Pompey's inability to obtain his wishes demonstrates that he lacked

---

53. Plut. *Pomp.* 25.2 and App. *Mith.* 94.

54. Tac. *Ann.* 15.25.3 (Woodman, trans.): *Suriaeque executio C. Cestio, copiae militares Corbuloni permissae, et quinta decuma legio ducente Mario Celso e Pannonia adiecta est. Scribitur tetrarchis ac regibus praefectisque et procuratoribus et qui praetorum finitimas provincias regebant, iussis Corbulonis obsequi, in tantum ferme modum aucta potestate, quem populus Romanus Cn. Pompeio bellum piraticum gesturo dederat.*

authority superior to that of his fellow commanders. On Crete, Metellus Creticus attacked and repulsed Pompey's legate when the latter tried to interfere in Metellus's campaigns against pirates on Crete, and in Gaul the consul Piso prevented Pompey from raising levies and funds.[55] In both cases, Pompey was authorized to take such steps by the *lex Gabinia*, but when he encountered resistance from the local commander he was unable to enforce his will, which he certainly would have been able to do if he had been invested with *imperium maius*. Both conflicts created significant problems for Rome: in one, a civil war nearly broke out on Crete because both commanders claimed precedence — based on different rights — in the same coastal space, and in the other a Roman fleet was unable to obtain supplies authorized by the state because the commander holding the land resented the intrusion into his *provincia* by the commander of the fleet. Whereas Antonius Creticus had apparently been careful not to offend his fellow commanders, Pompey was precisely the type of person who would take advantage of the overlapping of *provinciae* to claim authority in another man's *provincia*, thereby giving insult when tactful diplomacy was needed. Because there was no method for determining precedence of *imperium* within overlapping *provinciae*, the commanders fell into paralyzing conflict with one another, to Rome's disadvantage. Thus, although many scholars have argued that Pompey was given some form of *imperium maius* in 67 BC, it is more likely that he possessed only normal (*aequum*) *imperium*.[56] The importance of these piracy commands was their potential to blur the lines between the *provinciae* held by different men, weakening Rome's most

---

55. When pirates on Crete were facing defeat at the hands of Metellus, they offered to hand themselves over to Pompey, who was known to give generous terms to pirates who surrendered. Pompey — whose *provincia* certainly included coastal Crete — sent a legate to accept their surrender, but Metellus repulsed the legate and continued his own subjugation of the pirates on the island (*MRR* 2.145, and see Roddaz [1992] 191–93). Likewise, when Pompey sought to raise money and levies in Piso's *provincia* in Gaul, Piso's obstructions and resistance prevented Pompey from acquiring the needed commodities (Plut. *Pomp.* 27.1, Dio 36.37.2–3, and see Larsen [1931] 428 n. 1, Jameson [1970] 551, and Vervaet [2011] 284–90).

56. Jashemski (1950) 93 and Ehrenberg (1953) 117–20 believe that Pompey held *imperium pro consule*, Loader (1940) 134–36 and Beck, Duplá, Jehne, and Pina Polo (2011) 7 believe he held *imperium maius*, while Boak (1918) 19, Last (1947) 161, and Scullard (1982) 100 all argue for some kind of *imperium infinitum aequum*. Cobban (1935), Siber (1940) (cited and refuted by Syme [1946] 149–58), Staveley (1963) 480–81, and Girardet (1992a) 177–88, all argue for some kind of *imperium aequum*. Badian (1980) 105 states in a definitive manner that *imperium maius* was inconceivable in Pompey's day, and that "there is simply no evidence" for any argument on the existence of an *imperium* greater than *aequum*.

ancient and important method for avoiding conflicts between commanders in the field.

The temptation to look for *imperium maius* in Pompey's great eastern command against Mithridates also collapses quickly. In 66 BC the *lex Manilia* assigned to Pompey the standing *provinciae* of Cilicia and Bithynia, as well as the war against Mithridates in Pontus.[57] By the time he celebrated a triumph for this victory in 61 BC, however, he claimed to be triumphing *ex Asia Ponto Armenia Paphlagonia Cappadocia Cilicia Syria Scytheis Iudaeis Albania pirateis*.[58] While most of these areas and peoples were either subdued in some way or added to Pompey's *provincia* during his tenure of command, the first one — Asia — raises a problem. Jameson has pointed out that Asia was receiving regular governors during Pompey's campaign, and, since it was not permitted for a commander to claim a triumph for victories in another's *provincia*, she believes that Pompey must have possessed *imperium maius* in order to have celebrated a triumph for victories in Asia legally.[59] On the other hand, the sources do not say that Pompey was given *imperium maius* but seem to indicate that he had the same *imperium* that Roman commanders had always possessed. Although no source explicitly qualifies Pompey's *imperium* in this command, Appian records that he was given the same autocratic prerogatives as he had possessed and wielded against the pirates.[60] Because the *lex Gabinia* had given Pompey a three-year command in 67 BC[61] and there is no indication that he returned to Rome to lay down his pirate command before taking up the Mithridatic command, the practical effect of the *lex Manilia* must have been to change his provincial assignment from fighting pirates in the Mediterranean to fighting Mithridates in the eastern provinces. As discussed in chapter 3, the Roman state had always been able to adjust a commander's *provincia* while he was in

57. Cic. *Leg. Man.*, *Phil.* 11.18, *Mur.* 34, *Orat.* 102, Vell. 2.33.1, Ascon. 65 C, Plut. *Pomp.* 30.1–3, *Luc.* 35.7, App. *Mith.* 97, Dio 36.42.4–43.1.

58. *Inscr. Ital.* 13¹, 84–85, 566 (also *CIL* 1² 179). This text was restored in accordance with Pliny *NH* 7.98: *triumphi vero, quem duxit a.d. III kal. Oct. M. Pisone Messala coss., praefatio haec fuit: cum oram maritimam praedonibus liberasset et imperium maris populo Romano restituisset ex Asia Ponto Armenia Paphlagonia Cappadocia Cilicia Syria Scythis Iudaeis Albanis Hiberia insula Creta Basternis et super haec de rege Mithridate atque Tigrane triumphavit.*

59. Jameson (1970) 559 (cf. Ferrary [2000] #5). Girardet (1991) 201–15 and (1992a) 177–84 suggested that — in order to prevent conflict — the other commanders sent to Asia during Pompey's campaign against Mithridates were given only praetorian *imperium minus*. However, it was possession of the *provincia*, and not levels of *imperium*, that determined priority of command in a sphere.

60. App. *Mith.* 97.

61. *MRR* 2.144.

the field. In the East, therefore, Pompey used the same *imperium* he had taken up in Rome in 67 BC to fight the pirates; only his *provincia* had changed, which is why he celebrated a single triumph over the pirates and his eastern foes—he had conquered them all with the same *imperium* and *auspicium*. Cicero described the *lex Manilia* frequently and at length, and his failure to mention something as noteworthy as a grant of *imperium maius* for Pompey suggests that no such grant existed, especially since he was so quick to discuss the idea of *imperium maius* when it was proposed by the tribune Messius in 57 BC. Logically, Pompey's *imperium* in 66 BC should have been the same as it had been in 67 BC, which was specifically defined as being no greater than that of any other commander.

How then do we deal with Jameson's point that Pompey must have possessed *imperium maius* in order to have triumphed legally over Asia, which had its own, independent Roman commander at the time? The answer lies in understanding the changing nature of the *provincia*. Jameson only employs the geographic definition of the *provincia* in her argument and reasonably argues that two men cannot have held the same authority (*imperium*) over the same land (*provincia*). More likely, however, Pompey thought of his *provincia* as a task or war, which meant he was entitled to pursue Mithridates' forces anywhere they went, including into permanent provinces held by other Roman commanders. Indeed, in his speech on the *lex Manilia*, Cicero repeatedly refers to the eastern command as a war (*bellum*), and he emphasizes again and again that Pompey should be given the command to conquer Mithridates (not to govern peaceful territory).[62] As had been the case in the two piracy commands—where one commander's task of hunting pirates overlapped with another commander's supervision over a specific territory—the splitting of the *provincia* into the two concepts of task and territory made it possible for two men to claim legitimate authority over the same physical space. Thus Pompey's claim to triumph over Asia meant that his *provincia* of fighting Mithridates had wandered into Asia as well as into other territories. Although it would have been more polite and proper for Pompey to refrain from including Asia in his list of territories "conquered," he was never known as a restrained or humble man, and Asia was the most famous and prestigious of the eastern provinces. Indeed, Pompey was precisely the type of person who would exploit the ambiguity of the situation to claim an even greater accomplishment than he had actually achieved. Down to Pompey's triumph in 61 BC, therefore, there is no evidence that *imperium maius* had ever existed as a real con-

62. Cic. *Leg. Man.* 4–5, 7–8, 11–12, 19–22, 28, 36–39, 49–50, 64–68.

cept in Rome, but the changing nature of the *provincia* was decreasing the role of provincial assignment in separating commanders and preventing them from coming into conflict with one another.[63] Pompey's career had made this development painfully obvious — in particular his tendency to interfere in his colleagues' *provinciae* whenever the vagaries of provincial assignment made this possible. As the *provincia* lost its ability to separate supreme authority into different military spheres, some Romans must have begun looking for another mechanism to establish priority.

The theoretical possibility that a Roman commander could be given a greater level or degree of *imperium* than that possessed by every other *imperium*-bearing commander was first proposed publicly in 57 BC. In this year a prolonged grain shortage drove the senate (led by Cicero) to propose a special *provincia* for Pompey, which would confer on him complete authority over Rome's grain supply throughout the entire world for five years (*per quinquennium omnis potestas rei frumentariae toto orbe terrarum*).[64] Because the purpose behind this bill was to organize the collection and transport of grain throughout the empire, Cicero may have considered this a civilian position and not really a military command; Pompey had displayed a real talent for organization during his Mediterranean-wide piracy command a decade earlier, and his experience was what Rome needed. Before the people voted on this measure, however, a tribune named C. Messius proposed an expanded version of this legislation, in which Pompey would additionally be given an army as well as a navy, complete control over Rome's finances, and greater *imperium* than that held by other commanders (*maius imperium in provinciis quam sit eorum qui eas obtineant*).[65] The senate as a whole was vehemently opposed to Messius's proposal, and Cicero referred to it as an unbearable proposition: *haec [lex] Messi non ferenda*. Ehrenberg correctly notes that the senators objected to this proposal specifically because it was an unacceptable innovation to Roman custom, and Balsdon argued that Messius was proposing an unprecedented idea.[66] The proposed innovation that stimulated such hostility

63. In his survey of Pompey's extraordinary commands, Girardet ([1992a] 177–88) found that Pompey's *imperium* and *provinciae* did not depart significantly from traditional republican practice.

64. Cic. *Att.* 4.1.7 (cf. Livy *Per.* 104, Plut. *Rom. Q.* 204, App. *BC* 2.18, Dio 39.9.3). See Girardet (1992a) 184 and (2000) 183–85.

65. Cic. *Att.* 4.1.7.

66. Ehrenberg (1953) 121 and Balsdon (1957) 17. Mommsen (1887–88) 2.655 n. 2 suggested that the proposal was meant to confer the rank and authority of a consul on Pompey, who would otherwise have been a proconsul, but Ehrenberg pointed out that the senate's opposition was far too aggressive to be explained by such an argument.

among the senate was the idea that *imperium* could exist in different degrees or levels, and that Pompey could invoke this greater authority wherever he went, which was a radical departure from tradition and a fundamental change to the Roman concept of authority. The other aspects of Messius's proposal are unlikely to have caused such an outcry: Cicero had already supported giving Pompey *omnis potestas rei frumentaris toto orbe terrarum*, so the geographic scope of the proposed *cura annonae* cannot have been an objection, and Messius's suggestion that Pompey should also have an army, a navy, and great fiscal powers was really no different from the powers he had held under the *lex Gabinia* in 67 BC. In other words, the only true novelty or innovation in Messius's proposal was that Pompey was also to have *maius imperium*.

The idea that *imperium* could exist in greater and lesser degrees was still unacceptable to the Romans, and according to Cicero it was violently rejected as being contrary to tradition. Although it never became law, the proposal represents the first documented appearance of an actual innovation in the concept of *imperium*, which up to that time had been a single, indivisible, and absolute idea. The great attention Cicero gives to discussing this proposal highlights its novelty and innovation to tradition. Unlike Cicero's earlier reference to Antonius's *imperium infinitum*, which was mere rhetorical hyperbole in a heated public speech, Cicero's discussion of Messius's proposal appears in a letter to his friend Atticus and defines in clear language what this proposed *imperium maius* would be (*maius imperium in provinciis quam sit eorum qui eas obtineant*). Because this proposal of *imperium maius* was a new and unprecedented idea, Cicero's language may even be drawn from the actual wording of Messius's proposal. In other words, Cicero's letter preserves what may be the first fully articulated definition of a new Roman concept regarding the nature of military authority.

Exactly what Messius had in mind when he proposed *maius imperium* for Pompey is unclear. Perhaps he intended to empower Pompey to take whatever unilateral action he wished, although Seager suggests the possibility that Messius's proposal was meant to be rejected by Pompey—a straw man whose defeat was meant to make Pompey appear to be the champion of traditional republican values.[67] Staveley believed that Pompey's altercation with Metellus Creticus had demonstrated a need for an *imperium* that could override that of other governors.[68] It is even possible that Messius made his unusual proposal

---

67. Stockton (1971) 195 suggests that Pompey may have wanted to take control of Egypt and its vast agricultural resources. Seager (2002) 108 makes this suggestion with reservation. See also Miltner (1952) 2138.

68. Staveley (1963) 480–81.

in order to make Cicero's proposal (which was already very large and grand) look conservative by comparison. Cicero makes clear that this was indeed the result and that Messius's proposal was thought to be intolerable (*illa nostra lex consularis nunc modesta videtur, haec Messi non ferenda*).[69] Neither Messius nor anyone else may have fully considered what *imperium maius* might be or how it would function in Roman government; perhaps it was introduced simply as a political tactic that was never meant to be realized, or perhaps Messius wanted Pompey to have more power or authority than any other provincial commander he encountered. The breakdown of the *provincia* as a means of determining precedence may have forced Rome's leaders to imagine other ways of preventing conflicts of authority between commanders, or perhaps this innovative concept of a supreme commander in chief was adopted or absorbed from the eastern monarchies that Rome had encountered in the past century. Messius may also have been trying to increase the prestige of the grain *provincia* by giving it the trappings of a mighty military command. He may have thought the civilian task of grain supervision was too humble for Pompey, especially since his work would bring him into contact with proconsuls in the provinces, but equipped as he was with a large army and navy and with the new power of *imperium maius*, Pompey could stand toe-to-toe with any commander. Finally, it is possible that Messius imagined that *imperium maius* would only be used to resolve in-person disagreements between Pompey and other commanders. In traditional republican practice, many types of official actions could be exercised only in person: the tribunician powers of veto and *intercessio*, proposals of legislation, taking of auspices, prosecutions, voting, and even declaring one's candidacy for election all required the physical presence of the individual actor. If this was also the case in Messius's thinking, then his suggestion of *imperium maius* may have been intended only to establish Pompey's precedence when he was physically present with another commander, but it would not have allowed him to give orders to other governors by letter or messenger. In other words, this proposal of *imperium maius* may have been intended only to resolve in-person disagreements or conflicts, but not to establish one man as the supreme leader of the empire with simultaneous authority over all Roman commanders. Whatever Messius was thinking, however, his plan was not realized, but 57 BC seems to be the year when the concept of *imperium maius* finally entered Roman political thinking.

In an astounding paradox, it was Cicero who finally set in motion the creation of a real *imperium maius* that would culminate in that of Augustus's

69. Cic. *Att.* 4.1.7.

principate. In 43 BC, with a civil war looming between the Caesarians and the Liberators led by Brutus and Cassius, Cicero proposed to the senate that Cassius not only be named the provincial commander of Syria but also be given *maius imperium* in any eastern province he should enter for the purpose of raising troops and money for war with the Caesarians:

> *utique, quamcumque in provinciam eius belli gerendi causa advenerit, ibi maius imperium C. Cassi pro consule sit, quam eius erit, qui eam provinciam tum obtinebit, cum C. Cassius pro consule in eam provinciam venerit.*[70]

> In whatever *provincia* he should enter for the purpose of waging his war, in that place there will be *maius imperium* for the proconsul C. Cassius than there is for the man who is currently holding that *provincia* when the proconsul C. Cassius comes to the *provincia*.

The language of this proposal is striking, for it closely mirrors the phrasing of Messius's proposal fourteen years earlier. Cicero called this *imperium maius* "the best power to enable action," although he does not explain exactly what he meant by this.[71] Like all grants of *imperium* to this time, Cassius was to use his *imperium maius* only in the performance of his assigned *provincia*, which was the permanent *provincia* of Syria as well as supreme command in the war against the Caesarians (*belli gerendi causa*). Thus Cassius could not order other provincial commanders around at his whim like a monarch, but within the context of waging war against the Caesarians his *imperium* would always take precedence.[72] Although we cannot be certain of Cicero's intentions, his wording seems quite careful: he is essentially urging that—in addition to the permanent province of Syria—Cassius be given an additional *provincia* of waging war against the Caesarians, which is to say he should be the supreme commander in the war against the Caesarians and his decisions should take precedence over all other *imperium*-bearing commanders working with him.

Cicero's suggestion, however, had an obvious danger, since this *provincia* of waging war against the Caesarians would necessarily overlap with any num-

---

70. Cic. *Phil.* 11.30 (Drogula, trans.). See also Cic. *Phil.* 10.25, 11.28–31. See also Girardet (1993) and (2000) 185–89, and Roddaz (1992) for discussion and bibliography.

71. Cic. *Phil.* 11.30.

72. Appian—who lived under the *imperium maius* of the Roman emperors—described it (*BC* 4.58) thus: "The senate instructed all of the others who were commanding Roman provinces and armies—from the Ionian Sea to Syria—that they were to comply with the orders of Cassius and Brutus" (Drogula, trans.) (τοῖς τε ἄλλοις πᾶσιν ἐκέλευσαν, ὅσοι Ῥωμαίοις ἡγεμονεύουσιν ἐθνῶν ἢ στρατοπέδων ἀπὸ τοῦ Ἰονίου μέχρι Συρίας, ὑπακούειν, ἐς ὅ τι κελεύοι Κάσσιος ἢ Βροῦτος).

ber of permanent provinces, all of which were the *provinciae* of other men who might resent any intrusion into their sphere of authority. Making Cassius the commander in chief of a war against the Caesarians would likely create many situations in which two *provinciae* existed in the same geographic space, and other commanders might refuse to acknowledge Cassius's leadership. Cicero and others could guess that a battle against the Caesarians (who held the West) would not be fought in Cassius's *provincia* of Syria far off in the East, but probably in a more central location, like the *provincia* of Macedonia, which was currently under Brutus's command. If that happened, an awkward situation might arise in which Cassius—who held the *provincia* of the war— might have to claim priority of *imperium* in Brutus's *provincia* of Macedonia, an imposition that could offend Brutus. And even if Brutus and Cassius did not fight over the question of priority of *imperium* (as had Metellus Creticus and Pompey's legate on Crete in 67 BC), it still might prove difficult for Cassius to exercise effective command over Brutus and other proud aristocratic commanders. A few years earlier, Cicero and his colleagues had watched in horror as Pompey and the senate lost their civil war against Caesar largely because the traditionally republican, blue-blooded aristocrats had repeatedly refused to follow the advice of their commander in chief Pompey. Despite holding the *provincia* of the war, Pompey had been unable to marshal the senate's forces effectively, in large part because many of his aristocratic allies insisted on acting as independent commanders rather than as Pompey's lieutenants or *adiutores*.[73] Caesar, on the other hand, had been the absolute and unchallenged commander of his army, had fewer aristocratic peers to keep in check, and his orders had been obeyed with great speed and alacrity. The survivors of that civil war would have seen that Caesar's unified and unchallenged authority had been a key ingredient of his success, just as the weak and decentralized authority of the senatorial forces had directly contributed to their defeat.

By suggesting *imperium maius* for Cassius within the context of his *provincia* of waging war against the Caesarians, Cicero probably sought to anticipate and avoid any debilitating conflict between the anti-Caesarian commanders by clearly stipulating that, whenever Cassius's war *provincia* overlapped in a particular geographic space with the territorial *provincia* of another commander, Cassius's *imperium* would take precedence in all matters pertaining to his

---

73. Most famously, the proconsul L. Domitius Ahenobarbus ignored Pompey's urgent appeals to combine their forces, engaged Caesar on his own, and lost his entire army to Caesar (Cic. *Att.* 8.12a.1, 12b.1–2, and 12d.1–2). For a recent discussion of Pompey's official status during this civil war with Caesar, see Vervaet (2006b) 928–53.

leadership of the war. Cicero recognized the potential inability of commanders to determine precedence of *imperium* when two *provinciae* overlapped in the same space, and he realized that this type of situation would be created by an empirewide civil war against the Caesarians, so he proposed that Cassius specifically and explicitly be given precedence of *imperium* in such situations to ensure the effective mobilization of forces against the Caesarians.

Rather than intending to invent a new type of *imperium* that was somehow greater than normal *imperium* in absolute or even relative terms, Cicero was acknowledging that traditional methods of distinguishing precedence through provincial assignment were no longer sufficient, and in the dire situation of civil war he wanted to ensure effective military leadership. This is emphasized by Cicero's stipulation that Cassius actually had to be present in another man's *provincia* to utilize his *imperium maius* and could not merely send legates to order proconsuls around (*cum C. Cassius pro consule in eam provinciam venerit*). Cassius was not to be in command of other commanders but simply to have undiminished and unchallenged authority over all matters that pertained to the war against the Caesarians. Of course, Cicero may not have given much thought to his proposed innovation of *imperium maius*, and Staveley emphasized that Cicero's ideas may not have been fully articulated when he first suggested them.[74] The senate did not accept Cicero's proposal right away, but several months later it bowed to circumstances and granted both Brutus and Cassius such commands over all *transmarinae provinciae*.[75] Given the outrage that had accompanied Messius's proposal in 57 BC, it is surprising that the senate should now be willing to approve the creation of *imperium maius*. Indeed, Cicero was aware of the significance of his proposal and acknowledged to the senate that he was proposing a *dominatum et principatum* for Cassius, who, Cicero assured them, was worthy of the honor and power.[76] Naturally, Cicero could not have appreciated the irony of his statement, although the connection he made between *imperium maius* and *principatum* was certainly not lost on the young Octavian.

Although the senate had been hostile to Messius's proposal of *imperium maius* in 57 BC, several additional points help explain why it embraced the concept in 43 BC. First, the intervening fourteen years had produced several unusual events in Roman politics: Pompey's sole consulship and command *in absentia* of Spain; his appointment as defender of the state against Caesar;

74. Staveley (1963) 481–83.
75. Cic. *ad Brut.* 1.5.1; Livy *Per.* 122; Vell. 2.62.2; App. *BC* 3.63, 4.58; Dio 47.28.5–29.6.
76. Cic. *Phil.* 11.36.

Caesar's series of dictatorships ending in his appointment as dictator for life; and, most important, the creation of the Second Triumvirate as a legal body—*triumviri rei publicae constituendae*—with vast prerogatives over the empire. All of these events had no doubt acclimatized the senate to the domination of a few men with tremendous and highly unusual capabilities. Furthermore, the great men of the late republic had changed the nature and scale of commands and power, and the senate had to adapt its traditions in order to counter these men effectively. Cicero and his senatorial supporters were probably more willing in 43 BC to take decisive steps to establish clearly the absolute and centralized authority of Brutus and Cassius in the approaching civil war against the Caesarians, and to this end they introduced an idea that had perhaps been floating around in aristocratic thought for many years—*imperium maius*. Finally, the fact that *imperium maius* was a legal and traditional-sounding entitlement probably made it tolerable in the senate's eyes. Although it was highly unusual, *imperium maius* was still *imperium*: it was an official source of authority that the state could grant and rescind as it wished, and it sounded far better than tyranny or despotism. The senate needed to create a commander who could contend with—and defeat—the Caesarians, but they did not want simply to replace one tyrant with another. The power of the Second Triumvirate was in its loyal legions, the wealth of its provinces, and its extensive patronage and popularity in Rome, all of which were beyond the ability of the senate to control. Cassius's supreme authority, on the other hand, would be dependent on his receipt of *imperium maius* and a *provincia* from the state, which could be extended or revoked as the senate and people wished.

In summary, Cicero and the senate first invested a commander with *imperium maius* in an effort to defeat the Caesarians in 43 BC, but they probably did not think of it as the supreme authority it would become under Augustus and his successors. Assuming the senate adopted the definition of *imperium maius* that Cicero had articulated months earlier, its purpose was not to change Rome's system of provincial command into a hierarchy of authority but to resolve potential problems in that system that had arisen as a result of the evolution of the *provincia*. Cicero had not wanted or intended to make Cassius the absolute master of all eastern provinces and the *imperium*-bearing commanders who held them; recognizing that *provinciae* could overlap in geographic space, he wished to ensure that—should such an overlap occur—Cassius's authority over the war against the Caesarians would not be impeded or challenged in any way. While it is tempting to interpret *maius* as meaning greater in absolute terms of measure (i.e., Cassius having more or greater *imperium* than other commanders), the qualifications Cicero places on the use of this *imperium* indicate that the traditional concept of precedence — rather than a substantive difference — is intended. Had Brutus and Cassius succeeded, *imperium maius* might have been discarded and never utilized again by the senate. As things turned out, however, Augustus would take up the idea of *imperium maius* when he was seeking a traditional-sounding method for retaining monarchical control over the empire. Although Cicero had proposed the use of *imperium maius* as a means to defeat the Caesarians' challenge to the republican government, Augustus would make it the backbone of his military control over the entire empire, and the fact that it had been conceived by the great republican champions Cicero, Brutus, and Cassius no doubt gave it the patina of republicanism that made it more tolerable to Romans in the 20s BC.

Further Developments in *Imperium* during the Late Republic

The arguments about the nature, development, and relationship of *imperium* and the *provincia* presented in this study make it possible to approach certain phenomena of the late republic from a new perspective. Because these two concepts were absolutely fundamental in the definition and capacity of a Roman commander, the reinterpretations of these ideas provide new explanations for how or why certain events in the late republic happened as they did. This section uses the preceding arguments about *imperium* and the *provincia* to reconsider three such phenomena and to suggest new understandings of them.

THE *LEGATI CUM IMPERIO* OF POMPEY AND CAESAR

Throughout the republic, Roman commanders had been accompanied by special assistants called *legati*. Normally, a commander selected his legates from Rome's aristocracy — usually from his friends or family — and these individuals served as the commander's helpers, companions, and advisers.[77] Furthermore, legates were unique in the Roman army because they exercised considerable authority over the soldiers without having been elected to an office that conferred *potestas* or *imperium*; they derived their authority directly from the commander and operated as his personal lieutenants, but they did not possess official authority in their own right.[78] This seems to have been largely an in-

---

77. For a general discussion on Roman military *legati*, see Schleussner (1978) 101–203 and Linderski (1990a) 53–58.

78. All regular military officers were normally elected by the people (consuls, praetors, quaestors) or by the soldiers themselves (military tribunes and centurions).

formal arrangement; soldiers accepted the authority of a legate so long as they understood that he was following the directions of the commander in chief, but if the soldiers or junior officers had good reason to believe that a legate was *not* following the directions of the commander, they could probably ignore his orders completely, since the legate was not himself invested with any official authority to command.[79] As discussed in chapter 4, commanders could even direct a legate (or a quaestor) to act "as a commander" (*pro praetore*), which was essentially a battlefield promotion that gave the legate a higher degree of authority in the eyes of the soldiers but was not a legal conferral of *imperium*. Such a legate operated under the aegis of his commander's *imperium* and partook of the commander's *imperium*, but did not actually possess *imperium* in his own right and could not receive a triumph for victories he achieved.

In the late republic, the senate made an innovation to the practice of assigning legates that was relatively small at the time but would have a substantial long-term effect on the Roman Empire. When the *lex Gabinia* gave Pompey the war against pirates in 67 BC, it contained an unusual provision that he was permitted to select twenty-four legates with *imperium*, to whom he gave the insignia of praetors.[80] The investiture of the legates with praetorian insignia strongly suggests that they had *imperium* before they left Rome. The decision to assign so many legates to Pompey and to invest them with *imperium* was a considerable innovation, and certainly was a consequence of the logistics that would be required in the piracy command, since many fleets would need to operate independently throughout the Mediterranean. Pompey intended to send squadrons of ships all over the Mediterranean, and these legates with *imperium* would need the authority to operate as commanders in their own right — to have *imperium* and act *pro praetore*. They were something of a hybrid between the traditional legates (who normally had no official authority) and the *privati cum imperio* who had been used as substitutes for regular commanders in Spain and elsewhere over a century earlier.

If Pompey's legates were hybrids, from what source did they receive their *imperium*: from the state through a *lex curiata*, or through some exceptional

---

79. When the two Scipio brothers were killed fighting in Spain in 211 BC, their surviving soldiers did not accept Cn. Scipio's legate Fonteius as their new leader but instead selected a military tribune to lead them (Livy 25.37.1–7, Val. Max. 2.7.15a). Since Cn. Scipio died in an ambush, he probably did not have time to appoint Fronteius (who had remained in the camp) *pro praetore*, leaving Fronteius with insufficient authority to claim command of the army.

80. App. *Mith.* 94 (cf. Dio 36.36.1–2). Plutarch (*Pomp.* 25.3) says that the *lex Gabinia* originally gave Pompey fifteen such *legati*, but this number was subsequently raised to twenty-four. See Schleussner (1978) 179–84, 198–201, Brennan (2000) 425–26, Seager (2002) 206 n. 63.

process? Appian says Pompey gave the praetorian insignia (στρατηγίας σημεῖα περικεῖσθαι) to his legates, but this must mean either that Pompey selected his legates or that he played a role in their *lex curiata*.[81] Given the tremendous restrictions on the conferral of *imperium*, it seems impossible that one man could have usurped the state's prerogative to confer *imperium*. Furthermore, the fact that the question of Pompey's legates was written into the *lex Gabinia* suggests that something was unusual about them beyond simply their number. Antonius Creticus had eight or more legates in his piracy command from 74 to 71 BC, and no special law is known to have authorized their appointment.[82] Thus the need to include Pompey's legates in the legislation suggests that there was something different about them that required a vote of the people (or the *comitia curiata*) to authorize. Pompey's legates probably received special grants of *imperium* from the state, just as *privati cum imperio* had a century earlier. Since legates were *privati* (they held no office), this was essentially a revival of the older practice that had gone out of use in 197 BC, enabling each legate to have full and independent *imperium*, but they all had to recognize the precedence of Pompey's *imperium* because he held the *provincia* in which they were operating (the legates did not have *provinciae* of their own). Pompey was the commander in chief of his *provincia* and could claim all victories and glory won in that sphere as his own, but the capacity of his legates to exercise authority and command independently was much higher because they possessed *imperium* in their own right.

There are good reasons why Pompey as well as his opponents would have been willing to take this extraordinary step of legislating that he receive legates with independent grants of *imperium*. Pompey's motives are probably easy: it would increase his own prestige and status greatly to have so many men with independent *imperium* under his command. Such men were more like *adiutores* than mere *legati*, and it would have increased Pompey's appearance of power to have precedence over so many men with *imperium*. As his senatorial friends would remark years later — it was a prestigious and glorious thing to have bearers of *imperium* under your command.[83] In real terms, it probably made little difference to Pompey whether he instructed his legates to act *pro praetore* under the aegis of his *imperium*, or whether they were individually invested with *imperium* by the state; either way, because the *provincia* had been assigned to him, he enjoyed precedence of authority over everyone in that

81. App. *Mith.* 94.
82. See *MRR* 2.105–13 for references.
83. Plut. *Pomp.* 67.2–3, App. *BC* 2.67.

sphere, including other bearers of *imperium*. Although the senate as a whole had resisted the *lex Gabinia*, Pompey's opponents may have found something good about these *legati cum imperio*. In their opposition to the *lex Gabinia*, Q. Hortensius and Q. Catulus had argued that the proposed piracy command was too great for any one man, and they feared that wielding so much power and having so many men under one's command could corrupt the best men.[84] It was obvious that Pompey was going to need an extraordinarily large number of legates for this command — far more than the six that M. Antonius had used seven years earlier — and the senate may have sought to exert greater control over the choice (or at least approval) of those legates by arranging that they would receive a grant of *imperium* from the state. Though pleasing to Pompey's pride, such a grant would also mean that his legates owed their authority to the senate, which presumably could abrogate their *imperium* if it so wished (thereby delivering a blow to Pompey's prestige).

That the senate was behind (or at least complicit in) the decision to confer *imperium* on the legates may be indicated by the number of lictors they received. According to Appian, Pompey's legates possessed praetorian insignia, which presumably included six lictors bearing *fasces*. Badian, however, pointed out that no source confirms this number, and he suggested that republican *legati pro praetore* probably received only five lictors and *fasces* each, as was later the case under Augustus.[85] Naturally, the number of lictors and *fasces* a commander possessed meant nothing in regard to his capacity to command — the *imperium* of a praetor was every bit as complete and potent as the *imperium* of a consul. It was, however, a powerful visual statement that the *legati cum imperio* were not quite as important or prestigious as a praetor (or propraetor). This would have been an important symbolic point when Pompey's legates spread throughout the Mediterranean and began operating on and along the coasts of other commanders' *provinciae*. To reduce the insult Pompey's *provincia* was likely to give those other commanders, his *legati pro praetore* may have been given a smaller number of *fasces* to establish clearly their lesser status and the expectation that they would show willing deference to the more important proconsuls and propraetors. Of course, this depended on the legates' respect for higher office rather than on a real difference in authority, as was demonstrated when Pompey's legate on Crete refused to yield to the wishes of Metellus Creticus. Because the number of lictors and *fasces* a commander received

84. Dio (36.31.3–4) holds Marius and Sulla up for comparison as commanders who exercised too many and too great commands (cf. Dio 36.31.1–36.4).

85. Badian (1965) 112 n. 18.

normally was not variable, the decision to give Pompey's legates only five *fasces* each was probably established by the *lex Gabinia* to give Pompey the powerful lieutenants he needed without giving unnecessary insult or irritation to Rome's other provincial commanders.

That these *legati cum imperio* derived from a special compromise is also suggested by the fact that other provincial commanders did not start requesting such special legates for themselves. In fact, only one other such legate is known in the republic: T. Labienus, who served as Caesar's *legatus cum imperio* in his Gallic command.[86] Although Caesar is known to have made special use of *legati* by appointing one to assume executive responsibilities over each of his legions (a *legatus legionis*),[87] Labienus's unique position *cum imperio* seems to have been determined by the *lex Vatinia* that gave Caesar his command. While the possession of a *legatus cum imperio* was a special privilege, this aspect of the *lex Vatinia* may have been a concession to Caesar's political ally Pompey, since Labienus may well have been one of Pompey's men.[88] Perhaps the assignment originated from negotiations with Pompey or other senators who sought to influence Caesar's command by providing him with a legate who already possessed *imperium* by decree of the state (i.e., *imperium* that Caesar could not abrogate himself). In this manner the senate acted as it had with Pompey less than a decade earlier: it attempted to restrain the ambition of a commander who had received a large province by vote of the people. Furthermore, since the senate may have exerted influence over the selection of Caesar's *legatus cum imperio*, it was able to put forward men friendly to its interests (or at least men who were not unquestioningly loyal to Caesar). Although much of this is speculation, the fact remains that Labienus was the only significant officer in Caesar's army to abandon him when he marched into Italy in 49 BC,[89] suggesting that Labienus's primary loyalties had always rested with the senate and not Caesar.

While the senate may have hoped that this use of *legati cum imperio* would improve its position vis-à-vis Pompey and Caesar, its efforts had an impor-

---

86. Caes. *BG* 1.21, Plut. *Caes.* 34.5, *Pomp.* 64.3, App. *Celt.* 15.

87. Caes. *BG* 1.52.

88. Syme (1938) 113–25 argues convincingly that Labienus was a supporter of Pompey and had acquired his military experience serving in Pompey's great commands in the 60s BC. Pompey's "loan" of an experienced lieutenant can certainly be seen as a sign of friendship between the two men (who were, after all, related by Pompey's marriage to Julia). That Labienus was a known supporter of both Caesar and Pompey makes it even more unlikely that the senate wished to honor Caesar (or Labienus) through the authorization of a special legate.

89. Caes. *BC* 8.52 (solicited to desert Caesar), Cic. *Att.* 7.11.1, 12.5, 13.1, 13a.3 (deserts Caesar).

tant side effect: providing a clear example of one independent holder of *imperium* being subordinated to another. In the past, praetors and proconsuls had served as secondary commanders in the *provinciae* of consuls, consuls had yielded precedence of *imperium* to their colleague on alternate days in a shared *provincia*, and consuls had even served as secondary commanders in the *provinciae* of dictators, but never before had an *imperium*-bearing commander been specifically created for the sole purpose of acting as the subordinate of another commander. Pompey's *legati* formed something of a subclass of military commander that until that time was unknown in Rome: they had the same *imperium* as all other commanders, but their status as *legati* meant they held a subordinate status to the commander they served. Since the *legati* were never expected to have their own *provinciae*, they could never be fully independent commanders, as were praetors or promagistrates who operated as *adiutores* in the *provincia* of another commander; *legati cum imperio* were clear subordinates who happened to receive a grant of *imperium*. This new thinking about the subordination of one *imperium*-bearing commander to another may have influenced the tribune Messius, who would first suggest giving Pompey a greater level of *imperium* (*maius imperium*) in 57 BC. Thus the *legati cum imperio* given to Pompey (and Caesar) may have been a direct influence on the creation of *imperium maius* at the end of the republic, and they would provide the future emperor Augustus with ideas for how to control the Roman Empire.

CAESAR'S CHOICE OF THE DICTATORSHIP

As is well known, Julius Caesar chose to assume the office of dictator after he crossed the Rubicon in 49 BC and drove his enemies (including much of the senate) from Italy. He then made the dictatorship his primary source of authority for suppressing his opponents and bringing about his desired reforms for the state, holding the extraordinary office several times until his assassination in 44 BC. Although the tenure of the dictatorship had traditionally been limited to six months, Sulla's use of the office from 82 to 79 BC had provided a precedent (albeit not a very good one) for retaining the dictatorship for longer periods. While there were advantages to using the dictatorship in this way, it was also a dangerous choice, since it was certain to bring Caesar much odium from the senate and people of Rome: the office had been out of use for more than 150 years (since 202 BC), and Sulla's brief revival of it had stained it with the horror of the bloodshed and the proscriptions of Roman citizens. Furthermore, Caesar had used an unusual (and possibly illegal) process to be named dictator, which caused still more concerns about the legitimacy of his office.[90] Although Caesar was generally reserved in his exercise of authority and made clemency one of his watchwords, the dictatorship continued to be a hated office during his tenure, so much so that Mark Antony had the office formally abolished following Caesar's assassination in 44 BC.[91] From this perspective, one could say that holding the dictatorship did Caesar more harm than good, which someone as politically astute as he should have been able to anticipate. Jehne may well be correct that Caesar was aiming at some kind of monarchy and that the dictatorship was a preliminary step toward this goal, but what advantages did the dictatorship give him that he did not already have at his command?[92] He did not lack the *imperium, provincia,* and *auspicium* he needed to exercise legitimate legal command, and he laid down his first dictatorship after a mere eleven days, indicating that it did not give him a legal or a tactical or strategic advantage in fighting his enemies at Pharsalus.[93] The dictatorship did not allow him to outrank his rivals, because the dictatorship had no more authority than the consulship; the high prestige of the office would be little use in a civil war; and dictators were hampered by not being allowed to leave Italy, which Caesar needed to do very soon.[94] Given all of these problems — which he certainly could have anticipated — why did Caesar decide to work through this office?

The dictatorship possessed one important benefit that Caesar must have wanted badly enough to risk inspiring the general aversion that came with that office: the ability to hold and exercise *imperium* within the *pomerium* of Rome. The appointment of a dictator seems to have been the equivalent of a declaration of martial law in early Rome, for which reason the dictator was authorized to use his military authority within the civilian sphere of the city, where *imperium* was normally forbidden. When the dictatorship fell into abeyance after the Second Punic War, the Romans had turned to the *senatus consultum ultimum*, which achieved the same end by encouraging the consuls to use *imperium* within the city. This was not an option for Caesar, however, because the majority of the senate was against him and had already passed a *senatus con-*

90. Since the sitting consuls had fled Rome before Caesar's arrival, he had himself named dictator by a praetor. Cicero (*Att.* 9.9.3) seems to have believed this was illegal but could not prove it beyond saying it was unprecedented.

91. Cic. *Phil.* 1.3, 2.91; Livy *Per.* 116; App. *BC* 3.25; Dio 44.51.2.

92. See Jehne (1987) and (2010) for the possibility that Caesar used the dictatorship to establish some type of monarchy. Vervaet (2012) 133–46 also believes Caesar sought to use the dictatorship to subvert the traditional government.

93. Caes. *BC* 3.1-2, Plut. *Caes.* 37.2, App. *BC* 2.48, Dio 41.36.1-4.

94. Livy *Per.* 19, Dio 36.34.2.

sultum ultimum to authorize Pompey to move against him. Holding the dictatorship was probably the only legal way Caesar could enter the city—which he very much wanted to do, if only for eleven days—without automatically forfeiting his *auspicium militiae*, his *imperium*, his *provincia*, and his claims for a triumph for his conquests in Gaul and Britain.[95] In that time of civil war, he might have ignored the legal ban on *imperium* within the *pomerium*, but Caesar generally was careful about the legality of his actions; he was willing to bend laws when necessary, but he usually tried to avoid breaking them outright. Affairs in Rome demanded his presence, since both consuls and most of the senators had fled the city leaving public business up in the air, particularly the elections for 48 BC, in which Caesar intended to stand for the consulship. By using the dictatorship, Caesar was able to enter the city and take care of this business without laying down his *imperium*, which meant he retained his legions, his *provincia*, and his claims on a future triumph over Gaul and Britain. Sulla had certainly used the dictatorship to hold *imperium* inside the city, but unlike Caesar he also used his *imperium* to ignore the rights of *provocatio* and the other protections of civil law, and he carried out bloody purges of citizens. Caesar does not seem to have been interested in this aspect of the dictatorship, which means the only real benefit of the office was its ability to keep *auspicium* and *imperium*—and with them his claims on his triumphs—when crossing the *pomerium* and entering the city.

Once Caesar had achieved his aims in the city, he laid down his dictatorship, since it no longer served any purpose for him, and began his pursuit of Pompey in the East. Only after news of Caesar's victory at Pharsalus in October 48 BC reached Rome did his consular colleague and ally P. Servilius Isauricus name him dictator a second time (this time for a year), no doubt in the expectation that Caesar would be returning to Rome soon (Servilius may not have been aware that Caesar was en route to Egypt).[96] Caesar did little with this dictatorship, returning only briefly to Rome in September 47 BC to resolve some internal problems—all without laying down his *imperium*, thanks

95. Caesar may have been influenced by the difficulties Pompey surely faced following his consulship in 55 BC, when he had to remain outside the *pomerium* to retain his *imperium* and *provincia* of Spain (he had a brief respite from this during his consulship in 52 BC). Unable to enter the heart of the city, Pompey could not attend meetings of the senate and other public business unless the senators agreed to meet outside the *pomerium* (as they did several times to accommodate him: Cic. *Fam.* 8.4.4, *QFr* 2.3.3, Caes. *BC* 1.6).

96. *ILS* 70, Cic. *Phil.* 2.62, Livy *Per.* 112, Plut. *Caes.* 51.1, *Ant.* 8.3, Dio 42.20.3–21.1. On the date of this dictatorship, see *MRR* 2.284–85 n. 1. Since dictators were not supposed to leave Italy (Dio 36.34.2), it is possible this dictatorship was only to begin when Caesar returned from the East.

to his position as dictator—before setting out for Africa before the end of the year.[97] Caesar was consul again in 46 BC while fighting the Pompeians in Africa, but only when those enemies were defeated and he planned his return to Rome was he again appointed dictator in April 46 BC, and he was probably designated dictator for the next nine years.[98] The pattern is clear: Caesar sought dictatorships when he wanted to enter Rome without forfeiting his *imperium*, *provincia*, and his right to triumph for past victories. As consul and dictator, Caesar returned to Rome in July of that year and famously celebrated four triumphs between September 21 and October 2. It is also likely that possession of the dictatorship was necessary for Caesar to celebrate all four triumphs: although triumphators were normally exempted from the ban on *imperium* within the city, their *imperium* automatically expired at the end of their triumph, which means Caesar might have forfeited his claim on subsequent triumphs at the end of his first triumphal celebration. As a dictator entitled to possess and use *imperium* in the city, Caesar could claim that his *imperium* did not expire at the end of his triumphs, thereby retaining his legal right to celebrate subsequent triumphs. This use of the dictatorship was manipulative and contrary to tradition, but it gave Caesar the legal cover he needed to pursue his plans in Rome. Because Caesar probably needed the dictator's ability to hold *imperium* within the *pomerium*, he was willing to endure the popular odium the office created in order to achieve his goals.

OCTAVIAN'S *IMPERIUM PRO PRAETORE* IN 43 BC

A small incident in the early career of Augustus (Octavian at the time) sheds valuable light on the Roman concept of *imperium* and rank at the end of the republic. Shortly after Julius Caesar's assassination in 44 BC, his great nephew, primary heir, and adopted son Octavian began gathering an army of Caesar's veterans in southern Italy, and by the end of the year he had built up a sizable private army. At the time, Octavian held neither *imperium* nor any kind of official office, but the senate was too preoccupied with its efforts to support D. Junius Brutus against Mark Antony to worry about suppressing an inactive private army in the south. Cicero even sought to use Octavian's army against Mark Antony, although the senior statesman was surely galled at having to ask for help from the brash and youthful Octavian. In January 43 BC, Cicero

---

97. See references in *MRR* 2.286.

98. *Act. Trium.* for 45 and 44 BC, *BHisp.* 2.1, Dio 43.14.3–5. He was probably named dictator for the year, and designated dictator for future years (see Broughton's remarks in *MRR* 2.295).

convinced the senate to give Octavian a special grant of *imperium pro praetore* in an effort to win the young man's loyalty to the senate.[99] While many historians have tended to see *imperium pro consule* and *imperium pro praetore* as two different levels or ranks of *imperium*, this was not at all the case. Consuls and praetors always had the exact same level of *imperium*, so the only difference between a proconsul and a propraetor was the title: proconsul was a more prestigious title than propraetor, but there was nothing a proconsul could do that a propraetor could not do, and a proconsul could not claim precedence of *imperium* over a propraetor unless the latter was in the former's *provincia*. While the proconsul commanded more prestige, had a higher status in society, and possessed twelve *fasces* instead of the propraetor's six, legally they possessed the exact same *imperium* and capacity to command. When the senate offered Octavian the title *pro praetore* instead of *pro consule*, therefore, it was offering him a less prestigious title but not an inferior level of *imperium*. This was nevertheless a notable snub because it had become common for praetors to be prorogued with the augmented title *pro consule*. Indeed, by the end of the republic it had become extremely rare for a praetor *not* to be prorogued *pro consule*. It would have escaped no one's notice that the senate's offer to Caesar's heir of *imperium* with the title *pro praetore* was deliberately very modest indeed.

In all likelihood, the senate's offer was an effort to assert its moral authority over a precocious young aristocrat and was possibly a thinly disguised insult. In that year (43 BC) no fewer than eleven former praetors are believed to have been functioning *pro consule*, but Octavian was the only one recorded as serving *pro praetore*.[100] Receiving *imperium* and the title *pro praetore* without actually having reached the praetorship was naturally a signal achievement and a great honor for Octavian, but it must have been bittersweet on account of the obviously patronizing decision to give him a lower title than any other current commander. Likewise, the senate granted Octavian the prestigious status of a former consul in the senate, but this was a civilian status and had no bearing on his military rank as a promagistrate, and the paradox of being a consular senator but only a praetorian commander must have stung. Cicero seems to have expressed the backhanded nature of these compliments well, telling the senate that propraetorian rank was appropriate for Octavian's

99. Cic. *Ad Brut.* 1.15.7, *Phil.* 5.45–46, 13.22, 14.6; Aug. *RG* 1; Livy *Per.* 118; Vell. 2.61.3; Suet. *Aug.* 10.3; Dio 46.29.1–6.

100. See *MRR* 2.342–50 for references.

youth, and making the famous quip—much to Octavian's annoyance—that he was merely a youth to be praised, honored, and then discarded.[101] Since there was no real difference between *imperium pro consule* and *imperium pro praetore*, the senate's choice to offer Octavian the lowest title possible must surely be taken as a strong reprimand or a tacit insult—Octavian ultimately took it as the latter. There was certainly no legal reason for assigning him this rank; in a similar situation in 77 BC the senate had given Pompey a command in Spain with proconsular rank, even though he had held no office and was too young for the consulship.[102] Of course, Octavian was annoying the senate precisely at the moment in which it was working hard to reassert its control of the republic. Although the senate chose to make use of this young and arrogant man, it must have given him propraetorian rank specifically to deny him the higher honor, status, and more numerous *fasces* he would have received as *pro consule*.

This short glimpse at Octavian's first official title is useful, because it illustrates that *imperium* was still a single, absolute, and indivisible idea at the start of 43 BC. While the tribune Messius had proposed *imperium maius* many years earlier, the idea had not yet been realized, and it would not be realized until Cicero's speech later in 43 BC. All of the ex-praetors holding *provinciae* in that year had been prorogued with the augmented title *pro consule*, which—if one believes in different levels of *imperium*—means their *imperium* had been increased to consular *imperium maius*. Since all commanders in that year were either proconsuls *pro consule* or propraetors *pro consule*, that would mean all commanders in the empire had consular *imperium maius* and that no commanders had been given praetorian *imperium minus* until Octavian's unusual case. This is not realistic or possible. The Romans were using only one level of *imperium* at the start of 43 BC, which means the distinction between the two different levels of *imperium* was not important to the Romans, or—far more likely—the distinction did not yet exist. Octavian was the only person acting *pro praetore* in the entire empire not because the senate wanted him to have less *imperium* than the other commanders, but because it wanted to dress him down and give him a barely hidden insult. The only use the senate could find for the title *pro praetore* in 43 BC was to put down an annoying young man.

101. Cic. *Phil.* 5.45: *sit pro praetore eo iure, quo qui optimo. Qui honos quamquam est magnus illi aetati*, and *Fam.* 11.20.1, *Labeo Segulius . . . narravit . . . ipsum Caesarem nihil sane de te questum nisi dictum quod diceret te dixisse laudandum adulescentem, ornandum, tollendum.* The final verb *tollere* carried the double meaning of "raise up" and "remove."

102. Plut. *Pomp.* 17.3–4. Earlier in that year Pompey had been assigned a special command *pro praetore* against M. Aemilius Lepidus, but this low rank probably indicated that he was intended to be a helper (*adiutor*) to the proconsul Q. Lutatius Catulus, who was leading the resistance to Lepidus.

Conclusion

In the late republic, the rapidly accelerating competition for high office and military commands, the growing ambitions of the aristocracy, and the tremendous influence wielded by a small number of the senatorial elite drove men to experiment with the ideas of *imperium* and the *provincia* in their search for political advantage and success. When Gaius Gracchus tried to reduce the manipulation of provincial assignments by promulgating the *lex Sempronia* that required consular *provinciae* to be announced before consular elections, he initiated a shift in Roman thinking about how the *provincia* was assigned, which in time would cause new ideas about *imperium* to arise. Since it was difficult for the senate to determine many months in advance what wars or military campaigns would be most pressing after the new consuls had been elected and entered office, it became more practical for them to assign the consuls to permanent *provinciae* near foreign enemies who were likely to pose some threat to Rome. In the past, the senate had assigned consuls only to permanent *provinciae* when there was already an obvious need for major campaigning in or near that territory, but after the *lex Sempronia* it eventually became normal to assign all consuls to permanent *provinciae* whether or not there was an immediate and obvious need for major fighting in the region; it became rare for consuls to receive a *provincia* that did not involve command of a permanent *provincia*.

Because the *lex Sempronia* prevented sitting consuls from using their leadership of the senate to influence provincial assignments, some exceptionally popular or important men began using the popular assemblies as an alternative way to get the commands they wanted. Marius was the first to do this, but Pompey and Caesar took his example and expanded it, using tribunes to custom-build commands that were perfectly designed to win unprecedented glory, wealth, and status for the commanders. Since it had become normal for consuls to receive permanent *provinciae*, Pompey and Caesar arranged to receive command over multiple permanent *provinciae* at once, ensuring their proximity to a large number of enemies to fight, and providing them with the military resources necessary to build up and maintain large armies. By using the popular assemblies to acquire these vast commands, the great commanders thwarted the senate's traditional effort to keep the ambitions of its members in check by limiting the size and duration of their *provincia*. The shift in thinking about the *provincia* enabled the great generals to acquire commands of unprecedented size and scope, which in turn gave them the political power they needed to challenge the senate.

Finally, the evolution of the *provincia* eventually led to new thinking about *imperium* and the nature of authority. As the *provincia* had gradually split into two different concepts, provincial assignment had lost its ability to separate commanders into different spheres on every occasion. The pirate commands were the best example of this development because they created situations in which two *provinciae*—one a military task and the other a territory— overlapped in the same space. The shifting nature of the *provincia* made it difficult at times to determine which commander with *imperium* took precedence in what sphere. Rome's system of provincial command had always worked on the principle that commanders in chief were to be separated into different spheres or commissions, so that each commander had supreme authority over his own assigned task or area of responsibility. As the lines between these spheres began to blur, an alternative means of avoiding conflict was needed, leading some to contemplate fracturing *imperium* into different levels or degrees. Pompey's use of *legati cum imperio* in his pirate command created the unprecedented situation in which one *imperium*-bearing commander was a true subordinate of another *imperium*-bearing commander. Finally, the idea of *imperium maius* was raised and proposed in 57 BC, and it was first realized in 43 BC when Cicero and the senate needed a method to unify many different commanders with *imperium* under the supreme authority of one or two leaders to put down the Caesarians. On Cicero's suggestion, Brutus and Cassius were the first people to possess *imperium maius*, an innovation the senate no doubt expected would be a one-time, short-lived exception to their traditional understanding of *imperium*. Manipulations in the concept of the *provincia* had enabled Caesar to acquire unprecedented power and resources, so the senate manipulated the idea of *imperium* to enable Brutus and Cassius to amass and control a force capable of suppressing his successors.

7

AUGUSTAN MANIPULATION OF
TRADITIONAL IDEAS OF PROVINCIAL
GOVERNANCE

When Augustus (Octavian at the time) defeated Antony and became the sole ruler of the Roman Empire, the young *princeps* began searching for the means to retain his predominance without incurring the hatred of the ruling elite that had cost Julius Caesar his life. Over the next eight years (31 to 23 BC) Augustus crafted for himself a unique position in Roman society and government that enabled him to exercise unprecedented power and centralized authority over the entire Roman Empire without blatantly appearing to be a monarch. Although these Augustan reforms touched nearly every aspect of Roman life, this chapter examines only one aspect of these reforms: Augustus's role as a provincial commander and his contribution to the evolution of Roman provincial command.[1]

While Augustus's use of traditional terms and ideas to describe his near monopolization of military command is well known, this chapter argues that his manipulation of traditional concepts was much deeper and more intricate than has been previously recognized. In particular, Augustus took advantage of changes in the fundamental, underlying concepts that had shaped and defined provincial command to give himself a radically new but traditional-sounding position as Rome's main commander or *imperator*. This was possible because the growth of the Roman Empire in the second and (especially) first century BC had led the Romans to expand and diversify their traditional

---

1. A full discussion of the Augustan Reforms is beyond the scope of the current work. For a survey of the topic, see Mommsen (1887–88) 2.745–47, Last (1947), Salmon (1956) 457–59, Lacey (1974), Brunt (1984), Talbert (1984a), Brunt (1990), Raaflaub and Toher (1990), Girardet (1993) 202–5, Turpin (1994), Lacey (1996), Bleicken (1998), Eck (1998) 41–66, Giovannini (1999), Kearsley (1999), Meyer-Zwiffelhoffer (2002), Drogula (2011b), Southern (2014).

thinking about provincial command, so ideas that had once seemed simple—
like *imperium* and *provincia*—had acquired multiple meanings or interpretations. This complexity and diversity of definitions enabled Augustus to select
those interpretations that best served his purposes and combine them to form
a system of provincial governance that looked and sounded very traditional
but actually gave one man unprecedented control over Rome's *provinciae*. In
this respect, Augustus actually did follow Republican traditions of provincial
command, although only a very particular interpretation of those traditions.

Augustus did not create his principate in one stroke but gradually. This
chapter examines Augustus's provincial reforms by examining his different attempts to work within Roman tradition to secure his domination over Rome's
empire. By looking at his different combinations of conventional terms and
ideas, one can better understand how his principate was the product of centuries of development in Roman thought, and why his reforms and unique
position as *princeps* were acceptable to most of the senatorial aristocracy.

Augustus's Position in 32 BC

The nature of Augustus's position and authority in 32 BC is an intriguing problem, because it seems that he was running the western half of the Roman Empire without any kind of legitimate authority. For the previous decade (43 BC
to 33 BC), Augustus had legitimized his control over his provinces and armies
by holding the position *triumvir rei publicae constituendae*. The triumvirate
had been created in 43 BC for five years and renewed in 37 BC for another five
years, but at the end of this extension Augustus seems to have allowed this law-
based authority to expire, probably at the end of 33 BC.[2] In 32 BC, Augustus
was no longer legally a triumvir, although in his propaganda against Antony he
made several offers to lay down his (now expired) triumviral authority. In the
East, Antony continued to call himself a *triumvir* in spite of the legal expiration of his office. So what exactly was the nature of Augustus's (and Antony's)
authority and position in 32 BC?

There is no evidence that Augustus held a legal office between the expira-

---

2. The *lex Titia* of 43 BC: Aug. *RG* 7, App. *BC* 4.2–3 and 7, Dio 46.55.3 and 47.2.1–2; the extension in 37 BC: App. *BC* 5.95, Dio 48.54.6. There is some question of when the second five-year
term of the triumvirate ended, but Syme (1986) 29 and Lange (2009) 54–55 provide solid arguments
for accepting that it expired at the end of 33 BC. See also Southern (2014) 155–57 for recent discussion and bibliography. On the equality of consular *imperium* with triumviral *imperium*, see Girardet
(2000) 190. On the vagueness of the powers held by the *triumviri*, see Millar (1973) 50–67.

tion of his triumvirate at the end of 33 BC and the start of his next consulship in 31 BC, but he continued to exercise authority and perform official responsibilities throughout the intervening period: he convened the senate and sat between the two consuls on their official dais, he declared war against Cleopatra, and for that war he raised taxes and mobilized forces.[3] Although some scholars have suggested this exercise of power was — strictly speaking — an overthrow of legal government, others have suggested that Augustus was essentially a proconsul in 32 BC, since he still had *imperium* outside the *pomerium* even though his magisterial authority in Rome had expired.[4] This argument explains Dio's statement that Augustus stayed out of Rome during this year, which in turn suggests that the senate meeting that Augustus presided over in 32 BC was held outside the *pomerium*.[5] Other scholars have argued that Augustus could not possibly have been a proconsul, because his actions exceeded the normal authority of proconsuls. Of this latter group, Lange has recently revived Mommsen's argument that the triumvirate was an exceptional office that did not automatically expire but had to be laid down, meaning Augustus and Antony were still *triumviri* in 32 BC, and Augustus would remain a *triumvir* until 27 BC, although he chose not to use that title.[6] This seems unlikely, and the arguments presented in previous chapters give further support to the suggestion that Augustus was essentially a promagistrate.

Lange based this argument on the belief that "duration to abdication was characteristic of all those magistracies which were held not for the year, but for specific purposes, such as the dictatorship or censorship, although specific terms were often assigned."[7] Two assumptions underlie this argument: that a dictator or censor could retain his office beyond the maximum terms allotted to his magistracy, and that the triumvirate created by the *lex Titia* in 32 BC used the dictatorship or censorship as a paradigm rather than one of Rome's other boards of *triumviri*. The first assumption seems wrong, since there is no good evidence that dictators and censors could remain in office beyond

3. Convene the senate: Dio 50.2.5; declared war: Dio 50.4.3–6.1, 21.1–2, and 26.3–4; raised taxes: Plut. *Ant.* 58.1–2, Dio 50.10.4–5, 16.3, 20.3, 53.2.3; mobilized forces: Plut. *Ant.* 62.2–3.

4. Kromayer (1888) 2–21, Syme (1939) 225, 270–71, Millar (1973) and (1998), Gruen (1974), Bringmann (1988) 38, Reinhold (1998) 93, Bleicken (1990) 38–39, 57–62, and 68, Girardet (1990b) 338–42 and (1995) 150–61, Lewis (1991) 61, Pelling (1996) 52, Vervaet (2004) 65, Ungern-Sternberg (2004), Sumi (2005) 212, Lange (2009) 53–60.

5. Dio 50.2.4.

6. Lange (2009) 58. Lange also builds on arguments made by Coli (1953) 413–15 and Vervaet (2008).

7. Lange (2009) 58–59 and 181, citing work by Coli and Vervaet (note 6).

their allotted terms. To the contrary, Livy's account indicates that the maximum tenure of the censorship was set at eighteen months by a *lex Aemilia* of 434 BC,[8] and Julius Caesar surely would not have sought the provocative title of "dictator for life" (*dictator perpetuus*) if he could have simply retained his normal dictatorship indefinitely. What was the point of the qualifier *perpetuus* if not to prevent the automatic expiration of his dictatorship? While dictators (and, to a lesser degree, censors) could and did lay down their office voluntarily before the end of their allotted term, they generally did so only when they had completed their appointed task; thus they resigned because their job was finished, not because their office would continue indefinitely unless they formally resigned.

Second, it seems a mistake to assume that the *triumviri rei publicae constituendae* were modeled after the dictatorship or censorship instead of after Rome's other boards of *triumviri*, which generally had one-year terms. The best known of these boards were the *triumviri capitales* (in charge of Rome's jail and various police functions) and the *triumviri monetales* (in charge of Rome's mint), both of which belonged to the group of annual junior magistracies that young aristocrats usually held before the quaestorship.[9] Even extraordinary panels of *triumviri* seem to have held fixed terms: the three members of the Gracchan land commission set up in 133 BC (*triumviri agris iudicandis assignandis*) appear to have been appointed for single-year terms (although reappointment was permitted).[10] Although the panel of *triumviri rei publicae constituendae* established by the *lex Titia* had far greater powers and prerogatives than other boards of *triumviri*, there is no reason to imagine that it was fundamentally different in structure or conception from those other boards, or that its members could hold their office indefinitely whereas other *triumviri* had fixed terms. The sources are clear that the *lex Titia* established a five-year term for the triumvirate, and the fact that Augustus and his colleagues felt the need to acquire a renewal for a second five-year term in 37 BC seems solid evidence that their office would have expired without that extension. In short, the suggestion that Augustus legally could have retained his position as *triumvir* into 32 BC does not seem likely.

Third, the argument that Augustus must have been a *triumvir* in 32 BC be-

8. Livy 4.24.4–7, 9.33.9 and 34.9.

9. These *triumviri* were elected annually by the *comitia tributa*, and so their terms must have been one year. *RS* 45, Fest. 468L (cf. Cic. *Leg.* 3.6). See Pink (1952) 53–55, Jolowicz and Nicholas (1972) 56–57, and Lintott (1999a) 138.

10. Cic. *Leg. Agr.* 2.31, App. *BC* 1.9.

cause his actions in that year exceeded the normal prerogatives of a promagistrate also fails to convince. To support his argument that Augustus was a *triumvir*, Lange offers the following points: he sat between the two consuls at a senate meeting in 32 BC, which promagistrates were not supposed to do; he described his powers in that year as *potitus rerum omnium*, which seems too great a claim for a proconsul; and a *triumvir* would not have accepted the degradation of being demoted to the proconsulship.[11] As to the first of these objections, while it may have been presumptuous for Augustus as a promagistrate to sit between the two consuls at a senate meeting, our source on this event specifically states that Augustus attended that senate meeting surrounded by a guard of soldiers, as well as a group of friends carrying concealed daggers, and that this action frightened and intimidated the two sitting consuls (who were supporters of Antony).[12] Thus accompanied, Augustus was probably assuming prerogatives not specifically given to him by any law or office. While it may not have been proper procedure and behavior for a promagistrate, Dio points out that no one objected or tried to enforce normal etiquette, a qualification intended to point out that Augustus's action was not actually appropriate given his position. Furthermore, the fact that Augustus used the phrase *potitus rerum omnium* in his *Res Gestae* to describe his position in 32 BC need not be taken as a legal articulation of triumviral authority, but rather as a grandiose but vague statement of the power he had held at one point fifty-five years before the composition of the inscription. The *Res Gestae* was a key piece of Augustan propaganda, so one should not expect legal precision in place of magnificent-sounding but imprecise ideas, especially if telling the exact truth may have been a source of embarrassment for the emperor. Finally, it was not a degradation of his *dignitas* for Augustus to move from the position of a triumvir to what was essentially a proconsulship or even some sort of *protriumvir*. With the expiration of the triumvirate, the highest remaining military titles in the empire were proconsul and *imperator*, both of which Augustus possessed.[13] Furthermore, in 32 BC titles were probably less important to Augustus than the raw power he had at his command: he controlled half the empire and was preparing his legions for a civil war against Antony, so there is little reason to expect that he adhered strictly to the law or customary practice. The promagistracy had always been poorly defined in Roman law, so it provided Augustus the military authority he wanted to justify his command over his army.

---

11. Aug. *RG* 34.1. See Lange (2009) 57–58.
12. Dio 50.2.5–7.
13. Augustus was first proclaimed *imperator* by his soldiers in 43 BC (Cic. *Phil.* 14.11).

In all likelihood, Augustus was some sort of proconsul or even a protrium-vir in 32 BC, which suited his goals perfectly at the time. Being a promagis-trate enabled him to retain his *imperium*, *auspicium*, and provincial command indefinitely, and it was his control of his legions in his provinces that would ultimately decide whether he or Antony retained preeminence in Rome. To prevent his authority from lapsing, he seems to have been careful to remain outside the *pomerium* as Pompey had done when he governed his Spanish provinces from Rome. Since Augustus was not yet the cautious politician he would become later in his life, he probably broke Roman tradition by exercis-ing more authority than was proper for a promagistrate, such as presiding over the senate along with the consuls, but such excessive actions do not undermine the fact that he was essentially a proconsul or protriumvir.

Augustus the Consul: *Imperium* vs. the *Pomerium*

When Augustus and Antony faced each other at Actium in 31 BC, they did so as Rome's two consuls, each invested with *imperium* and *provinciae* that com-prised nearly half of the empire. When Antony lost that battle and afterward committed suicide in Egypt, Augustus was left the unrivaled leader of the Ro-man world. Naturally, his position rested primarily on the loyalty of his legions and the control they gave him over the provinces, but a blatant military dic-tatorship was not his preferred method for retaining power. His dilemma was how to retain autocratic control over Rome's military resources without look-ing too much like the autocrat he was and intended to remain. He also faced the same problem that his great-uncle Caesar had encountered eighteen years earlier: how could a military commander (*imperator*) exercise legitimate, long-term authority within the city of Rome, where military authority was forbid-den by ancient tradition? Caesar had elected to make use of the dictatorship and its capacity to hold *imperium* inside the *pomerium*, but his career (and that of Sulla before him) had made the dictatorship tremendously unpopular, and the office had been outlawed shortly after Caesar's assassination. Augustus's first solution, therefore, was to hold repeated consulships to guarantee that he would always be one of the two most important men in the government.

Repeated consulships gave Augustus what he most dearly needed: the legal ability to cross the *pomerium* and enter the city without forfeiting his military command. Provincial assignments to sitting magistrates were valid both inside and outside the city, so a consul did not forfeit his *provincia* when he crossed the *pomerium*. The evidence for this is clear: consuls and praetors in the repub-lic were usually given their military assignments shortly after entering office, although normally they did not leave Rome and take up their commands until weeks or months later. Furthermore, it often happened that a sitting consul on campaign in the field would leave his *provincia* and return to Rome to conduct necessary business in the city, and — when the tasks were complete — he would return to his *provincia* without hindrance and would continue his campaign for the remainder of his term in office (and longer, if prorogued).[14] Although a consul or praetor laid down his *imperium* automatically when he entered the city, he could take it up again when crossing the *pomerium* and exiting the city, and thereby resume active command of his *provincia* without difficulty or other delay (albeit under new auspices). The office and legal standing of the sitting magistrate were the same inside and outside Rome (a consul was a consul both inside and outside the *pomerium*), his possession of a *provincia* was unaffected if he crossed the *pomerium*, and he could take up and lay down his *imperium* as often as he wished. A promagistrate, on the other hand, had no office or legal status in Rome and therefore had no right to take up *imperium* again once he had laid it down by crossing the *pomerium* and entering the city. When Pompey decided to remain at Rome and command his *provincia* of Spain *in absentia* through legates from 54 to 49 BC, he had to remain outside the *pomerium* in order to retain his authority and status as proconsul (except during his third consulship in 52 BC), which meant that the senate had to meet outside the *pomerium* if it wanted to permit Pompey to attend.[15]

Augustus improved on Pompey's arrangement by holding consecutive consulships from 31 to 23 BC, enabling him to enter and exit the city as often as he wished without ever forfeiting his *provincia*. Unlike a promagistrate, he could act as the leader of the senate within the city, engage with the *comitia tributa* and the priestly colleges, and fully participate in civic life. He presumably followed tradition and allowed his *imperium* to lapse when he was in the city, but this would not have been a problem for him: his armies were under handpicked lieutenants who would obey Augustus's instructions whether or not he had *imperium*, and he could take up his *imperium* again simply by performing the necessary rituals upon exiting the city. To be sure, this must have been time-consuming and bothersome for him, but it enabled him to present himself as a thoroughly traditional consul, and he probably did not have to go through the process of performing the rituals often, since he spent much

14. For example, see Ti. Sempronius Longus in 218 BC (Livy 21.57.4) and C. Terentius Varro in 216 BC (Livy 23.23.9).

15. The senate had met outside the *pomerium* when it wanted Pompey to attend (Cic. *Fam.* 8.4.4, *QFr* 2.3.3, Caes. *BC* 1.6).

of the period between 27 and 23 BC campaigning in the provinces away from Rome. It was not a perfect solution, but it was an effective means to be simultaneously a magistrate and commander for several years.

As consul, Augustus had the same *imperium* as all other Roman commanders, but this is unlikely to have been a serious concern at the time because no one could rival the resources at his command. Control of provinces and their resources — and not levels of *imperium* — determined power. Augustus may have monopolized command of the provinces by (improperly) using the triumviral powers he had laid down years earlier (very few would have been so bold as to insist that those powers had expired), or he may have claimed that his appointment as Rome's leader against Antony and Cleopatra had made him the supreme commander of the entire empire, with priority of *imperium* in every province.[16] Most important, he had many ways to ensure that the senate assigned provinces as he wished, so that — through influence, bribery, coercion, or threat — he and his most trusted allies received command over the provinces that contained most of Rome's legions. And, since it was tradition that consuls receive the most important commands each year, the fact that he held the consulship every year from 31 to 23 BC prevented any other man from having a higher claim on those provinces that Augustus wanted to control. Whether or not his methods were entirely legal, Augustus said in his *Res Gestae* that he had acquired absolute power over the republic, although the fact that other men held triumphs between 31 and 27 BC indicates that he did not claim (or did not enforce his claim) that all provinces fell under his *auspicium*.[17] Most likely, Augustus carefully controlled consular elections and provincial assignments to prevent any rival from obtaining sufficient power to threaten him and to ensure that other provincial commanders were likely to defer voluntarily to his will.[18] Thus it was his control of (or influence over) provincial assignment that enabled him to control the empire and its legions during this period.

Augustus's encounter with M. Licinius Crassus (cos. 30 BC) illustrates how the emperor was thinking about ways to use the *provincia* and provincial

16. Augustus states in his *Res Gestae* (25) that all of Italy and the provinces in Spain, Gaul, Africa, Sicily, and Sardinia, chose him as commander and swore an oath of obedience to him (*iuravit in mea verba tota Italia sponte sua et me belli quo vici ad Actium ducem depoposcit*). See Syme (1939) 284–93 and Southern (2013) 161–62.

17. Aug. *RG* 34. The *Fasti Triumphales* show two proconsuls celebrating triumphs in 28 BC and two in 27 BC, which means they must have had possession of a *provincia*, *imperium*, and *auspicium*.

18. Millar (1973) 62, provides evidence for Augustus appointing provincial governors from 31 to 27 BC.

assignment to maintain his domination of the empire. After his consulship, Crassus had conducted aggressive campaigns in Macedonia, and when he returned to Rome in 27 BC he requested both a triumph for his victory and the right to dedicate the *spolia opima* because he had slain the enemy chieftain in hand-to-hand combat.[19] Augustus did not deny that Crassus had a solid legal claim on the triumph (i.e., he had independent *imperium* and *auspicium*, and possession of the *provincia*), but not wishing his own glory to be eclipsed by Crassus's accomplishments, he arranged it that they both received triumphs for Crassus's victories and that he (Augustus) received the title *imperator*. The question of the *spolia opima* was dropped, probably because Augustus's opposition was insurmountable. On what grounds — if any — did Augustus claim that he deserved a triumph and acclamation as *imperator* for Crassus's victory? Since Crassus was permitted to triumph, there can be no doubt that he was the supreme commander of his *provincia* and thus was not serving under Augustus's auspices. This may be a simple case of naked force, with Augustus appropriating honors that were not his due in Roman tradition and law. On the other hand, he may have been thinking about how *provinciae* and authority had overlapped during the second triumvirate: each triumvir had held command over a block of Roman provinces, but proconsuls of individual provinces within a triumvir's block were still able to celebrate triumphs.[20] In other words, the authority and *provinciae* of the triumvirs seem to have overlapped with the authority and *provinciae* of the individual proconsuls, but this overlap did not make the proconsuls into subordinates or lieutenants of the triumvirs, as demonstrated by the fact that proconsuls could still triumph. This type of thinking, in which two commanders could claim authority over a single *provincia*, may explain Augustus's action: he may have asserted that because he *also* held authority over Macedonia (perhaps as a consequence of his supreme command against Mark Antony), he also deserved the honors that came from victories in that *provincia*. This was certainly a heavy-handed assertion of authority, and Augustus's claims were probably weak and relied more on his influence than on legal principle, but it demonstrates clearly how Augustus was already thinking about how Roman conceptions of the *provincia* might be manipulated for his benefit.

19. Dio 51.23.2–27.3. See Syme (1939) 310, Raaflaub and Samons (1990) 423, Rich (1996), Southern (2014) 198–200.

20. The *Fasti Triumphales* show ten men who were not triumvirs celebrating triumphs in 43, 42, 41, 39, 38, 36, and 34 BC. All of these were after the passage of the *lex Titia* creating the second triumvirate.

Finally, although consuls had no greater *imperium* than other military commanders, Augustus could use his consular role as leader of the senate to exert a powerful influence on other commanders. It had traditionally been the job of the consuls (or, in their absence, the praetors) to act as the voice of the senate when communicating with commanders in the field and with foreign powers.[21] Using his role as spokesman for the senate — over which he exerted considerable influence — Augustus was certainly able to blur the line between his personal wishes and the official instructions of the senate when writing other Roman commanders as well as foreign states. While he did not yet have *imperium maius* over other commanders, his position as consul gave him not only considerable *auctoritas* but also a method for presenting his own desires as being the will of the senate.

Augustus's First Settlement: Manipulating Provincial Assignment

Although he may have been considering the situation for some time, Augustus finally decided to reorganize and restructure his provincial assignment at the start of 27 BC — several months before his encounter with Crassus (cos. 30 BC). In a grand gesture, he formally returned control of the provinces and legions to the senate, laying down his vast command that (as he later claimed) encompassed the entire empire.[22] In practical terms, this probably means that Augustus declared that he had completed the task given him — either by the *lex Titia* or by "all of Italy" when he went to war with Antony — and therefore the senate should resume its role of assigning *provinciae* to commanders. Augustus was still a sitting consul when he laid down his provinces, meaning he still held *imperium* outside the city, and he still had the capacity to be given another *provincia* by the state. In what was certainly a well-orchestrated meeting of the senate, therefore, the consul Augustus was given a new provincial assignment comprising the permanent provinces in Spain, Gaul, Syria, Cilicia, Cyprus, and Egypt, which he was instructed to hold for a period of ten years.[23] These regions contained the most important military theaters (includ-

---

21. In 172 BC, for example, the senate instructed the praetor C. Licinius Crassus to write a letter *ex auctoritate senatus* ordering the consul C. Popillius Laenas to hand over much of his army to a propraetor (Livy 42.27.5), and in the *lex de provinciis praetoriis* of 100 BC the senior consul is instructed by the senate to write to Hellenistic kingdoms in the East announcing the establishment of Cilicia as a Roman *provincia* (*RS* 12 Cnidos Copy, col. III, ll. 28–41).

22. Aug. *RG* 34.1.

23. Dio 53.12.3–9 and 13.1 (cf. Strabo 17.3.25, Suet. *Aug.* 47.1). See Lacey (1974), Scullard (1982)

ing the *provinciae* chosen by the members of the so-called First Triumvirate) and after the Battle of Actium Augustus had positioned twenty-two of Rome's twenty-eight legions in permanent camps in these provinces. The new provincial assignment, containing nearly 80 percent of Rome's legions, gave Augustus such a preponderant command of military strength that no other Roman commander could ever hope to challenge him in open war. Furthermore, since the provinces he held made him responsible for most of Rome's expansionary campaigning, he usually incorporated newly conquered territories into his command, just as Pompey had added Pontus and Syria to his *provincia* during his campaigns against Mithridates, and Caesar had vastly expanded the territory contained within the province of Transalpine Gaul. This creation of a special provincial assignment encompassing the most important military *provinciae* in the empire resembled the *popularis* legislation of the late republic that had enabled ambitious commanders to acquire extraordinary super commands by combining multiple provinces into a single provincial command. Unlike those *populares*, Augustus had acquired enough power and influence to get the command he wanted from the senate, instead of through the popular assemblies, but the pattern of crafting provincial commands for personal gain was an innovation that Augustus adopted easily.

This settlement simplified and clarified Augustus's control of the provinces. As consul he would keep some of the provinces as his consular command (the imperial provinces), but the rest of the provinces (the public provinces) would follow traditional practice and receive proconsular commanders chosen by the senate.[24] Since Augustus could not be in all of his provinces at once, he continued to appoint men to exercise direct command over each of his provinces, but instead of giving these men the title of proconsul (which he had done up to that time), he appointed them as legates with the unusual title *legatus Augusti pro praetore*.[25] This made it clear that Augustus was the sole commander in chief of the imperial provinces, since *legati* had always been subordinate lieu-

---

451 n. 4, and Southern (2014) 190–95. Lacey (1996) 89–91 suggests that Augustus selected Spain, Gaul, and Syria because these had been the provinces assigned to the members of the first triumvirate, and the emperor's sole possession of these provinces and the military resources they contained was meant to assure the Romans that another civil war was henceforth impossible.

24. Dio (53.13.2–4) says senatorial proconsuls drew lots for the public provinces. Millar (1989a) 93–97 emphasizes that all of Rome's provinces technically and legally belonged to the Roman people.

25. Millar (1973) 62 and n. 86 points out that the commanders of imperial provinces lost the title proconsul and instead became *legati Augusti pro praetore* in or shortly after the First Settlement of 27 BC, although the new title is not attested until a few years later.

tenants in Roman tradition, although they could—in certain situations—act *pro praetore* under the aegis of their commander's *imperium*. In doing this, he was probably following the precedent established by Pompey, who had governed the two Spanish *provinciae* through legates from 54 to 49 BC while he remained at Rome. Yet these *legati Augusti pro praetore* were almost certainly based on the *legati pro praetore* used by Pompey and Caesar, meaning they were probably invested with *imperium* by the state and therefore could perform all the duties and responsibilities of traditional provincial commanders, but the fact they held neither the *provincia* nor the *auspicium* meant they were subordinate lieutenants who had no claim on the victories they achieved.[26] Thus *legati Augusti* enjoyed the prestige of possessing independent *imperium* and the trappings that went with it, and they could operate as competent military commanders and manage all of the day-to-day responsibilities of provincial command, but as *legati cum imperio* they could not claim any glory or profit they achieved (they could not triumph), and they were always under the authority of the emperor, who could assume direct command at any time, or send a member of his elite circle to exercise supreme authority in his name.[27]

Although few Romans could have been deceived into thinking that Augustus was merely a consul, the language and ideas he used in this First Settlement were conventional. Indeed, his creative interpretation of Rome's traditional concept of the *provincia* enabled him to say with justice that he held no extraordinary power or authority during this period. Although his consecutive consulships were unusual, they were not unprecedented, and he did not hold any more *potestas* or *imperium* as consul than had any previous consul. And while the size and scope of his provincial assignment was vast, it could—at the very least—point to republican precedents like Pompey's piracy command,

26. Whether the *legati Augusti* received their *imperium* from the state through a *lex curiata* or from the emperor by delegation is debated. The *lex de imperio Vespasiani* (*RS* 39 = *ILS* 244) records some of the powers and prerogatives exercised by the Julio-Claudian emperors, and one section (ll.10–12) states that whomever the emperor recommended for a magistracy, power, *imperium*, or a supervisory position (*magistratum, potestatem, imperium, curationemve*) should receive it. This may indicate the senate was accustomed to conveying *imperium* on whomever the emperor named as his *legati Augusti*. Mommsen (1887–88) 2.244 and Millar (1966) 157 support the idea that *legati Augusti* received *imperium* from the state, but Galsterer (1996) 411 and Ewald and Norena (2010) 92 believe that *legati Augusti* held only delegated *imperium*.

27. Tacitus (*Ann.* 1.31.2) gives a good example of this in his account of AD 14: "There were two armies on the bank of the Rhine. One, named 'the upper' was under the legate C. Silius; the lower was the concern of A. Caecina; direction of the whole lay with Germanicus, who at the time was intent on conducting a census of the Galliae" (Woodman, trans.).

the Mithridatic commands of Lucullus and Pompey, and Caesar's Gallic command, all of which had been an amassing of multiple permanent *provinciae* in a single provincial assignment. Even the long, ten-year tenure he was given was not entirely unprecedented—Caesar, Pompey, and Crassus had all received five-year provincial commands, as had Augustus and his fellow triumvirs in the Second Triumvirate.

In the eyes of the *mos maiorum*, Augustus could justifiably present his position as solidly based on precedents in republican tradition. That Augustus hoped to deceive the Romans into believing that he had turned back the clock and restored the republic is unlikely—few (if any) informed Romans could have believed that he was *just* a consul. Still, an argument does not have to be true to be socially and politically useful. More important, Augustus's presentation of his position in legal and traditional language enabled most Romans to allow themselves to overlook the deeper truths of his command. The new *imperator* controlled tremendous resources and unheard-of power, and it was impossible to struggle against him, but his traditional presentation of his position relieved Romans from the moral requirement to rise up against him. It may not have been a true façade but simply a method of soothing the concerns of the aristocracy and letting them know that his autocracy would not be rubbed in their faces. The concept of the *provincia* had undergone considerable evolution in the late republic, and Augustus was able to select those interpretations that best served his political goals.

The Second Settlement: Augustus and the Manipulation of *Imperium* and the *Provincia*

For five years Augustus successfully used the consulship as the underpinning of his domination over the Roman Empire, but in 23 BC he decided to make a change. The product of this reorganization is known as the Second Settlement, which created the Augustan principate and would come to define the position and powers of the *princeps* in the Julio-Claudian Dynasty. Although the Second Settlement involved a substantial rearrangement of Augustus's civilian authority (such as his adoption of tribunician *potestas*), the present work is concerned only with the changes it made to his position as a provincial commander, and how he used and manipulated traditional ideas of provincial command to create his new position. From this perspective, the most important change Augustus made in 23 BC was to stop using the consulship as the legitimizing foundation of his military authority and his control over much of

Rome's empire, and instead to take on the status of a proconsul, although he appears to have used this title (*pro consule*) only in the provinces.[28]

Augustus probably had many reasons for making this change: holding the consulship required him to invest too much time in the day-to-day administration of the city; the senatorial aristocracy was probably frustrated and angered that he was monopolizing one-half of the available consulships each year (thereby cutting in half the number of senators who could attain consular status each year); his perpetual retention of the consulship may have resembled too closely Caesar's despised position as dictator-for-life; and he may have become annoyed by his constant need to lay down his *imperium* every time he wished to enter the *pomerium*, as well as by the time-consuming ceremonies he needed to perform when he wished to once again take up his *imperium* when leaving the city. He solved all of these difficulties by giving up the consulship and instead acting like a proconsul once again, but he was confronted with the same problem he had faced before: proconsuls could not enter Rome without forfeiting their *imperium* and with it their provincial command. So long as he remained outside the *pomerium*, the proconsulship enabled Augustus to retain his *imperium* and provincial command indefinitely, and although the senate had the authority to strip him of both, his control over that body was strong (especially after he acquired the tribunician power of veto), and the senators probably knew that his armies and *legati* were likely to obey him no matter what the senate said or did. The proconsulship was less burdensome than the consulship, and it provided Augustus with the *imperium* and provincial command he needed to maintain his domination of the empire, but to be an effective long-term solution, he needed a way to enter the city without forfeiting his *imperium* (and command).

Instead of solving this problem through an innovation that could be construed as tyranny, Augustus looked to the manipulation of traditional concepts to reach his goals. Since holding the dictatorship was no longer an option, he instead determined to separate the dictator's ability to hold *imperium* within the *pomerium* from the office itself by arranging to receive a special dispensation from the prohibition on *imperium* inside the *pomerium*. Although this prohibition had been rigorously maintained throughout the republic, the senate and people of Rome had always been able to grant exemptions when they

---

28. Augustus is referred to as a proconsul—*pro co(n)s(ule)*—in an edict dating to 15 BC (*AE* 1999, 915 = 2000, 760). Germanicus also had the title *pro consule* during his eastern command under Tiberius (*AE* 1996, 885 ll. 30–36). See Alföldy (2000) 192–96. Dio (53.32.5) states that the senate gave Augustus the power of a proconsul permanently (τήν τε ἀρχὴν τὴν ἀνθύπατον ἐσαεὶ καθάπαξ ἔχειν).

wished, such as to enable a victorious general to march his army through the streets of Rome in triumph, or to suppress an internal crisis by appointing a dictator. The senate did not change the law on such occasions, but merely granted specific and individual exceptions to the general rule. It was this practice of making exceptions that Augustus sought to exploit. He arranged to receive a special and perpetual exemption from the laws that prohibited *imperium* within the city, enabling him — and only him — to cross the *pomerium* and enter the city without forfeiting his *imperium*, his status as a promagistrate, or his possession of his *provincia*. According to Dio, the senate "allowed Augustus to have *imperium pro consule* permanently so that he neither had to lay it down when going inside the *pomerium* nor did he have to take it up again when going out."[29] Equipped with this exemption, he exited the city on July 1 in 23 BC and went to the Alban Mount, which was more than ten miles away from the city, where he resigned his consulship.[30] The reason for the distance was to make it perfectly clear that, although he had resigned the consulship, he still retained his *imperium* and his provincial command, because these did not automatically expire when he laid down his office. Dio's comment indicates that the senate had authorized Augustus to exercise his *imperium* as a proconsul (*pro consule*), so when he resigned his consulship he became a proconsul who could cross the *pomerium* and enter Rome freely without forfeiting his *imperium*.

In arranging this, Augustus had before him the examples of Sulla and Caesar, both of whom had used the dictatorship to avoid laying down their *imperium* in Rome. Although the dictatorship had been abolished, Augustus acquired for himself its ability to hold *imperium* in the city while shunning the actual title of dictator. This tactic of acquiring one important aspect of a magistracy without holding the office itself was a hallmark of Augustan political machinations (in that same year he also received tribunician *potestas* without actually being a plebeian tribune). For the rest of his life, Augustus was able to cross the *pomerium* and enter the city without laying down his *imperium*. He would also be careful to retain his provincial command: the senate had given

---

29. Dio 53.32.5: τήν τε ἀρχὴν τὴν ἀνθύπατον ἐσαεὶ καθάπαξ ἔχειν ὥστε μήτε ἐν τῇ ἐσόδῳ τῇ εἴσω τοῦ πωμηρίου κατατίθεσθαι αὐτὴν μήτ᾽ αὖθις ἀνανεοῦσθαι (Drogula, trans). Some scholars have suggested he did not receive *imperium* in Rome until 19 BC: Jones (1951) 118 and (1970) 60, Cotton and Yakobson (2002) 195–96, 201, and Girardet (1990a) 118. For further discussion on this grant of *imperium*, including its validity inside the *pomerium*, see also Jones (1951) 113–15, Lowenstein (1973) 250–51, Brunt (1977) 96–97, Bleicken (1990) 96–97 and (1998) 730, Hurlet (1994) 258–61, Girardet (2000) 197–200, Ferrary (2001a) 9–21 and (2001b) 101–54.

30. Dio 53.32.2–3.

him a ten-year command of his provinces back in 27 BC, and Augustus would receive regular ten-year extensions of his command until his death.[31] It is unlikely that Augustus intended to make much use his *imperium* within the city; it legitimized his command of the Praetorian Guard within the *pomerium*, but otherwise he seems to have played down the fact that he was transgressing tradition by being an *imperator* and proconsul inside Rome's civilian sphere. Augustus thus achieved his ends by manipulating some of the traditional ideas that had defined the Roman commander. Although it was probably an unintended consequence, Augustus's ability to retain his *imperium* and *provincia* inside the *pomerium* made his proconsulship resemble a real office (although it was not). In the past, proconsuls had held no magisterial standing — they stood in place of a consul (*pro consule*) and acted like a consul in the sphere *militiae*, but they were not actually consuls, and thus lost all authority and existence in Rome, which was the traditional responsibility of the consuls themselves. Although his position most resembled that of a proconsul (he held military command but not public office), the fact that he could possess and use some consular prerogatives in Rome gave Augustus official-looking status that was almost (but not quite) magisterial.[32]

A second aspect of this rearrangement of his position was his decision to receive from the senate a special grant of *imperium maius*. According to Dio, "the senate gave [Augustus] more authority to command in the subject territory than that of the commanders of each place."[33] Although Dio's language

31. In 27 BC Augustus had received his provincial command for ten years (Dio 53.13.1), and he received ten-year extensions of his command in 18 BC (Dio 54.12.4–5), 8 BC (Dio 55.6.1), AD 3 (Dio 55.12.2–3), and in AD 13 (Dio 56.28.1).

32. In addition to receiving a special grant of tribunician *potestas* in 23 BC (Dio 53.32.5; his statement [51.19.6] that Augustus also received this *potestas* in 30 BC is probably an error), Augustus also seems to have received some consular prerogatives as well (Dio 54.10.5). Jones (1951) 113 argues that it was in this settlement that Augustus was given the right to declare war and make treaties mentioned by the *lex de imperio Vespasiani* (*RS* 39 = *ILS* 244). Augustus had also been chosen *princeps senatus* in 29–28 BC and given the right to speak first in all meetings of the senate (Aug. *RG* 7.2, Dio 53.1.3), which — given his tremendous influence — was probably sufficient to guide senatorial decisions much of the time. Ferrary (2001b) 101–54 gives a good survey of Augustus's powers.

33. Dio 53.32.5: καὶ διὰ ταῦθ' ἡ γερουσία ... καὶ ἐν τῷ ὑπηκόῳ τὸ πλεῖον τῶν ἑκασταχόθι ἀρχόντων ἰσχύειν ἐπέτρεψεν (trans. Drogula). Much ink has been spilled on the question of whether Augustus received *maius imperium proconsulare* or *maius imperium consulare*, but this debate is based on the mistaken assumption that consuls possessed a fundamentally different type of *imperium* from that held by proconsuls, an error that has been addressed in the preceding chapters. For bibliography and summary of the positions of this debate, see Bringmann (1977) 219–38, Eder (1990) 106–7, Girardet (1992b), (2000) 200–202, and (2001) 158, Potter (1996) 274 n. 9, Hurlet (1997) 31, Giovannini (1999) 97, Ferrary (2001b) and (2003), Roddaz (2003) 411, Southern (2014) 206–8.

is not as clear as we would like, two other descriptions of *imperium maius* give more detail. When Agrippa was given *imperium maius* a few years later, it was described as: "In whatever of the provinces to which the public affairs of the Romans might take you, it was established in law that no one's *imperium* in those places would be greater than yours"; and much later the *senatus consultum de Pisone patre* (AD 20) described Germanicus's *imperium maius* as: "In whatever province to which he should come, let him have greater *imperium* than he who holds the province as a proconsul, although greater *imperium* in every matter shall be to Tiberius Caesar Augustus than to Germanicus Caesar."[34] Lacey suggested that Dio was using a shorthand description of Augustus's *imperium* and that the actual formula was something closer either to what Cicero suggested for Cassius (*maius imperium in provinciis quam sit eorum qui eas obtineant*), or to what Tacitus records regarding Germanicus (*maiusque imperium, quoquo adisset, quam iis qui sorte aut missu principis obtinerent*).[35] If Lacey is correct, then the original purpose of Augustus's *imperium maius* as created in 23 BC was not to make him the overlord of all other commanders in the empire but to establish his superiority in any conflict with another provincial governor. In other words, Augustus's *imperium maius* was not (originally) intended to subordinate other commanders to his authority but to establish the priority of his *imperium* in case of dispute. Ferrary has argued convincingly that the emperor's *imperium maius* was not originally understood as being greater than the *imperium* of all other commanders in the empire, but this idea developed over several decades and became evident only in the early years of Tiberius's reign.[36] Thus Augustus's *imperium maius* achieved the same purpose as provincial assignment in the republic: it established priority or precedence, but did not subordinate one commander to another.

Although the idea of *imperium maius* was highly unusual, it had an impeccable republican pedigree: the great republican Cicero had proposed grants of *maius imperium* for the tyrannicides and champions of the republic, Brutus

---

34. *P. Köln* 249.7–14: καὶ εἰς ἃς δήποτέ σε ὑπαρχείας τὰ κοινὰ τῶν Ῥωμαίων ἐφέλκοιτο, μηθενὸς ἐν ἐκείναις ἐξουσίαν <εἶναι> μείζω τῆς σῆς ἐν νόμωι ἐκυρώθη, ἀλλὰ σὺ εἰς πλεῖστον ὑοὺς καὶ ἡμετέραι [σ]πουδῆ καὶ ἀρεταῖς ἰδίαις κα[θ'] ὁμοφροσύνην συμπάντων ἀνθρώπων διαράμενος; *SC de Pisone patre* (ll. 34–36): *ut in quamcumque provinciam venisset, maius ei imperium quam ei, qui eam provinciam proconsule optineret, esset, dum in omni re maius imperium Ti. Caesari Augusto quam Germanico Caesari esset.*

35. Lacey (1996) 100, Cic. *Att.* 4.1.7, and Tac. *Ann.* 2.43.1.

36. Ferrary (2001b) 130–41. In particular, he argues that the *imperium maius* given to Germanicus in AD 17—which is described as greater than that of other proconsuls but lesser than the emperor's own *imperium*—demonstrates that it had become understood that the emperor's *imperium* was absolutely greater that of all other commanders.

and Cassius. Unlike the dictatorship, which had been tainted by its unfavorable association with Sulla and Caesar, the concept of *imperium maius* carried the unimpeachable imprimatur of three paragons of traditional republican virtue, which may explain why Augustus felt comfortable making it a foundation of his control over other republican commanders. There is no way to know if Augustus (or anyone else for that matter) really understood what *imperium maius* was or how it would operate when it was introduced in 23 BC; it had a good republican pedigree but little foundation or exactness in Roman law. Since he acquired it as part of the arrangement that included his resignation of the consulship, he must have believed *imperium maius* would compensate him in some way for the authority he had wielded as consul. Because he did not need *imperium maius* to command his own provinces, he must have believed it would assist him in interfering in the public provinces of independent proconsuls. From his subsequent actions, Augustus clearly intended to rule the entire empire (imperial and public provinces alike): Dio records that he gave instructions or *mandata* to proconsuls of public provinces as well as to his own *legati Augusti*; in 21 BC he arranged important affairs in Sicily and Greece, including founding colonies and changing boundaries; in 20 BC he instituted various reforms in Asia and Bithynia; and in 7–6 BC he published several edicts regulating affairs in Crete and Cyrene.[37] Whether Augustus believed that he achieved these actions through the legal force of his *imperium maius* or that proconsuls of public provinces should simply show social deference to his tremendous *auctoritas* is unclear. The truth is probably somewhere in the middle: his *auctoritas* was normally sufficient to gain his objectives, but if necessary he had *imperium maius* with which to compel obedience to his will. Although *imperium maius* was not a fully formed idea in 23 BC, Augustus probably wanted it because he believed it would provide the legal capacity (or at least legal justification) for him to interfere in affairs not directly related to his own command. This is subtly different from what Cicero had intended. Knowing that overlapping *provinciae* could cause confusion, conflict, and non-cooperation between commanders, Cicero had suggested a grant of *imperium maius* for Cassius to distinguish clearly and without doubt that Cassius was the supreme commander in the war against the Caesarians, even if that war took place in another man's province. Augustus, on the other hand, wanted *imperium maius* specifically because his provincial command did *not* overlap with other men's *provinciae* as it had during the triumvirate, and he wanted some means to legitimize his intention to influence affairs in provinces not

37. Dio 53.15.4–16.1, 54.7.1 and 4–5; for Crete and Cyrene, see Oliver # 8–12.

given to him by the state. While Cicero had been concerned with distinguishing and separating *provinciae*, Augustus was interested in blurring the lines between *provinciae* so he could exert his authority more broadly.

This manipulation and use of the concept of *imperium* was one underlying factor in his success, and his manipulation of the concept of the *provincia* was another. The division of provinces in 27 BC had given Augustus control over the majority of legions and military campaigns, which was necessary for his own security and the stability of the empire but was sure to provoke the aristocracy over time. By hoarding most of Rome's military commands for himself, Augustus made it difficult for senators to win military glory and status-building reputation for themselves. For centuries, Rome's ruling elite had defined itself through the exercise of military command, and senatorial families had acquired honor, status, and influence in the republic by leading Rome's armies to victory. After 27 BC, only three of the public provinces came with legions and opportunities for military command, and those senators who agreed to lead armies in one of Augustus's provinces did so as subordinate commanders who had no right to any victory and glory they achieved. This unequal sharing of military opportunities not only threatened to insult the senatorial elites; it also endangered their *dignitas* and social structure, which would no longer be bolstered and renewed with fresh military glory. To relieve some of this pressure, Augustus manipulated the traditional republican ideas of consular and praetorian *provinciae* to present his provincial arrangements in terms more likely to be satisfactory—if not pleasing—to the senatorial elites. This recasting of the traditional republican definitions of the *provincia* was an important aspect of his reforms that helped the aristocracy accept his domination of the empire.

The provinces under Augustus's command were clearly based on the consular *provinciae* of the late republic: they were permanent provinces that bordered foreign lands where major wars or other campaigning would usually be needed. Like consular commanders in the late republic, Augustus and his lieutenants had large armies under their command, and they freely exited their permanent provinces to campaign against hostile neighbors when necessary or desired. Imperial provinces were the launching pads for all major wars and expansionary campaigning, just as consular *provinciae* had been in the late republic. Although the civilian population in each of his provinces probably demanded some level of governance from its commander in chief, he could easily delegate this responsibility to his *legati Augusti*, taking a personal interest only in major domestic problems and military campaigns outside of the provinces. The periodic changes Augustus made in his provincial assignment illustrate that he wanted only the military commands that would have been considered consular in the republic: if one of his provinces became pacified and therefore focused more on governance than conquest (i.e., if it became praetorian in nature), he generally handed that province over to senatorial control, whereas he was quick to claim for himself any previously-pacified territory that suddenly became the theater of major war (and therefore consular in nature). Thus Augustus eventually made Cyprus, Baetica, and Narbonese Gaul public provinces, but he took over Illyricum when preparing his Balkan campaign, and he also temporarily made Corsica an imperial province when a major military effort was needed to suppress piracy in the area.[38] Thus the imperial provinces followed the tradition of the consular command.

The public provinces, on the other hand, would mostly have been considered praetorian commands in the late republic. Whether by accident or by design, the provinces that Augustus returned to the authority of the senate shared three key traits with the praetorian commands of the late republic: they offered substantially fewer and smaller opportunities for military command than consular *provinciae*, they expected governors to perform extensive administrative responsibilities, and they comprised — and were limited to — a specific territory with defined geographic borders within which the governor was expected to remain. Because of these fundamental qualities, the praetorian province of the late republic had become more of an administrative unit than a sphere of expansionary warfare, and this became the model for the public province of the Augustan Age. The permanent provinces that Augustus returned to the senate in 27 BC included Africa, Asia, Bithynia, Cilicia, Crete with Cyrene, Illyricum, Macedonia, Pontus, Sardinia with Corsica, and Sicily.[39] Most of these provinces had been pacified during the republic, so much so that Augustus thought only three of them — Africa, Illyricum, and Macedonia — required a Roman military presence in 31 BC, and after the completion of his Balkan campaigns, Africa was the only public province that required a legion.[40] Tacitus refers to the public provinces as "unarmed," and

38. Dio 53.12.4 and 7, 54.4.1 and 34.4, and 55.28.1.

39. Dio 53.12.4, Strabo 17.3.25.

40. Augustus began his Balkan campaigns even before the Battle of Actium (Sherk [1957] 52), and made Illyricum (Dalmatia) an imperial province and took over its legions in 12 or 11 BC (Dio 53.12.7, 54.34.4), and after he conquered the Balkans up to the Danube and created the new imperial provinces of Moesia and Pannonia, Macedonia ceased to be a frontier province, so its legions were moved north into the new imperial province of Moesia (Vanderspoel [2010] 269). Public provinces occasionally received detachments of soldiers when needed — see Ritterling (1927) 28–32, Sherk (1955) 400–413 and (1957) 52–62, and Eck (1972) 429–36.

even Rome's fleets were stationed in Italy under prefects rather than in public provinces under proconsuls.[41] Lacking legions and opportunities for significant military campaigning, the public provinces were mainly administrative posts, where governors would exercise jurisdiction and other peaceful responsibilities of government. To emphasize this, governors of public provinces were expected to remain in civilian dress rather than in the military uniforms that Roman commanders had worn in their *provinciae* since time immemorial.[42]

The public provinces under Augustus also resembled the praetorian commands of the late republic in their geographic definition. Whereas imperial commanders and *legati Augusti* regularly marched their armies beyond the borders of the imperial provinces to attack hostile enemies in territories not yet subject to Rome, the governors who held public provinces were normally confined within fixed borders that defined their province and limited or confined their authority. These borders were well defined under Augustus: the limits of the island provinces were obvious; the borders of Rome's Africa province were repeatedly redefined by Julius Caesar and Augustus; the territory of Cyrene had been identified and ownership of it transferred three times between 74 and circa 31 BC; the borders of the Roman provinces and client kingdoms in Asia Minor had been adjusted and confirmed following the Battle of Actium; and the creation of the new province of Achaea in 27 BC formalized the borders of Macedonia and Illyricum.[43] Strabo—who as an adult observed Augustus's organization of the empire—illustrates the geographic definition of the public provinces in his listing of them:

> But at the outset Caesar organized the Provinces of the People by creating, first, two consular provinces; I mean (1) Libya [Africa], in so far as it was subject to the Romans, except the part which was formerly subject to Juba and is now subject to Ptolemy his son, and (2) the part of Asia that lies this side of the Halys River and the Taurus, except the countries of the Gala-

41. Tac. *Ann.* 14.3.3 and *Hist.* 1.11 (cf. *ILS* 1,327).

42. Dio 53.13.3.

43. The boundaries of most public provinces had been established back in the republic, and most senators would know exactly where their authority began and ended. See Raven (1993) 49–58 on the various rearrangements of the Africa province, Jones (1937) 360 and 485 n. 12 on Cyrene, Magie (1950) 427–67 on the borders in Asia Minor, and Vanderspoel (2010) 269 on the borders of Macedonia, Illyria, and Achaea. Purcell (1990 [2002]) 14 argues that descriptions in Strabo (7.5 and 3.39) indicate that the *via Egnatia* marked the eastern border of Macedonia and the *via Domitia* marked the border between Narbonese Gaul and Nearer Spain. Syme (1939) 217 identifies the river Drin as marked the border between Macedonia and Illyricum (see also Purcell [1990 (2002)] 22 on rivers as borders).

tians and of the tribes which had been subject to Amyntas, and also of Bithynia and the Propontis; and, secondly, ten praetorial provinces, first, in Europe and the islands near it, I mean (1) Iberia Ulterior, as it is called, in the neighbourhood of the Baetis and Anas Rivers, (2) Narbonitis in Celtica, (3) Sardo together with Cyrnus, (4) Sicily, (5 and 6) Macedonia and, in Illyria, the country next to Epeirus, (7) Achaea as far as Thessaly and Aetolia and Acarnania and certain Epeirotic tribes which border on Macedonia, (8) Crete along with Cyrenaea, (9) Cyprus, and (10) Bithynia along with the Propontis and certain parts of the Pontus.[44]

As Rome's provinces swelled to incorporate nearly the entire Mediterranean world, and as Augustus established new provinces in freshly conquered territory, the empire became a single cohesive and unbroken entity of contiguous provinces, each one touching the next and each province helping to establish the borders of its neighboring provinces.[45] Although the northern borders of Illyricum and Macedonia were probably open or undefined when Augustus returned those provinces to senatorial control in 27 BC, his takeover of Illyricum, his Balkan campaigns, and his creation of Moesia and Pannonia soon reduced Macedonia to an interior province that was entirely surrounded and contained by the sea and other Roman territories. The southern border of Africa and Cyrene remained open, and Africa even retained a legion for defense against nomadic raiders, but the harsh climate of the Sahara Desert formed a very real southern border. The public provinces closely resembled the praetorian provinces of the republic, particularly in their clear geographic definition that limited the governor's exercise of authority and prevented him from leaving their provinces to conduct military campaigns.

The aristocracy should have been appalled at this division of the empire, since it gave senators only second-rate administrative posts to hold as their commands while Augustus monopolized nearly all of the traditional consular commands. While Augustus's military power gave him the naked force to impose this arrangement on an unwilling aristocracy, he attempted to make it palatable by manipulating the traditional concepts of provincial command.

44. Strabo 17.3.25 (Jones, trans.).
45. Talbert (2004) 23–24, noted the significance of Augustus's arrangement of the provinces: "The notion of provinces as ready-made, well established components for creating a vision of the Roman world hardly seems likely to predate Augustus' rule. Only from that date is the empire a single cohesive entity from the Iberian peninsula to Egypt, subdivided into provinces that are each defined units adjoining one another (or large islands). From then onwards, however, a comprehensive framework is established."

Although he gave the senate praetorian-type provinces to govern and sent his *legati Augusti* to rule the consular-type provinces in his name, he inverted the prestige traditionally accorded to each type of command, so that public provinces became the more prestigious and important type of command in the eyes of the Romans. In a move of shrewd political calculation, he gambled that — if Rome's aristocracy could not enjoy traditional consular commands — it would be content with the prestige and honors that normally derived from possession of a consular *provincia*. He recognized that one of the main reasons for wanting a consular *provincia* in the republic was to achieve the prestige and benefits that raised one's *dignitas* and status in Roman society and politics, and so he guessed that many senators would not mind forgoing the demands (and dangers) of leading a major military campaign so long as they received the all-important benefits of a consular *provincia*. Augustus arranged that senatorial governors of public provinces — both ex-praetors and ex-consuls — would hold the high title of proconsul as well as independent grants of *imperium* and *auspicium*. Invested with these sources of authority and possession of a *provincia* (even a peaceful one), these proconsuls were fully independent commanders and enjoyed all the trappings and authority of Rome's ancient consuls, which would have been appealing to the status-conscious Romans.[46]

When a proconsul returned to Rome and reentered civilian life, his status in domestic society was significantly elevated by his tenure of a proconsular command with its time-honored regalia. Because real military glory was no longer generally available to proconsuls (except the emperor and his family), the trappings of military glory became the next-best choice for status-conscious aristocrats. This guarantee of rank and status would have held an irresistible allure for the members of Rome's great families, who, as Tacitus would later describe them, were more concerned about the security of their current rank than they were ambitious to acquire real power.[47] Sumi has recently argued that Augustus established a hierarchy of military honors to create a court society around his principate, which demonstrates how the appearance of military glory — but not necessarily the glory itself — was highly desired by the Augustan aristocracy.[48] Since proconsuls of public provinces held *imperium* and *auspicium* in

---

46. Proconsuls who had held the consulship in Rome were entitled to twelve lictors and *fasces*, while those proconsuls who had only reached the praetorship were invested with six lictors and *fasces* (Dio 53.13.2–4).

47. Tac. *Hist.* 4.48.2: *proconsulum splendidissimus quisque securitati magis quam potentiae consulebant.*

48. Sumi (2011) 81–102.

their own right, they were able to perform the impressive, public ceremonies when leaving Rome for their provinces in full consular regalia, and they enjoyed the prestige of holding the authority of Rome's ancient kings. Augustus seemed to have gambled correctly that the ruling elite would tolerate his virtual monopoly on consular commands so long as they received consular symbols and trappings, which were essential to justify their claims to nobility and position in civilian society.

Augustus's manipulation of the prestige attached to public provinces is particularly evident in his treatment of Africa and Asia. These were old, famous, and wealthy provinces filled with prestigious cities, but in the late republic they had been almost exclusively assigned to praetors: between 100 and 50 BC, no consul is known to have been assigned to Africa, and Asia was assigned to consuls only during the Mithridatic wars. Because they were pacified, geographically confined, and offered little to no opportunities for military glory, both provinces clearly had been considered second-choice assignments in the late republic, and thus they were normally assigned to praetors, who spent their time in administrative pursuits. In the political and military calculus of the late republic, Africa and Asia were not particularly desirable provinces, because they normally offered few opportunities to enhance one's status back in Rome. Augustus changed this by declaring that these two public provinces should be especially reserved for ex-consuls, making them the hardest public provinces to acquire and endowing them with the consular ranking or identity.[49] By denying the provinces to ex-praetors, the exclusivity of these two provinces made them more desirable and gave them a cachet that made them particularly attractive to status-conscious senators, such that the proconsulship of Africa or Asia soon became the pinnacle of a senator's career. This was a dramatic reversal in the traditional valuation of provinces, and it was achieved by transferring consular honors, titles, and regalia to two provinces that had been considered praetorian in the republic.

Augustus also sought to placate the aristocracy by ensuring that the honors and titles given to his *legati Augusti pro praetore* were less desirable than those of the proconsuls of public provinces. In the reckoning of traditional markers of honor, the public provinces elevated a man's status in Rome more than the imperial provinces (although this would change over time). In the first place, *legati* were mere lieutenants and did not have the distinction of having been the supreme governor of a province. Second, *legati Augusti* held the lesser title of propraetor (*legatus Augusti pro praetore*), which had practi-

49. Strabo 17.3.25, Dio 53.14.2.

cally gone out of use by the end of the republic. Augustus knew well the inferiority of this title: although all the praetors in 43 BC had been prorogued *pro consule*, the senate chose to give him the lesser title *pro praetore* as a subtle insult to curb his pride and ambition.[50] Augustus had certainly been insulted by receiving the lowly title of propraetor, so his decision to give the same low title to his *legati* was clearly an effort to reduce their prestige and status in comparison to the proconsuls of the public provinces. Furthermore, whereas propraetors in the republic were normally entitled to six *fasces* (the normal complement for a praetor), *legati Augusti pro praetore* were accompanied by only five lictors with *fasces*, visually emphasizing their lower rank.[51] Unlike proconsuls of public provinces, the subordinate status of the *legati Augusti* was advertised in their title and regalia, which helps to explain why the men who first sought service as legates in imperial provinces tended to be from new and unknown senatorial families.[52] Since they could not compete against the men from more famous families who were pursuing the more prestigious and independent commands in public provinces, the less desirable post of propraetor was an attractive stepping-stone for their political career. In this way Augustus increased the importance of the visible signs of governorship but separated them from their traditional associations with military command, so that the ancient and coveted symbols of consular prestige and status would henceforth be invested in permanent, pacified provinces that had traditionally been assigned to praetors in the republic. As the Roman aristocracy gradually became accustomed to Augustus's administration of the empire, the liabilities of the *legati Augusti* would appear less serious and the prestige of their office would gradually rise.[53] In 27 BC, however, the five *fasces* and the title *pro praetore* would have seemed significantly less distinguished than the regalia given to proconsuls of public provinces. By inverting the titles and prestige of the two types of republican *provinciae*, Augustus made his autocratic rule more tolerable to the Roman nobility.

50. Cic. *Ad Brut.* 1.15.7, *Phil.* 5.45–46, 13.22, 14.6; Aug. *RG* 1; Livy *Per.* 118; Vell. 2.61.3; Suet. *Aug.* 10.3; Dio 46.29.5–6.

51. Dio 53.13.8. See Cotton (2000) 217–34. It is possible that these *legati Augusti* were modeled after the *legati cum imperio* that Pompey and Caesar possessed in the final decades of the republic (see chapter 4), in which case they may have had independent grants of *imperium* (although Augustus's possession of the *provincia* made him the commander in chief).

52. Syme (1939) 502 and (1986) 32–49.

53. Talbert (1984b) 393, who indicates that the post of *legati Augusti pro praetore* eventually ranked above proconsuls who were merely ex-praetors, although the proconsulship of Africa and Asia (available only to ex-consuls) remained the most prestigious post.

Nowhere is this inversion of prestige and military responsibility so apparent as the emperor's arrangement of the governance of Egypt, which was one of the great commands in the empire. After it became an imperial province in 30 BC, Egypt hosted a large army of three legions, good opportunities for military campaigning in the South, tremendous wealth, a topography that made the province easy to defend against outside invasion, and an ancient and prestigious history. Any Roman commander might long for a powerful command like Egypt, and its resources made it an ideal base for an aristocrat who wanted to start a rebellion against the emperor (Augustus even forbade senators to enter Egypt without his express permission).[54] For these reasons, Augustus took the unusual step of placing an equestrian prefect in command of the province, instead of a *legatus Augusti pro praetore* chosen from the (lesser) senatorial aristocracy. This decision meant that the governor of Egypt held a very low title indeed, since prefects were normally low-ranking officers, and an equestrian was not even a member of Rome's office-holding elite.[55] By making the governor of Egypt an equestrian with such a low title, Augustus solved two problems: such a man probably lacked the *dignitas* and *auctoritas* necessary to be a credible figurehead in a revolt against the emperor, and it gave the prefecture of Egypt low status and prestige in comparison with the proconsular provinces controlled by the senate. Thus one of the most powerful and important military commands in the empire was given the lowest and least desirable title of any provincial governor.

While Augustus did an impressive job of wrapping his new provincial arrangements in the cloak of republican tradition, we should not think that he genuinely tricked the aristocracy into believing they were living in a restored republic. Aristocrats knew that Rome had changed and that their opportunities for provincial command had changed as well.[56] The Augustan system was

54. Tac. *Ann.* 2.59.3 and Dio 51.17.1. See Drogula (2011b).

55. Prefects had always been minor officials in Rome's government (such as those sent to hear legal cases in Cumae and Capua), and as low-level officers in the army (such as the prefect of the camp or leaders of cavalry units — see Keppie [1984]). On Augustus's decision to place Egypt under a prefect, see Brunt (1975)124–47. On Augustus's other use of prefects, see Jolowicz and Nicholas (1972) 334–36.

56. Millar (1973) 63–64 and Roddaz (2003) 415 have demonstrated that Augustus never claimed to have restored traditional Roman government, nor did the Romans actually believe that he had made such a restoration (*contra*: Ferrary [2003] 419–28). Ovid (*Fasti* 1.589: *redditaque est omnis populo provincia nostro*), a contemporary, recorded the incorrect (but perhaps widespread) opinion that Augustus had returned all of the provinces to the people of Rome. This should not, however, be mistaken for a popular belief that Augustus had "restored" the republic. Eder (1990) 105: "The final settlement of 27 BC bears the earmarks of a practical distribution, approximately equal in terms of

accepted because it offered greater and more attractive rewards than had been available to most senators for much of the late republic, and it did so in a way that protected the honor and status of the aristocracy. Although Augustus's retention of most of Rome's legions and military campaigns seems like a dramatic departure from republican government, few senators likely judged the situation so simply. Senatorial politics had become quite complicated in the late republic, and senators had a range of goals and objectives. The senatorial elites probably judged the offered First Settlement against their own immediate experience, in which a few great men had manipulated the government and dominated provincial commands for decades. Starting in 59 BC, the members of the so-called First Triumvirate not only manipulated the assemblies to obtain the provinces they wanted but also made sure that choice commands went to their most important supporters.[57] As dictator, Caesar had handed out provinces as he saw fit, and the members of the Second Triumvirate (including Augustus) had held complete control of the empire and all its provinces for over twelve years.[58] By 27 BC, great men had been influencing—if not outright controlling—Rome's system of provincial assignment for more than thirty years, and few senators would remember a time when the senate had complete control over the provinces and provincial assignment.

While Augustus retained control of several important provinces in 27 BC, therefore, the senators would not register this as a loss or anything other than the status quo, and only the most naïve senators could have been surprised that Augustus decided to keep the most important military provinces for himself. On the other hand, the return of so many provinces to the senate's control— three of which (at the time) came with legions and real opportunities for mili-

---

square area, in which the division of troops produced no military monopoly for Augustus; and yet it fell in with the *princeps'* declared purpose of securing the peace, since the restless provinces with most troops were allotted to him. A senator thinking in republican terms could live comfortably with this adjustment, since Augustus promised to give his provinces back to the senate once they were pacified."

57. The *lex Vatinia* of 59 BC placed Caesar in command of Gaul (*MRR* 2.190) and the *lex Trebonia* of 55 BC placed Crassus in command of Syria and Pompey in command of Spain (*MRR* 2.217); the *lex Clodia* of 58 BC for Piso and Gabinius (*MRR* 2.196).

58. For example, Caesar appointed M. Antonius to exercise command in Italy in 49 BC (*MRR* 2.260); he left Q. Cassius Longinus in command of Farther Spain in 49 BC (*MRR* 2.261); he had the senate give C. Scribonius Curio command of Sicily in 49 BC (*MRR* 2.263); he placed Cn. Domitius Calvinus in command of Asia Minor in 48 BC (*MRR* 2.277, 289); he placed C. Sallustius Crispus in command of the new province of Africa Nova in 46 BC (*MRR* 2.298); he placed M. Junius Brutus in command of Cisalpine Gaul in 46 BC (*MRR* 2.297); and he placed Ser. Sulpicius Rufus in command of Achaea in 46 BC (*MRR* 2.299).

tary command—was probably seen as a tremendous improvement to senatorial prerogatives. From the senatorial perspective, Augustus's retention of some provinces would not have been nearly as surprising as was his return of the rest of the empire (including three military provinces) to public control. This event would have been all the more tolerable when it was realized that governors of public provinces received much higher titles, independent *imperium*, full curule regalia, and greater honor and status than the men sent to hold imperial provinces in Augustus's name. The senators must also have been pleased when Augustus ceased holding consecutive consulships in 23 BC, thereby giving other aristocrats the opportunity to reach that prestigious office. In these ways, Augustus arranged that public provinces would provide senators with what all but a few of them needed and wanted most: status-enhancing prestige that augmented their standing among their peers in Rome.

Conclusion

Augustus's consolidation of his position following the Battle of Actium brought about a fundamental and far-reaching restructuring of the Roman Empire that permanently transformed Rome's system of provincial command. While his preponderant control of military force gave him the raw power he needed to enact his reforms, it was his skillful manipulation of the traditional ideas of *imperium* and the *provincia* that enabled the long-term success of his reorganization of provincial command. His two settlements with the aristocracy were not radical new ideas, but neither were they strictly traditional. The gradual evolution of Roman thinking about *imperium* and the *provincia* in the last two centuries of the republic gave Augustus different interpretations of each concept to choose from, and selecting those ideas that best served his purposes, he was able to establish what would become the imperial monarchy. Finding the responsibilities of repeated consulships too burdensome, and the limitations of the proconsulship too confining, Augustus constructed for himself a hybrid method of provincial command: he had the proconsul's capacity to hold *imperium* and a *provincia* outside Rome indefinitely, but he also had the magistrate's capacity to enter Rome without forfeiting his *provincia* and a dictator's capacity to hold *imperium* inside the *pomerium*. Furthermore, he adopted for himself the unusual authority of *imperium maius*, which may still have been a largely theoretical concept with little legal definition at the time, but had a solid republican pedigree. Whereas provincial assignment had determined priority of *imperium* in the *provinciae* during the republic, Augustus used his *imperium maius* to circumvent this implication of provincial assignment by enabling him to claim priority of *imperium* in any province if and when he wished. Provincial assignment would still define the spheres of authority for proconsuls and *legati Augusti*, but *imperium maius* was a new overlying concept that provided an alternative structure for determining precedence of authority.

His manipulation of the *provincia* was even more extensive: to forestall aristocratic anger at his monopolization of most of Rome's military commands, he inverted the prestige traditionally associated with different types of *provinciae* in order to make the aristocracy content with holding mostly peaceful provinces. By giving consular honors, prestige, and status to what would have been considered a praetorian command in the republic, and by simultaneously reducing the prestige and status of his legates by giving them the lesser title of *propraetores* and the unusually small number of five lictors and *fasces*, he induced the aristocracy to prefer (or at least be satisfied with) receiving the trappings, honor, and prestige of traditional consular commands rather than leadership of the armies and campaigns that used to comprise the consular *provincia*. They received the social benefits of a consular province without actually holding military command. Although few senators were likely tricked into believing that the republic had truly been restored, Augustus's efforts to preserve their honor and status intact gave them good reason to accept the new regime. The manipulation of traditional ideas, rather than the imposition of new ones, enabled Augustus to satisfy (if not please) the senatorial aristocracy.

CONCLUSION

Change was normal in the Roman Republic: words and ideas evolved over time as Rome grew from a village to a Mediterranean-wide empire. Because of this, provincial command was not a static conceptual monolith that remained unchanged throughout the republic, but a complex idea that was defined or made up by simpler ideas like *imperium, auspicium, magistratus,* and *provincia,* all of which evolved over time. Although the military commander and his command were ancient and fundamental notions in the Roman mind, they were nevertheless malleable intellectual constructs that changed and became more complex as successive generations of Romans experimented with their underlying principles, especially with *imperium* and the *provincia*. As these fundamental ideas of authority and responsibility individually evolved over time, they caused the larger idea of military command to change as well. In this respect, Rome's concept of provincial command was highly reactive, in that it developed in response to Rome's military needs.

After the expulsion of the monarchy, military command in the early republic was probably an unregulated process in which influential and wealthy aristocrats could use their personal resources to wage private wars against Rome's neighbors. A man's capacity to command derived from his ability to assemble and lead a war band and — if he wished to consult the auspices — from his own interpretation of divine will. When these aristocrats needed to combine their resources to fight larger and more dangerous foes, they may well have used augury to select a single commander in chief from among their number, as the passage from Cincius in chapter 1 suggests, but this was an ad hoc arrangement used only as needed. In this reconstruction, military authority was controlled by powerful aristocrats and had little to do with the developing concepts of civilian government in Rome. Because military authority was thus decentralized and separate from state control, it was common for multiple military commanders to exist and operate independently of one another at any given time, because every aristocrat had a certain right or claim to exercise sole and absolute command over his own personal army. This way of thinking continued throughout the republic, when Rome could dispatch any number of independent military commanders into the field at once, and each was directed to a specific *provincia* in which his *imperium* and *auspicium* took precedence over that of any other commander.

Because commanders were all independent of one another and separated into different *provinciae*, the Romans did not need or employ the concept of military rank or the idea that supreme military authority could exist in different levels or degrees. Just as individual aristocratic clans or tribes had probably claimed precedence in their own "turf" or sphere of primary influence (the lands controlled by their clan and their retainers), Roman commanders in the later republic could recognize that each of them enjoyed precedence within a defined sphere. This was a system of deference rather than obedience, whereby a commander reciprocated for the priority he enjoyed in his own *provincia* by showing willing deference to other commanders in their respective *provinciae*. Instead of a hierarchy of command, the Romans saw their military operations as a patchwork quilt of individual and separate spheres of authority. This method of dividing commanders into different spheres was basic and even primitive compared to the systematic chains of command used elsewhere, which could combine the full resources of a state under a single leader's authority. The diffused and shared nature of military command in the republic—based on a sharing out of *imperium* into different *provinciae* rather than a unification of all resources under a single man's *imperium*—seems to have grown organically from a period of aristocratic rule rather than being a holdover from Rome's monarchy or a constitutional construct at the birth of the republic.

As the democratic element in Rome's government grew stronger, aristocratic traditions of military command were probably subjected to greater public control and regulation. This was probably aided by the expansion of Roman territory and the resultant need for larger armies, which the aristocratic clans could not produce from their individual resources. As the plebeian tribunes and popular assemblies gained greater influence, it became necessary for aristocrats to receive their official authority to command (*imperium* and *auspicium*) from the state, and eventually the assemblies also gained the prerogative to select (through election) which aristocrats would exercise military command in a given year. Since military campaigns were increasingly large wars that required the participation of thousands of Roman soldiers, the citizens in their assemblies acquired the ability to determine which commanders they would follow and what enemies they would fight, although this latter decision could easily be left to the wisdom of the senate, and often was. From this process of bringing the exercise of military command under state control, the familiar republican government gradually arose. While the shortage of evidence from the early republic means that this reconstruction is largely based on deductive reasoning, it does fit what evidence we have better than the traditional Roman belief that the classical republican government was spontaneously created at the expulsion of the monarchy.

These origins of Roman provincial command are a challenge to modern thinking, which is steeped in two thousand years of imperial, regal, or constitutional commanders in chief. The chain of command and the hierarchy of ranks are ubiquitous in modern military thinking, making it difficult to imagine that every Roman commander possessed the same *imperium* as his colleagues in absolute and relative terms. Nevertheless, the evidence presented in the preceding chapters makes it difficult to accept that any notion of *imperium maius* (or *minus*) existed before the end of the republic. Instead, the concept of the *provincia* was far more important to the definition and organization of early Roman military campaigns, and it was probably an older concept as well, since early aristocratic warlords probably respected each other's "turf" (*provinciae*) long before they acknowledged that they needed the state's authority (*imperium* and *auspicium*) to lead soldiers in battle. The likely agreement among early aristocrats that each commander would mind his own business and not interfere in one another's raids against hostile neighbors established a fundamental belief that military commands were separate and individual endeavors, and not interconnected activities that fit within a hierarchy of relative status. Since each commander expected to wield unchallenged military authority in his *provincia*, any question of levels or degrees of *imperium* (or *auspicium*) would have been nonsensical and a waste of time; it was only possession of *imperium* and *auspicium* that mattered, not possession of a particular level of *imperium* or *auspicium*. In other words, the simple grant of *imperium* and *auspicium* defined a man as having the authority to exercise military command in the later republic, and this was a simple yes or no vote by the people. The far more dynamic and variable question was the *provincia* to which each commander would be assigned, since this established a real difference between the men authorized to hold *imperium*. Indeed, the granting of *imperium* became such a boring and routine action that the *comitia curiata* (which authorized the conferral of *imperium*) eventually devolved from a major assembly of citizens into a small committee of lictors who represented the *curiae* of the people. Even the duration of *imperium* was not a variable. The granting of *imperium* was important and necessary, but it involved no variables or decision making that differentiated one *imperium*-bearer from another.

Provincial assignment, on the other hand, was a complex decision-making process that separated commanders into distinct activities and determined which of them would take precedence in which spheres. The specific purpose of provincial assignment was to create differences between commanders, and the state could adjust or change a man's *provincia* even after he had taken up *imperium* and left the city. The *provincia* was the main concept that defined — and therefore limited — the scope of each commander's use of his authority, and as such it was a far more dynamic and malleable idea than *imperium*. Even on those occasions when a particularly large threat forced the state to assign two commanders to a single *provincia*, the commanders did not share the *provincia* as much as they divided it either by breaking it into two smaller *provinciae* or by alternating sole possession of the *provincia*, so that only one man could claim precedence of authority in the *provincia* at any given time. The *provincia*, therefore, was the decisive attribute that determined which commander took precedence in what sphere.

Given this critical role played by the *provincia*, it is not surprising that most of the important developments in provincial command that occurred during the republic derived from experiments with (or manipulation of) the concept of the *provincia*. Since provincial assignment determined precedence of command, the state could always change military leadership by transferring one commander's *provincia* to another commander. This was normally done at the end of each year when sitting magistrates retired and new magistrates were inaugurated, but it could also be done midyear: the *provincia* of a dead, ill, or defeated consul could be transferred to another consul, to a praetor, or even to a dictator. Likewise, the relationship between a consul and a praetor in the field was established by their relative provincial assignments: each claimed supreme authority over his own *provincia*, although a praetor might willingly choose to defer to requests for assistance or coordination made by the more senior consuls. Prorogation is also better explained as an extension of a commander's possession of a *provincia* (which could be done by simple senatorial decree) rather than some kind of renewal or extension of *imperium*, which was entirely unnecessary, since *imperium* did not automatically expire, and which would have been impractical since the ceremonies concerning *imperium* generally needed the presence of the *imperium* holder in Rome. The relationship between consuls and praetors and the prorogation of commanders are difficult and awkward to explain in terms of authority (*imperium* or *auspicium*) but easy to explain in terms of provincial assignment.

Finally, the structure and development of the Roman Empire are also illuminated by the evolution of the concept of the *provincia*. Although the *provin-*

cia was originally a short-term military campaign against a particular enemy, the Romans adapted the concept to provide a structure to control their overseas conquests. Whereas Rome had absorbed most of Italy by establishing colonies and extending partial Roman citizenship to its conquered enemies, it decided to retain control of territories taken from Carthage by making them permanent *provinciae*, which meant assigning them to commanders as *provinciae* whether or not active campaigning was needed. In addition to a temporary war focused on the conquest of a particular enemy, the *provincia* very gradually came to signify the defense and management of a specific area. This was probably seen as a small and not-particularly-significant expansion of the traditional meaning of the *provincia* at the time, but the development of a second and fundamentally different type of *provincia* would have profound and far-reaching significance for the republic. The decision to expand the praetorian college to provide commanders for the permanent *provinciae* would further differentiate the praetorship from the consulship, making the praetorship substantially more common and less desirable and respected than the consulship. While the two offices continued to have the same *imperium* and almost identical prerogatives in Rome, the consulship would increasingly be seen as the more important of the two, exponentially increasing the competition among praetors to reach the exalted consulship. Thus, while the praetorship and consulship continued to possess the exact same *imperium* and capacity for command, the Romans were increasingly thinking of them as higher and lower commanders.

This distinction was amplified as the Roman people imposed more and more regulation on their provincial commanders. Over the course of the second century BC, the Romans passed several pieces of legislation intended to punish those provincial commanders who did not show proper self-restraint in their commands, and these new regulations overwhelmingly fell on the shoulders of the praetors in permanent provinces. This was probably intentional: whereas consuls normally received wars as their *provinciae*, giving them ample opportunities to enrich themselves through legitimate plunder, praetors frequently found themselves holding peaceful permanent provinces with no obvious way to acquire the glory and wealth they needed to advance further up the *cursus honorum*. As a result, praetors were probably more tempted than consuls to abuse their authority and extort riches from peaceful provincials, and in response the Roman people passed laws trying to prevent (or at least limit) this abuse. The *lex Porcia* of 100 BC was of particular importance, because it not only imposed further regulation against extortion but also sought to prevent unauthorized triumph hunting by requiring commanders to remain inside the boundaries of their *provinciae*. Since consular *provinciae* were normally military campaigns that were not subject to boundaries (or had vague boundaries), this requirement probably had little de facto influence on consular commands. Praetors, on the other hand, probably felt the full weight of the *lex Porcia*. Because it had become normal for praetorian *provinciae* to be geographically recognizable places, it was much harder for praetors to justify leaving their assigned *provincia* in violation of the *lex Porcia*. By imposing limits on praetors' use of authority and their ability to actually function like military commanders, this legislation increased further the distinction between consuls and praetors. Whereas consuls remained generals, the legislation attempted to make the praetors into provincial governors, and whereas consular *provinciae* remained wars of conquest, praetorian *provinciae* were being transformed into zones of administration and governance.

Part of this legislation was the *lex Sempronia* of Gaius Gracchus, which attempted to reduce corruption by requiring the senate to name consular provincial assignments before the consular elections. An unintended consequence of this *lex* was a change in the pattern of provincial assignment: because the *lex* forced the senators to name provincial commands several months early, they began sending consuls to permanent provinces near potentially dangerous neighbors, which placed consular commanders and armies in the regions where major campaigning was most likely to be needed or useful. Whereas permanent provinces had overwhelmingly gone to praetors before 123 BC, the Gracchan legislation made it much more common for consuls to receive those permanent provinces that might serve as launching platforms for aggressive campaigning. Permanent provinces thus became the backbone of Rome's system of provincial assignment. While it was still possible for the senate to give a commander a task as his *provincia* (such as the war with Spartacus or Pompey's piracy command), it became much more common to give consuls permanent *provinciae* from which a task might be accomplished (such as Asia or Cilicia with the war against Mithridates, or Macedonia with the opportunity to campaign against untamed northern tribes). It was ancient tradition that consuls received important military campaigns as their *provinciae*, so they were expected to exit their permanent *provinciae* to attack hostile neighbors. These consuls were also expected to manage the administrative needs of provincials in their permanent *provincia*; they prioritized their military activity, but assignment to a permanent *provincia* meant consular commanders needed to be (occasional) governors as well as generals.

Praetors, on the other hand, had developed into junior or secondary commanders who did not have the same traditional prerogative to seek out glory.

Although they had the same capacity to command as consuls, praetors were generally assigned to permanent provinces that contained smaller armies or no legions at all. Indeed, since consuls were increasingly assigned to the permanent provinces that offered the best opportunities for campaigning, the praetors were generally left with the provinces that required only minimal or no military activity. While the patterns of provincial assignment in the second century BC had usually ensured that a few praetors might be given real opportunities for military command, praetors in the first century BC rarely received significant military commands and came to operate more as governors than generals. Thus the changing patterns in provincial assignment further underscored the de facto (but not de jure) difference between the consulship and praetorship. Whereas the creation of the permanent *provincia* in the third century BC had been a remarkable innovation, by the late republic permanent *provinciae* made up most of Rome's empire, a development that significantly changed the Romans' conception of the *provincia* and the commander.

In the late republic, powerful and ambitious men would use the malleable concept of the *provincia* to acquire unprecedented personal power. Marius used the popular assemblies to circumvent the senate's by-now traditional prerogative of assigning provinces, while Pompey and Caesar used the same assemblies to acquire provincial commands of unprecedented size and importance, often combining several permanent provinces into a single provincial command. By accident or design, Pompey's piracy campaign created a situation in which two different *provinciae* existed in the same geographic space, a condition that other men might have handled with restraint, but which Pompey seized upon as an opportunity to win personal glory at the expense of another commander. The tables would be turned on Pompey eighteen years later, when his supporters refused to obey his instructions during his civil war with Caesar.

As military commands grew in size and scope, the *provincia* and provincial assignment lost some of its capacity to separate commanders into separate and distinct spheres. Amid this breakdown in the traditional effectiveness of provincial assignment, certain Romans probably began contemplating other methods for determining precedence of command, such as the hierarchical authority used by eastern monarchs. Although a tribune first mentioned the idea of *imperium maius* in 57 BC, it was Cicero in 43 BC who formally suggested the radical step of giving Cassius *imperium maius* to make him the unchallenged commander in chief in the war against Caesar's lieutenants. Cicero probably intended *imperium maius* to perform the same task that the *provincia* had performed for centuries: establish precedence in a particular sphere between two equal commanders. *Imperium maius* was meant not to subordinate one *imperium*-bearing commander to another (a very un-republican idea) but simply to give the orders of one commander priority over those of any other commander within a particular *provincia*. In this respect, Cicero's *imperium maius* was probably intended to reinforce provincial assignment and to prevent the confusion caused by overlapping *provinciae*; he wanted Cassius to be the supreme commander in the *provincia* against the Caesarians, regardless of where Cassius was or what permanent province he entered, but he did not mean to make Cassius the superior of all other commanders.

Few Romans were better at manipulating traditional ideas than Augustus, and he used successive interpretations of the *provincia* and *imperium* to craft his principate. Although he went through several stages in establishing his preeminence, he ultimately grounded his position as a provincial commander in Cicero's *imperium maius* and in the control of key *provinciae* that had given Pompey, Caesar, and the Second Triumvirate so much military power. Yet Augustus seems to have expanded on Cicero's thinking about *imperium*: whereas Cicero had probably seen *imperium maius* as a means of reinforcing the traditional ability of provincial assignment to separate commanders into different spheres, Augustus interpreted it as giving him the authority to interfere in provinces clearly not assigned to him. While Cicero had wanted to protect the independence of commanders in their respective *provinciae*, Augustus wanted to weaken this role of provincial assignment. Furthermore, Augustus selected some traditional aspects of military command to provide some justification for his untraditional actions, such as acquiring for himself the dictator's ability to retain *imperium* in the *pomerium* without actually holding the dictatorship. Finally, he sought to mollify the aristocracy and further secure his position by manipulating the honor and prestige given to the different types of *provinciae* in the empire. In particular, he inverted the prestige given to provincial commanders by giving consular honors to holders of public provinces (which would have been considered praetorian in the republic) while giving his lieutenants in individual imperial provinces comparatively low honors and titles to dilute the prestige they received for holding what would have been considered consular provinces in the republic. He did this because the prestige of a provincial command had traditionally been consistent with the prestige of its holder, such that the most important commanders (consuls) had received the best and most prestigious commands. By increasing the prestige of peaceful provinces with consular trappings, and reducing the prestige of militarized provinces with lower titles, Augustus tried to give the aristocracy some reason to tolerate his reforms. Although none of Augustus's contemporaries could have been deluded into thinking that he had actually restored the republic, his efforts to confer the greatest prestige and honor on the proconsuls of the public provinces illustrate how he tried to manipulate Roman thinking about the *provincia* to assuage aristocratic feelings about his principate.

The *provincia* was the most important and dynamic aspect of military command in the republic because it allowed for Rome's aristocrats to share the exercise of authority and leadership in war. Rome's system of provincial assignment enabled many men simultaneously to exercise military command equally and independently of one another, so it was a sharing of power that enabled many aristocrats to enjoy the benefits of command and prevented any single aristocrat from gaining too much power or influence. In the late republic, however, the oversized ambition of a handful of men drove them to seek greater personal power and prestige by manipulating the idea of the *provincia* to create vast commands; rather than a sharing of military opportunities, these great men sought to hoard the most important military commands for themselves. For men with autocratic tendencies like Caesar, the *provincia* was a malleable concept that enabled him to fold several important provinces into a single gigantic command. His aristocratic opponents, on the other hand, declined to combine their individual *provinciae* under a single leader (Pompey) and were defeated, largely because they continued to think of provincial assignment as an equal sharing of command opportunities. In the next civil war against the Second Triumvirate, Cicero proposed *imperium maius* as a way for Cassius to hold supreme authority in the war against the Caesarians without forcing individual commanders to relinquish control of their own *provinciae*. Cicero had proposed an innovation to *imperium* in order to preserve the aristocratic sharing of *provinciae*, but Augustus would see *imperium maius* as a tool of monarchy that would enable him to control any province he wished. Although he did not emphasize the full monarchical nature of his *imperium maius* during his principate, provincial assignment became less important in the imperial era because it no longer determined which commander exercised supreme authority in what sphere; provincial command had shifted from an aristocratic sharing of independent *provinciae* to an imperial monarchy in which all *provinciae* fell under the *imperium maius* of the emperor. The evolution of provincial command — particularly of *imperium* and the *provincia* — is in large part the history of Rome itself.

Bibliography

Abbott, F. F. 1901. *A History and Description of Roman Political Institutions*. Boston and London.

Adcock, F. E. 1959. "Consular Tribunes and Their Successors," *JRS* 47: 9–14.

Ager, S. 1996. *Interstate Arbitrations in the Greek World, 337–90 BC*. Berkeley, Los Angeles, and London.

Alföldi, A. 1965. *Early Rome and the Latins*. Ann Arbor, Mich.

———. 1972. Review of *The Archaic Community of the Romans* by Robert E. A. Palmer, *Gnomon* 44: 787–99.

Alföldy, G. 2000. "Das neue Edikt des Augustus aus El Bierzo in Hispanien," *ZPE* 131: 177–205.

Allen, W., Jr. 1952. "Cicero's Provincial Governorship in 63 BC," *TAPA* 83: 233–41.

Allison, J. E., and J. D. Cloud. 1962. "The *Lex Julia Maiestatis*," *Latomus* 21: 711–31.

Ando, C. 1999. "Was Rome a Polis?," *Cl. Ant.* 18: 5–34.

———. 2000. *Imperial Ideology and Provincial Loyalty in the Roman Empire*. Berkeley and Los Angeles.

Arangio-Ruiz, V., and G. Pugliese Carratelli. 1954. "*Tabulae Herculanenses* IV," *Parola del Passato* 9: 54–74.

Astin, A. E. 1958. *The Lex Annalis before Sulla*. Brussels.

———. 1963. "Augustus and *Censoria Potestas*," *Latomus* 22: 226–35.

———. 1964. "The Roman Commander in Hispania Ulterior," *Historia* 13: 245–54.

———. 1967. *Scipio Aemilianus*. Oxford.

Avidov, A. 1997. "Were the Cilicians a Nation of Pirates?," *Mediterranean Historical Review* 10: 5–55.

Awerbuch, M. 1981. "*Imperium*," *Archiv für Begriffsgeschichte* 25: 162–84.

Badian, E. 1952. "The Treaty between Rome and the Achaean League," *JRS* 42: 76–80.

———. 1964. *Studies in Greek and Roman History*. Oxford.

———. 1965. "M. Porcius Cato and the Annexation and Early Administration of Cyprus," *JRS* 55: 110–21.

———. 1966. "Notes on *Provincia Gallia* in the Late Republic," in R. Chevallier (ed.) *Mélanges d'archéologie et d'histoire offerts à André Piganiol*. Paris: 901–18.

———. 1968. *Roman Imperialism in the Late Republic*. Ithaca, N.Y.

———. 1976. "Lucius Sulla: The Deadly Reformer," in A. J. Dunstan (ed.) *Essays on Roman Culture*. The Todd Memorial Lectures. Toronto: 35–74.

———. 1980. "Notes on the Laudatio of Agrippa," *CJ* 76: 97–109.

———. 1990. "Magistratur und Gesellschaft," in W. Eder (ed.) *Staat und Staatlichkeit in der frühen römischen Republik*. Stuttgart: 458–75.

Balsdon, J. P. V. D. 1939. "Consular Provinces under the Late Republic, I. General Considerations," *JRS* 29: 57–73.

———. 1957. "Roman History, 58–56 BC: Three Ciceronian Problems," *JRS* 47: 15–20.

———. 1962. "Roman History, 65–50 BC: Five Problems," *JRS* 52: 134–41.

Barker, G., and T. Rasmussen. 2000. *The Etruscans*. Oxford.

Barlow, C. T. 1980. "The Roman Government and the Roman Economy, 92–80 BC," *AJPh* 101: 202–19.

Baronowski, D. W. 1988. "The Provincial Status of Mainland Greece after 146 BC: A Criticism of Erich Gruen's Views," *Klio* 70: 448–60.

———. 1991. "The Romans' Awareness of Their Imperialism in the Second Century B.C.," in E. Hermon (ed.) *Gouvernants et gouvernés dans l'Imperium Romanum*. Quebec: 173–81.

Bauman, R. A. 1967. *The Crimen Maiestatis in the Roman Republic and Augustan Principate*. Johannesburg.

———. 1973. "The Lex Valeria de provocatione of 300 BC," *Historia* 22: 34–47.

———. 1974a. "Criminal Prosecutions by the Aediles," *Latomus* 33: 245–64.

———. 1974b. *Impietas in Principem*. Munich.

———. 1996. *Crime and Punishment in Ancient Rome*. London and New York.

Baumgarten, A. I. 2002. *Sacrifice in Religious Experience*. Leiden.

Beard, M. 2007. *The Roman Triumph*. Cambridge, Mass., and London.

Beard, M., J. North, and S. Price. 1998. *Religions of Rome*. 2 vols. Cambridge.

Beck, H. 2005. *Karriere und Hierarchie: Die römische Aristokratie und die Anfänge des cursus honorum in der mittleren Republik*. Berlin.

———. 2011. "Consular Power and the Roman Constitution: The Case of *imperium* Reconsidered," in H. Beck, A. Duplá, M. Jehne, and F. Pina Polo (eds.) *Consuls and the Res Publica: Holding High Office in the Roman Republic*. Cambridge: 77–96.

Beck, H., A. Duplá, M. Jehne, and F. Pina Polo (eds.). 2011. *Consuls and the Res Publica: Holding High Office in the Roman Republic*. Cambridge.

Beloch, K. J. 1926. *Römische Geschichte*. Berlin and Leipzig.

Beltrán Lloris, F. 2011. "Les colonies latines d'Hispanie (IIe siècle av. n. E.): émigration italique et intégration politique," in N. Barradon and F. Kirbihler (eds.) *Les gouverneurs et les provinciaux sous la République romaine*. Rennes: 131–44.

Béranger, J. 1948. "A propos d'un *imperium infinitum*. Histoire et stylistique," in J. Ernst (ed.) *Mélanges de philologie, de littérature et d'histoire anciennes offerts à J. Marouzeau par ses collègues et élèves étrangers*. Paris: 19–27.

———. 1977. "*Imperium*, expression et conception du pouvoir impérial," *Rev. Ét. Lat.* 55: 325–44.

Bergk, A. 2011. "The Development of the Praetorship in the Third century BC," in H. Beck, A. Duplá, M. Jehne, and F. Pina Polo (eds.) *Consuls and the Res Publica: Holding High Office in the Roman Republic*. Cambridge: 61–74.

Bernardi, A. 1988. "La Roma dei re fra storia e leggenda," in A. Momigliano and A. Schiavone (eds.) *Storia di Roma*. Turin: 181–202.

Bernhardt, R. 1985. *Polis und römische Herrschaft in der späten Republik (149–31 v. Chr.)*. Berlin and New York.

Bertrand, J.-M. 1982. "Langue grecque et administration romaine: de l'ἐπαρχεία τῶν Ῥωμαίων à l'ἐπαρχεία τῶν Θράκων," *Ktema* 7: 167–76.

———. 1989. "A propos du mot provincia: Étude sur les modes d'élaboration du langage politique," *Journal des Savants* 191–215.

Billows, R. 1989. "Legal Fiction and Political Reform at Rome in the Early Second Century BC," *Phoenix* 43: 112–33.

Birks, P., A. Rodger, and J. S. Richardson. 1984. "Further Aspects of the Tabula Contrebiensis," *JRS* 74: 45–73.

Birley, A. R. 2000. "Senators as Generals," in G. Alföldy, B. Dobson, and W. Eck (eds.) *Kaiser, Heer und Gesellschaft in der Römischen Kaiserzeit.* Stuttgart: 97–119.

Bispham, E. 2010. "Literary Sources," in N. Rosenstein and R. Morstein-Marx (eds.) *A Companion to the Roman Republic.* West Sussex: 29–50.

Bleicken, J. 1955. *Das Volkstribunat der klassischen Republik.* Munich.

———. 1959. "Ursprung und Bedeutung der Provocation," *ZRG* 76: 324–77.

———. 1967. *"Imperium,"* in *Der Kleine Pauly* II. Stuttgart: 1381–83.

———. 1975. *Lex Publica: Gesetz und Recht in der römischen Republik.* Berlin.

———. 1980. *Geschichte der römischen Republik.* Munich.

———. 1981. *Verfassungs- und Sozialgeschichte des Römischen Kaiserreiches.* Paderborn.

———. 1990. *Zwischen Republik und Prinzipat: Zum Charakter des zweiten Triumvirats.* Göttingen.

———. 1993. *"Imperium consulare/proconsulare* im Übergang von der Republik zum Prinzipat," in J. Bleicken (ed.) *Colloquium aus Anlass des 80. Geburtstages von Alfred Heuss.* Kallmünz: 117–33.

———. 1995. *Die Verfassung der Römischen Republik.* Paderborn.

———. 1998. *Augustus: Eine Biographie.* Berlin.

Blösel, W. 2003. "Die memoria der gentes als Rückgrat der kollektiven Erinnerung im republikanischen Rom," in U. Eigler, U. Gotter, N. Luraghi, and U. Walter (eds.) *Formen römischer Geschichtsschreibung von den Anfängen bis Livius: Gattungen, Autoren, Kontexte.* Darmstadt: 53–72.

Boak, A. E. R. 1918. "The Extraordinary Commands from 80 to 48 BC: A Study in the Origins of the Principate," *American Historical Review* 24: 1–25.

Boddington, A. 1959. "The Original Nature of the Consular Tribunate," *Historia* 8: 356–64.

Bonfante-Warren, L. 1970a. "Roman Triumphs and Etruscan Kings: The Changing Face of the Triumph," *JRS* 60: 49–66.

———. 1970b. "Roman Triumphs and the Etruscan Kings: The Latin Word *Triumphus,"* in R. C. Lugton and M. G. Saltzer (eds.) *Studies in Honor of J. Alexander Kerns.* The Hague: 108–20.

Botsford, G. W. 1909. *The Roman Assemblies.* New York.

Bouchier, E. S. 1917. *Sardinia in Ancient Times.* Oxford.

Brand, C. E. 1968. *Roman Military Law.* Austin.

Bremmer, J. 1982. "The Suodales of Poplios Valesios," *ZPE* 47: 133–47.

Brennan, T. C. 1994. "M.' Curius Dentatus and the Praetor's Right to Triumph," *Historia* 43: 423–39.

———. 2000. *The Praetorship in the Roman Republic.* 2 vols. Oxford.

———. 2004. "Power and Process under the Republican 'Constitution,'" in H. Flower (ed.) *The Cambridge Companion to the Roman Republic.* Cambridge: 31–65.

Bringmann, K. 1977. "Imperium Proconsulare und Mitregentschaft im frühen Prinzipat," *Chiron* 7: 219–38.

———. 1988. "Das zweite Triumvirat. Bemerkungen zu Mommsens Lehre von der außerordentlichen konstituierenden Gewalt," in P. Kneissl and V. Losemann (eds.) *Alte Geschichte und Wissenschaftsgeschichte. Festschrift Karl Christ zum 65. Geburtstag*, Darmstadt, 22–38.

Bringmann, K., and T. Schäfer. 2002. *Augustus und die Begründung des römischen Kaisertums*. Berlin.

Briscoe, J. 1973. *A Commentary on Livy Books XXXI–XXXIII*. Oxford.

———. 1981. *A Commentary on Livy Books XXXIV–XXXVIII*. Oxford.

Broughton, T. R. S. 1946. "Notes on Roman Magistrates. I. The Command of M. Antonius in Cilicia. II. Lucullus' Commission and Pompey's Acta," *TAPA* 77: 35–43.

———. 1948. "More Notes on Roman Magistrates," *TAPA* 79: 63–78.

———. 1951. *Magistrates of the Roman Republic*. 2 vols. New York.

Brunt, P. A. 1961. "The *Lex Valeria Cornelia*," *JRS* 51: 71–83.

———. 1962. "The Army and the Land in the Roman Revolution," *JRS* 52: 69–86.

———. 1971. *Italian Manpower: 225 BC–AD 14*. Oxford.

———. 1975. "The Administrators of Roman Egypt," *JRS* 65: 124–47.

———. 1977. "Lex de Imperio Vespasiani," *JRS* 67: 95–116.

———. 1984. "The Role of the Senate in the Augustan Regime," *CQ* 34: 423–44.

———. 1987. *Italian Manpower: 225 BC–AD 14*. 2nd ed. Oxford.

———. 1988. *The Fall of the Roman Republic and Related Essays*. Oxford.

———. 1990. *Roman Imperial Themes*. Oxford.

Bruun, C. 2000. "'What every man in the street used to know': M. Furius Camillus, Italic Legends and Roman Historiography," in C. Bruun (ed.) *The Roman Middle Republic: Politics, Religion, and Historiography, c. 400–133 BC*. Rome: 41–68.

Bucher, G. S. 1987. "The Annales Maximi in the Light of Roman Methods of Keeping Records," *American Journal of Ancient History* 12: 3–61.

Buckland, W. W. 1934. "L'Edictum provinciale," *RHDFE* 13: 81–96.

———. 1937. "Civil Proceedings against Ex-magistrates in the Republic," *JRS* 27: 37–47.

———. 1963. *A Text-Book of Roman Law: From Augustus to Justinian*. Cambridge.

Bunse, R. 1998. *Das römische Oberamt in der frühen Republik und das Problem der Konsulartribunen*. Trier.

———. 2001. "Die frühe Zensur und die Entstehung der Kollegialität," *Historia* 50: 145–62.

———. 2002a. "Entstehung und Funktion der Losung ("sortitio") under den "magistratus maiores" der römischen Republik," *Hermes* 130: 416–32.

———. 2002b. "Die klassische Prätur und die Kollegialität (par potestas)," *ZRG* 119: 29–43.

Buonauro, C. 2002. "La Responsabilità dei magistrati," *Labeo* 1: 138–46.

Burton, G. P. 1976. "The Issuing of *Mandata* to Proconsuls and a New Inscription from Cos," *ZPE* 21: 63–68.

———. 2002. "The Roman Imperial State (AD 14–235): Evidence and Reality," *Chiron* 32: 249–80.

Burton, P. J. 2011. *Friendship and Empire: Roman Diplomacy and Imperialism in the Middle Republic*. Cambridge.

Campanile, E. (ed.) 1988. *Alle Origini di Roma*. Pisa.

Campanile, E., and C. Letta. 1979. *Studi sulle magistrature indigene e municipali in area italica*. Pisa.

Campbell, J. B. 1975. "Who Were the 'Viri Militares'?," *JRS* 65: 11–31.

Cancik, H. 1983. "*Libri Fatales*. Römische Offenbarungsliteratur und Geschichtstheologie," in D. Hellholm (ed.) *Apocalypticism in the Mediterranean World and the Near East.* Tübingen: 549–76.

Carey, W. L. 1996. "Nullus Videtur Dolo Facere: The Roman Seizure of Sardinia in 237 BC," *CPh* 91: 203–22.

Cary, M. 1919. "A Forgotten Treaty between Rome and Carthage," *JRS*: 9: 67–77.

Cascione, C. 1999. *Tresviri capitales: Storia di una magistratura minore.* Naples.

Castro, J. L. L. 2013. "The Spains, 205–72 BC," in D. Hoyos (ed.) *A Companion to Roman Imperialism.* Leiden: 67–78.

Catalano, P. 1960. *Contributi allo studio del diritto augurale I.* Turin.

———. 1978. "Aspetti spaziali del sistema giuridico-religioso romano," *ANRW* 2.16.1: 440–553.

Chaplin, J. 2000. *Livy's Exemplary History.* Oxford.

Churchill, J. B. 1999. "Ex qua quod vellent facerent: Roman magistrates' Authority over Praeda and Manubiae," *TAPA* 129: 85–116.

Clemente, G. 1988. "Sicily and Rome: The Impact of Empire on a Roman Province," in T. Yuge and M. Doi (eds.) *Forms of Control and Subordination in Antiquity.* Leiden: 105–20.

Coarelli, F. 1972. "Il sepolcro degli Scipioni," *DArch* 6: 36–106.

———. 1982. "Su alcuni proconsoli d'Asia tra la fine del II e gli inizi del I secolo a. C. e sulla politica di Mario in Oriente," *Tituli* 4: 435–51.

Cobban, J. M. 1935. *Senate and Provinces, 78–49 BC: Some Aspects of the Foreign Policy and Provincial Relations of the Senate during the Closing Years of the Roman Republic.* Cambridge.

Cohen, D. 1957. "The Origin of the Roman Dictatorship," *Mnemosyne* 10: 300–318.

Coli, U. 1951. *Regnum.* Studia et Documenta Historiae et Iuris 17. Pavia.

———. 1953. "Sui limiti durata delle magistrature romane," *Studi in onore di Vincenzo Arangio-Ruiz nel XLV anno del suo insegnamento.* Naples: 395–418.

Cornell, T. J. 1982. Review of Wiseman, *Clio's Cosmetics* (1979), *JRS* 72: 203–6.

———. 1988. "La Guerra e lo stato in Roma archaica (VII–V sec.)," in E. Campanile (ed.) *Alle Origini di Roma.* Pisa: 89–100.

———. 1989. "Rome and Latium," *CAH²* 7.2: 243–308.

———. 1995. *The Beginnings of Rome.* London.

———. 2000. "The City-States of Latium," in M. H. Hansen (ed.) *A Comparative Study of Thirty City-State Cultures.* Copenhagen: 209–28.

———. 2003. "Coriolanus: Myth, History and Performance," in D. Braund and C. Gill (eds.) *Myth, History and Culture in Republican Rome.* Exeter: 73–97.

———. 2005. "The Value of the Literary Tradition Concerning Archaic Rome," in K. A. Raaflaub (ed.) *Social Struggles in Archaic Rome.* 2nd ed. Malden, Mass., Oxford, and Victoria: 47–74.

Cotton, H. M. 2000. "Cassius Dio, Mommsen and the quinquefascales," *Chiron* 30: 217–34.

Cotton, H. M., and A. Yakobson. 2002. "Arcanum Imperii: The Powers of Augustus," in G. Clark and T. Rajak (eds.) *Philosophy and Power in the Graeco-Roman World.* Oxford: 193–209.

Cowles, F. H. 1917. "Gaius Verres: An Historical Study." Ph.D. diss. Cornell University.

Crawford, M. H. 1996. *Roman Statutes*. 2 vols. London.

Cristofani, M. 1986. "C. Genucius Cleusina pretore a Caere," *Archeologia nella Tuscia* 2: 24–26.

———. 1987. *Saggi di storia etrusca arcaica*. Rome.

———. 1989. "C. Genucius Cleusina pretore a Caere," in G. Bretschneider (ed.) *Secondo Congresso Internazionale Etrusco (Firenze 1985)*, I, 167–70. Rome.

———. 1990. *La grande Roma dei Tarquini*. Rome.

Culham, P. 1989. "Archives and Alternatives in Republican Rome," *CPh* 84: 100–115.

Curchin, L. A. 1991. *Roman Spain: Conquest and Assimilation*. London and New York.

Dahlheim, W. 1977. *Gewalt und Herrschaft*. Berlin and New York.

Daube, D. 1951. "The Peregrine Praetor," *JRS* 41: 66–70.

———. 1956. *Forms of Roman Legislation*. Oxford.

———. 1969. *Roman Law*. Edinburgh.

Daubner, F. 2007. "Die *lex Porcia*, das Ehrendekret für Menippos von Kolophon und die römische Provinzverwaltung der 120er Jahre," *Göttinger Forum für Altertumswissenshaft* 10: 9–20.

David, J.-M. 1994 [1996]. *The Roman Conquest of Italy* (A. Nevill, trans.). Oxford.

Dawson, D. 1996. *The Origins of Western Warfare*. Boulder, Colo.

de Francisci, P. 1944. "Dal regnum alia 'res publica,'" *Studia et Documenta Historiae et Iuris* 10: 150–66.

———. 1948. *Arcana Imperii*. Rome.

———. 1953. "Intorno alla natura e alla storia dell'auspicium imperiumque," in V. Arangio-Ruiz (ed.) *Studi in memoria di E. Albertario I*, 399–432. Milan.

de Martino, F. 1958. *Storia della costituzione romana, I*. Naples.

———. 1972a. *Storia della costituzione romana*. 2 vols. Naples.

———. 1972b. "Intorno all'origine della repubblica romana e delle magistrature," *ANRW* 1.1: 217–49.

———. 1988. "La costituzione della città-stato," in A. Momigliano and A. Schiavone (eds.) *Storia di Roma*. Turin: 345–65.

———. 1990. *Storia della costituzione romana*. 2nd ed. 2 vols. Naples.

de Sanctis, G. 1956–67. *Storia dei Romani, I–III.1*. Florence.

de Souza, P. 1997. "Romans and Pirates in a Late Hellenistic Oracle from Pamphylia," *CQ* 47: 477–81.

———. 1999. *Piracy in the Graeco-Roman World*. Cambridge.

Deubner, L. 1934. "Die Tracht des römischen Triumphators," *Hermes* 69: 316–23.

Develin, R. 1975. "Prorogation of Imperium before the Hannibalic War," *Latomus* 34: 716–22.

———. 1977. "Lex Curiata and the Competence of Magistrates," *Mnemosyne* 30: 49–65.

———. 1978a. "Provocatio and plebiscites. Early Roman Legislation and the Historical Tradition," *Mnemosyne* 31: 45–60.

———. 1978b. "Tradition and Development of Triumphal Regulations in Rome," *Klio* 60: 429–38.

———. 1978c. "Scipio Aemilianus and the Consular Elections of 148 BC," *Latomus* 37: 484–88.

———. 1979. *Patterns in Office-Holding, 366–49 BC*. Brussels.

————. 1980. "The Roman Command Structure and Spain, 218–190 BC," *Klio* 62: 355–67.

————. 1985. *The Practice of Politics in Rome, 366–167 BC*. Brussels.

————. 2005. "The Integration of the Plebeians after 366 BC," in K. A. Raaflaub (ed.) *Social Struggles in Archaic Rome*. 2nd ed. Berkeley: 293–311.

Dillon, M., and L. Garland. 2005. *Ancient Rome: From the Early Republic to the Assassination of Julius Caesar*. London and New York.

Dmitriev, S. 2005. "The History and Geography of the Province of Asia during Its First Hundred Years and the Provincialization of Asia Minor," *Athenaeum* 93: 71–133.

Drews, R. C. 1988. "Pontiffs, Prodigies, and the Disappearance of the *Annales Maximi*," *CP* 83: 289–99.

Drogula, F. 2007. "*Imperium, Potestas*, and the *Pomerium* in the Roman Republic," *Historia* 56: 419–52.

————. 2011a. "The *Lex Porcia* and the Development of Legal Restraints on Roman Governors," *Chiron* 41: 91–124.

————. 2011b. "Controlling Travel: Deportation, Islands and the Regulation of Senatorial Mobility in the Augustan Principate," *CQ* 61: 230–66.

Drummond, A. 1974. *The History and Reliability of the Early Fasti Consulares: With Special Reference to the So-Called Plebeian Consuls*. D.Phil Thesis. Oxford.

————. 1978a. "The Dictator Years," *Historia* 27: 550–72.

————. 1978b. "Some Observations on the Order of Consuls' Names," *Athenaeum* 56: 80–108.

————. 1980. "Consular Tribunes in Livy and Diodorus," *Athenaeum* 58: 57–72.

————. 1995. *Law, Politics and Power*. Stuttgart.

Dumézil, G. 1966 [1996]. *Fêtes romaines d'été et d'automne: suivi de dix questions romaines*. Paris.

Duplá, A. 1990. *Videant consules. Las medidas de excepción en la crisis de la República romana*. Saragossa.

Durante, M. 1951. "*Triumphe e triumphus*: un capitolo del più antico culto dionisiaco latino," *Maia* 4: 138–44.

Duyvendak, N. 1946. "Restraining Regulations for Roman Officials in the Roman Provinces," in M. David, B. A. van Groningen, and E. M. Meijers (eds.) *Symbolae ad Jus et Historiam Antiquitatis Pertinentes Julio Christiano van Oven Dedicatae*. Leiden: 333–48.

Dyson, S. L. 1985. *The Creation of the Roman Frontier*. Princeton.

Eck, W. 1972. "Bemerkungen zum Militärkommando in den Senatsprovinzen der Kaiserzeit," *Chiron* 2: 429–36.

————. 1995. "Provinz—Ihre Definition unter politisch-administrativem Aspekt," in H. von Hesberg (ed.) *Was ist eigentlich Provinz? Zur Beschreibung eines Bewusstseins*. Cologne: 15–32.

————. 1998. *Augustus und seine Zeit*. Munich.

Eckstein, A. M. 1987. *Senate and General*. Berkeley, Los Angeles, and London.

————. 1995. *Moral Vision in the Histories of Polybius*. Berkeley, Los Angeles, and London.

————. 2009. *Mediterranean Anarchy, Interstate War, and the Rise of Rome*. Berkeley, Los Angeles, and London.

————. 2010. "Macedonia and Rome, 221–146 BC," in J. Roisman and I. Worthington (eds.) *A Companion to Ancient Macedonia*. Oxford: 225–51.

———. 2012. *Rome Enters the Greek East: From Anarchy to Hierarchy in the Hellenistic Mediterranean, 230–170 BC*. Malden, Mass., and Oxford.

———. 2013. "Hegemony and Annexation beyond the Adriatic, 230–146 BC," in D. Hoyos (ed.) *A Companion to Roman Imperialism*. Leiden and Boston: 79–98.

Eder, W. 1969. "Vorsullanische Repetundenverfahren." Diss. Munich.

———. 1990. "Augustus and the Power of Tradition: The Augustan Principate as Binding Link between Republic and Empire," in K. A. Raaflaub and M. Toher (eds.) *Between Republic and Empire*. Berkeley, Los Angeles, and London: 71–122.

———. 2005. "The Political Significance of the Codification of Law in Archaic Societies: An Unconventional Hypothesis," in K. A. Raaflaub (ed.) *Social Struggles in Archaic Rome*. 2nd ed. Malden, Mass., Oxford, and Victoria: 239–67.

Edwell, P. W. 2013. "Definitions of Roman Imperialism," in D. Hoyos (ed.) *A Companion to Roman Imperialism*. Leiden and Boston: 39–52.

Ehrenberg, V. 1953. "Imperium Maius in the Roman Republic," *AJPh* 74: 113–36.

Eilers, C. 2002. *Roman Patrons of Greek Cities*. Oxford.

Errington, R. M. 1972. *The Dawn of Empire: Rome's Rise to World Power*. Ithaca, N.Y.

Evans, R. J., and M. Kleijwegt. 1992. "Did the Romans like Young Men? A Study of the *Lex Villia Annalis*: Causes and Effects," *ZPE* 92: 181–95.

Ewald, B. C., and C. F. Norena. 2010. *The Emperor and Rome: Space, Representation, and Ritual*. Cambridge.

Facchetti, V. 1981. "Le 'Lex de Imperio': Struttura giuridica, ragioni politiche, significato storico," in B. Riposati (ed.) *Atti del Congresso Internazionale di Studi Vespasianei*. Rieti: 399–410.

Feeney, D. 2007. *Caesar's Calendar*. Berkeley, Los Angeles, and London.

Ferenczy, E. 1976. *From the Patrician State to the Patricio-Plebeian State*. Budapest.

Ferrary, J.-L. 1977. "Recherches sur la legislation de Saturninus et de Glaucia," *MEFRA* 89: 619–60.

———. 1985. "La Lex Antonia de Termessibus," *Athenaeum* 73: 419–57.

———. 1990. "Traités et domination romaine dans le monde hellénique," in L. Canfora, M. Liverani, and C. Zaccagnini (eds.) *I trattati nel mondo antico forma ideologia funzione*. Rome: 217–35.

———. 1991. "Le statut des cités libres dans l'Empire romain à la lumière des inscriptions de Claros," *CRAI* 135: 557–77.

———. 1998. "Chapitres tralatices et références à des lois antérieures dans les lois romaines," in M. Humbert and Y. Thomas (eds.) *Mélanges de droit romain et d'histoire ancienne: homage à la mémoire de André Magdelain*. Paris: 151–67.

———. 2000. "Les Gouverneurs des provinces romaines d'Asie Mineure (Asie et Cilicie), depuis l'organisation de la province d'Asie jusqu'à la première guerre de Mithridate (126–88 av. J.-C.)," *Chiron* 30: 161–93.

———. 2001a. "Les Pouvoirs d'Auguste: l'affranchissement de la limite du pomerium," in N. Belayche (ed.) *Rome, les Césars et la Ville*. Rennes: 9–22.

———. 2001b. "A propos des pouvoirs d'Auguste," *CGG* 12: 101–54.

———. 2002. "Le création de la province d'Asie et la présence italienne en Asie Mineure," *Bulletin de Correspondance Hellénique Suppl.* 41: 133–46.

———. 2003. "Res publica restituta et les pouvoirs d'Auguste," in S. F. d'Espèrey,

V. Fromentin, S. Gotteland, and J.-M. Roddaz (eds.) *Fondements et Crises du Pouvoir*. Paris: 419–28.

———. 2006. "Les lois de répression de la brigue et leurs consequences sur la creation et le gouvernement des provinces," *Revista Storica dell' Antichità* 36: 9–21.

———. 2008. "Provinces, magistratures, et lois: la création des provinces sous la République," in I. Piso (ed.) *Die Römischen Provinzen: Begriff und Gründung*. Cluj-Napoca: 7–18.

———. 2010. "La législation comitiale en matière de création, d'assignation et de gouvernement des provinces," in N. Barrandon and F. Kirbihler (eds.) *Administrer les provinces de la République romaine*. Rennes: 33–44.

Ferriès, M.-C., and F. Delrieux. 2011. "Quintus Mucius Scaevola, un gouverneur modèle pour les Grecs de la province d'Asie?," in N. Barradon and F. Kirbihler (eds.) *Les gouverneurs et les provinciaux sous la République romaine*. Rennes: 207–30.

Finer, S. E. 1997. *The History of Government from the Earliest Times*. Oxford.

Finley, M. I. 1979. *Ancient Sicily*. Totowa, N.J.

Fischer, T. 1995. "Ist Provinz gleich Provinz?," in H. von Hesberg (ed.) *Was ist eigentlich Provinz? Zur Beschreibung eines Bewußtseins*. Cologne: 107–17.

Flower, H. 1996. *Ancestor Masks and Aristocratic Power in Roman Culture*. Oxford.

———. 2004. "Spectacle and Political Culture in the Roman Republic," in H. Flower (ed.) *The Cambridge Companion to the Roman Republic*. Cambridge: 322–43.

———. 2010. *Roman Republics*. Princeton and Oxford.

Forsythe, G. 1994. *The Historian L. Calpurnius Piso Frugi and the Roman Annalistic Tradition*. Lanham, Md.

———. 1999. *Livy and Early Rome: A Study in Historical Method and Judgment*. Stuttgart.

———. 2000. "The Roman Historians of the Second Century BC," in C. Bruun (ed.) *The Roman Middle Republic: Politics, Religion, and Historiography, c. 400–133 BC*. Rome: 1–11.

———. 2005. *A Critical History of Early Rome*. Berkeley, Los Angeles, and London.

———. 2007. "The Army and Centuriate Organization in Early Rome," in P. Erdkamp (ed.) *A Companion to the Roman Army*. Malden, Mass., Oxford, and Victoria: 24–42.

Fraccaro, P. 1957. "The History of Rome in the Regal Period," *JRS* 47: 59–65.

Fraschetti, A. 2005. *The Foundation of Rome* (M. Hill and K. Windle, trans.). Edinburgh.

Frederiksen, M. W., and N. Purcell. 1984. *Campania*. London.

Freyburger-Galland, M.-L. 1996. "La Notion de 'provincia' chez Dion Cassius," in E. Hermon (ed.) *Pouvoir et Imperium*. Naples: 97–104.

Frezouls, E. 1991. "Perception des rapports gouvernants/gouvernés à la fin de la république: quelques exemples," in E. Hermon (ed.) *Gouvernants et gouvernés dans l'Imperium Romanum*. Trois Rivières: 95–113.

Frier, B. W. 1983. "Urban Praetors and Rural Violence: The Legal Background of Cicero's Pro Caecina," *TAPA* 113: 221–41.

———. 1985. *The Rise of the Roman Jurists*. Princeton.

———. 1999. *Libri Annales Pontificum Maximorum: The Origins of the Annalistic Tradition*. Ann Arbor, Mich.

Fronda, M. P. 2010. *Between Rome and Carthage: Southern Italy during the Second Punic War*. Cambridge.

Gabba, E. 1982. "La 'Storia di Roma archaica' di Dionigi d'Alicarnasso," *ANRW* 2.30.1: 799–816.

———. 1984. "The Historians and Augustus," in F. Millar and E. Segal (eds.) *Caesar Augustus: Seven Aspects*. Oxford: 189–218.

———. 1991. *Dionysius and "The History of Archaic Rome."* Berkeley.

Gagé, J. 1970. "La ligne pomériale et les catégories sociales de la Rome primitive," *RD* 1: 162–84.

———. 1973. "Une consultation d'haruspices: sur les tabous étrusques de la statue dite d'Horatius Coclès," *Latomus* 32: 1–22.

Galsterer, H. 1976. *Herrschaft und Verwaltung im republikanischen Italien. Die Beziehungen Roms zu den italischen Gemeinden von Latinerfrieden 338 v. Chr. bis zum Bundesgenossenkrieg 91 v. Chr.* Munich.

———. 1986. "Roman Law in the Provinces: Some Problems of Transmission," in M. Crawford (ed.) *L'impero romano e le strutture economiche e sociali delle province.* Como: 13–27.

———. 1996. "The Administration of Justice," *CAH*² 10: 397–413.

Gardner, J. F. 2009. "The Dictator," in M. Griffin (ed.) *A Companion to Julius Caesar.* Oxford: 57–71.

Garlan, Y. 1972 [1975]. *War in the Ancient World* (J. Lloyd, trans.). New York.

Garnsey, P. 1968. "The Criminal Jurisdiction of Governors," *JRS* 58: 51–59.

———. 1988. *Famine and Food Supply in the Graeco-Roman World.* Cambridge.

Gaughan, J. E. 2010. *Murder Was Not a Crime.* Austin.

Gibson, B. J. 1997. "Horace, Carm. 3.30.1–5," *CQ* 47: 312–14.

Giovannini, A. 1978. "La solde des troupes à l'epoque républicaine," *MH* 35: 258–63.

———. 1983. *Consulare Imperium.* Basel.

———. 1984. "Les Origines des magistratures romaines," *Museum Helveticum* 41: 15–30.

———. 1990. "Magistratur und Volk: Ein Beitrag zur Entstehungsgeschichte des Staatsrechts," in W. Eder (ed.) *Staat und Staatlichkeit in der frühen Römischen Republik.* Stuttgart: 406–36.

———. 1999. "Les Pouvoirs d'Auguste de 27 à 23 av. J.-C. Une relecture de l'ordonnance de Kymè de l'an 27 (IK 5, no. 17)," *ZPE* 124: 95–106.

———. 2008. "Date and objectifs de la *lex de provinciis praetoriis*," *Historia* 57: 92–107.

Giovannini, A., and E. Grzybek. 1978. "La lex de piratis persequendis," *Museum Helveticum* 35: 33–47.

Girardet, K. M. 1990a. "Die Entmachtung des Konsulates im Übergang von der Republik zur Monarchie und die Rechtgrundlagen des augusteischen Prinzipats," in W. Görler and S. Koster (eds.) *Pratum Saraviense: Festschrift für P. Steinmetz.* Stuttgart: 89–126.

———. 1990b. "Der Rechtsstatus Oktavians im Jahre 32 v. Chr.," *RhM.* 133: 322–50.

———. 1991. "Der Triumph des Pompeius im Jahre 61 v. Chr. — Ex Asia?," *ZPE* 89: 201–15.

———. 1992a. "Imperium und provinciae des Pompeius seit 67 v. Chr.," *CGG* 2: 177–88.

———. 1992b. "Zur Diskussion um das imperium consulare militae im 1. Jh. v. Chr.," *CGG* 2: 213–20.

———. 1993. "Die Rechtsstellung der Caesarattentäter Brutus und Cassius in den Jahren 44–42 v. Chr.," *Chiron* 23: 207–32.

———. 1995. "Per continuos annos decem (res gestae divi Augusti 7,1): Zur Frage nach dem Endtermin des Triumvirats," *Chiron* 25: 147–61.

———. 2000. "Imperium 'maius': Politische und verfassungsrechtliche Aspekte. Versuch einer Klärung," in A. Giovannini and B. Grange (eds.) *La Révolution Romaine après Ronald Syme*. Genève: 167–227.

——. 2001. "Imperia und provinciae des Pompeius 82 bis 48 v. Chr.," *Chiron* 31: 153–209.

Gjerstad, E. 1953–73. *Early Rome*. 6 vols. Lund.

——. 1967. "Discussions concerning Early Rome, 3," *Historia* 16: 257–78.

——. 1972. "Innenpolitische und militärische Organisation in frührömischer Zeit," *ANRW* 1.1.136–88.

Golden, G. K. 2013. *Crisis Management during the Roman Republic*. Cambridge.

Goldsworthy, A. 2000. *The Punic Wars*. London.

Goodyear, F. R. D. 1981. *The Annals of Tacitus: Book Two*. Cambridge.

Gordon, R., and J. Reynolds. 2003. "Roman Inscriptions," *JRS* 93: 212–94.

Grandazzi, A. 1991 [1997]. *The Foundation of Rome: Myth and History* (J. M. Todd, trans.) Ithaca, N.Y.

——. 2008. *Alba Longa: histoire d'une légende; recherches sur l'archéologie, la religion, les traditions de l'ancien Latium, I–II*. Rome.

Grant, M. 1969. *From Imperium to Auctoritas*. Cambridge.

Green, C. M. C. 2007. *Roman Religion and the Cult of Diana at Aricia*. Cambridge.

Greenidge, A. H. J. 1895. "The Title 'Quaestor Pro Praetore,'" *CR* 9: 258–59.

——. 1901. *The Legal Procedure of Cicero's Time*. Oxford.

Griffin, M. 1973. "The Tribune C. Cornelius," *JRS* 63: 196–213.

Gruen, E. S. 1968. *Roman Politics and the Criminal Courts*. Cambridge, Mass.

——. 1974. *The Last Generation of the Roman Republic*. Berkeley and Los Angeles.

——. 1975. "Rome and Rhodes in the Second Century BC: A Historiographical Inquiry," *CQ* 25: 58–81.

——. 1978. "The Consular Elections for 216 BC and the Veracity of Livy," *California Studies in Classical Antiquity* 11: 61–74.

——. 1984. *The Hellenistic World and the Coming of Rome*. Berkeley.

——. 1990. "The Imperial Policy of Augustus," in K. A. Raaflaub and M. Toher (eds.) *Between Republic and Empire*. Berkeley, Los Angeles, and London: 395–416.

——. 1992. "The Exercise of Power in the Roman Republic," in A. Molho, K. Raaflaub and J. Emlen (eds.) *City States in Classical Antiquity and Medieval Italy*. Ann Arbor, Mich.: 251–67.

Guarino, A. 1969. "Praetor Maximus," *Labeo* 15: 199–201.

Guichard, L. 2011. "*Iidem ubique Di immortales*: les activités religieuses des gouverneurs romains de la deuxième Guerre punique à la fin de la République," in N. Barrandon and F. Kirbihler (eds.) *Les gouverneurs et les provinciaux sous la République romaine*. Rennes: 29–52.

Habel, T. 1958. "Adiutor," *RE* 1: 364–66.

Hackl, U. 1982. *Senat und Magistratur in Rom von der Mitte des 2. Jahrhunderts v. Chr. bis zur Diktatur Sullas*. Kallmünz.

Hahm, D. 2009. "The Mixed Constitution in Greek Thought," in R. K. Balot (ed.) *A Companion to Greek and Roman Political Thought*. West Sussex: 178–98.

Hamel, D. 1998. *Athenian Generals: Military Authority in the Classical Period*. Leiden.

Hardy, E. G. 1917. "Consular Provinces between 67 and 52 BC," *CR* 31: 11–15.

Harris, W. V. 1976. "The Development of the Quaestorship, 267–81 BC," *CQ* 26: 92–106.

————. 1979. *War and Imperialism in Republican Rome*. Oxford.

————. 1990. "Roman Warfare in the Economic and Social Context of the 4th Century BC," in W. Eder (ed.) *Staat und Staatlichkeit in der frühen römischen Republik*. Stuttgart: 494–510.

————. 1991. *Ancient Literacy*. Cambridge, Mass.

Hartfield, M. 1982. "The Roman Dictatorship: Its Character and Its Evolution." Ph.D. diss., University of California, Berkeley.

Haslam, M. W. 1980. "Augustus' Funeral Oration for Agrippa," *CJ* 75: 193–99.

Hassall, M., M. Crawford, and J. Reynolds. 1974. "Rome and the Eastern Provinces at the End of the Second Century BC," *JRS* 64: 195–220.

Hellegouarc'h, J. 1972. *Le Vocabulaire Latin des relations et des partis politiques sous la république*. Paris.

Henderson, M. I. 1957. "Potestas Regia," *JRS* 47: 82–87.

Hermon, E. 1982. "La place de la loi curiate dans l'histoire constitutionnelle de la fin de la république romaine," *Ktema* 7: 297–307.

Heurgon, J. 1964. "L. Cincius et la loi du *clavus annalis*," *Athenaeum* 42: 432–37.

————. 1967. "Magistratures romaines et étrusques," in *Les origins de la république romaine: neuf exposés suivis de discussions*. Geneva: 99–127.

————. 1973. *The Rise of Rome to 264 BC* (J. Willis, trans.). Berkeley.

Heuss, A. 1944. "Zur Entwicklung des Imperiums der römischen Oberbeamten," *ZRG* 64: 57–133.

Hillman, T. P. 1998. "Pompeius' Imperium in the War with Lepidus," *Klio* 80: 91–110.

Hoffman, J. 1976. "Civil Law Procedures in the Provinces of the Late Roman Republic," *Irish Jurist* 11: 355–74.

Hofmann-Löbl, I. 1996. *Die Calpurnii: Politisches Wirken und familiäre Kontinuität*. Frankfurt am Main and New York.

Hölkeskamp, K.-J. 1987. *Die Entstehung der Nobilität: Studien zur sozialen und politischen Geschichte der Römischen Republik im 4. Jhdt. v. Chr.* Stuttgart.

————. 1993. "Conquest, Competition and Consensus: Roman Expansion in Italy and the Rise of the 'Nobilitas,'" *Historia* 42: 12–39.

————. 1996. "Exempla und mos maiorum. Überlegungen zum kollektiven Gedächtnis der Nobilität," in H.-J. Gehrke and A. Möller (eds.) *Vergangenheit und Lebenswelt. Soziale Kommunikation, Traditionsbildung und historisches Bewußtein*. Tübingen: 301–38.

————. 2001. "Capitol, Comitium und Forum: Öffentliche Räume, sakrale Topographie und Erinnerungslandschaften der römischen Republik," in S. Faller (ed.) *Studien zu antiken Identitäten*. Würzburg: 97–132.

————. 2004. *Senatus Populusque Romanus: Die politische Kultur der Republik: Dimensionen und Deutungen*. Stuttgart.

————. 2006. "Der Triumph: 'Erinnere Dich, daß Du ein Mensch bist," in E. Stein-Hölkeskamp and K.-J. Hölkeskamp (eds.) *Erinnerungsorte der Antike: Die römische Welt*. Munich: 258–76, 745–47.

————. 2010. *Reconstructing the Roman Republic*. Princeton.

————. 2011. "The Roman Republic as Theatre of Power: The Consuls as Leading Actors," in H. Beck, A. Duplá, M. Jehne, and F. Pina Polo (eds.) *Consuls and the Res Publica: Holding High Office in the Roman Republic*. Cambridge: 161–81.

Holloway, R. R. 1994. *The Archaeology of Early Rome and Latium*. London.

———. 2008. "Who Were the Tribuni Militum Consulari Potestate?," *Ant. Clas.* 77: 107–25.

———. 2009. "Praetor Maximus and Consul," in G. Uggeri, C. Marangio, and G. Laudizi (eds.) *Palaia philia: studi di topografia antica in onore di Giovanni Uggeri*. Galatina: 71–75.

Hoyos, D. 1973. "Lex Provinciae and Governor's Edict," *Antichthon* 7:4: 7–53.

———. 2003. *Hannibal's Dynasty: Power and Politics in the Western Mediterranean, 247–183 BC*. London and New York.

Humm, M. 2012. "The Curiate Law and the Religious Nature of the Power of Roman Magistrates," in O. Tellegen-Couperus (eds.) *Law and Religion in the Roman Republic*. Leiden and Boston: 57–84.

Hurlet, F. 1994. "Recherches sur la durée de l'imperium des 'co-régents' sous les principats d'Auguste et de Tibère," *CGG* 5: 255–89.

———. 1997. *Les Collègues du Prince sous Auguste et Tibère*. Rome.

———. 2010. "Recherches sur la *profectio* de la dictature de Sylla à la *lex Pompeia* (82–52): le cas des gouverneurs de rang prétorien," in N. Barrandon and F. Kirbihler (eds.) *Administrer les provinces de la République romaine*. Rennes: 45–72.

Itgenshorst, T. 2005. *Tota illa pompa: Der Triumph in der römischen Republik*. Göttingen.

Jameson, S. 1970. "Pompey's Imperium in 67: Some Constitutional Fictions," *Historia* 19: 539–60.

———. 1975. "Augustus and Agrippa Postumus," *Historia* 24: 287–314.

Jashemski, W. F. 1950. *The Origins and History of the Proconsular and the Propraetorian Imperium to 27 BC*. Chicago.

Jehne, M. 1987. *Der Staat des Dictators Caesar*. Cologne.

———. 1989. "Die Dictatur optima lege," *ZRG* 106: 557–72.

———. 2002. "Die Geltung der Provocation und die Konstruktion der römischen Republik als Freiheitsgemeinschaft," in G. Melville and H. Vorländre (eds.) *Geltungsgeschichten: Über die Stabilisierung und Legitimierung institutioneller Ordnungen*. Cologne: 55–74.

———. 2010. "Der Dictator und die Republik. Wurzeln, Formen und Perspektiven von Caesars Monarchie," in B. Linke, M. Meier, and M. Strothmann (eds.), *Zwischen Monarchie und Republik*. Stuttgart: 187–211.

———. 2011. "The Rise of the Consular as a Social Type in the Third and Second Centuries BC," in H. Beck, A. Duplá, M. Jehne, and F. Pina Polo (eds.) *Consuls and the* Res Publica: *Holding High Office in the Roman Republic*. Cambridge: 211–31.

Jolowicz, H. F., and B. Nicholas. 1972. *Historical Introduction to the Study of Roman Law*. Cambridge.

Jones, A. H. M. 1937. *Cities of the Eastern Roman Provinces*. Oxford.

———. 1951. "The Imperium of Augustus," *JRS* 41: 112–19.

———. 1970. *Augustus*. London.

———. 1972. *The Criminal Courts of the Roman Republic and Principate*. Oxford.

Jördens, A. 1999. "Das Verhältnis der römischen Amtsträger in Ägypten zu den 'Städten' in der Provinz," in W. Eck (ed.) *Lokale Autonomie und römische Ordnungsmacht in den kaiserzeitlichen Provinzen vom 1. bis 3. Jahrhundert*. Munich: 141–80.

Judge, E. A. 1974. "'Res Publica Restituta': A Modern Illusion?," in J. A. S. Evans (ed.) *Polis and Imperium: Studies in Honour of Edward Togo Salmon*. Toronto: 279–311.

Kallet-Marx, R. 1995. *Hegemony to Empire*. Berkeley and Los Angeles.

Kaplan, A. 1973-74. "Religious Dictators of the Roman Republic," *CW* 67: 172-75.

———. 1977. *Dictatorships and "Ultimate" Decrees in the Early Roman Republic, 501-202 BC.* New York.

Kaser, M., and K. Hackl. 1996. *Das römische Zivilprozessrecht.* 2nd ed. Handbuch der Altertumswissenschaft 10.3.4. Munich.

Kaster, R. A. 1995. *Suetonius: De Grammaticis et Rhetoribus.* Oxford.

Kearsley, R. A. 1999. "A Bilingual Epitaph from Ephesos for the Son of a *Tabularius* in the *Familia Caesaris*," in P. Scherrer, H. Taeuber, and H. Thür (eds.) *Steine und Wege. Festschrift für D. Knibbe zum 65. Geburtstag.* Vienna: 77-88.

Keaveney, A. 1987. *Rome and the Unification of Italy.* Exeter.

Keay, S. 1990. "Processes in the Development of the Coastal Communities of Hispania Citerior in the Republican Period," in T. Blagg and M. Millett (eds.) *The Early Roman Empire in the West.* Oxford: 120-50.

Keppie, L. 1984. *The Making of the Roman Army.* Norman, Okla.

Kirby, V. 1976. "The Consular Tribunate and the Roman Oligarchy," in *Mundus Antiquus* 1: 24-29.

Kloft, H. 1977. *Prorogation und Außerordentliche Imperien 326-81 v. Chr.* Meisenheim am Glan.

Knapp, R. C. 1980. "Festus 262L and Praefecturae in Italy," *Athenaeum* 58: 14-38.

Konrad, C. F. 2004. *"Vellere signa,"* in C. F. Konrad (ed.) *Augusto Augurio: Rerum Humanarum et Divinarum Commentationes.* Stuttgart: 169-203.

Kromayer, J. 1888. *Die rechtliche Begründung des Prinzipats.* Marburg.

Kunkel, W. 1962. *Untersuchungen zur Entwicklung des römischen Kriminalverfahrens in vorsullanischer Zeit.* Munich.

———. 1973. *An Introduction to Roman Legal and Constitutional History* (J. M. Kelly trans.). Oxford.

Kunkel, W., and R. Wittmann. 1995. *Staatsordnung und Staatspraxis der römischen Republik.* Munich.

Künzl, E. 1988. "Romanisierung am Rhein-Germanische Fürstengräber als Dokument des römischen Einflusses nach der gescheiterten Expansionspolitik," in *Kaiser Augustus und die verlorene Republik.* Berlin: 546-605.

Lacey, W. K. 1974. "Octavian in the Senate, January 27 BC," *JRS* 64: 176-84.

———. 1996. *Augustus and the Principate: The Evolution of the System.* Trowbridge, Wiltshire.

Lange, C. H. 2009. *Res Publica Constituta: Actium, Apollo and the Accomplishment of the Triumviral Assignment.* Leiden.

Larsen, J. A. O. 1931. "Were Narbonensis and Gallia Cisalpina under One Governor from 67 to 65 BC?," *CPh* 26: 427-29.

Last, H. 1932. "The Wars of the Age of Marius," *CAH* 9: 102-57.

———. 1945. "The Servian Reforms," *JRS* 35: 30-48.

———. 1947. "Imperium Maius: A Note," *JRS* 37: 157-64.

Latte, K. 1934-36. *"Lex Curiata* und *coniuratio,"* *Nachr. Ges. d. Wiss. Gött.* 1: 59-77.

Lauria, M. 1930. *"Iurisdictio,"* *Studi Bonfante II,* 479-538. Milan.

Lazenby, J. F. 1998. *Hannibal's War: A Military History of the Second Punic War.* Norman, Okla.

———. 2004. "Rome and Carthage," in H. Flower (ed.) *The Cambridge Companion to the Roman Republic*. Cambridge: 224–40.

Lehmann, G. A. 1996. *"Römischer Tod" in Kolophon/Klaros: Neue Quellen zum Status der "freien" Polisstaaten an der Westküste Kleinasiens im Späten zweiten Jahrhundert v. Chr.* Göttingen.

Leifer, F. 1914. *Die Einheit des Gewaltgedankens im römischen Staatsrecht*. Munich.

Lendon, J. E. 1997. *Empire of Honour*. Oxford.

le Roux, P. 1984. "Pouvoir central et provinces," *Revue des Études Anciennes* 86: 31–53.

———. 1985. "Legal Fiction and Political Reform at Rome in the Early Second Century BC," *Gerión* 3: 411–22.

Lewis, R. G. 1991. *"Rechtsfrage II: Octavian's Powers in 32 BC," LCM* 16: 57–62.

Liebeschuetz, J. H. W. G. 1979. *Continuity and Change in Roman Religion*. Oxford.

Liebs, D. 1975. *Römisches Recht*. Göttingen.

———. 1976. "Römische Provinzialjurisprudenz," *ANRW* 2.15: 288–362.

Linderski, J. 1965. "Constitutional Aspects of the Consular Elections in 59 BC," *Historia* 14: 423–42.

———. 1979. *"Legibus praefecti mittebantur* (Mommsen and Festus 262, 5, 13 L)," *Historia* 28: 247–50.

———. 1986. "The Augural Law," *ANRW* 2.16: 2146–2312.

———. 1990a. "Roman Officers in the Year of Pydna," *AJPh* 111: 53–71.

———. 1990b. "The Auspices and the Struggle of the Orders," in W. Eder (ed.) *Staat und Staatlichkeit in der frühen römischen Republik*. Stuttgart: 34–48.

———. 1995. "Ambassadors Go to Rome," in E. Frezouls and A. Jacquemin (eds.) *Les relations internationales: Actes de Colloque de Strasbourg, 15–17 juin 1999*. Paris: 453–78.

Lintott, A. W. 1970. "The Tradition of Violence in the Annals of the Early Roman Republic," *Historia* 19: 12–29.

———. 1972. *"Provocatio* from the Struggle of the Orders to the Principate," *ANRW* 1.2: 226–67. Berlin and New York.

———. 1974. "Cicero and Milo," *JRS* 64: 62–78.

———. 1976. "Notes on the Roman Law Inscribed at Delphi and Cnidos," *ZPE* 20: 65–82.

———. 1981a. "What Was the 'Imperium Romanum?,'" *G&R* 28: 53–67.

———. 1981b. "The *Leges de Repetundis* and Associate Measures under the Republic," *ZSav* 98, 162–212.

———. 1992. *Judicial Reform and Land Reform in the Roman Republic*. Cambridge.

———. 1993. *Imperium Romanum*. London and New York.

———. 1999a. *The Constitution of the Roman Republic*. Oxford.

———. 1999b. *Violence in Republican Rome*. 2nd ed. Oxford.

Liou-Gille, B. 1993. "Le Pomerium," *Museum Helveticum* 50: 94–106.

———. 1997. "Les rois de Rome et la Ligue Latine: définitions et interprétations," *Latomus* 56: 729–64.

Loader, W. R. 1940. "Pompey's Command under the *Lex Gabinia*," *CR* 54: 134–36.

Loreto, L. 2011. "Roman Politics and Expansion, 241–219," in D. Hoyos (ed.) *A Companion to the Punic Wars*. Oxford: 184–203.

Lowenstein, K. 1973. *The Governance of Rome*. The Hague.

Luce, T. J. 1965. "The Dating of Livy's First Decade," *TAPA* 96: 209–40.

MacKay, Ch. S. 2004. *Ancient Rome: A Military and Political History*. Cambridge.

Magdelain, A. 1964a. "Auspicia ad patres redeunt," in M. Renard and R. Schilling (eds.) *Hommages à Jean Bayet*. Coll. Latomus 70. Brussels: 427–73.

———. 1964b. "Note sur la loi curiate et les auspices des magistrats," *RHD* 62: 198–203.

———. 1968. *Recherches sur l'"Imperium," la loi curiate et les auspices d'investiture*. Paris.

———. 1977a. "L'inauguration de l'urbs et l'imperium," *MEFRA* 89: 11–29.

———. 1977b. "Le Pomerium Archaïque et le Mundus," *Revue des Études Latines* 54: 71–109.

———. 1984. "Quirinus et le droit. Spolia opima, ius fetiale, ius Quiritium," *MEFRA* 96: 195–237.

———. 1986. "Le ius archaïque," *MEFRA* 98: 265–358.

———. 1987. "De la coercition capitale du magistrat supérieur au tribunal du people," *Labeo* 32: 139–66.

———. 1990. *Ius, imperium, auctoritas: Études de droit romain*. Rome.

Magie, D. 1905. *De Romanorum Iuris Publici Sacrique Vocabulis Sollemnibus in Graecum Sermonem Conversis*. Leipzig.

———. 1950. *Roman Rule in Asia Minor*. 2 vols. Princeton.

Mamoojee, A.-H. 1998. "Cicero's Choice of a Deputy in Cilicia," *Ancient History Bulletin* 12: 19–28.

Maróti, E. 1971. "On the Problem of M. Antonius Creticus' Imperium Infinitum," *Acta Antiqua* 19: 259–72.

Marshall, A. J. 1967. "Verres and Judicial Corruption," *CQ* 17: 408–13.

———. 1972. "The Lex Pompeia de provinciis (52 BC) and Cicero's Imperium in 51–50 BC: Constitutional Aspects," *ANRW* 1.1: 887–921. Berlin and London.

———. 1984. "Symbols and Showmanship in Roman Public Life: The Fasces," 38: 120–41.

Martini, R. 1969. *Ricerche in tema di editto provinciale*. Milan.

Mattern, S. P. 1999. *Rome and the Enemy*. Berkeley and Los Angeles.

Martin, J. 1970. "Die Provokation in der klassischen und späten Republik," *Hermes* 98: 72–96.

———. 1990. "Aspekte antiker Staatlichkeit," in W. Eder (ed.) *Staat und Staatlichkeit in der frühen römischen Republik*. Stuttgart: 220–32.

Mason, H. J. 1974. *Greek Terms for Roman Institutions*. Toronto.

McDonald, A. H. 1944. "Rome and the Italian Confederation (200–186 BC)," *JRS* 34: 11–33.

———. 1953. Review of *Magistrates of the Roman Republic* by T. Robert S. Broughton and Marcia L. Patteron, *JRS* 43: 142–45.

McFayden, D. 1921. "The Princeps and the Senatorial Provinces," *CPh* 16: 34–50.

———. 1928. "The Newly Discovered Cyrenaean Inscription and the Alleged Imperium Maius Proconsulare of Augustus," *CPh* 23: 388–93.

McGushin, P. 1977. *C. Sallustius Crispus, Bellum Catilinae: A Commentary*. Leiden.

Mellano, L. D. 1977. *Sui rapporti tra governatore provinciale e guidici locali alla luce delle Verrine*. Milan.

Ménager, L. R. 1980. "Systèmes onomastiques, structures familiales et classes sociales dans le monde gréco-Romain," *SDHI* 46: 147–235.

Meyer, E. 1924. *Kleine Schriften II*. Halle.

Meyer, E. A. 2006. "The Justice of the Roman Governor and the Performance of Prestige," in A. Kolb (ed.) *Herrschaftspraxis und Herrschaftstrukturen. Konzepte, Prinzipien und Strategien der Administration im römischen Kaiserreich. Akten der Tagung an der Universität Zürich 18–20. Oktober 2004.* Berlin: 167–80.

Meyer-Zwiffelhoffer, E. 2002. *Politikos Archein: Zum Regierungsstil der senatorischen Statthalter in den kaiserzeitlichen griechischen Provinzen.* Stuttgart.

Miles, G. B. 1995. *Livy: Reconstructing Early Rome.* Ithaca and London.

Millar, F. 1966. "The Emperor, the Senate and the Provinces," *JRS* 56: 156–66.

———. 1973. "Triumvirate and Principate," *JRS* 63: 50–67.

———. 1982. "Emperors, Frontiers and Foreign Relations, 31 BC to AD 378," *Britannia* 13: 1–23.

———. 1984a. "The Political Character of the Classical Roman Republic, 200–151 BC," *JRS* 74: 1–19.

———. 1984b. "State and Subject: The Impact of Monarchy," in F. Millar and E. Segal (eds.) *Caesar Augustus: Seven Aspects.* Oxford: 37–60.

———. 1986. "Government and Diplomacy in the Roman Empire during the First Three Centuries," *International History Review* 10: 345–77.

———. 1989a. "'Senatorial' Provinces: An Institutionalized Ghost," *Ancient World* 20: 93–97.

———. 1989b. "Political Power in Mid-Republican Rome: Curia or Comitium?," *JRS* 79: 138–50.

———. 1995. "Popular Politics at Rome," in I. Malkin and Z. W. Rubinsohn (eds.) *Leaders and Masses in the Roman World: Studies in Honour of Zvi Yavetz.* Tel Aviv: 91–113.

———. 1998. *The Crowd in Rome in the Late Republic.* Ann Arbor, Mich.

Miltner, F. 1952. "Cn. Pompeius Magnus," *RE* 21 (2): 2062–2213.

Mineo, B. 2011. "Principal Literary Sources for the Punic Wars (apart from Polybius)," in D. Hoyos (ed.) *A Companion to the Punic Wars.* Oxford: 111–28.

Mitchell, R. E. 1990. *Patricians and Plebeians.* Ithaca and London.

———. 2005. "The Definition of *patres* and *plebs*: An End to the Struggle of the Orders," in K. A. Raaflaub (ed.) *Social Struggles in Archaic Rome.* 2nd ed. Malden, Mass., Oxford, and Victoria: 128–67.

Mitchell, S. 1971. "Roman-Carthaginian Treaties: 306 and 279/8 BC," *Historia* 20: 633–55.

———. 1999. "The Administration of Roman Asia from 133 BC to AD 250," in W. Eck (ed.) *Lokale Autonomie und römische Ordnungsmacht in den kaiserzeitlichen Provinzen vom 1. bis 3. Jahrhundert.* Munich: 17–46.

Momigliano, A. 1963. "An Interim Report on the Origins of Rome," *JRS* 53: 95–121.

———. 1989. "The Origins of Rome," in *CAH* [2] 7.2: 52–112.

Mommsen, Th. 1887–88. *Römisches Staatsrecht.* 3rd ed. 3 vols. Leipzig.

Mommsen, Th., B. Demandt, and A. Demandt. 1992. *Römische Kaisergeschichte: Nach den Vorlesungs-Mitschriften von Sebastian und Paul Hensel 1882/86.* Munich.

Mora, F. 1999. *Fasti e schemi cronologici: la riorganizzazione annalistica del passato remoto romano.* Stuttgart.

Morgan, M. G. 1969. "Metellus Macedonicus and the Province Macedonia," *Historia* 18: 422–46.

Morstein-Marx, R. 2000. "*Res Publica Res Populi*," *SCI* 19: 224–33.

———. 2007. "Caesar's Alleged Fear of Prosecution and His *Ratio Absentis* in the Approach to the Civil War," *Historia* 56: 159–78.

Morstein-Marx, R., and N. Rosenstein. 2006. "The Transformation of the Republic," in N. Rosenstein and R. Morstein-Marx (eds.) *A Companion to the Roman Republic*. Oxford: 625–37.

Mousourakis, G. 2003. *The Historical and Institutional Context of Roman Law*. Hampshire.

———. 2007. *A Legal History of Rome*. London and New York.

Nedergaard, E. 2001. "Facts and Fiction about the Fasti Capitolini," *Analecta Romana* 27: 107–27.

Nicolet, C. 1980. *The World of the Citizen in Republican Rome*. Berkeley and Los Angeles.

———. 1992. "Autour de l'Imperium," *CGG* 3: 163–66.

Nicholls, J. J. 1956. "The Reform of the Comitia Centuriata," *AJPh* 77: 225–54.

———. 1967. "The Content of the Lex Curiata," *AJPh* 88: 257–78.

Nippel, W. 1984. "Policing Rome," *JRS* 74: 20–29.

———. 1995. *Public Order in Ancient Rome*. Cambridge.

Oakley, S. P. 1997–2004. *A Commentary on Livy: Books VI–X*. 4 vols. Oxford.

———. 2004. "The Early Republic," in H. Flower (ed.) *The Cambridge Companion to the Roman Republic*. Cambridge: 15–30.

Ogilvie, R. M. 1965. *A Commentary on Livy. Books 1–5*. Oxford.

———. 1969. *The Romans and Their Gods*. London.

———. 1976. *Early Rome and the Etruscans*. Trowbridge, Wiltshire.

Oost, S. I. 1955. "Cato Uticensis and the Annexation of Cyprus," *CPh* 50: 98–112.

———. 1963. "Cyrene, 96–74 BC," *CPh* 58: 11–25.

Östenberg, I. 2009. *Staging the World: Spoils, Captives, and Representations in the Roman Triumphal Procession*. Oxford.

Pallottino, M. 1991. *A History of Earliest Italy*. Ann Arbor, Mich.

Palmer, R. E. A. 1970 [2009]. *The Archaic Community of the Romans*. Cambridge.

Pareti, L. 1952. *Storia di Roma e del mondo romano, I*. Turin.

———. 1953. *Storia di Roma e del mondo romano, II*. Turin.

Patterson, J. 2000. *Political Life in the City of Rome*. London.

Payne, R. 1962. *The Roman Triumph*. London.

Pelling, C. B. R. 1996. "The Triumviral Period," *CAH*[2] 10: 1–69.

Phang, S. E. 2008. *Roman Military Service: Ideologies of Discipline in the Late Republic and Early Principate*. Cambridge.

Pina Polo, F. 2011. *The Consul at Rome*. Cambridge.

———. 2011. "Consuls as *curatores pacis deorum*," in H. Beck, A. Duplá, M. Jehne, and F. Pina Polo (eds.) *Consuls and the Res Publica: Holding High Office in the Roman Republic*. Cambridge: 97–115.

Pink, K. 1952. *The Triumviri Monetales and the Structure of the Coinage of the Roman Republic*. New York.

Pinsent, J. 1975. *Military Tribunes and Plebeian Consuls: The Fasti from 444 V to 342 V*. Wiesbaden.

Pittenger, M. R. P. 2008. *Contested Triumphs: Politics, Pageantry, and Performance in Livy's Republican Rome*. Berkeley, Los Angeles, and London.

Poe, J. P. 1984. "The Secular Games, the Aventine, and the Pomerium in the Campus Martius," *CQ* 3: 57–81.

Pohl, H. 1993. *Die römische Politik und die Piraterie im östlichen Mittelmeer vom 3. bis zum 1. Jh. v. Chr.* Berlin.

Polia, M. 2001. *Imperium: Origine e funzione del potere regale nella Roma archaica.* Rimini.

Poma, G. 1990. "Considerazioni sul processo di formazione della tradizione annalistica: il caso della sedizione militare del 342 a. C.," in W. Eder (ed.) *Staat und Staatlichkeit in der frühen römischen Republik.* Stuttgart: 139–57.

Potter, D. 1996a. "Performance, Power and Justice in the High Empire," in W. J. Slater (ed.) *Roman Theater and Society,* 129–59. Ann Arbor, Mich.

———. 1996b. "Palmyra and Rome: Odaenathus' Titulature and the Use of *Imperium Maius*," *ZPE* 113: 271–85.

Prag, J. 2011. "Provincial Governors and Auxiliary Soldiers," in N. Barrandon and F. Kirbihler (eds.) *Les gouverners et les provinciaux sous la République romaine.* Rennes: 15–28.

———. 2013. "Sicily and Sardinia-Corsica: The First Provinces," in D. Hoyos (ed.) *A Companion to Roman Imperialism.* Leiden and Boston: 53–66.

Pritchard, R. T. 1971. "Gaius Verres and the Sicilian Farmers," *Historia* 20: 224–38.

Purcell, N. 1990 [2002]. "The Creation of the Provincial Landscape: the Roman Impact on Cisalpine Gaul," in T. Blagg and M. Millet (eds.) *The Early Roman Empire in the West.* Oxford: 7–29.

Raaflaub, K. A. 1974. *Dignitatis contentio: Studien zur Motivation und politischen Taktik im Bürgerkrieg zwischen Caesar und Pompeius.* Vestigia 20. Munich.

———. 2005a. "The Conflict of the Orders in Archaic Rome: A Comprehensive and Comparative Approach," in K. A. Raaflaub (ed.) *Social Struggles in Archaic Rome.* 2nd ed. Malden, Mass., Oxford, and Victoria: 1–46.

———. 2005b. "From Protection and Defense to Offense and Participation: Stages in the Conflict of the Orders," in K. A. Raaflaub (ed.) *Social Struggles in Archaic Rome.* 2nd ed. Malden, Mass., Oxford, and Victoria: 185–222.

———. 2010. "Between Myth and History: Rome's Rise from Village to Empire (the Eighth Century to 264)," in N. S. Rosenstein and R. Morstein-Marx (eds.) *A Companion to the Roman Republic.* Oxford: 125–46.

Raaflaub, K. A., and L. J. Samons II. 1990. "Opposition to Augustus," in K. A. Raaflaub and M. Toher (eds.) *Between Republic and Empire.* Berkeley, Los Angeles, and London: 417–54.

Raaflaub, K. A., and M. Toher (eds.). 1990. *Between Republic and Empire.* Berkeley, Los Angeles, and London.

Rasmussen, S. W. 2003. *Public Portents in Republican Rome.* Rome.

Rauh, N. K., R. F. Townsend, M. Hoff, and L. Wandsnider. 2000. "Pirates in the Bay of Pamphylia: An Archaeological Inquiry," in G. J. Oliver, R. Brock, T. J. Cornell, and S. Hodkinson (eds.) *The Sea in Antiquity.* BAR International Series 899. Oxford: 151–77.

Raven, S. 1993. *Rome in Africa.* London and New York.

Rawlings, L. 1999. "Condottieri and Clansmen: Early Italian Raiding, Warfare and the State," in K. Hopwood (ed.) *Organised Crime in Antiquity.* London: 97–127.

Rawson, E. 1971. "Prodigy Lists and the Use of the Annales Maximi," *CQ* 21: 158–69.

———. 1990. "The Antiquarian Tradition: Spoils and Representations of Foreign Armour," in W. Eder (ed.) *Staat und Staatlichkeit in der frühen römischen Republik.* Stuttgart: 158–73.

Reinhold, M. 1988. *From Republic to Principate: An Historical Commentary on Cassius Dio's Roman History Books 49–52 (36–29 BC).* Atlanta.

Reynolds, J. 1982. *Aphrodisias and Rome*. London.

Rich, J. W. 1983. "The Supposed Manpower Shortage of the Later Second Century BC," *Historia* 32: 287–331.

———. 1988. Review of *Hispaniae: Spain and the Development of Roman Imperialism, 218–82 BC* by J. S. Richardson, *JRS* 78: 212–14.

———. 1993. "Fear, Greed, and Glory: The Causes of Roman War-Making in the Middle Republic," in J. Rich and G. Shipley (eds.) *War and Society in the Roman World*. London and New York: 38–68.

———. 1996. "Augustus and the Spolia Opima," *Chiron* 26: 85–127.

———. 1997. "Structuring Roman History: The Consular Year and the Roman Historical Tradition," *Histos* 1 (= *Histos* 5 [2011] 1–43).

———. 1999. "Drusus and the Spolia Opima," *CQ* 49: 544–55.

———. 2007. "Warfare and the Army in Early Rome," in P. Erdkamp (ed.) *A Companion to the Roman Army*. Malden, Mass., Oxford, and Victoria: 7–23.

———. 2011. "The Fetiales and Roman International Relations," in J. Richardson and F. Santangelo (eds.) *Priests and State in the Roman World*. Stuttgart: 187–242.

Richard, J.-C. 1978. *Les origines de la plebe romaine: essai sur la formation du dualisme patricio-plébéien*. Rome and Paris.

———. 1982. "Praetor collega consulis est: contribution à l'histoire de la préture," *Revue de Philologie* 56: 19–31.

———. 1990. "Historiographie et histoire: l'expédition des Fabii à la Crémère," in W. Eder (ed.) *Staat und Staatlichkeit in der frühen römischen Republik*. Stuttgart: 174–99.

———. 2001. "Annalistique et fastes: l'histoire d'une invention?," *Rev. étud. lat.* 79: 19–25.

———. 2005. "Patricians and Plebeians: The Origins of a Social Dichotomy," in K. A. Raaflaub (ed.) *Social Struggles in Archaic Rome*. 2nd ed. Malden, Mass., Oxford, and Victoria: 107–28.

Richardson, J. S. 1975. "The Triumph, the Praetors and the Senate in the Early Second Century BC," *JRS* 65: 50–63.

———. 1976a. *Roman Provincial Administration, 227 BC to AD 117*. London.

———. 1976b. "The Spanish Mines and the Development of Provincial Taxation in the Second Century BC," *JRS* 66: 139–52.

———. 1979. "Ea Quae Fiunt in Provinciis," *JRS* 69: 156–61.

———. 1983. "The *Tabula Contrebiensis*: Roman Law in Spain in the Early First Century BC," *JRS* 73: 33–41.

———. 1986. *Hispaniae: Spain and the Development of Roman Imperialism, 218–82 BC*. Cambridge.

———. 1991. "Imperium Romanum: Empire and the Language of Power," *JRS* 81: 1–9.

———. 1994. "The Administration of the Empire," *CAH*² 9, 564–598. Cambridge.

———. 1996a. *The Romans in Spain*. Oxford.

———. 1996b. "The Reception of Roman Law in the West: The Epigraphic Evidence," in E. Hermon (ed.) *Pouvoir et Imperium*. Naples: 65–75.

———. 2008. *The Language of Empire*. Cambridge.

———. 2011a. "Spain, Africa, and Rome after Carthage," in D. Hoyos (ed.) *A Companion to the Punic Wars*. Oxford: 467–82.

———. 2011b. "*Fines Provinciae*," in O. Hekster and T. Kaizer (eds.) *Frontiers in the Roman*

World. Proceedings of the Ninth Workshop of the International Network Impact of Empire (Durham, 16–19 April 2009). Leiden and Boston: 1–11.

Ridley, R. T. 1979. "The Origin of the Roman Dictatorship: An Overlooked Opinion," *RhM* 122: 303–9.

———. 1981. "The Extraordinary Commands of the Late Republic: A Matter of Definition," *Historia* 30: 280–97.

———. 1983. "Falsi triumphi, plures consulares," *Latomus* 43: 372–82.

———. 1986. "The 'Consular Tribunate': The Testimony of Livy," *Klio* 68: 444–65.

———. 2000. "Livy and the Hannibalic War," in C. Bruun (ed.) *The Roman Middle Republic: Politics, Religion, and Historiography, c. 400–133 BC.* Rome: 13–40.

Rigsby, K. J. 1988. "Provincia Asia," *TAPA* 118: 123–53.

Ritterling, E. 1927. "Military Forces in the Senatorial Provinces," *JRS* 17: 28–32.

Robert, J., and L. Robert. 1989. *Claros I: Décrets hellénistiques.* Paris.

Robinson, O. F. 1995. *The Criminal Law of Ancient Rome.* Baltimore.

———. 1997. *The Sources of Roman Law.* London and New York.

Roddaz, J.-M. 1992. "Imperium: nature et compétences à la fin de la République et au début de l'Empire," *CGG* 3: 189–211.

———. 1996. "Les Triumvirs et les provinces," in E. Hermon (ed.) *Pouvoir et Imperium.* Naples: 77–96.

———. 2003. "La Métamorphose: d'Octavien a Auguste," in S. F. d'Espèrey, V. Fromentin, S. Gotteland and J.-M. Roddaz (eds.) *Fondements et crises du pouvoir.* Paris: 397–418.

Rödl, B. 1968. *Das senatus consultum ultimum und der Tod der Gracchen.* Bonn.

Rogers, R. S. 1959. "Treason in the Early Empire," *JRS* 49: 90–94.

Rosenstein, N. 1986. "'*Imperatores Victi*': The Case of C. Hostilius Mancinus," *Classical Antiquity* 5: 230–52.

———. 1990. *Imperatores Victi: Military Defeat and Aristocratic Competition in the Middle and Late Republic.* Berkeley, Los Angeles, and Oxford.

———. 1995. "Sorting out the Lot in Republican Rome," *AJPh* 116: 43–75.

———. 2009. "General and Imperialist," in M. Griffin (ed.) *A Companion to Julius Caesar.* Malden, Mass., and Oxford: 85–99.

———. 2011. "War, Wealth and Consuls," in H. Beck, A. Duplá, M. Jehne, and F. Pina Polo (eds.) *Consuls and the* Res Publica*: Holding High Office in the Roman Republic.* Cambridge: 133–58.

———. 2012. *Rome and the Mediterranean 290 to 146 BC: The Imperial Republic.* Edinburgh.

Rowe, G. 2002. *Princes and Political Cultures: The New Tiberian Senatorial Decrees.* Ann Arbor, Mich.

Rüpke, J. 1990. *Domi militiae: Die religiöse Konstruktion des Krieges.* Stuttgart.

———. 1993. "Livius, Priesternamen, und die *Annales Maximi*," *Klio* 75: 155–79.

———. 1995a. "Fasti: Quellen oder Produkte römischer Geschichtsschreibung?," *Klio* 77: 184–202.

———. 1995b. *Kalender und Öffentlichkeit: Die Geschichte der Repräsentation und religiösen Qualifikation von Zeit in Rome.* Berlin.

———. 2004. "Roman Religion," in H. Flower (eds.) *The Cambridge Companion to the Roman Republic.* Cambridge: 179–98.

Ryan, F. X. 1998. *Rank and Participation in the Republican Senate.* Stuttgart.

Salmon, E. T. 1956. "The Evolution of Augustus' Principate," *Historia* 5: 456–78.

———. 1967. *Samnium and the Samnites*. Cambridge.

———. 1970. *Roman Colonization under the Republic*. Ithaca, N.Y.

———. 1982. *The Making of Roman Italy*. London.

Sandberg, K. 2000. "Tribunician and Non-Tribunician Legislation in Mid-Republican Rome," in C. Bruun (ed.) *The Roman Middle Republic: Politics, Religion, and Historiography, c. 400–133 BC*. Rome: 121–40.

———. 2001. *Magistrates and Assemblies: A Study of Legislative Practice in Republican Rome*. Rome.

Santangelo, F. 2007. *Sulla, the Elites and the Empire: A Study of Roman Policies in Italy and the Greek East*. Leiden.

Schäfer, T. 1989. *Imperii Insignia: Sella curulis und Fasces; Zur Repräsentation römischer Magistrate*. Mainz.

Scheid J. 2003. *An Introduction to Roman Religion*. Trans. J. Lloyd. Bloomington, Ind.

Schiavone, A. 2012. *The Invention of Law in the West*. Cambridge, Mass., and London.

Schiller, A. A. 1978. *Roman Law: Mechanisms of Development*. The Hague, Paris, and New York.

Schleussner, B. 1978. *Die Legaten der römischen Republik*. Munich.

Scullard, H. H. 1981. *Festivals and Ceremonies of the Roman Republic*. Ithaca, N.Y.

———. 1982. *From the Gracchi to Nero*. 5th ed. London.

Schulz, R. 1997. *Herrschaft und Regierung: Roms Regiment in den Provinzen in der Zeit der Republik*. Paderborn.

Seager, R. 2002. *Pompey the Great*. Oxford.

Sealey, R. 1959. "Consular Tribunes Once More," *Latomus* 18: 521–30.

Serrati, J. 2000a. "The Coming of the Romans: Sicily from the Fourth to the First Century BC," in C. Smith and J. Serrati (eds.) *Sicily from Aeneas to Augustus*. Edinburgh: 109–14.

———. 2000b. "Garrisons and Grain: Sicily between the Punic Wars," in C. Smith and J. Serrati (eds.) *Sicily from Aeneas to Augustus*. Edinburgh: 115–33.

———. 2011. "The Rise of Rome to 264 BC," in D. Hoyos (ed.) *A Companion to the Punic Wars*. Oxford: 11–27.

Sherk, R. K. 1955. "The *Inermes Provinciae* of Asia Minor," *AJP* 76: 400–413.

———. 1957. "Roman Imperial Troops in Macedonia and Achaea," *AJP* 78: 52–62.

Sherwin-White, A. N. 1972. "The Date of the *Lex Repetundarum* and Its Consequences," *JRS* 62: 83–99.

———. 1973. *The Roman Citizenship*. Oxford.

———. 1976. "Rome, Pamphylia and Cilicia, 133–70 BC," *JRS* 66: 1–14.

———. 1982. "The *Lex Repetundarum* and the Political Ideas of Gaius Gracchus," *JRS* 72: 18–31.

———. 1984. *Roman Foreign Policy in the East: 168 BC to AD 1*. London.

Siber, H. 1940. *Das Führeramt des Augustus*. Leipzig.

Simón, F. M. 2011. "The *Feriae Latinae* as Religious Legitimation of the Consuls' *Imperium*," in H. Beck, A. Duplá, M. Jehne, and F. Pina Polo (eds.) *Consuls and the Res Publica: Holding High Office in the Roman Republic*. Cambridge: 116–32.

Smith, C. J. 1996. *Early Rome and Latium: Economy and Society, c. 1000 to 500 BC*. Oxford.

———. 2006. *The Roman Clan*. Cambridge.

————. 2011. "The Magistrates of the Early Roman Republic," in H. Beck, A. Duplá, M. Jehne, and F. Pina Polo (eds.) *Consuls and the Res Publica: Holding High Office in the Roman Republic.* Cambridge: 19–40.

Smith, R. E. 1960. "Pompey's Conduct in 80 and 77 BC," *Phoenix* 14: 1–13.

Sohlberg, D. 1991. "Militärtribunen und verwandte Probleme der frühen römischen Republik," *Historia* 40: 257–74.

Southern, P. 2007. *The Roman Army: A Social and Institutional History.* Oxford.

————. 2013. *Augustus.* 2nd ed. London and New York.

Spaeth, B. S. 1996. *The Roman Goddess Ceres.* Austin.

Staedler, E. 1942a. "Das römisch-rechtliche Element in den Augusteischen Regesten," *ZRG* 62: 82–121.

————. 1942b. "Über Rechtsnatur und Rechtsinhalt der Augusteischen Regesten," *ZRG* 61: 77–122.

Staveley, E. S. 1953. "The Significance of the Consular Tribunate," *JRS* 43: 30–46.

————. 1955. "*Provocatio* during the Fifth and Fourth Centuries BC," *Historia* 3: 412–28.

————. 1956. "The Constitution of the Roman Republic, 1940–1954," *Historia* 5: 74–122.

————. 1963. "The Fasces and Imperium Maius," *Historia* 12: 458–83.

Stephenson, A. 1992. *A History of Roman Law.* Littleton, Colo.

Stevenson, G. H. 1939. *Roman Provincial Administration.* Oxford.

Stewart, R. 1998. *Public Office in Early Rome.* Ann Arbor, Mich.

Stibbe, C. M., G. Colonna, C. de Simone, and H. S. Versnel. 1980. *Lapis Satricanus.* The Hague.

Stockton, D. 1971. *Cicero: A Political Biography.* Oxford.

————. 1979. *The Gracchi.* Oxford.

Stone, M. 2013. "The Genesis of Roman Imperialism," in D. Hoyos (ed.) *A Companion to Roman Imperialism.* Leiden: 23–38.

Sumi, G. S. 2005. *Ceremony and Power: Performing Politics in Rome between Republic and Empire.* Ann Arbor, Mich.

————. 2011. "Ceremony and the Emergence of Court Society in the Augustan Principate," *AJPh* 132: 81–102.

Sumner, G. V. 1970. "Proconsuls and Provinciae in Spain, 218/7–196/5 BC," *Arethusa* 3: 85–102.

————. 1977. "Notes on Provinciae in Spain (197–133 BC)," *CPh* 72: 126–30.

————. 1978. "Governors of Asia in the Nineties BC," *GRBS* 19: 147–53.

————. 1982. "The Coitio of 54 BC, or Waiting for Caesar," *HSCP* 86: 133–39.

Suolahti, J. 1955. *The Junior Officers of the Roman Army in the Republican Period.* Helsinki.

Syme, R. 1934. "Lentulus and the Origin of Moesia," *JRS* 24: 113–37.

————. 1938. "The Allegiance of Labienus," *JRS* 28: 113–25.

————. 1939. *The Roman Revolution.* Oxford.

————. 1946. Review of *Das Führeramt des Augustus* by H. Siber, *JRS* 36: 149–58.

————. 1986. *The Augustan Aristocracy.* Oxford.

Szramkiewicz, R. 1974. *Les Gouverneurs de province à l'époque Augustéenne.* 2 vols. Paris.

Takács, S. A. 2008. *Vestal Virgins, Sibyls, and Matrons.* Austin.

Talbert, R. J. A. 1984a. "Augustus and the Senate," *G&R* 31: 55–63.

————. 1984b. *The Senate of Imperial Rome.* Princeton.

———. 1985. *Atlas of Classical History*. London and New York.

———. 2004. "Rome's Provinces as Framework for World-View," in L. de Ligt, E. A. Hemelrijk, and H. W. Singor (eds.) *Roman Rule and Civic Life: Local and Regional Perspectives*. Amsterdam: 21–37.

Taylor, L. R. 1946. "The Date of the Capitoline Fasti," *CPh* 41: 1–11.

———. 1949. *Party Politics in the Age of Caesar*. Berkeley, Los Angeles, and London.

———. 1950. "Annals of the Roman Consulship on the Arch of Augustus," *TAPA* 94: 511–16.

———. 1960. *The Voting Districts of the Roman Republic*. Rome.

———. 1966. *Roman Voting Assemblies*. Ann Arbor, Mich.

Taylor, L. R., and T. R. S. Broughton. 1949. "The Order of the Two Consuls' Names in the Yearly Lists," *MAAR* 19: 3–14.

———. 1968. "The Order of the Consuls' Names in Official Republican Lists," *Historia* 17: 166–72.

Taylor, R. 2000. "Watching the Skies: Janus, Auspication, and the Shrine in the Roman Forum," *Memoirs of the American Academy of Rome* 45: 1–40.

Tellegen-Couperus, O. 2001. "The So-Called *Consilium* of the Praetor and the Development of Roman Law," *Legal History Review* 69: 11–20.

———. 2006. "Pontiff, Praetor, and *Iurisdictio* in the Roman Republic," *Legal History Review* 74: 31–44.

Thiel, J. H. 1954. *A History of Roman Sea-Power before the Second Punic War*. Amsterdam.

Thomasson, B. E. 1991. *Legatus: Beiträge zur römischen Verwaltungsgeschichte*. Stockholm.

Thompson, L. A. 1962. "The Relationship between Provincial Quaestors and Their Commanders-in-Chief," *Historia* 11: 339–55.

Torelli, M. 1968. "Il Donario di M. Fulvio Flacco nell' Area Sacra di S. Omobono," *Quad. Ist. Top. Ant. Univ. Roma* 5: 71–76.

———. 1974–75. "Tre studi di storia etrusca," *DdA* 8: 3–78.

———. 1989. "Archaic Rome between Latium and Etruria," in *CAH*² 7.1: 30–51.

———. 2000. "*C. Genucio(s) Clousin(s) prai(fectos)*. La fondazione della praefectura Caeritum," in C. Bruun (ed.) *The Roman Middle Republic: Politics, Religion, and Historiography, c. 400–133 BC*. Rome: 141–76.

Turpin, W. 1994. "Res Gestae 34.1 and the Settlement of 27 BC," *CQ* 44: 427–37.

Ungern-Sternberg, J. von. 1970. *Untersuchungen zum spätrepublikanischen Notstandsrecht: Senatus consultum ultimum und hostis-Erklärung*. Munich.

———. 1975. *Capua im zweiten punischen Krieg: Untersuchungen zur römischen Annalistik*. Munich.

———. 1988. "Überlegungen zur frühen römischen Überlieferung im Lichte der Oral-Tradition-Forschung," in J. von Ungern-Sternberg and H. Reinau (eds.) *Vergangenheit in mündlicher Überlieferung*. Stuttgart: 237–65.

———. 1990. "Die Wahrnehmung des 'Ständekampfes' in der römischen Geschichtsschreibung," in W. Eder (ed.) *Staat und Staatlichkeit in der frühen römischen Republik*. Stuttgart: 92–102.

———. 2000. "Eine Katastrophe wird verarbeitet: Die Gallier in Rom," in C. Bruun (ed.) *The Roman Middle Republic*. Rome: 207–22.

———. 2004. "The Crisis of the Republic," in H. Flower (ed.) *The Cambridge Companion to the Roman Republic*. Cambridge: 89–112.

———. 2005. "The Formation of the 'Annalistic Tradition': The Example of the Decemvirate," in K. A. Raaflaub (ed.) *Social Struggles in Archaic Rome*. 2nd ed. Malden, Mass., Oxford, and Victoria: 75–97.

———. 2006. *Römische Studien: Geschichtsbewußtsein, Zeitalter der Gracchen, Krise der Republik*. Leipzig.

Urso, G. 2011. "The Origin of the Consulship in Cassius Dio's *Roman History*," in H. Beck, A. Duplá, M. Jehne, and F. Pina Polo (eds.) *Consuls and the* Res Publica: *Holding High Office in the Roman Republic*. Cambridge: 41–60.

Valgaeren, J. H. 2012. "The Jurisdiction of the Pontiffs at the End of the Fourth Century BC," in O. Tellegen-Couperus (ed.) *Law and Religion in the Roman Republic*. Leiden and Boston: 107–18.

Valgiglio, E. 1956. *Silla e la crisi repubblicana*. Florence.

Vanderspoel, J. 2010. "*Provincia Macedonia*," in J. Roisman and I. Worthington (eds.) *A Companion to Ancient Macedonia*. Oxford: 251–75.

van Der Vliet, E. Ch.-L. 1990. "Early Rome and the Early State," in W. Eder (ed.) *Staat und Staatlichkeit in der frühen römischen Republik*. Stuttgart: 233–57.

Van Sickle, J. 1987. "The Elogia of the Cornelii Scipiones and the Origin of Epigram at Rome," *AJPh* 108: 41–55.

Vansina, J. 1985. *Oral Tradition as History*. Madison, Wisc.

Verbrugghe, G. P. 1972. "Sicily 210–70 BC: Livy, Cicero and Diodorus," *TAPA* 103: 535–59.

Versnel, H. S. 1970. *Triumphus: An Inquiry into the Origin, Development and Meaning of the Roman Triumph*. Leiden.

———. 1980. "Historical Implications," in C. M. Stibbe, G. Colonna, C. de Simone, and H. S. Versnel (eds.) *Lapis Satricanus*. The Hague: 95–150.

———. 2006. "Red (Herring?) Comments on a New Theory concerning the Origin of the Triumph," *Numen* 53: 290–326.

Vervaet, F. 2004. "The *lex Valeria* and Sulla's Empowerment as Dictator (82–79 BCE)," *CCGG* 15: 37–84.

———. 2006a. "The Scope of the *lex Sempronia* concerning the Assignment of the Consular Provinces (123 BCE)," *Athenaeum* 94: 625–54.

———. 2006b. "The Official Position of Cn. Pompeius in 49 and 48 BCE," *Latomus* 65: 928–53.

———. 2008. "The Secret History: The Official Position of Imperator Caesar Divi Filius from 31 to 27 BCE," *Anc. Soc.* 40: 79–152.

———. 2009. "Pompeius' Career from 79 to 70 BCE: Constitutional, Political and Historical Considerations," *Klio* 91: 406–34.

———. 2011. "Reducing Senatorial Control over Provincial Commanders: A Forgotten Gabinian Law of 67 BCE," in O. Hekster and T. Kaizer (eds.) *Frontiers in the Roman World. Proceedings of the Ninth Workshop of the International Network Impact of Empire (Durham, 16–19 April 2009)*. Leiden and Boston: 265–90.

———. 2012. "The Monopolisation of the *Summum Imperium Auspiciumque* from Cornelius Sulla Felix to Imperator Caesar (82–44 BCE)," in Y. Rivière (ed.) *Des Réformes Augustéennes*. École Francaise de Rome. Rome: 123–47.

Vishnia, R. F. 1996. *State, Society and Popular Leaders in Mid-Republican Rome, 241–167 BC*. London.

von Fritz, K. 1950. "The Reorganisation of the Roman Government in 366 BC," *Historia* 1: 3–44.

von Lübtow, U. 1952. "Die *Lex curiata de Imperio*," *ZRG* 69: 154–71.

Wachter, R. 1987. *Altlateinische Inschriften. Sprachliche und epigraphische Untersuchungen zu den Dokumenten bis etwa 150 v. Chr.* Bern and Frankfurt.

Walbank, F. W. 1957–79. *A Historical Commentary on Polybius.* 3 vols. Oxford.

Watson, A. 1970. "The Development of the Praetor's Edict," *JRS* 60: 105–19.

———. 1972. "Roman Private Law and the *Leges Regiae*," *JRS* 62: 100–105.

———. 1993. *International Law in Archaic Rome: War and Religion.* Baltimore and London.

Weinrib, E. J. 1968. "The Prosecution of Roman Magistrates," *Phoenix* 22: 32–56.

Werner, R. 1963. *Der Beginn der römischen Republik: Historisch-chronologische Untersuchungen über die Anfangszeit der libera res publica.* Munich and Vienna.

Wesch-Klein, G. 2008. *Provincia: Okkupation und Verwaltung der Provinzen des Imperium Romanum von der Inbesitznahme Siziliens bis auf Diokletian.* Zurich and Münster.

Wieacker, F. 1988. *Römische Rechtsgeschichte* I. Munich.

Willems, P. 1880. *Le droit public romain depuis la fondation de Rome jusqu'á Justinien.* Paris and Bonn.

Williamson, C. 1990. "The Roman Aristocracy and Positive Law," *CPh* 4: 266–76.

———. 2005. *The Laws of the Roman People.* Ann Arbor, Mich.

Wilson, A. J. N. 1966. *Emigration from Italy in the Republican Age of Rome.* Manchester.

Wiseman, T. P. 1983. "The Wife and Children of Romulus," *CQ* 33: 445–52.

———. 1989. "Roman Legend and Oral Tradition," *JRS* 79: 129–37.

———. 1994. "The Senate and the *Populares*, 69–60 BC," *CAH*² 9: 327–67.

———. 1995. *Remus: A Roman Myth.* Cambridge.

———. 1998. *Roman Drama and Roman History.* Exeter.

Woodman, A. J. 1977. *Velleius Paterculus: The Tiberian Narrative (2.94–131).* Cambridge.

Woolf, G. 1993. "Roman Peace," in J. Rich (ed.) *War and Society in the Roman World.* London: 171–94.

Wörrle, M. 1988. *Stadt und Fest im kaiserzeitlichen Kleinasien. Studien zu einer agonistischen Stiftung aus Oinoanda.* Munich.

Yakobson, A. 1999. *Elections and Electioneering in Rome: A Study in the Political System of the Late Republic.* Stuttgart.

Yavetz, Z. 1991. "Towards a Further Step into the Study of Roman Imperialism," in *CEA* 26: 3–22.

Ziolkowski, A. 1992. *The Temples of Mid-Republican Rome and Their Historical and Topographical Context.* Rome.

———. 2011. "The Capitol and the 'Auspices of Departure,'" in S. Rucinski, C. Balbuza, and C. Królczyk (eds.) *Studia Lesco Mrozewicz.* Poznan: 465–71.

Index

Chalcis, 278

Cilicia (Roman Province), 108, 127, 132–33, 134 (n. 9), 139, 254, 270 (n. 118), 286 (n. 147), 287, 290 (n. 155), 310–11, 316–17, 323, 354, 364, 379

Cimbri, 125, 150 (n. 68, 157), 216, 287–88, 313 (n. 37), 318

Citizenship, Roman, 51, 235, 238 (n. 9), 241, 243, 265, 274–75, 277, 294, 300 (n. 6), 378

Civitas foederata, 241

Civitas foedere immunis ac libera, 241

Claudia (vestal virgin) (143 BC), 104

Claudius Caecus, Ap. (91) (cos. 307, 296 BC), 147–48, 186 (n. 12)

Claudius Crassinus Inregillensis Sabinus, Ap. (123) (cos. 471, 451 BC), 83, 159

Claudius Marcellus, C. (214) (pr. 80 BC), 228 (n. 116)

Claudius Marcellus, M. (220) (cos. 222, 215, 214, 210, 208 BC), 82 (n. 120), 112, 125 (n. 260), 135 (n. 16), 147, 186 (n. 12), 198, 221–22, 224, 225 (n. 107), 276

Claudius Marcellus, M. (229) (cos. 51 BC), 288

Claudius Nero, C. (246) (cos. 207 BC), 139–40, 146–47, 198, 263 (n. 94)

Claudius Nero, C. (247) (pr. 81 BC), 228 (n. 116)

Claudius Nero, Ti. (251) (pr. 178 BC), 229 (n. 123)

Claudius Pulcher, Ap. (293) (cos. 212 BC), 198

Claudius Pulcher, Ap. (295) (cos. 143 BC), 104, 113 (n. 223)

Claudius Pulcher, Ap. (297) (cos. 54 BC), 74, 75 (n. 95), 107–9, 270 (n. 118)

Claudius Pulcher, C. (300) (cos. 177 BC), 109–10

Claudius Pulcher, P. (304) (cos. 249 BC), 81 (n. 114)

Clodius Pulcher, P. (48) (aed. 56 BC), 74, 107, 122, 134 (n. 12)

Coercitio, 82 (n. 122), 88, 99–101, 107, 117–18, 168

Colony, 96, 235–36, 238–39, 241, 243–44, 250, 254, 312, 362, 378

Colophon, 279

Comitia calata, 53, 75

Comitia centuriata, 24, 36 (n. 94), 39–40, 49 (n. 8), 50, 53, 55, 70–71, 75–78, 83, 105–6, 109 (n. 207), 152, 186, 209, 217, 304 (n. 15)

Comitia curiata, 36, 38, 39, 40 (n. 104), 53, 71–78, 92 (n. 151), 106–7, 215, 226, 334, 376

Comitia tributa, 24, 55, 71, 76, 78, 106, 134, 278, 348 (n. 9), 351

Commagene, 286 (n. 147), 311

Concilium plebis, 36 (n. 94), 37 (n. 96), 55, 64, 135

Conflict of the orders, 37–38, 88 (n. 138), 123, 183

Consul/consulship: not (originally) civilian magistrates, 18–20, 31–44; collegiality with praetors, 2, 116, 184–209, 230–31, 247, 277, 284, 289, 341–42; developed from praetorship, 185–89, 209, 230, 232, 247, 255–63, 378; elections of, 30, 34, 38–43, 69, 71–78, 82–83, 106, 184, 186 (n. 10), 190–91, 192 (n. 28), 260, 298–99, 343, 375; liable to arrest in Rome, 102–3, 121, 128, 136 (n. 20), 138; originally called praetors, 2, 15, 19 (n. 35), 20, 144, 184; seniority to praetors traditional rather than legal, 68, 183, 185–92, 201, 209, 223, 230–31, 234, 236, 247, 255–63, 296, 313, 377, 379–80

Cornelius, P. (42) (pr. 234 BC), 258 (n. 75)

Cornelius Arvina, P. (66) (cos. 306 BC), 147

Cornelius Blasio, Cn. (74) (pr. 194 BC), 223 (n. 106)

Cornelius Cethegus, C. (88) (cos. 197 BC), 149–50, 173, 223 (n. 106), 253 (n. 58)

Cornelius Cethegus, M. (92) (cos. 204 BC), 200, 208

Cornelius Cethegus, P. (96) (pr. 184 BC), 259

Cornelius Cossus, A. (112) (cos. 428 BC), 41 (n. 110)

Cornelius Cossus Arvina, A. (122) (cos. 343 BC), 164

Cornelius Dolabella, Cn. (135) (pr. 81 BC), 139

Cornelius Dolabella, P. (141) (cos. suff. 44 BC), 140

Cornelius Lentulus, Cn. (176) (cos. 201 BC), 298 (n. 4)

Cornelius Lentulus, L. (188) (cos. 199 BC), 222 (n. 105), 225 (n. 108)

Cornelius Lentulus Sura, P. (240) (cos. 71 BC), 122

Cornelius Scipio, Cn. (345) (cos. 222 BC), 160–61, 221–22, 224, 227, 248, 333 (n. 79)

Cornelius Scipio, P. (330) (cos. 218 BC), 139, 160–61, 200–201, 221–22, 227, 248, 333 (n. 79)

Cornelius Scipio Aemilianus, P. (335) (cos. 147, 134 BC), 134 (n. 12), 285 (n. 145), 304 (n. 15)

Cornelius Scipio Africanus, P. (336) (cos. 205, 194), 83, 125 (n. 260), 134 (nn. 9, 11, 12), 136, 139–40, 161 (n. 98), 199, 203, 211 (n. 75), 213, 222, 225, 249–50, 251 (n. 53), 267, 285, 298 (n. 4), 304 (n. 13), 308, 313 (n. 38)

Cornelius Scipio Asiaticus, L. (337) (cos. 190 BC), 285

Cornelius Scipio Barbatus, L. (343) (cos. 298 BC), 41, 188 (n. 17), 217

Cornelius Scipio Nasica, P. (350) (cos. 191 BC), 140, 229 (n. 120)

Cornelius Sulla, L. (392) (cos. 88, 80 BC), 81, 82 (n. 119), 108 (n. 203), 119 (n. 239), 124, 156, 162 (n. 100), 163, 179–80, 237, 259 (n. 82), 286 (nn. 147, 148), 292 (n. 162), 309–10, 313–14, 335 (n. 84), 337, 339, 350, 359, 362

Cornell, T., 9–12, 25, 46

Corsica (Roman province), 136, 229 (n. 121), 233, 239–40, 244, 246–48, 251, 255 (n. 65), 266, 272, 364, 366

Crawford, M. H., 65

Crete (Roman province), 268 (n. 107), 278, 300 (n. 6), 307, 321–22, 329, 335, 362, 364, 366

Cursus honorum, 188, 208, 378

Curule regalia, 13, 93–97, 110, 119, 126–27, 223, 227, 231, 335, 372

Cyprus (Roman province), 354, 364, 366

Cyrene (Roman province), 362, 364–66

Dacia, 301, 316

Dates magistrates enter office, 32, 72, 76, 143 (n. 48), 162

Daube, D., 87

Decemviri consulari imperio legibus scribundis, 34–36, 73 (n. 86), 89, 93 (n. 152), 103–4, 159

Decemviri stlitibus iudicandis, 63

Decimation (fustuarium), 49, 83

Decimus Flavus, C. (9) (pr. 184 BC), 259

Decius, P. (9) (pr. 115 BC), 67–68

Decius Mus, P. (16) (cos. 312, 308, 297, 295), 159–60, 217

Deditio in fidem, 238

Develin, R., 72, 113, 221

Dictator, 14, 25, 27–8, 30, 41 (n. 108), 42, 55 (n. 24), 60–61, 64 (n. 53), 65, 73 (n. 86), 76, 86, 89–90, 102, 114, 118–25, 130, 138, 144, 154 (n. 81), 159, 161–82, 185, 191, 218–21, 331, 337–40, 347–48, 350, 358–59, 362, 371–72, 377, 381; had same imperium as consuls and praetors, 89–90, 161–80; Latin, 30; liable to prosecution, 120–21, 175; permitted to use imperium inside the pomerium, 118–25, 168–69, 381; and the provincia, 169–80

Didius, T. (5) (cos. 98 BC), 229 (n. 124), 287, 289

Dignitas, 95, 122, 186, 189, 195, 198, 201–2, 207–9, 316, 349, 363, 367, 370

Domi militiaeque, 5–6, 47–56, 61–63, 76, 80, 83–87, 90–93, 101, 104–6, 117–19, 121–25, 129–31, 169, 241, 265, 269–77, 290, 314; and the pomerium, 50–4

Domitius Ahenobarbus, Cn. (20) (cos. 122 BC), 149 (n. 66)

Domitius Ahenobarbus, L. (27) (cos. 54 BC), 108 (n. 203), 261, 329 (n. 73)

Domitius Calvinus, Cn. (43) (cos. 53 BC), 371 (n. 58)

Domitius Corbulo, Cn. 321

Drepana (battle), 81

Drummond, A., 16

Duplá, A., 5

Eckstein, A. M., 138, 263, 276

Edict, 62–63, 70, 270–72, 362

Egypt, 326 (n. 67), 339, 350, 354, 366 (n. 45), 370

Ehrenberg, V., 325

Extortion, 278, 280–81, 283–84, 289, 293, 378

Fabian clan fights Veii, 12, 21–22, 32

Fabius, Caeso (159) (cos. 479 BC), 32

Hadrian (emperor), 271 (n. 122)

Hamilcar Barca, 244

Hannibal Barca, 44 (n. 120), 82 (n. 120), 83, 90, 110, 125, 133, 136, 139, 146, 154–56, 169 (n. 129), 170, 174, 176, 200–202, 221, 237–38

Hasdrubal Barca (brother of Hannibal), 140, 146

Hasdrubal Barca (son-in-law of Hamilcar), 244

Helvius, M. (4) (pr. 197 BC), 79–80, 145, 253

Henderson, M. I., 167

Herdonius, Ap., 22

Heuss, A., 34, 86

Hiero (king of Syracuse), 240, 271

Holloway, R. R., 19, 23

Honos, 66, 189

Horatii and Curatii, 22

Hortensius, L. (4) (pr. 170 BC), 278

Hortensius Hortalus, Q. (13) (cos. 69 BC), 315 (n. 46), 335

Hostilius Mancinus, A. (16) (cos. 170 BC), 128

Hostilius Tubulus, C. (25) (pr. 209 BC), 227 (n. 113)

Illyricum (Roman province), 134, 300 (n. 6), 301, 302 (n. 7), 308, 312, 316, 364–66

Imperator, 14, 82, 106 (n. 197), 111, 113, 158–60, 218, 222, 345, 349, 353, 360

Imperii dies, 153

Imperii insignia, 93–95

Imperii prorogatio, 211, 214–17

Imperii vis, 193–94

Imperium: abrogation of, 125–26, 128, 138, 215, 335; *aequum*, 319–20, 322; and Augustus, 7, 346 (n. 2), 347, 350–54, 357–63, 372–73, 381–82; and civilian governance, 56–68, 84, 97–102; *consulare*, 85, 88 (n. 138), 360 (n. 33); and dictators, 118–25, 168–69, 172, 175, 338–40, 358–60, 372, 381; not originally divisible into greater and lesser degrees, 86, 142–47, 153–54, 158–61, 165–81, 187–209, 216, 223–26, 247, 291, 295–96, 318–26, 341–42, 346 (n. 2), 352, 354, 375–78; *domi*, 59, 85–87, 90–93, 97, 101–3, 106, 113–17, 130, 190, 196–97, 314; duration of, 126–28, 209–10, 214, 219, 376; expires inside the *pomerium*, 104, 110–15, 125–26, 128, 210, 214,

347, 350–51, 358–60; and the *fasces*, 13, 86, 93–97, 119, 126–27, 153, 216; and immunity from prosecution, 62, 103, 128–29, 131 (n. 1), 180, 278; *infinitum*, 319, 322 (n. 56), 326; and the *lex curiata*, 36, 38, 39 (n. 101), 42, 75–76, 78, 101, 105–10, 118 (n. 234), 162, 186, 215, 217–18, 226, 333–34, 356 (n. 26), 376; limited to assigned *provincia*, 125, 127, 131–42, 291; limits on commanders' use of, 36, 42, 125–29, 278–94, 303; *maius*, 59 (n. 32), 86, 153–54, 165–68, 171–74, 181, 186 (n. 9), 189–209, 216, 226–27, 230–31, 296, 318–32, 337, 342, 344, 354, 360–62, 372–73, 376, 380–82; military authority only, 6, 32–34, 47, 52, 77–78, 81–130; *militiae*, 85–86, 92–93, 114, 116, 314; *minus*, 153–54, 181, 189–209, 226–27, 296, 318, 323 (n. 59), 326, 342, 361 (n. 36), 376; with modifiers (*summum, maximum, totum, omne*), 88–89, 153–54, 165, 167; origins of, 13, 33–34, 36–38; and *potestas*, 32, 57–68, 81–84; and precedence of command, 325–32, 372–73; prohibited inside the *pomerium*, 50–52, 54–6, 105, 110–18, 121–25, 126, 128, 130, 168, 338–40, 347, 350, 358–60; range of meanings of, 87–90; and the *senatus consultum ultimum*, 121–25, 338–39; taken up outside the *pomerium*, 50, 83, 92 (n. 151), 93, 106, 109–10, 113, 115, 136, 138, 351, 358–60, 368; and the triumph, 62, 74 (n. 90), 86, 92 (n. 151), 104, 107–18, 122, 127, 132, 173, 194–96, 202, 204–6, 214–16, 220, 323–24, 333, 339–40, 353, 358–59

Intercessio (magisterial intercession), 48, 64–65, 327

Interrex, 43, 70

Italica, 250–51

Iudicia imperio continentia, 98–99

Iudicia legitima, 98–99

Iustitium, 117 (n. 232), 124 (n. 258)

Jameson, S., 319, 323–24

Jashemski, W. F., 213, 221

Jehne, M., 5, 338

Jolowicz, H. F., 61

Judaea, 286 (n. 147), 311

Otacilius Crassus, T. (12) (pr. 217, 214 BC), 82, 177–78

Ovation (*ovatio*), 79–80, 112, 228, 250 (n. 49)

Paludatus, 105, 109–10

Pannonia (Roman province), 321, 364 (n. 40), 366

Papirius Carbo, Cn. (37) (cos. 113 BC), 305 (n. 16)

Papirius Cursor, L. (52) (cos. 326, 320, 319, 315, 313 BC), 120–21, 177, 179, 186 (n. 12)

Parthian Empire, 73 (n. 86), 286 (n. 147), 302, 311

Paterfamilias, 275–76

Patrum auctoritas, 39, 40 (n. 104)

Pergamum, 253–54

Perseus (king of Macedon), 198, 234, 278, 319

Pharsalus (battle), 206, 338–39

Philip (king of Macedon), 136 (n. 21), 304 (n. 12), 313 (n. 38)

Pina Polo, F., 5, 87, 315

Pinarius Rusca, M. (10) (pr. 181 BC), 266 (n. 102)

Pinsent, J., 194

Pirates and piracy commands, 245–46, 248, 288, 297, 300 (n. 6), 306–10, 318–25, 333–35, 344, 356, 364, 379–80

Plautius, C. (2) (cos. 341 BC), 43 (n. 117)

Plautius, L. (2 or 5) (pr. 322 BC), 164

Poetelius Libo Visolus, C. (dict. 313 BC), 164

πολέμαρχος, 23

Pomerium, 49 (n. 8), 50–55, 57 (n. 27), 58, 62, 75 (n. 97), 77, 82, 85, 87, 93–94, 97, 102–28, 132, 168–69, 172, 180–81, 210, 214–15, 228, 338–40, 347, 350–51, 358–60, 372, 381; *imperium* normally forbidden inside of, 50–51, 54–55, 93, 110–17, 121–25, 130, 168, 338, 350, 358–60; and the first milestone outside the city, 52 (n. 16), 82 (n. 122), 85 (n. 127), 98 (n. 168)

Pompeius Magnus, Cn. (15) (cos. 70, 55, 52 BC), 74, 82 (n. 119), 102 (n. 183), 122, 127–28, 132, 134 (n. 12), 195, 206, 211 (n. 75), 286 (n. 148), 288, 301–2, 306–12, 315 (n. 46), 317, 319–39, 342–44, 350–51, 355–57, 369 (n. 51), 371 (n. 57), 379–82

Pomponius, M. (9) (pr. 216 BC), 198

Pomponius Matho, M'. (5) (cos. 233 BC), 258 (nn. 75)

Pomponius Matho, M. (6) (cos. 231 BC), 258 (n. 76)

Pomptinus, C. (1) (pr. 63 BC), 74 (n. 90), 101, 107–9

Pontifex Maximus, 66, 75–76, 102, 136 (n. 20)

Pontus (Roman province), 254, 286 (n. 147), 297, 311, 323, 355, 364, 366

Popillius Laenas, C. (7) (cos. 172 BC), 136 (n. 20), 354 (n. 21)

Popillius Laenas, M. (6) (cos. 173 BC), 138

Popularis politics, 124, 295, 304–14, 343, 355

Porcius Cato, M. (10) (cos. 195 BC), 80, 203, 258, 263

Porcius Cato, M. (pr. c. 100 BC), 281–82

Porcius Cato, M. (20) (pr. 54 BC), 74 (n. 90), 206–9

Postumius Albinus, L. (22) (cos. 234, 229, 215 BC), 186 (n. 12), 221

Postumius Megellus, L. (19) (cos. 305, 294, 291 BC), 132, 139, 146, 186 (n. 12), 217

Potestas, 6, 32, 47, 52, 54, 57–58, 61–68, 70, 78, 81–84, 88–89, 92, 95, 97, 99–101, 103, 106–7, 109, 116–18, 126, 129, 131, 143, 168, 172, 209–10, 332–33, 356–57, 359, 360 (n. 32); as authority of civilian governance, 57–68, 83–84, 99–101

Praetor, praetorship: collegiality with consuls, 2, 68, 116, 183–209, 224, 230–31, 246–47, 293, 300–301, 341–42, 377; development of classical form, 183–209, 246–47, 255–63; lack protections of *imperium* in Rome, 102–3, 121, 128; lower status emphasized by provincial assignment, 187–89, 246–47, 255–63, 293, 300–301; lower status than consuls traditional rather than legal, 68, 183, 185–92, 201, 209, 223, 230–31, 234, 236, 247, 255–63, 296, 313, 377, 379–80; originally a generic term for commander, 19–20, 23–24, 28, 31, 34–35, 184; *maximus*, 15, 27–28, 166; not originally civilian magistrates, 18–20, 31–44, 183–92; *urbanus*, 64 (n. 50), 103, 138 (n. 30), 189, 191 (n. 25), 194, 247, 255

Praetorian college expanded for provincial

command, 185, 187, 223, 242–47, 249–50, 272–73, 293, 378

Praetorian commanders more constrained by new restrictions, 279–81, 284–90, 293–94, 301, 378

Praetorian Guard, 360

Prag, J., 269

Precedence of command among equals, 144–47, 151–52, 155–59, 181, 192–94, 198–204, 206–9, 216, 223–24, 252, 291, 295–96, 318, 325, 361, 380

Prefect of Capua and Cumae, 238–39, 245, 370 (n. 55)

Prefect of Egypt, 370

Price, S., 54

Prior consul, 151

Privati cum imperio, 73 (n. 86), 183, 206, 220–30, 206, 210, 212–13, 220–31, 249, 333–34

Prorogation/promagistrates, 27, 61–63, 79–80, 93, 113, 160, 175–76, 183, 209–31, 255, 290, 295–96, 306–8, 313–14, 317, 341–42, 347–51, 369, 377; duration of, 213, 308; extends possession of *provincia*, 214–17; senate assumes full control of, 255, 306, 308, 317

Prosecution of ex-commanders, 51 (n. 15), 62 (n. 43), 83, 103, 120–23, 125–28, 132, 136 (n. 20), 138 (n. 30), 145–46, 158, 175, 180, 277–84, 293–94

Provincia: assignment of, 131–42, 161, 180–81, 200–203, 208, 215, 233–37, 243, 246, 254–63, 298–318, 320, 325, 330, 350, 354–57; assignment establishes precedence of command authority, 142–61, 198–209, 252–53, 295–96, 318, 328–32, 334, 337, 341, 344, 361, 372–73, 377; Augustan manipulation of prestige relating to, 363–70, 381; borders or boundaries of, 156, 247–48, 250–54, 263, 271, 283–87, 290–91, 364–66, 379; commanders expected to remain in, 138–42, 250, 272, 283–89, 292, 301, 364–65, 378–79; consular and praetorian types, 255–63, 299–313, 363–70, 373, 379–81; defines sphere in which a commander uses *imperium*, 131–42, 169–80, 328–32, 375, 377; and dictators, 169–80; flexible and dynamic concept, 125, 135–37, 154, 200, 215, 246, 279, 294–98,

302, 305, 310, 314–15, 323, 345, 368–70, 376–77, 380, 382; original definition as a task (especially a military campaign), 58, 131–42, 144, 146, 159, 162, 169–72, 180, 232–40, 246, 248–51, 254–60, 262–63, 273–74, 276, 284–88, 292–94, 297–98, 302, 306–7, 318, 324, 328, 344, 351, 354, 377–78; shared/divided by two commanders, 141, 148–58, 176, 251–52, 306, 309–10, 312–13, 317, 320, 337, 377; short-term assignment (originally), 141–42, 218, 232–33, 235–38, 251, 271, 287–88, 292, 378; overlapping, 308, 318–25, 328–31, 344, 353, 362–63, 380–81

Province (permanent Roman possession): abuse of peaceful provincials resulted in new regulations on commanders, 272–94; Augustan manipulation of prestige relating to, 363–70, 381; become attractive to consuls, 295–96, 300–304, 315–17, 343; become zones of administration and governance, 288–92, 294, 300, 303–4; borders or boundaries of, 156, 247–48, 250–54, 263, 271, 283–87, 290–91, 364–66, 379; created demand for governance, 263–73; defensive nature of, 234–39, 243 (n. 30), 245–50, 254–58, 262–63, 292–93, 297, 300–301, 306, 318, 378; defined by geography, 233–64, 268 (n. 107), 271, 283–89, 291–94, 297–311, 318, 324, 329, 331, 363–68, 378–80; initially given to praetors, 246–47, 255–63, 295–96, 300, 368, 378–79; loses ability to separate commanders, 318–25, 327–30, 380; often given to consuls after 123 BC, 255–63, 295–96, 298–304, 315–17, 343, 379; originally less desirable, 209, 246–47, 255–63, 293, 295, 368; overlapping, 308, 318–25, 328–31, 344, 353, 362–63, 380–81; separates commanders, 144–51, 176, 250–54, 318–25, 344, 375; ten senators sent to advise on creation, 240, 268 (n. 107); used differently by consuls, 257–63, 301–4, 363–64, 379

Provincial governance, 233–36, 238–39, 263–94, 302–4, 363–65, 379–80

Provincial maladministration, state efforts to control, 234–35, 273–94, 378; commanders expected to show restraint, 275–77, 280–81,

Tribunes able to arrest and prosecute sitting
consuls and praetors, 102, 121, 128, 136
(n. 20), 138
Tribunician veto, 55, 64, 67, 85, 104, 107, 119,
121 (n. 245), 124, 261 (n. 90), 298, 327, 358
Tribune (*tribunus*), 14, 19, 24–25, 27, 65 (n. 58);
tribunus militum, 14, 24, 65, 84, 128, 139,
142, 158, 197, 332 (n. 78), 333 (n. 79); *tribunus militum consulari potestate*, 14, 22,
24–27, 35, 37–38, 41 (n. 108), 48, 73 (n. 86),
89, 144, 159, 167; *tribunus plebis*, 14, 31–32,
36, 37 (n. 96), 48, 50, 52, 55, 58, 60 (n. 37),
63, 65, 67, 68 (n. 64), 78, 88, 99, 101–4,
112, 119–21, 134 (n. 11), 136 (n. 20), 138, 149,
172, 175 (n. 145), 197, 211, 217, 232, 278,
298 (n. 4), 304 (n. 12), 305, 317, 327, 343,
359, 375
Triumph, 17, 43 (n. 117), 62, 79–81, 86, 104–9,
111–18, 122, 126–28, 139–41, 145–47, 149–
50, 172–73, 186, 194–96, 198–99, 202, 204–
6, 210–12, 214–15, 218, 220, 228, 253, 257,
262, 273, 287, 296, 319, 323–24, 333, 339–40,
352–53, 356, 359, 378; celebrant must remain
outside *pomerium* until triumph, 52 (n. 16),
62, 86, 105, 107–8, 112–16, 127, 214–15;
Etruscan, 114–15; an exception to the ban
on *imperium* inside the *pomerium*, 111–18,
125, 340, 358–59; hunting, 287, 378
Triumphator's banquet, 113 (n. 222), 194–96
Triumviri agris iudicandis assignandis, 348
Triumviri monetales, 348
Triumviri rei publicae constituendae, 73 (n. 86),
331, 346–49
Triumvirate (First), 107 (n. 201), 301, 355, 371
Triumvirate (Second), 306, 309, 312, 331, 346–
49, 353, 357, 362, 371, 381–82
Tuccius, M. (5) (pr. 190 BC), 227 (n. 113)
Tullius Cicero, M. (29) (cos. 63 BC), 74, 127,
132–33, 135, 270 (n. 118), 294, 298 (n. 2), 315
(n. 46), 316, 326–32, 340–42, 344, 361–63,
380–82
Tullius Cicero, Q. (31) (pr. 62 BC), 228 (n. 116)
Tumultus, 90, 117 (n. 232)

Τυραννίς, 163
Twelve tables, 15, 63 (n. 46)

Ungern-Sternberg, J. von, 9, 35
Ύπατος, 165–66
Urso, G., 35

Valerius Corvus, M. (137) (cos. 348, 346, 343,
335, 300, 299 BC), 43 (n. 117), 177, 179, 186
(n. 12), 238
Valerius Falto, Q. (157) (cos. 239 BC), 201,
204–6, 227
Valerius Flaccus, L. (176) (cos. 100 BC), 289
(n. 154)
Valerius Laevinus, M. (211) (cos. 210 BC), 136
(n. 21), 138, 198
Valerius Maximus, M'. (243) (dict. 494 BC),
171
Valerius Messala Rufus, M. (77) (cos. 53 BC),
75–76
Valerius Poplicola, P. (300) (cos. 352 BC), 186
(n. 12)
Valerius Publicola, P. (302) (cos. 508, 507,
504 BC), 23, 119, 179
Valgaeren, J. H., 61
Veii, 12, 21, 32, 141
Vercellae (battle), 288
Verres, C. (1) (pr. 74 BC), 51 (n. 15), 89, 110–11,
139, 145–46, 270 (n. 117), 272 (n. 123), 274
(n. 125), 294
Versnel, H. S., 72, 74–75, 87
Vervaet, F., 298, 308
Vibenna brothers, 22
Vipsanius Agrippa, M., 361
Vocatio (summons), 101–2
Volumnius Flamma Violens, L. (3) (cos. 307,
296 BC), 148

War bands, 12, 21–23, 26, 31, 43, 58, 68, 80
Wesch-Klein, G., 5

Ziolkowski, A., 30